THE BOOK

YAR/ST

Vauxhall/Opel Astra and Zafira
Service and Repair Manual

A K Legg LAE MIMI and Martynn Randall

Models covered

(3758-368-7AJ3)

Astra Hatchback, Saloon & Estate and Zafira MPV models with petrol engines,
including special/limited editions
1.4 litre (1389cc), 1.6 litre (1598cc), 1.8 litre (1796cc), 2.0 litre (1998cc) & 2.2 litre (2198cc)

For coverage of diesel models, see manual no. 3797
Does NOT cover bi-fuel models, 1.6 litre 'Twinport' or 2.0 litre turbo engines
Does NOT cover Coupe or Convertible models, or new range introduced May 2004

© Haynes Publishing 2005

ABCDE
FGHI

A book in the **Haynes Service and Repair Manual Series**

ISBN 1 84425 165 9

British Library Cataloguing in Publication Data
A catalogue record for this book is available from the British Library.

Printed in the USA

Haynes Publishing
Sparkford, Yeovil, Somerset BA22 7JJ, England

Haynes North America, Inc
861 Lawrence Drive, Newbury Park, California 91320, USA

Editions Haynes
4, Rue de l'Abreuvoir
92415 COURBEVOIE CEDEX, France

Haynes Publishing Nordiska AB
Box 1504, 751 45 UPPSALA, Sverige

Contents

LIVING WITH YOUR VAUXHALL ASTRA/ZAFIRA

Safety first!	Page	0•5
Introduction	Page	0•6

Roadside Repairs
If your car won't start	Page	0•7
Jump starting	Page	0•8
Wheel changing	Page	0•9
Identifying leaks	Page	0•10
Towing	Page	0•10

Weekly Checks
Introduction	Page	0•11
Underbonnet check points	Page	0•11
Engine oil level	Page	0•13
Coolant level	Page	0•13
Tyre condition and pressure	Page	0•14
Brake (and clutch) fluid level	Page	0•15
Power steering fluid level	Page	0•15
Screen washer fluid level	Page	0•16
Battery	Page	0•16
Wiper blades	Page	0•17
Electrical systems	Page	0•17

Lubricants and fluids
	Page	0•18

Tyre pressures
	Page	0•18

MAINTENANCE

Routine Maintenance and Servicing

Servicing specifications	Page	1•2
Maintenance schedule	Page	1•3
Maintenance procedures	Page	1•9

Contents

REPAIRS AND OVERHAUL

Engine and Associated Systems

1.6 litre SOHC engine in-car repair procedures .... Page **2A•1**

1.4, 1.6, 1.8 and 2.0 litre DOHC engine in-car repair procedures .... Page **2B•1**

2.2 litre DOHC engine in-car repair procedures .... Page **2C•1**

Engine removal and overhaul procedures .... Page **2D•1**

Cooling, heating and air conditioning systems .... Page **3•1**

Fuel and exhaust systems .... Page **4A•1**

Emission control systems .... Page **4B•0**

Starting and charging systems .... Page **5A•1**

Ignition system .... Page **5B•1**

Transmission

Clutch .... Page **6•1**

Manual transmission .... Page **7A•1**

Automatic transmission .... Page **7B•1**

Driveshafts .... Page **8•1**

Brakes and suspension

Braking system .... Page **9•1**

Suspension and steering .... Page **10•1**

Body equipment

Bodywork and fittings .... Page **11•1**

Body electrical system .... Page **12•1**

Wiring Diagrams

Vauxhall Astra .... Page **12•26**

Vauxhall Zafira .... Page **12•46**

REFERENCE

Dimensions and weights .... Page **REF•1**

Conversion factors .... Page **REF•2**

Buying spare parts .... Page **REF•3**

Vehicle identification .... Page **REF•3**

General repair procedures .... Page **REF•4**

Jacking and vehicle support .... Page **REF•5**

Disconnecting the battery .... Page **REF•5**

Tools and working facilities .... Page **REF•6**

MOT test checks .... Page **REF•8**

Fault finding .... Page **REF•12**

Glossary of technical terms .... Page **REF•19**

Index

Index .... Page **REF•23**

Advanced driving

Many people see the words 'advanced driving' and believe that it won't interest them or that it is a style of driving beyond their own abilities. Nothing could be further from the truth. Advanced driving is straightforward safe, sensible driving - the sort of driving we should all do every time we get behind the wheel.

An average of 10 people are killed every day on UK roads and 870 more are injured, some seriously. Lives are ruined daily, usually because somebody did something stupid. Something like 95% of all accidents are due to human error, mostly driver failure. Sometimes we make genuine mistakes - everyone does. Sometimes we have lapses of concentration. Sometimes we deliberately take risks.

For many people, the process of 'learning to drive' doesn't go much further than learning how to pass the driving test because of a common belief that good drivers are made by 'experience'.

Learning to drive by 'experience' teaches three driving skills:

- ☐ Quick reactions. (Whoops, that was close!)
- ☐ Good handling skills. (Horn, swerve, brake, horn).
- ☐ Reliance on vehicle technology. (Great stuff this ABS, stop in no distance even in the wet...)

Drivers whose skills are 'experience based' generally have a lot of near misses and the odd accident. The results can be seen every day in our courts and our hospital casualty departments.

Advanced drivers have learnt to control the risks by controlling the position and speed of their vehicle. They avoid accidents and near misses, even if the drivers around them make mistakes.

The key skills of advanced driving are **concentration,** effective all-round **observation, anticipation** and **planning.** When **good vehicle handling** is added to

these skills, all driving situations can be approached and negotiated in a safe, methodical way, leaving nothing to chance.

Concentration means applying your mind to safe driving, completely excluding anything that's not relevant. Driving is usually the most dangerous activity that most of us undertake in our daily routines. It deserves our full attention.

Observation means not just looking, but seeing and seeking out the information found in the driving environment.

Anticipation means asking yourself what is happening, what you can reasonably expect to happen and what could happen unexpectedly. (One of the commonest words used in compiling accident reports is 'suddenly'.)

Planning is the link between seeing something and taking the appropriate action. For many drivers, planning is the missing link.

If you want to become a safer and more skilful driver and you want to enjoy your driving more, contact the Institute of Advanced Motorists at www.iam.org.uk, phone 0208 996 9600, or write to IAM House, 510 Chiswick High Road, London W ⁵RG for an information pack.

Working on your car can be dangerous. This page shows just some of the potential risks and hazards, with the aim of creating a safety-conscious attitude.

General hazards

Scalding

• Don't remove the radiator or expansion tank cap while the engine is hot.
• Engine oil, automatic transmission fluid or power steering fluid may also be dangerously hot if the engine has recently been running.

Burning

• Beware of burns from the exhaust system and from any part of the engine. Brake discs and drums can also be extremely hot immediately after use.

Crushing

• When working under or near a raised vehicle, always supplement the jack with axle stands, or use drive-on ramps. *Never venture under a car which is only supported by a jack.*
• Take care if loosening or tightening high-torque nuts when the vehicle is on stands. Initial loosening and final tightening should be done with the wheels on the ground.

Fire

• Fuel is highly flammable; fuel vapour is explosive.
• Don't let fuel spill onto a hot engine.
• Do not smoke or allow naked lights (including pilot lights) anywhere near a vehicle being worked on. Also beware of creating sparks (electrically or by use of tools).
• Fuel vapour is heavier than air, so don't work on the fuel system with the vehicle over an inspection pit.
• Another cause of fire is an electrical overload or short-circuit. Take care when repairing or modifying the vehicle wiring.
• Keep a fire extinguisher handy, of a type suitable for use on fuel and electrical fires.

Electric shock

• Ignition HT voltage can be dangerous, especially to people with heart problems or a pacemaker. Don't work on or near the ignition system with the engine running or the ignition switched on.

• Mains voltage is also dangerous. Make sure that any mains-operated equipment is correctly earthed. Mains power points should be protected by a residual current device (RCD) circuit breaker.

Fume or gas intoxication

• Exhaust fumes are poisonous; they often contain carbon monoxide, which is rapidly fatal if inhaled. Never run the engine in a confined space such as a garage with the doors shut.
• Fuel vapour is also poisonous, as are the vapours from some cleaning solvents and paint thinners.

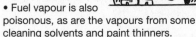

Poisonous or irritant substances

• Avoid skin contact with battery acid and with any fuel, fluid or lubricant, especially antifreeze, brake hydraulic fluid and Diesel fuel. Don't syphon them by mouth. If such a substance is swallowed or gets into the eyes, seek medical advice.
• Prolonged contact with used engine oil can cause skin cancer. Wear gloves or use a barrier cream if necessary. Change out of oil-soaked clothes and do not keep oily rags in your pocket.
• Air conditioning refrigerant forms a poisonous gas if exposed to a naked flame (including a cigarette). It can also cause skin burns on contact.

Asbestos

• Asbestos dust can cause cancer if inhaled or swallowed. Asbestos may be found in gaskets and in brake and clutch linings. When dealing with such components it is safest to assume that they contain asbestos.

Special hazards

Hydrofluoric acid

• This extremely corrosive acid is formed when certain types of synthetic rubber, found in some O-rings, oil seals, fuel hoses etc, are exposed to temperatures above 400°C. The rubber changes into a charred or sticky substance containing the acid. *Once formed, the acid remains dangerous for years. If it gets onto the skin, it may be necessary to amputate the limb concerned.*
• When dealing with a vehicle which has suffered a fire, or with components salvaged from such a vehicle, wear protective gloves and discard them after use.

The battery

• Batteries contain sulphuric acid, which attacks clothing, eyes and skin. Take care when topping-up or carrying the battery.
• The hydrogen gas given off by the battery is highly explosive. Never cause a spark or allow a naked light nearby. Be careful when connecting and disconnecting battery chargers or jump leads.

Air bags

• Air bags can cause injury if they go off accidentally. Take care when removing the steering wheel and/or facia. Special storage instructions may apply.

Diesel injection equipment

• Diesel injection pumps supply fuel at very high pressure. Take care when working on the fuel injectors and fuel pipes.

⚠ *Warning: Never expose the hands, face or any other part of the body to injector spray; the fuel can penetrate the skin with potentially fatal results.*

Remember...

DO

• Do use eye protection when using power tools, and when working under the vehicle.

• Do wear gloves or use barrier cream to protect your hands when necessary.

• Do get someone to check periodically that all is well when working alone on the vehicle.

• Do keep loose clothing and long hair well out of the way of moving mechanical parts.

• Do remove rings, wristwatch etc, before working on the vehicle – especially the electrical system.

• Do ensure that any lifting or jacking equipment has a safe working load rating adequate for the job.

DON'T

• Don't attempt to lift a heavy component which may be beyond your capability – get assistance.

• Don't rush to finish a job, or take unverified short cuts.

• Don't use ill-fitting tools which may slip and cause injury.

• Don't leave tools or parts lying around where someone can trip over them. Mop up oil and fuel spills at once.

• Don't allow children or pets to play in or near a vehicle being worked on.

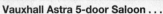
Vauxhall Astra 5-door Saloon . . .

. . . and Estate models

The Vauxhall Astra-G model was introduced in the UK in February 1998 as a replacement for the previous Astra, the 'F' model. It was available in Saloon, Hatchback and Estate versions with 1.4, 1.6, 1.8 and 2.0 litre petrol engines. The 1.6 litre engines are in either 8-valve or 16-valve form, and the 1.4, 1.8 and 2.0 litre engines are all 16-valve units.

In February 2000, a 2.2 litre petrol engine was introduced for both the Astra and Zafira, whilst from October 2000, Astra models were also available with a 2.0 litre turbocharged petrol engine. This engine, along with the various diesel engines fitted to the Astra and Zafira range, are not covered in this manual.

Models may be fitted with a five-speed manual transmission or four-speed automatic transmission mounted on the left-hand side of the engine.

All models have front-wheel-drive with fully-independent front suspension, and semi-independent rear suspension with a torsion beam and trailing arms.

Electro/Hydraulic power steering (PAS) is fitted as standard to all models, whilst Anti-Lock Braking (ABS) is available as an option.

The Zafira range was launched in June 1999, available with 1.6 and 1.8 litre DOHC 16-valve petrol engines. Whilst the Zafira shares the same drive train and suspension as the Astra, the body is that of a Multi Personnel Vehicle (MPV). Not only does the Zafira have 7 seats arranged in three rows, it quickly converts to a spacious load carrier – thanks to the 'Flex 7' system, which allows the rear seats to fold completely flat into the floor giving an uninterrupted load space.

Both models have a full-sized driver's side airbag fitted as standard, and side impact air-bags available as an option. Passenger's side airbags became standard equipment from January 1999. Cruise control is available as an option on certain models.

For the home mechanic, the Vauxhall Astra/Zafira is a straightforward vehicle to maintain and repair since design features have been incorporated to reduce the actual cost of ownership to a minimum, and most of the items requiring frequent attention are easily accessible.

Your Vauxhall Astra and Zafira manual

The aim of this manual is to help you get the best value from your vehicle. It can do so in several ways. It can help you decide what work must be done (even should you choose to get it done by a garage), provide information on routine maintenance and servicing, and give a logical course of action and diagnosis when random faults occur. However, it is hoped that you will use the manual by tackling the work yourself. On simpler jobs, it may even be quicker than booking the car into a garage and going there twice, to leave and collect it. Perhaps most important, a lot of money can be saved by avoiding the costs a garage must charge to cover its labour and overheads.

The manual has drawings and descriptions to show the function of the various components, so that their layout can be understood. Then the tasks are described and photographed in a clear step-by-step sequence.

References to the 'left' or 'right' are in the sense of a person in the driver's seat, facing forward.

Acknowledgements

Certain illustrations are the copyright of Vauxhall Motors Limited, and are used with their permission. Thanks are also due to Draper Tools Limited, who provided some of the workshop tools, and to all those people at Sparkford who helped in the production of this manual.

We take great pride in the accuracy of information given in this manual, but vehicle manufacturers make alterations and design changes during the production run of a particular vehicle of which they do not inform us. No liability can be accepted by the authors or publishers for loss, damage or injury caused by any errors in, or omissions from, the information given.

Project vehicles

The main vehicle used in the preparation of this manual, and which appears in many of the photographic sequences, was a Zafira fitted with a 1.8 litre engine. Other vehicles used included 1.6 litre SOHC and DOHC models.

Vauxhall Zafira

The following pages are intended to help in dealing with common roadside emergencies and breakdowns. You will find more detailed fault finding information at the back of the manual, and repair information in the main chapters.

If your car won't start and the starter motor doesn't turn

☐ If it's a model with automatic transmission, make sure the selector is in P or N.
☐ Open the bonnet and make sure that the battery terminals are clean and tight.
☐ Switch on the headlights and try to start the engine. If the headlights go very dim when you're trying to start, the battery is probably flat. Get out of trouble by jump starting (see next page) using a friend's car.

If your car won't start even though the starter motor turns as normal

☐ Is there fuel in the tank?
☐ Is there moisture on electrical components under the bonnet? Switch off the ignition, then wipe off any obvious dampness with a dry cloth. Spray a water-repellent aerosol product (WD-40 or equivalent) on ignition and fuel system electrical connectors like those shown in the photos. Pay special attention to the ignition coil wiring connector and HT leads.

A Check the condition and security of the battery connections.

B Check the engine wiring harness at the left-hand rear of the engine compartment.

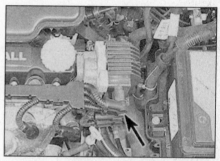

C Check the wiring to the DIS ignition module (1.6 engine).

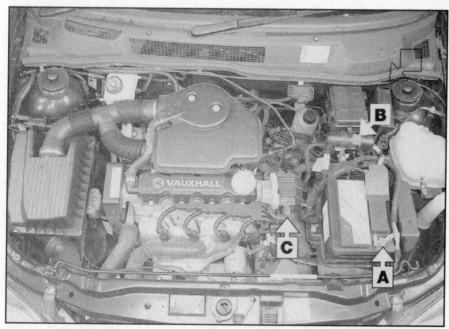

Check that electrical connections are secure (with the ignition switched off) and spray them with a water dispersant spray like WD-40 if you suspect a problem due to damp.

D Check the wiring to the airflow meter (1.8 engine).

E Remove the engine top cover, and check the wiring for the ignition coils (1.8 engine).

Jump starting

When jump-starting a car using a booster battery, observe the following precautions:

✔ Before connecting the booster battery, make sure that the ignition is switched off.

✔ Ensure that all electrical equipment (lights, heater, wipers, etc) is switched off.

✔ Take note of any special precautions printed on the battery case.

✔ Make sure that the booster battery is the same voltage as the discharged one in the vehicle.

✔ If the battery is being jump-started from the battery in another vehicle, the two vehicles MUST NOT TOUCH each other.

✔ Make sure that the transmission is in neutral (or PARK, in the case of automatic transmission).

> **HAYNES HiNT** *Jump starting will get you out of trouble, but you must correct whatever made the battery go flat in the first place. There are three possibilities:*
>
> **1** *The battery has been drained by repeated attempts to start, or by leaving the lights on.*
>
> **2** *The charging system is not working properly (alternator drivebelt slack or broken, alternator wiring fault or alternator itself faulty).*
>
> **3** *The battery itself is at fault (electrolyte low, or battery worn out).*

1 Connect one end of the red jump lead to the positive (+) terminal of the flat battery

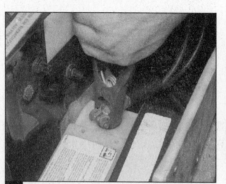

2 Connect the other end of the red lead to the positive (+) terminal of the booster battery.

3 Connect one end of the black jump lead to the negative (-) terminal of the booster battery

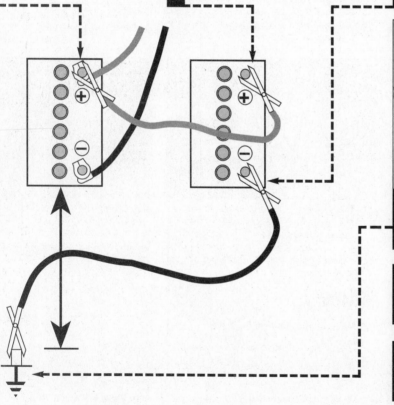

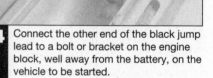

4 Connect the other end of the black jump lead to a bolt or bracket on the engine block, well away from the battery, on the vehicle to be started.

5 Make sure that the jump leads will not come into contact with the fan, drive-belts or other moving parts of the engine.

6 Start the engine using the booster battery and run it at idle speed. Switch on the lights, rear window demister and heater blower motor, then disconnect the jump leads in the reverse order of connection. Turn off the lights etc.

Wheel changing

Some of the details shown here will vary according to model. For instance, the location of the spare wheel and jack is not the same on all cars. However, the basic principles apply to all vehicles.

⚠️ *Warning: Do not change a wheel in a situation where you risk being hit by another vehicle. On busy roads, try to stop in a lay-by or a gateway. Be wary of passing traffic while changing the wheel – it is easy to become distracted by the job in hand.*

Preparation

- [ ] When a puncture occurs, stop as soon as it is safe to do so.
- [ ] Park on firm level ground, if possible, and well out of the way of other traffic.
- [ ] Use hazard warning lights if necessary.
- [ ] If you have one, use a warning triangle to alert other drivers of your presence.
- [ ] Apply the handbrake and engage first or reverse gear (or Park on models with automatic transmission).
- [ ] Chock the wheel diagonally opposite the one being removed – a couple of large stones will do for this.
- [ ] If the ground is soft, use a flat piece of wood to spread the load under the jack.

Changing the wheel

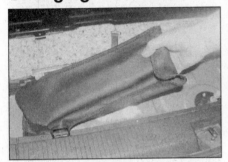

1 On Astra models the jack and wheel brace are stowed under the spare wheel beneath the luggage compartment floor. On Zafira models they are beneath a cover at the rear of the luggage compartment floor.

2 The spare wheel is beneath a cover in the luggage compartment on Astra models. Raise the cover, remove the screw and lift out the spare wheel. Place it beneath the sill as a precaution against the jack failing. On Zafira models, the spare wheel is under the rear of the vehicle. Lift the rear of the luggage compartment floor, and slacken the bolt in the floor, using the wheel brace. Unhook the catch, lower the spare, and detach the cable. The spare can now be lifted out.

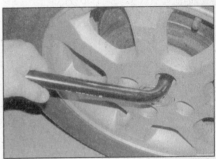

3 On models with steel wheels, use the special tool to pull the wheel trim from the wheel. On models with alloy wheels, use the screwdriver provided inserted at the wheel bolt holes, to prise off the trim. Where an anti-theft device is fitted, use the tool provided to remove the trim. Loosen each wheel bolt by half a turn.

4 All models have depressions in the sill vertical web, which indicate the points at which the jack head is to be attached. On Astra models, the depressions are concealed by flaps in the outer sill bodywork. Prise out the flaps to access the jacking points. Position the jack head under the jacking point and make sure that the slot in the head engages correctly with the vertical web of the sill. Turn the handle until the base of the jack touches the ground then make sure that the base is located directly below the sill. Raise the vehicle until the wheel is clear of the ground. If the tyre is flat make sure that the vehicle is raised sufficiently to allow the spare wheel to be fitted.

5 Remove the bolts and lift the wheel from the vehicle. Place it beneath the sill in place of the spare as a precaution against the jack failing. Fit the spare wheel and tighten the bolts moderately with the wheel brace.

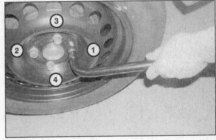

6 Lower the vehicle to the ground, then finally tighten the wheel bolts in a diagonal sequence. Refit the wheel trim. Note that the wheel bolts should be tightened to the specified torque at the earliest opportunity.

Finally...

- [ ] Remove the wheel chocks.
- [ ] Stow the jack and tools in the correct locations in the car.
- [ ] Check the tyre pressure on the wheel just fitted. If it is low, or if you don't have a pressure gauge with you, drive slowly to the nearest garage and inflate the tyre to the right pressure.
- [ ] Have the damaged tyre or wheel repaired as soon as possible.

Identifying leaks

Puddles on the garage floor or drive, or obvious wetness under the bonnet or underneath the car, suggest a leak that needs investigating. It can sometimes be difficult to decide where the leak is coming from, especially if the engine bay is very dirty already. Leaking oil or fluid can also be blown rearwards by the passage of air under the car, giving a false impression of where the problem lies.

 Warning: Most automotive oils and fluids are poisonous. Wash them off skin, and change out of contaminated clothing, without delay.

 HAYNES HiNT *The smell of a fluid leaking from the car may provide a clue to what's leaking. Some fluids are distinctively coloured. It may help to clean the car carefully and to park it over some clean paper overnight as an aid to locating the source of the leak.*
Remember that some leaks may only occur while the engine is running.

Sump oil

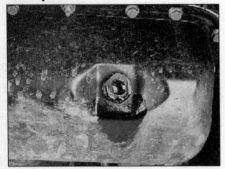

Engine oil may leak from the drain plug...

Oil from filter

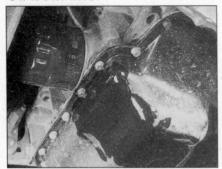

...or from the base of the oil filter.

Gearbox oil

Gearbox oil can leak from the seals at the inboard ends of the driveshafts.

Antifreeze

Leaking antifreeze often leaves a crystalline deposit like this.

Brake fluid

A leak occurring at a wheel is almost certainly brake fluid.

Power steering fluid

Power steering fluid may leak from the pipe connectors on the steering rack.

Towing

When all else fails, you may find yourself having to get a tow home – or of course you may be helping somebody else. Long-distance recovery should only be done by a garage or breakdown service. For shorter distances, DIY towing using another car is easy enough, but observe the following points:

The towing eye has a left-hand thread

☐ A towing eye is provided with the warning triangle in the luggage compartment.
☐ To fit the towing eye, prise the cover from the front bumper, then screw in the towing eye anti-clockwise as far as it will go using the handle of the wheel brace to turn the eye. Note that the towing eye has a **left-hand thread (see illustration)**. A rear towing eye is provided beneath the rear of the vehicle.
☐ Use a proper tow-rope – they are not expensive. The vehicle being towed must display an ON TOW sign in its rear window.
☐ Always turn the ignition key to the 'on' position when the vehicle is being towed, so that the steering lock is released, and that the direction indicator and brake lights will work.
☐ Before being towed, release the handbrake and select neutral on the transmission.
☐ On models with automatic transmission, only tow with the vehicle facing forwards, at less than

50 mph, and no further than 60 miles. If in doubt, do not tow, or transmission damage may result.
☐ Note that greater-than-usual pedal pressure will be required to operate the brakes, since the vacuum servo unit is only operational with the engine running.
☐ The driver of the car being towed must keep the tow-rope taut at all times to avoid snatching.
☐ Make sure that both drivers know the route before setting off.
☐ Only drive at moderate speeds and keep the distance towed to a minimum. Drive smoothly and allow plenty of time for slowing down at junctions.

⚠ **Warning: To prevent damage to the catalytic converter, a vehicle must not be push-started, or started by towing, when the engine is at operating temperature. Use jump leads (see Jump starting).**

Introduction

There are some very simple checks which need only take a few minutes to carry out, but which could save you a lot of inconvenience and expense.

These *Weekly checks* require no great skill or special tools, and the small amount of time they take to perform could prove to be very well spent, for example:

☐ Keeping an eye on tyre condition and pressures, will not only help to stop them wearing out prematurely, but could also save your life.

☐ Many breakdowns are caused by electrical problems. Battery-related faults are particularly common, and a quick check on a regular basis will often prevent the majority of these.

☐ If your car develops a brake fluid leak, the first time you might know about it is when your brakes don't work properly. Checking the level regularly will give advance warning of this kind of problem.

☐ If the oil or coolant levels run low, the cost of repairing any engine damage will be far greater than fixing the leak, for example.

Underbonnet check points

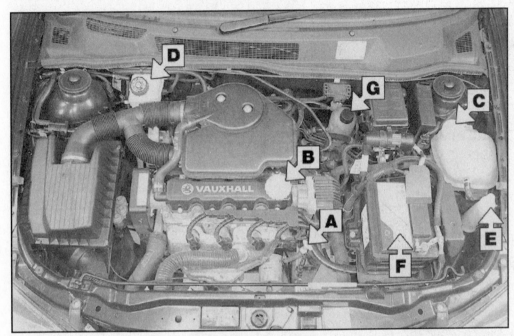

◀ 1.6 litre SOHC

A *Engine oil level dipstick*

B *Engine oil filler cap*

C *Coolant reservoir (expansion tank)*

D *Brake and clutch fluid reservoir*

E *Washer fluid reservoir*

F *Battery*

G *Power steering fluid reservoir*

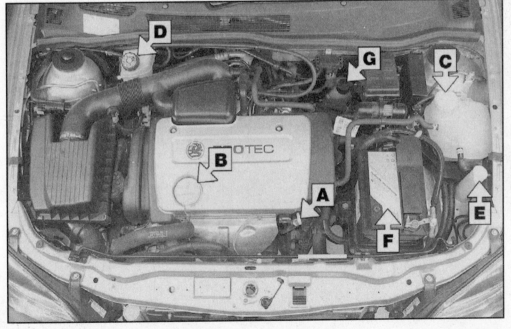

◀ 1.4 & 1.6 litre DOHC

A *Engine oil level dipstick*

B *Engine oil filler cap*

C *Coolant reservoir (expansion tank)*

D *Brake and clutch fluid reservoir*

E *Washer fluid reservoir*

F *Battery*

G *Power steering fluid reservoir*

◀ **1.8 litre DOHC**

A *Engine oil level dipstick*

B *Engine oil filler cap*

C *Coolant reservoir (expansion tank)*

D *Brake and clutch fluid reservoir*

E *Washer fluid reservoir*

F *Battery*

G *Power steering fluid reservoir*

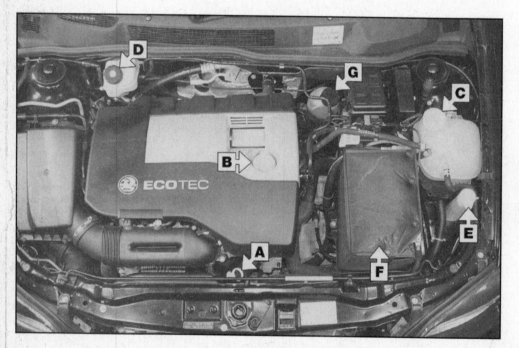

◀ **2.2 litre DOHC**

A *Engine oil level dipstick*

B *Engine oil filler cap*

C *Coolant reservoir (expansion tank)*

D *Brake and clutch fluid reservoir*

E *Washer fluid reservoir*

F *Battery*

G *Power steering fluid reservoir*

Engine oil level

Before you start

✔ Make sure that your car is on level ground.
✔ Check the oil level before the car is driven, or at least 5 minutes after the engine has been switched off.

 HAYNES HiNT *If the oil is checked immediately after driving the vehicle, some of the oil will remain in the upper engine components, resulting in an inaccurate reading on the dipstick.*

The correct oil

● Modern engines place great demands on their oil. It is very important that the correct oil for your car is used (see *Lubricants and fluids*).

Car Care

● If you have to add oil frequently, you should check whether you have any oil leaks. Place some clean paper under the car overnight, and check for stains in the morning. If there are no leaks, the engine may be burning oil.

● Always maintain the level between the upper and lower dipstick marks (see photo 3). If the level is too low severe engine damage may occur. Oil seal failure may result if the engine is overfilled by adding too much oil.

1 The dipstick is located on the front of the engine (see *Underbonnet Check Points* for exact location). Withdraw the dipstick.

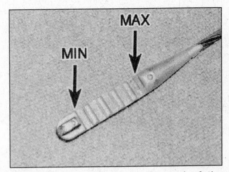

3 Note the oil level on the end of the dipstick, which should be between the upper (MAX) mark and lower (MIN) mark. Approximately 1.0 litre of oil will raise the level from the lower mark to the upper mark.

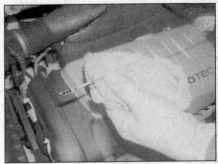

2 Using a clean rag or paper towel remove all oil from the dipstick. Insert the clean dipstick into the tube as far as it will go, then withdraw it again.

4 Oil is added through the filler cap. Rotate the cap through a quarter-turn anti-clockwise and withdraw it. Top-up the level. A funnel may help to reduce spillage. Add the oil slowly, checking the level on the dipstick often. Do not overfill.

Coolant level

 Warning: DO NOT attempt to remove the expansion tank pressure cap when the engine is hot, as there is a very great risk of scalding. Do not leave open containers of coolant about, as it is poisonous.

Car Care

● With a sealed-type cooling system, adding coolant should not be necessary on a regular basis. If frequent topping-up is required, it is likely there is a leak. Check the radiator, all hoses and joint faces for signs of staining or wetness, and rectify as necessary.

● It is important that antifreeze is used in the cooling system all year round, not just during the winter months. Don't top-up with water alone, as the antifreeze will become too diluted.

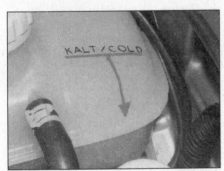

1 The coolant level varies with the temperature of the engine. When the engine is cold, the coolant level should be slightly above the KALT/COLD mark on the side of the tank. When the engine is hot, the level will rise.

2 If topping-up is necessary, **wait until the engine is cold**. Slowly unscrew the expansion tank cap, to release any pressure present in the cooling system, and remove it.

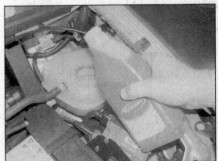

3 Add a mixture of water and antifreeze to the expansion tank until the coolant is up to the MAX level mark. Refit the cap and tighten it securely.

Tyre condition and pressure

It is very important that tyres are in good condition, and at the correct pressure - having a tyre failure at any speed is highly dangerous. Tyre wear is influenced by driving style - harsh braking and acceleration, or fast cornering, will all produce more rapid tyre wear. As a general rule, the front tyres wear out faster than the rears. Interchanging the tyres from front to rear ("rotating" the tyres) may result in more even wear. However, if this is completely effective, you may have the expense of replacing all four tyres at once!
Remove any nails or stones embedded in the tread before they penetrate the tyre to cause deflation. If removal of a nail does reveal that the tyre has been punctured, refit the nail so that its point of penetration is marked. Then immediately change the wheel, and have the tyre repaired by a tyre dealer.

Regularly check the tyres for damage in the form of cuts or bulges, especially in the sidewalls. Periodically remove the wheels, and clean any dirt or mud from the inside and outside surfaces. Examine the wheel rims for signs of rusting, corrosion or other damage. Light alloy wheels are easily damaged by "kerbing" whilst parking; steel wheels may also become dented or buckled. A new wheel is very often the only way to overcome severe damage.

New tyres should be balanced when they are fitted, but it may become necessary to re-balance them as they wear, or if the balance weights fitted to the wheel rim should fall off. Unbalanced tyres will wear more quickly, as will the steering and suspension components. Wheel imbalance is normally signified by vibration, particularly at a certain speed (typically around 50 mph). If this vibration is felt only through the steering, then it is likely that just the front wheels need balancing. If, however, the vibration is felt through the whole car, the rear wheels could be out of balance. Wheel balancing should be carried out by a tyre dealer or garage.

1 Tread Depth - visual check
The original tyres have tread wear safety bands (B), which will appear when the tread depth reaches approximately 1.6 mm. The band positions are indicated by a triangular mark on the tyre sidewall (A).

2 Tread Depth - manual check
Alternatively, tread wear can be monitored with a simple, inexpensive device known as a tread depth indicator gauge.

3 Tyre Pressure Check
Check the tyre pressures regularly with the tyres cold. Do not adjust the tyre pressures immediately after the vehicle has been used, or an inaccurate setting will result.

Tyre tread wear patterns

Shoulder Wear

Underinflation (wear on both sides)
Under-inflation will cause overheating of the tyre, because the tyre will flex too much, and the tread will not sit correctly on the road surface. This will cause a loss of grip and excessive wear, not to mention the danger of sudden tyre failure due to heat build-up.
Check and adjust pressures
Incorrect wheel camber (wear on one side)
Repair or renew suspension parts
Hard cornering
Reduce speed!

Centre Wear

Overinflation
Over-inflation will cause rapid wear of the centre part of the tyre tread, coupled with reduced grip, harsher ride, and the danger of shock damage occurring in the tyre casing.
Check and adjust pressures

If you sometimes have to inflate your car's tyres to the higher pressures specified for maximum load or sustained high speed, don't forget to reduce the pressures to normal afterwards.

Uneven Wear

Front tyres may wear unevenly as a result of wheel misalignment. Most tyre dealers and garages can check and adjust the wheel alignment (or "tracking") for a modest charge.
Incorrect camber or castor
Repair or renew suspension parts
Malfunctioning suspension
Repair or renew suspension parts
Unbalanced wheel
Balance tyres
Incorrect toe setting
Adjust front wheel alignment
Note: *The feathered edge of the tread which typifies toe wear is best checked by feel.*

Brake (and clutch) fluid level

Warning:
● *Brake fluid can harm your eyes and damage painted surfaces, so use extreme caution when handling and pouring it.*
● *Do not use fluid that has been standing open for some time, as it absorbs moisture from the air, which can cause a dangerous loss of braking effectiveness.*

● *Make sure that your car is on level ground.*
● *The fluid level in the reservoir will drop slightly as the brake pads wear down, but the fluid level must never be allowed to drop below the MIN mark.*

Safety First!
● If the reservoir requires repeated topping-up this is an indication of a fluid leak somewhere in the system, which should be investigated immediately.

● If a leak is suspected, the car should not be driven until the braking system has been checked. Never take any risks where brakes

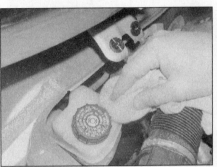

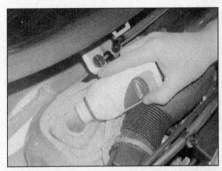

1 The MAX and MIN marks are indicated on the front of the reservoir. The fluid level must be kept between the marks at all times. **Note:** *On Zafira models, first remove the plastic water deflector from in front of the windscreen.*

2 If topping-up is necessary, first wipe clean the area around the filler cap to prevent dirt entering the hydraulic system.

3 Carefully add fluid, taking care not to spill it onto the surrounding components. Use only the specified fluid; mixing different types can cause damage to the system. After topping-up to the correct level, securely refit the cap and wipe off any spilt fluid.

Power steering fluid level

Before you start
✔ Park the vehicle on level ground.
✔ With the engine idling, turn the steering wheel slowly from lock to lock 2 or 3 times and set the front wheels at the straight-ahead position, then stop the engine.

For the check to be accurate, the steering must not be turned once the engine has been stopped.

Safety First!
● The need for frequent topping-up indicates a leak, which should be investigated immediately.

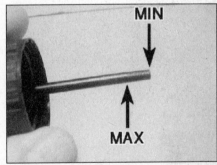

1 The power steering fluid reservoir is located on RHD vehicles on the left-hand side of the engine compartment between the transmission and the bulkhead. On LHD vehicles, the reservoir is located between the engine and bulkhead on the right-hand side of the engine compartment. The fluid level should be checked with the engine stopped. **Note:** *On Zafira models, first remove the plastic water deflector from in front of the windscreen.*

2 Unscrew the filler cap from the top of the reservoir. On TRW manufactured units, the dipstick is incorporated into the filler cap, whilst Delphi manufactured units have the dipstick incorporated into the filler immediately below the filler cap. Wipe all fluid from the dipstick with a clean rag. Refit the dipstick, then remove it again. Note the fluid level on the dipstick.

3 When the engine is cold, the fluid level should be between the upper and lower marks on the dipstick. Top up the fluid level using the specified type of fluid (do not overfill the reservoir), then refit and tighten the filler cap.

Screen washer fluid level

Screenwash additives not only keep the windscreen clean during foul weather, they also prevent the washer system freezing in cold weather – which is when you are likely to need it most. Don't top up using plain water as the screenwash will become too diluted, and will freeze during cold weather. *On no account use coolant antifreeze in the washer system – this could discolour or damage paintwork.*

1 The reservoir for the windscreen and rear window (where applicable) washer systems is located on the front left-hand side of the engine compartment. If topping-up is necessary, open the cap.

2 When topping-up the reservoir(s) a screenwash additive should be added in the quantities recommended on the bottle.

Battery

Caution: Before carrying out any work on the vehicle battery, read the precautions given in 'Safety first!' at the start of this manual.

✔ Make sure that the battery tray is in good condition, and that the clamp is tight. Corrosion on the tray, retaining clamp and the battery itself can be removed with a solution of water and baking soda. Thoroughly rinse all cleaned areas with water. Any metal parts damaged by corrosion should be covered with a zinc-based primer, then painted.

✔ Periodically (approximately every three months), check the charge condition of the battery as described in Chapter 5A.

✔ If the battery is flat, and you need to jump start your vehicle, see *Roadside Repairs*.

1 The battery is located on the left-hand side of the engine compartment. Unclip the fabric cover from the top of the battery (if fitted) for access to the terminals. The exterior of the battery should be inspected periodically for damage such as a cracked case or cover.

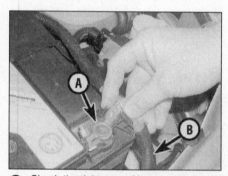

2 Check the tightness of battery clamps (A) to ensure good electrical connections. You should not be able to move them. Also check each cable (B) for cracks and frayed conductors.

HAYNES HINT

Battery corrosion can be kept to a minimum by applying a layer of petroleum jelly to the clamps and terminals after they are reconnected.

3 If corrosion (white, fluffy deposits) is evident, remove the cables from the battery terminals, clean them with a small wire brush, then refit them. Automotive stores sell a tool for cleaning the battery post . . .

4 . . . as well as the battery cable clamps

Wiper blades

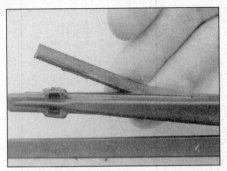

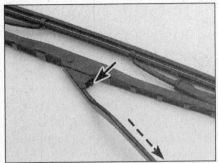

1 Check the condition of the wiper blades; if they are cracked or show any signs of deterioration, or if the glass swept area is smeared, renew them. Wiper blades should be renewed annually.

2 To remove a wiper blade, pull the arm fully away from the glass until it locks. Swivel the blade through 90°, then squeeze the locking clip, and detach the blade from the arm. When fitting the new blade, make sure that the blade locks securely into the arm, and that the blade is orientated correctly.

Electrical systems

✔ Check all external lights and the horn. Refer to the appropriate Sections of Chapter 12 for details if any of the circuits are found to be inoperative.

✔ Visually check all accessible wiring connectors, harnesses and retaining clips for security, and for signs of chafing or damage.

HAYNES HiNT *If you need to check your brake lights and indicators unaided, back up to a wall or garage door and operate the lights. The reflected light should show if they are working properly.*

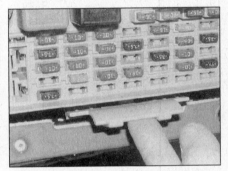

1 If a single indicator light, stop-light or headlight has failed, it is likely that a bulb has blown and will need to be renewed. Refer to Chapter 12 for details. If both stop-lights have failed, it is possible that the switch has failed (see Chapter 9).

2 If more than one indicator light or headlight has failed, it is likely that either a fuse has blown or that there is a fault in the circuit (see Chapter 12). On Zafira models, the main fuses are located beneath a cover on the driver's side of the facia between the steering column and the driver's door. Pull out and remove the cover, then pull out the bottom of the fusebox. On Astra models, the main fuses are located next to the steering column behind the storage compartment. Open the compartment, squeeze the lugs at each side, pull the compartment down to its full extent and detach it. Remove the fixing screws and remove the storage compartment frame, then pull out the bottom of the fusebox. Additional fuses and relays are located in the left-hand side of the engine compartment.

3 To renew a blown fuse, remove it, where applicable, using the plastic tool provided. Fit a new fuse of the same rating, available from car accessory shops. It is important that you find the reason that the fuse blew (see *Electrical fault finding* in Chapter 12).

Lubricants and fluids

Engine	Multigrade engine oil, viscosity SAE 5W/40, 10W/40 or 15W/40, to ACEA A3 or higher
Cooling system	
Up to Model Year 2001	'Blue' antifreeze, Vauxhall part number 90 297 545
From Model Year 2001	'Red' antifreeze, Vauxhall part number 09 194 431
Manual gearbox	Gear oil, Vauxhall part number 09 120 541
Automatic transmission	Automatic transmission oil, Vauxhall part number 09 117 946
Power steering reservoir	Special steering fluid, Vauxhall part number 90 544 116
Brake and clutch fluid reservoir	Hydraulic fluid to SAE J1703, DOT 4

Choosing your engine oil

Engines need oil, not only to lubricate moving parts and minimise wear, but also to maximise power output and to improve fuel economy.

HOW ENGINE OIL WORKS

• Beating friction

Without oil, the moving surfaces inside your engine will rub together, heat up and melt, quickly causing the engine to seize. Engine oil creates a film which separates these moving parts, preventing wear and heat build-up.

• Cooling hot-spots

Temperatures inside the engine can exceed 1000° C. The engine oil circulates and acts as a coolant, transferring heat from the hot-spots to the sump.

• Cleaning the engine internally

Good quality engine oils clean the inside of your engine, collecting and dispersing combustion deposits and controlling them until they are trapped by the oil filter or flushed out at oil change.

OIL CARE - FOLLOW THE CODE

To handle and dispose of used engine oil safely, always:

• *Avoid skin contact with used engine oil. Repeated or prolonged contact can be harmful.*
• *Dispose of used oil and empty packs in a responsible manner in an authorised disposal site. Call 0800 663366 to find the one nearest to you. Never tip oil down drains or onto the ground.*

Tyre pressures (cold)

Note: *Pressures apply to original-equipment tyres, and may vary if any other make or type of tyre is fitted; check with the tyre manufacturer or supplier for correct pressures if necessary. The pressures are given on the inside of the fuel filler flap.*

Astra	Front	Rear
All models except 2.0 and 2.2 litre engines (all tyre sizes):		
Up to 3 persons	2.2 bar (32 psi)	1.9 bar (28 psi)
Full load	2.4 bar (35 psi)	2.8 bar (41 psi)
2.0 litre engine models:		
195/60 tyres:		
Up to 3 persons	2.2 bar (32 psi)	1.9 bar (28 psi)
Full load	2.3 bar (33 psi)	2.8 bar (41 psi)
205/50 tyres:		
Up to 3 persons	2.3 bar (33 psi)	2.0 bar (29 psi)
Full load	2.5 bar (36 psi)	2.9 bar (42 psi)
2.2 litre engine models (all tyre sizes):		
Up to 3 persons	2.4 bar (35 psi)	2.1 bar (30 psi)
Full load	2.5 bar (36 psi)	2.9 bar (42 psi)
Zafira		
All tyre sizes:		
Up to 3 persons	2.2 bar (32 psi)	2.2 bar (32 psi)
Full load	2.6 bar (38 psi)	3.0 bar (44 psi)

Chapter 1
Routine maintenance and servicing

Contents

Air cleaner element renewal 22
Automatic transmission fluid level check 21
Auxiliary drivebelt check and renewal 5
Body corrosion check 9
Brake (and clutch) fluid renewal 26
Coolant renewal 28
Electrical systems check 7
Engine oil and filter renewal 4
Exhaust emission check 6
Front brake pad and disc check 10
Fuel filter renewal 23
General information 1
Handbrake adjustment check 12
Headlight beam alignment check 8
Hinge and lock lubrication 18
Hose and fluid leak check 13
Pollen filter renewal 16
Rear brake pad and disc check 11
Rear brake shoe and drum check 19
Rear suspension level control system check 15
Regular maintenance 2
Remote control battery renewal 27
Road test 17
Service indicator reset 3
Spark plug renewal and ignition system check 24
Suspension, steering and driveshaft gaiter check 20
Timing belt renewal 25
Wheel bolt tightness check 14

Degrees of difficulty

Easy, suitable for novice with little experience | **Fairly easy,** suitable for beginner with some experience | **Fairly difficult,** suitable for competent DIY mechanic | **Difficult,** suitable for experienced DIY mechanic | **Very difficult,** suitable for expert DIY or professional

Lubricants and fluids .... Refer to *Weekly checks*

Capacities

Engine oil (including filter)
1.4 and 1.6 litre engines .... 3.5 litres
1.8 and 2.0 litre engines .... 4.25 litres
2.2 litre engines .... 5.0 litres
Difference between MIN and MAX on dipstick .... 1.0 litre

Cooling system (approximate)	Without air conditioning	With air conditioning
Astra models:		
1.4 litre engines	6.3 litres	6.6 litres
1.6 litre SOHC engines	5.9 litres	6.2 litres
1.6 litre DOHC engines	6.3 litres	6.6 litres
1.8 litre engines	6.8 litres	7.0 litres
2.0 litre engines	7.0 litres	7.2 litres
2.2 litre engines	6.8 litres	7.1 litres
Zafira models:		
1.6 litre engines	6.3 litres	6.6 litres
1.8 litre engines	6.5 litres	6.8 litres
2.2 litre engines	6.8 litres	7.1 litres

Transmission
Manual transmission:
F13 and F17 transmissions .... 1.6 litres
F18 transmissions .... 1.8 litres
F23 transmissions .... 1.75 litres
Automatic transmission (at fluid change) .... 4.0 litres

Washer fluid reservoir
Without headlight washers .... 2.3 litres
With headlight washers .... 4.5 litres

Fuel tank
Astra models .... 52 litres
Zafira models .... 58 litres

Cooling system

Antifreeze mixture:
50% antifreeze .... Protection down to –37°C
55% antifreeze .... Protection down to –45°C
Note: *Refer to antifreeze manufacturer for latest recommendations.*

Ignition system

Spark plugs:	Type	Electrode gap
All except 2.2 litre engines	Bosch FLR 8 LD+U	1.0 mm
2.2 litre engines	Bosch HLR 8 STEX	1.1 mm

Brakes

Friction material minimum thickness:
Front and rear brake pads .... 2.0 mm
Rear brake shoes .... 1.0 mm

Torque wrench settings	Nm	lbf ft
Engine oil filter (spin-on canister type)	15	11
Engine oil filter housing cap (element type)	15	11
Engine oil filter housing-to-block bolt (element type)	45	33
Ignition module retaining screws	8	6
Roadwheel bolts	110	81
Spark plugs	25	18
Sump drain plug:		
SOHC engines:		
Models without air conditioning (pressed-steel sump)	55	41
Models with air conditioning (alloy sump)	45	33
DOHC engines:		
1.4, 1.6 and 1.8 litre engines:		
Inner Torx type (rubber seal ring)	14	10
Hexagon type (metal seal ring)	45	33
2.0 litre engines	10	7
2.2 litre engines	25	18

1 The maintenance intervals in this manual are provided with the assumption that you, not the dealer, will be carrying out the work. These are the minimum maintenance intervals recommended by us for vehicles driven daily. If you wish to keep your vehicle in peak condition at all times, you may wish to perform some of these procedures more often. We encourage frequent maintenance, because it enhances the efficiency, performance and resale value of your vehicle.

2 If the vehicle is driven in dusty areas, used to tow a trailer, or driven frequently at slow speeds (idling in traffic) or on short journeys, more frequent maintenance intervals are recommended.

3 When the vehicle is new, it should be serviced by a factory-authorised dealer service department, in order to preserve the factory warranty.

Note: *From Model Year 2001 the 10 000 mile (15 000 km) service interval is extended to 20 000 miles (30 000 km). The time interval remains the same at 12 months.*

Every 5000 miles (7500 km) or 6 months, whichever comes first

☐ Renew the engine oil and filter (Section 4)

Note: *Vauxhall recommend that the engine oil and filter are changed every 10 000 miles (15 000 km) or 12 months. However, oil and filter changes are good for the engine and we recommend that the oil and filter are renewed more frequently, especially if the vehicle is used on a lot of short journeys.*

Every 10 000 miles (15 000 km) or 12 months, whichever comes first

☐ Check the condition and tension of the auxiliary drivebelts (Section 5)*
☐ Exhaust emission test (Section 6)
☐ Check the operation of all electrical systems (Section 7)
☐ Check and if necessary adjust the headlight beam alignment (Section 8)*
☐ Check the body and underbody for corrosion protection (Section 9)*
☐ Check the front brake pads and discs for wear (Section 10)
☐ Check the rear brake pads and discs (where applicable) for wear (Section 11)
☐ Check and if necessary adjust the handbrake (Section 12)*
☐ Check all components, pipes and hoses for fluid leaks (Section 13)*
☐ Check the roadwheel bolts are tightened to the specified torque (Section 14)
☐ Check the rear suspension level control system (Section 15)
☐ Renew the pollen filter (Section 16)

Note: *If the vehicle is used in dusty conditions, the pollen filter should be renewed more frequently.*

☐ Carry out a road test (Section 17)

* *On vehicles covering a high mileage (more than 20 000 miles/ 30 000 km annually) carry out the items marked with an asterisk every 20 000 miles (30 000 km).*

Every 20 000 miles (30 000 km) or 2 years, whichever comes first

☐ Lubricate all door locks and hinges, door stops, bonnet lock and release, and tailgate lock and hinges (Section 18)
☐ Check the rear brake shoes and drums (where applicable) for wear (Section 19)
☐ Check the steering and suspension components for condition and security (Section 20)
☐ Check the condition of the driveshaft gaiters (Section 20)
☐ Check the automatic transmission fluid level (Section 21)

Every 40 000 miles (60 000 km) or 4 years, whichever comes first

☐ Renew the air cleaner element (Section 22)
☐ Renew the fuel filter (Section 23)
☐ Renew the spark plugs and check the ignition system (Section 24)
☐ Renew the timing belt (Section 25)

Note: *The manufacturer's timing belt renewal interval ranges from 40 000 miles (60 000 km) or 4 years, to 80 000 miles (120 000 km) or 8 years, depending on engine type and year of manufacture. We recommend that the timing belt is renewed at the 40 000 mile (60 000 km) or 4 year interval on all models and, in particular, those which are subjected to intensive use, ie, mainly short journeys or a lot of stop-start driving. The actual belt renewal interval is therefore very much up to the individual owner, but bear in mind that severe engine damage will result if the belt breaks.*

Every 2 years, regardless of mileage

☐ Renew the brake (and clutch) fluid (Section 26)
☐ Renew the remote control batteries (Section 27)
☐ Renew the coolant (Section 28)*

* *Vehicles using Vauxhall antifreeze do not need the coolant renewed on a regular basis.*

Underbonnet view of a 1.6 litre 8-valve Astra

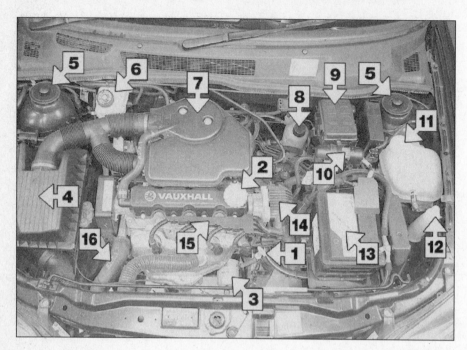

1 Engine oil level dipstick
2 Engine oil filler cap
3 Oil filter
4 Air cleaner
5 Front suspension strut upper mountings
6 Brake fluid reservoir
7 Air inlet duct
8 Electric/hydraulic power steering fluid reservoir
9 Engine related fusebox
10 Engine wiring harness connection
11 Coolant expansion tank
12 Windscreen/headlamp washer fluid reservoir
13 Battery
14 Ignition DIS module
15 HT leads to spark plugs
16 Radiator top hose

Front underbody view of a 1.6 litre 8-valve Astra

1 Oil filter
2 Engine oil drain plug
3 Manual transmission
4 Exhaust downpipe with flexible section
5 Driveshaft
6 Washer fluid reservoir
7 Subframe
8 Front suspension lower arms
9 Rear engine mounting
10 Steering gear
11 Track rod ends
12 Horns

Rear underbody view of a 1.6 litre 8-valve Astra

1 Rear exhaust silencer and tailpipe
2 Rear suspension torsion beam and trailing arms
3 Brake proportioning valve
4 Fuel tank
5 Handbrake cables
6 Spare wheel well
7 Rear coil springs
8 Rear shock absorber lower mountings

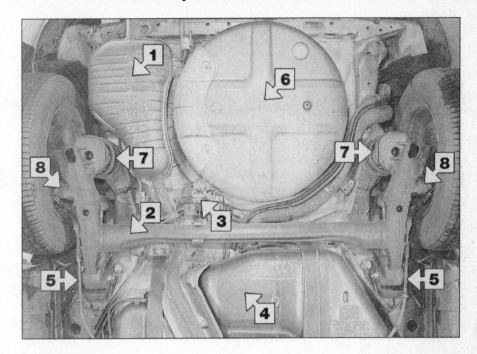

Underbonnet view of a 1.6 litre 16-valve Astra

1 Engine oil level dipstick
2 Engine oil filler cap
3 Timing belt cover
4 Air cleaner
5 Front suspension strut upper mountings
6 Brake fluid reservoir
7 Air inlet duct
8 Electric/hydraulic power steering fluid reservoir
9 Engine related fusebox
10 Engine wiring harness connection
11 Coolant expansion tank
12 Windscreen/headlamp washer fluid reservoir
13 Battery
14 Ignition module
15 Radiator top hose

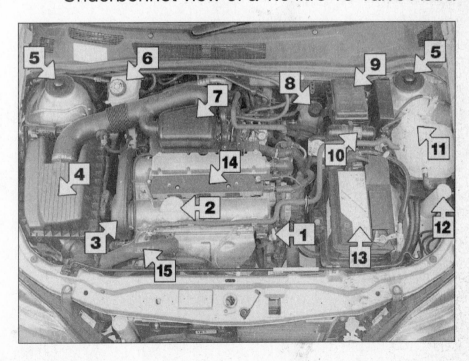

Front underbody view of a 1.6 litre 16-valve Astra

1 Oil filter
2 Engine oil drain plug
3 Manual transmission
4 Exhaust downpipe with flexible section
5 Driveshaft
6 Cooling system wiring multiplugs
7 Subframe
8 Front suspension lower arms
9 Rear engine mounting
10 Steering gear
11 Track rod ends
12 Horns

Underbonnet view of a 1.8 litre 16-valve Zafira

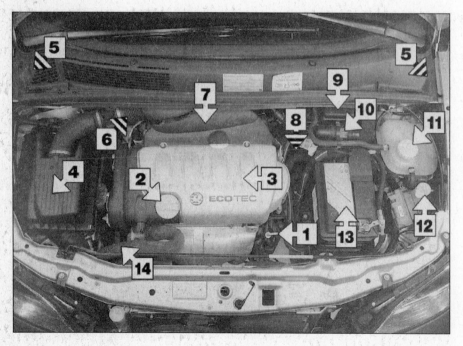

1 Engine oil level dipstick
2 Engine oil filler cap
3 Engine top cover
4 Air cleaner
5 Front suspension strut upper mountings
6 Brake fluid reservoir
7 Air inlet duct
8 Electric/hydraulic power steering fluid reservoir
9 Engine related fusebox
10 Engine wiring harness connection
11 Coolant expansion tank
12 Windscreen/headlamp washer fluid reservoir
13 Battery
14 Radiator top hose

Front underbody view of a 1.8 litre 16-valve Zafira

1 Oil filter
2 Engine oil drain plug
3 Manual transmission
4 Exhaust downpipe with flexible section
5 Driveshaft
6 Front engine mounting
7 Subframe
8 Front suspension lower arms
9 Rear engine mounting
10 Steering gear
11 Track rod ends
12 Front brake calipers

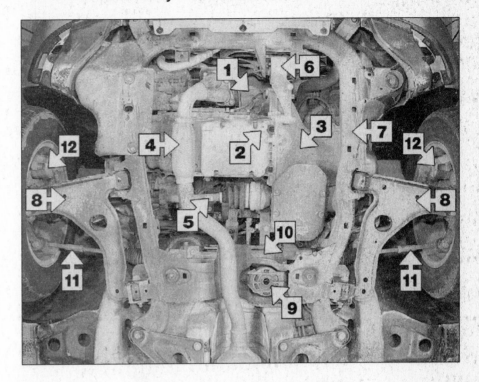

Rear underbody view of a 1.8 litre 16-valve Zafira

1 Rear exhaust silencer and tailpipe
2 Rear suspension torsion beam and trailing arms
3 Rear brake calipers
4 Fuel tank
5 Handbrake cables
6 Spare wheel and cover
7 Rear coil springs
8 Rear shock absorber lower mountings
9 Fuel tank filler and vent pipes
10 Intermediate exhaust pipe

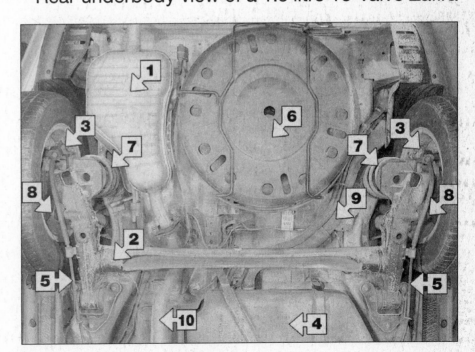

Underbonnet view of a 2.2 litre 16-valve Astra

1 Engine oil level dipstick
2 Engine oil filler cap
3 Oil filter
4 Air cleaner
5 Front suspension strut upper
  mountings
6 Brake fluid reservoir
7 Air inlet duct
8 Electric/hydraulic power steering
  fluid reservoir
9 Engine related fusebox
10 Engine wiring harness connection
11 Coolant expansion tank
12 Windscreen/headlamp washer fluid
   reservoir
13 Battery
14 Ignition module

Front underbody view of a 2.2 litre 16-valve Astra

1 Air conditioning compressor
2 Engine oil drain plug
3 Manual transmission
4 Exhaust downpipe
5 Driveshaft
6 Front engine mounting
7 Subframe
8 Front suspension lower arms
9 Rear engine mounting
10 Steering gear
11 Track rod ends
12 Front brake calipers

1 General information

1 This Chapter is designed to help the home mechanic maintain his/her vehicle for safety, economy, long life and peak performance.

2 The Chapter contains a master maintenance schedule, followed by Sections dealing specifically with each task in the schedule. Visual checks, adjustments, component renewal and other helpful items are included. Refer to the accompanying illustrations of the engine compartment and the underside of the vehicle for the locations of the various components.

3 Servicing your vehicle in accordance with the mileage/time maintenance schedule and the following Sections will provide a planned maintenance programme, which should result in a long and reliable service life. This is a comprehensive plan, so maintaining some items but not others at the specified service intervals will not produce the same results.

4 As you service your vehicle, you will discover that many of the procedures can – and should – be grouped together, because of the particular procedure being performed, or because of the proximity of two otherwise-unrelated components to one another. For example, if the vehicle is raised for any reason, the exhaust can be inspected at the same time as the suspension and steering components.

5 The first step in this maintenance programme is to prepare yourself before the actual work begins. Read through all the Sections relevant to the work to be carried out, then make a list and gather all the parts and tools required. If a problem is encountered, seek advice from a parts specialist, or a dealer service department.

2 Regular maintenance

1 If, from the time the vehicle is new, the routine maintenance schedule is followed closely, and frequent checks are made of fluid levels and high-wear items, as suggested throughout this manual, the engine will be kept in relatively good running condition, and the need for additional work will be minimised.

2 It is possible that there will be times when the engine is running poorly due to the lack of regular maintenance. This is even more likely if a used vehicle, which has not received regular and frequent maintenance checks, is purchased. In such cases, additional work may need to be carried out, outside of the regular maintenance intervals.

3 If engine wear is suspected, a compression test (refer to Chapter 2A, 2B or 2C, as applicable) will provide valuable information regarding the overall performance of the main internal components. Such a test can be used as a basis to decide on the extent of the work to be carried out. If, for example, a compression test indicates serious internal engine wear, conventional maintenance as described in this Chapter will not greatly improve the performance of the engine, and may prove a waste of time and money, unless extensive overhaul work is carried out first.

4 The following series of operations are those most often required to improve the performance of a generally poor-running engine:

Primary operations

a) Clean, inspect and test the battery (refer to *Weekly checks*).

b) Check all the engine-related fluids (refer to *Weekly checks*).

c) Check the condition and tension of the auxiliary drivebelt (Section 5).

d) Renew the spark plugs (Section 24).

e) Check the condition of the air filter, and renew if necessary (Section 22).

f) Renew the fuel filter (Section 23).

g) Check the condition of all hoses, and check for fluid leaks (Section 13).

5 If the above operations do not prove fully effective, carry out the following secondary operations:

Secondary operations

All items listed under *Primary operations*, plus the following:

a) Check the charging system (refer to Chapter 5A).

b) Check the ignition system (refer to Chapter 5B).

c) Check the fuel system (refer to Chapter 4A).

3 Service indicator reset

1 Astra & Zafira models are equipped with a Service Interval Display (SID), mounted in the lower half of the speedometer in the instrument panel. The liquid crystal display will change to INSP when a service is due within one week or 300 miles. After having carried out the required service, the SID can be reset using the following procedure.

2 With the ignition turned off, press and hold-in the odometer trip reset button.

3 Switch the ignition on. Continue to hold-in the trip reset button for at least 3 seconds.

4 The SID will flash a few times and reset. Release the button.

Every 5000 miles (7500 km) or 6 months

4 Engine oil and filter renewal

1 Frequent oil and filter changes are the most important preventative maintenance procedures which can be undertaken by the DIY owner. As engine oil ages, it becomes diluted and contaminated, which leads to premature engine wear.

2 Before starting this procedure, gather together all the necessary tools and materials. Also make sure that you have plenty of clean rags and newspapers handy, to mop up any spills. Ideally, the engine oil should be warm, as it will drain more easily, and more built-up sludge will be removed with it. Take care not to touch the exhaust or any other hot parts of the engine when working under the vehicle. To avoid any possibility of scalding, and to protect yourself from possible skin irritants and other harmful contaminants in used engine oils, it is advisable to wear gloves when carrying out this work.

3 Firmly apply the handbrake then jack up the front of the vehicle and support it on axle stands (see *Jacking and vehicle support*).

4 Remove the oil filler cap **(see illustration)**.

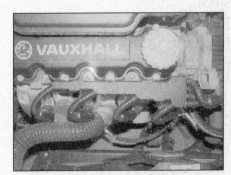

4.4 Oil filler cap – 1.6 SOHC engine

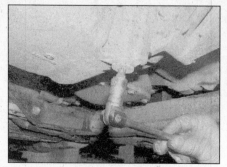

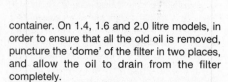

4.7 **Tighten the sump plug**

4.8 **Oil filter – 1.4 and 1.6 litre engines**

As the drain plug releases from the threads, move it away sharply so the stream of oil issuing from the sump runs into the container, not up your sleeve.

5 Using a suitable socket and bar, or Torx tool, slacken the drain plug about half a turn. Position the draining container under the drain plug, then remove the plug completely **(see Haynes Hint)**.

6 Allow some time for the oil to drain, noting that it may be necessary to reposition the container as the oil flow slows to a trickle.

7 After all the oil has drained, wipe the drain plug and the sealing washer with a clean rag. Examine the condition of the sealing washer, and renew it if it shows signs of scoring or other damage which may prevent an oil-tight seal. Clean the area around the drain plug opening, and refit the plug complete with the washer and tighten it to the specified torque **(see illustration)**.

8 Move the container into position under the oil filter. On 1.4, 1.6, 1.8 and 2.2 litre models the filter is located on the front of the cylinder block **(see illustration)**, on 2.0 litre engines it is located on the right-hand end of the rear of the engine, where it is screwed onto the oil pump housing.

9 On 1.4, 1.6 and 2.0 litre models, use an oil filter removal tool to slacken the filter initially, then unscrew it by hand the rest of the way. On 1.8 and 2.2 litre models, undo and remove the oil filter housing cap along with the filter element. Discard the O-ring **(see illustration)**. Empty the oil from the old filter into the

container. On 1.4, 1.6 and 2.0 litre models, in order to ensure that all the old oil is removed, puncture the 'dome' of the filter in two places, and allow the oil to drain from the filter completely.

10 Use a clean rag to remove all oil, dirt and sludge from the filter sealing area on the engine. On 1.8 litre models, if required, the oil filter housing can be removed from the cylinder block by unscrewing the retaining bolt. The housing can then be thoroughly cleaned and refitted to the block with a new sealing ring **(see illustration)**. Tighten the retaining bolt to the specified torque.

11 On 1.4, 1.6 and 2.0 litre models, apply a light coating of clean engine oil to the sealing ring on the new filter, then screw the filter into position on the engine. Tighten the filter firmly by hand only – **do not** use any tools. If a genuine filter is being fitted and the special oil filter tool (a socket which fits over the end of the filter) is available, tighten the filter to the specified torque. On 1.8 and 2.2 litre models, insert the new filter element into the housing cap and, using a new O-ring, screw the cap into the housing, and tighten the cap to the specified torque **(see illustration)**.

12 Remove the old oil and all tools from under the vehicle then lower the vehicle to the ground.

13 Fill the engine through the filler hole, using the correct grade and type of oil (refer to *Weekly Checks* for details of topping-up). Pour in half the specified quantity of oil first, then wait a few minutes for the oil to drain into the sump. Continue to add oil, a small

quantity at a time, until the level is up to the lower mark on the dipstick. Adding approximately a further 1.0 litre will bring the level up to the upper mark on the dipstick.

14 Start the engine and run it for a few minutes, while checking for leaks around the oil filter seal and the sump drain plug. Note that there may be a delay of a few seconds before the low oil pressure warning light goes out when the engine is first started, as the oil circulates through the new oil filter and the engine oil galleries before the pressure builds-up.

15 Stop the engine, and wait a few minutes for the oil to settle in the sump once more. With the new oil circulated and the filter now completely full, recheck the level on the dipstick, and add more oil as necessary.

16 Dispose of the used engine oil safely with reference to *General repair procedures*. It should be noted that used oil filters should not be included with domestic waste. Most local authority used oil 'banks' also have used filter disposal points alongside.

OIL CARE FOLLOW THE CODE

OIL BANK LINE
0800 66 33 66
www.oilbankline.org.uk

Note: It is antisocial and illegal to dump oil down the drain. To find the location of your local oil recycling bank, call this number free.

4.9 **Oil filter cap O-ring – 1.8 litre engine**

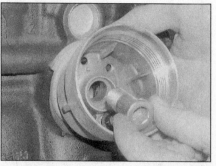

4.10 **Oil filter housing bolt – 1.8 litre engine**

4.11 **Insert the filter into the cap – 1.8 litre engine**

Every 10 000 miles (15 000 km) or 12 months

5 Auxiliary drivebelt check and renewal

Checking

1 Due to their function and material makeup, drivebelts are prone to failure after a long period of time and should therefore be inspected regularly.

2 With the engine stopped, inspect the full length of the drivebelt for cracks and separation of the belt plies. It will be necessary to turn the engine (using a spanner or socket and bar on the crankshaft pulley bolt) in order to move the belt from the pulleys so that the belt can be inspected thoroughly. Twist the belt between the pulleys so that both sides can be viewed. Also check for fraying, and glazing which gives the belt a shiny appearance. Check the pulleys for nicks, cracks, distortion and corrosion.

3 Check the position of the drivebelt tensioner assembly arm, the arm should be in between the stops on the backplate and should be free to move **(see illustrations)**.

4 Renew the belt if it shows any sign of wear or damage. If the tensioner arm is against the stop, the belt and tensioner must be renewed.

Renewal

5 Firmly apply the handbrake, then jack up the front of the car and support it securely on axle stands (see *Jacking and vehicle support*). Remove the right-hand roadwheel, and the lower wheelarch liner.

6 Remove the air cleaner housing as described in Chapter 4A.

7 Prior to removal, make a note of the correct routing of the belt around the various pulleys. If the belt is to be re-used, also mark the direction of rotation on the belt to ensure the belt is refitted the same way around.

8 Using a suitable spanner or socket fitted to

the tensioner pulley centre bolt, lever the tensioner away from the belt until there is sufficient slack to enable the belt to be slipped off the pulleys. Carefully release the tensioner pulley until it is against its stop then remove the belt from the vehicle.

9 As stated in paragraph 4, if the tensioner arm was against the stop with the belt fitted, then the tensioner and belt must be renewed. Remove and refit the tensioner as described in Chapter 5A.

10 Manoeuvre the belt into position, routing it correctly around the pulleys; if the original belt is being fitted use the marks made prior to removal to ensure it is fitted the correct way around.

11 Lever the tensioner roller back against is spring, and seat the belt on the pulleys. Ensure the belt is centrally located on all pulleys then slowly release the tensioner pulley until the belt is correctly tensioned. **Do not** allow the tensioner to spring back and stress the belt.

12 Refit the air cleaner housing as described in Chapter 4A, then refit the lower wheelarch liner and roadwheel.

6 Exhaust emission check

1 Vauxhall specify that this check should be carried out annually on vehicles which are subject to intensive use (eg, taxis/hire cars) and every 3 years on other vehicles. The check involves checking the engine management system operation by plugging an electronic tester into the system diagnostic socket to check the electronic control unit (ECU) memory for faults (see Chapter 4A, Section 7).

2 In reality, if the vehicle is running correctly and the engine management warning light in the instrument panel is functioning normally, then this check need not be carried out.

7 Electrical systems check

1 Check the operation of all electrical equipment, ie, lights, direction indicators, horn, wash/wipe system, etc. Refer to the appropriate Sections of Chapter 12 for details if any of the circuits are found to be inoperative.

2 Visually check all accessible wiring connectors, harnesses and retaining clips for security, and for signs of chafing or damage. Rectify any faults found.

8 Headlight beam alignment check

Refer to Chapter 12.

9 Body corrosion check

This work should be carried out by a Vauxhall dealer in order to validate the vehicle warranty. The work includes a thorough inspection of the vehicle paintwork and underbody for damage and corrosion.

10 Front brake pad and disc check

1 Firmly apply the handbrake, then jack up the front of the vehicle and support it securely on axle stands (see *Jacking and vehicle support*). Remove the front roadwheels.

2 For a quick check, the pad thickness can be carried out via the inspection hole on the front of the caliper **(see Haynes Hint)**. Using a

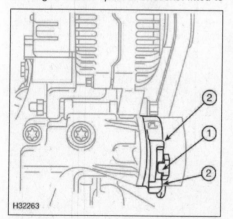

5.3a Auxiliary belt tensioner arm (1) and stops (2) – models without air conditioning

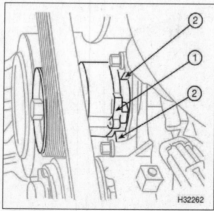

5.3b Auxiliary belt tensioner arm (1) and stops (2) – models with air conditioning

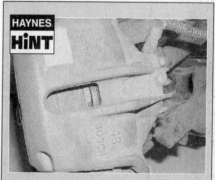

For a quick check, the thickness of friction material on each brake pad can be measured through the aperture in the caliper body.

steel rule, measure the thickness of the pad lining. This must not be less than that indicated in the Specifications.

3 The view through the caliper inspection hole gives a rough indication of the state of the brake pads. For a comprehensive check, the brake pads should be removed and cleaned. The operation of the caliper can then also be checked, and the condition of the brake disc itself can be fully examined on both sides. Chapter 9 contains a detailed description of how the brake disc should be checked for wear and/or damage.

4 If any pad's friction material is worn to the specified thickness or less, *all four pads must be renewed as a set*. Refer to Chapter 9 for details.

5 On completion, refit the roadwheels and lower the vehicle to the ground.

11 Rear brake pad and disc check

1 Chock the front wheels, then jack up the rear of the vehicle and support it securely on axle stands (see *Jacking and vehicle support*). Remove the rear roadwheels.

2 For a quick check, the pad thickness can be carried out via the inspection hole on the rear of the caliper. Using a steel rule, measure the thickness of the pad lining. This must not be less than that indicated in the Specifications.

3 The view through the caliper inspection hole gives a rough indication of the state of the brake pads. For a comprehensive check, the brake pads should be removed and cleaned. The operation of the caliper can then also be checked, and the condition of the brake disc itself can be fully examined on both sides. Chapter 9 contains a detailed description of how the brake disc should be checked for wear and/or damage.

4 If any pad's friction material is worn to the specified thickness or less, *all four pads must be renewed as a set*. Refer to Chapter 9 for details.

5 On completion, refit the roadwheels and lower the vehicle to the ground.

12 Handbrake adjustment check

Refer to Chapter 9.

13 Hose and fluid leak check

1 Visually inspect the engine joint faces, gaskets and seals for any signs of water or oil leaks. Pay particular attention to the areas around the cylinder head cover, cylinder head,

oil filter and sump joint faces. Bear in mind that, over a period of time, some very slight seepage from these areas is to be expected – what you are really looking for is any indication of a serious leak. Should a leak be found, renew the offending gasket or oil seal by referring to the appropriate Chapters in this manual.

2 Also check the security and condition of all the engine-related pipes and hoses, and all braking system pipes and hoses and fuel lines. Ensure that all cable ties or securing clips are in place, and in good condition. Clips which are broken or missing can lead to chafing of the hoses, pipes or wiring, which could cause more serious problems in the future.

3 Carefully check the radiator hoses and heater hoses along their entire length. Renew any hose which is cracked, swollen or deteriorated. Cracks will show up better if the hose is squeezed. Pay close attention to the hose clips that secure the hoses to the cooling system components. Hose clips can pinch and puncture hoses, resulting in cooling system leaks. If the crimped-type hose clips are used, it may be a good idea to replace them with standard worm-drive clips.

4 Inspect all the cooling system components (hoses, joint faces, etc) for leaks.

5 Where any problems are found on system components, renew the component or gasket with reference to Chapter 3.

6 With the vehicle raised, inspect the fuel tank and filler neck for punctures, cracks and other damage. The connection between the filler neck and tank is especially critical. Sometimes a rubber filler neck or connecting hose will leak due to loose retaining clamps or deteriorated rubber.

7 Carefully check all rubber hoses and metal fuel lines leading away from the fuel tank. Check for loose connections, deteriorated hoses, crimped lines, and other damage. Pay particular attention to the vent pipes and hoses, which often loop up around the filler neck and can become blocked or crimped. Follow the lines to the front of the vehicle, carefully inspecting them all the way. Renew damaged sections as necessary. Similarly, while the vehicle is raised, take the opportunity to inspect all underbody brake fluid pipes and hoses.

8 From within the engine compartment, check the security of all fuel, vacuum and brake hose attachments and pipe unions, and inspect all hoses for kinks, chafing and deterioration.

9 Check the condition of the power steering and, where applicable, the automatic transmission fluid pipes and hoses.

14 Wheel bolt tightness check

1 Remove the wheel trims and check the tightness of all the wheel bolts, using a torque wrench.

2 Refit the wheel trims on completion.

15 Rear suspension level control system check

Where fitted on Estate models, check that the rear suspension level control system operates correctly with reference to Chapter 10. In the event of a fault, have the system checked by a Vauxhall dealer.

16 Pollen filter renewal

1 With reference to Chapter 11, remove the passenger side glovebox and lower facia panel. Remove the passenger side footwell air duct (see Chapter 3, Section 10).

2 The pollen filter is built into the heater distribution housing. Two types of filter housing are fitted: One has the filter cover secured by two locking pins, and on the other housing the cover is secured by two bolts and two clamps. Release the clamps/pin and bolts where applicable and open the cover. Pull the filter from the housing **(see illustrations)**.

3 Fit the new filter using a reversal of the removal procedure; some filters have an arrow marking visible on the end of the filter. Make sure that this arrow points to the front of the car with the cover open.

16.2a Remove the cover . . .

16.2b . . . and pull out the pollen filter

17 Road test

Instruments and electrical equipment

1 Check the operation of all instruments and electrical equipment.
2 Make sure that all instruments read correctly, and switch on all electrical equipment in turn, to check that it functions properly.

Steering and suspension

3 Check for any abnormalities in the steering, suspension, handling or road 'feel'.
4 Drive the vehicle, and check that there are no unusual vibrations or noises.
5 Check that the steering feels positive, with no excessive 'sloppiness', or roughness, and check for any suspension noises when cornering and driving over bumps.

Drivetrain

6 Check the performance of the engine, clutch, transmission and driveshafts.

7 Listen for any unusual noises from the engine, clutch and transmission.
8 Make sure that the engine runs smoothly when idling, and that there is no hesitation when accelerating.
9 Check that, where applicable, the clutch action is smooth and progressive, that the drive is taken up smoothly, and that the pedal travel is not excessive. Also listen for any noises when the clutch pedal is depressed.
10 Check that all gears can be engaged smoothly without noise, and that the gear lever action is smooth and not abnormally vague or 'notchy'.
11 On automatic transmission models, make sure that all gearchanges occur smoothly, without snatching, and without an increase in engine speed between changes. Check that all of the gear positions can be selected with the vehicle at rest. If any problems are found, they should be referred to a Vauxhall dealer or specialist.
12 Listen for a metallic clicking sound from the front of the vehicle, as the vehicle is driven slowly in a circle with the steering on full-lock. Carry out this check in both directions. If a clicking noise is heard, this indicates wear in a driveshaft joint (see Chapter 8).

Braking system

13 Make sure that the vehicle does not pull to one side when braking, and that the wheels do not lock when braking hard.
14 Check that there is no vibration through the steering when braking.
15 Check that the handbrake operates correctly, without excessive movement of the lever, and that it holds the vehicle stationary on a slope.
16 Test the operation of the brake servo unit as follows. Depress the footbrake four or five times to exhaust the vacuum, then start the engine. As the engine starts, there should be a noticeable 'give' in the brake pedal as vacuum builds-up. Allow the engine to run for at least two minutes, and then switch it off. If the brake pedal is now depressed again, it should be possible to detect a hiss from the servo as the pedal is depressed. After about four or five applications, no further hissing should be heard, and the pedal should feel considerably harder.

Every 20 000 miles (30 000 km) or 2 years

18 Hinge and lock lubrication

1 Work around the vehicle and lubricate the hinges of the bonnet, doors and tailgate with a light machine oil.
2 Lightly lubricate the bonnet release mechanism and exposed section of inner cable with a smear of grease.
3 Check the security and operation of all hinges, latches and locks, adjusting them where required. Check the operation of the central locking system.
4 Check the condition and operation of the tailgate struts, renewing them both if either is leaking or no longer able to support the tailgate securely when raised.

19 Rear brake shoe and drum check

Refer to Chapter 9.

20 Suspension, steering and driveshaft gaiter check

Front suspension and steering

1 Raise the front of the vehicle, and securely support it on axle stands (see Jacking and vehicle support).

2 Visually inspect the balljoint dust covers and the steering rack-and-pinion gaiters for splits, chafing or deterioration. Any wear of these components will cause loss of lubricant, together with dirt and water entry, resulting in rapid deterioration of the balljoints or steering gear.
3 Check the power steering fluid hoses for chafing or deterioration, and the pipe and hose unions for fluid leaks. Also check for signs of fluid leakage under pressure from the steering gear rubber gaiters, which would indicate failed fluid seals within the steering gear.
4 Grasp the roadwheel at the 12 o'clock and 6 o'clock positions, and try to rock it (see illustration). Very slight free play may be felt, but if the movement is appreciable, further investigation is necessary to determine the source. Continue rocking the wheel while an assistant depresses the footbrake. If the movement is now eliminated or significantly reduced, it is likely that the hub bearings are at fault. If the free play is still evident with the footbrake depressed, then there is wear in the suspension joints or mountings.
5 Now grasp the wheel at the 9 o'clock and 3 o'clock positions, and try to rock it as before. Any movement felt now may again be caused by wear in the hub bearings or the steering track rod balljoints. If the outer balljoint is worn, the visual movement will be obvious. If the inner joint is suspect, it can be felt by placing a hand over the rack-and-pinion rubber gaiter and gripping the track rod. If the wheel is now rocked, movement will be felt at the inner joint if wear has taken place.

6 Using a large screwdriver or flat bar, check for wear in the suspension mounting bushes by levering between the relevant suspension component and its attachment point. Some movement is to be expected, as the mountings are made of rubber, but excessive wear should be obvious. Also check the condition of any visible rubber bushes, looking for splits, cracks or contamination of the rubber.
7 With the car standing on its wheels, have an assistant turn the steering wheel back-and-forth about an eighth of a turn each way. There should be very little, if any, lost movement between the steering wheel and roadwheels. If this is not the case, closely observe the joints and mountings previously described. In addition, check the steering column universal joints for wear, and also check the rack-and-pinion steering gear itself.

20.4 Check for wear in the hub bearings by grasping the wheel and trying to rock it

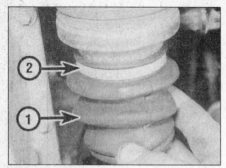

20.12 Check the condition of the driveshaft gaiters (1) and the retaining clips (2)

21.3a The automatic transmission dipstick is located between the engine and battery

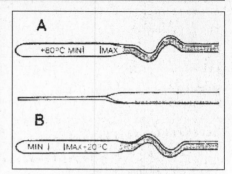

21.3b Automatic transmission dipstick fluid markings

A Markings for use when fluid is at operating temperature
B Markings for use when fluid is cold

Rear suspension

8 Chock the front wheels, then jack up the rear of the vehicle and support securely on axle stands (see Jacking and vehicle support).
9 Working as described previously for the front suspension, check the rear hub bearings, the suspension bushes and the shock absorber mountings for wear.

Shock absorber

10 Check for any signs of fluid leakage around the shock absorber body, or from the rubber gaiter around the piston rod. Should any fluid be noticed, the shock absorber is defective internally, and should be renewed. Note: Shock absorbers should always be renewed in pairs on the same axle.
11 The efficiency of the shock absorber may be checked by bouncing the vehicle at each corner. Generally speaking, the body will return to its normal position and stop after being depressed. If it rises and returns on a rebound, the shock absorber is probably suspect. Also examine the shock absorber upper and lower mountings for any signs of wear.

Driveshaft gaiter

12 With the vehicle raised and securely supported on stands, turn the steering onto full lock then slowly rotate the roadwheel. Inspect the condition of the outer constant velocity (CV) joint rubber gaiters while squeezing the gaiters to open out the folds

(see illustration). Check for signs of cracking, splits or deterioration of the rubber which may allow the grease to escape and lead to water and grit entry into the joint. Also check the security and condition of the retaining clips. Repeat these checks on the inner CV joints. If any damage or deterioration is found, the gaiters should be renewed as described in Chapter 8.
13 At the same time, check the general condition of the CV joints themselves by first holding the driveshaft and attempting to rotate the wheel. Repeat this check by holding the inner joint and attempting to rotate the driveshaft. Any appreciable movement indicates wear in the joints, wear in the driveshaft splines or loose driveshaft retaining nut.

21 Automatic transmission fluid level check

1 Park the vehicle on level ground and firmly apply the handbrake. The fluid level is checked using the dipstick which is situated on the top of the transmission unit and is positioned between the battery and engine unit.
2 Start the engine and allow it to idle for a couple of minutes with the selector lever in the P position.
3 With the engine idling, withdraw the

dipstick from the tube, and wipe all the fluid from its end with a clean rag or paper towel. Insert the clean dipstick back into the tube as far as it will go, then withdraw it once more. Note the fluid level on the end of the dipstick and ensure it is between the upper (MAX) and lower (MIN) level markings (see illustrations). If the transmission fluid is cold, use the markings on the side of the dipstick marked +20°C and if the transmission fluid is at operating temperature, use the markings on the +80°C side of the dipstick.
4 If topping-up is necessary, add the required quantity of the specified fluid to the transmission via the dipstick tube. Use a funnel with a fine mesh gauze, to avoid spillage, and to ensure that no foreign matter enters the transmission. Note: Never overfill the transmission so that the fluid level is above the relevant upper (MAX) mark.
5 After topping-up, take the vehicle on a short run to distribute the fresh fluid, then recheck the level, topping-up if necessary.
6 Always maintain the level between the two dipstick marks. If the level is allowed to fall below the lower mark, fluid starvation may result, which could lead to severe transmission damage.
7 Frequent need for topping-up indicates that there is a leak, which should be found and corrected before it becomes serious.

Every 40 000 miles (60 000 km) or 4 years

22 Air cleaner element renewal

1 The air cleaner is located in the front right-hand corner of the engine compartment.

1.4, 1.6, 1.8 and 2.0 litre engines

2 Release the securing clips, or undo the

retaining screws (as applicable) and lift the air cleaner cover sufficiently to enable removal of the filter element (see illustrations). Take care not to strain the wiring for the airflow meter/intake air temperature sensor wiring (as applicable) as the cover is lifted.
3 Lift out the filter element.
4 Wipe out the air cleaner housing and the cover. Fit the new filter, noting that the rubber locating flange should be uppermost, and secure the cover with the clips or screws.

22.2a Release the retaining clips . . .

**22.2b ... and remove the filter element –
1.4, 1.6, 1.8 and 2.0 litre engines**

**22.5a Release the fuel vapour hose clips
from the side of the air cleaner cover ...**

**22.5b ... and release the hose from the
clip at the rear of the cover**

2.2 litre engines

5 Release the fuel vapour hose support clips from the lugs on the side of the air cleaner cover, and release the hose from the clip at the rear of the cover **(see illustrations)**.

6 Slacken the retaining clip securing the air inlet trunking to the air cleaner cover **(see illustration)**.

7 Release the securing clips, or undo the retaining screws (as applicable) securing the air cleaner cover to the housing **(see illustration)**.

8 Lift the cover off the air cleaner housing and detach it from the inlet trunking **(see illustration)**.

9 Lift out the filter element then wipe out the housing and the cover **(see illustration)**. Fit the new filter, noting that the rubber locating flange should be uppermost

10 Refit the cover to the inlet trunking and air

cleaner housing and secure the cover with the securing clips or screws. Tighten the inlet trunking retaining clip and resecure the fuel vapour hose.

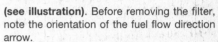

23 Fuel filter renewal

1 The fuel filter is located under the rear of the vehicle where it is clipped or screwed onto the fuel tank retaining strap.

2 Depressurise the fuel system as described in Chapter 4A.

3 Chock the front wheels, then jack up the rear of the vehicle and support on axle stands (see *Jacking and vehicle support*).

4 Release the retaining clip or undo the screw holding the filter bracket to the fuel tank strap

(see illustration). Before removing the filter, note the orientation of the fuel flow direction arrow.

5 Be prepared for fuel spillage, and take adequate fire precautions. Position a suitable container below the fuel filter, to catch spilt fuel.

6 Release the connectors and disconnect the fuel hoses from the fuel filter, noting their locations to ensure correct refitting. A Vauxhall special tool is available to disconnect the hose connectors, but provided care is taken, the connections can be released using a pair of pliers or a screwdriver.

7 Withdraw the filter from under the vehicle.

8 Fitting the new filter is a reversal of removal, bearing in mind the following points.

a) *Slide the fuel pipe connector clips from the old filter onto the new filter* **(see illustration)**.

**22.6 Slacken the clip securing the air inlet
trunking to the air cleaner cover**

**22.7 Release the clips, or undo the screws
securing the air cleaner cover to the housing**

**22.8 Lift off the air cleaner cover and
detach it from the inlet trunking**

**22.9 Lift out the filter element then wipe
out the housing and the cover**

**23.4 Undo the screw holding the filter to
the bracket**

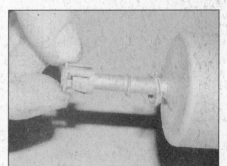

**23.8 Transfer the pipe clips from the old
filter to the new filter**

b) Ensure that the filter is fitted with the flow direction arrow on the filter body pointing in the direction of fuel flow.

c) Ensure that the hoses are reconnected to their correct locations, as noted before removal.

d) On completion, run the engine and check for leaks. If leakage is evident, stop the engine immediately and rectify the problem without delay.

24 Spark plug renewal and ignition system check

Spark plug renewal

1 The correct functioning of the spark plugs is vital for the correct running and efficiency of the engine. It is essential that the plugs fitted are appropriate for the engine; suitable types are specified at the beginning of this Chapter, or in the vehicle's Owner's Handbook. If the correct type is used and the engine is in good condition, the spark plugs should not need attention between scheduled renewal intervals. Spark plug cleaning is rarely necessary, and should not be attempted unless specialised equipment is available, as damage can easily be caused to the firing ends.

1.4, 1.6 DOHC, 1.8 and 2.2 litre engines

2 Remove the oil filler cap then undo the retaining screws and remove the cover from the top of the engine (see illustration). Refit the oil filler cap.

3 The ignition module is fitted directly above the spark plugs between the inlet and exhaust camshaft casings. Disconnect the ignition module wiring plug, undo the screws that secure the module to the cylinder head, and lift the module up and out of position. If the module proves reluctant to separate from the spark plugs, insert two long 8 mm bolts into the threaded holes in the top of the module, and pull up on the bolts to free the module from the plugs (see illustration).

24.2 Undo the retaining screws and remove the engine cover

2.0 litre engines

4 Undo the retaining screws and lift off the spark plug cover from the top of the camshaft cover (see illustration).

1.6 SOHC and 2.0 litre engines

5 If the marks on the original-equipment spark plug (HT) leads cannot be seen, mark the leads to correspond to the cylinder the lead serves. Pull the leads from the plugs by gripping the end fitting, not the lead, otherwise the lead connection may be fractured (see illustration).

All engines

6 It is advisable to remove the dirt from the spark plug recesses using a clean brush, vacuum cleaner or compressed air before removing the plugs, to prevent dirt dropping into the cylinders.

7 Unscrew the plugs from the cylinder head using a spark plug spanner, suitable box spanner or a deep socket and extension bar. Keep the socket aligned with the spark plug – if it is forcibly moved to one side, the ceramic insulator may be broken off.

8 Examination of the spark plugs will give a good indication of the condition of the engine. As each plug is removed, examine it as follows. If the insulator nose of the spark plug is clean and white, with no deposits, this is indicative of a weak mixture or too hot a plug (a hot plug transfers heat away from the

24.3 Lift the ignition module from the spark plugs

electrode slowly, a cold plug transfers heat away quickly).

9 If the tip and insulator nose are covered with hard black-looking deposits, then this is indicative that the mixture is too rich. Should the plug be black and oily, then it is likely that the engine is fairly worn, as well as the mixture being too rich.

10 If the insulator nose is covered with light tan to greyish-brown deposits, then the mixture is correct and it is likely that the engine is in good condition.

11 All engines are fitted with multi-electrode plugs as standard by Vauxhall (see illustration). On these plugs, the electrode gaps are all preset and no attempt should be made to bend the electrodes.

12 If non-standard single electrode plugs are to be installed, the spark plug electrode gap is of considerable importance. If the gap is too large or too small, the size of the spark and its efficiency will be seriously impaired and it will not perform correctly under all engine speed and load conditions. The gap should be set to the value specified by the spark plug manufacturer.

13 To set the gap, measure it with a feeler blade or spark plug gap gauge and then carefully bend the outer plug electrode until the correct gap is achieved. The centre electrode should never be bent, as this may crack the insulator and cause plug failure, if nothing worse. If using feeler blades, the gap

24.4 On 2.0 litre engines undo the retaining screws (arrowed) and remove the spark plug cover

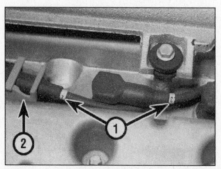

24.5 The HT leads should be numbered (1) for identification purposes. Note the HT lead removal tool (2) clipped to the cap

24.11 The multi-electrode plugs fitted as standard should not be adjusted

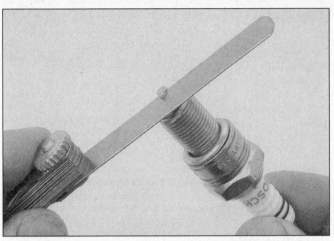

24.13a If single electrode plugs are being fitted, check the electrode gap using a feeler gauge . . .

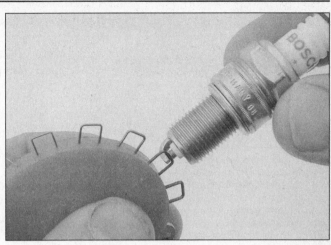

24.13b . . . or a wire gauge . . .

is correct when the appropriate-size blade is a firm sliding fit **(see illustrations)**.

14 Special spark plug electrode gap adjusting tools are available from most motor accessory shops, or from some spark plug manufacturers **(see illustration)**.

15 Before fitting the spark plugs, check that the threaded connector sleeves are tight, and that the plug exterior surfaces and threads are clean **(see Haynes Hint)**.

16 Remove the rubber hose (if used), and tighten the plug to the specified torque using the spark plug socket and a torque wrench. Refit the remaining spark plugs in the same manner **(see illustration)**.

17 Where applicable, reconnect the HT leads to their original locations, or refit the ignition module to the top of the spark plugs. Tighten the ignition module retaining screws to the specified torque.

Ignition system check

Note: *The following applies to 1.6 SOHC and 2.0 litre engines only.*

⚠️ *Warning: Voltages produced by an electronic ignition system are considerably higher than those produced by conventional ignition systems. Extreme care must be taken when working on the system with the ignition switched on. Persons with surgically-implanted cardiac pacemaker devices should keep well clear of the ignition circuits, components and test equipment.*

18 The spark plug (HT) leads should be checked whenever new spark plugs are fitted.

19 Ensure that the leads are numbered before removing them, to avoid confusion when refitting. Pull the leads from the plugs by gripping the end fitting, not the lead, otherwise the lead connection may be fractured.

20 Check inside the end fitting for signs of corrosion, which will look like a white crusty powder. Push the end fitting back onto the spark plug, ensuring that it is a tight fit on the plug. If not, remove the lead again and use pliers to carefully crimp the metal connector inside the end fitting until it fits securely on the end of the spark plug.

21 Using a clean rag, wipe the entire length of the lead to remove any built-up dirt and grease. Once the lead is clean, check for burns, cracks and other damage. Do not bend the lead excessively, nor pull the lead lengthwise – the conductor inside might break.

22 Disconnect the other end of the lead from the DIS module and check for corrosion and a tight fit in the same manner as the spark plug end. Refit the lead securely on completion.

23 Check the remaining leads one at a time, in the same way.

24 If new spark plug (HT) leads are required, purchase a set for your car and engine.

25 Even with the ignition system in first-class condition, some engines may still occasionally experience poor starting attributable to damp ignition components. To disperse moisture, a water-dispersant aerosol can be very effective.

25 Timing belt renewal

1 Refer to the information given in Chapter 2A, 2B or 2C as applicable.

24.14 . . . and if necessary adjust the gap by bending the electrode

HAYNES HINT

It is very often difficult to insert spark plugs into their holes without cross-threading them. To avoid this possibility, fit a short length of 5/16 inch internal diameter rubber hose over the end of the spark plug. The flexible hose acts as a universal joint to help align the plug with the plug hole. Should the plug begin to cross-thread, the hose will slip on the spark plug, preventing thread damage to the cylinder head.

24.16 Tighten the spark plugs to the specified torque

Every 2 years, regardless of mileage

26 Brake (and clutch) fluid renewal

⚠️ **Warning: Hydraulic fluid can harm your eyes and damage painted surfaces, so use extreme caution when handling and pouring it. Do not use fluid that has been standing open for some time, as it absorbs moisture from the air. Excess moisture can cause a dangerous loss of braking effectiveness.**

Note: *On manual transmission models, the clutch hydraulic fluid should also be renewed (See Chapter 6).*

1 The procedure is similar to that for the bleeding of the hydraulic system as described in Chapter 9.
2 Working as described in Chapter 9, open the first bleed screw in the sequence, and pump the brake pedal gently until nearly all the old fluid has been emptied from the master cylinder reservoir. Top-up to the MAX level with new fluid, and continue pumping until only the new fluid remains in the reservoir, and new fluid can be seen emerging from the bleed screw. Tighten the screw, and top the reservoir level up to the MAX level line.
3 Work through all the remaining bleed screws in the sequence until new fluid can be seen at all of them. Be careful to keep the master cylinder reservoir topped-up to above the MIN level at all times, or air may enter the system and greatly increase the length of the task.
4 When the operation is complete, check that all bleed screws are securely tightened, and that their dust caps are refitted. Wash off all traces of spilt fluid, and recheck the master cylinder reservoir fluid level.
5 Check the operation of the brakes before taking the car on the road.

27 Remote control battery renewal

Note: *The following procedure must be performed within 3 minutes, otherwise the remote control unit will have to be reprogrammed.*
1 Using a screwdriver inserted as shown prise the key section from the remote control unit. Then prise the battery cover from the remote control unit **(see illustrations)**.
2 Note how the battery is fitted, then carefully remove it from the contacts.
3 Fit the new battery and refit the cover making sure that it clips fully onto the base. Refit the key section.

28 Coolant renewal

Refer to Chapter 3.

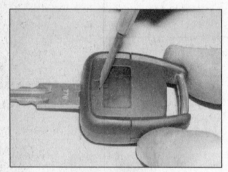

27.1a Prise the key section away . . .

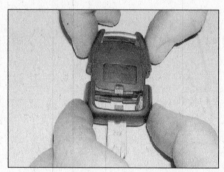

27.1b . . . from the remote control . . .

27.1c . . . and open the battery cover

Chapter 2 Part A:
1.6 litre SOHC engine in-car repair procedures

Contents

Camshaft cover – removal and refitting 4
Camshaft followers and hydraulic tappets – removal,
  inspection and refitting 11
Camshaft housing and camshaft – removal, inspection and refitting 10
Camshaft oil seal – renewal 9
Compression test – description and interpretation 2
Crankshaft oil seals – renewal 16
Crankshaft pulley – removal and refitting 5
Cylinder head – removal and refitting 12
Engine oil and filter – renewal .See Chapter 1

Engine oil level check . . . . .See Weekly checks
Engine/transmission mountings – inspection and renewal 17
Flywheel/driveplate – removal, inspection and refitting 15
General information 1
Oil pump – removal, overhaul and refitting 14
Sump – removal and refitting 13
Timing belt – removal and refitting 7
Timing belt covers – removal and refitting 6
Timing belt tensioner and sprockets – removal and refitting 8
Top dead centre (TDC) for No 1 piston – locating 3

Degrees of difficulty

Easy, suitable for novice with little experience	Fairly easy, suitable for beginner with some experience	Fairly difficult, suitable for competent DIY mechanic	Difficult, suitable for experienced DIY mechanic	Very difficult, suitable for expert DIY or professional

Specifications

General

Engine type . . . . Four-cylinder, in-line, water-cooled. Single overhead camshaft, belt-driven, acting on hydraulic tappets

Manufacturer's engine code:
Single-point injection engines X16SZR
Multi-point injection engines Z16SE
Bore . . . . 79.0 mm
Stroke . . . . 81.5 mm
Capacity . . . . 1598 cc
Firing order . . . . 1-3-4-2 (No 1 cylinder at timing belt end)
Direction of crankshaft rotation . . . . Clockwise (viewed from timing belt end of engine)
Compression ratio 9.6:1
Maximum power:
X16SZR . . . . 55 kW at 5200 rpm
Z16SE . . . . 62 kW at 5400 rpm
Maximum torque:
X16SZR . . . . 128 Nm at 2800 rpm
Z16SE . . . . 138 Nm at 2600 rpm

Compression pressures

Standard . . . . 12 to 15 bar (174 to 218 psi)
Maximum difference between any two cylinders . . . . 1 bar (15 psi)

Camshaft

Endfloat	0.09 to 0.21 mm
Maximum permissible radial run-out	0.040 mm
Cam lift:	
Inlet valve	5.61 mm
Exhaust valve	6.12 mm

Lubrication system

Oil pump type	Gear type, driven directly from crankshaft
Minimum permissible oil pressure at idle speed, with engine at operating temperature (oil temperature of at least 80°C)	1.5 bar (22 psi)
Oil pump clearances:	
Gear teeth clearance	0.08 to 0.15 mm
Gear endfloat	0.10 to 0.20 mm

Torque wrench settings

	Nm	lbf ft
Camshaft cover bolts	8	6
Camshaft sprocket bolt	45	33
Camshaft thrustplate bolts	8	6
Camshaft housing end cover bolts	8	6
Connecting rod big-end bearing cap bolt*:		
Stage 1	25	18
Stage 2	Angle-tighten a further 30°	
Coolant pump bolts	8	6
Crankshaft pulley bolt*:		
Stage 1	95	70
Stage 2	Angle-tighten a further 30°	
Stage 3	Angle-tighten a further 15°	
Crankshaft sensor mounting bracket bolt	8	6
Cylinder head bolts*:		
Stage 1	25	18
Stage 2	Angle-tighten a further 85°	
Stage 3	Angle-tighten a further 85°	
Stage 4	Angle-tighten a further 20°	
Driveplate bolts*:		
Stage 1	55	41
Stage 2	Angle-tighten a further 30°	
Stage 3	Angle-tighten a further 15°	
Driveplate cover plate	8	6
Engine/transmission mounting bolts:		
Left-hand mounting:		
Mounting bracket-to-adapter bolts	55	41
Mounting-to-bracket bolts	55	41
Mounting-to-body bolts	20	15
Bracket-to-adapter bolts	35	26
Battery support-to-body bolts	15	11
Front mounting:		
Mounting-to-transmission bolts	60	44
Mounting-to-body bolt	55	41
Rear mounting:		
Mounting-to-bracket bolts	55	41
Mounting-to-subframe bolts	55	41
Bracket-to-transmission bolts	60	44
Right-hand mounting:		
Mounting-to-bracket bolts	55	41
Mounting-to-body bolts	35	26
Bracket-to-cylinder head bolts	50	37
Engine-to-transmission unit bolts:		
M12 bolts	60	44
Flywheel bolts*:		
Stage 1	35	26
Stage 2	Angle-tighten a further 30°	
Stage 3	Angle-tighten a further 15°	
Flywheel cover plate	8	6
Front subframe bolts*		
Stage 1	90	66
Stage 2	Angle-tighten a further 45°	
Stage 3	Angle-tighten a further 15°	

Torque wrench settings (continued)

	Nm	lbf ft
Main bearing cap bolts*:		
Stage 1	50	37
Stage 2	Angle-tighten a further 45°	
Stage 3	Angle-tighten a further 15°	
Oil pressure switch	30	22
Oil pump:		
Retaining bolts	8	6
Pump cover screws	6	4
Oil pressure relief valve bolt	50	37
Oil pump pick-up/strainer bolts	8	6
Sump bolts:		
Models without air conditioning (steel sump):		
Sump-to-cylinder block/oil pump bolts	10	7
Drain plug	55	41
Models with air conditioning (alloy sump):		
Sump-to-cylinder block/oil pump bolts	10	7
Sump flange-to-transmission (M10) bolts	40	30
Drain plug	45	33
Roadwheel bolts	110	81
Timing belt cover bolts:		
Upper and lower covers	4	3
Rear cover	6	4
Timing belt tensioner bolt	20	15

Use new bolts

1 General information

How to use this Chapter

1 This Part of Chapter 2 is devoted to in-car repair procedures for the engine. All procedures concerning engine removal and refitting, and engine block/cylinder head overhaul can be found in Chapter 2D.

2 Most of the operations included in this Part are based on the assumption that the engine is still installed in the car. Therefore, if this information is being used during a complete engine overhaul, with the engine already removed, many of the steps included here will not apply.

Engine description

3 The engine is a single overhead camshaft, four-cylinder, in-line unit, mounted transversely at the front of the car, with the clutch and transmission on its left-hand end.

4 The aluminium alloy cylinder block is of the dry-liner type. The crankshaft is supported within the cylinder block on five shell-type main bearings. Thrustwashers are fitted to number 3 main bearing, to control crankshaft endfloat.

5 The connecting rods are attached to the crankshaft by horizontally split shell-type big-end bearings, and to the pistons by interference-fit gudgeon pins. The aluminium alloy pistons are of the slipper type, and are fitted with three piston rings, comprising two compression rings and a scraper-type oil control ring.

6 The camshaft runs directly in the camshaft housing, which is mounted on top of the cylinder head, and driven by the crankshaft via a toothed rubber timing belt (which also drives the coolant pump). The camshaft operates each valve via a follower. Each follower pivots on a hydraulic self-adjusting valve lifter (tappet) which automatically adjust the valve clearances.

7 Lubrication is by pressure-feed from a gear-type oil pump, which is mounted on the right-hand end of the crankshaft. It draws oil through a strainer located in the sump, and then forces it through an externally-mounted full-flow cartridge-type filter. The oil flows into galleries in the main bearing cap bridge arrangement and cylinder block/crankcase, from where it is distributed to the crankshaft (main bearings) and camshaft. The big-end bearings are supplied with oil via internal drillings in the crankshaft, while the camshaft bearings also receive a pressurised supply. The camshaft lobes and valves are lubricated by splash, as are all other engine components.

8 A semi-closed crankcase ventilation system is employed; crankcase fumes are drawn from the cylinder head cover, and passed via a hose to the inlet manifold.

Operations with engine in car

9 The following operations can be carried out without having to remove the engine from the vehicle:

a) *Removal and refitting of the cylinder head.*
b) *Removal and refitting of the timing belt and sprockets.*
c) *Renewal of the camshaft oil seal.*
d) *Removal and refitting of the camshaft housing and camshaft.*
e) *Removal and refitting of the sump.*
f) *Removal and refitting of the connecting rods and pistons*.*
g) *Removal and refitting of the oil pump.*
h) *Renewal of the crankshaft oil seals.*
i) *Renewal of the engine mountings.*
j) *Removal and refitting of the flywheel/driveplate.*

* Although the operation marked with an asterisk can be carried out with the engine in the car after removal of the sump, it is better for the engine to be removed, in the interests of cleanliness and improved access. For this reason, the procedure is described in Chapter 2D.

2 Compression test – description and interpretation

1 When engine performance is down, or if misfiring occurs which cannot be attributed to the ignition or fuel systems, a compression test can provide diagnostic clues as to the engine's condition. If the test is performed regularly, it can give warning of trouble before any other symptoms become apparent.

2 The engine must be fully warmed-up to normal operating temperature, the battery must be fully-charged, and the spark plugs must be removed (see Chapter 1). The aid of an assistant will also be required.

3 Disable the ignition system by disconnecting the wiring connector from the ignition module (see Chapter 5B) and the fuel system by removing the fuel pump relay from

2.4 Compression tester fitted to No 1 spark plug hole

3.5a Align the camshaft sprocket timing mark with the cut-out on the timing belt cover . . .

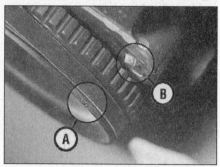

3.5b . . . and align the crankshaft pulley notch (A) with the timing mark pointer (B) to position No 1 piston at TDC on its compression stroke

the engine compartment relay box (see Chapter 4A).

4 Fit a compression tester to the number 1 cylinder spark plug hole. The type of tester which screws into the plug thread is to be preferred **(see illustration)**.

5 Have the assistant hold the throttle wide open and crank the engine on the starter motor; after one or two revolutions, the compression pressure should build-up to a maximum figure, and then stabilise. Record the highest reading obtained.

6 Repeat the test on the remaining cylinders, recording the pressure in each.

7 All cylinders should produce very similar pressures; any difference greater than that specified indicates the existence of a fault. Note that the compression should build-up quickly in a healthy engine. Low compression on the first stroke, followed by gradually-increasing pressure on successive strokes, indicates worn piston rings. A low compression reading on the first stroke, which does not build-up during successive strokes, indicates leaking valves or a blown head gasket (a cracked head could also be the cause). Deposits on the undersides of the valve heads can also cause low compression.

8 If the pressure in any cylinder is the specified minimum or less, carry out the following test to isolate the cause. Introduce a teaspoonful of clean oil into that cylinder through its spark plug hole, and repeat the test.

9 If the addition of oil temporarily improves the compression pressure, this indicates that bore or piston wear is responsible for the pressure loss. No improvement suggests that leaking or burnt valves, or a blown head gasket, may be to blame.

10 A low reading from two adjacent cylinders is almost certainly due to the head gasket having blown between them; the presence of coolant in the engine oil will confirm this.

11 If one cylinder is about 20 per cent lower than the others, and the engine has a slightly rough idle, a worn camshaft lobe could be the cause.

12 If the compression reading is unusually high, the combustion chambers are probably coated with carbon deposits. If this is the case, the cylinder head should be removed and decarbonised.

13 On completion of the test, refit the spark plugs (see Chapter 1), refit the fuel pump relay and reconnect the wiring connector to the ignition module.

3 Top dead centre (TDC) for No 1 piston – locating

1 In its travel up and down its cylinder bore, Top Dead Centre (TDC) is the highest point that each piston reaches as the crankshaft rotates. While each piston reaches TDC both

at the top of the compression stroke, and again at the top of the exhaust stroke, for the purpose of timing the engine TDC refers to the piston position (usually number 1) at the top of its compression stroke.

2 Number 1 piston (and cylinder) is at the right-hand (timing belt) end of the engine, and its TDC position is located as follows. Note that the crankshaft rotates clockwise when viewed from the right-hand side of the car.

3 Disconnect the battery negative terminal (refer to *Disconnecting the battery* in the Reference Chapter). If necessary, remove all the spark plugs as described in Chapter 1 to enable the engine to be easily turned over.

4 To gain access to the camshaft sprocket timing mark, remove the timing belt upper cover as described in Section 6.

5 Using a socket and extension bar on the crankshaft pulley bolt, turn the crankshaft whilst keeping an eye on the camshaft sprocket. Rotate the crankshaft until the timing mark on the camshaft sprocket is correctly aligned with the cut-out on the top of the timing belt rear cover and the notch on the crankshaft pulley rim is correctly aligned with the pointer on the timing belt lower cover **(see illustrations)**.

6 With the crankshaft pulley and camshaft sprocket timing marks positioned as described, the engine is positioned with No 1 piston at TDC on its compression stroke.

4 Camshaft cover – removal and refitting

Removal

1 On single-point injection engines, remove the air inlet cover from the top of the throttle body, as described in Chapter 4A.

2 Release the retaining clips and disconnect the breather hoses from the camshaft cover **(see illustrations)**.

3 Slacken and remove the retaining bolts, noting the correct fitted location of any clips or brackets retained by the bolts then lift the camshaft cover from the camshaft housing

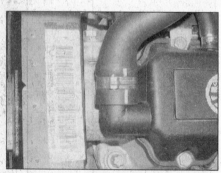

4.2a Slacken the retaining clips and disconnect the large . . .

4.2b . . . and small breather pipes from the rear of the camshaft cover

(see illustration). If the cover is stuck, do not lever between the cover and camshaft housing mating surfaces – if necessary, gently tap the cover sideways to free it. Recover the gasket; if it shows signs of damage or deterioration it must be renewed.

Refitting

4 Prior to refitting, examine the inside of the cover for a build-up of oil sludge or any other contamination, and if necessary clean the cover with paraffin, or a water-soluble solvent. Examine the condition of the crankcase ventilation filter inside the camshaft cover, and clean as described for the inside of the cover if clogging is evident (if desired, the filter can be removed from the cover, after removing the securing bolts). Dry the cover thoroughly before refitting.

5 Ensure the cover is clean and dry and seat the gasket in the cover recess then refit the cover to the camshaft housing, ensuring the gasket remains correctly seated **(see illustration)**.

6 Refit the retaining bolts, ensuring all relevant clips/brackets are correctly positioned, and tighten them to the specified torque working in a diagonal sequence.

7 Reconnect the breather hoses securely to the camshaft cover, and refit the air inlet cover (where applicable).

4.3 Removing the camshaft cover from the engine

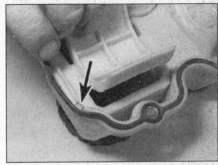

4.5 Ensure the gasket is correctly located in the camshaft cover recess (arrowed)

| 5 | Crankshaft pulley – removal and refitting | 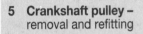 |

Note: *A new pulley retaining bolt will be required on refitting.*

Removal

1 Firmly apply the handbrake, then jack up the front of the car and support it securely on axle stands (see *Jacking and vehicle support*). Remove the right-hand roadwheel.

2 Remove the auxiliary drivebelt as described in Chapter 1. Prior to removal, mark the direction of rotation on the belt to ensure the belt is refitted the same way around.

3 Slacken the crankshaft pulley retaining bolt. To prevent crankshaft rotation on manual transmission models, have an assistant select

top gear and apply the brakes firmly. On automatic transmission models prevent rotation by removing one of the torque converter retaining bolts and bolting the driveplate to the transmission housing using a metal bar, spacers and suitable bolts. If the engine is removed from the vehicle it will be necessary to lock the flywheel/driveplate (see Section 15).

4 Unscrew the retaining bolt and washer and remove the crankshaft pulley from the end of the crankshaft, taking care not to damage the crankshaft sensor.

Refitting

5 Refit the crankshaft pulley, aligning the pulley cut-out with the raised notch on the timing belt sprocket, then fit the washer and new retaining bolt **(see illustration)**.

6 Lock the crankshaft by the method used on removal, and tighten the pulley retaining bolt to the specified Stage 1 torque setting then angle-tighten the bolt through the specified Stage 2 angle, using a socket and extension bar, and finally through the specified Stage 3 angle. It is recommended that an angle-measuring gauge is used during the final stages of the tightening, to ensure accuracy **(see illustration)**. If a gauge is not available, use white paint to make alignment marks between the bolt head and pulley prior to tightening; the marks can then be used to check that the bolt has been rotated through the correct angle.

7 If necessary, remove the metal bar securing the driveplate to the transmission housing.

Refit the auxiliary drivebelt as described in Chapter 1 using the mark made prior to removal to ensure the belt is fitted the correct way around.

8 Refit the roadwheel then lower the car to the ground and tighten the wheel bolts to the specified torque.

| 6 | Timing belt covers – removal and refitting | |

Upper cover

Removal

1 Remove the air cleaner housing as described in Chapter 4A.

2 Undo the retaining bolts then unclip the timing belt upper cover and remove it from the engine **(see illustration)**.

Refitting

3 Refitting is the reverse of removal. Tighten the cover retaining bolts to the specified torque.

Lower cover

Removal

4 Remove the crankshaft pulley (see Section 5).

5 With reference to Chapter 5A, remove the alternator (auxiliary) drivebelt tensioner.

6 Remove the upper cover (see paragraphs 1 and 2) then undo the retaining screws and

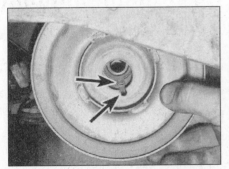

5.5 Refit the crankshaft pulley aligning the cut-out with the raised notch on the crankshaft sprocket (arrowed)

5.6 Fit the new retaining bolt and tighten it as described in the text

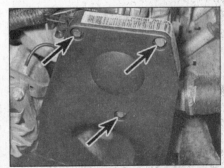

6.2 Timing belt upper cover retaining bolts (arrowed)

remove the lower cover from the engine (see illustration).

Refitting

7 Refitting is the reverse of removal, using a new crankshaft pulley retaining bolt. Tighten all bolts to the specified torques.

Rear cover

Removal

8 Remove the camshaft and crankshaft timing belt sprockets and the timing belt tensioner as described in Section 8.
9 Support the weight of the engine using a trolley jack with a block of wood placed on its head.
10 Remove the three bolts securing the right-hand engine mounting bracket to the cylinder block.
11 Undo the bolts securing the mounting to the body, and withdraw the bracket with the mounting.
12 Note the cable routing, and unclip the crankshaft position sensor cable from the rear cover.
13 Slacken and remove the bolts securing the rear cover to the camshaft housing and oil pump housing, and remove the cover from the engine (see illustration).

Refitting

14 Refitting is the reverse of removal, tightening the cover retaining bolts and engine mounting bolts to the specified torque.

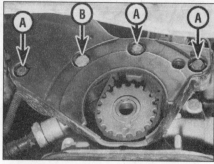

6.6 Timing belt lower cover retaining bolts (A) and timing belt tensioner bolt (B)

7 Timing belt –
removal and refitting

Note: The timing belt must be removed and refitted with the engine cold.

Removal

1 Remove the timing belt upper cover as described in Section 6.
2 Position No 1 cylinder at TDC on its compression stroke as described in Section 3.
3 Remove the crankshaft pulley as described in Section 5.
4 Support the weight of the engine using a trolley jack with a block of wood placed on its head.

6.13 Slacken and remove the retaining bolts and remove the timing belt rear cover

5 Remove the three bolts securing the right-hand engine mounting to the bracket on the cylinder block.
6 Undo the bolts securing the mounting to the body, and withdraw the mounting.
7 Unbolt the timing belt lower cover and remove it from the engine (see Section 6).
8 Insert a suitable tool (such as a pin punch) into the hole in the timing belt tensioner arm, then lever the arm clockwise to its stop, and lock it in position by inserting the tool into the corresponding hole in the tensioner backplate (see illustrations). Leave the tool in position to lock the tensioner in position until the belt is refitted.
9 Check the camshaft and crankshaft sprocket timing marks are correctly aligned with the marks on the belt rear cover and oil pump housing.
10 Slacken the coolant pump retaining bolts then, using an open-ended spanner, carefully rotate the pump to relieve the tension in the timing belt. Adapters to fit the pump are available from most tool shops and allow the pump to be easily turned using a ratchet or extension bar (see illustrations).
11 Slide the timing belt off its sprockets and remove it from the engine (see illustration). If the belt is to be re-used, use white paint or similar to mark the direction of rotation on the belt. **Do not** rotate the crankshaft until the timing belt has been refitted.
12 Check the timing belt carefully for any signs of uneven wear, splitting or oil contamination, and renew it if there is the slightest doubt about its condition. If the

7.8a Insert a tool (such as a punch) into the hole (arrowed) in the tensioner arm . . .

7.8b . . . then lever the arm clockwise and lock the tensioner in the position by locating the tool in the backplate hole

7.10a Slacken the coolant pump bolts . . .

7.10b . . . and relieve the timing belt tension by rotating the pump with a suitable adapter

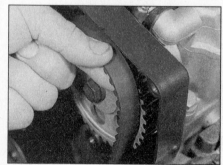

7.11 Slip the timing belt from the sprockets and remove it from the engine

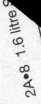
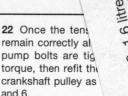
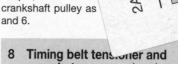
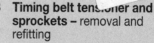

7.13 Ensure the timing mark on the crankshaft sprocket is correctly aligned with the mark on the oil pump housing

engine is undergoing an overhaul and the vehicle is approaching 40 000 miles (see Chapter 1) renew the belt as a matter of course, regardless of its apparent condition. If signs of oil contamination are found, trace the source of the oil leak and rectify it, then wash down the engine timing belt area and all related components to remove all traces of oil.

Refitting

13 On reassembly, thoroughly clean the timing belt sprockets then check that the camshaft sprocket timing mark is still correctly aligned with the cover cut-out and the crankshaft sprocket mark is still aligned with the mark on the oil pump housing **(see illustration)**.
14 Fit the timing belt over the crankshaft and camshaft sprockets, ensuring that the belt front run is taut (ie, all slack is on the tensioner pulley side of the belt), then fit the belt over the coolant pump sprocket and tensioner pulley. Do not twist the belt sharply while refitting it. Ensure that the belt teeth are correctly seated centrally in the sprockets, and that the timing marks remain in alignment. If a used belt is being refitted, ensure that the arrow mark made on removal points in the normal direction of rotation, as before.
15 Carefully remove the punch from the timing belt tensioner to release the tensioner spring.
16 Refit the engine mounting to the body and cylinder head bracket, tightening the securing bolts to the specified torque.

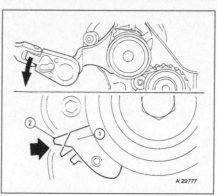

7.20 Rotate the coolant pump until the tensioner arm pointer (1) is correctly aligned with the cut-out (2) on the backplate

17 Check the sprocket timing marks are still correctly aligned. If adjustment is necessary, lock the tensioner in position again then disengage the belt from the sprockets and make any necessary adjustments.
18 If the marks are still correctly positioned, tension the timing belt by rotating the coolant pump whilst observing the movement of the tensioner arm. Position the pump so that the tensioner arm is fully over against its stop, without exerting any excess strain on the belt, then tighten the coolant pump retaining bolts.
19 Temporarily refit the crankshaft pulley bolt then rotate the crankshaft smoothly through two complete turns (720°) in the normal direction of rotation to settle the timing belt in position.
20 Check that both the camshaft and crankshaft sprocket timing marks are realigned then slacken the coolant pump bolts. Adjust the pump so that the tensioner arm pointer is aligned with the cut-out on the backplate then tighten the coolant pump bolts to the specified torque **(see illustration)**. Rotate the crankshaft smoothly through another two complete turns in the normal direction of rotation, to bring the sprocket timing marks back into alignment. Check that the tensioner arm pointer is still aligned with the backplate cut-out.
21 If the tensioner arm is not correctly aligned with the backplate, repeat the procedure.

22 Once the ten... remain correctly al... pump bolts are tig... torque, then refit th... crankshaft pulley as... and 6.

8 Timing belt tensioner and sprockets – removal and refitting

Camshaft sprocket

Removal

1 Remove the timing belt as described in Section 7.
2 The camshaft must be prevented from turning as the sprocket bolt is unscrewed, and this can be achieved in one of two ways as follows.
a) *Make up a sprocket-holding tool using two lengths of steel strip (one long, the other short), and three nuts and bolts; one nut and bolt forms the pivot of a forked tool, with the remaining two nuts and bolts at the tips of the 'forks' to engage with the sprocket spokes (see illustration).*
b) *Remove the camshaft cover as described in Section 4 and hold the camshaft with an open-ended spanner on the flats provided.*
3 Unscrew the retaining bolt and washer and remove the sprocket from the end of the camshaft.

Refitting

4 Prior to refitting check the oil seal for signs of damage or leakage, if necessary, renewing it as described in Section 9.
5 Refit the sprocket to the end of the camshaft, aligning its cut-out with the camshaft locating pin, then refit the retaining bolt and washer **(see illustration)**.
6 Tighten the sprocket retaining bolt to the specified torque whilst preventing rotation using the method employed on removal **(see illustration)**.
7 Refit the timing belt as described in Section 7 then (where necessary) refit the camshaft cover as described in Section 4.

8.2 Using a home-made sprocket holding tool to retain the camshaft whilst the bolt is slackened

8.5 Refit the camshaft sprocket making sure the locating pin (1) engages with the sprocket hole (2)

8.6 Using an open-ended spanner to retain the camshaft whilst the sprocket retaining bolt is tightened to the specified torque

8.11 Refit the crankshaft sprocket making sure its timing marks are facing outwards

8.14 Slacken and remove the retaining bolt and remove the timing belt tensioner assembly

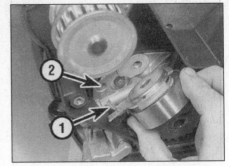

8.15 On refitting, ensure the tensioner backplate lug (1) is correctly located in the oil pump housing hole (2)

Crankshaft sprocket

Removal

8 Remove the timing belt (see Section 7).
9 Slide the sprocket off the end of the crankshaft, noting which way around it is fitted.

Refitting

10 Ensure the Woodruff key is correctly fitted to the crankshaft.
11 Align the sprocket with the crankshaft groove then slide the sprocket into position, making sure its timing mark is facing outwards **(see illustration)**.
12 Refit the timing belt (see Section 7).

Tensioner assembly

Removal

13 Remove the timing belt (see Section 7).
14 Slacken and remove the retaining bolt and remove the tensioner assembly from the oil pump **(see illustration)**.

Refitting

15 Fit the tensioner to the oil pump housing, making sure that the lug on the backplate is correctly located in the oil pump housing hole **(see illustration)**. Ensure the tensioner is correctly seated then refit the retaining bolt and tighten it to the specified torque.

9 Camshaft oil seal – renewal

1 Remove the camshaft sprocket as described in Section 8.
2 Carefully punch or drill two small holes opposite each other in the oil seal. Screw a self-tapping screw into each, and pull on the screws with pliers to extract the seal **(see illustration)**.
3 Clean the seal housing, and polish off any burrs or raised edges which may have caused the seal to fail in the first place.
4 Lubricate the lips of the new seal with clean engine oil, and press it into position using a suitable tubular drift (such as a socket) which bears only on the hard outer edge of the seal

(see illustration). Take care not to damage the seal lips during fitting; note that the seal lips should face inwards.
5 Refit the camshaft sprocket as described in Section 8.

10 Camshaft housing and camshaft – removal, inspection and refitting

Removal

Using Vauxhall tool MKM 891

Caution: Prior to fitting the special tool, rotate the crankshaft clockwise 90° past the TDC position (see Section 3). This will position the pistons approximately mid-way in the bores and prevent the valves contacting them when the tool is fitted.
1 If access to the special service tool can be gained, the camshaft can be removed from the engine without disturbing the camshaft housing. The tool is fitted to the top of the camshaft housing, once the cover has been removed (see Section 4), and depresses the cam followers. This allows the camshaft to be withdrawn from the left-hand end of the housing once the timing belt sprocket has been removed (see Section 8) and the cover and thrustplate have been unbolted (see paragraphs 3 to 5).

Without Vauxhall tool

2 Assuming that such a tool is not available,

the camshaft can only be removed once the camshaft housing has been removed from the engine. Since the camshaft housing is secured in position by the cylinder head bolts, it is not possible to remove the camshaft without removing the cylinder head (see Section 12).
Note: *In theory it is possible to remove the camshaft housing once the cylinder head bolts have been removed, and leave the head in position. However, this procedure carries a high risk of disturbing the head gasket, resulting in the head gasket 'blowing' once the camshaft and housing are refitted. If you wish to attempt this, remove the camshaft housing, as described in Section 12, noting that it will not be necessary to remove the manifolds, etc. Be warned though that, after refitting, you may find the head gasket will need renewing, meaning that the cylinder head will have to be removed after all and need another set of bolts. The decision is yours as to whether this is a chance worth taking.*
3 With the camshaft housing removed, unbolt the ignition module and remove it from the end of the housing.
4 Undo the retaining bolts and remove the end cover from the left-hand end of the housing **(see illustration)**. Remove the sealing ring from the cover and discard it, a new one should be used on refitting.
5 Measure the camshaft endfloat by inserting feeler gauges between the thrustplate and the camshaft; if the endfloat is not within the limits given in the Specifications then the thrustplate will need to be renewed. Unscrew the two

9.2 Removing the camshaft oil seal

9.4 Fitting a new camshaft oil seal

10.4 Remove the cover from the left-hand end of the camshaft housing (sealing ring arrowed)

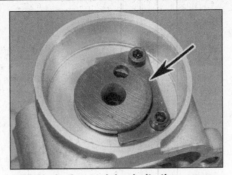

10.5 Undo the retaining bolts then remove the thrustplate (arrowed) . . .

10.6 . . . and slide the camshaft out from the housing

retaining bolts then slide out the camshaft thrustplate, noting which way round it is fitted **(see illustration)**.

6 Carefully withdraw the camshaft from the left-hand end of the housing, taking care not to damage the bearing journals **(see illustration)**.

Inspection

7 With the camshaft removed, examine the bearings in the camshaft housing for signs of obvious wear or pitting. If evident, a new camshaft housing will probably be required. Also check that the oil supply holes in the camshaft housing are free from obstructions.

8 The camshaft itself should show no marks or scoring on the journal or cam lobe surfaces. If evident, renew the camshaft. If the camshaft lobes show signs of wear also examine the followers (see Section 11).

9 Check the camshaft thrustplate for signs of wear or grooves, and renew if necessary.

Refitting

10 Carefully prise the old seal out of from the camshaft housing, using a suitable screwdriver. Ensure the housing is clean then press the in new seal, ensuring its sealing lip is facing inwards, until it is flush with the housing.

11 Liberally lubricate the camshaft and housing bearings and the oil seal lip with fresh engine oil.

12 Carefully insert the camshaft into the housing, taking care not to mark the bearing surfaces or damage the oil seal lip.

13 Slide the thrustplate into position, engaging it with the camshaft slot, and tighten its

retaining bolts to the specified torque. Check the camshaft endfloat (see paragraph 5).

14 Fit a new sealing ring to the end cover recess then refit the cover to the camshaft housing and tighten its retaining bolts to the specified torque. Refit the ignition module to the housing cover.

15 If work is being carried out using the special service tool, remove the tool and refit the camshaft sprocket. Return the crankshaft to TDC and refit the timing belt (see Sections 7 and 8).

16 If the tool is not being used, refit the camshaft housing as described in Section 12.

11 Camshaft followers and hydraulic tappets – removal, inspection and refitting

Using Vauxhall tool KM-565

Removal

1 If access to the special tool (KM-565) or a suitable equivalent can be gained, the cam followers and tappets can be removed as follows, without disturbing the camshaft.

2 Firmly apply the handbrake then jack up the front of the vehicle and support it on axle stands. Remove the right-hand front roadwheel.

3 Remove the camshaft cover (see Section 4).

4 Using a socket and extension bar, rotate the crankshaft in the normal direction of rotation until the camshaft lobe of the first follower/tappet to be removed is pointing straight upwards.

5 Fit the service tool to the top of the

camshaft housing, making sure the tool end is correctly engaged with the top of the valve. Screw the tool stud into one of the housing bolt holes until the valve is sufficiently depressed to allow the follower to be slid out from underneath the camshaft. The hydraulic tappet can then also be removed, as can the thrust pad from the top of the valve. Inspect the components (see paragraphs 10 and 11) and renew if worn or damaged.

Refitting

6 Lubricate the tappet and follower with fresh engine oil then slide the tappet into its bore in the cylinder head. Manoeuvre the follower into position, ensuring it is correctly engaged with the tappet and valve stem, then carefully remove the service tool.

7 Repeat the operation on the remaining followers and tappets.

Without Vauxhall tool

Removal

8 Without the use of the special tool, it will be necessary to remove the camshaft housing to allow the followers and tappets to be removed (see Section 10, paragraph 2).

9 With the housing removed, obtain eight small, clean plastic containers, and number them 1 to 8; alternatively, divide a larger container into eight compartments. Lift out each follower, thrust pad and hydraulic tappet in turn, and place them in their respective container. Do not interchange the cam followers, or the rate of wear will be much-increased **(see illustrations)**.

11.9a Remove each follower . . .

11.9b . . . thrust pad . . .

11.9c . . . and hydraulic tappet from the cylinder head

Inspection

10 Examine the cam follower bearing surfaces which contact the camshaft lobes for wear ridges and scoring. Renew any follower on which these conditions are apparent. If a follower bearing surface is badly scored, also examine the corresponding lobe on the camshaft for wear, as it is likely that both will be worn. Also check the thrust pad for signs of wear or damage. Renew worn components as necessary.

11 If the hydraulic tappets are thought to be faulty they should be renewed; testing of the tappets is not possible.

Refitting

12 Lubricate the hydraulic tappets and their cylinder head bores with clean engine oil. Refit the tappets to the cylinder head, making sure they are fitted in their original locations.

13 Fit the thrust pads to the top of its respective valves.

14 Lubricate the followers with clean engine oil. Fit each follower, making sure it is correctly located with both the tappet and thrust pad, then refit the camshaft housing (see Section 12).

---

12 Cylinder head – removal and refitting

Note: *The engine must be cold when removing the cylinder head. New cylinder head bolts must be used on refitting.*

Removal

1 Depressurise the fuel system as described in Chapter 4A, then disconnect the battery negative terminal (refer to *Disconnecting the battery* in the Reference Chapter).

2 Drain the cooling system as described in Chapter 3, and remove the spark plugs as described in Chapter 1.

3 Remove the timing belt as described in Section 7.

4 Unscrew the retaining bolts, and remove the engine mounting bracket from the right-hand end of the cylinder head.

5 Remove the inlet and exhaust manifolds as described in Chapter 4A. If no work is to be carried out on the cylinder head, the head can be removed complete with manifolds once the following operations have been carried out.
  a) *Disconnect the various wiring connectors from the throttle body and manifold.*
  b) *Disconnect the fuel hoses from the throttle body and the various vacuum and coolant hoses from the inlet manifold.*
  c) *Unbolt the inlet manifold support bracket and the alternator upper bracket.*
  d) *Disconnect the accelerator cable (where fitted).*
  e) *Unbolt the exhaust front pipe from manifold and disconnect the oxygen sensor wiring connector.*

6 Remove the camshaft cover as described in Section 4.

7 Remove the camshaft sprocket as described in Section 8.

8 Undo the retaining bolts securing the timing belt rear cover to the camshaft housing.

9 Disconnect the wiring connectors from the ignition module, purge valve and the coolant temperature sender unit on the left-hand end of the cylinder head. Remove the cable guide from the camshaft cover, and position it clear of the cylinder head.

10 Slacken the retaining clip and disconnect the coolant hose from the thermostat housing.

11 Make a final check to ensure that all relevant hoses, pipes and wires, etc, have been disconnected.

12 Working in the **reverse** of the tightening sequence **(see illustration 12.30a)**, progressively slacken the cylinder head bolts by a third of a turn at a time until all bolts can be unscrewed by hand. Remove each bolt in turn, along with its washer.

13 Lift the camshaft housing from the cylinder head **(see illustration)**. If necessary, tap the housing gently with a soft-faced mallet to free it from the cylinder head, but **do not** lever at

the mating faces. Note the fitted positions of the two locating dowels, and remove them for safe-keeping if they are loose.

14 Lift the cylinder head from the cylinder block, taking care not to dislodge the cam followers or thrust pads **(see illustration)**. If necessary, tap the cylinder head gently with a soft-faced mallet to free it from the block, but **do not** lever at the mating faces. Note the fitted positions of the two locating dowels, and remove them for safe-keeping if they are loose.

15 Recover the cylinder head gasket, and discard it.

Preparation for refitting

16 The mating faces of the cylinder head and block must be perfectly clean before refitting the head. Use a scraper to remove all traces of gasket and carbon, and also clean the tops of the pistons. Take particular care with the aluminium surfaces, as the soft metal is damaged easily. Also, make sure that debris is not allowed to enter the oil and water channels – this is particularly important for the oil circuit, as carbon could block the oil supply to the camshaft or crankshaft bearings. Using adhesive tape and paper, seal the water, oil and bolt holes in the cylinder block. To prevent carbon entering the gap between the pistons and bores, smear a little grease in the gap. After cleaning the piston, rotate the crankshaft so that the piston moves down the bore, then wipe out the grease and carbon with a cloth rag. Clean the other piston crowns in the same way.

17 Check the block and head for nicks, deep scratches and other damage. If slight, they may be removed carefully with a file. More serious damage may be repaired by machining, but this is a specialist job.

18 If warpage of the cylinder head is suspected, use a straight-edge to check it for distortion. Refer to Chapter 2D if necessary.

19 Ensure that the cylinder head bolt holes in the crankcase are clean and free of oil. Syringe or soak up any oil left in the bolt

12.13 Removing the camshaft housing

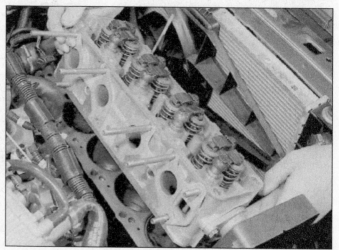
12.14 Removing the cylinder head

12.23a Fit the new gasket to the cylinder block, engaging it with the locating dowels (arrowed) . . .

12.23b . . . making sure its OBEN/TOP marking is uppermost

12.26 Apply sealant to the cylinder head upper mating surface then refit the camshaft housing

holes. This is most important in order that the correct bolt tightening torque can be applied and to prevent the possibility of the block being cracked by hydraulic pressure when the bolts are tightened.

20 Renew the cylinder head bolts regardless of their apparent condition.

Refitting

21 Position number 1 piston at TDC, and wipe clean the mating faces of the head and block.

22 Ensure that the two locating dowels are in position at each end of the cylinder block/crankcase surface.

23 Fit the new cylinder head gasket to the block, making sure it is fitted with the correct way up with its OBEN/TOP mark uppermost **(see illustrations)**.

24 Carefully refit the cylinder head, locating it on the dowels.

25 Ensure the mating surfaces of the cylinder head and camshaft housing are clean and dry. Check the camshaft is still correctly positioned by temporarily fitting the camshaft sprocket and checking that the sprocket timing mark is still uppermost.

26 Apply a bead of suitable sealant to the cylinder head upper mating surface **(see illustration)**.

27 Ensure the two locating dowels are in position then lubricate the camshaft followers with clean engine oil.

28 Carefully lower the camshaft housing assembly into position, locating it on the dowels.

29 Fit the washers to the new cylinder head bolts then carefully insert them into position (**do not drop**), tightening them finger-tight only at this stage **(see illustration)**.

30 Working progressively and in sequence, first tighten all the cylinder head bolts to the Stage 1 torque setting **(see illustrations)**.

31 Once all bolts have been tightened to the Stage 1 torque, again working in sequence, tighten each bolt through its specified Stage 2 angle, using a socket and extension bar. It is recommended that an angle-measuring gauge is used during this stage of the tightening, to ensure accuracy **(see illustration)**.

32 Working in the specified sequence, go around again and tighten all bolts through the specified Stage 3 angle.

33 Finally go around in the specified sequence again and tighten all bolts through the specified Stage 4 angle.

34 Refit the bolts securing the timing belt rear cover to the camshaft housing and tighten them to the specified torque.

35 Ensure the right-hand engine mounting bracket is correctly positioned, and tighten the retaining bolts to the specified torque.

36 Refit the camshaft sprocket as described in Section 8 then fit the timing belt as described in Section 7.

37 Reconnect the wiring connectors to the

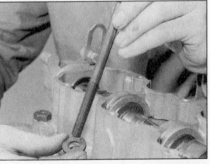

12.29 Fit the washers to the new cylinder head bolts and screw the bolts into position

cylinder head components, ensuring all wiring is correctly routed, and secure it in position with the necessary clips.

38 Reconnect the coolant hose to the thermostat housing and securely tighten its retaining clip.

39 Refit/reconnect the manifolds as described in Chapter 4A (as applicable).

40 Refit the roadwheel then lower the vehicle to the floor and tighten the wheel bolts to the specified torque.

41 Ensure all pipes and hoses are securely reconnected then refill the cooling system (Chapter 3) and refit the spark plugs (Chapter 1).

42 Reconnect the battery then start the engine and check for signs of leaks.

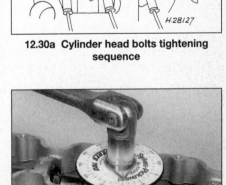

12.30a Cylinder head bolts tightening sequence

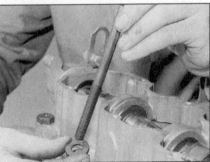

12.30b Working in the specified sequence, tighten the cylinder head bolts to the specified Stage 1 torque setting . . .

12.31 . . . and then through the various specified angles (see text)

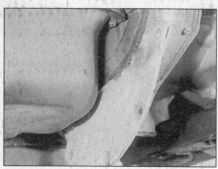

13.6 Removing the flywheel/driveplate lower cover plate – models without air conditioning

13.7 Removing the pressed steel sump – models without air conditioning

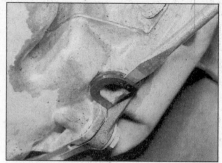

13.10 On models with air conditioning remove the rubber plugs from the sump flange to access the remaining bolts

13 Sump –
removal and refitting

Removal

1 Disconnect the battery negative terminal (refer to *Disconnecting the battery* in the Reference Chapter).
2 Firmly apply the handbrake, then jack up the front of the car and support it securely on axle stands (see *Jacking and vehicle support*).
3 Drain the engine oil as described in Chapter 1, then fit a new sealing washer and refit the drain plug, tightening it to the specified torque.
4 Remove the exhaust system front pipe as described in Chapter 4A.
5 Where necessary, disconnect the wiring connector from the oil level sender unit on the sump.

Models without air conditioning

6 Slacken and remove the flywheel/driveplate lower cover retaining bolts and remove the cover from the base of the transmission unit **(see illustration)**.
7 Progressively slacken and remove the bolts securing the sump to the base of the cylinder block/oil pump. Break the sump joint by striking the sump with the palm of the hand, then lower the sump from the engine and

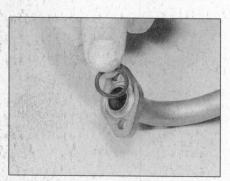

13.12 Fit a new sealing ring to the oil pump pick-up/strainer

withdraw it **(see illustration)**. Remove the gasket and discard it.
8 While the sump is removed, take the opportunity to check the oil pump pick-up/strainer for signs of clogging or splitting. If necessary, unbolt the pick-up/strainer and remove it from the base of the oil pump housing along with its sealing ring. The strainer can then be cleaned easily in solvent or renewed.

Models with air conditioning

9 Slacken and remove the bolts securing the sump flange to the transmission housing.
10 Progressively slacken and remove the bolts securing the sump to the base of the cylinder block/oil pump. Note that the bolts securing the transmission end of the sump to the cylinder block are accessed through the cut-outs in the sump flange, once the rubber plugs have been removed **(see illustration)**. Break the sump joint by striking the sump with the palm of the hand, then lower the sump from the engine and withdraw it. Remove the gasket and discard it. While the sump is removed, take the opportunity to check the oil pump pick-up/strainer for signs of clogging or splitting. If necessary, unbolt the pick-up/strainer and remove it from the base of the oil pump housing along with its sealing ring. The strainer can then be cleaned easily in solvent or renewed.

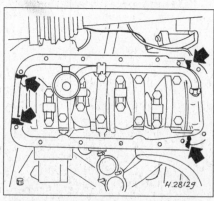

13.13 Apply sealant to the oil pump and rear main bearing cap joints (arrowed) before the sump is refitted

Refitting

Models without air conditioning

11 Remove all traces of dirt and oil from the mating surfaces of the sump and cylinder block and (where removed) the pick-up/strainer and oil pump housing. Also remove all traces of locking compound from the pick-up bolts (where removed).
12 Where necessary, position a new sealing ring on top of the oil pump pick-up/strainer and fit the strainer **(see illustration)**. Apply locking compound to the threads of the retaining bolts then fit the bolts and tighten to the specified torque.
13 Apply a smear of suitable sealant to the areas of the cylinder block mating surface around the areas of the of the oil housing and rear main bearing cap joints **(see illustration)**.
14 Fit a new gasket to the sump then offer up the sump to the cylinder block and refit the retaining bolts. Working out from the centre in a diagonal sequence, progressively tighten the sump retaining bolts to their specified torque setting.
15 Refit the cover plate to the transmission housing, tightening its retaining bolts to the specified torque.
16 Refit the exhaust front pipe (see Chapter 4A) and reconnect the oil level sender wiring connector (where fitted).
17 Lower the vehicle to the ground then fill the engine with fresh oil, with reference to Chapter 1.

Models with air conditioning

18 Where necessary, refit the oil pump pick-up/strainer as described in paragraphs 11 and 12.
19 Ensure the sump and cylinder block mating surfaces are clean and dry and remove all traces of locking compound from the sump bolts.
20 Apply a smear of suitable sealant to the areas of the cylinder block mating surface around the areas of the of the oil housing and rear main bearing cap joints.
21 Fit a new gasket to the sump and apply a few drops of locking compound to the threads of the sump to cylinder block/oil pump bolts.
22 Offer up the sump, ensuring the gasket

14.8 Undo the retaining screws and remove the oil pump cover

14.10 Removal of pump outer gear – outer face identification punch mark arrowed

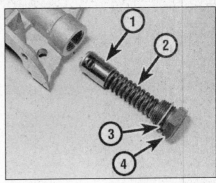

14.11 Oil pressure relief valve components

1 Plunger
2 Spring
3 Sealing washer
4 Valve bolt

remains correctly positioned, and loosely refit all the retaining bolts. Working out from the centre in a diagonal sequence, progressively tighten the bolts securing the sump to the cylinder block/oil pump to their specified torque setting.
23 Tighten the bolts securing the sump flange to the transmission housing to their specified torque setting. Refit the rubber plugs to the sump flange cut-outs.
24 Refit the exhaust front pipe (see Chapter 4A) and reconnect the oil level sender wiring connector (where fitted).
25 Lower the vehicle to the ground then fill the engine with fresh oil, with reference to Chapter 1.

14 Oil pump – removal, overhaul and refitting

Note: *The pressure relief valve can be removed with pump in position on the engine.*

Removal

1 Remove the timing belt (see Section 7).
2 Remove the camshaft and crankshaft timing belt sprockets and the tensioner as described in Section 8.
3 Unbolt the timing belt rear cover from the camshaft housing and oil pump and remove it from the engine.
4 Remove the sump and oil pump pickup/strainer as described in Section 13.
5 Disconnect the wiring connector from the oil pressure switch.

6 Unbolt the crankshaft sensor mounting bracket and position it clear of the oil pump.
7 Slacken and remove the retaining bolts then slide the oil pump housing assembly off the end of the crankshaft, taking great care not to lose the locating dowels. Remove the housing gasket and discard it.

Overhaul

8 Undo the retaining screws and lift off the pump cover from the rear of the housing **(see illustration)**.
9 Using a suitable marker pen, mark the surface of both the pump inner and outer gears; the marks can then be used to ensure the rotors are refitted the correct way around.
10 Lift out the inner and outer gears from the pump housing **(see illustration)**.
11 Unscrew the oil pressure relief valve bolt from the front of the housing and withdraw the spring and plunger from the housing, noting which way around the plunger is fitted **(see illustration)**. Remove the sealing washer from the valve bolt.
12 Clean the components, and carefully examine the gears, pump body and relief valve plunger for any signs of scoring or wear. Renew any component which shows signs of wear or damage; if the gears or pump housing are marked then the complete pump assembly should be renewed.
13 If the components appear serviceable, measure the clearance between the inner gear and outer gear using feeler blades. Also measure the gear endfloat, and check the flatness of the end cover **(see illustrations)**. If

the clearances exceed the specified tolerances, the pump must be renewed.
14 If the pump is satisfactory, reassemble the components in the reverse order of removal, noting the following.
a) *Ensure both gears are fitted the correct way around.*
b) *Fit a new sealing washer to the pressure relief valve bolt and tighten the bolt to the specified torque.*
c) *Remove all traces of locking compound from the cover screws. Apply a drop of fresh locking compound to each screw and tighten the screws to the specified torque.*
d) *On completion prime the oil pump by filling it with clean engine oil whilst rotating the inner gear.*

Refitting

15 Prior to refitting, carefully lever out the crankshaft oil seal using a flat-bladed screwdriver. Fit the new oil seal, ensuring its sealing lip is facing inwards, and press it squarely into the housing using a tubular drift which bears only on the hard outer edge of the seal **(see illustration)**. Press the seal into position so that it is flush with the housing and lubricate the oil seal lip with clean engine oil.
16 Ensure the mating surfaces of the oil pump and cylinder block are clean and dry and the locating dowels are in position.
17 Fit a new gasket to the cylinder block.

14.13a Using a feeler blade to check gear clearance

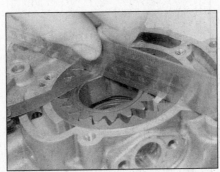

14.13b Using a straight-edge and feeler blade to measure gear endfloat

14.15 Fitting a new crankshaft oil seal to the oil pump housing

18 Carefully manoeuvre the oil pump into position and engage the inner gear with the crankshaft end (see illustration). Locate the pump on the dowels, taking great care not damage the oil seal lip.

19 Refit the pump housing retaining bolts in their original locations and tighten them to the specified torque.

20 Refit the crankshaft sensor bracket to the pump housing and tighten its mounting bolt to the specified torque. Reconnect the oil pressure sensor wiring connector.

21 Refit the oil pump pick-up/strainer and sump as described in Section 13.

22 Refit the rear timing belt cover to the engine, tightening its retaining bolts to the specified torque.

23 Refit the timing belt sprockets and tensioner then refit the belt as described in Sections 7 and 8.

24 On completion refill the engine with clean oil as described in Chapter 1.

15 Flywheel/driveplate –
removal, inspection and refitting

Note: *New flywheel/driveplate retaining bolts will be required on refitting.*

Removal

Manual transmission models

1 Remove the transmission as described in Chapter 7A then remove the clutch assembly as described in Chapter 6.

2 Prevent the flywheel from turning by locking the ring gear teeth (see illustration). Alternatively, bolt a strap between the flywheel and the cylinder block/crankcase. Make alignment marks between the flywheel and crankshaft using paint or a suitable marker pen.

3 Slacken and remove the retaining bolts and remove the flywheel. Do not drop it, as it is very heavy.

Automatic transmission models

4 Remove the transmission as described in

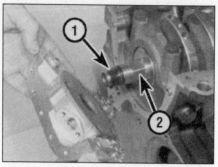

14.18 Take care not to damage the oil seal on the crankshaft lip (1) and engage the inner gear with the crankshaft flats (2)

Chapter 7B then remove the driveplate as described in paragraphs 2 and 3, noting that there is a retaining plate fitted between the retaining bolts and driveplate.

Inspection

5 On manual transmission models, examine the flywheel for scoring of the clutch face. If the clutch face is scored, the flywheel may be surface-ground, but renewal is preferable. Check for wear or chipping of the ring gear teeth. Renewal of the ring gear is also possible, but is not a task for the home mechanic; renewal requires the new ring gear to be heated (up to 230°C) to allow it to be fitted.

6 On automatic transmission models closely examine the driveplate and ring gear teeth for signs of wear or damage and check the driveplate surface for any signs of cracks.

7 If there is any doubt about the condition of the flywheel/driveplate, seek the advice of a Vauxhall dealer or engine reconditioning specialist. They will be able to advise if it is possible to recondition it or whether renewal is necessary.

Refitting

Manual transmission models

8 Clean the mating surfaces of the flywheel and crankshaft.

9 Offer up the flywheel and fit the new retaining bolts with a little locking compound. If the original is being refitted align the marks made prior to removal.

10 Lock the flywheel by the method used on removal, and tighten the retaining bolts to the specified Stage 1 torque setting then angle-tighten the bolts through the specified Stage 2 angle, using a socket and extension bar, and finally through the specified Stage 3 angle (see illustrations). It is recommended that an angle-measuring gauge is used during the final stages of the tightening, to ensure accuracy. If a gauge is not available, use white paint to make alignment marks between the bolt head and flywheel prior to tightening; the marks can then be used to check that the bolt has been rotated through the correct angle.

11 Refit the clutch as described in Chapter 6 then remove the locking tool, and refit the transmission as described in Chapter 7A.

Automatic transmission models

12 Clean the mating surfaces of the driveplate and crankshaft and remove all traces of locking compound from the driveplate retaining bolt threads.

13 Apply a drop of locking compound to each of the retaining bolt threads then offer up the driveplate, if the original is being refitted align the marks made prior to removal. Refit the retaining plate and screw in the retaining bolts.

14 Lock the driveplate by the method used on removal, and tighten the retaining bolts to the specified Stage 1 torque setting then angle-tighten the bolts through the specified Stage 2 angle, using a socket and extension bar, and finally through the specified Stage 3 angle. It is recommended that an angle-measuring gauge is used during the final stages of the tightening, to ensure accuracy. If a gauge is not available, use white paint to make alignment marks between the bolt head and flywheel prior to tightening; the marks can then be used to check that the bolt has been rotated through the correct angle.

15 Remove the locking tool and refit the transmission as described in Chapter 7B.

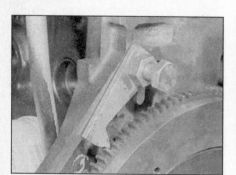

15.2 Lock the flywheel/driveplate ring gear with a suitable tool

15.10a On manual transmission models, tighten the flywheel bolts to the specified Stage 1 torque setting . . .

15.10b . . . then tighten them through the specified Stage 2 and 3 angles

16 Crankshaft oil seals – renewal

Timing belt end oil seal

1 Remove the crankshaft sprocket as described in Section 8.
2 Carefully punch or drill two small holes opposite each other in the oil seal. Screw a self-tapping screw into each and pull on the screws with pliers to extract the seal (see illustration).
Caution: Great care must be taken to avoid damage to the oil pump
3 Clean the seal housing and polish off any burrs or raised edges which may have caused the seal to fail in the first place.
4 Lubricate the lips of the new seal with clean engine oil and ease it into position on the end of the shaft. Press the seal squarely into position until it is flush with the housing. If necessary, a suitable tubular drift, such as a socket, which bears only on the hard outer edge of the seal can be used to tap the seal into position (see illustration). Take great care not to damage the seal lips during fitting and ensure that the seal lips face inwards.
5 Wash off any traces of oil, then refit the crankshaft sprocket as described in Section 8.

Flywheel/driveplate end oil seal

6 Remove the flywheel/driveplate as described in Section 15.
7 Renew the seal as described in paragraphs 2 to 4.
8 Refit the flywheel/driveplate as described in Section 15.

17 Engine/transmission mountings – inspection and renewal

Inspection

1 If improved access is required, firmly apply the handbrake, then jack up the front of the car and support it securely on axle stands (see *Jacking and vehicle support*). Where

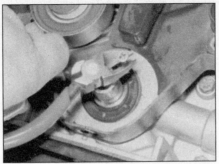
16.2 Removing the crankshaft right-hand oil seal

necessary, undo the retaining bolts and remove the undercover from beneath the engine/transmission unit.
2 Check the mounting rubber to see if it is cracked, hardened or separated from the metal at any point; renew the mounting if any such damage or deterioration is evident.
3 Check that all the mounting's fasteners are securely tightened; use a torque wrench to check if possible.
4 Using a large screwdriver or a pry bar, check for wear in the mounting by carefully levering against it to check for free play; where this is not possible, enlist the aid of an assistant to move the engine/transmission unit back-and-forth, or from side-to-side, while you watch the mounting. While some free play is to be expected even from new components, excessive wear should be obvious. If excessive free play is found, check first that the fasteners are correctly secured, then renew any worn components as described below.

Renewal

Note: *Before slackening any of the engine mounting bolts/nuts, the relative positions of the mountings to their various brackets should be marked to ensure correct alignment upon refitting.*

Right-hand mounting

5 Remove the air cleaner assembly as described in Chapter 4A.
6 Support the weight of the engine using a trolley jack with a block of wood placed on its head. Remove the three bolts securing the

16.4 Fitting a new crankshaft right-hand oil seal

right-hand engine mounting bracket to the cylinder block bracket (see illustration).
7 Undo the bolts securing the mounting to the body, and withdraw the bracket with the mounting (see illustration).

Front mounting

8 Firmly apply the handbrake, then jack up the front of the car and support it securely on axle stands (see *Jacking and vehicle support*).
9 Support the weight of the engine/transmission using a trolley jack with a block of wood placed on its head.
10 Slacken and remove the nut and washer securing the mounting to the bracket. Withdraw the bolt (see illustration)
11 Undo the bolts securing the mounting bracket to the transmission, then manoeuvre the mounting and bracket out of position. **Note:** *Take great care not to place any excess stress on the exhaust system when raising or lowering the engine. If necessary, disconnect the front pipe from the manifold (see Chapter 4A).*
12 Check all components for signs of wear or damage, and renew as necessary.
13 On reassembly, refit the mounting bracket and tighten its bolts to the specified torque.
14 Locate the mounting in the subframe, ensuring it is fitted the correct way up, and manoeuvre the engine/transmission into position. Refit the mounting bolts and new nuts. Tighten them to the specified torque.
15 Lower the vehicle to the ground.

Rear mounting

16 Firmly apply the handbrake, then jack up the front of the car and support it securely on

17.6 Remove the mounting bracket-to-cylinder head bracket bolts

17.7 Remove the right-hand engine mounting

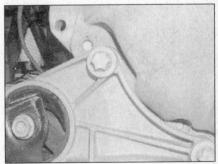
17.10 Front engine mounting

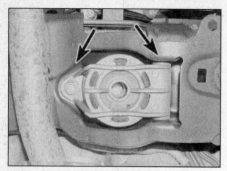

17.18 Rear engine mounting and retaining bolts (arrowed)

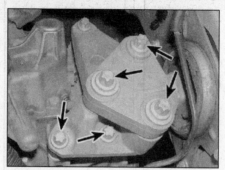

17.25 Undo the five or six (depending on model) mounting/bracket bolts

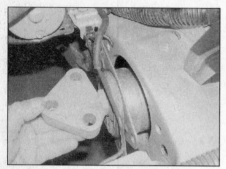

17.26 Undo the four Torx screws and remove the left-hand mounting

17.27 Remove the Torx bolt to separate the mounting elements

axle stands (see *Jacking and vehicle support*).
17 Support the weight of the engine/ transmission using a trolley jack with a block of wood placed on its head. Position the jack underneath the transmission and raise the

transmission slightly to remove all load from the rear mounting.
18 Slacken and remove the two bolts securing the rear mounting to the subframe, and the nut securing the mounting to the

transmission bracket, then manoeuvre the assembly out from underneath the vehicle **(see illustration)**.
19 On refitting, manoeuvre the mounting into position and refit the bolts/nuts securing it to the subframe. Ensure that the mounting is correctly engaged with the transmission bracket and fit the new mounting-to-bracket retaining nut. Tighten the mounting bolts/nuts to their specified torque settings. Remove the jack from underneath the engine/ transmission.
20 Lower the vehicle to the ground.

Left-hand mounting

21 Support the weight of the transmission using a trolley jack with a block of wood placed on its head.
22 Remove the battery as described in Chapter 5A.
23 Undo the retaining bolts, and remove the battery support from the body.
24 Remove the left-hand lower wheelarch panel.
25 Undo the six (automatic transmission: five) retaining bolts, and withdraw the mounting bracket from the transmission **(see illustration)**.
26 Slacken and remove the four Torx screws and manoeuvre the mounting out from the inner wing **(see illustration)**.
27 If required, separate the rubber element from the bracket by unscrewing the single retaining bolt **(see illustration)**.
28 Refitting is a reversal of removal. Ensure all bolts/nuts are tightened to their specified torques.

Chapter 2 Part B:
1.4, 1.6, 1.8 and 2.0 litre DOHC engine in-car repair procedures

Contents

Balancer unit (2.0 litre engine) – removal and refitting 18
Camshaft and followers – removal, inspection and refitting 10
Camshaft cover – removal and refitting 4
Camshaft oil seals – renewal 9
Compression test – description and interpretation 2
Crankshaft oil seals – renewal 16
Crankshaft pulley – removal and refitting 5
Cylinder head – removal and refitting 11
Engine oil and filter – renewal .See Chapter 1
Engine oil level check . . . . .See Weekly checks
Engine/transmission mountings – inspection and renewal 17
Flywheel/driveplate – removal, inspection and refitting 15
General information 1
Oil pump – removal, overhaul and refitting 14
Oil level sensor – removal and refitting. 13
Sump – removal and refitting 12
Timing belt – removal and refitting 7
Timing belt covers – removal and refitting 6
Timing belt sprockets, tensioner and idler pulleys – removal and
  refitting 8
Top dead centre (TDC) for No 1 piston – locating 3

Degrees of difficulty

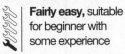

Easy, suitable for novice with little experience	**Fairly easy,** suitable for beginner with some experience	**Fairly difficult,** suitable for competent DIY mechanic	**Difficult,** suitable for experienced DIY mechanic	**Very difficult,** suitable for expert DIY or professional

Specifications

General

Engine type	Four-cylinder, in-line, water-cooled. Double overhead camshaft, belt-driven

Manufacturer's engine codes:

1.4 litre	X14XE, Z14XE
1.6 litre	X16XEL, Z16XE
1.8 litre	X18XE1, Z18XE, Z18XEL
2.0 litre	X20XEV

Bore:

1.4 litre	77.6 mm
1.6 litre	79.0 mm
1.8 litre	80.5 mm
2.0 litre	86.0 mm

Stroke:

1.4 litre	73.4 mm
1.6 litre	81.5 mm
1.8 litre	88.2 mm
2.0 litre	86.0 mm
Firing order	1-3-4-2 (No 1 cylinder at timing belt end)
Direction of crankshaft rotation	Clockwise (viewed from timing belt end of engine)

Capacity:

1.4 litre	1389 cc
1.6 litre	1598 cc
1.8 litre	1796 cc
2.0 litre	1998 cc

Compression ratio:

1.4, 1.6 and 1.8 litre	10.5:1
2.0 litre	10.8:1

General (continued)

Maximum power (kW):

1.4 litre	66 at 6000 rpm
1.6 litre	74 at 6200 rpm

1.8 litre:

X18XE1 and Z18XEL	85 at 5400 rpm
Z18XE	92 at 5600 rpm
2.0 litre	100 at 5600 rpm

Maximum torque (Nm):

1.4 litre	125 at 4000 rpm
1.6 litre	150 at 3200 rpm
1.8 litre	170 at 3600 rpm
2.0 litre	188 at 3200 rpm

Compression pressures

Standard	12 to 15 bar (174 to 218 psi)
Maximum difference between any two cylinders	1 bar (15 psi)

Camshaft

Endfloat	0.04 to 0.15 mm
Maximum permissible radial run-out	0.040 mm

Cam lift:

	Inlet	Exhaust
1.4, 1.6 and 1.8 litre engines	8.5 mm	8.0 mm
2.0 litre engines	10.0 mm	10.0 mm

Balancer shaft unit (2.0 DOHC engine)

Permissible backlash	0.02 to 0.06 mm

Shim code number:	Shim thickness
55	0.535 to 0.565 mm
58	0.565 to 0.595 mm
61	0.595 to 0.625 mm
64	0.625 to 0.655 mm
67	0.655 to 0.685 mm
70	0.685 to 0.715 mm
73	0.715 to 0.745 mm
76	0.745 to 0.775 mm
79	0.775 to 0.805 mm
82	0.805 to 0.835 mm
85	0.835 to 0.865 mm

Lubrication system

Oil pump type	Gear-type, driven directly from crankshaft
Minimum permissible oil pressure at idle speed, with engine at operating temperature (oil temperature of at least 80°C)	1.5 bar (22 psi)

Oil pump clearances:

Inner-to-outer gear teeth clearance	0.10 to 0.20 mm
Gear endfloat	0.03 to 0.10 mm

Torque wrench settings

	Nm	lbf ft

1.4, 1.6 and 1.8 litre models

	Nm	lbf ft
Auxiliary drivebelt tensioner-to-alternator support bolt	35	26
Baffle plate bolts	8	6
Camshaft bearing cap bolts	8	6
Camshaft cover bolts	8	6
Camshaft sensor bolts	8	6
Camshaft sprocket bolt*:		
Stage 1	50	37
Stage 2	Angle-tighten a further 60°	
Stage 3	Angle-tighten a further 15°	
Connecting rod big-end bearing cap bolt*:		
Stage 1	25	18
Stage 2	Angle-tighten a further 30°	
Crankshaft pulley bolt*:		
Stage 1	95	70
Stage 2	Angle-tighten a further 30°	
Stage 3	Angle-tighten a further 15°	
Crankshaft sensor mounting bracket bolt	8	6

Torque wrench settings (continued)

	Nm	lbf ft
1.4, 1.6 and 1.8 litre models (continued)		
Cylinder head bolts*:		
Stage 1	25	18
Stage 2	Angle-tighten a further 90°	
Stage 3	Angle-tighten a further 90°	
Stage 4	Angle-tighten a further 90°	
Stage 5	Angle-tighten a further 45°	
Driveplate bolts*	60	44
Engine/transmission mounting bolts:		
Front mounting:		
Mounting-to-transmission bolts	60	44
Mounting-to-subframe	55	41
Left-hand mounting:		
Mounting-to-body bolts	20	15
Bracket-to-transmission bolts	35	26
Mounting-to-bracket bolts	55	41
Rear mounting:		
Mounting-to-bracket bolts	55	41
Mounting-to-subframe bolts	55	41
Bracket-to-transmission bolts	60	44
Right-hand mounting:		
Bracket-to-engine bolts	50	37
Mounting-to-body nuts	45	33
Mounting-to-adapter bolt	55	41
Adapter-to-cylinder block bracket	55	41
Engine-to-transmission unit bolts:		
M12 bolts	60	44
Front subframe bolts*:		
Stage 1	90	66
Stage 2	Angle-tighten a further 45°	
Stage 3	Angle-tighten a further 15°	
Flywheel bolts*:		
Stage 1	35	26
Stage 2	Angle-tighten a further 30°	
Stage 3	Angle-tighten a further 15°	
Main bearing cap bolts*:		
Stage 1	50	37
Stage 2	Angle-tighten a further 45°	
Stage 3	Angle-tighten a further 15°	
Oil level sensor Torx screws	8	6
Oil pump:		
Retaining bolts	10	7
Pump cover screws	6	4
Oil pressure relief valve bolt	50	37
Oil pressure switch	30	22
Oil pump pick-up/strainer bolts	8	6
Roadwheel bolts	110	81
Sump bolts:		
Sump to cylinder block/oil pump bolts	10	7
Sump flange-to-transmission (M10) bolts	40	30
Drain plug:		
Inner Torx type (rubber seal ring)	14	10
Hexagon type (metal seal ring)	45	33
Timing belt cover bolts:		
Upper and lower covers	3	2
Rear cover	6	4
Timing belt idler pulley bolt	25	18
Timing belt tensioner bolt	20	15
2.0 litre models		
Auxiliary drivebelt tensioner-to-alternator support:		
Models without air conditioning	35	26
Models with air conditioning	25	18
Baffle plate bolts	8	6
Balancer unit-to-cylinder block bolts:		
Stage 1	20	15
Stage 2	Angle-tighten a further 45°	

Torque wrench settings (continued)

	Nm	lbf ft
2.0 litre models (continued)		
Camshaft bearing cap bolts	8	6
Camshaft cover bolts	8	6
Camshaft sensor bolts	6	4
Camshaft sprocket bolt*:		
Stage 1	50	37
Stage 2	Angle-tighten a further 60°	
Stage 3	Angle-tighten a further 15°	
Connecting rod big-end bearing cap bolt*:		
Stage 1	35	25
Stage 2	Angle-tighten a further 45°	
Stage 3	Angle-tighten a further 15°	
Crankshaft pulley bolts	20	15
Crankshaft sprocket bolt:		
Stage 1	130	96
Stage 2	Angle-tighten a further 40 to 50°	
Cylinder head bolts*:		
Stage 1	25	18
Stage 2	Angle-tighten a further 90°	
Stage 3	Angle-tighten a further 90°	
Stage 4	Angle-tighten a further 90°	
Stage 5	Angle-tighten a further 15°	
Driveplate bolts*:		
Stage 1	55	41
Stage 2	Angle-tighten a further 30°	
Stage 3	Angle-tighten a further 15°	
Engine/transmission mounting bolts:		
Front mounting:		
Mounting-to-transmission bolts	60	44
Mounting-to-subframe	55	41
Left-hand mounting:		
Mounting-to-body bolts	20	15
Bracket-to-transmission bolts	35	26
Mounting-to-bracket bolts	55	41
Right-hand mounting:		
Bracket-to-engine bolts	50	37
Mounting-to-body nuts	45	33
Mounting-to-adapter bolt	55	41
Adapter-to-cylinder block bracket	55	41
Rear mounting:		
Mounting-to-bracket bolts	55	41
Mounting-to-subframe bolts	55	41
Bracket-to-transmission bolts	60	44
Engine-to-transmission unit bolts:		
M12 bolts	60	44
Flywheel bolts*:		
Stage 1	65	48
Stage 2	Angle-tighten a further 30°	
Stage 3	Angle-tighten a further 15°	
Main bearing bridge-to-cylinder block:		
Stage 1	20	15
Stage 2	Angle tighten a further 45°	
Main bearing cap bolts*:		
Stage 1	50	37
Stage 2	Angle-tighten a further 45°	
Stage 3	Angle-tighten a further 15°	
Main bearing ladder casting bolts	20	15
Oil level sensor Torx screws	8	6
Oil pump:		
Retaining bolts	8	6
Pump cover screws	6	4
Pressure relief valve bolt	50	41
Oil pump pick-up/strainer bolts:		
Pick-up-to-oil pump housing bolts	8	6
Pick-up-to-main bearing cap casting bolt	20	15
Roadwheel bolts	110	81

Torque wrench settings (continued)

	Nm	lbf ft
2.0 litre models (continued)		
Sump bolts:		
Sump pan bolts:		
Stage 1	8	6
Stage 2	Angle-tighten a further 30°	
Main casting bolts:		
Sump-to-cylinder block/oil pump bolts	20	15
Sump flange-to-transmission bolts	40	30
Drain plug	10	7
Timing belt cover bolts	6	4
Timing belt idler pulley:		
Pulley bolt	25	18
Mounting bracket bolts	25	18
Timing belt tensioner bolt	20	15

Use new bolts/nuts

1 General information

How to use this Chapter

1 This Part of Chapter 2 is devoted to in-car repair procedures for the engine. All procedures concerning engine removal and refitting, and engine block/cylinder head overhaul can be found in Chapter 2D.

2 Most of the operations included in this Part are based on the assumption that the engine is still installed in the car. Therefore, if this information is being used during a complete engine overhaul, with the engine already removed, many of the steps included here will not apply.

Engine description

3 The engine is a double overhead camshaft, four-cylinder, in-line unit, mounted transversely at the front of the car, with the clutch and transmission on its left-hand end.

4 The aluminium alloy cylinder block is of the dry-liner type. The crankshaft is supported within the cylinder block on five shell-type main bearings. Thrustwashers are fitted to number 3 main bearing, to control crankshaft endfloat.

5 The connecting rods are attached to the crankshaft by horizontally split shell-type big-end bearings, and to the pistons by interference-fit gudgeon pins. The aluminium alloy pistons are of the slipper type, and are fitted with three piston rings, comprising two compression rings and a scraper-type oil control ring.

6 The camshafts run directly in the cylinder head, and driven by the crankshaft via a toothed rubber timing belt (which also drives the coolant pump). The camshafts operate each valve via a follower. Each follower incorporates a hydraulic self-adjusting valve which automatically adjust the valve clearances.

7 Lubrication is by pressure-feed from a gear-type oil pump, which is mounted on the right-hand end of the crankshaft. It draws oil through a strainer located in the sump, and then forces it through an externally mounted full-flow cartridge-type filter. The oil flows into galleries in the main bearing cap bridge arrangement and cylinder block/crankcase, from where it is distributed to the crankshaft (main bearings) and camshaft(s). The big-end bearings are supplied with oil via internal drillings in the crankshaft, while the camshaft bearings also receive a pressurised supply. The camshaft lobes and valves are lubricated by splash, as are all other engine components.

8 A semi-closed crankcase ventilation system is employed; crankcase fumes are drawn from the cylinder head cover, and passed via a hose to the inlet manifold.

Operations with engine in car

9 The following operations can be carried out without having to remove the engine from the vehicle.
a) *Removal and refitting of the cylinder head.*
b) *Removal and refitting of the timing belt and sprockets.*
c) *Renewal of the camshaft oil seals.*
d) *Removal and refitting of the camshafts and followers.*
e) *Removal and refitting of the sump.*
f) *Removal and refitting of the connecting rods and pistons*.*
g) *Removal and refitting of the oil pump.*
h) *Renewal of the crankshaft oil seals.*
i) *Renewal of the engine mountings.*
j) *Removal and refitting of the flywheel/driveplate.*

* *Although the operation marked with an asterisk can be carried out with the engine in the car after removal of the sump, it is better for the engine to be removed, in the interests of cleanliness and improved access. For this reason, the procedure is described in Chapter 2D.*

2 Compression test – description and interpretation

Refer to Chapter 2A, Section 2.

3 Top dead centre (TDC) for No 1 piston – locating

1 In its travel up and down its cylinder bore, Top Dead Centre (TDC) is the highest point that each piston reaches as the crankshaft rotates. While each piston reaches TDC both at the top of the compression stroke, and again at the top of the exhaust stroke, for the purpose of timing the engine, TDC refers to the piston position (usually number 1) at the top of its compression stroke.

2 Number 1 piston (and cylinder) is at the right-hand (timing belt) end of the engine, and its TDC position is located as follows. Note that the crankshaft rotates clockwise when viewed from the right-hand side of the car.

3 Disconnect the battery negative terminal (refer to *Disconnecting the battery* in the Reference Chapter). If necessary, remove all the spark plugs as described in Chapter 1 to enable the engine to be easily turned over.

1.4, 1.6 and 1.8 litre models

4 To gain access to the camshaft sprocket timing marks, remove the timing belt upper cover as described in Section 6.

5 Using a socket and extension bar on the crankshaft pulley bolt, rotate the crankshaft until the timing marks on the camshaft sprockets are facing towards each other, and an imaginary straight line can be drawn through the camshaft sprocket bolts and the timing marks. With the camshaft sprocket marks correctly positioned, align the notch on

3.5a Align the camshaft timing marks . . .

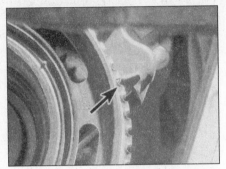

3.5b . . . and the crankshaft timing mark

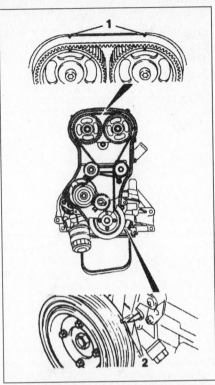

3.7 On 2.0 litre engines align the camshaft sprocket timing marks with the marks (1) on the cylinder head cover, and the crankshaft pulley notch with the pointer (2)

the crankshaft pulley rim with the mark on the timing belt lower cover (see illustrations). The engine is now positioned with No 1 piston at TDC on its compression stroke.

2.0 litre models

6 To gain access to the camshaft sprocket timing marks, remove the timing belt outer cover as described in Section 6.

7 Using a socket and extension bar on the crankshaft sprocket bolt, rotate the crankshaft until the timing marks on the camshaft sprockets are both at the top and are correctly aligned with the marks on the camshaft cover. With the camshaft sprocket marks correctly positioned, align the notch on the crankshaft pulley rim with the pointer on the cover (see illustration). The engine is now positioned with No 1 piston at TDC on its compression stroke.

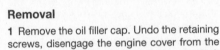

4 Camshaft cover – removal and refitting

1.4 and 1.6 litre models

Removal

1 Remove the oil filler cap. Undo the retaining screws, disengage the engine cover from the locating lugs at the front of the camshaft cover, and remove the cover from the engine compartment (see illustration).

2 Disconnect the wiring plug, remove the retaining screws, and remove the ignition module. If necessary, refer to Chapter 5B.

3 Release the retaining clips and disconnect the breather hoses from the left-hand end of the camshaft cover (see illustration).

4 Evenly and progressively slacken and remove the camshaft cover retaining bolts.

5 Lift the camshaft cover away from the cylinder head and recover the cover's seals and the sealing rings which are fitted to each of the retaining bolt holes (see illustration). Examine the seals and sealing rings for signs of wear or damage and renew if necessary.

Refitting

6 Ensure the cover and cylinder head surfaces are clean and dry then fit the camshaft seals securely to the cover grooves. Fit the sealing rings to the recesses around each retaining bolt hole, holding them in position with a smear of grease (see illustrations).

4.1 Undo the two screws and disengage the locating lugs to remove the engine cover

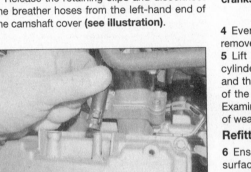

4.3 Disconnect the breather hoses

4.5 Lift the camshaft cover away from the engine

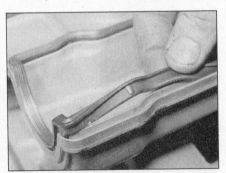

4.6a Ensure the seals are correctly seated in the cover recesses . . .

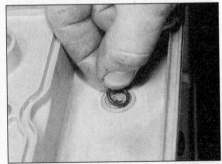

4.6b . . . and fit the sealing rings to the recess around each retaining bolt hole

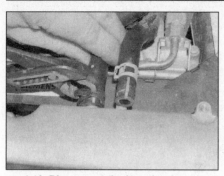

4.13 Disconnect the breather hoses

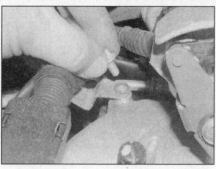

4.16 Remove the bolt supporting the coolant pipe across the camshaft cover

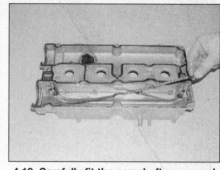

4.19 Carefully fit the camshaft cover seal

7 Apply a smear of suitable sealant to areas of the cylinder head surface around the right-hand end inlet and exhaust camshaft bearing caps and also to the semi-circular cut-outs on the left-hand end of the head.

8 Carefully manoeuvre the camshaft cover into position, taking great care to ensure all the sealing rings remain correctly seated. Refit the cover retaining bolts and tighten the retaining bolts to the specified torque, working in a spiral pattern from the centre outwards.

9 Reconnect the breather hoses, securing them in position with the retaining clips.

10 Refit the ignition module with reference to Chapter 5B.

11 Refit the engine cover.

1.8 litre models

Removal

12 Remove the engine cover as described in paragraph 1.

13 Slacken the retaining clips and disconnect the breather hoses from the left-hand rear of the cover (see illustration).

14 Disconnect the wiring plug, undo the retaining screws, and remove the ignition module. Refer to Chapter 5B if necessary.

15 Disconnect the wiring plug from the coolant temperature sensor.

16 Disconnect the coolant pipe from the thermostat housing. Unbolt the retaining bracket from the camshaft cover and inlet manifold, release the retaining clip and move the pipe to one side (see illustration). Be prepared for coolant spillage.

17 Evenly and progressively slacken and remove the camshaft cover retaining bolts.

18 Lift the camshaft cover away from the cylinder head and recover the rubber seal. Examine the seal for signs of wear or damage and renew if necessary.

Refitting

19 Ensure the cover and cylinder head surfaces are clean and dry then fit the camshaft seal securely to the cover groove (see illustration).

20 Carefully manoeuvre the camshaft cover into position, taking great care to ensure the sealing ring remains correctly seated. Refit the cover retaining bolts and tighten the retaining

bolts to the specified torque, working in a spiral pattern from the centre outwards.

21 Reconnect the coolant pipe to the thermostat housing, making sure it is secured by the retaining bracket on the camshaft cover and inlet manifold (see illustration). Top up the cooling system as described in *Weekly checks*.

22 Refit the wiring plug to the coolant temperature sensor.

23 Reconnect the breather hoses, securing them in position with the retaining clips.

24 Refit the ignition module with reference to Chapter 5B.

25 Refit the engine cover.

2.0 litre models

Removal

26 With reference to Chapter 4A, remove the air cleaner assembly.

27 Remove the timing belt upper cover as described in Section 6.

28 Disconnect the engine breather hoses from the right-hand rear and left-hand front of the cover (see illustration).

29 Undo the retaining screws and remove the spark plug cover. Disconnect the plug caps from the plugs then unclip the HT leads and position them clear of the cover.

30 Disconnect the wiring plug from the camshaft position sensor. Unclip the wiring harness from the cover.

31 Evenly and progressively slacken and remove the camshaft cover retaining bolts.

32 Lift the camshaft cover away from the

cylinder head and recover the cover's seal and the sealing rings which are fitted to each of the retaining bolts holes. Examine the seal and sealing rings for signs of wear or damage and renew if necessary.

Refitting

33 Ensure the cover and cylinder head surfaces are clean and dry then fit the camshaft seals securely to the cover grooves. Fit the sealing rings to the recesses around each retaining bolt hole, holding them in position with a smear of grease.

34 Apply a smear of suitable sealant to areas of the cylinder head surface around the right-hand end inlet and exhaust camshaft bearing caps and also to the semi-circular cut-outs on the left-hand end of the head.

35 Carefully manoeuvre the camshaft cover into position, taking great care to ensure all the sealing rings remain correctly seated. Refit the cover retaining bolts and tighten the retaining bolts to the specified torque, working in a spiral pattern from the centre outwards.

36 Reconnect the breather hoses, securing them in position with the retaining clips.

37 Refit the plug caps to the spark plugs, and reposition the HT leads.

38 Position the spark plug cover in the centre of the camshaft cover, and tighten the retaining screws securely.

39 Refit the timing belt upper cover as described in Section 6.

40 Refit the air cleaner assembly (see Chapter 4A).

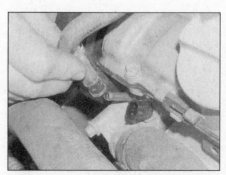

4.21 Reconnect the pipe to the thermostat housing

4.28 Disconnect the breather hoses from the cover (arrowed)

5.5 Align the pulley cut-out with the raised notch

5 Crankshaft pulley –
removal and refitting

1.4, 1.6 and 1.8 litre models

Note: *A new crankshaft pulley retaining bolt will be required on refitting.*

Removal

1 Firmly apply the handbrake, then jack up the front of the car and support it securely on axle stands (see *Jacking and vehicle support*). Remove the right-hand roadwheel, and lower wheelarch liner.
2 Using a spanner, hold the auxiliary drivebelt tensioner against the spring pressure and lift the drivebelt from the pulleys. Refer to Chapter 1 if necessary. Prior to removal, mark the direction of rotation on the belt to ensure the belt is refitted the same way around.
3 Slacken the crankshaft pulley retaining bolt. To prevent crankshaft rotation on manual transmission models, have an assistant select top gear and apply the brakes firmly. On automatic transmission models prevent rotation by removing one of the torque converter retaining bolts and bolting the driveplate to the transmission housing using a metal bar, spacers and suitable bolts (see Chapter 7B). If the engine is removed from the vehicle it will be necessary to lock the flywheel/driveplate (see Section 15).

4 Unscrew the retaining bolt and washer and remove the crankshaft pulley from the end of the crankshaft, taking care not to damage the crankshaft sensor (where applicable).

Refitting

5 Refit the crankshaft pulley, aligning the pulley cut-out with the raised notch on the timing belt sprocket, then fit the washer and new retaining bolt **(see illustration)**.
6 Lock the crankshaft by the method used on removal, and tighten the pulley retaining bolt to the specified Stage 1 torque setting then angle-tighten the bolt through the specified Stage 2 angle, using a socket and extension bar, and finally through the specified Stage 3 angle. It is recommended that an angle-measuring gauge is used during the final stages of the tightening, to ensure accuracy. If a gauge is not available, use white paint to make alignment marks between the bolt head and pulley prior to tightening; the marks can then be used to check that the bolt has been rotated through the correct angle.
7 Refit the auxiliary drivebelt as described in Chapter 1 using the mark made prior to removal to ensure the belt is fitted the correct way around.
8 Refit the lower wheelarch liner and roadwheel, then lower the car to the ground and tighten the wheel bolts to the specified torque.

2.0 litre models

Removal

9 Carry out the operations described in paragraphs 1 and 2.
10 Using a socket and extension bar on the crankshaft sprocket bolt, turn the crankshaft until the notch on the pulley rim is correctly aligned with the pointer on the cover.
11 Slacken and remove the small retaining bolts securing the pulley to the crankshaft sprocket and remove the pulley from the engine. If necessary, prevent crankshaft rotation by holding the sprocket retaining bolt with a suitable socket.

Refitting

12 Check that the crankshaft sprocket mark

is still aligned with the mark on the housing then manoeuvre the crankshaft pulley into position. Align the notch on the pulley rim with the pointer then seat the pulley on the sprocket and tighten its retaining bolts to the specified torque.
13 Carry out the operations described in paragraphs 7 and 8.

6 Timing belt covers –
removal and refitting

1.4, 1.6 and 1.8 litre models

Upper cover

1 Remove the air cleaner assembly as described in Chapter 4A.
2 Release the camshaft position sensor wiring from the retaining clip on the upper cover. Undo the three retaining screws then unclip the upper cover from the rear cover and remove it from the engine compartment **(see illustration)**.
3 Refitting is the reverse of removal, ensure that the camshaft position sensor wiring is correctly routed, and tighten the retaining bolts to the specified torque **(see illustration)**.

Lower cover

4 Remove the upper cover as described in paragraphs 1 and 2.
5 Hold the tensioner against the spring pressure, and disengage the auxiliary drivebelt from the pulleys (refer to Chapter 1 if necessary). Prior to removal, mark the direction of rotation on the belt to ensure the belt is refitted the same way around.
6 Firmly apply the handbrake, then jack up the front of the car and support it securely on axle stands (see *Jacking and vehicle support*). Remove the right-hand roadwheel.
7 Remove the right-hand front lower wheelarch panel, as described in Chapter 11.
8 Undo the retaining bolt and remove the auxiliary drivebelt tensioner **(see illustration)**.
9 Remove the crankshaft pulley as described in Section 5.
10 Undo the retaining bolt then unclip the

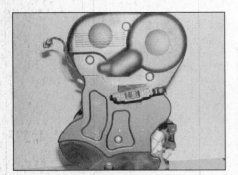

6.2 Undo the three upper cover screws

6.3 Ensure that the camshaft position sensor wiring is correctly routed

6.8 Remove the auxiliary drivebelt tensioner

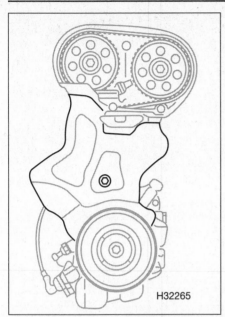

6.10 On 1.4, 1.6 and 1.8 litre engines, undo the centre retaining bolt

6.11 Clip the cover back into position

6.15 Engine mounting-to-cylinder block bracket retaining bolts

cover from the rear cover and manoeuvre it out of position **(see illustration)**.

11 Refitting is the reverse of removal, clip the cover into position and tighten the cover bolts to the specified torque **(see illustration)**.

Rear cover

12 Remove the timing belt as described in Section 7.

13 Remove the camshaft cover as described in Section 4.

14 Remove the camshaft sprockets, crankshaft sprocket, timing belt tensioner, front idler pulley and the rear idler pulley as described in Section 8.

15 Slacken and remove the three retaining bolts, and withdraw the engine mounting bracket bolted to the cylinder block **(see illustration)**.

16 Undo the four retaining bolts and remove the rear cover upwards and away from the engine **(see illustration)**.

17 Refitting is the reverse of removal. Refit and tighten the cover bolts to the specified torque.

2.0 litre models

Upper cover

18 Remove the air cleaner assembly as described in Chapter 4A.

19 Slacken and remove the two upper cover retaining bolts.

20 Lift away the upper cover.

21 Refitting is a reversal of removal. Tighten the cover retaining bolts to the specified torque.

Lower cover

22 Remove the upper cover as described in paragraphs 18 to 20.

23 Hold the tensioner against the spring pressure, and disengage the auxiliary drivebelt from the pulleys (refer to Chapter 1 if necessary). Prior to removal, mark the direction of rotation on the belt to ensure the belt is refitted the same way around.

24 On models with air conditioning, firmly apply the handbrake, then jack up the front of the car and support it securely on axle stands (see *Jacking and vehicle support*). Remove the right-hand roadwheel, then remove the right-hand front lower wheelarch panel, as described in Chapter 11.

25 Undo the retaining bolt(s), and remove the

auxiliary drivebelt tensioner from the alternator support bracket.

26 Remove the crankshaft pulley, as described in Section 5.

27 Slacken and remove the two retaining bolts, release the retaining clips and remove the cover from the engine unit along with its seal **(see illustration)**.

28 Refitting is the reverse of removal, ensure the cover seal is correctly fitted. Tighten all bolts to the specified torque.

Rear cover

29 Remove the timing belt as described in Section 7.

30 With reference to Section 4, remove the camshaft cover.

31 Remove the camshaft sprockets, crankshaft sprocket, the timing belt tensioner and the idler pulleys as described in Section 8.

32 Unbolt the camshaft sensor from the cylinder head.

33 Unscrew the retaining bolts and remove the engine mounting bracket from the cylinder block.

34 Undo the four retaining bolts and remove the rear cover from the engine unit.

35 Refitting is the reverse of removal, tightening all bolts to the specified torque.

---

7 Timing belt – removal and refitting

Note: *The timing belt must be removed and refitted with the engine cold.*

Removal

1 Position No 1 cylinder at TDC on its compression stroke as described in Section 3.

2 Remove the engine oil filler cap, and undo the screws securing the engine cover to the camshaft cover. Remove the cover from the engine compartment.

3 Unbolt the timing belt upper and lower covers and remove them from the engine (see Section 6).

4 Support the weight of the engine using a trolley jack with a block of wood placed on its head.

5 Remove the three bolts securing the right-

6.16 Lift the rear cover away

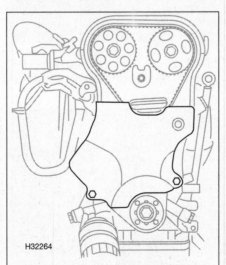

6.27 Lower cover retaining bolts – 2.0 litre engines

7.5 Right-hand engine mounting bolts

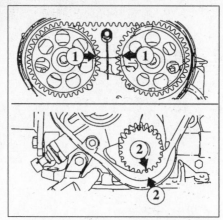

7.6a Camshaft and crankshaft timing marks – 1.4, 1.6 and 1.8 litre engines

1 *Camshaft and crankshaft timing marks aligned with the cylinder head upper surface*
2 *Crankshaft timing mark aligned with mark on oil pump housing*

7.6b Unbolt the camshaft sensor

hand engine mounting to the bracket on the cylinder block, and the three bolts securing the mounting to the inner wing. Withdraw the mounting **(see illustration)**.

6 On 1.4, 1.6 and 1.8 litre models, check the camshaft sprocket timing marks are correctly aligned with the cylinder head surface and the crankshaft sprocket timing mark is aligned with the mark on the cover. Undo the two bolts securing the camshaft sensor to the cylinder head and position it clear of the engine **(see illustrations)**. If available, insert Vauxhall tool KM852 to lock the camshafts in place.

7 On 2.0 litre models, check the camshaft sprocket timing marks are correctly aligned with the camshaft cover marks and the crankshaft sprocket timing mark is aligned with the pointer at the base of the cover **(see illustration)**. If available, insert Vauxhall tool

KM853 to lock the camshaft sprockets in place.

8 On all models, slacken the timing belt tensioner retaining bolt. Using an Allen key, rotate the tensioner arm clockwise until the roller is as far away from the belt as possible to relieve the tension in the timing belt, hold it in position and securely tighten the retaining bolt **(see illustration)**.

9 Slide the timing belt from its sprockets and remove it from the engine **(see illustration)**. If the belt is to be re-used, use white paint or similar to mark the direction of rotation on the belt. **Do not** rotate the crankshaft or camshafts until the timing belt has been refitted.

10 Check the timing belt carefully for any signs of uneven wear, splitting or oil contamination, and renew it if there is the slightest doubt about its condition. If the engine is undergoing an overhaul and is approaching 40 000 miles (60 000km) in service, renew the belt as a matter of course, regardless of its apparent condition. If signs of oil contamination are found, trace the source of the oil leak and rectify it, then wash down the engine timing belt area and all related components to remove all traces of oil.

Refitting

11 On reassembly, thoroughly clean the timing belt sprockets and tensioner/idler pulleys.

12 Check that the camshaft sprocket timing marks are still correctly aligned with the cylinder head surface (1.4, 1.6 and 1.8 litre models) or the camshaft cover marks (2.0 litre models) and the crankshaft sprocket mark is still aligned with the mark on the cover **(see illustration)**.

13 Fit the timing belt over the crankshaft and camshaft sprockets and around the idler pulleys, ensuring that the belt front run is taut (ie, all slack is on the tensioner side of the belt), then fit the belt over the coolant pump sprocket and tensioner pulley **(see illustration)**. Do not

7.7 On 2.0 litre engines ensure the camshaft sprocket marks are correctly aligned with the marks on the camshaft cover (arrowed)

7.8 Slacken the timing belt tensioner bolt (1) and rotate the tensioner clockwise using an Allen key in the arm cut-out (2)

7.9 Removing the timing belt

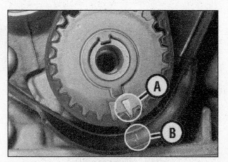

7.12 Crankshaft sprocket (A) and belt cover (B) timing marks – 1.4, 1.6 and 1.8 litre engines

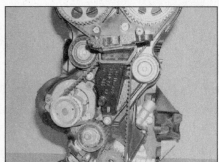

7.13 Timing belt routing – 1.8 litre engines

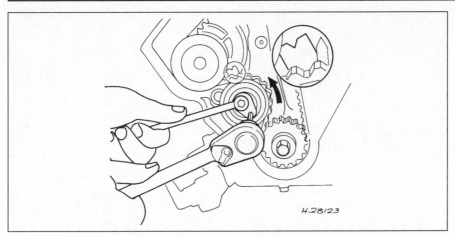

7.14 Tension the belt by rotating the tensioner arm fully anti-clockwise until the pointer is positioned as shown

twist the belt sharply while refitting it. Ensure that the belt teeth are correctly seated centrally in the sprockets, and that the timing marks remain in alignment. If a used belt is being refitted, ensure that the arrow mark made on removal points in the normal direction of rotation, as before.

14 Slacken the timing belt tensioner bolt to release the tensioner spring. Rotate the tensioner arm anti-clockwise until the tensioner pointer is fully over to the right,

without exerting any excess strain on the belt. Hold the tensioner in position and securely tighten its retaining bolt **(see illustration)**.

15 Check the sprocket timing marks are still correctly aligned. If adjustment is necessary, release the tensioner again then disengage the belt from the sprockets and make any necessary adjustments. If previously fitted, remove Vauxhall tool KM852 or KM853 to 'unlock' the camshaft sprockets.

16 Using a socket on the crankshaft

pulley/sprocket bolt (as applicable), rotate the crankshaft smoothly through two complete turns (720°) in the normal direction of rotation to settle the timing belt in position.

17 Check that both the camshaft and crankshaft sprocket timing marks are correctly realigned then slacken the tensioner bolt again.

18 If a new timing belt is being fitted, adjust the tensioner so that the pointer is aligned with the cut-out on the backplate **(see illustration)**. Hold the tensioner in the correct position and tighten its retaining bolt to the specified torque. Rotate the crankshaft smoothly through another two complete turns in the normal direction of rotation, to bring the sprocket timing marks back into alignment. Check that the tensioner pointer is still aligned with the backplate cut-out.

19 If the original belt is being refitted on 1.4, 1.6 and 2.0 litre engines, adjust the tensioner so that the pointer is positioned 4.0 mm to the left of the cut-out on the backplate. On 1.8 litre engines, adjust the tensioner so that the pointer is positioned in line with the USED mark on the backplate **(see illustration)**. Hold the tensioner in the correct position and tighten its retaining bolt to the specified torque. Rotate the crankshaft smoothly through another two complete turns in the normal direction of rotation, to bring the sprocket timing marks back into alignment. Check that the tensioner pointer is still correctly positioned in relation to the backplate cut-out.

20 If the tensioner pointer is not correctly positioned in relation to the backplate, repeat the procedure in paragraph 18 (new belt) or 19 (original belt), as applicable.

21 Once the tensioner pointer and backplate remain correctly aligned, the remainder of the refitment procedure is a reversal of removal, noting the following:

a) *Refit the right-hand engine mounting before refitting the crankshaft pulley.*

b) *Tighten all nuts and bolts to the specified torque.*

c) *After the vehicle has been lowered to the ground, tighten the roadwheel bolts to the specified torque.*

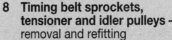

8 Timing belt sprockets, tensioner and idler pulleys – removal and refitting

Camshaft sprockets

Note: *New sprocket retaining bolt(s) will be required on refitting.*

1 Remove the timing belt as described in Section 7.

2 Turn the crankshaft 60° anti-clockwise away from TDC, to move the pistons away from the valves in the cylinder head. This is purely a precaution to prevent valve-to-piston contact if the camshafts are inadvertently rotated during the sprocket bolt removal/refitting procedure.

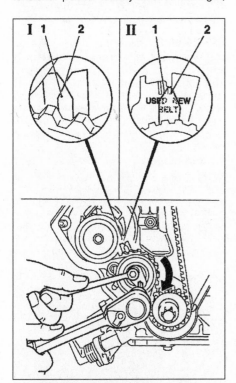

7.18 Timing belt tensioner pointer positions

I *1.4, 1.6 and 2.0 litre engines: Pointer (1) and backplate (2) for new belts*

II *1.8 litre engines: Pointer (1) and backplate (2) for new belt*

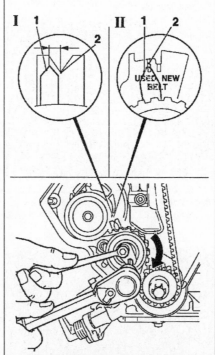

7.19 Timing belt tensioner pointer positions

I *1.4, 1.6 and 2.0 litre engines: Pointer (1) and backplate (2) for used belts*

II *1.8 litre engines: Pointer (1) and backplate (2) for used belts*

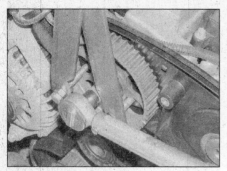

8.3a Hold the camshaft sprocket using a home-made tool . . .

8.3b . . . or use an open-ended spanner to hold the camshaft whilst the sprocket bolt is slackened

3 The camshaft must be prevented from turning as the sprocket bolt is unscrewed, and this can be achieved in one of two ways as follows.
  a) *Make up a sprocket-holding tool using two lengths of steel strip (one long, the other short), and three nuts and bolts; one nut and bolt forms the pivot of a forked tool, with the remaining two nuts and bolts at the tips of the 'forks' to engage with the sprocket spokes (see illustration).*
  b) *Remove the camshaft cover as described in Section 4 and hold the camshaft with an open-ended spanner on the flats provided (see illustration).*
4 Unscrew the retaining bolt and washer and remove the sprocket from the end of the

8.8a On 1.4, 1.6 and 1.8 litre engines ensure that the camshaft sprocket cut-out (arrowed) is correctly engaged with the locating pin

camshaft. If the sprocket locating pin is a loose fit in the camshaft end, remove it and store it with the sprocket for safe-keeping.
5 If necessary, remove the remaining sprocket using the same method. On 1.4, 1.6 and 1.8 litre models the exhaust camshaft sprocket can be easily identified by the lugs which activate the camshaft position sensor. On 2.0 litre models the exhaust sprocket has four spokes and is marked EXHAUST.
6 Prior to refitting check the oil seals for signs of damage or leakage. If necessary, renew as described in Section 9.
7 Ensure the locating pin is in position in the camshaft end.
8 Refit the sprocket to the camshaft end, aligning its cut-out with the locating pin, and fit the washer and new retaining bolt. If both sprockets have been removed, ensure each sprocket is fitted to the correct shaft: on 1.4,

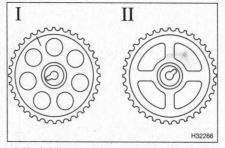

8.8b 2.0 litre engine camshaft sprockets

I   Inlet camshaft sprocket
II Exhaust camshaft sprocket

1.6 and 1.8 litre models the exhaust camshaft sprocket can be identified by the raised sections on the sprocket outer face which trigger the camshaft position sensor. On 2.0 litre models the exhaust sprocket has four spokes and is marked EXHAUST **(see illustrations)**.
9 On all models, retain the sprocket by the method used on removal, and tighten the pulley retaining bolt to the specified Stage 1 torque setting then angle-tighten the bolt through the specified Stage 2 angle, using a socket and extension bar, and finally through the specified Stage 3 angle **(see illustration)**. It is recommended that an angle-measuring gauge is used during the final stages of the tightening, to ensure accuracy. If a gauge is not available, use white paint to make alignment marks between the bolt head and pulley prior to tightening; the marks can then be used to check that the bolt has been rotated through the correct angle.
10 Carefully rotate the crankshaft 60° clockwise until the mark on the crankshaft sprocket aligns with the mark at the base of the cover **(see illustration)**. Refit the timing belt as described in Section 7 then (where necessary) refit the camshaft cover as described in Section 4.

Crankshaft sprocket

1.4, 1.6 and 1.8 litre models

11 Remove the timing belt as described in Section 7.
12 Slide the sprocket off from the end of the crankshaft, noting which way around it is fitted.
13 Align the sprocket locating key with the crankshaft groove then slide the sprocket into position, making sure its timing mark is facing outwards **(see illustration)**.
14 Refit the timing belt as described in Section 7.

2.0 litre models

Note: *A new crankshaft sprocket retaining bolt will be required on refitting.*
15 Remove the timing belt as described in Section 7.
16 Slacken the crankshaft sprocket retaining bolt. To prevent crankshaft rotation on manual transmission models, have an assistant select

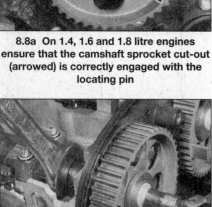

8.9 Tighten the camshaft sprocket

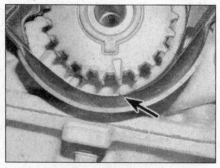

8.10 Align the crankshaft timing mark (arrowed)

8.13 Refit the crankshaft sprocket with the timing mark facing outwards

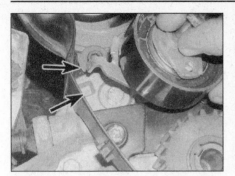

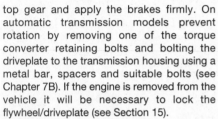

8.23a Engage the tensioner backplate lug with the locating hole in the oil pump housing . . .

8.23b . . . and rotate the tensioner arm clockwise until the roller is as far away from the belt run as possible

8.26 Idler pulley retaining bolt

top gear and apply the brakes firmly. On automatic transmission models prevent rotation by removing one of the torque converter retaining bolts and bolting the driveplate to the transmission housing using a metal bar, spacers and suitable bolts (see Chapter 7B). If the engine is removed from the vehicle it will be necessary to lock the flywheel/driveplate (see Section 15).

17 Unscrew the retaining bolt and washer and remove the crankshaft sprocket from the end of the crankshaft.

18 Align the sprocket location key with the crankshaft groove and slide the sprocket into position, ensuring its timing mark is facing outwards. Fit the washer and new retaining bolt.

19 Lock the crankshaft by the method used on removal, and tighten the sprocket retaining bolt to the specified Stage 1 torque setting then angle-tighten the bolt through the specified Stage 2 angle, using a socket and extension bar. It is recommended that an angle-measuring gauge is used during the final stages of the tightening, to ensure accuracy. If a gauge is not available, use white paint to make alignment marks between the bolt head and sprocket prior to tightening; the marks can then be used to check that the bolt has been rotated through the correct angle.

20 Refit the timing belt as described in Section 7.

Tensioner assembly

21 Remove the timing belt as described in Section 7.

22 Slacken and remove the retaining bolt and remove the tensioner assembly from the engine.

23 Fit the tensioner to the engine, making sure that the lug on the backplate is correctly located in the oil pump housing hole. Ensure the tensioner is correctly seated then refit the retaining bolt. Using an Allen key, rotate the tensioner arm clockwise until the roller is as far away from the belt run as possible, then securely tighten the retaining bolt **(see illustrations)**.

24 Refit the timing belt as described in Section 7.

Idler pulleys

25 Remove the timing belt as described in Section 7.

26 Slacken and remove the retaining bolt(s) and remove the idler pulley(s) from the engine **(see illustration)**.

27 Refit the idler pulley(s) and tighten the retaining bolt(s) to the specified torque.

28 Refit the timing belt as described in Section 7.

9 Camshaft oil seals – renewal

1 Remove the relevant camshaft sprocket as described in Section 8.

2 Carefully punch or drill two small holes opposite each other in the oil seal. Screw a self-tapping screw into each, and pull on the

screws with pliers to extract the seal **(see illustration)**.

3 Clean the seal housing, and polish off any burrs or raised edges which may have caused the seal to fail in the first place.

4 Lubricate the lips of the new seal with clean engine oil, and press it into position using a suitable tubular drift (such as a socket) which bears only on the hard outer edge of the seal **(see illustration)**. Take care not to damage the seal lips during fitting; note that the seal lips should face inwards.

5 Refit the camshaft sprocket as described in Section 8.

10 Camshaft and followers – removal, inspection and refitting

Removal

1 Remove the timing belt as described in Section 7. Prior to releasing the timing belt tension and removing the belt, rotate the crankshaft **backwards** by approximately 60°; this will position the camshafts so that the valve spring pressure is evenly exerted along the complete length of the shaft, reducing the risk of the bearing caps being damaged on removal/refitting **(see illustration)**.

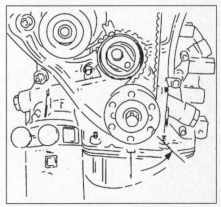

10.1 Prior to removing the timing belt, rotate the crankshaft 60° backwards to ensure the camshafts are correctly positioned – 2.0 litre engine

9.2 Camshaft oil seal removal method

9.4 Refit the camshaft oil seal with a tool that bears only on the hard outer edge of the seal

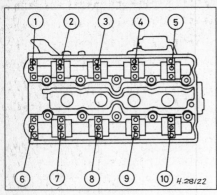

10.3a Camshaft bearing cap numbering sequence

10.3b The identification numbers should be marked on both the bearing caps and the cylinder head (arrowed)

10.6 Use a valve lapping tool to remove the cam followers

2 Remove the camshaft sprockets as described in Section 8.

3 Starting on the inlet camshaft, working in a spiral pattern from the outside inwards (the reverse of illustration 10.15), slacken the camshaft bearing cap retaining bolts by one turn at a time, to relieve the pressure of the valve springs on the bearing caps gradually and evenly. Once the valve spring pressure has been relieved, the bolts can be fully unscrewed and removed along with the caps; the bearing caps and the cylinder head are numbered (inlet camshaft 1 to 5, exhaust camshaft 6 to 10) to ensure the caps are correctly positioned on refitting **(see illustrations)**. Take care not to loose the locating dowels (where fitted).

Caution: If the bearing cap bolts are carelessly slackened, the bearing caps might break. If any bearing cap breaks then the complete cylinder head assembly must be renewed; the bearing caps are matched to the head and are not available separately.

4 Lift the camshaft out of the cylinder head and slide off the oil seal.

5 Repeat the operations described in paragraphs 3 and 4 and remove the exhaust camshaft.

6 Obtain sixteen small, clean plastic containers, and label them for identification. Alternatively, divide a larger container into compartments. Lift the followers out from the top of the cylinder head and store each one in its respective fitted position **(see illustration)**. Note: *Store all the followers the correct way up to prevent the oil draining from the hydraulic valve adjustment mechanisms.*

Inspection

7 Examine the camshaft bearing surfaces and cam lobes for signs of wear ridges and scoring. Renew the camshaft if any of these conditions are apparent. Examine the condition of the bearing surfaces both on the camshaft journals and in the cylinder head. If the head bearing surfaces are worn excessively, the cylinder head will need to be renewed.

8 Support the camshaft end journals on V-blocks, and measure the run-out at the centre journal using a dial gauge. If the run-out exceeds the specified limit, the camshaft should be renewed.

9 Examine the follower bearing surfaces which contact the camshaft lobes for wear ridges and scoring. Check the followers and their bores in the cylinder head for signs of wear or damage. If any follower is thought to be faulty or is visibly worn it should be renewed.

Refitting

10 Where removed, lubricate the followers with clean engine oil and carefully insert each one into its original location in the cylinder head.

11 Lubricate the camshaft followers with MoS₂ (Molybdenum Disulphide) paste then lay the camshafts in position. On 1.8 litre models, the inlet camshaft is marked C3, and the exhaust camshaft is marked T3. Ensure the crankshaft is still positioned approximately 60° BTDC and position each camshaft so that the lobes of No 1 cylinder are pointing upwards **(see illustrations)**. Temporarily refit the sprockets to the camshafts and position each one so that its sprocket timing mark is approximately at its TDC alignment position.

12 Ensure the mating surfaces of the bearing caps and cylinder head are clean and dry and lubricate the camshaft journals and lobes with clean engine oil.

13 Apply a smear of sealant to the mating surfaces of both the inlet (No 1) and exhaust (No 6) camshaft right-hand bearing caps **(see illustration)**.

14 Ensure the locating dowels (where fitted) are in position then refit the camshaft bearing caps and the retaining bolts in their original locations on the cylinder head **(see illustration)**. The caps are numbered (inlet camshaft 1 to 5, exhaust

10.11a Camshaft identification marks – 1.8 litre engine

C3 for inlet camshaft and T3 for the exhaust camshaft

10.11b Prior to refitting the camshaft, lubricate the cam followers with molybdenum disulphide (MoS₂) paste

10.13 Apply sealant to the right-hand bearing caps

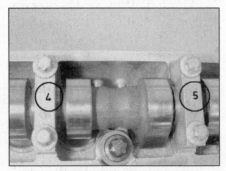

10.14 Camshaft bearing cap numbers

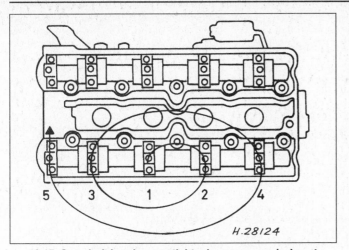

10.15 Camshaft bearing cap tightening sequence (exhaust camshaft shown – inlet the same)

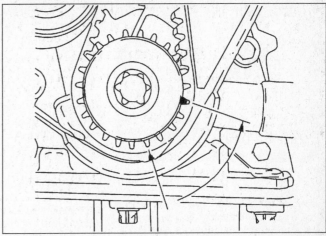

11.3 Prior to remove the timing belt, rotate the crankshaft 60° backwards to ensure the camshafts are correctly positioned

camshaft 6 to 10) from right to left and the corresponding numbers are marked on the cylinder head upper surface. All bearing cap numbers should be the right way up when viewed from the front of the engine.

15 Working on the inlet camshaft, tighten the bearing cap bolts by hand only then, working in a spiral pattern from the centre outwards, tighten the bolts by one turn at a time to gradually impose the pressure of the valve springs on the bearing caps **(see illustration)**. Repeat this sequence until all bearing caps are in contact with the cylinder head then go around and tighten the camshaft bearing cap bolts to the specified torque.

Caution: If the bearing cap bolts are carelessly tightened, the bearing caps might break. If any cap breaks then the complete cylinder head assembly must be renewed; the bearing caps are matched to the head and are not available separately.

16 Tighten the exhaust camshaft bearing cap bolts as described in paragraph 15.

17 Fit new camshaft oil seals as described in Section 9.

18 Refit the camshaft sprockets as described in Section 8.

19 Align the camshaft sprocket timing marks, and then the crankshaft timing marks to bring them back to TDC. Refit the timing belt as described in Section 7.

20 Refit the camshaft cover and timing belt cover(s) as described in Sections 4 and 6.

11 Cylinder head – removal and refitting

Note: *The engine must be cold when removing the cylinder head. New cylinder head bolts must be used on refitting.*

Removal

1 Depressurise the fuel system as described in Chapter 4A then disconnect the battery negative terminal (refer to *Disconnecting the battery* in the *Reference Chapter*).

2 Drain the cooling system as described in Chapter 3, and remove the spark plugs as described in Chapter 1.

3 Remove the timing belt as described in Section 7. Prior to releasing the timing belt tension and removing the belt, rotate the crankshaft **backwards** by approximately 60°; this will position the camshafts so that the valve spring pressure is evenly exerted along the complete length of the shafts, preventing the shafts turning and reducing the risk of the valves contacting the pistons **(see illustration)**. Proceed as described under the relevant sub-heading.

1.4, 1.6 and 1.8 litre models

4 Remove the complete inlet manifold as described in Chapter 4A. Remove the exhaust manifold as described in Chapter 4A. If no work is to be carried out on the cylinder head, the head can be removed complete with the manifold once the following operations have been carried out (see Chapter 4A).
a) Unbolt the exhaust front pipe from manifold.
b) Disconnect the oxygen sensor wiring connector.
c) Disconnect the wiring plug for the crankshaft position sensor.

5 Remove the camshaft cover as described in Section 4.

6 Remove the camshaft sprockets and the timing belt idler pulleys as described in Section 8.

7 Undo the retaining bolts securing the timing belt rear cover to the cylinder head.

8 If not already removed, disconnect the wiring connectors from the ECU (Electronic Control Unit) at the left-hand end of the cylinder head.

9 Disconnect the two hoses from the thermostat housing.

10 Referring to Chapter 3, unclip the heater matrix-to-intake manifold hoses to drain the coolant from the cylinder block. Once the flow of coolant has stopped, reconnect both hoses and mop up any spilt coolant. Undo the two Torx bolts, and disconnect the coolant hose flange from the rear of the cylinder head **(see illustrations)**.

11 On 1.4 and 1.6 litre models, detach the engine breather pipe from the control unit bracket at the left-hand end of the cylinder head.

12 On 1.8 litre models, remove the oil dipstick retaining bolt and turn the dipstick guide tube to one side.

13 Make a final check to ensure that all relevant hoses, pipes and wires, etc, have been disconnected.

14 Working in the **reverse** of the tightening sequence **(see illustration 11.42)**,

11.10a Coolant flange – 1.8 litre engine

11.10b Coolant flange – 1.4 and 1.6 litre engine

11.14 Remove each bolt along with its washer

progressively slacken the cylinder head bolts by a third of a turn at a time until all bolts can be unscrewed by hand. Remove each bolt in turn, along with its washer **(see illustration)**.

15 Lift the cylinder head from the cylinder block. If necessary, tap the cylinder head gently with a soft-faced mallet to free it from the block, but **do not** lever at the mating faces.

16 Note the fitted positions of the two locating dowels, and remove them for safe-keeping if they are loose. Recover the cylinder head gasket, and discard it.

2.0 litre models

17 Remove the inlet and exhaust manifolds as described in Chapter 4A. If no work is to be carried out on the cylinder head, the head can be removed complete with manifolds once all

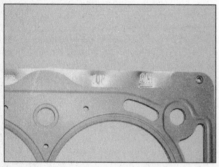

11.39a Fit the new cylinder head gasket with the OBEN/TOP marking uppermost . . .

the hoses/wiring, etc, have been disconnected (see Chapter 4A).

18 Remove the camshaft cover as described in Section 4.

19 Remove the camshaft sprockets as described in Section 8.

20 Undo the retaining bolts securing the timing belt rear cover to the cylinder head.

21 If the inlet manifold is to remain attached to the cylinder head, remove the alternator-to-manifold support brackets, and allow the alternator to swing back out of the way.

22 Disconnect the accelerator cable with reference to Chapter 4A.

23 Disconnect the brake servo vacuum hose from the inlet manifold.

24 Detach the fuel supply and return pipes from the fuel distributor pipe.

25 Release the retaining clips and disconnect the coolant hoses from the heater matrix and throttle body.

26 If not already carried out, disconnect the wiring plugs from the injectors and place the wiring to one side.

27 Remove the exhaust camshaft, as described in Section 10.

28 Make a final check to ensure that all relevant hoses, pipes and wires, etc, have been disconnected.

29 Working in the **reverse** of the tightening sequence **(see illustration 11.42)**, using a T55 splined tool such as Vauxhall tool KM2355, progressively slacken the cylinder head bolts by a third of a turn at a time until all bolts can be unscrewed by hand. Remove each bolt in turn, along with its washer.

30 Lift the cylinder head from the cylinder block. If necessary, tap the cylinder head gently with a soft-faced mallet to free it from the block, but **do not** lever at the mating faces. Note the fitted positions of the two locating dowels, and remove them for safe-keeping if they are loose.

31 Recover the cylinder head gasket, and discard it.

Preparation for refitting

32 The mating faces of the cylinder head and block must be perfectly clean before refitting the head. Use a wooden or plastic scraper to

remove all traces of gasket and carbon, and also clean the tops of the pistons. Take particular care with the aluminium surfaces, as the soft metal is damaged easily. Also, make sure that debris is not allowed to enter the oil and water channels – this is particularly important for the oil circuit, as carbon could block the oil supply to the camshaft or crankshaft bearings. Using adhesive tape and paper, seal the water, oil and bolt holes in the cylinder block. To prevent carbon entering the gap between the pistons and bores, smear a little grease in the gap. After cleaning the piston, rotate the crankshaft so that the piston moves down the bore, then wipe out the grease and carbon with a cloth rag. Clean the other piston crowns in the same way.

33 Check the block and head for nicks, deep scratches and other damage. If slight, they may be removed carefully with a file. More serious damage may be repaired by machining, but this is a specialist job.

34 If warpage of the cylinder head is suspected, use a straight-edge to check it for distortion. Refer to Chapter 2D if necessary.

35 Ensure that the cylinder head bolt holes in the crankcase are clean and free of oil. Syringe or soak up any oil left in the bolt holes. This is most important in order that the correct bolt tightening torque can be applied and to prevent the possibility of the block being cracked by hydraulic pressure when the bolts are tightened.

36 Renew the cylinder head bolts regardless of their apparent condition.

Refitting

37 Ensure the crankshaft is positioned approximately 60° BTDC and wipe clean the mating faces of the head and block.

38 Ensure that the two locating dowels are in position at each end of the cylinder block/crankcase surface.

39 Fit the new cylinder head gasket to the block, making sure it is fitted with the correct way up with its OBEN/TOP mark uppermost **(see illustrations)**.

40 Carefully refit the cylinder head, locating it on the dowels **(see illustration)**.

41 Fit the washers to the new cylinder head

11.39b . . . over the locating dowels

11.40 Engage the cylinder head with the locating dowels

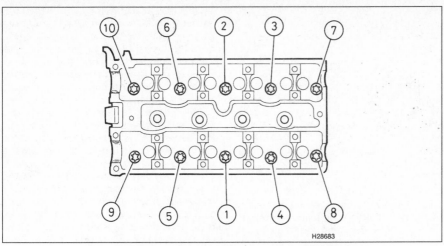

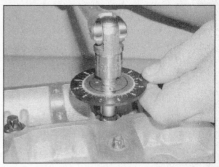

11.43 Tighten the cylinder head bolts through the various angle-tightening sequences

11.42 Cylinder head bolt tightening sequence – 2.0 litre engine (1.4, 1.6 and 1.8 litre engines are the same)

bolts then carefully insert them into position (**do not drop**), tightening them finger-tight only at this stage. Note that on some models, the new bolts come with washers already fitted.

42 Working progressively and in sequence, first tighten all the cylinder head bolts to the Stage 1 torque setting (**see illustration**).

43 Once all bolts have been tightened to the Stage 1 torque, again working in sequence, tighten each bolt through its specified Stage 2 angle, using a socket and extension bar. It is recommended that an angle-measuring gauge is used during this stage of the tightening, to ensure accuracy (**see illustration**).

44 Working in the specified sequence, go around again and tighten all bolts through the specified Stage 3 angle.

45 Working again in the specified sequence, go around and tighten all bolts through the specified Stage 4 angle.

46 Finally go around in the specified sequence again and tighten all bolts through the specified Stage 5 angle.

1.4, 1.6 and 1.8 litre models

47 Reconnect the coolant hoses, securing them in position with the retaining clips. Reconnect the coolant hose flange at the rear of the cylinder head using a new rubber seal/gasket.

48 Reconnect the wiring connectors to the cylinder head, ensuring the harness is correctly routed and retained by all the necessary clips.

49 Refit the timing belt rear cover retaining bolts and tighten them to the specified torque.

50 Refit the camshaft sprockets and idler pulleys as described in Section 8.

51 Align all the sprocket timing marks to bring the camshafts and crankshaft back to TDC then refit the timing belt as described in Section 7.

52 Refit the camshaft cover and timing belt cover(s) as described in Sections 4 and 6.

53 Refit/reconnect the inlet and exhaust manifolds (see Chapter 4A).

54 Refit the roadwheel then lower the vehicle to the floor and tighten the wheel bolts to the specified torque.

55 Ensure all pipes and hoses are securely reconnected then refill the cooling system and refit the spark plugs as described in Chapters 1 and 3.

56 Refit the ignition module, engine cover, and air filter housing/trunking.

57 Reconnect the battery then start the engine and check for signs of leaks.

2.0 litre models

58 Refit the exhaust camshaft with reference to Section 10.

59 Reconnect the coolant hoses, securing them in position with the retaining clips.

60 Refit the timing belt rear cover retaining bolts and tighten them to the specified torque.

61 Refit the camshaft sprockets as described in Section 8.

62 Carry out the procedures described in paragraphs 51 to 57.

12 Sump – removal and refitting

1.4, 1.6 and 1.8 litre models

Removal

1 Disconnect the battery negative terminal (refer to *Disconnecting the battery* in the Reference Chapter).

2 Firmly apply the handbrake, then jack up the front of the car and support it securely on axle stands (see *Jacking and vehicle support*). Where necessary, undo the retaining screws and remove the undercover from beneath the engine/transmission unit.

3 Drain the engine oil as described in Chapter 1, then fit a new sealing washer and refit

the drain plug, tightening it to the specified torque.

4 Remove the exhaust system front pipe as described in Chapter 4A.

5 Disconnect the wiring connector from the oil level sensor (where fitted).

6 Slacken and remove the bolts securing the sump flange to the transmission housing.

7 Remove the rubber plugs from the transmission end of the sump flange to gain access to the sump end retaining bolts (**see illustration**).

8 Progressively slacken and remove the bolts securing the sump to the base of the cylinder block/oil pump. Break the sump joint by striking the sump with the palm of the hand, then lower the sump away from the engine and withdraw it. On 1.4 and 1.6 litre models, remove the gasket and discard it.

9 While the sump is removed, take the opportunity to check the oil pump pick-up/strainer for signs of clogging or splitting. If necessary, unbolt the pick-up/strainer and remove it from the engine along with its sealing ring. The strainer can then be cleaned easily in solvent or renewed.

Refitting

10 Remove all traces of dirt and oil from the mating surfaces of the sump and cylinder block and (where removed) the pick-up/strainer. Also remove all traces of locking compound from the pick-up bolts (where removed).

11 Where necessary, position a new gasket/seal on top of the oil pump pick-

12.7 Remove the rubber plugs to gain access to the sump retaining bolts

12.11 Oil pump pick-up pipe

up/strainer and fit the strainer. Apply locking compound to the threads of the retaining bolts then fit the bolts and tighten to the specified torque **(see illustration)**.

12 Ensure the sump and cylinder block mating surfaces are clean and dry and remove all traces of locking compound from the sump bolts.

13 On 1.4 and 1.6 litre models, apply a smear of suitable sealant (available form Vauxhall dealers) to the areas of the cylinder block mating surface around the areas of the of the oil pump housing and rear main bearing cap joints **(see illustration)**.

14 On 1.4 and 1.6 litre models, fit a new gasket to the sump and apply a few drops of locking compound to the threads of the sump to cylinder block/oil pump bolts.

15 On 1.8 litre models, apply a bead of suitable sealant (available from Vauxhall dealers) approximately 2.5 mm thick to the sealing surface of the oil pan. Around the No 5 main bearing cap area, increase the thickness of the bead to 3.5 mm **(see illustration)**.

16 Offer up the sump, ensuring the gasket remains correctly positioned, and loosely refit all the retaining bolts. If the sump is being refitted to an engine block with the transmission removed, use a straight-edge to ensure that the transmission flange of the sump is flush with the transmission flange of the block. Working out from the centre in a diagonal sequence, progressively tighten the bolts securing the sump to the cylinder

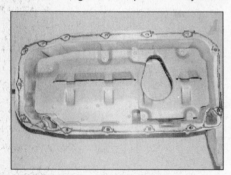

12.15 Apply a 2.5 mm thick bead of sealant to the sump sealing surface – increase the thickness to 3.5 mm around the No 5 main bearing cap area – 1.8 litre engines

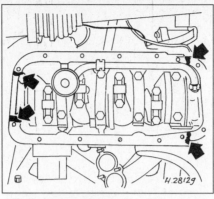

12.13 Apply sealant to the oil pump and rear main bearing cap joints (arrowed) before the sump is refitted

block/oil pump to their specified torque setting.

17 Tighten the bolts securing the sump flange to the transmission housing to their specified torque settings. Refit the rubber plugs to the sump flange cut-outs **(see illustration)**.

18 Refit the exhaust front pipe (see Chapter 4A) and reconnect the oil level sender wiring connector (where fitted).

19 Lower the vehicle to the ground then fill the engine with fresh oil, with reference to Chapter 1.

2.0 litre models

Note: *New lower sump retaining bolts will be required on refitting.*

Removal

20 Carry out the operations described in paragraphs 1 to 4.

21 Disconnect the wiring connector from the oil level sensor then slide off the retaining clip and push the sensor connector into the sump.

22 Slacken and remove the bolts securing the lower sump pan to the main casting then free the sump pan from the main casting and remove it along with its gasket. Take care not to damage the oil level sensor wiring as the pan is removed.

23 To remove the main casting from the engine, remove the oil filter (see Chapter 1). If the oil filter is damaged on removal (which is

12.17 Sump retaining bolts – transmission end flange

likely), a new one should be used on refitting and the engine should be filled with fresh oil.

24 On manual transmission models, disconnect the right-hand driveshaft from the transmission as described in Chapter 8. Remove the right-hand driveshaft bearing flange from the transmission to provide sufficient clearance.

25 Slacken and remove the bolts securing the sump flange to the transmission housing.

26 Remove the oil pump pick-up pipe-to-main bearing bridge retaining bolts, and the pick-up pipe-to-oil pump bolts.

27 Progressively slacken and remove the bolts securing the main casting to the base of the cylinder block/oil pump. Break the joint by striking the casting with the palm of the hand, then lower it away from the engine and withdraw it complete with the oil pick-up pipe. Remove the gasket and discard it.

Refitting

28 Remove all traces of dirt and oil from the mating surfaces of the sump main casting and pan, the cylinder block and the pick-up/strainer. Also remove all traces of locking compound from the threads of the sump pan holes.

29 Position a new seal ring on top of the oil pump pick-up/strainer.

30 Ensure the main casting and cylinder block mating surfaces are clean and dry and remove all traces of locking compound from the retaining bolts.

31 Apply a smear of suitable sealant (available from Vauxhall dealers) to the areas of the cylinder block mating surface around the areas of the oil pump housing and rear main bearing cap joints.

32 Fit a new gasket to the main casting and apply a few drops of locking compound to the threads of the casting to cylinder block/oil pump bolts.

33 Offer up the main casting with the oil pick-up pipe, ensuring the gasket remains correctly positioned, and loosely refit all the retaining bolts. Working out from the centre in a diagonal sequence, progressively tighten the bolts securing it to the cylinder block/oil pump to their specified torque setting. Tighten the oil pick-up pipe-to-bearing bridge and pipe-to-oil pump bolts to the specified torque setting.

34 Tighten the bolts securing the main casting flange to the transmission housing to their specified torque settings.

35 Refit the exhaust front pipe (see Chapter 4A) and, refit the driveshaft bearing flange.

36 With reference to Chapter 8, refit the right-hand driveshaft.

37 Ensure the sump pan and main casting surfaces are clean and dry, place a new gasket on the top of the pan and offer it up to the main casting. Fit a new sealing ring to the oil level sensor wiring connector and seat the wiring connector in the main casting, securing it in position with the retaining clip, prior to seating the sump pan on the main casting.

13.4 Manoeuvre the oil level sensor from the sump – renew the seal

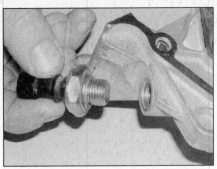

14.4 Disconnect and remove the oil pressure switch

14.6 Undo the pump retaining bolts

38 Fit the new sump pan retaining bolts then go around in a diagonal sequence and tighten them to the specified Stage 1 torque setting. Once all bolts have been tightened go around again and angle-tighten them through the specified Stage 2 angle.

39 Fit a new oil filter and reconnect the oil level sender wiring connector.

40 Lower the vehicle to the ground then fill the engine with fresh oil, with reference to Chapter 1.

13 Oil level sensor – removal and refitting

1.4, 1.6 and 1.8 litre models

Removal

1 Firmly apply the handbrake, then jack up the front of the car and support it securely on axle stands (see *Jacking and vehicle support*). Where necessary, undo the retaining screws and remove the undercover from beneath the engine/transmission unit.

2 Drain the engine oil as described in Chapter 1, then fit a new sealing washer and refit the drain plug, tightening it to the specified torque.

3 Disconnect the oil level sensor wiring plug.

4 Slacken and remove the four screws, and manoeuvre the sensor out from the sump **(see illustration)**.

Refitting

5 If the original sensor is to be re-used, renew the sealing ring.

6 Refit the sensor to the sump, apply a little

locking compound to the retaining screws, and tighten the screws to the specified torque setting.

7 Lower the vehicle to the ground then fill the engine with fresh oil, with reference to Chapter 1.

2.0 litre models

Removal

8 Firmly apply the handbrake, then jack up the front of the car and support it securely on axle stands (see *Jacking and vehicle support*). Where necessary, undo the retaining screws and remove the undercover from beneath the engine/transmission unit.

9 Drain the engine oil as described in Chapter 1, then fit a new sealing washer and refit the drain plug, tightening it to the specified torque.

10 Disconnect the wiring connector from the oil level sensor then slide off the retaining clip and push the sensor connector into the sump.

11 Slacken and remove the bolts securing the lower sump pan to the main casting then free the sump pan from the main casting and remove it along with its gasket. Take care not to damage the oil level sensor wiring as the pan is removed.

12 Undo the two Torx screws and remove the sensor from the sump.

Refitting

13 Fit the sensor to the sump and tighten the Torx screws to the specified torque setting.

14 Ensure the sump pan and main casting surfaces are clean and dry, place a new gasket on the top of the pan and offer it up to the main casting. Fit a new sealing ring to the oil level sensor wiring connector and seat the

wiring connector in the main casting, securing it in position with the retaining clip, prior to seating the sump pan on the main casting.

15 Fit the new sump pan retaining bolts then go around in a diagonal sequence and tighten them to the specified Stage 1 torque setting. Once all bolts have been tightened go around again and angle-tighten them through the specified Stage 2 angle.

16 Lower the vehicle to the ground then fill the engine with fresh oil, with reference to Chapter 1.

14 Oil pump – removal, overhaul and refitting

Note: *The pressure relief valve can be removed with pump in position on the engine unit, although on some models it will be necessary to unbolt the mounting bracket assembly from the block to allow the valve to be removed.*

Removal

1 Remove the timing belt as described in Section 7.

2 Remove the rear timing belt cover as described in Section 6.

3 Remove the sump and oil pump pick-up/strainer as described in Section 12.

4 Disconnect the wiring connector and the oil pressure switch **(see illustration)**.

5 Where applicable, unbolt the crankshaft sensor from the mounting bracket and position it clear of the oil pump.

6 Slacken and remove the retaining bolts then slide the oil pump housing assembly off of the end of the crankshaft, taking great care not to lose the locating dowels. Remove the housing gasket and discard it **(see illustration)**.

Overhaul

7 Undo the retaining screws and lift off the pump cover from the rear of the housing **(see illustration)**.

8 Note any marks identifying the outer faces of the pump gears. If none can be seen, using a suitable marker pen, mark the surface of both the pump inner and outer gears; the marks can then be used to ensure the gears are refitted the correct way around **(see illustration)**.

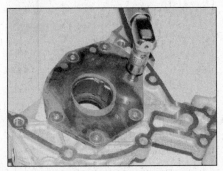

14.7 Oil pump cover screws

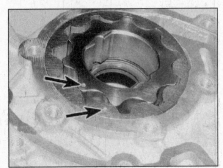

14.8 Oil pump gears identifying marks

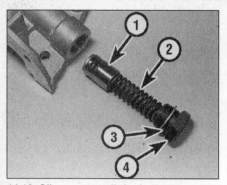

14.10 Oil pressure relief valve components

1 Plunger
2 Spring
3 Sealing washer
4 Valve bolt

14.12a Using a feeler gauge to check gear clearance

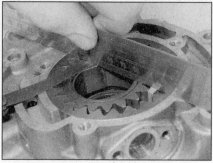

14.12b Using a straight-edge and feeler gauge to measure gear endfloat

9 Lift out the inner and outer gears from the pump housing.

10 Unscrew the oil pressure relief valve bolt from the front of the housing and withdraw the spring and plunger from the housing, noting which way around the plunger is fitted. Remove the sealing washer from the valve bolt **(see illustration)**.

11 Clean the components, and carefully examine the gears, pump body and relief valve plunger for any signs of scoring or wear. Renew any component which shows signs of wear or damage; if the gears or pump housing are marked, then the complete pump assembly should be renewed.

12 If the components appear serviceable, measure the clearance between the inner and outer gears using feeler blades. Also measure the gear endfloat, and check the flatness of the end cover **(see illustrations)**. If the clearances exceed the specified tolerances, the pump must be renewed.

13 If the pump is satisfactory, reassemble the components in the reverse order of removal, noting the following.

a) *Ensure both gears are fitted the correct way around.*
b) *Fit a new sealing ring to the pressure relief valve bolt and tighten the bolt to the specified torque.*
c) *Apply a little locking compound to the threads, and tighten the pump cover*

screws to the specified torque **(see illustration)**.
d) *On completion prime the oil pump by filling it with clean engine oil whilst rotating the inner gear.*

Refitting

14 Prior to refitting, carefully lever out the crankshaft oil seal using a flat-bladed screwdriver. Fit the new oil seal, ensuring its sealing lip is facing inwards, and press it squarely into the housing using a tubular drift which bears only on the hard outer edge of the seal **(see illustration)**. Press the seal into position so that it is flush with the housing and lubricate the oil seal lip with clean engine oil.

15 Ensure the mating surfaces of the oil pump and cylinder block are clean and dry and the locating dowels are in position.

16 Fit a new gasket to the cylinder block.

17 Carefully manoeuvre the oil pump into position and engage the inner gear with the crankshaft end **(see illustration)**. Locate the pump on the dowels, taking great care not damage the oil seal lip.

18 Refit the pump housing retaining bolts in their original locations and tighten them to the specified torque.

19 Refit the crankshaft sensor bracket and tighten its mounting bolt to the specified torque (where given).

20 Reconnect the oil pressure sensor wiring connector.

21 Refit the oil pump pick-up/strainer and sump as described in Section 12.

22 Refit the rear timing belt cover to the engine, tightening its retaining bolts to the specified torque.

23 Refit the timing belt sprockets, idler pulleys and tensioner then refit the belt as described in Sections 7 and 8.

24 On completion, fit a new oil filter and fill the engine with clean oil as described in Chapter 1.

15 Flywheel/driveplate – removal, inspection and refitting

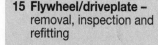

Note: *New flywheel/driveplate retaining bolts will be required on refitting.*

Removal

Manual transmission models

1 Remove the transmission as described in Chapter 7A then remove the clutch assembly as described in Chapter 6.

2 Prevent the flywheel from turning by locking the ring gear teeth. Alternatively, bolt a strap between the flywheel and the cylinder block/crankcase. Make alignment marks between the flywheel and crankshaft using

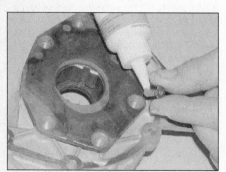

14.13 Apply thread locking compound to the oil pump cover screws

14.14 Fitting a new crankshaft oil seal to the oil pump housing

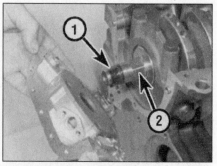

14.17 On refitting take care not to damage the oil seal on the crankshaft lip (1) and engage the inner gear with the crankshaft flats (2)

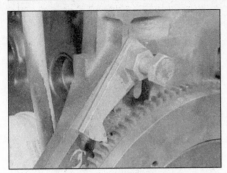

15.2a Lock the flywheel/driveplate ring gear with a suitable tool

15.2b Make alignment marks between the flywheel and crankshaft

15.10 Use an angle-gauge to tighten the flywheel bolts accurately

paint or a suitable marker pen (see illustrations).

3 Slacken and remove the retaining bolts and remove the flywheel. Do not drop it, as it is very heavy.

Automatic transmission models

4 Remove the transmission as described in Chapter 7B then remove the driveplate as described in paragraphs 2 and 3, noting that there is a retaining plate fitted between the retaining bolts and driveplate.

Inspection

5 On manual transmission models, examine the flywheel for scoring of the clutch face. If the clutch face is scored, the flywheel may be surface-ground, but renewal is preferable. Check for wear or chipping of the ring gear teeth. Renewal of the ring gear is also possible, but is not a task for the home mechanic; renewal requires the new ring gear to be heated (to 230ºC) to allow it to be fitted.

6 On automatic transmission models closely examine the driveplate and ring gear teeth for signs of wear or damage and check the driveplate surface for any signs of cracks.

7 If there is any doubt about the condition of the flywheel/driveplate, seek the advice of a Vauxhall dealer or engine reconditioning specialist. They will be able to advise if it is possible to recondition it or whether renewal is necessary.

Refitting

Manual transmission models

8 Clean the mating surfaces of the flywheel and crankshaft.

9 Offer up the flywheel and fit the new retaining bolts with a little locking compound. If the original is being refitted align the marks made prior to removal.

10 Lock the flywheel by the method used on removal, and tighten the retaining bolts to the specified Stage 1 torque setting then angle-tighten the bolts through the specified Stage 2 angle, using a socket and extension bar, and finally through the specified Stage 3 angle. It is recommended that an angle-measuring gauge is used during the final stages of the tightening, to ensure accuracy (see illustration). If a gauge is not available, use white paint to make alignment marks between the bolt head and flywheel prior to tightening; the marks can then be used to check that the bolt has been rotated through the correct angle.

11 Refit the clutch as described in Chapter 6 then remove the locking tool, and refit the transmission as described in Chapter 7A.

Automatic transmission models

12 Clean the mating surfaces of the driveplate and crankshaft and remove all traces of locking compound from the driveplate retaining bolt threads.

13 Apply a drop of locking compound to each of the retaining bolt threads then offer up the driveplate, if the original is being refitted

align the marks made prior to removal. Refit the retaining plate and screw in the retaining bolts.

14 Lock the driveplate using the method employed on dismantling then, working in a diagonal sequence, evenly and progressively tighten the retaining bolts to the specified torque (and angle-tighten where necessary).

15 Remove the locking tool and refit the transmission as described in Chapter 7B.

16 Crankshaft oil seals – renewal

Timing belt end oil seal

1 Remove the crankshaft sprocket as described in Section 8.

2 Carefully punch or drill two small holes opposite each other in the oil seal. Screw a self-tapping screw into each and pull on the screws with pliers to extract the seal (see illustration).

Caution: Great care must be taken to avoid damage to the oil pump.

3 Clean the seal housing and polish off any burrs or raised edges which may have caused the seal to fail in the first place.

4 Lubricate the lips of the new seal with clean engine oil and ease it into position on the end of the shaft. Press the seal squarely into position until it is flush with the housing. If necessary, a suitable tubular drift, such as a socket, which bears only on the hard outer edge of the seal can be used to tap the seal into position (see illustration). Take great care not to damage the seal lips during fitting and ensure that the seal lips face inwards.

5 Wash off any traces of oil, then refit the crankshaft sprocket as described in Section 8.

Flywheel/driveplate end oil seal

6 Remove the flywheel/driveplate as described in Section 15.

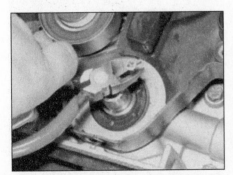

16.2 Removing the crankshaft right-hand oil seal

16.4 Fitting a new crankshaft right-hand oil seal

7 Renew the seal as described in paragraphs 2 to 4 **(see illustration)**.
8 Refit the flywheel/driveplate as described in Section 15.

17 Engine/transmission mountings – inspection and renewal

Refer to Chapter 2A, Section 17.

18 Balancer unit (2.0 litre engine) – removal and refitting

Removal

1 Some models fitted with the 2.0 litre DOHC engine are equipped with a balancer unit fitted between the cylinder block and the main sump casting. The unit consists of two counter-rotating balance shafts driven by the crankshaft **(see illustration)**.
2 Remove the sump main casting as described in Section 12.
3 Slacken the retaining bolts, and remove the balancer unit and shim.

Refitting

4 If operations have been carried out that might affect the backlash between the balancer shafts and the crankshaft (crankshaft, bearing cap or balancer unit replacement), then the backlash must be measured and, if necessary, adjusted. If none of theses mentioned operations have been carried out, the original shim can be re-used.
5 In order to carry out the measurement and adjustment procedure, Vauxhall tool KM 949 must be used. If this tool is not available, take the cylinder block and balancer unit to a Vauxhall dealer or specialist to have the backlash measured and adjusted. If the tool is available, proceed as follows.

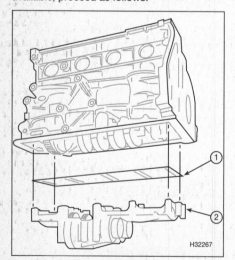

18.1 Balancer unit (2) and shim (1) – 2.0 litre engine

16.7 Left-hand crankshaft oil seal

6 With reference to Section 3 if necessary, set the crankshaft at TDC on No 1 cylinder at the end of the compression stroke.
7 Position the two balance shafts so that when viewed from the right-hand of the engine, the two flat machined surfaces are exactly horizontal **(see illustration)**.
8 Fit the existing shim and balancer unit to the cylinder block. Insert the retaining bolts and tighten them to the specified torque.
9 Screw Vauxhall tool KM 949 with the long knurled bolt into the end of the inlet side balancer shaft. Position the measuring arm so that it points to the 9 o'clock position, when viewed from the end of the engine. Hand tighten the bolt.
10 Screw the short knurled bolt of tool KM 949 into the exhaust side balancer shaft. Hand tighten the bolt.
11 Mount a dial gauge onto the balancer unit or cylinder block, so that the gauge probe acts vertically against the measuring arm between the notches of the flat machined surface **(see illustration)**.
12 Determine the 'beginning' and 'end' of the backlash by turning the exhaust side knurled bolt backwards and forwards. Position this balancer shaft at the 'beginning' of the backlash and zero the dial gauge.
13 Turn the exhaust side balancer shaft to the 'end' of the backlash, and read off the measurement from the dial gauge.
14 The backlash should be measured at four different balancer shaft positions. Using the crankshaft timing sprocket bolt, turn the crankshaft clockwise until the measuring arm

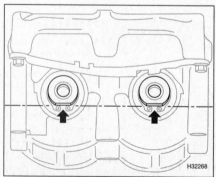

18.7 Position the balancer shafts so that the two flat machined surfaces are horizontal

on the inlet side balancer shaft points to the 6 o'clock position. Loosen the knurled bolt and reposition the arm back to the 9 o'clock position. Repeat the backlash measurement procedure in this position, and take two further readings repositioning the balancer shaft each time.
15 If any of the four reading are outside the value given in the Specifications, the backlash must be adjusted. Adjustment is achieved by inserting a shim of various thicknesses between the balancer unit and the cylinder block. Each shim is given a code number to represent its thickness (see Specifications). This code is also stamped onto the shim.
16 Having established the backlash, and the thickness of the existing shim (from the code number), it is then possible to determine the thickness (and code number) of the shim required to adjust the backlash to within the given tolerance. The next larger or smaller shim changes the backlash by approximately 0.02 mm. For example: The measured backlash with a shim code number '70' fitted was 0.08 mm. If this shim is substituted by one with the code number '67', the backlash is reduced to 0.06 mm. Only one shim may be fitted at a time.
17 After selecting the correct shim, and refitting the balancer unit and shim as described in paragraphs 6 to 8, repeat the measurement procedure to ensure the backlash is within tolerance.
18 Remove the dial gauge and the two knurled bolts of tool KM 949.
19 Refit the sump as described in Section 12.

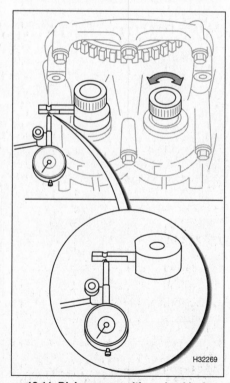

18.11 Dial gauge position – backlash adjustment

Chapter 2 Part C:
2.2 litre DOHC engine in-car repair procedures

Contents

Balance shaft – removal and refitting 14
Camshaft and followers – removal, inspection and refitting 10
Camshaft cover – removal and refitting 5
Compression test – description and interpretation 2
Crankshaft oil seals – renewal 15
Crankshaft pulley/vibration damper – removal and refitting 6
Cylinder head – removal and refitting 11
Engine oil and filter renewal ....See Chapter 1
Engine oil level check ....See *Weekly checks*
Engine/transmission mountings – inspection and renewal 17

Flywheel/driveplate – removal, inspection and refitting 16
General information 1
Oil pump – removal, inspection and refitting 13
Sump – removal and refitting 12
Timing chain cover – removal and refitting 7
Timing chain tensioners – removal and refitting 8
Timing chains and sprockets – removal, inspection and refitting ... 9
Top dead centre (TDC) for No 1 piston – locating 3
Valve timing – checking and adjustment 4

Degrees of difficulty

Easy, suitable for novice with little experience	**Fairly easy,** suitable for beginner with some experience	**Fairly difficult,** suitable for competent DIY mechanic	**Difficult,** suitable for experienced DIY mechanic	**Very difficult,** suitable for expert DIY or professional

Specifications

General

Engine type	Four-cylinder, in-line, water-cooled. Chain-driven double overhead camshaft, acting on hydraulic tappets, 16 valves
Manufacturer's engine code	Z22SE
Bore	86.0 mm
Stroke	94.6 mm
Capacity	2198 cc
Injection sequence	1-3-4-2 (No 1 cylinder at timing chain end of engine)
Direction of crankshaft rotation	Clockwise (viewed from timing chain end of engine)
Compression ratio	10:1
Maximum power	108 kW at 5800 rpm
Maximum torque	203 Nm at 4000 rpm

Compression pressures

Standard	12 to 15 bar (174 to 218 psi)
Maximum difference between any two cylinders	1 bar (15 psi)
Pressure loss	Not more than 25% max per cylinder

Camshaft

Endfloat	0.04 to 0.14 mm
Maximum permissible radial run-out	0.06 mm
Cam lift (inlet and exhaust)	8.0 mm

Lubrication system

Oil pump type	Rotor-type, driven by crankshaft pulley/vibration damper from crankshaft
Minimum permissible oil pressure at idle speed, with engine at operating temperature (oil temperature of at least 80°C)	1.5 bar (22 psi)
Oil pump clearances:	
Between outer rotor and oil pump housing	0.350 mm (max)
Between inner and outer rotor	0.150 mm (max)
Indentation/endfloat (rotor-to-upper edge of timing case cover)	0.080 mm (max)

Torque wrench settings

	Nm	lbf ft
Auxiliary drivebelt tensioner bolt	42	31
Balance shaft retaining bracket bolts	10	7
Balance shaft sprocket bolts*:		
Stage 1	8	6
Stage 2	Angle-tighten a further 30°	
Camshaft bearing cap bolts:		
Caps 1 to 10	8	6
Cap 11	20	15
Camshaft cover bolts	10	7
Camshaft sprocket bolt*:		
Stage 1	85	63
Stage 2	Angle-tighten a further 30°	
Stage 3	Angle-tighten a further 15°	
Connecting rod big-end bearing cap bolt*:		
Stage 1	25	18
Stage 2	Angle-tighten a further 50°	
Stage 3	Angle-tighten a further 50°	
Coolant drain bolt in coolant pump	20	15
Coolant pump sprocket access cover bolts	8	6
Coolant pump sprocket bolts	10	7
Coolant pump-to-cylinder block bolts	25	18
Crankshaft pulley/vibration damper bolt*:		
Stage 1	100	74
Stage 2	Angle-tighten a further 75°	
Stage 3	Angle-tighten a further 15°	
Cylinder head x10 (main) bolts*:		
Stage 1	30	22
Stage 2	Angle-tighten a further 75°	
Stage 3	Angle-tighten a further 75°	
Stage 4	Angle-tighten a further 15°	
Cylinder head x4 (timing chain end) bolts*	35	26
Driveplate bolts*:		
Stage 1	53	39
Stage 2	Angle-tighten a further 25°	
Engine/transmission mounting bolts:		
Right-hand mounting:		
Mounting-to-bracket bolts	55	41
Mounting-to-body bolts	35	26
Bracket-to-cylinder head bolts	50	37
Left-hand mounting:		
Mounting-to-body bolts	20	15
Bracket-to-transmission bolts	35	26
Mounting-to-bracket bolts	55	41
Rear mounting:		
Mounting-to-bracket bolts	45	33
Mounting-to-subframe bolts	60	44
Bracket-to-transmission bolts	60	44
Front mounting:		
Mounting-to-transmission bolts	60	44
Mounting to subframe	55	41
Flywheel bolts*:		
Stage 1	53	39
Stage 2	Angle-tighten a further 25°	
Lower main bearing cylinder block casing:		
M8 bolts	25	18
M10 bolts (main bearing bolts)*:		
Stage 1	20	15
Stage 2	Angle-tighten a further 70°	
Oil dipstick tube to intake manifold	10	7
Oil pump:		
Oil pressure control valve plug	40	30
Oil pump cover plate-to-timing cover bolts	6	4
Roadwheel bolts	110	81
Sump drain plug	25	18
Sump-to-cylinder block baseplate	25	18
Sump-to-transmission bolts	25	18

Torque wrench settings (continued)	Nm	lbf ft
Timing chain cover bolts	25	18
Timing chain guide bolts	10	7
Timing chain oil spray/injector nozzle	10	7
Timing chain sliding rail bolt*	10	7
Timing chain tensioner:		
Camshaft	75	55
Balance shafts	10	7
Timing chain tensioner rail pivot bolt	10	7
Transmission-to-cylinder block bolts	60	44

Use new fasteners

1 General information

How to use this Chapter

1 This Part of Chapter 2 is devoted to in-car repair procedures for the engine. All procedures concerning engine removal and refitting, and engine block/cylinder head overhaul can be found in Chapter 2D.

2 Most of the operations included in this Part are based on the assumption that the engine is still installed in the car. Therefore, if this information is being used during a complete engine overhaul, with the engine already removed, many of the steps included here will not apply.

Engine description

3 The 2.2 litre (2198 cc) engine is a completely new engine designed by Vauxhall. It is of the sixteen-valve, in-line four-cylinder, double overhead camshaft (DOHC) type, mounted transversely at the front of the car with the transmission attached to its left-hand end.

4 The aluminium alloy cylinder block is of the dry-liner type. The crankshaft is supported within the cylinder block on five shell-type main bearings. Thrustwashers are fitted to number 2 main bearing, to control crankshaft endfloat.

5 The connecting rods rotate on horizontally-split bearing shells at their big-ends. The pistons are attached to the connecting rods by gudgeon pins, which are an interference fit in the connecting rod small-end, and retained by circlips. The aluminium-alloy pistons are fitted with three piston rings – two compression rings and scraper-type oil control ring.

6 The inlet and exhaust valves are each closed by coil springs, and operate in guides pressed into the cylinder head.

7 The camshafts are driven by the crankshaft via a timing chain arrangement; there is also a lower timing chain which links the crankshaft to the balance shafts and coolant pump. The camshafts rotate directly in the head and operate the sixteen valves via followers and hydraulic tappets. The followers are situated directly below the camshafts, each one operating a separate valve. Valve clearances are automatically adjusted by the hydraulic tappets.

8 Lubrication is by means of an oil pump, which is driven off the right-hand end of the crankshaft. It draws oil from the sump, and then forces it through an externally-mounted filter into galleries in the cylinder block/crankcase. From there, the oil is distributed to the crankshaft (main bearings) and camshaft. The big-end bearings are supplied with oil via internal drillings in the crankshaft, while the camshaft bearings also receive a pressurised supply. The camshaft lobes and valves are lubricated by splash, as are all other engine components. The timing chain is lubricated by an oil spray nozzle.

9 A semi-closed crankcase ventilation system is employed; crankcase fumes are drawn from cylinder head cover, and passed via a hose to the inlet manifold.

Operations with engine in car

10 The following operations can be carried out without having to remove the engine from the vehicle.

a) *Compression pressure testing.*
b) *Camshaft cover – removal and refitting.*
c) *Timing chain cover – removal and refitting.*
d) *Timing chains – removal and refitting.*
e) *Timing chain tensioners, guides and sprockets – removal and refitting.*
f) *Camshaft and followers – removal, inspection and refitting.*
g) *Cylinder head – removal and refitting.*
h) *Connecting rods and pistons – removal and refitting*.*
i) *Sump – removal and refitting.*
j) *Oil pump – removal, overhaul and refitting.*
k) *Crankshaft oil seals – renewal.*
l) *Engine/transmission mountings – inspection and renewal.*
m) *Flywheel – removal, inspection and refitting.*

* *Although the operation marked with an asterisk can be carried out with the engine in the car after removal of the sump, it is better for the engine to be removed, in the interests* of cleanliness and improved access. For this reason, the procedure is described in Chapter 2D.

2 Compression test – description and interpretation

Refer to Chapter 2A, Section 2.

3 Top dead centre (TDC) for No 1 piston – locating

1 In its travel up and down its cylinder bore, Top Dead Centre (TDC) is the highest point that each piston reaches as the crankshaft rotates. While each piston reaches TDC both at the top of the compression stroke and again at the top of the exhaust stroke, for the purpose of timing the engine, TDC refers to the piston position (usually number 1) at the top of its compression stroke.

2 Number 1 piston is at the right-hand (timing chain) end of the engine, and its TDC position is located as follows. Note that the crankshaft rotates clockwise when viewed from the right-hand side of the car.

3 Disconnect the battery negative terminal (refer to *Disconnecting the battery* in the Reference Chapter).

4 Firmly apply the handbrake, then jack up the front of the car and support it securely on axle stands (see *Jacking and vehicle support*). Remove the retaining screws/clips and remove the right-hand wheelarch liner and engine undertray (where fitted).

5 To gain access to the camshaft sprocket timing marks, remove the camshaft cover as described in Section 5.

6 Using a socket and extension bar on the crankshaft sprocket bolt, rotate the crankshaft until the timing marks on the camshaft sprockets are both correctly aligned (see Section 4). With the camshaft sprocket alignment marks correctly positioned, the notch on the crankshaft pulley rim should align with the pointer on the timing chain cover. The engine is now positioned with No 1 piston at TDC.

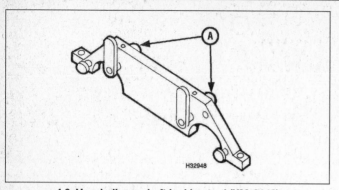

4.0 Vauxhall camshaft locking tool (KM-6148)

A   *Camshaft sprocket locating pins*

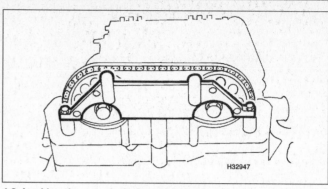

4.3 Locking the camshaft sprockets in position using the Vauxhall tool KM-6148

4 Valve timing – checking and adjustment

Note: *To check the valve timing, it will be necessary to use the following Vauxhall special tool (or suitable equivalent); the camshaft locking tool number is KM-6148 (see illustration). If access to this tool cannot be gained, this task must be entrusted to a Vauxhall dealer. The camshaft locking tool has locating pins that locate in the holes in the camshaft sprockets, to ensure that the camshafts remain correctly positioned.*

1 Remove the camshaft cover as described in Section 5.

2 Position No 1 cylinder at TDC as described in Section 3, ensuring the crankshaft pulley notch is correctly aligned with the timing mark on the timing chain cover.

3 With the crankshaft in position, insert the camshaft locking tool into position on the right-hand end of the camshaft sprockets **(see illustration).**

4 If the locking tool can be correctly fitted, the valve timing is correctly set and no adjustment is necessary.

5 Refit the camshaft cover as described In Section 5

6 If the camshaft tool cannot be inserted correctly into the camshaft sprockets, the timing will need to be reset. See Section 9 for the removal, inspection and refitting of the timing chain and sprockets.

5 Camshaft cover – removal and refitting

Removal

1 Unclip and remove the plastic cover from the top of the engine.

2 Release the securing clip from the wiring plug on the ignition module and disconnect the plug.

3 Undo the four retaining bolts from the ignition module assembly and lift upwards to release from the spark plugs **(see illustration).**

4 Disconnect the breather hose from the front of the camshaft cover.

5 Unclip the wiring harness from along the front edge and left-hand side of the camshaft cover.

6 Disconnect the wiring plug from the EGR (exhaust gas recirculation) valve.

7 Unclip the brake servo vacuum pipe and coolant expansion tank hose from the wiring brackets along the front edge and left-hand side of the camshaft cover.

8 Undo the two retaining nuts and lift off the wiring trough from along the front of the camshaft cover **(see illustration).**

9 Undo the two retaining nuts and remove the wiring bracket from the left-hand side of the camshaft cover. With the bracket removed, undo the right-hand stud to release the earth strap.

10 Undo the two retaining bolts from the timing chain end of the camshaft cover to release the fuel pipe support bracket.

11 Slacken and remove the camshaft cover retaining bolts along with their sealing washers then lift the camshaft cover and gasket/seals away from the cylinder head. Renew the cover gasket/seals and retaining bolt sealing washers.

Refitting

12 Refitting is a reversal of removal noting the following points:

a) *Use new camshaft cover gasket/seals.*

b) *Once the cover is in position, first tighten all the bolts hand-tight, then go around and tighten them all to the specified torque setting.*

c) *Make sure the securing clip is fitted correctly to the wiring plug on the ignition module.*

6 Crankshaft pulley/vibration damper – removal and refitting

Note: *A new pulley retaining bolt will be required on refitting.*

Removal

1 Firmly apply the handbrake, then jack up the front of the car and support it securely on axle stands (see *Jacking and vehicle support*). Remove the right-hand roadwheel.

2 Undo the retaining screws/clips and remove the engine undertray and wheelarch liner if required.

3 Remove the auxiliary drivebelt as described in Chapter 1. Prior to removal, mark the direction of rotation on the belt to ensure the belt is refitted the same way around.

4 Slacken the crankshaft pulley retaining bolt. To prevent crankshaft rotation on manual transmission models, have an assistant select top gear and apply the brakes firmly. On automatic transmission models prevent rotation by removing one of the torque converter retaining bolts and bolting the driveplate to the transmission housing using a metal bar, spacers and suitable bolts. If the

5.3 Removing the ignition module assembly from the spark plugs

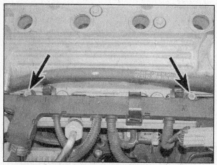

5.8 Undo the two retaining nuts (arrowed) to remove the wiring trough

6.6a Turn the pulley until the flat on the centre hub locates with the oil pump drive . . .

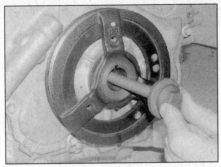

6.6b . . . then fit a new securing bolt to the pulley

6.7 Using an angle-measuring gauge to tighten the crankshaft pulley (engine removed for photo)

engine is removed from the vehicle it will be necessary to lock the flywheel/driveplate (see Section 16).

5 Unscrew the retaining bolt and washer and remove the crankshaft pulley from the end of the crankshaft. Whilst the pulley is removed check the oil seal for signs of wear or damage and, if necessary, renew as described in Section 15.

Refitting

6 Carefully locate the crankshaft pulley on the crankshaft end. Align the flats on the pulley with the oil pump, then turn the pulley to align the slot in the pulley with the crankshaft key. Slide the pulley fully into position, taking great care not to damage the oil seal, then fit the washer and new retaining bolt **(see illustrations)**.

7 Lock the crankshaft by the method used on removal, and tighten the pulley retaining bolt to the specified Stage 1 torque setting then angle-tighten the bolt through the specified Stage 2 angle, using a socket and extension bar, and finally through the specified Stage 3 angle. It is recommended that an angle-measuring gauge is used during the final stages of the tightening, to ensure accuracy **(see illustration)**. If a gauge is not available, use white paint to make alignment marks between the bolt head and pulley prior to tightening; the marks can then be used to check that the bolt has been rotated through the correct angle.

8 Refit the auxiliary drivebelt as described in

Chapter 1 using the mark made prior to removal to ensure the belt is fitted the correct way around.

9 Position the engine undertray and wheelarch liner, then refit the retaining clips/screws.

10 Refit the roadwheel then lower the car to the ground and tighten the wheel bolts to the specified torque.

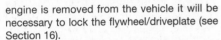

7 Timing chain cover – removal and refitting

Removal

1 Firmly apply the handbrake, then jack up the front of the car and support it securely on axle stands (see *Jacking and vehicle support*). Where necessary, undo the retaining clips/screws and remove the engine undertray.

2 Referring to Section 17, support the engine/transmission unit and unbolt the right-hand mounting assembly from the cylinder head.

3 Mark the running direction of the auxiliary drivebelt, then slacken the tensioner and remove the belt as described in Chapter 1.

4 Undo the securing bolt from the auxiliary drivebelt tensioner and remove the tensioner from the cylinder block.

5 For better access remove the right-hand side front wheelarch liner, then remove the

crankshaft pulley/vibration damper (see Section 6).

6 Drain the engine oil as described in Chapter 1.

7 Noting each bolt's correct fitted location (one bolt is also securing the coolant pump), slacken and remove all the bolts securing the timing chain cover to the cylinder block **(see illustration)**.

8 Carefully ease the timing cover squarely away from the cylinder block and manoeuvre it out of position, noting the correct fitted positions of its locating dowels. If the locating dowels are a loose fit, remove them and store with the cover for safe-keeping.

9 Remove the gasket and ensure the mating surfaces are clean, renew the gasket as required.

Refitting

10 Prior to refitting the cover, it is recommended that the crankshaft oil seal should be renewed. Carefully lever the old seal out of the cover using a large flat-bladed screwdriver. Fit the new seal to the cover, making sure its sealing lip is facing inwards. Press/tap the seal into position until it is flush with the cover, using a suitable tubular drift, such as a socket, which bears only on the hard outer edge of the seal **(see illustrations)**.

11 Ensure the mating surfaces of the cover and cylinder block are clean and dry and the locating dowels are in position.

12 Manoeuvre the gasket into position and locate it on the dowels.

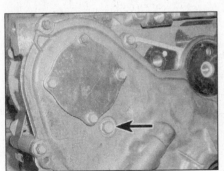

7.7 Note retaining bolt (arrowed) on the inner part of the timing chain cover casing

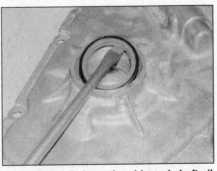

7.10a Carefully lever the old crankshaft oil seal out of the cover . . .

7.10b . . . then using a suitable drift, tap in the new oil seal

7.16 Refit the tensioner, making sure the dowel is located in the hole in the casing

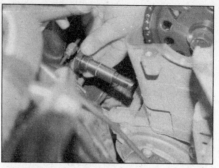

8.2 Removing the timing chain tensioner assembly

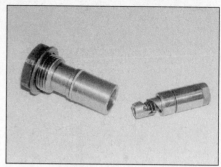

8.3 Inner piston removed to check for wear or damage

13 Manoeuvre the timing cover into position, locating it on the dowels. Refit the cover retaining bolts, ensuring each one is fitted in its original location, and tighten them evenly and progressively to the specified torque.
14 Refit the crankshaft pulley as described in Section 6.
15 Refit the oil drain plug with new sealing washer, and tighten to the specified torque.
16 Refit the auxiliary drivebelt tensioner making sure the dowel in the rear of the tensioner is aligned, then tighten the securing bolt to the specified torque (see illustration).
17 Refit the auxiliary drivebelt (see Chapter 1).
18 Refit the engine/transmission right-hand mounting assembly (see Section 17).
19 Refit the undertray (where fitted) then lower the vehicle to the ground.
20 On completion refill the engine with oil as described in Chapter 1. Start the engine and check for signs of oil leaks.

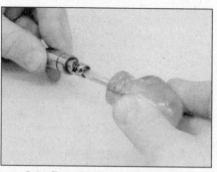

8.4a Turn the inner piston screw clockwise until it locks in position . . .

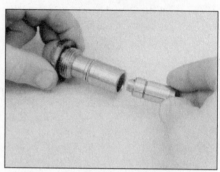

8.4b . . . then fit the inner piston to the outer tensioner assembly

8 Timing chain tensioners – removal and refitting

Camshaft chain tensioner

Note: If a new camshaft timing chain tensioner is being fitted, then a new tension rail should be fitted at the same time. Under no circumstances should the old tension rail be fitted with a new tensioner.

Removal

1 Remove the camshaft cover as described in Section 5.
2 Unscrew the camshaft timing chain tensioner from the rear of the cylinder head, and remove the inner piston assembly (see illustration) Remove the sealing rings and discard them, new ones should be used on refitting.
Caution: Do not rotate the engine whilst the tensioner is removed.
3 Dismantle the tensioner (see illustration), and inspect the tensioner piston for signs of wear or damage and renew if necessary.

Refitting

4 Pretension the timing chain tensioner, by

turning the inner piston clockwise (see illustrations) and allow it to lock in position. Lubricate the inner piston, then reassemble the timing chain tensioner.
5 Replace the sealing rings, then lubricate the timing chain tensioner/piston with clean engine oil and insert it into the cylinder head. Note: Check the threads are clean on the

tensioner and in the cylinder head before refitting.
6 Tighten the tensioner to the specified torque.
7 Release the tensioner by pressing on the tension rail/timing chain with a rounded bar (see illustration). This will press against the inner piston of the tensioner to unlock it, when

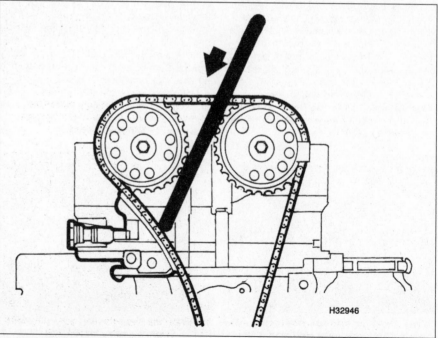

8.7 Press the bar against the tension rail to release the tensioner inner piston

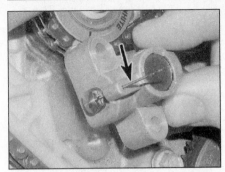

8.13 1.0 mm drill bit (arrowed) used to lock the tensioner piston in place

it releases the spring-loaded piston will take up the slack in the timing chain.

Caution: This procedure must be carried out correctly, otherwise the chain may be left slack and skip a tooth on the sprockets. This will result in engine damage.

8 Rotate the crankshaft through two complete rotations (720°) in the correct direction of rotation and check that all the timing marks re-align up at TDC, see Section 3.

9 Refit the camshaft cover as described in Section 5.

Balance shaft chain tensioner

Removal

10 Remove the timing chain cover as

9.0a Align the silver link (arrowed) with the triangular timing mark on the exhaust sprocket . . .

9.0c . . . and the second silver-coloured link (arrowed) with the timing mark (white dot) on the crankshaft sprocket

8.15 Removing the locking pin to release the tensioner

described in Section 7.

11 Undo the two retaining bolts and remove the balancer shaft chain tensioner from the cylinder block.

Caution: Do not rotate the engine whilst the tensioner is removed.

12 Inspect the tensioner piston for signs of wear or damage and renew if necessary.

Refitting

13 Pretension the balance shaft chain tensioner, by turning the piston clockwise approximately 45° and push it back into the tensioner housing. Insert a 1.0 mm locking pin or drill bit into the hole in the piston housing, which will lock the piston in position **(see illustration)**.

14 Lubricate the tensioner piston with clean engine oil, then refit it onto the cylinder block

9.0b . . . the copper-coloured link (arrowed) with the diamond timing mark on the intake sprocket . . .

9.5 Undo the two retaining bolts (arrowed) from the chain sliding rail

tightening the bolts to there specified torque.

15 Once the tensioner is in position, remove the locking pin to release the tensioner piston **(see illustration)**. Make sure the piston engages with the tension rail correctly and takes up any slack in the balancer shaft timing chain.

Caution: This procedure must be carried out correctly, otherwise the chain may be left slack and skip a tooth on the sprockets. This could result in engine vibration or damage.

16 Refit the timing chain cover as described in Section 7.

Chain tensioner and guide rails

17 Tensioner and guide rail removal and refitting is part of the timing chain and sprockets removal and refitting procedure **(see Section 9)**. They must be renewed if they show signs of wear or damage on their chain surfaces.

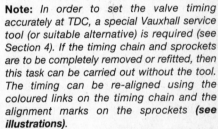

9 Timing chains and sprockets – removal, inspection and refitting

Note: In order to set the valve timing accurately at TDC, a special Vauxhall service tool (or suitable alternative) is required (see Section 4). If the timing chain and sprockets are to be completely removed or refitted, then this task can be carried out without the tool. The timing can be re-aligned using the coloured links on the timing chain and the alignment marks on the sprockets (see illustrations).

Caution: Prior to removal, ensure the camshaft sprockets are suitably marked as they are identical and can be refitted to either camshaft.

Note: If there is any wear on the camshaft timing chain, tension rails, guides or crankshaft sprocket the components must always be renewed as a complete assembly.

Removal

Camshaft chain and sprockets

Note: New camshaft sprocket retaining bolts and new timing chain sliding rail retaining bolts will be required on refitting.

1 Disconnect the battery negative terminal (refer to *Disconnecting the battery* in the Reference Chapter).

2 Position No 1 cylinder at TDC, as described in Section 3. The mark on the crankshaft pulley/vibration damper should be aligned with the mark on the timing cover casing.

3 Remove the timing chain cover as described in Section 7.

4 Remove the camshaft timing chain tensioner as described in Section 8.

5 Undo the two retaining bolts from the camshaft timing chain sliding rail on the top of the cylinder head **(see illustration)**.

6 Remove the access plug from the cylinder

9.6a Remove the access plug from the cylinder head . . .

9.6b . . . and remove the guide rail upper securing bolt

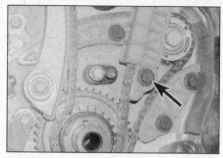

9.7 Undo the lower guide rail securing bolt (arrowed) and remove the guide rail downwards

head and undo the upper securing bolt for the timing chain guide rail **(see illustrations)**.

7 Undo the lower securing bolt for the timing chain guide rail and remove downwards out from the engine **(see illustration)**.

8 Hold the camshafts in turn using an open-ended spanner on the flats provided, then slacken and remove the camshaft sprocket retaining bolts **(see illustration)**.

9 Remove the exhaust camshaft sprocket, making sure it is marked for refitting as they are identical.

10 Undo the lower securing bolt from the timing chain tension rail, then remove it downwards and out from the engine **(see illustration)**.

11 Lift the timing chain off the crankshaft sprocket and remove the intake camshaft sprocket, complete with timing chain, out through the top of the cylinder head.

9.8 Undo the camshaft sprocket retaining bolts – hold the camshafts using an open-ended spanner

9.10 Undo the retaining bolt and remove the tension rail from the engine

12 Slide the crankshaft drivegear/sprocket (and spring washer, where fitted) off the Woodruff key on the crankshaft. **Note:** *FRONT is marked on the outer face of the gear.*

Balance shaft chain and sprockets

Note: *If there is any wear on the balancer shaft timing chain, tension rail and guides, balance shaft chain tensioner or the drivegears/sprockets the components must always be renewed as a complete assembly.*

13 Remove the camshaft timing chain and sprockets as described in paragraphs 1 to 12.

14 Undo the two retaining bolts and remove the balancer shaft chain tensioner from the cylinder block.

15 Undo the securing bolts and remove the tension rail and the two guide rails from the cylinder block **(see illustration)**.

16 Lift the balancer shaft timing chain from the sprockets and remove.

17 Using a suitable drift, lock the balance shaft sprockets and undo the retaining bolts, then remove the sprocket from the balance shaft **(see illustration)**. Use new bolts when refitting.

18 Slide the crankshaft drivegear/sprocket (and spring washer, where fitted) off the Woodruff key on the crankshaft. **Note:** *FRONT is marked on the outer face of the gear.*

19 Lock the coolant pump drivegear with a suitable screwdriver, and undo the three securing bolts. Remove the drivegear from the coolant pump.

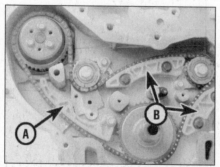

9.15 Undo the retaining bolts and remove the tension rail and guide rails

A Tension rail   B Guide rails

Inspection

20 Examine the teeth on the sprockets for any sign of wear or damage such as chipped, hooked or missing teeth. If there is any sign of wear or damage on any sprocket/gear, all the sprockets/gears and the relevant chain should be renewed as a set.

21 Inspect the links of each timing chain for signs of wear or damage on the rollers. The extent of wear can be judged by checking the amount by which the chain can be bent sideways; a new chain will have very little sideways movement. If there is an excessive amount of side play in a timing chain, it must be renewed.

22 Note that it is a sensible precaution to renew the timing chains, regardless of their apparent condition, if the engine has covered a high mileage, or if it has been noted that the chain(s) have sounded noisy when the engine running. It is advised renewing the chains and sprockets as a matched set, since it is false economy to run a new chain on worn sprockets and *vice-versa*. If there is any doubt about the condition of the timing chains and sprockets, seek the advice of a Vauxhall dealer service department, who will be able to advise you as to the best course of action, based on their previous knowledge of the engine.

23 Examine the chain guide(s) and tensioner rail(s) for signs of wear or damage to their chain contact faces, renewing any which are badly marked.

9.17 Using a drift to lock the balance shaft sprocket

9.26 Refit the timing chain crankshaft sprocket, noting FRONT is marked on the outer face

9.29 Turning the camshaft slightly using an open-ended spanner to locate the sprocket in the correct position

9.36 Use new retaining bolts when refitting the sliding rail

Refitting

Camshaft chain and sprockets

24 If any new components are being fitted, transfer any alignment marks you have made from the original components to aid refitting. Ensure the crankshaft is still in the TDC position.

25 If not already fitted, refit the balance shaft timing chain and sprockets as described in paragraphs 40 to 47.

26 Slide the crankshaft drive sprocket (and spring washer, where fitted) onto the Woodruff key on the crankshaft. **Note:** *FRONT is marked on the outer face of the sprocket (see illustration).*

27 Refit the intake camshaft sprocket complete with timing chain down through the top of the cylinder head. The copper-coloured link should line up with the INT mark on the intake sprocket (a cable tie can be used to keep the chain in position – **see illustration 9.0b**). Attach the sprocket to the camshaft using a new securing bolt, tightening it hand-tight at this stage.

28 Insert the timing chain tension rail up through the engine casing into position for the tensioner. (Do not refit the lower securing bolt until the timing chain is in position.)

29 Insert the exhaust camshaft sprocket into the timing chain, making sure the silver link on the timing chain lines up with the EXH mark on the sprocket (a cable tie can be used to keep the chain in position – **see illustration 9.0a**). Attach the sprocket to the camshaft using a new securing bolt, tightening it hand-tight at this stage. **Note:** *One or both of the camshafts*

may have moved slightly, due to valve spring pressure. It may be necessary to turn the camshafts slightly to locate the sprockets in the correct position, use an open-ended spanner on the camshaft if required (see illustration). Do not turn the camshafts too far as the engine is set at TDC and the valves could hit the pistons.

30 Locate the timing chain onto the crankshaft drive sprocket, aligning the silver link with the mark on the sprocket **(see illustration 9.0c)**.

31 The lower securing bolt can now be fitted to the tension rail and tightened to its specified torque.

32 Insert the guide rail and fit lower securing bolt, tightening it to its specified torque.

33 Refit the guide rail upper securing bolt and access bolt in the cylinder head, tightening them to there specified torque. *Caution: All the timing marks (coloured chain links) must be aligned with the corresponding marks on the sprockets. This procedure must be carried out correctly, otherwise the timing being offset by one tooth will result in engine damage.*

34 Refit the timing chain cover as described in Section 7.

35 Remove the cable ties from camshaft sprockets. Hold the camshafts in turn using an open-ended spanner on the flats provided, then tighten the new securing bolts to their specified torque.

36 Attach the sliding rail for the camshaft timing chain to the top of the cylinder head, using new retaining bolts tighten them to their specified torque **(see illustration)**.

37 Refit the camshaft timing chain tensioner as described in Section 8.

38 Rotate the crankshaft through two complete rotations (720°) in the correct direction of rotation (to bring number 1 piston back to TDC on its compression stroke). If the special tool is available, check the valve timing as described in Section 4.

39 Refit the camshaft cover as described in Section 5, then reconnect the battery negative terminal.

Balance shaft chain and sprockets

40 Refit the drivegear to the coolant pump, and tighten the three securing bolts to the specified torque.

41 Slide the crankshaft drivegear/sprocket (and spring washer, where fitted) onto the Woodruff key on the crankshaft. **Note:** *FRONT is marked on the outer face of the gear (see illustration).* The timing mark on the drivegear should be pointing downwards to align with the silver-coloured link on the timing chain.

42 Refit the exhaust sprocket to the balance shaft, using a new securing bolt **(see illustration)**. The sprocket is marked EXHAUST and has an arrow which points downwards to align with the silver-coloured link on the timing chain. Tighten the bolts to the specified torque, locking the balance shaft sprockets as on removal.

43 Refit the intake sprocket to the balance shaft, using a new securing bolt. The sprocket is marked INTAKE and has an arrow which points upwards to align with the copper-coloured link on the timing chain **(see illustration)**. Tighten

9.41 Refit the balance shaft crankshaft sprocket, noting FRONT is marked on the outer face

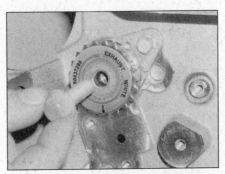

9.42 Refit the balance shaft sprockets using new securing bolts

9.43 The arrow points upwards on the intake sprocket

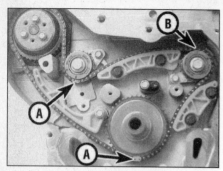

9.44 Balance shaft timing chain layout

A *Silver-coloured chain links aligned with timing marks*
B *Copper-coloured chain link aligned with timing mark*

the bolts to the specified torque, locking the balance shaft sprockets as on removal.

44 Refit the balancer shaft timing chain to the sprockets/gears and align the timing marks (coloured chain links) with the marks on the appropriate sprockets as mentioned above **(see illustration)**.

45 Refit the tension rail and two guide rails to the cylinder block, tightening the securing bolts to the specified torque.

46 Refit the balancer shaft chain tensioner as described in Section 8.

47 Refit the camshaft timing chain and sprockets as described above.

10 Camshaft and followers – removal, inspection and refitting

Note: *New camshaft sprocket retaining bolts and new timing chain sliding rail retaining bolts will be required on refitting.*

Removal

1 Disconnect the battery negative terminal (refer to *Disconnecting the battery* in the Reference Chapter).

2 Remove the camshaft cover as described in Section 5.

3 Position No 1 cylinder at TDC as described in Section 3.

4 Undo the two retaining bolts and remove

the camshaft timing chain sliding rail on the top of the cylinder head **(see illustration 9.5)**.

5 If the special tool mentioned in Section 4 is not available, make sure No 1 cylinder is at TDC then cable tie the timing chain to the camshaft sprockets and mark the sprockets in relation to the cylinder head **(see illustration)**.

6 To prevent crankshaft rotation on manual transmission models, if the vehicle is still on axle stands, lower it back onto the ground making sure the handbrake is on and 1st gear is engaged. On automatic transmission models prevent rotation by removing one of the torque converter retaining bolts and bolting the driveplate to the transmission housing using a metal bar, spacers and suitable bolts.

7 Remove the camshaft timing chain tensioner as described in Section 8.

8 Hold the camshafts, using an open-ended spanner on the flats provided, then slacken and remove the camshaft sprocket retaining bolts **(see illustration 9.8)**.

Caution: Prior to removal ensure the camshaft sprockets are suitably marked as they are identical and can be refitted to either camshaft.

9 Disengage the camshaft sprockets (complete with chain) from the camshafts, keeping the chain under tension. Use a suitable screwdriver, bar or bolt to pass through the sprockets and rest on the upper surface of the cylinder head to prevent the timing chain falling down and coming off the crankshaft drivegear/sprocket.

10 Note the identification markings on the camshaft bearing caps. The caps are numbered 1 to 10 with all numbers being the right way up when viewed from the driver's seat; numbers 1 to 5 on the exhaust camshaft starting from the timing chain end of the engine, and numbers 6 to 10 on the intake camshaft starting at the timing chain end. **Note:** *There is also an 11th cap on the intake camshaft, at the flywheel end of the cylinder head.* If the markings are not clearly visible, make identification marks to ensure each cap is fitted correctly on refitting.

11 Undo the two bolts and remove the cover plate and gasket from the 11th bearing cap on the intake camshaft. Working in a spiral

pattern from the outside inwards, slacken the camshaft bearing cap retaining bolts by one turn at a time, to relieve the pressure of the valve springs on the bearing caps gradually and evenly. Once the valve spring pressure has been relieved, the bolts can be fully unscrewed and removed, along with the caps. Take care not to loose any locating dowels which may be fitted to some of the bearing caps and lift the camshaft out from the head, noting the position of the lobes on the camshaft.

Caution: If the bearing cap bolts are carelessly slackened, the bearing caps might break. If any bearing cap breaks then the complete cylinder head assembly must be renewed; the bearing caps are matched to the head and are not available separately.

12 Obtain 16 small, clean plastic containers, and label them for identification. Alternatively, divide a larger container into compartments. Lift the followers out from the top of the cylinder head and store each one in its respective fitted position **(see illustration)**.

13 If the hydraulic tappets are also to be removed, withdraw each hydraulic tappet and place them in small containers with clean engine oil. This will keep them primed ready for refitting **(see illustration)**.

Inspection

14 Examine the camshaft bearing surfaces and cam lobes for signs of wear ridges and scoring. Renew the camshaft if any of these conditions are apparent. Examine the condition of the bearing surfaces both on the camshaft journals and in the cylinder head. If the head bearing surfaces are worn excessively, the cylinder head will need to be renewed.

15 Support the camshaft end journals on V-blocks, and measure the run-out at the centre journal using a dial gauge. If the run-out exceeds the specified limit, the camshaft should be renewed.

16 Examine the follower bearing surfaces which contact the camshaft lobes for wear ridges and scoring. Renew any followers on which these conditions are apparent.

17 Check the hydraulic tappets (where removed) and their bores in the cylinder head

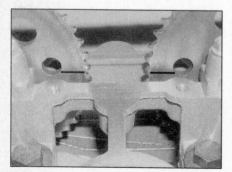

10.5 Alignment marks made on camshaft sprockets for refitting

10.12 A container used to keep the followers and hydraulic tappets in order

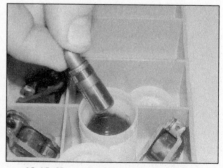

10.13 Keep the hydraulic tappets in labelled containers with clean engine oil

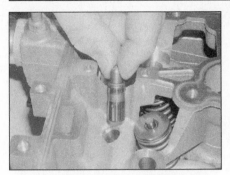

10.18 Lubricate the tappets with clean engine oil before refitting

10.19 Refit the camshaft followers in their original position

10.22 Apply silicone sealing compound thinly to the surface areas arrowed

for signs of wear or damage. If any tappet is thought to be faulty it should be renewed.

Refitting

18 Where removed, lubricate the hydraulic tappets with clean engine oil and carefully insert each one into its original location in the cylinder head **(see illustration)**.
19 Refit the camshaft followers to the cylinder head, ensuring each follower is fitted in its original location **(see illustration)**.
20 Lubricate the camshaft followers with clean engine oil then lay the camshafts into position. Ensure the crankshaft is still aligned in position, and position the camshaft so that the lobes are pointing in the direction noted on removal.
21 Ensure the mating surfaces of the bearing caps and cylinder head are clean and dry and lubricate the camshaft journals and lobes with clean engine oil.
22 Apply a smear of sealant to the cylinder head mating surface at the transmission end of the intake camshaft (No 11) bearing cap **(see illustration)**. Refit the cap locating dowels to the cap if they have been removed.
23 Refit the camshaft bearing caps and the retaining bolts in their original locations on the cylinder head. The caps are numbered 1 to 10 with all numbers being the right way up when viewed from the driver's seat; numbers 1 to 5 on the exhaust camshaft starting from the timing chain end of the engine, and numbers 6 to 10 on the intake camshaft starting at the timing chain end. Refit the 11th cap on the

intake camshaft, at the transmission end of the cylinder head **(see illustration)**.
24 Tighten all bolts by hand only then, working in a spiral pattern from the centre outwards, tighten the bolts by one turn at a time to gradually impose the pressure of the valve springs on the bearing caps. Repeat this sequence until all bearing caps are in contact with the cylinder head then go around and tighten the camshaft bearing cap bolts to the specified torque.
Caution: If the bearing cap bolts are carelessly tightened, the bearing caps might break. If any bearing cap breaks then the complete cylinder head assembly must be renewed; the bearing caps are matched to the head and are not available separately.
25 Using the marks made on removal, ensure that the timing chain is still correctly engaged with the sprockets then refit the camshaft sprockets to the camshaft. Locate the sprockets on the end of the camshaft and fit the new retaining bolts hand-tight at this stage **(see illustration)**. Remove the cable ties from the camshaft chain and sprockets.
26 Refit the camshaft timing chain tensioner as described in Section 8.
27 If the special tool is available, check that No 1 cylinder is correctly set at TDC, as described in Section 3.
28 If the special tool is not available, align the marks made prior to removal on the camshaft and sprockets. Hold the camshaft with an open-ended spanner and tighten the sprocket bolt to the specified Stage 1 torque setting.

Ensure the marks have remained in alignment then tighten the bolt through the specified Stage 2 and Stage 3 angles. It is recommended that an angle-measuring gauge is used during the final stages of the tightening, to ensure accuracy. If a gauge is not available, use white paint to make alignment marks prior to tightening; the marks can then be used to check that the bolt has been rotated through the correct angle.
29 Refit the camshaft timing chain sliding rail using new retaining bolts, then tighten to the specified torque.
30 Using a new gasket, refit the cover plate to the 11th bearing cap on the intake camshaft, and tighten the two bolts securely.
31 Turn the crankshaft pulley/vibration damper in the direction of rotation a two full revolutions. Check that the timing marks on the crankshaft pulley line up with the mark on the casing, and the special tool lines up with the camshaft sprockets (or the marks in relation to the cylinder head, made prior to removal).
32 Refit the camshaft cover as described in Section 5.
33 Reconnect the battery negative terminal and lower the vehicle to the ground (where applicable).

11 Cylinder head – removal and refitting

Caution: Be careful not to allow dirt into the fuel injection pump or injector pipes during this procedure.
Note: *New cylinder head bolts, camshaft timing chain sliding rail bolts and camshaft sprocket retaining bolts will be required on refitting.*

Removal

1 Drain the cooling system as described in Chapter 3.
2 Carry out the operations described in paragraphs 1 to 8 of Section 10.
3 Depressurise the fuel system as described in Chapter 4A.
4 Wipe clean the area around the fuel hose unions then slacken and remove the union

10.23 Refitting No 11 bearing cap to the intake camshaft

10.25 Refit new retaining bolts to the camshaft sprockets

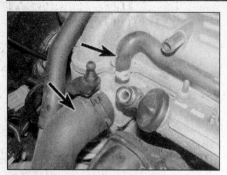

11.7 Remove the two coolant hoses (arrowed) from the front of the cylinder head

bolts and sealing washers. Release the hoses from their retaining clips, and position them clear of the cylinder head.

5 Remove the inlet and exhaust manifolds as described in Chapter 4A.

6 Remove the air cleaner assembly as described in Chapter 4A.

7 Release the retaining clips and disconnect the coolant hoses from the front of the right-hand end of the cylinder head **(see illustration)**.

8 On vehicles with air conditioning, release the hoses/pipes from their retaining clips and move to one side. If the system requires disconnecting, see Chapter 3 for further information.

9 Remove the access bolt from the cylinder head and undo the upper securing bolt for the timing chain guide rail **(see illustrations 9.6a and 9.6b)**.
Caution: Prior to removal ensure the camshaft sprockets are suitably marked as they are identical and can be refitted to either camshaft.

10 Remove the camshaft sprockets from the timing chain. Hold the timing chain up, to prevent it dropping down into the cylinder block, keeping the timing chain located onto the crankshaft sprocket.

11 Slacken and remove the four retaining bolts from the timing chain end of the cylinder head **(see illustration 11.27)**.

12 Working in the **reverse** of the tightening

sequence **(see illustration 11.27)**, progressively slacken the ten main cylinder head bolts by half a turn at a time, until all bolts can be unscrewed by hand.

13 Lift out the cylinder head bolts and where applicable recover the washers.

14 Lift the cylinder head away; seek assistance if possible, as it is a heavy assembly (especially if complete with manifolds). Also assistance will be required to guide the timing chain out through the cylinder head while keeping the chain under tension.

15 Remove the gasket, noting the locating dowels fitted to the top of the cylinder block. If they are a loose fit, remove the locating dowels and store them with the head for safe-keeping.
Caution: Do not lay the head on its lower mating surface; support the head on wooden blocks as it may be damaged if the head is placed directly onto a bench.

16 If the cylinder head is to be dismantled for overhaul, refer to Part D of this Chapter.

Preparation for refitting

17 The mating faces of the cylinder head and cylinder block/crankcase must be perfectly clean before refitting the head. Use a hard plastic or wood scraper to remove all traces of gasket and carbon; also clean the piston crowns. Take particular care, as the surfaces are damaged easily. Also, make sure that the carbon is not allowed to enter the oil and water passages – this is particularly important for the lubrication system, as carbon could block the oil supply to any of the engine's components. Using adhesive tape and paper, seal the water, oil and bolt holes in the cylinder block/crankcase. To prevent carbon entering the gap between the pistons and bores, smear a little grease in the gap. After cleaning each piston, use a small brush to remove all traces of grease and carbon from the gap, then wipe away the remainder with a clean rag. Clean all the pistons in the same way.

18 Check the mating surfaces of the cylinder block/crankcase and the cylinder head for nicks, deep scratches and other damage. If

slight, they may be removed carefully with a file, but if excessive, machining may be the only alternative to renewal (see your local specialist for machining).

19 Ensure that the cylinder head bolt holes in the crankcase are clean and free of oil. Syringe or soak up any oil left in the bolt holes. This is most important in order that the correct bolt tightening torque can be applied and to prevent the possibility of the block being cracked by hydraulic pressure when the bolts are tightened.

20 The cylinder head bolts must be discarded and renewed, regardless of their apparent condition.

21 If warpage of the cylinder head gasket surface is suspected, use a straight-edge to check it for distortion. Refer to Part D of this Chapter if necessary.

Refitting

22 Using a tap, clean out the thread in the four bolt holes at the timing chain end of the cylinder block **(see illustration)**. Wipe clean the mating surfaces of the cylinder head and cylinder block/crankcase.

23 Check that the locating dowels are in position then fit the new gasket to the cylinder block **(see illustrations)**.

24 Ensure the crankshaft is positioned approx 60° BTDC (this is to prevent any damage to the valves or pistons when refitting the cylinder head).

25 With the aid of an assistant, carefully refit the cylinder head assembly to the block, aligning it with the locating dowels. As the head is fitted, pass the timing chain up through the cylinder head, holding it in position by passing a suitable tool/screwdriver through the chain and resting it on the head upper surface. Note: *Keep the chain taut to prevent it coming off the crankshaft sprocket.*

26 Apply a smear of oil to the threads and the underside of the heads of the new cylinder head bolts and carefully enter each bolt into its relevant hole (*do not drop them in*). Screw all bolts in, by hand only, until finger-tight.

27 Working progressively and in sequence, tighten the cylinder head bolts to their Stage 1

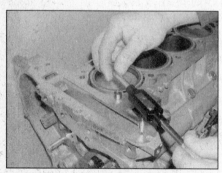

11.22 Using a tap to clean out the threads in the cylinder block

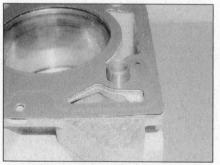

11.23a Check the dowels are in position to locate the cylinder head gasket . . .

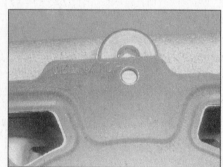

11.23b . . . ensuring the gasket is fitted with its OBEN/TOP marking uppermost

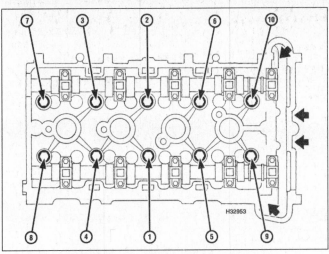

11.27 Cylinder head bolt tightening sequence

11.28 Tightening the cylinder head down through its stages, using an angle gauge

torque setting, using a torque wrench and suitable socket (see illustration).

28 Once all bolts have been tightened to the Stage 1 torque, working again in the specified sequence, go around and tighten all bolts through the specified Stage 2 angle. It is recommended that an angle-measuring gauge is used to ensure accuracy (see illustration). If a gauge is not available, use white paint to make alignment marks prior to tightening; the marks can then be used to check that the bolt has been rotated through the correct angle.

29 Go around again in the specified sequence and angle tighten the bolts through the specified Stage 3 angle.

30 Finally go around in the specified sequence and angle tighten the bolts through the specified Stage 4 angle.

31 Refit the four bolts securing the right-hand end of the cylinder head to the block (timing chain end) and tighten them to the specified torque setting (see illustrations).

32 Re-align the camshaft sprockets, then turn the crankshaft carefully in the direction of engine rotation, to bring No 1 cylinder back to TDC.

33 Refit the camshaft sprockets to the camshafts as described in Section 10, paragraphs 25 to 33.

34 Reconnect the coolant hoses to the cylinder head and secure them in position with the retaining clips.

35 Refit/reconnect the inlet and exhaust manifolds and associated components as described in Chapter 4A.

36 Position a new sealing washer on each side of the fuel hose unions then refit union bolts and tighten them to the specified torque (for further information refer to Chapter 4A).

37 On completion refill the cooling system (and air conditioning if required) as described in Chapter 3.

12 Sump – removal and refitting

Removal

1 Disconnect the battery negative terminal (refer to *Disconnecting the battery* in the Reference Chapter).

2 Firmly apply the handbrake, then jack up the front of the car and support it securely on axle stands (see *Jacking and vehicle support*). Where necessary, undo the retaining clips/screws and remove the engine undertray and right-hand wheelarch cover.

3 Drain the engine oil as described in Chapter 1, then fit a new sealing washer and refit the drain plug, tightening it to the specified torque.

4 Where fitted, disconnect the wiring connector from the oil level sensor (see Chapter 5A).

5 Mark the running direction of the auxiliary drivebelt, then slacken the tensioner and remove the belt as described in Chapter 1.

6 Remove the lower mounting bolt for the air conditioning compressor. Slacken (do not remove) the upper two mounting bolts and use a block of wood (or similar) to wedge the compressor away from the sump. **Note:** *Take care not to damage the bolts or alloy mounting point when inserting the wedge; do not use excessive force.*

7 Slacken and remove the bolts securing the sump flange to the transmission housing (see illustration).

8 Progressively slacken and remove the bolts securing the sump to the base of the cylinder block lower casing (there is one long bolt at

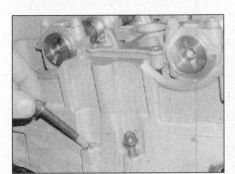

11.31a Fit four new retaining bolts to the timing chain end of the cylinder head . . .

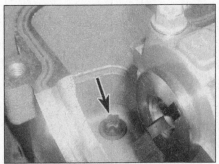

11.31b . . . two of the bolts are inside the timing chain housing (bolt arrowed on exhaust side of head)

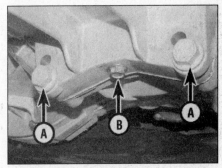

12.7 Undo the two sump to transmission bolts (A) and also the sump-to-lower cylinder block bolt (B)

12.11a Apply a continuous bead of silicone sealer around the sump . . .

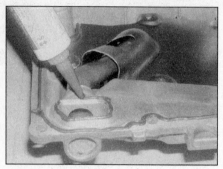

12.11b . . . and also around the oil intake pipe area

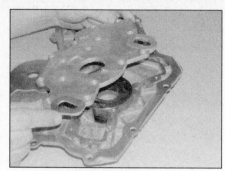

13.2 Undo the retaining screws and remove the pump cover plate

the transmission end of the sump) **(see illustration 12.7)**. To break the sump joint it may be necessary to cut the silicone sealer using a suitable knife, taking care not to damage any surfaces. Lower the sump away from the engine.

9 While the sump is removed, take the opportunity to check the oil pump pick-up/strainer (if possible) for signs of clogging or splitting. **Note:** *The pick-up/strainer cannot be removed from the sump as it is riveted in position.*

Refitting

10 Remove all traces of silicone sealer and oil from the mating surfaces of the sump and cylinder block.

11 Apply a continuous bead of silicone sealing compound (available from your Vauxhall dealer) at approximately 1.0 mm from the inner edge of the sump. The bead of sealant should be between 2.0 and 2.5 mm in diameter. Also apply a bead of sealant (2.0 to 2.5 mm) around the oil intake pipe area of the sump mating surface **(see illustrations)**.

12 Offer up the sump to the cylinder block and loosely refit all the retaining bolts.

13 Working out from the centre in a diagonal sequence, progressively tighten the bolts securing the sump to the cylinder block lower casing. Tighten all the bolts to their specified torque setting.

14 Tighten the bolts securing the sump flange to the transmission housing to their specified torque settings.

15 Remove the wedge-shaped block from

the air conditioning compressor and refit the lower mounting bolt. Tighten the three compressor mounting bolts to their specified torque (Chapter 3).

16 Refit the auxiliary drivebelt (see Chapter 1).

17 Reconnect the oil level sensor wiring connector (as applicable). Where necessary refit the engine undertray and wheelarch cover.

18 Lower the vehicle to the ground then fill the engine with fresh engine oil (see Chapter 1).

13 Oil pump – removal, inspection and refitting

Note: *The oil pump pressure control valve can be removed with the timing chain cover in position on the engine (see paragraph 5 below).*

Removal

1 The oil pump assembly is built into the timing chain cover. Removal and refitting of the cover is described in Section 7.

Inspection

2 Undo the retaining screws and lift off the pump cover plate from the inside of the timing chain cover **(see illustration)**.

3 Note any marks identifying the outer faces of the pump rotors. If none can be seen, use a suitable marker pen and mark the surface of

both the pump inner and outer rotors; the marks can then be used to ensure the rotors are refitted the correct way around.

4 Lift out the inner and outer rotors from the cover **(see illustration)**.

5 Unscrew the oil pressure control valve plug from the timing chain cover and withdraw the spring and plunger, noting which way around the plunger is fitted. Remove the sealing ring from the valve bolt **(see illustrations)**.

6 Clean the components, and carefully examine the rotors, pump body and valve plungers for any signs of scoring or wear. Renew any component which shows signs of wear or damage; if the rotors or pump housing are marked then the complete pump assembly should be renewed.

7 If the components appear serviceable, measure the clearances (using feeler blades) between:

a) The inner rotor and the outer rotor.
b) The outer rotor and oil pump housing.
c) The rotor endfloat.
d) The flatness of the end cover.

If the clearances exceed the specified tolerances (see Specifications at the beginning of this Chapter), the pump must be renewed **(see illustrations)**.

8 If the pump is satisfactory, reassemble the components in the reverse order of removal, noting the following.

a) Ensure both rotors and the valve plunger are fitted the correct way around.
b) Fit new sealing rings to the pressure control valve and tighten to the specified torque setting.

13.4 Removing the inner and outer rotors

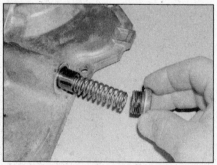

13.5a Undo and remove the oil pressure control valve plug . . .

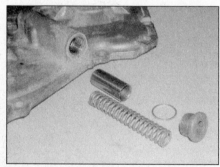

13.5b . . . and remove the oil pressure valve spring and plunger

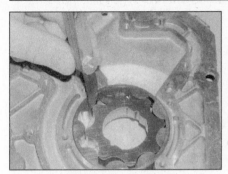

13.7a Using a feeler blade to check the inner-to-outer rotor clearance . . .

13.7b . . . the outer rotor to oil pump housing . . .

13.7c . . . and also using a straight-edge to check the endfloat

c) *Refit the pump cover tightening the cover screws to the specified torque.*
d) *On completion prime the oil pump by filling it with clean engine oil whilst rotating the inner rotor.*

Refitting

9 Refit the timing chain cover as described in Section 7.

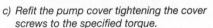

14 Balance shaft – removal and refitting

Removal

1 Remove the balance shaft timing chain and sprockets as described in Section 9.
2 If the balance shaft sprockets are removed, mark the shafts to identify the intake shaft from the exhaust shaft for refitting.
3 Undo the securing nut from the balance shaft retaining plate and slide the balance shaft out from the cylinder block **(see illustrations)**.

Refitting

4 Refitting is the reverse of removal, tighten the retaining plate bolts to their specified torque.
5 Refit the balance shaft timing chain and sprockets as described in Section 9.

14.3a Undo the retaining bolt (arrowed) . . .

15 Crankshaft oil seals – renewal

Timing chain end oil seal

1 Remove the crankshaft pulley as described in Section 6.
2 Using a large flat-bladed screwdriver, carefully lever the seal out from the timing chain cover.
3 Clean the seal housing and polish off any burrs or raised edges which may have caused the seal to fail in the first place.
4 Lubricate the lips of the new seal with clean engine oil and press/tap it squarely into

14.3b . . . and withdraw the balance shaft assembly

position until it sits into the recess in the cover **(see illustration)**. If necessary, a suitable tubular drift, such as a socket, which bears only on the hard outer edge of the seal can be used to tap the seal into position. Take great care not to damage the seal lips during fitting and ensure that the seal lips face inwards.
5 Wash off any traces of oil, then refit the crankshaft pulley as described in Section 6.

Flywheel/driveplate end oil seal

6 Remove the flywheel/driveplate as described in Section 16.
7 Carefully punch or drill two small holes opposite each other in the oil seal. Screw a self-tapping screw into each and pull on the screws with pliers to extract the seal **(see illustration)**.

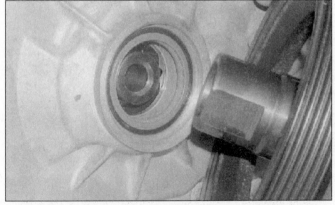

15.4 Make sure the seal seats squarely into the timing chain cover

15.7 Removing a crankshaft left-hand oil seal, using a pair of pliers and a screw

15.9 Carefully ease the oil seal over the end of the crankshaft and tap/press it squarely into position

8 Clean the seal housing and polish off any burrs or raised edges which may have caused the seal to fail in the first place. **Note:** *Insulation tape can be put around the crankshaft flange to help fit the oil seal.*

9 Lubricate the lips of the new seal with clean engine oil and ease it into position on the end of the crankshaft. Press the seal squarely into position until it is flush with the bearing cap. If necessary, a suitable tubular drift, such as a socket, which bears only on the hard outer edge of the seal can be used to tap the seal into position. Take great care not to damage the seal lips during fitting and ensure that the seal lips face inwards **(see illustration)**.

10 If insulation tape was used around the crankshaft flange, remove it, taking care not to damage the oil seal. Refit the flywheel as described in Section 16.

16 Flywheel/driveplate – removal, inspection and refitting

Refer to Chapter 2B, Section 15.

17 Engine/transmission mountings – inspection and renewal

Refer to Chapter 2A, Section 17.

Chapter 2 Part D:
Engine removal and overhaul procedures

Contents

Crankshaft – inspection 13
Crankshaft – refitting and main bearing clearance check 17
Crankshaft – removal 10
Cylinder block – cleaning and inspection 11
Cylinder head – dismantling 6
Cylinder head – reassembly 8
Cylinder head and valves – cleaning and inspection 7
Engine and transmission unit – removal, separation and refitting . . . 4
Engine – initial start up after overhaul 19
Engine overhaul – dismantling sequence 5
Engine overhaul – general information 2
Engine overhaul – reassembly sequence 15
Engine removal – methods and precautions 3
General information 1
Main and big-end bearings – inspection 14
Piston rings – refitting 16
Piston/connecting rod assembly – inspection 12
Piston/connecting rod assembly – refitting and big-end clearance
    check 18
Piston/connecting rod assembly – removal 9

Degrees of difficulty

Easy, suitable for novice with little experience	Fairly easy, suitable for beginner with some experience	Fairly difficult, suitable for competent DIY mechanic	Difficult, suitable for experienced DIY mechanic	Very difficult, suitable for expert DIY or professional

Specifications

Note: *Where specifications are given as N/A, no information was available at the time of writing. Refer to your Vauxhall dealer for the latest information available.*

1.6 litre SOHC engines

Cylinder head

Maximum gasket face distortion	0.05 mm
Cylinder head height	95.90 to 96.10 mm
Valve seat width:	
Inlet	1.3 to 1.5 mm
Exhaust	1.6 to 1.8 mm

Valves and guides

	Inlet	Exhaust
Valve guide height in cylinder head . . . . 80.85 to 81.25 mm		
Valve stem diameter*:	**Inlet**	**Exhaust**
Standard (K)	6.998 to 7.012 mm	6.978 to 6.992 mm
1st oversize (0.075 mm – K1)	7.073 to 7.087 mm	7.053 to 7.067 mm
2nd oversize (0.150 mm – K2)	7.148 to 7.162 mm	7.128 to 7.142 mm
Valve stem run-out	Less than 0.03 mm	
Valve guide bore diameter*:		
Standard (K)	7.030 to 7.050 mm	
1st oversize (0.075 mm – K1)	7.105 to 7.125 mm	
2nd oversize (0.150 mm – K2)	7.180 to 7.200 mm	
Stem-to-guide clearance:		
Inlet	0.018 to 0.052 mm	
Exhaust	0.038 to 0.072 mm	
Valve length:		
Inlet	99.35 mm	
Exhaust	99.65 mm	
Valve stem fitted height	13.75 to 14.35 mm	
Valve head diameter:		
Inlet	38 mm	
Exhaust	31 mm	

* Identification marking in brackets

1.6 litre SOHC engines (continued)

Cylinder block

Maximum gasket face distortion	0.05 mm
Cylinder bore diameter:	
Standard:	
Size group 8	78.975 to 78.985 mm
Size group 99	78.985 to 78.995 mm
Size group 00	78.995 to 79.005 mm
Size group 01	79.005 to 79.015 mm
Size group 02	79.015 to 79.025 mm
Oversize (0.5 mm)	79.465 to 79.475 mm
Maximum cylinder bore ovality	0.013 mm
Maximum cylinder bore taper	0.013 mm

Pistons and rings

Piston diameter:	
Standard:	
Size group 8	78.955 to 78.965 mm
Size group 9	78.965 to 78.975 mm
Size group 00	78.975 to 78.985 mm
Size group 01	78.985 to 78.995 mm
Size group 02	78.995 to 79.005 mm
Oversize (0.5 mm) – size group 7 + 0.5	79.445 to 79.455 mm
Piston-to-bore clearance	0.02 to 0.04 mm
Piston ring end gaps (fitted in bore):	
Top and second compression rings	0.3 to 0.5 mm
Oil control ring	0.4 to 1.4 mm
Piston ring thickness:	
Top compression ring	1.2 mm
Second compression ring	1.5 mm
Oil control ring	3.0 mm
Piston ring-to-groove clearance:	
Top compression ring:	0.02 to 0.04 mm
Second compression ring	0.04 to 0.06 mm
Oil control ring	0.01 to 0.03 mm

Gudgeon pins

Diameter	17.997 to 18 mm
Length	55 mm
Gudgeon pin-to-piston clearance	0.009 to 0.012 mm

Connecting rod

Big-end side clearance	0.07 to 0.24 mm

Crankshaft

Endfloat	0.1 to 0.2 mm
Main bearing journal diameter:	
Standard	54.980 to 54.997 mm
1st (0.25 mm) undersize	54.730 to 54.747 mm
2nd (0.50 mm) undersize	54.482 to 54.495 mm
Big-end bearing journal (crankpin) diameter:	
Standard	42.971 to 42.987 mm
1st (0.25 mm) undersize	42.721 to 42.737 mm
2nd (0.50 mm) undersize	42.471 to 42.487 mm
Journal out-of-round	0.04 mm
Journal taper	N/A
Crankshaft run-out	Less than 0.03 mm
Main bearing running clearance	0.017 to 0.047 mm
Big-end bearing (crankpin) running clearance	0.019 to 0.071 mm

Torque wrench settings

Refer to Chapter 2A Specifications

1.4, 1.6 and 1.8 litre DOHC engines

Cylinder head

Maximum gasket face distortion	0.05 mm
Cylinder head height:	
1.4 and 1.6 litre	134.9 to 135.1 mm
1.8 litre	135.85 to 136.0 mm
Valve seat width:	
Inlet	1.0 to 1.4 mm
Exhaust	1.4 to 1.8 mm

1.4, 1.6 and 1.8 litre DOHC engines (continued)

Valves and guides

Valve guide height in cylinder head	10.70 to 11.00 mm	

Valve stem diameter*:

	Inlet	Exhaust
1.4 and 1.6 litre engines:		
Standard (GM)	5.995 to 5.970 mm	5.935 to 5.950 mm
1st oversize (0.075 mm – K1)	6.030 to 6.045 mm	6.010 to 6.025 mm
2nd oversize (0.150 mm – K2)	6.105 to 6.120 mm	6.085 to 6.100 mm
1.8 litre engines:		
Standard (GM)	4.955 to 4.970 mm	4.935 to 4.950 mm

Valve stem run-out	Less than 0.03 mm

Valve guide bore diameter*:

1.4 and 1.6 litre engines:	
Standard	6.000 to 6.012 mm
1st oversize (0.075 mm)	6.075 to 6.090 mm
2nd oversize (0.150 mm)	6.150 to 6.165 mm
1.8 litre engines:	
Standard	5.000 to 5.012 mm
1st oversize (0.075 mm)	5.075 to 5.087 mm
2nd oversize (0.15 mm)	5.150 to 5.162 mm
Stem-to-guide clearance	N/A

Valve length:

1.4 and 1.6 litre engines:	
Inlet	101.51 to 101.93 mm
Exhaust	100.55 to 100.97 mm
1.8 litre engines:	
Inlet	100.1 to 100.3 mm
Exhaust	99.4 to 99.6 mm

Valve head diameter:

1.4 and 1.6 litre engines:	
Inlet	31.0 mm
Exhaust	27.5 mm
1.8 litre engines:	
Inlet	31.2 mm
Exhaust	27.5 mm

* Identification marking in brackets

Cylinder block

Maximum gasket face distortion	0.05 mm

Cylinder bore diameter:

1.4 litre engines:	
Standard:	
Size group 8	77.575 to 77.585 mm
Size group 99	77.585 to 77.595 mm
Size group 00	77.595 to 77.605 mm
Size group 01	77.605 to 77.615 mm
Size group 02	77.615 to 77.625 mm
Oversize:	
Size group 7 + 0.5 mm	78.065 to 78.075 mm
1.6 litre engines:	
Standard:	
Size group 8	78.975 to 78.985 mm
Size group 99	78.985 to 78.995 mm
Size group 00	78.995 to 79.005 mm
Size group 01	79.005 to 79.015 mm
Size group 02	79.015 to 79.025 mm
Oversize:	
Size group 7 + 0.5 mm	79.465 to 79.475 mm
1.8 litre engines:	
Standard:	
Size group 99	80.485 to 80.495 mm
Size group 00	80.495 to 80.505 mm
Size group 01	80.505 to 80.515 mm
Size group 05	80.545 to 80.555 mm
Oversize:	
Size group 00 + 0.5 mm	80.995 to 81.005 mm
Maximum cylinder bore ovality and taper	0.013 mm

1.4, 1.6 and 1.8 litre DOHC engines (continued)

Pistons and rings
Piston diameter:
  1.4 litre engines:
    Standard:
      Size group 8 .... 77.555 to 77.565 mm
      Size group 99 .... 77.565 to 77.575 mm
      Size group 00 .... 77.575 to 77.585 mm
      Size group 01 .... 77.585 to 77.595 mm
      Size group 02 .... 77.595 to 77.605 mm
    Oversize:
      Size group 7 + 0.5 mm .... 78.045 to 78.055 mm
  1.6 litre engines:
    Standard:
      Size group 8 .... 78.955 to 78.965 mm
      Size group 99 .... 78.965 to 78.075 mm
      Size group 00 .... 78.075 to 78.085 mm
      Size group 01 .... 78.085 to 78.095 mm
      Size group 02 .... 78.095 to 79.005 mm
    Oversize:
      Size group 7 + 0.5 mm .... 79.445 to 79.455 mm
  1.8 litre engines:
    Standard:
      Size group 99 .... 80.455 to 80.465 mm
      Size group 00 .... 80.465 to 80.475 mm
      Size group 01 .... 80.475 to 80.485 mm
      Size group 05 .... 80.515 to 80.525 mm
    Oversize:
      Size group 00 + 0.5 mm .... 80.965 to 80.975 mm
Piston-to-bore clearance .... 0.02 to 0.04 mm
Piston ring end gaps (fitted in bore):
  Top and second compression rings .... 0.3 to 0.5 mm
  Oil control ring .... 0.4 to 1.4 mm
Piston ring thickness:
  1.4 litre engines:
    Top compression ring .... 1.2 mm
    Second compression ring .... 1.5 mm
    Oil control ring .... 3.0 mm
  1.6 litre engines:
    Top compression ring .... 1.5 mm
    Second compression ring .... 1.5 mm
    Oil control ring .... 3.0 mm
  1.8 litre engines:
    Top compression ring .... 1.2 mm
    Second compression ring .... 1.2 mm
    Oil control ring .... 2.0 mm
Piston ring-to-groove clearance:
  Top compression ring .... 0.02 to 0.04 mm
  Second compression ring .... 0.04 to 0.06 mm
  Oil control ring .... 0.01 to 0.03 mm

Gudgeon pins
Diameter .... 17.997 to 18.0 mm
Length .... 55 mm
Gudgeon pin-to-piston clearance .... 0.007 to 0.010 mm

Connecting rod
Big-end side clearance .... 0.11 to 0.24 mm

Crankshaft
Endfloat .... 0.1 to 0.2 mm
Main bearing journal diameter:
  Standard (brown) .... 54.980 to 54.997 mm
  1st (0.25 mm) undersize (brown/blue) .... 54.730 to 54.747 mm
  2nd (0.50 mm) undersize (brown/white) .... 54.482 to 54.495 mm
Big-end bearing journal (crankpin) diameter:
  Standard .... 42.971 to 42.987 mm
  1st (0.25 mm) undersize .... 42.721 to 42.737 mm
  2nd (0.50 mm) undersize .... 42.471 to 42.487 mm

1.4, 1.6 and 1.8 litre DOHC engines (continued)

Crankshaft (continued)

Journal out-of-round	0.04 mm
Journal taper	N/A
Crankshaft run-out	Less than 0.03 mm
Main bearing running clearance	0.017 to 0.047 mm
Big-end bearing (crankpin) running clearance	0.019 to 0.071 mm

Torque wrench settings

Refer to Chapter 2B Specifications

2.0 litre DOHC engines

Cylinder head

Maximum gasket face distortion	0.05 mm
Cylinder head height	134 mm
Valve seat width:	
Inlet	1.0 to 1.4 mm
Exhaust	1.4 to 1.8 mm

Valves and guides

	Inlet	Exhaust
Valve guide height in cylinder head	13.70 to 14.00 mm	
Valve stem diameter*:	**Inlet**	**Exhaust**
Standard (GM)	5.955 to 5.970 mm	5.945 to 5.960 mm
1st oversize (0.075 mm – K1)	6.030 to 6.045 mm	6.020 to 6.035 mm
2nd oversize (0.150 mm – K2)	6.105 to 6.120 mm	6.095 to 6.110 mm
Valve stem run-out	Less than 0.03 mm	
Valve guide bore diameter*:		
Standard (GM)	6.000 to 6.012 mm	
1st oversize (0.075 mm – K1)	6.075 to 6.090 mm	
2nd oversize (0.150 mm – K2)	6.150 to 6.165 mm	
Stem-to-guide clearance:		
Inlet	0.030 to 0.057 mm	
Exhaust	0.040 to 0.067 mm	
Valve length:		
Inlet	102.0 to 102.2 mm	
Exhaust	92.15 to 92.35 mm	
Valve head diameter:		
Inlet	31.9 to 32.1 mm	
Exhaust	28.9 to 29.1 mm	

* Identification marking in brackets

Cylinder block

Maximum gasket face distortion	0.05 mm
Cylinder bore diameter:	
Standard:	
Size group 8	85.975 to 85.985 mm
Size group 99	85.985 to 85.995 mm
Size group 00	85.995 to 86.005 mm
Size group 01	86.005 to 86.015 mm
Size group 02	86.015 to 86.025 mm
Oversize (0.5 mm)	86.465 to 86.475 mm
Maximum cylinder bore ovality	0.013 mm
Maximum cylinder bore taper	0.013 mm

Pistons and rings

Piston diameter:	
Standard:	
Size group 8	85.945 to 85.955 mm
Size group 99	85.955 to 85.965 mm
Size group 00	85.965 to 85.975 mm
Size group 01	85.975 to 85.985 mm
Size group 02	85.985 to 85.995 mm
Oversize (0.5 mm) – size group 7 + 0.5	86.435 to 86.445 mm
Piston-to-bore clearance	0.02 to 0.04 mm
Piston ring end gaps (fitted in bore):	
Top and second compression rings	0.3 to 0.5 mm
Oil control ring	0.4 to 1.4 mm

2.0 litre DOHC engines (continued)

Pistons and rings (continued)

Piston ring thickness:
Top and second compression ring	1.5 mm
Oil control ring	3.0 mm

Piston ring-to-groove clearance:
Top and second compression ring	0.02 to 0.04 mm
Oil control ring	0.01 to 0.03 mm

Gudgeon pins

Diameter	21 mm
Length	57.7 to 58.0 mm
Gudgeon pin-to-piston clearance	0.011 to 0.014 mm

Connecting rod

Big-end side clearance	0.07 to 0.24 mm

Crankshaft

Endfloat	0.05 to 0.15 mm

Main bearing journal diameter:
  Standard:
1st size group (white)	57.974 to 57.981 mm
2nd size group (green)	57.981 to 57.988 mm
3rd size group (brown)	57.988 to 57.995 mm
1st (0.25 mm) undersize	57.732 to 57.745 mm
2nd (0.50 mm) undersize	57.482 to 57.495 mm

Big-end bearing journal (crankpin) diameter:
Standard	48.970 to 48.988 mm
1st (0.25 mm) undersize	48.720 to 48.738 mm
2nd (0.50 mm) undersize	48.470 to 48.488 mm
Journal out-of-round	0.04 mm
Journal taper	N/A
Crankshaft run-out	Less than 0.03 mm
Main bearing running clearance	0.015 to 0.040 mm
Big-end bearing (crankpin) running clearance	0.006 to 0.031 mm

Torque wrench settings

Refer to Chapter 2B Specifications

2.2 litre DOHC engines

Cylinder head

Maximum gasket face distortion	0.05 mm
Cylinder head height (resurfacing is not permitted)	129 mm

Cam lift:
Inlet	5.87 mm
Exhaust	5.99 mm
Valve seat angle in cylinder head	90°
Valve seat angle at valve head	90° 40'

Valve seat width in cylinder head:
Inlet	1.1 to 1.3 mm
Exhaust	1.4 to 1.8 mm

Valves and guides

Installation height of valve guide	11.20 to 11.50 mm
Installation height of valves	40.10

Valve guide bore diameter:
Standard	6.000 to 6.012 mm
Oversize	N/A
Length of valve guides	36 mm

Valve stem diameter*:	**Inlet**	**Exhaust**
Standard	5.955 to 5.970 mm	5.945 to 5.960 mm
Oversize – 0.075 mm (K1)	6.030 to 6.045 mm	6.020 to 6.035 mm
Valve length*:	**Inlet**	**Exhaust**
Standard	101.995 to 102.545	100.685 to 101.235
Oversize – 0.075 mm (K1)	101.595 to 102.145	100.285 to 100.835

Stem-to-guide clearance:
Inlet	0.042 to 0.045 mm
Exhaust	0.052 to 0.055 mm
Valve stem run-out	Less than 0.03 mm

Valve head diameter:
Inlet	34.95 to 35.25 mm
Exhaust	29.95 to 30.25 mm

2.2 litre DOHC engines (continued)

Cylinder block
Maximum gasket face distortion	0.05 mm
Cylinder bore diameter:	
Standard	85.992 to 86.008 mm
Oversize	86.117 to 86.133 mm
Maximum cylinder bore ovality	0.013 mm
Maximum cylinder bore taper	0.013 mm

Pistons and rings
Piston diameter:	
Standard	85.967 to 85.982 mm
Oversize	86.092 to 86.107 mm
Piston-to-bore clearance	0.025 to 0.026 mm
Piston rings:	
Top (rectangular) compression ring:	
Height (thickness)	1.17 to 1.19 mm
Gap	0.20 to 0.40 mm
Vertical play	0.06 mm
Middle (tapered) compression ring:	
Height (thickness)	1.471 to 1.490 mm
Gap	0.35 to 0.55 mm
Vertical play	0.05 mm
Bottom oil scraper ring:	
Height (thickness)	2.348 to 2.477 mm
Gap	0.25 to 0.76 mm
Vertical play	0.063 to 0.172 mm
Piston ring gap arrangement in cylinder	120°
Piston ring-to-groove clearance	N/A

Gudgeon pins
Diameter	19.995 to 20.000 mm
Length	62.59 to 63.09 mm
Gudgeon pin clearance:	
In connecting rod	0.012 to 0.021 mm
In piston	0.007 mm

Crankshaft
Main bearing journal diameter:	
Standard size	55.994 to 56.008 mm
1st undersize – 0.25 mm	55.744 to 55.758 mm
2nd undersize – 0.50 mm	55.494 to 55.508 mm
Main bearing shell thickness (Nos 1, 3, 4 and 5):	
Standard	4.030 to 4.037 mm
1st undersize – 0.25 mm	4.155 to 4.162 mm
2nd undersize – 0.50 mm	4.280 to 4.287 mm
Main bearing/thrust shell thickness (No 2):	
Standard	4.036 to 4.043 mm
1st undersize – 0.25 mm	4.161 to 4.168 mm
2nd undersize – 0.50 mm	4.268 to 4.293 mm
Main bearing/thrust shell width (No 2)	26.26 to 26.46 mm
Main bearing running clearance	0.007 to 0.014 mm
Big-end bearing journal (crankpin) diameter:	
Standard	49.000 to 49.014 mm
1st undersize – 0.25 mm	48.750 to 48.764 mm
2nd undersize – 0.50 mm	48.500 to 48.514 mm
Big-end bearing journal shell thickness:	
Standard	1.539 to 1.545 mm
1st undersize – 0.25 mm	1.664 to 1.670 mm
2nd undersize – 0.50 mm	1.795 to 1.798 mm
Big-end bearing (crankpin) running clearance	0.041 to 0.043 mm
Big-end side clearance	0.07 to 0.24 mm
Crankshaft endfloat	0.09 to 0.24 mm
Crankshaft run-out	Less than 0.03 mm
Journal out-of-round	0.04 mm
Journal taper	N/A

Torque wrench settings
Refer to Chapter 2C Specifications

1 General information

1 Included in this Part of Chapter 2 are details of removing the engine/transmission from the car and general overhaul procedures for the cylinder head, cylinder block and all other engine internal components.

2 The information given ranges from advice concerning preparation for an overhaul and the purchase of new parts, to detailed step-by-step procedures covering removal, inspection, renovation and refitting of engine internal components.

3 After Section 8, all instructions are based on the assumption that the engine has been removed from the car. For information concerning in-car engine repair, as well as the removal and refitting of those external components necessary for full overhaul, refer to the relevant in-car repair procedure in Part A, B or C of this Chapter and to Section 5. Ignore any preliminary dismantling operations described in the relevant in-car repair sections that are no longer relevant once the engine has been removed from the car.

4 Apart from torque wrench settings, which are given at the beginning of Part A, B and C, all specifications relating to engine overhaul are at the beginning of this Part of Chapter 2.

2 Engine overhaul – general information

1 It is not always easy to determine if an engine should be completely overhauled, as a number of factors must be considered.

2 High mileage is not necessarily an indication that an overhaul is needed, while low mileage does not preclude the need for an overhaul. Frequency of servicing is probably the most important consideration. An engine which has had regular and frequent oil and filter changes, as well as other required maintenance, should give many thousands of miles of reliable service. Conversely, a neglected engine may require an overhaul very early in its life.

3 Excessive oil consumption is an indication that piston rings, valve seals and/or valve guides are in need of attention. Make sure that oil leaks are not responsible before deciding that the rings and/or guides are worn. Perform a compression test, as described in the relevant Part of this Chapter, to determine the likely cause of the problem.

4 Check the oil pressure with a gauge fitted in place of the oil pressure switch, and compare it with that specified. If it is extremely low, the main and big-end bearings, and/or the oil pump, are probably worn out.

5 Loss of power, rough running, knocking or metallic engine noises, excessive valve gear noise, and high fuel consumption may also point to the need for an overhaul, especially if they are all present at the same time. If a complete service does not remedy the situation, major mechanical work is the only solution.

6 An engine overhaul involves restoring all internal parts to the specification of a new engine. During an overhaul, the pistons and the piston rings are renewed. New main and big-end bearings are generally fitted; if necessary, the crankshaft may be renewed, to restore the journals. The valves are also serviced as well, since they are usually in less-than-perfect condition at this point. While the engine is being overhauled, other components, such as the starter and alternator, can be overhauled as well. The end result should be an as-new engine that will give many trouble-free miles. **Note:** *Critical cooling system components such as the hoses, thermostat and coolant pump should be renewed when an engine is overhauled. The radiator should be checked carefully, to ensure that it is not clogged or leaking. Also, it is a good idea to renew the oil pump whenever the engine is overhauled.*

7 Before beginning the engine overhaul, read through the entire procedure, to familiarise yourself with the scope and requirements of the job. Overhauling an engine is not difficult if you follow carefully all of the instructions, have the necessary tools and equipment, and pay close attention to all specifications. It can, however, be time-consuming. Plan on the car being off the road for a minimum of two weeks, especially if parts must be taken to an engineering works for repair or reconditioning. Check on the availability of parts and make sure that any necessary special tools and equipment are obtained in advance. Most work can be done with typical hand tools, although a number of precision measuring tools are required for inspecting parts to determine if they must be renewed. Often the engineering works will handle the inspection of parts and offer advice concerning reconditioning and renewal. **Note:** *Always wait until the engine has been completely dismantled, and until all components (especially the cylinder block and the crankshaft) have been inspected, before deciding what service and repair operations must be performed by an engineering works. The condition of these components will be the major factor to consider when determining whether to overhaul the original engine, or to buy a reconditioned unit. Do not, therefore, purchase parts or have overhaul work done on other components until they have been thoroughly inspected.* As a general rule, time is the primary cost of an overhaul, so it does not pay to fit worn or sub-standard parts.

8 As a final note, to ensure maximum life and minimum trouble from a reconditioned engine, everything must be assembled with care, in a spotlessly-clean environment.

3 Engine removal – methods and precautions

1 If you have decided that the engine must be removed for overhaul or major repair work, several preliminary steps should be taken.

2 Locating a suitable place to work is extremely important. Adequate work space, along with storage space for the car, will be needed. If a workshop or garage is not available, at the very least a flat, level, clean work surface is required.

3 Cleaning the engine compartment and engine/transmission before beginning the removal procedure will help keep tools clean and organised.

4 An engine hoist or A-frame will also be necessary. Make sure the equipment is rated in excess of the combined weight of the engine and transmission. Safety is of primary importance, considering the potential hazards involved in lifting the engine/transmission out of the car.

5 If this is the first time you have removed an engine, an assistant should ideally be available. Advice and aid from someone more experienced would also be helpful. There are many instances when one person cannot simultaneously perform all of the operations required when lifting the engine out of the vehicle.

6 Plan the operation ahead of time. Before starting work, arrange for the hire of or obtain all of the tools and equipment you will need. Some of the equipment necessary to perform engine/transmission removal and installation safely and with relative ease (in addition to an engine hoist) is as follows: a heavy duty trolley jack, complete sets of spanners and sockets as described in the back of this manual, wooden blocks, and plenty of rags and cleaning solvent for mopping-up spilled oil, coolant and fuel. If the hoist must be hired, make sure that you arrange for it in advance, and perform all of the operations possible without it beforehand. This will save you money and time.

7 Plan for the car to be out of use for quite a while. An engineering works will be required to perform some of the work which the do-it-yourselfer cannot accomplish without special equipment. These places often have a busy schedule, so it would be a good idea to consult them before removing the engine, in order to accurately estimate the amount of time required to rebuild or repair components that may need work.

8 Always be extremely careful when removing and refitting the engine/transmission. Serious injury can result from careless actions. Plan ahead and take your time, and a job of this nature, although major, can be accomplished successfully.

4 Engine and transmission unit – removal, separation and refitting

Note: *The engine can be removed from the car only as a complete unit with the transmission; the two are then separated for overhaul. The engine/transmission unit is lowered out of position, and withdrawn from under the vehicle. Bearing this in mind, ensure the vehicle is raised sufficiently so that there is enough clearance between the front of the vehicle and the floor to allow the engine/transmission assembly to be slid out once it has been lowered out of position.*

Removal

1 Park the vehicle on firm, level ground then remove the bonnet as described in Chapter 11.

2 Depressurise the fuel system (see Chapter 4A) then remove the battery and mounting plate as described in Chapter 5A.

3 Firmly apply the handbrake, then jack up the front of the car and support it securely on axle stands bearing in mind the note at the start of this Section (see *Jacking and vehicle support*). Remove the front roadwheels. Where necessary, undo the retaining screws and remove the undercover from beneath the engine/transmission unit.

4 If the engine is to be dismantled, working as described in Chapter 1, first drain the engine oil and remove the oil filter. Also drain the cooling system (see Chapter 3).

5 Referring to Chapter 4A, carry out the following procedures.
 a) Remove the air cleaner assembly and associated components.
 b) Remove the exhaust front pipe.
 c) Disconnect the fuel hose(s) from the fuel rail/throttle housing.
 d) Disconnect the accelerator and cruise control cable (where fitted) and position it clear of the engine.
 e) Disconnect the brake servo hose and various vacuum hoses and from the inlet manifold, noting each hoses correct fitted location.
 f) Detach the fuel tank vent valve hose from the throttle body.

6 Remove the front bumper as described in Chapter 11.

7 Referring to Chapter 3, carry out the following procedures.
 a) Release the retaining clips and disconnect the various coolant hoses from the cylinder head and the block.
 b) At the engine compartment bulkhead, disconnect the heater coolant hoses by depressing the clip, pulling forward the collar, and pulling the hose from the connection.
 c) Release the coolant/air-conditioning hoses/pipes (as applicable) from any relevant clips and ties and position them clear of the engine unit.
 d) Secure the radiator/air conditioning condenser in place by inserting suitable bolts or rods through the holes in the radiator mounting brackets **(see illustration)**.

8 Disconnect the engine wiring loom large multi-plug, and any other wiring connectors between the engine wiring loom and the engine compartment wiring loom **(see illustrations)**. Unbolt any relevant earth leads from the cylinder block/transmission.

9 On models with a manual transmission unit, carry out the following procedures.
 a) Drain the transmission oil (see Chapter 7A) or be prepared for oil spillage as the engine/transmission unit is removed.
 b) Disconnect the wiring connector from the reversing light switch.
 c) On all except 2.2 litre models, working underneath the vehicle, undo the clamp bolt and disconnect the selector rod **(see illustration)**. On 2.2 litre models, remove the gearchange linkage assembly from the top of the transmission unit (see Chapter 7A).
 d) Clamp the flexible hose next to the connection and, using a screwdriver, release the clutch pressure hose connector retaining clip from the clutch bellhousing, and withdraw the pressure hose with the connector from the bellhousing.

10 On models with an automatic transmission unit, carry out the following procedures as described in Chapter 7B.
 a) Drain the transmission fluid.
 b) Disconnect the selector cable from the selector lever and support bracket – position the cable clear of the transmission.
 c) Disconnect the transmission unit wiring connectors by pulling the locking mechanism out from the connector.
 d) Disconnect the fluid cooler hoses from the transmission.

11 Manoeuvre the engine hoist into position, and attach it to the lifting brackets bolted onto the engine/transmission. Raise the hoist until it is supporting the weight of the engine.

12 Refer to Chapter 8 and remove both driveshafts.

13 With the engine securely supported, remove the front suspension subframe assembly as described in Chapter 10.

14 Make a final check that any components which would prevent the removal of the engine/transmission from the car have been removed or disconnected.

15 Mark the relative positions of the left and right-hand engine/transmission mounting brackets to the cylinder block bracket/transmission adapter plate. Slacken and remove the three bolts securing the right-hand engine mounting bracket to the cylinder head bracket, and the three bolts securing the mounting to the body. Slacken and remove the three bolts securing the left-hand transmission mounting to transmission

4.7 Secure the radiator in place with two bolts or rods

4.8a Disconnect the large engine wiring loom plug . . .

4.8b . . . and the grey connector

4.9 Undo the selector rod clamp bolt

4.15a Right-hand engine mounting bolts

4.15b Undo the three left-hand mounting bracket bolts (arrowed)

Refitting

Manual transmission models

29 If the engine and transmission have been separated, perform the operations described below in paragraphs 30 to 33. If not, proceed as described from paragraph 34 onwards.

30 Ensure the locating dowels are correctly positioned then carefully offer the transmission to the engine, until the locating dowels are engaged **(see illustration)**. Ensure that the weight of the transmission is not allowed to hang on the input shaft as it is engaged with the clutch friction plate.

31 Refit the engine-to-transmission housing bolts, ensuring that all the necessary brackets are correctly positioned, and tighten them to the specified torque setting.

32 Refit the starter motor and tighten its mounting bolts to the specified torque (see Chapter 5A).

33 On models with a pressed-steel sump, refit the flywheel lower cover plate to the transmission, and tighten its retaining bolts to the specified torque (Chapter 7A).

34 Slide the engine/transmission unit into position and reconnect the hoist and lifting tackle to the engine lifting brackets.

35 With the aid of an assistant, carefully lift the assembly into position in the engine compartment, manipulating the hoist and lifting tackle as necessary, taking great care not to trap any components.

36 Align the engine with the right-hand side of the engine compartment then refit the engine mounting and bracket. Tighten the bolts by hand only at this stage. Align the transmission with the left-hand engine mounting, and refit the three bolts securing the mounting bracket to the adapter plate on the transmission. On models equipped with air conditioning, manoeuvre the compressor into place. Refit and tighten the compressor retaining bolts to the specified torque (Chapter 3).

37 Renew the driveshaft oil seals (see Chapter 7A) then carefully refit the driveshafts (see Chapter 8).

38 Refit the front suspension subframe as described in Chapter 10.

39 With the subframe assembly correctly installed, align the previously-made marks and tighten the right and left-hand engine/transmission mounting bolts to the specified torque.

40 The remainder of the refitting procedure is a direct reversal of the removal sequence, noting the following points:

a) Ensure that all wiring is correctly routed and retained by all the relevant retaining clips and that all connectors are correctly and securely reconnected.

b) Ensure that all disturbed hoses are correctly reconnected, and securely retained by their retaining clips. Engage the heater hoses over the raised ridges on the heater pipes at the engine compartment bulkhead, and then push the locking collars to the rear **(see illustration)**.

adapter plate **(see illustrations)**. On models with air conditioning, disconnect the wiring plug, unbolt the compressor and position it clear of the engine. **Do not** open the refrigerant circuit.

16 If available, a low trolley should be placed under the engine/transmission assembly, to facilitate its easy removal from under the vehicle. Lower the engine/transmission assembly, making sure that nothing is trapped, taking great care not to damage the radiator/cooling fan assembly. Enlist the help of an assistant during this procedure, as it may be necessary to tilt the assembly slightly to clear the body panels. Great care must be taken to ensure that no components are trapped and damaged during the removal procedure.

17 Detach the hoist and withdraw the engine/transmission unit from under the vehicle.

Separation

Manual transmission models

18 With the engine/transmission assembly removed, support the assembly on suitable blocks of wood, on a workbench (or failing that, on a clean area of the workshop floor).

19 On models with a pressed-steel sump, undo the retaining bolts and remove the flywheel lower cover plate from the transmission.

20 Undo the retaining bolts and remove the starter motor from the transmission (see Chapter 5A).

21 Ensure that both engine and transmission are adequately supported, then slacken and remove the remaining bolts securing the transmission housing to the engine. Note the correct fitted positions of each bolt (and the relevant brackets) as they are removed, to use as a reference on refitting.

22 Carefully withdraw the transmission from the engine, ensuring that the weight of the transmission is not allowed to hang on the input shaft while it is engaged with the clutch friction plate.

23 If they are loose, remove the locating dowels from the engine or transmission, and keep them in a safe place.

Automatic transmission models

24 With the engine/transmission assembly removed, support the assembly on suitable blocks of wood, on a workbench (or failing that, on a clean area of the workshop floor).

25 Undo the retaining bolts and remove the starter motor from the transmission (see Chapter 5A).

26 Remove the rubber cover(s) from the cylinder block/sump flange to gain access to the torque converter retaining bolts. Slacken and remove the visible bolt(s) then, using a socket and extension bar to rotate the crankshaft pulley, undo the remaining bolts securing the torque converter to the driveplate as they become accessible. On 1.4, 1.6, 1.8 and 2.2 litre models there are three retaining bolts, whilst on 2.0 litre models six retaining bolts are fitted. Discard the bolts, new ones must be used on refitting.

27 To ensure that the torque converter does not fall out as the transmission is removed, slide the converter along the shaft and fully into the transmission housing.

28 Separate the engine and transmission as described in paragraphs 21 to 23.

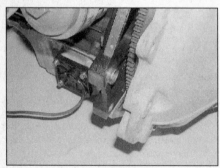

4.30 Ensure the locating dowels are correctly engaged

4.40 Engage the heater hoses over the raised ridges, and push the locking collars to the rear

c) Fit a new sealing ring to the clutch hose end fitting on the transmission unit and reconnect the end fitting, ensuring it is securely retained by the clip. On completion, bleed the hydraulic system as described in Chapter 6.

d) Refit the gearchange selector rod or linkage assembly, as applicable, and adjust as described in Chapter 7A.

e) Refit the front bumper and bonnet as described in Chapter 11.

f) Adjust the accelerator cable (where applicable) as described in the Chapter 4A.

g) Refill the transmission with correct quantity and type of oil, as described in Chapter 7A. If the oil was not drained, top-up the level as described in Chapter 7A.

h) Refill the engine with oil as described in Chapter 1 and also refill the cooling system (Chapter 3).

Automatic transmission models

41 If the engine and transmission have been separated, perform the operations described below in paragraphs 42 to 46. If not, proceed as described from paragraph 47 onwards.

42 Remove all traces of old locking compound from the torque converter threads by running a tap of the correct thread diameter and pitch down the holes. In the absence of a suitable tap, use one of the old bolts with slots cut in its threads.

43 Ensure the engine/transmission locating dowels are correctly positioned and apply a smear of molybdenum disulphide grease to the torque converter locating pin and its centring bush in the crankshaft end.

44 Carefully offer the transmission to the engine, until the locating dowels are engaged. Refit the engine-to-transmission housing bolts, ensuring that all the necessary brackets are correctly positioned, and tighten them to the specified torque setting.

45 Fit the new torque converter-to-driveplate bolts and tighten them lightly only to start then go around and tighten them to the specified torque setting in a diagonal sequence (Chapter 7B). Refit the rubber covers to the transmission flange.

46 Refit the starter motor and tighten its mounting bolts to the specified torque (see Chapter 5A).

47 Slide the engine/transmission unit into position and reconnect the hoist and lifting tackle to the engine lifting brackets.

48 With the aid of an assistant, carefully lift the assembly into position the engine compartment, manipulating the hoist and lifting tackle as necessary, taking great care not to trap any components.

49 Align the engine with the right-hand side of the engine compartment then refit the engine mounting and bracket. Tighten the bolts by hand only at this stage. Align the transmission with the left-hand engine mounting, and refit the three bolts securing

the mounting bracket to the adapter plate on the transmission.

50 Renew the driveshaft oil seals (see Chapter 7B) then carefully refit the driveshafts (see Chapter 8).

51 Refit the front suspension subframe as described in Chapter 10.

52 With the subframe assembly correctly installed, tighten the right and left-hand mounting bolts to the specified torque.

53 The remainder of the refitting procedure is a direct reversal of the removal sequence, noting the following points:

a) Ensure that all wiring is correctly routed and retained by all the relevant retaining clips and that all connectors are correctly and securely reconnected.

b) Ensure that all disturbed hoses are correctly reconnected, and securely retained by their retaining clips.

c) Fit new sealing rings to the transmission fluid cooler hose unions and ensure both unions are securely retained by their clips.

d) Refit the front bumper and bonnet as described in Chapter 11.

e) Adjust the accelerator cable as described in the Chapter 4A.

f) Refill the transmission with the specified type and quantity of fluid and adjust the selector cable as described in Chapter 7B.

g) Refill the engine with correct quantity and type of oil, as described in Chapter 1.

h) Refill the cooling system as described in Chapter 3.

5 Engine overhaul – dismantling sequence

1 It is much easier to dismantle and work on the engine if it is mounted on a portable engine stand. These stands can often be hired from a tool hire shop. Before the engine is mounted on a stand, the flywheel/driveplate should be removed, so that the stand bolts can be tightened into the end of the cylinder block.

2 If a stand is not available, it is possible to dismantle the engine with it blocked up on a sturdy workbench, or on the floor. Be extra-careful not to tip or drop the engine when working without a stand.

3 If you are going to obtain a reconditioned engine, all the external components must be removed first, to be transferred to the replacement engine (just as they will if you are doing a complete engine overhaul yourself). These components include the following:

a) Inlet and exhaust manifolds (Chapter 4A).

b) Alternator/air conditioning compressor bracket(s) (as applicable).

c) Coolant pump (Chapter 3).

d) Fuel system components (Chapter 4A).

e) Wiring harness and all electrical switches and sensors.

f) Oil filter (Chapter 1).

g) Flywheel/driveplate (relevant Part of this Chapter).

Note: When removing the external components from the engine, pay close attention to details that may be helpful or important during refitting. Note the fitted position of gaskets, seals, spacers, pins, washers, bolts and other small items.

4 If you are obtaining a 'short' engine (which consists of the engine cylinder block, crankshaft, pistons and connecting rods all assembled), then the cylinder head, sump, oil pump, and timing belt will have to be removed also.

5 If you are planning a complete overhaul, the engine can be dismantled, and the internal components removed, in the order given below, referring to the relevant Part of this Chapter unless otherwise stated.

a) Inlet and exhaust manifolds (Chapter 4A).

b) Timing belt/chain, sprockets and tensioner.

c) Cylinder head.

d) Flywheel/driveplate.

e) Sump.

f) Balancer unit (where fitted).

g) Oil pump.

h) Piston/connecting rod assemblies.

i) Crankshaft.

6 Before beginning the dismantling and overhaul procedures, make sure that you have all of the correct tools necessary. Refer to the *Tools and working facilities* Section of this manual for further information.

6 Cylinder head – dismantling

Note: *New and reconditioned cylinder heads are available from the manufacturer, and from engine overhaul specialists. Be aware that some specialist tools are required for the dismantling and inspection procedures, and new components may not be readily available. It may therefore be more practical and economical for the home mechanic to purchase a reconditioned head, rather than dismantle, inspect and recondition the original head.*

1 On 1.6 litre SOHC engines, referring to Part A of this Chapter, remove the cylinder head from the engine then lift the camshaft followers, thrust pads and hydraulic tappets out from the cylinder head.

2 On 1.4, 1.6, 1.8 and 2.0 litre DOHC engines remove the camshafts and followers as described in Part B of this Chapter then remove the cylinder head from the engine.

3 On 2.2 litre DOHC engines, working as described in Part C of this Chapter, remove the camshafts, followers and shims from the cylinder head, then remove the cylinder head from the engine.

4 On all models, using a valve spring compressor, compress each valve spring in turn until the split collets can be removed.

6.4a Using a valve spring compressor . . .

6.4b . . . compress the valve spring until the collets can be removed from the valve

6.4c Remove the compressor then lift off the spring collar . . .

6.4d . . . and remove the valve spring

6.4e Pull the seal off the top of the valve guide . . .

6.4f . . . then remove the spring seat

Release the compressor, and lift off the spring retainer and spring. Using a pair of pliers, carefully extract the valve stem seal from the top of the guide then slide off the spring seat **(see illustrations)**.

5 If, when the valve spring compressor is screwed down, the spring retainer refuses to free and expose the split collets, gently tap the top of the tool, directly over the retainer, with a light hammer. This will free the retainer.

6 Withdraw the valve through the combustion chamber. It is essential that each valve is stored together with its collets, retainer, spring, and spring seat. The valves should also be kept in their correct sequence, unless they are so badly worn that they are to be renewed.

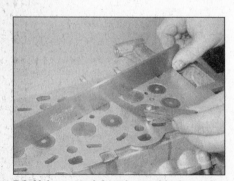

7.6 Using a straight-edge and feeler gauge to check cylinder head surface distortion

7 Cylinder head and valves – cleaning and inspection

1 Thorough cleaning of the cylinder head and valve components, followed by a detailed inspection, will enable you to decide how much valve service work must be carried out during the engine overhaul. **Note:** *If the engine has been severely overheated, it is best to assume that the cylinder head is warped – check carefully for signs of this.*

Cleaning

2 Scrape away all traces of old gasket material from the cylinder head.

3 Scrape away the carbon from the combustion chambers and ports, then wash the cylinder head thoroughly with paraffin or a suitable solvent.

4 Scrape off any heavy carbon deposits that may have formed on the valves, then use a power-operated wire brush to remove deposits from the valve heads and stems.

Inspection

Note: *Be sure to perform all the following inspection procedures before concluding that the services of a machine shop or engine overhaul specialist are required. Make a list of all items that require attention.*

Cylinder head

5 Inspect the head very carefully for cracks,

evidence of coolant leakage, and other damage. If cracks are found, a new cylinder head should be obtained.

6 Use a straight-edge and feeler gauge blade to check that the cylinder head surface is not distorted **(see illustration)**. If it is distorted beyond the specified value, the cylinder head must be renewed, as Vauxhall state that resurfacing of the head is not permitted.

7 Examine the valve seats in each of the combustion chambers. If they are severely pitted, cracked or burned, then they will need to be recut by an engine overhaul specialist. If they are only slightly pitted, this can be removed by grinding-in the valve heads and seats with fine valve grinding compound, as described below.

8 If the valve guides are worn (indicated by a side-to-side motion of the valve, and accompanied by excessive blue smoke in the exhaust when running) new guides must be fitted. Measure the diameter of the existing valve stems (see below) and the bore of the guides, then calculate the clearance and compare the result with the specified value. If the clearance is not within the specified limits, renew the valves and/or guides as necessary.

9 The renewal of valve guides should be carried out by an engine reconditioning specialist who will have the necessary tools and equipment available.

10 If renewing the valve guides, the valve seats should be recut or reground only *after* the guides have been fitted.

7.12 Measure the valve stem diameter using a micrometer

7.15 Grinding-in a valve

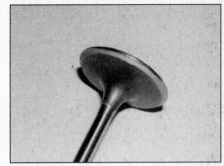

7.16 Grind the valve until a smooth unbroken ring of light grey matt finish is produced

Valves

11 Examine the head of each valve for pitting, burning, cracks and general wear, and check the valve stem for scoring and wear ridges. Rotate the valve, and check for any obvious indication that it is bent. Look for pitting and excessive wear on the tip of each valve stem. Renew any valve that shows any such signs of wear or damage.

12 If the valve appears satisfactory at this stage, measure the valve stem diameter at several points using a micrometer **(see illustration)**. Any significant difference in the readings obtained indicates wear of the valve stem. Should any of these conditions be apparent, the valve(s) must be renewed.

13 If the valves are in satisfactory condition, they should be ground (lapped) into their respective seats, to ensure a smooth gas-tight seal. If the seat is only lightly pitted, or if it has been recut, fine grinding compound **only** should be used to produce the required finish. Coarse valve-grinding compound should **not** be used unless a seat is badly burned or deeply pitted; if this is the case, the cylinder head and valves should be inspected by an expert to decide whether seat recutting, or even the renewal of the valve or seat insert, is required.

14 Valve grinding is carried out as follows. Place the cylinder head upside-down on a bench.

15 Smear a trace of the appropriate grade of valve-grinding compound on the seat face, and press a suction grinding tool onto the valve head. With a semi-rotary action, grind the valve head to its seat, lifting the valve occasionally to redistribute the grinding compound **(see illustration)**. A light spring placed under the valve head will greatly ease this operation.

16 If coarse grinding compound is being used, work only until a dull, matt even surface is produced on both the valve seat and the valve, then wipe off the used compound and repeat the process with fine compound. When a smooth unbroken ring of light grey matt finish is produced on both the valve and seat, the grinding operation is complete. **Do not** grind in the valves any further than absolutely necessary, or the seat will be

prematurely sunk into the cylinder head **(see illustration)**.

17 When all the valves have been ground-in, carefully wash off all traces of grinding compound using paraffin or a suitable solvent before reassembly of the cylinder head.

Valve components

18 Examine the valve springs for signs of damage and discoloration; if possible; also compare the existing spring free length with new components.

19 Stand each spring on a flat surface, and check it for squareness. If any of the springs are damaged, distorted or have lost their tension, obtain a complete new set of springs.

20 On 1.6 litre SOHC engines, the exhaust valve spring seats incorporate a bearing; the bearing rotates the valve which helps to keep the valve seat clean. If any spring seats bearing shows signs of wear or does not rotate smoothly then the seat should be renewed.

8.1a Fit the spring seat

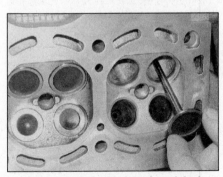

8.2 Insert the valve into the original location

8 Cylinder head – reassembly

1 Working on the first valve, refit the spring seat. Dip the new valve stem seal in fresh engine oil, then carefully locate onto the guide. Use a suitable socket or metal tube to press the seal firmly onto the guide **(see illustrations)**.

2 Lubricate the stems of the valves, and insert them into their original locations **(see illustration)**. If new valves are being fitted, insert them into the locations to which they have been ground. Take care not to damage the guide seal as the valve in inserted.

3 Locate the spring on the seat and fit the spring collar.

4 Compress the valve spring, and locate the split collets in the recess(es) in the valve stem **(see illustration)**. Release the compressor,

8.1b . . . and then the oil seal

8.4 Locate the collets into the recess in the valve stem

then repeat the procedure on the remaining valves.

5 With all the valves installed, place the cylinder head flat on the bench and, using a hammer and interposed block of wood, tap the end of each valve stem to settle the components.

6 On 1.6 litre SOHC engines, working as described in Part A, refit the hydraulic tappets, thrust pads and followers to the head then refit the cylinder head.

7 On 1.4, 1.6, 1.8 and 2.0 litre DOHC engines, working as described in Part B, refit the cylinder head to the engine and install the followers and camshafts.

8 On 2.2 litre DOHC engines, working as described in Part C, refit the cylinder head to the engine and install the followers, shims and camshafts.

9 Piston/connecting rod assembly – removal

Note: *New connecting rod big-end cap bolts will be needed on refitting.*

1 On 1.4, 1.6 and 1.8 litre engines, remove the cylinder head and sump. On 1.4 and 1.6 litre engines remove the baffle plate. Unbolt the pick-up/strainer from the base of the oil pump and the cylinder block. Refer to Part A for information on the SOHC engine and Part B for information on the DOHC engine.

2 On 2.0 litre engines, referring to Part B of this Chapter, remove the cylinder head and sump lower part. Slacken and remove the bolts securing the sump upper part, then unbolt the pick-up/strainer from the main bearing bridge or balancer unit (where fitted). Slide the sump upper part towards the front of the engine to expose the pick-up/strainer-to-oil pump retaining bolts. Undo these retaining bolts and remove the pick-up/strainer along with the sump upper part. Undo the retaining screws and remove the baffle plate from the base of the cylinder block. Evenly and progressively slacken the retaining bolts and remove the main bearing ladder or balancer unit casting (where fitted) from the base of the block.

3 On 2.2 litre engines, referring to Part C of

this Chapter, remove the cylinder head and sump then remove the cylinder block lower casing.

4 On all models, if there is a pronounced wear ridge at the top of any bore; it may be necessary to remove it with a scraper or ridge reamer, to avoid piston damage during removal. Such a ridge indicates excessive wear of the cylinder bore.

5 Prior to removal, using feeler blades, measuring the connecting rod big-end side clearance of each rod **(see illustration)**. If any rod exceeds the specified clearance, it must be renewed.

6 Using a hammer and centre-punch, paint or similar, mark each connecting rod and its bearing cap with its respective cylinder number on the flat machined surface provided; if the engine has been dismantled before, note carefully any identifying marks made previously **(see illustration)**. Note that No 1 cylinder is at the timing belt/chain (as applicable) end of the engine.

7 Turn the crankshaft to bring pistons 1 and 4 to BDC (bottom dead centre).

8 Unscrew the bolts from No 1 piston big-end bearing cap. Take off the cap and recover the bottom half bearing shell. If the bearing shells are to be re-used, tape the cap and the shell together.

Caution: On some engines, the connecting rod/bearing cap mating surfaces are not machined flat; the big-end bearing caps are 'cracked' off from the rod during production and left untouched to ensure the cap and rod mate perfectly. Where this type of connecting rod is fitted, great care must be taken to ensure the mating surfaces of the cap and rod are not marked or damaged in anyway. Any damage to the mating surfaces will adversely affect the strength of the connecting rod and could lead to premature failure.

9 Using a hammer handle, push the piston up through the bore, and remove it from the top of the cylinder block. Recover the bearing shell, and tape it to the connecting rod for safe-keeping.

10 Loosely refit the big-end cap to the

connecting rod, and secure with the nuts/bolts – this will help to keep the components in their correct order.

11 Remove No 4 piston assembly in the same way.

12 Turn the crankshaft through 180° to bring pistons 2 and 3 to BDC (bottom dead centre), and remove them in the same way.

10 Crankshaft – removal

Note: *New main bearing cap bolts will be required on refitting.*

1.4, 1.6 and 1.8 litre engines

1 Remove the oil pump and flywheel/driveplate. Refer to Part A for information on the SOHC engine and Part B for information on the DOHC engine.

2 Remove the piston and connecting rod assemblies as described in Section 9. If no work is to be done on the pistons and connecting rods, unbolt the caps and push the pistons far enough up the bores that the connecting rods are positioned clear of the crankshaft journals.

3 Check the crankshaft endfloat as described in Section 13, then proceed as follows.

4 The main bearing caps should be numbered 1 to 5 from the timing belt end of the engine and all identification numbers should be the right way up when read from the rear of the cylinder block **(see illustration)**. **Note:** *On some engines the flywheel/driveplate end (number 5) bearing cap may not be numbered but is easily identified anyway.* If the bearing caps are not marked, using a hammer and punch or a suitable marker pen, number the caps from 1 to 5 from the timing belt end of the engine and mark each cap to indicate its correct fitted direction to avoid confusion on refitting.

5 Working in a diagonal sequence, evenly and progressively slacken the ten main bearing cap retaining bolts by half a turn at a time until all bolts are loose. Remove all bolts.

6 Carefully remove each cap from the cylinder block, ensuring that the lower main bearing shell remains in position in the cap.

9.5 Checking connecting rod big-end side clearance

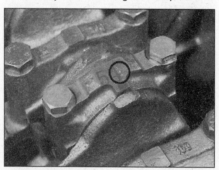

9.6 Prior to removal, make identification markings on the connecting rods and bearing caps (circled)

Note that lug on the bearing cap faces towards the flywheel/driveplate end of the engine

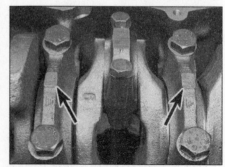

10.4 Main bearing cap identification markings (arrowed)

7 Carefully lift out the crankshaft, taking care not to displace the upper main bearing shells **(see illustration)**. Remove the oil seal and discard it.

8 Recover the upper bearing shells from the cylinder block, and tape them to their respective caps for safe-keeping.

2.0 litre engines

9 Remove the flywheel/driveplate and the oil pump as described in Part B of the Chapter.

10 Undo the retaining screws and remove the baffle plate from the base of the cylinder block. **Note:** *The oil baffle plate is only fitted to engines without a balancer unit.*

11 Evenly and progressively slacken the retaining bolts and remove the main bearing ladder casting or balancer unit (where fitted) from the base of the block.

12 Remove the crankshaft as described in paragraphs 2 to 8.

2.2 litre engines

13 Working as described in Part C of this Chapter, remove the flywheel/driveplate and unbolt the oil pump cover from the right-hand end of the cylinder block.

14 Evenly and progressively slacken the retaining bolts and unbolt the lower main bearing cylinder block casing and remove it from the cylinder block. If the housing locating dowels are a loose fit, remove them and store them with the housing for safe-keeping.

15 Remove the piston and connecting rod assemblies as described in Section 10. If no work is to be done on the pistons and connecting rods, unbolt the caps and push the pistons far enough up the bores that the connecting rods are positioned clear of the crankshaft journals.

16 Check the crankshaft endfloat as described in Section 13, then remove the crankshaft and upper bearing shells as described in paragraphs 7 and 8.

11 Cylinder block – cleaning and inspection

Cleaning

1 Remove all external components and electrical switches/sensors from the block. For complete cleaning, the core plugs should ideally be removed. Drill a small hole in the plugs, then insert a self-tapping screw into the hole. Pull out the plugs by pulling on the screw with a pair of grips, or by using a slide hammer.

2 Scrape all traces of gasket from the cylinder block, and from the main bearing casting (where fitted), taking care not to damage the gasket/sealing surfaces.

3 Remove all oil gallery plugs (where fitted). The plugs are usually very tight – they may have to be drilled out, and the holes retapped.

10.7 Removing the crankshaft

Use new plugs when the engine is reassembled.

4 If any of the castings are extremely dirty, all should be steam-cleaned.

5 After the castings are cleaned, clean all oil holes and oil galleries one more time. Flush all internal passages with warm water until the water runs clear. Dry thoroughly, and apply a light film of oil to all mating surfaces, to prevent rusting. Also oil the cylinder bores. If you have access to compressed air, use it to speed up the drying process, and to blow out all the oil holes and galleries.

> ⚠ *Warning: Wear eye protection when using compressed air.*

6 If the castings are not very dirty, you can do an adequate cleaning job with hot (as hot as you can stand), soapy water and a stiff brush. Take plenty of time, and do a thorough job. Regardless of the cleaning method used, be sure to clean all oil holes and galleries very thoroughly, and to dry all components well. Protect the cylinder bores as described above, to prevent rusting.

7 All threaded holes must be clean, to ensure accurate torque readings during reassembly. To clean the threads, run the correct-size tap into each of the holes to remove rust, corrosion, thread sealant or sludge, and to restore damaged threads. If possible, use compressed air to clear the holes of debris produced by this operation. A good alternative is to inject aerosol-applied water-dispersant lubricant into each hole, using the long spout usually supplied.

> ⚠ *Warning: Wear eye protection when cleaning out these holes in this way.*

8 Apply suitable sealant to the new oil gallery plugs, and insert them into the holes in the block. Tighten them securely. Similarly fit new core plugs.

9 If the engine is not going to be reassembled right away, cover it with a large plastic bag to keep it clean; protect all mating surfaces and the cylinder bores as described above, to prevent rusting.

Inspection

10 Visually check the castings for cracks and corrosion. Look for stripped threads in the threaded holes. If there has been any history of internal water leakage, it may be worthwhile having an engine overhaul specialist check the cylinder block/crankcase with special equipment. If defects are found, have them repaired if possible, or renew the assembly.

11 Check the bore of each cylinder for scuffing and scoring.

12 Measure the diameter of each cylinder bore at the top (just below the wear ridge), centre and bottom of the bore, both parallel to the crankshaft axis and at right angles to it, so that a total of six measurements are taken. Note that there are various size groups of standard bore diameter to allow for manufacturing tolerances; the size group markings are stamped on the cylinder block.

13 Compare the results with the Specifications at the beginning of this Chapter; if any measurement exceeds the service limit specified, the cylinder block must be rebored if possible, or renewed and new piston assemblies fitted.

14 If the cylinder bores are badly scuffed or scored, or if they are excessively worn, out-of-round or tapered, or if the piston-to-bore clearance is excessive (see Section 12), the cylinder block must be rebored (if possible) or renewed and new pistons fitted. Oversize (0.5 mm) pistons are available for all engines.

15 If the bores are in reasonably good condition and not worn to the specified limits, then the piston rings should be renewed. If this is the case, the bores should be honed to allow the new rings to bed in correctly and provide the best possible seal. The conventional type of hone has spring-loaded stones, and is used with a power drill. You will also need some paraffin (or honing oil) and rags. The hone should be moved up-and-down the bore to produce a crosshatch pattern, and plenty of honing oil should be used. Ideally, the crosshatch lines should intersect at approximately a 60° angle. Do not take off more material than is necessary to produce the required finish. If new pistons are being fitted, the piston manufacturers may specify a finish with a different angle, so their instructions should be followed. Do not withdraw the hone from the bore while it is still being turned – stop it first. After honing a bore, wipe out all traces of the honing oil. If equipment of this type is not available, or if you are not sure whether you are competent to undertake the task yourself, an engine reconditioning specialist will carry out the work at moderate cost.

12 Piston/connecting rod assembly – inspection

1 Before the inspection process can begin, the piston/connecting rod assemblies must be cleaned, and the original piston rings removed from the pistons.

2 Carefully expand the old rings over the top

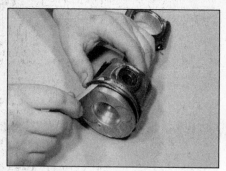

12.2 Using a feeler gauge to remove a piston ring

13.2 Check the crankshaft endfloat using a dial gauge . . .

13.3 . . . or feeler gauge

of the pistons. The use of two or three old feeler blades will be helpful in preventing the rings dropping into empty grooves (see illustration). Be careful not to scratch the piston with the ends of the ring. The rings are brittle, and will snap if they are spread too far. They're also very sharp – protect your hands and fingers. Note that the third (oil control) ring consists of a spacer and two side rails. Always remove the rings from the top of the piston. Keep each set of rings with its piston if the old rings are to be re-used.

3 Scrape away all traces of carbon from the top of the piston. A hand-held wire brush (or a piece of fine emery cloth) can be used, once the majority of the deposits have been scraped away. The piston identification markings should now be visible.

4 Remove the carbon from the ring grooves in the piston, using an old ring. Break the ring in half to do this (be careful not to cut your fingers – piston rings are sharp). Be careful to remove only the carbon deposits – do not remove any metal, and do not nick or scratch the sides of the ring grooves.

5 Once the deposits have been removed, clean the piston/connecting rod assembly with paraffin or a suitable solvent, and dry thoroughly. Make sure that the oil return holes in the ring grooves are clear.

6 If the cylinder bores are not damaged or worn excessively, and if the cylinder block does not need to be rebored (see Section 11), check the pistons as follows.

7 Carefully inspect each piston for cracks around the skirt, around the gudgeon pin holes, and at the piston ring 'lands' (between the ring grooves).

8 Look for scoring and scuffing on the piston skirt, holes in the piston crown, and burned areas at the edge of the crown. If the skirt is scored or scuffed, the engine may have been suffering from overheating, and/or abnormal combustion which caused excessively high operating temperatures. The cooling and lubrication systems should be checked thoroughly. Scorch marks on the sides of the pistons show that blow-by has occurred. A hole in the piston crown, or burned areas at the edge of the piston crown, indicates that abnormal combustion (pre-ignition, knocking, or detonation) has been occurring. If any of

the above problems exist, the causes must be investigated and corrected, or the damage will occur again. The causes may include incorrect ignition timing or a faulty injector.

9 Corrosion of the piston, in the form of pitting, indicates that coolant has been leaking into the combustion chamber and/or the crankcase. Again, the cause must be corrected, or the problem may persist in the rebuilt engine.

10 Measure the piston diameter at right-angles to the gudgeon pin axis; compare the results with the Specifications at the beginning of this Chapter. Note that there are various size groups of standard piston diameter to allow for manufacturing tolerances; the size group markings are stamped on the piston crown.

11 To measure the piston-to-bore clearance, either measure the bore (see Section 11) and piston skirt as described and subtract the skirt diameter from the bore measurement, or insert each piston into its original bore, then select a feeler gauge blade and slip it into the bore along with the piston. The piston must be aligned exactly in its normal attitude, and the feeler gauge blade must be between the piston and bore, on one of the thrust faces, just up from the bottom of the bore. Divide the measured clearance by two, to provide the clearance when the piston is central in the bore. If the clearance is excessive, a new piston will be required. If the piston binds at the lower end of the bore and is loose towards the top, the bore is tapered. If tight spots are encountered as the piston/feeler gauge blade is rotated in the bore, the bore is out-of-round.

12 Repeat this procedure for the remaining pistons and cylinder bores. Any piston which is worn beyond the specified limits must be renewed.

13 Examine each connecting rod carefully for signs of damage, such as cracks around the big-end and small-end bearings. Check that the rod is not bent or distorted. Damage is highly unlikely, unless the engine has been seized or badly overheated. Detailed checking of the connecting rod assembly can only be carried out by a Vauxhall dealer or engine reconditioning specialist with the necessary equipment.

14 On all but 2.2 litre engines, the gudgeon pins are an interference fit in the connecting rod small-end bearing. Therefore, piston and/or connecting rod renewal should be entrusted to a Vauxhall dealer or engine reconditioning specialist, who will have the necessary tooling to remove and install the gudgeon pins. If new pistons are to be fitted, ensure that the correct size group pistons are fitted to each bore. **Note:** *Vauxhall state that the piston/connecting rod assemblies should not be disassembled. If any components requires renewal, then the complete assembly must be renewed.*

13 Crankshaft – inspection

Checking crankshaft endfloat

1 If the crankshaft endfloat is to be checked, this must be done when the crankshaft is still installed in the cylinder block, but is free to move (see Section 10).

2 Check the endfloat using a dial gauge in contact with the end of the crankshaft. Push the crankshaft fully one way, and then zero the gauge. Push the crankshaft fully the other way, and check the endfloat (see illustration). The result can be compared with the specified amount, and will give an indication as to whether new main bearing shells are required.

3 If a dial gauge is not available, feeler gauges can be used. First push the crankshaft fully towards the flywheel/driveplate end of the engine, then use feeler gauges to measure the gap between the web of the crankpin and the side of thrustwasher (see illustration). The thrustwashers are incorporated into number 2 main bearing shell on 2.2 litre engines, and number 3 main bearing shells on all other engines.

Inspection

4 Clean the crankshaft using paraffin or a suitable solvent, and dry it, preferably with compressed air if available. Be sure to clean the oil holes with a pipe cleaner or similar probe, to ensure that they are not obstructed.

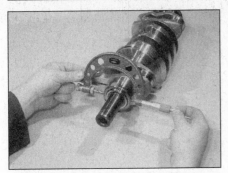

13.10 Using a micrometer to measure a crankshaft main bearing journal diameter

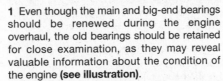

14.1 Typical main bearing shell identification markings

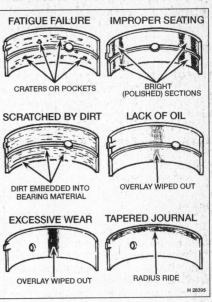

14.2 Typical bearing failures

 Warning: Wear eye protection when using compressed air.

5 Check the main and big-end bearing journals for uneven wear, scoring, pitting and cracking.

6 Big-end bearing wear is accompanied by distinct metallic knocking when the engine is running (particularly noticeable when the engine is pulling from low speed) and some loss of oil pressure.

7 Main bearing wear is accompanied by severe engine vibration and rumble – getting progressively worse as engine speed increases – and again by loss of oil pressure.

8 Check the bearing journal for roughness by running a finger lightly over the bearing surface. Any roughness (which will be accompanied by obvious bearing wear) indicates that the crankshaft requires regrinding (where possible) or renewal.

9 Check for burrs around the crankshaft oil holes (the holes are usually chamfered, so burrs should not be a problem unless regrinding has been carried out carelessly). Remove any burrs with a fine file or scraper, and thoroughly clean the oil holes as described previously.

10 Using a micrometer, measure the diameter of the main and big-end bearing journals, and compare the results with the Specifications **(see illustration)**. By measuring the diameter at a number of points around each journal's circumference, you will be able to determine whether or not the journal is out-of-round. Take the measurement at each end of the journal, near the webs, to determine if the journal is tapered. Compare the results obtained with those given in the Specifications.

11 Check the oil seal contact surfaces at each end of the crankshaft for wear and damage. If the seal has worn a deep groove in the surface of the crankshaft, consult an engine overhaul specialist; repair may be possible, but otherwise a new crankshaft will be required.

12 Set the crankshaft up in V-blocks, and position a dial gauge on the top of the crankshaft number 1 main bearing journal. Zero the dial gauge, then slowly rotate the crankshaft through two complete revolutions,

noting the journal run-out. Repeat the procedure on the remaining four main bearing journals, so that a run-out measurement is available for all main bearing journals. If the difference between the run-out of any two journals exceeds the service limit given in the Specifications, the crankshaft must be renewed.

13 Undersize (0.25 mm and 0.50 mm) big-end and main bearing shells are produced by Vauxhall for all engines. If the crankshaft journals have not already been reground, it may be possible to have the crankshaft reconditioned, and to fit undersize shells.

14 Main and big-end bearings – inspection

1 Even though the main and big-end bearings should be renewed during the engine overhaul, the old bearings should be retained for close examination, as they may reveal valuable information about the condition of the engine **(see illustration)**.

2 Bearing failure can occur due to lack of lubrication, the presence of dirt or other foreign particles, overloading the engine, or corrosion **(see illustration)**. Regardless of the cause of bearing failure, the cause must be corrected (where applicable) before the engine is reassembled, to prevent it from happening again.

3 When examining the bearing shells, remove them from the cylinder block, the main bearing caps, the connecting rods and the connecting rod big-end bearing caps. Lay them out on a clean surface in the same general position as their location in the engine. This will enable you to match any bearing problems with the corresponding crankshaft journal.

4 Dirt and other foreign matter gets into the engine in a variety of ways. It may be left in the engine during assembly, or it may pass through filters or the crankcase ventilation system. It may get into the oil, and from there into the bearings. Metal chips from machining operations and normal engine wear are often present. Abrasives are sometimes left in engine components after reconditioning,

especially when parts are not thoroughly cleaned using the proper cleaning methods. Whatever the source, these foreign objects often end up embedded in the soft bearing material, and are easily recognised. Large particles will not embed in the bearing, and will score or gouge the bearing and journal. The best prevention for this cause of bearing failure is to clean all parts thoroughly, and keep everything spotlessly-clean during engine assembly. Frequent and regular engine oil and filter changes are also recommended.

5 Lack of lubrication (or lubrication breakdown) has a number of interrelated causes. Excessive heat (which thins the oil), overloading (which squeezes the oil from the bearing face) and oil leakage (from excessive bearing clearances, worn oil pump or high engine speeds) all contribute to lubrication breakdown. Blocked oil passages, which usually are the result of misaligned oil holes in a bearing shell, will also oil-starve a bearing, and destroy it. When lack of lubrication is the cause of bearing failure, the bearing material is wiped or extruded from the steel backing of the bearing. Temperatures may increase to the point where the steel backing turns blue from overheating.

6 Driving habits can have a definite effect on bearing life. Full-throttle, low-speed operation (labouring the engine) puts very high loads on bearings, tending to squeeze out the oil film. These loads cause the bearings to flex, which produces fine cracks in the bearing face (fatigue failure). Eventually, the bearing material will loosen in pieces, and tear away from the steel backing.

7 Short-distance driving leads to corrosion of bearings, because insufficient engine heat is produced to drive off the condensed water and corrosive gases. These products collect in the engine oil, forming acid and sludge. As the oil is carried to the engine bearings, the acid attacks and corrodes the bearing material.

8 Incorrect bearing installation during engine assembly will lead to bearing failure as well. Tight-fitting bearings leave insufficient bearing running clearance, and will result in oil starvation. Dirt or foreign particles trapped behind a bearing shell result in high spots on the bearing, which lead to failure.

9 As mentioned at the beginning of this Section, the bearing shells should be renewed as a matter of course during engine overhaul; to do otherwise is false economy.

15 Engine overhaul –
reassembly sequence

1 Before reassembly begins, ensure that all new parts have been obtained, and that all necessary tools are available. Read through the entire procedure to familiarise yourself with the work involved, and to ensure that all items necessary for reassembly of the engine are at hand. In addition to all normal tools and materials, thread-locking compound will be needed. A good quality tube of liquid sealant will also be required for the joint faces that are fitted without gaskets.

2 In order to save time and avoid problems, engine reassembly can be carried out in the following order:
  a) Crankshaft.
  b) Piston/connecting rod assemblies.
  c) Oil pump.
  d) Balancer unit (where fitted)
  e) Main bearing ladder
  f) Sump.
  g) Flywheel/driveplate.
  h) Cylinder head.
  i) Timing chains and sprockets – 2.2 litre engines.
  j) Timing belt tensioner and sprockets, and belts – all except 2.2 litre engines.
  k) Inlet and exhaust manifolds (Chapter 4A).
  l) Engine external components.

3 At this stage, all engine components should be absolutely clean and dry, with all faults repaired. The components should be laid out (or in individual containers) on a completely clean work surface.

16.4 Measure a piston ring end gap using a feeler gauge

16 Piston rings – refitting

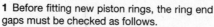

1 Before fitting new piston rings, the ring end gaps must be checked as follows.
2 Lay out the piston/connecting rod assemblies and the new piston ring sets, so that the ring sets will be matched with the same piston and cylinder during the end gap measurement and subsequent engine reassembly.
3 Insert the top ring into the first cylinder, and push it down the bore using the top of the piston. This will ensure that the ring remains square with the cylinder walls. Push the ring down into the bore until it is positioned 15 to 20 mm down from the top edge of the bore, then withdraw the piston.
4 Measure the end gap using feeler gauges, and compare the measurements with the figures given in the Specifications **(see illustration)**.
5 If the gap is too small (unlikely if genuine Vauxhall parts are used), it must be enlarged, or the ring ends may contact each other during engine operation, causing serious damage. Ideally, new piston rings providing the correct end gap should be fitted. As a last resort, the end gap can be increased by filing the ring ends very carefully with a fine file. Mount the file in a vice with soft jaws, slip the ring over the file with the ends contacting the file face, and slowly move the ring to remove material from the ends. Take care, as piston rings are sharp, and are easily broken.
6 With new piston rings, it is unlikely that the end gap will be too large. If the gaps are too

16.9 Install the oil control ring spacer and side rails first

large, check that you have the correct rings for your engine and for the particular cylinder bore size.
7 Repeat the checking procedure for each ring in the first cylinder, and then for the rings in the remaining cylinders. Remember to keep rings, pistons and cylinders matched up.
8 Once the ring end gaps have been checked and if necessary corrected, the rings can be fitted to the pistons.
9 Fit the piston rings using the same technique as for removal. Fit the bottom (oil control) spacer first then install both the side rails, noting that both the spacer and side rails can be installed either way up **(see illustration)**.
10 The second and top compression rings are different and can be identified by their cross-sections; the top ring is square whilst the second ring is tapered. Fit the second and top compression rings ensuring that each ring is fitted the correct way up with its identification (TOP) mark uppermost **(see illustrations)**.
Note: *Always follow any instructions supplied with the new piston ring sets – different manufacturers may specify different procedures. Do not mix up the top and second compression rings. On some engines the top ring will not have an identification marking and can be fitted either way up.*
11 With the piston rings correctly installed, check that each ring is free to rotate easily in its groove. Check the ring-to-groove clearance of each ring using feeler gauges and check that the clearance is within the specified range then position the ring end gaps as shown **(see illustration)**.

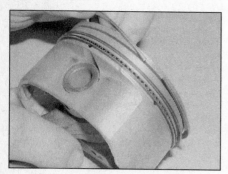

16.10a Install the second and top compression rings . . .

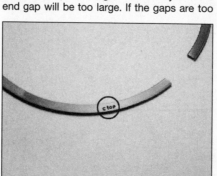

16.10b . . . with the identification marks (TOP) uppermost

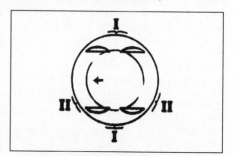

16.11 Piston ring end gap positions
I Top and second compression rings
II Oil control ring side rails

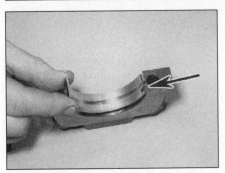

17.3 Fit the bearing shells making sure their tabs are correctly located in the slots on the bearing cap/block

17.7 Plastigauge in place on a crankshaft main bearing journal

17.9 Measure the width of the deformed Plastigauge using the scale on the card

17 Crankshaft – refitting and main bearing clearance check

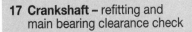

Note: *It is recommended that new main bearing shells are fitted regardless of the condition of the original ones.*

Selection of bearing shells

1 On all engines, although the original bearing shells fitted at the factory maybe of various grades, all new bearing shells sold are of the same grade. Vauxhall supply both standard size bearing shells and undersize shells for use when the crankshaft has been reground. The required size of shell required can be determined by measuring the crankshaft journals (see Section 13).

Main bearing clearance check

2 Clean the backs of the bearing shells and the bearing locations in both the cylinder block and the main bearing caps.
3 Press the bearing shells into their locations, ensuring that the tab on each shell engages in the notch in the cylinder block or main bearing cap **(see illustration)**. If the original bearing shells are being used for the check, ensure they are refitted in their original locations. The clearance can be checked in either of two ways.
4 One method (which will be difficult to achieve without a range of internal micrometers or internal/external expanding calipers) is to refit the main bearing caps to the cylinder block, with bearing shells in place. With the cap retaining bolts correctly tightened (use the original bolts for the check, not the new ones), measure the internal diameter of each assembled pair of bearing shells. If the diameter of each corresponding crankshaft journal is measured and then subtracted from the bearing internal diameter, the result will be the main bearing running clearance.
5 The second (and more accurate) method is to use a product known as Plastigauge. This

consists of a fine thread of perfectly round plastic which is compressed between the bearing shell and the journal. When the shell is removed, the plastic is deformed and can be measured with a special card gauge supplied with the kit. The running clearance is determined from this gauge. Plastigauge is sometimes difficult to obtain but enquiries at one of the larger specialist quality motor factors should produce the name of a stockist in your area. The procedure for using Plastigauge is as follows.
6 With the main bearing upper shells in place, carefully lay the crankshaft in position. Do not use any lubricant; the crankshaft journals and bearing shells must be perfectly clean and dry.
7 Cut several lengths of the appropriate size Plastigauge (they should be slightly shorter than the width of the main bearings) and place one length on each crankshaft journal axis **(see illustration)**.
8 With the main bearing lower shells in position, refit the main bearing caps, using the identification marks to ensure each one is correctly positioned. Refit the original retaining bolts and tighten them to the specified torque and angle settings in the Stages given in the Specifications (see paragraphs 22 to 24). Take care not to disturb the Plastigauge and **do not** rotate the crankshaft at any time during this operation. Evenly and progressively slacken and remove the main bearing cap bolts then

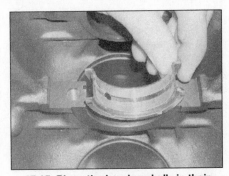

17.15 Place the bearing shells in their correct locations

lift off the caps again taking great care not to disturb the Plastigauge or rotate the crankshaft.
9 Compare the width of the crushed Plastigauge on each journal to the scale printed on the Plastigauge envelope to obtain the main bearing running clearance **(see illustration)**. Compare the clearance measured with that given in the Specifications at the start of this Chapter.
10 If the clearance is significantly different from that expected, the bearing shells may be the wrong size (or excessively worn if the original shells are being re-used). Before deciding that the crankshaft is worn, make sure that no dirt or oil was trapped between the bearing shells and the caps or block when the clearance was measured. If the Plastigauge was wider at one end than at the other, the crankshaft journal may be tapered.
11 Before condemning the components concerned, seek the advice of your Vauxhall dealer or suitable engine reconditioning specialist. They will also be able to inform as to the best course of action or whether renewal will be necessary.
12 Where necessary, obtain the correct size of bearing shell and repeat the running clearance checking procedure as described above.
13 On completion, carefully scrape away all traces of the Plastigauge material from the crankshaft and bearing shells using a fingernail or other object which is unlikely to score the bearing surfaces.

Final crankshaft refitting

1.4, 1.6 and 1.8 litre engines

14 Carefully lift the crankshaft out of the cylinder block.
15 Place the bearing shells in their locations as described above in paragraphs 2 and 3 **(see illustration)**. If new shells are being fitted, ensure that all traces of the protective grease are cleaned off using paraffin. Wipe dry the shells and caps with a lint-free cloth.
16 Lubricate the upper shells with clean

17.16a Lubricate the bearing shells . . .

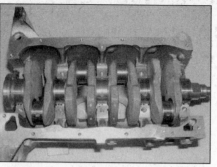

17.16b . . . and lower the crankshaft into position

17.18 The No 1 bearing cap is fitted at the timing belt end

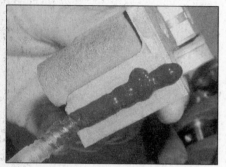

17.19 Fill the groove on each side of the No 5 bearing cap with sealant

17.20 Apply a continuous bead of silicone sealing compound (arrowed) around the edge of the cylinder block – 2.2 litre engines

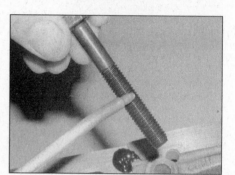

17.21 Oil the new bolts

engine oil then lower the crankshaft into position **(see illustrations)**.

17 Ensure the crankshaft is correctly seated then check the endfloat as described in Section 13.

18 On models with separate main bearing caps, ensure the bearing shells are correctly located in the caps and refit the caps number 1 to 4 to the cylinder block **(see illustration)**. Ensure the caps are fitted in their correct locations, with number 1 cap at the timing belt end, and are fitted the correct way around so that all the numbers are the correct way up when read from the rear of the cylinder block.

19 Ensure the left-hand (number 5) bearing cap is clean and dry then fill the groove on each side of the cap with sealing compound (Vauxhall recommend the use of sealant, part no 90485251, available from your Vauxhall dealer) **(see illustration)**. Fit the bearing cap to the engine, ensuring it is fitted the correct way around.

20 On models with a lower main bearing cylinder block casing, remove all traces of silicone sealer and oil from the mating surfaces of the cylinder block and lower main bearing casing. Apply a continuous bead of silicone sealing compound (available from your Vauxhall dealer) to the groove in the cylinder block mating surface **(see illustration)**. The bead of sealant should be between 2.0 and 2.5 mm in diameter. Carefully locate the casing in position on the cylinder block.

21 Apply a smear of clean engine to oil to the threads and underneath the heads of the new main bearing cap bolts. Fit the bolts, tightening them all by hand **(see illustration)**.

22 Working in a diagonal sequence from the centre outwards, tighten the main bearing cap/lower main bearing cylinder block casing (M10) bolts to the specified Stage 1 torque setting.

23 Once all bolts are tightened to the specified Stage 1 torque, go around again and tighten all bolts through the specified Stage 2 angle. On models with separate main bearing caps, go around for once more and tighten all bolts through the specified Stage 3 angle. It is

recommended that an angle-measuring gauge is used during the final stages of the tightening, to ensure accuracy **(see illustrations)**. If a gauge is not available, use white paint to make alignment marks between the bolt head and cap prior to tightening; the marks can then be used to check that the bolt has been rotated through the correct angle.

24 On models with a lower main bearing cylinder block casing, tighten the remaining M8 bolts to the specified torque, again working in a diagonal sequence.

25 Once all the bolts have been tightened, inject more sealant down the grooves in the main bearing cap until sealant is seen to be escaping through the joints. Once you are sure the cap grooves are full of sealant, wipe

17.23a Tighten the main bearing cap bolts through the various angle-tightening sequences

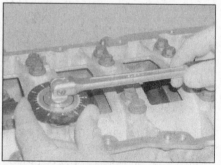

17.23b Tightening the lower main bearing cylinder block casing bolts through the specified angle-tightening sequence – 2.2 litre engines

17.25 Inject more sealant down into the grooves in the main bearing cap

off all excess sealant using a clean cloth (see illustration).

26 Check that the crankshaft is free to rotate smoothly; if excessive pressure is required to turn the crankshaft, investigate the cause before proceeding further.

27 Refit/reconnect the piston connecting rod assemblies to the crankshaft as described in Section 18.

28 Referring to Part A (SOHC engine) or Part B (DOHC engine), fit a new left-hand crankshaft oil seal, then refit the flywheel/driveplate, oil pump, baffle plate (where fitted), cylinder head, timing belt sprocket(s) and fit a new timing belt.

2.0 litre engines

29 Refit the crankshaft as described in paragraphs 14 to 25.

30 Ensure the bearing cap and main bearing ladder casting or balancer unit surfaces are clean and dry then refit the casting/unit to the engine. Refit the retaining bolts and tighten them to the specified torque, working in a diagonal sequence from the centre outwards.

31 Refit the baffle plate to the base of the cylinder block assembly and tighten its retaining bolts to the specified torque. **Note:** *The oil baffle plate is only fitted to engines without a balancer unit.*

32 Working as described in Part B of this Chapter, fit a new left-hand oil crankshaft oil seal then refit the flywheel/driveplate, oil pump, cylinder head, timing belt sprocket(s) and fit a new timing belt.

2.2 litre engines

33 Refit the crankshaft as described in paragraphs 14 to 25.

34 Working as described in Part C of this Chapter, fit a new left-hand oil crankshaft oil seal then refit the flywheel/driveplate, oil pump, cylinder head, timing chain sprocket(s) and fit a new timing chain.

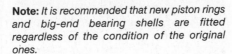

18 Piston/connecting rod assembly – refitting and big-end running clearance check

Note: *It is recommended that new piston rings and big-end bearing shells are fitted regardless of the condition of the original ones.*

Selection of bearing shells

1 On all engines, although the original bearing shells fitted at the factory maybe of various grades, all new bearing shells sold are of the same grade. Vauxhall supply both standard size bearing shells and undersize shells for use when the crankshaft has been reground. The required size of shell required can be determined by measuring the crankshaft journals (see Section 13).

Big-end bearing clearance check

2 Clean the backs of the bearing shells and the bearing locations in both the connecting rod and bearing cap.

3 Press the bearing shells into their locations, ensuring that the tab on each shell engages in the notch in the connecting rod and cap (see illustration). If the original bearing shells are being used for the check, ensure they are refitted in their original locations. The clearance can be checked in either of two ways.

4 One method is to refit the big-end bearing cap to the connecting rod, with bearing shells in place. With the cap retaining bolts/nuts (use the original bolts for the check) correctly

tightened, use an internal micrometer or vernier caliper to measure the internal diameter of each assembled pair of bearing shells. If the diameter of each corresponding crankshaft journal is measured and then subtracted from the bearing internal diameter, the result will be the big-end bearing running clearance.

5 The second method is to use Plastigauge as described in Section 17, paragraphs 5 to 13. Place a strand of Plastigauge on each (cleaned) crankpin journal and refit the (clean) piston/connecting rod assemblies, shells and big-end bearing caps. Tighten the bolts/nuts (as applicable) correctly taking care not to disturb the Plastigauge. Dismantle the assemblies without rotating the crankshaft and use the scale printed on the Plastigauge envelope to obtain the big-end bearing running clearance. On completion of the measurement, carefully scrape off all traces of Plastigauge from the journal and shells using a fingernail or other object which will not score the components.

Piston/connecting rod refitting

6 Ensure the bearing shells are correctly refitted as described above in paragraphs 2 and 3. If new shells are being fitted, ensure that all traces of the protective grease are cleaned off using paraffin. Wipe dry the shells and connecting rods with a lint-free cloth.

7 Lubricate the bores, the pistons and piston rings then lay out each piston/connecting rod assembly in its respective position (see illustration).

8 Starting with assembly number 1, make sure that the piston rings are still spaced as described in Section 16, then clamp them in position with a piston ring compressor (see illustration).

9 Insert the piston/connecting rod assembly into the top of cylinder No 1, ensuring that the arrow marking on the piston crown is pointing towards the timing belt/chain end of the engine. Using a block of wood or hammer handle against the piston crown, tap the assembly into the cylinder until the piston

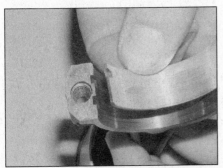

18.3 Ensure that the tab on each big-end shell locates in the notch in the connecting rod and cap

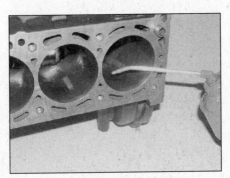

18.7 Oil the cylinder bores

18.8 Piston ring clamp

18.9a The arrow on the piston crown should point towards the timing belt end of the engine

18.9b Make sure the ring clamp is kept against the block face, and push the piston in

crown is flush with the top of the cylinder **(see illustrations)**.

10 Taking care not to mark the cylinder bore, liberally lubricate the crankpin and both bearing shells, then pull the piston/connecting rod assembly down the bore and onto the crankpin and refit the big-end bearing cap using the markings to ensure it is fitted the correct way around (the lug on the bearing cap base should be facing the flywheel/driveplate end of the engine) and screw in the new retaining bolts **(see illustrations)**.

11 On 1.4, 1.6 and 1.8 litre engines, tighten both bearing cap bolts to the specified Stage 1 torque setting and then tighten them through the specified Stage 2 angle. It is recommended that an angle-measuring gauge is used to ensure accuracy **(see illustration)**. If a gauge is not available, use white paint to make alignment marks between the bolt head and cap prior to tightening; the marks can then be used to check that the bolt has been rotated through the correct angle.

12 On 2.0 and 2.2 litre engines, tighten both bearing cap bolts to the specified Stage 1 torque setting then tighten them through the

specified Stage 2 angle, and finally through the specified Stage 3 angle. It is recommended that an angle-measuring gauge is used during the final stages of the tightening, to ensure accuracy. If a gauge is not available, use white paint to make alignment marks between the bolt head and cap prior to tightening; the marks can then be used to check that the bolt has been rotated through the correct angle.

13 Refit the remaining three piston and connecting rod assemblies in the same way.

14 Rotate the crankshaft, and check that it turns freely, with no signs of binding or tight spots.

15 On 2.0 and 2.2 litre engines, where removed, ensure that the surfaces of the bearing cap and main bearing ladder casting, lower main bearing cylinder casing, or balancer unit, as applicable, are clean and dry. Refit the casting/unit to the engine and tighten its retaining bolts to the specified torque, working in a diagonal sequence from the centre outwards. Refit the baffle plate (where fitted) to the base of the cylinder block and tighten its retaining bolts to the specified torque.

16 On all engines, refit the oil pump strainer, sump and the cylinder head as described in Part A, B, or C of this Chapter, according to engine type.

19 Engine – initial start up after overhaul

1 With the engine refitted in the vehicle, double-check the engine oil and coolant levels. Make a final check that everything has been reconnected, and that there are no tools or rags left in the engine compartment.

2 Disable the ignition system by disconnecting the wiring connector from the ignition module, and the fuel system by removing the fuel pump relay from the engine compartment relay box (see Chapter 4A). Turn the engine on the starter until the oil pressure warning light goes out then stop and reconnect the wiring connector and refit the relay.

3 Start the engine as normal noting that this may take a little longer than usual, due to the fuel system components having been disturbed.

4 While the engine is idling, check for fuel, water and oil leaks. Don't be alarmed if there are some odd smells and smoke from parts getting hot and burning off oil deposits.

5 Assuming all is well, keep the engine idling until hot water is felt circulating through the top hose, then switch off the engine.

6 Allow the engine to cool then recheck the oil and coolant levels as described in *Weekly Checks*, and top-up as necessary.

7 If new pistons, rings or crankshaft bearings have been fitted, the engine must be treated as new, and run-in for the first 500 miles (800 km). *Do not* operate the engine at full-throttle, or allow it to labour at low engine speeds in any gear. It is recommended that the oil and filter be changed at the end of this period.

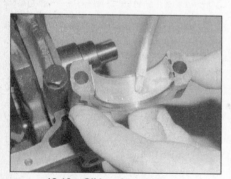

18.10a Oil bearing shells . . .

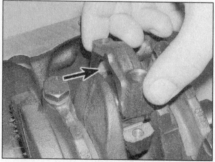

18.10b . . . and fit the caps with the lug on the base towards the flywheel/driveplate (arrowed)

18.11 Angle-tighten the big-end bolts

Chapter 3
Cooling, heating and air conditioning systems

Contents

Air conditioning system – general information and precautions 11
Air conditioning system components – removal and refitting 12
Auxiliary drivebelt check and renewal ....See Chapter 1
Coolant pump – removal and refitting 8
Cooling system – draining, flushing and refilling 2
Cooling system – general 1
Cooling system electrical switches and sensors – testing,
   removal and refitting 7

Cooling system hoses – disconnection and renewal 3
Electric cooling fan – testing, removal and refitting 6
Heater/ventilation system components – removal and refitting 10
Heating and ventilation system – general information 9
Hose and fluid leak check ....See Chapter 1
Pollen filter renewal ....See Chapter 1
Radiator – removal, inspection and refitting 4
Thermostat – removal, testing and refitting 5

Degrees of difficulty

Easy, suitable for novice with little experience	Fairly easy, suitable for beginner with some experience	Fairly difficult, suitable for competent DIY mechanic	Difficult, suitable for experienced DIY mechanic	Very difficult, suitable for expert DIY or professional

Specifications

System type .... Pressurised, with front-mounted radiator, remote expansion tank, and electric cooling fan

Thermostat
Type .... Wax
Start-to-open temperature:
  1.8 and 2.2 litre engines .... 80°C
  All other engines .... 92°C
Fully-open temperature:
  2.2 litre engines .... 97°C
  All other engines .... 107°C

Electric cooling fan
Switches on at .... 100°C
Switches off at .... 95°C

Air conditioning compressor
Lubricant capacity:
  1.6 and 2.2 litre DOHC engines .... 120 cc
  Except 1.6 and 2.2 litre DOHC engines .... 150 cc
Lubricant type .... Vauxhall part number 90509933/1949873

Torque wrench settings

	Nm	lbf ft
Air conditioning compressor mounting:		
1.6 litre SOHC engines	25	18
Except 1.6 litre SOHC engines	20	15
Air conditioning refrigerant line to receiver-dryer and condenser	20	15
Condensation drain to floor	5	4
Coolant pump:		
1.4 and 1.6 litre engines	8	6
1.8 and 2.0 litre engines	25	18
2.2 litre engines	22	16
Coolant pump drain plug:		
2.2 litre engines	20	15
Coolant pump sprocket:		
2.2 litre engines	10	7
Electric cooling fan assembly frame to radiator	5	4
Pressure pick-up to receiver-dryer	9	7
Steering crossmember to bulkhead	25	18
Temperature sensor:		
1.4 and 1.6 litre DOHC engines	14	10
1.6 litre SOHC engines	20	15
1.8 litre engines	20	15
2.0 litre engines	10	7
2.2 litre engines	20	15
Thermostat base housing to cylinder head/block:		
1.4 and 1.6 litre DOHC engines	20	15
2.2 litre engines	8	6
Thermostat cover:		
1.4 and 1.6 litre DOHC engines	8	6
1.6 litre SOHC engines	10	7
1.8 litre engines	20	15
2.0 litre engines	15	11
2.2 litre engines	8	6

1 Cooling system – general

General information

The cooling system is of pressurised type, comprising a coolant pump, a crossflow radiator, electric cooling fan, and thermostat. On 2.2 litre engines, the coolant pump is driven by the balancer shaft drive chain, whereas on all other engines the pump is driven by the timing belt.

The system functions as follows. Cold coolant from the radiator passes through the bottom hose to the coolant pump, where it is pumped around the cylinder block, head passages and heater matrix. After cooling the cylinder bores, combustion surfaces and valve seats, the coolant reaches the underside of the thermostat, which is initially closed. The coolant passes through the heater, and is returned to the coolant pump.

When the engine is cold, the coolant circulates only through the cylinder block, cylinder head and heater. When the coolant reaches a predetermined temperature, the thermostat opens and the coolant passes through to the radiator. As the coolant circulates through the radiator, it is cooled by the in-rush of air when the car is in forward motion. Airflow is supplemented by the action of the electric cooling fan when necessary.

Once the coolant has passed through the radiator, and has cooled, the cycle is repeated.

The electric cooling fan, mounted on the radiator, is controlled by a cooling module located behind the left-hand side of the front bumper. At a predetermined coolant temperature, the fan is actuated.

An expansion tank is fitted to the left-hand side of the engine compartment to accommodate expansion of the coolant when hot. The expansion tank is connected to the top of the radiator by a small bore rubber hose.

Precautions

 Warning: Do not attempt to remove the expansion tank filler cap, or disturb any part of the cooling system, while the engine is hot; there is a high risk of scalding. If the cap must be removed before the engine and radiator have fully cooled (even though this is not recommended) the pressure in the cooling system must first be relieved. Cover the cap with a thick layer of cloth, to avoid scalding, and slowly unscrew the filler cap until a hissing sound can be heard. When the hissing has stopped, indicating that the pressure has reduced, slowly unscrew the filler cap until it can be removed; if more hissing sounds are heard, wait until they have stopped before unscrewing the cap completely. At all times, keep well away from the filler cap opening.

 Warning: Do not allow antifreeze to come into contact with the skin, or with the painted surfaces of the vehicle. Rinse off spills immediately, with plenty of water.

Warning: If the engine is hot, the electric cooling fan may start rotating even if the engine is not running; be careful to keep hands, hair and loose clothing well clear when working in the engine compartment.

Warning: Refer to Section 11 for precautions to be observed when working on models equipped with air conditioning.

2 Cooling system – draining, flushing and refilling

 Warning: Wait until the engine is cold before starting this procedure. Do not allow antifreeze to come in contact with your skin, or with the painted surfaces of the vehicle. Rinse off spills immediately with plenty of water.

Draining

1 To drain the cooling system, first unscrew and remove the expansion tank filler cap (see

2.1 Removing the expansion tank filler cap

2.3a The drain tap is located on the right-hand side of the radiator

2.3b Connect a hose to the drain tap to drain the cooling system

2.4 Removing the coolant drain plug located under the coolant pump housing – 2.2 litre engines

illustration). If the engine is not completely cold, place a thick cloth over the cap, and unscrew it slowly to release any pressure.

2 Where necessary, remove the splash guard from under the radiator and engine.

3 Position a container beneath the right-hand side of the radiator and connect a short length of hose from the radiator drain tap to the container. Open the tap and allow the coolant to drain into the container (see illustrations).

4 On 2.2 litre engines, when the coolant has drained from the radiator, position the container beneath the coolant pump and unscrew the drain plug from the underside of the coolant pump housing (see illustration). On all other engines, as no cylinder block drain plug is fitted, the engine cannot be drained completely. Care should therefore be taken when refilling the system to maintain antifreeze strength.

5 If the coolant has been drained for a reason other than renewal, then provided it is clean and less than two years old, it can be re-used. Note: Vauxhall state that the coolant should be renewed after fitting a radiator, cylinder head, cylinder head gasket or engine. Vauxhall do not specify renewal intervals for the coolant installed in the system when the vehicle is new, so renewal is up to the discretion of the owner.

Flushing

6 If coolant renewal has been neglected, or if the antifreeze mixture has become diluted then, in time, the cooling system may gradually lose efficiency, as the coolant passages become restricted due to rust, scale deposits, and other sediment. The cooling system efficiency can be restored by flushing the system clean.

7 The radiator should be flushed independently of the engine, to avoid unnecessary contamination.

8 To flush the radiator, disconnect the top and bottom hoses from the radiator, then insert a garden hose into the radiator top inlet. Direct a flow of clean water through the radiator and continue flushing until clean water emerges from the radiator bottom outlet. If after a reasonable period, the water still does not run clear, the radiator can be flushed with a flushing solution, available at all good motorist outlets. It is important that the cleaning agent manufacturer's instructions are followed carefully. If the contamination is particularly bad, remove the radiator then insert the hose in the bottom outlet, and flush the radiator in reverse ('reverse-flushing').

9 To flush the engine, remove the thermostat as described in Section 5 and disconnect the bottom hose from the radiator.

10 Insert a hose in the thermostat housing or cylinder head and direct a flow of clean water through the engine until clean water emerges from the bottom hose.

11 On completion of flushing, refit the thermostat, referring to Section 5 and reconnect the hoses.

Refilling

12 Before attempting to fill the cooling system, make sure that all hoses and clips are in good condition, and that the clips are tight. Close the radiator drain tap and, on 2.2 litre engines, refit the drain plug to the base of the coolant pump housing. An antifreeze solution must be used all year round, to prevent corrosion of the alloy engine components.

13 Unscrew and remove the expansion tank cap, and fill the system slowly until the level reaches the KALT (or COLD) mark on the tank. During refilling, occasionally assist the purging of air locks by squeezing the radiator top and bottom hoses several times. If the coolant is being renewed, begin by pouring in a couple of litres of water, followed by the

correct quantity of antifreeze, then top-up with more water.

14 Refit and tighten the expansion tank cap.

15 Start the engine and run it until it reaches normal operating temperature, then stop the engine and allow it to cool.

16 Check for leaks, particularly around disturbed components. Check the coolant level in the expansion tank, and top-up if necessary. Note that the system must be cold before an accurate level is indicated in the expansion tank. If the expansion tank cap is removed while the engine is still warm, cover the cap with a thick cloth and unscrew the cap slowly to gradually relieve the system pressure (a hissing sound will normally be heard). Wait until any pressure remaining in the system is released, then continue to turn the cap until it can be removed.

17 Refit the cap, then where necessary, refit the splash guard beneath the radiator and engine.

3 Cooling system hoses – disconnection and renewal

Note: *Refer to the warnings given in Section 1 of this Chapter before proceeding. Do not attempt to disconnect any hose while the system is still hot.*

1 If the checks described in Chapter 1 reveal a faulty hose, it must be renewed as follows.

2 First drain the cooling system (see Section 2). If the coolant is not due for renewal, it may be re-used if it is collected in a clean container.

TOOL TIP

The hose clips fitted as original equipment are particularly difficult to remove with grips or pliers, a home-made tool can easily be fabricated out of a worm-drive clip. Cut the clip with reference to the photograph and bend over one end to hook around the square end of the original clip. Drill a hole in the other end to fit over the protruding end of the original clip.

3 Before disconnecting a hose, first note its routing in the engine compartment, and its fitted position. Loosen the clips then move the clips along the hose, clear of the relevant inlet/outlet union **(see Tool Tip)**. Carefully ease the hose free.

4 Note that the radiator inlet and outlet unions are fragile; do not use excessive force when attempting to remove the hoses. If a hose proves to be difficult to remove, try to release it by rotating the hose ends before attempting to free it.

5 When fitting a hose, first slide the clips onto the hose, then work the hose into position. If the hose is stiff, use a little soapy water (washing-up liquid is ideal) as a lubricant, or soften the hose by soaking it in hot water.

6 Slide each clip along the hose until it passes over the flared end of the relevant inlet/outlet union, before tightening the clips securely.

7 Refill the cooling system with reference to Section 2.

8 Check thoroughly for leaks as soon as possible after disturbing any part of the cooling system.

4 Radiator – removal, inspection and refitting

Removal

1 On models **without** air conditioning, disconnect the battery negative terminal (refer to *Disconnecting the battery* in the Reference Chapter).

2 On Astra models **with** air conditioning, remove the battery as described in Chapter 5A, then unbolt the battery tray from the inner wing panel. Also remove the air cleaner assembly and air ducts with reference to Chapter 4A.

3 On Zafira models **with** air conditioning, unbolt the air intake resonator from the front crossmember, and disconnect it from the air intake hose **(see illustrations)**.

4 Apply the handbrake, then jack up the front of the vehicle and support it on axle stands (see *Jacking and vehicle support*). Where necessary, remove the splash guard from the bottom of the engine compartment.

5 Drain the cooling system as described in Section 2.

6 Remove the electric fan assembly from the rear of the radiator as described in Section 6.

7 Loosen the clip and disconnect the top hose from the right-hand side of the radiator **(see illustration)**.

8 Loosen the clip and disconnect the bottom hose from the left-hand side of the radiator.

9 Loosen the clip and disconnect the air purge hose from the left-hand side of the radiator **(see illustration)**.

4.3a Unscrew the bolts . . .

4.3b . . . and remove the air intake resonator from the front crossmember

4.7 Disconnecting the top hose

4.9 Disconnecting the air purge hose

4.11 Removing the front bumper

4.14a Unscrew the bolts securing the condenser to the front of the radiator . . .

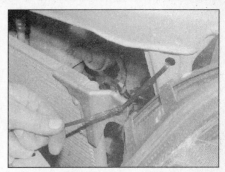

4.14b . . . then tie the condenser to the front crossmember with plastic ties

10 On models with automatic transmission, unscrew the union bolts and disconnect the fluid cooler hoses from the left-hand side of the radiator. Recover the copper washers. Be prepared for some loss of fluid by placing a suitable container beneath the hoses. Note the location of the hoses to ensure correct refitting.

11 Remove the front bumper as described in Chapter 11 **(see illustration)**.

12 Insert two lengths of welding rod or two screwdrivers through the radiator side mountings from inside the engine compartment in order to support the radiator while the bottom mounting brackets are removed.

13 Unbolt the bottom mounting brackets from the subframe and slide the brackets with rubbers from the extensions on the bottom of the radiator.

14 On models **with** air conditioning, unscrew the bolts securing the condenser to the front of the radiator, then tie the condenser to the front crossmember with plastic ties or wire **(see illustrations)**.

15 Support the radiator, then remove the rods or screwdrivers from the side mountings (paragraph 12), lower the radiator out of its mountings, and either lift it or lower it from the engine compartment **(see illustration)**.

16 If a new radiator is to be fitted, transfer the relevant parts from the old unit.

Inspection

17 If the radiator has been removed due to suspected blockage, reverse-flush it as

described in Section 2. Clean dirt and debris from the radiator fins, using an air line (in which case, wear eye protection) or a soft brush.
Caution: Be careful, as the fins are easily damaged, and are sharp.

18 If necessary, a radiator specialist can perform a 'flow test' on the radiator, to establish whether an internal blockage exists.

19 A leaking radiator must be referred to a specialist for permanent repair. Do not attempt to weld or solder a leaking radiator, as damage may result.

20 In an emergency, minor leaks from the radiator can be cured by using a suitable radiator sealant (in accordance with its manufacturer's instructions).

21 Inspect the radiator mounting rubbers, and renew them if necessary.

Refitting

22 Refitting is a reversal of removal, bearing in mind the following points.
   a) *Ensure that the lower mounting rubbers are correctly located in the bottom mounting brackets.*
   b) *Ensure that all hoses are correctly reconnected, and their retaining clips securely tightened.*
   c) *On completion, refill the cooling system as described in Section 2 and, on models with automatic transmission, check and if necessary top-up the automatic transmission fluid level as described in Chapter 1.*

4.15 Lifting the radiator from the engine compartment

5.8 Testing the thermostat opening temperature

5 Thermostat – removal, testing and refitting

1.6 litre SOHC engines

Removal

1 Disconnect the battery negative terminal (refer to *Disconnecting the battery* in the Reference Chapter).

2 Drain the cooling system as described in Section 2.

3 Remove the air cleaner assembly and air ducting as described in Chapter 4A.

4 Loosen the clip and disconnect the top hose from the thermostat cover on the right-hand side of the engine.

5 Remove the timing belt and idler, camshaft sprocket, and rear timing belt cover with reference to Chapter 2A.

6 Unscrew the mounting bolts and remove the thermostat cover from the cylinder head.

7 Carefully prise the thermostat from the cylinder head and remove the sealing ring.

Testing

8 A rough test of the thermostat's operation may be made by suspending it with a piece of string in a container full of water. Heat the water to bring it to the boil – the thermostat must open by the time the water boils. If not, renew it **(see illustration)**.

9 The opening temperature is usually marked on the thermostat. If a thermometer is available, the precise opening temperature of the thermostat may be determined, and compared with the value marked on the thermostat.

10 A thermostat which fails to close as the water cools must also be renewed.

Refitting

11 Thoroughly clean the mating faces of the thermostat cover and the cylinder head.

12 Locate the thermostat in the cylinder head together with a new sealing ring. Make sure that the spring and capsule end is facing into the head and position the thermostat with the outer bar vertical.

13 Refit the thermostat cover and tighten the bolts to the specified torque.

5.38 Removing the thermostat housing cover

5.39 Removing the thermostat from the housing

14 Refit the rear timing belt cover, camshaft sprocket, and timing belt and idler with reference to Chapter 2A.
15 Refit the air cleaner assembly and air ducting with reference to Chapter 4A.
16 Reconnect the top hose to the thermostat cover and tighten the clip.
17 Reconnect the battery negative terminal.
18 Refill the cooling system with reference to Section 2.

DOHC engines (not 2.2 litre)

Removal

19 Disconnect the battery negative terminal (refer to *Disconnecting the battery* in the Reference Chapter).
20 Drain the cooling system as described in Section 2.
21 Loosen the clip and disconnect the top hose from the thermostat cover on the right-hand side of the engine. On 1.4 and 1.6 litre engines the cover is attached to a further housing bolted to the right-hand end of the engine. On 1.8 and 2.0 litre engines the cover is bolted directly to the cylinder head and it is necessary to disconnect the small hose in addition to the top hose.
22 On 1.8 litre engines, disconnect the wiring from the temperature sensor.
23 Unscrew the bolts and remove the thermostat cover which has an integral thermostat. On 1.4 and 1.6 litre engines, remove the sealing ring. On 2.0 litre engines remove the gasket. On 1.8 litre engines the cover is sealed with sealant, and there is no gasket fitted.
24 If necessary on 1.4 and 1.6 litre engines, disconnect the wiring from the temperature sensor then unbolt the thermostat base housing from the cylinder head and remove the gasket. If required, unscrew and remove the sensor from the housing.
25 If necessary on 1.8 litre engines, unscrew and remove the temperature sensor.

Testing

26 Refer to paragraphs 8 to 10 inclusive.

Refitting

27 On 1.4 and 1.6 litre engines, where removed, thoroughly clean the mating faces of the thermostat base housing and cylinder head, then refit the housing together with a new gasket and tighten the mounting bolts to the specified torque. Screw in the temperature sensor and tighten to the specified torque (where given), then reconnect the wiring.
28 Thoroughly clean the mating faces of the thermostat cover and cylinder head or base housing. On 1.8 litre engines, apply sealant to the surfaces of the cover and cylinder head.
29 Fit the thermostat and cover, together with a new sealing ring (1.4 and1.6 litre engines) or gasket (2.0 litre engine). Tighten the bolts to the specified torque.
30 On 1.8 litre engines, insert the temperature sensor and tighten to the specified torque. Reconnect the wiring.
31 Reconnect the top hose (and small hose on 1.8 and 2.0 litre engines) to the thermostat cover and tighten the clip(s).
32 Reconnect the battery negative terminal. Refill the cooling system with reference to Section 2.

2.2 litre DOHC engines

Removal

33 The thermostat is located on the left-hand rear of the cylinder head, over the transmission.
34 Disconnect the battery negative terminal (refer to *Disconnecting the battery* in the Reference Chapter).
35 Apply the handbrake, then jack up the front of the vehicle and support it on axle stands (see *Jacking and vehicle support*). Remove the engine compartment undertray.
36 Drain the cooling system as described in Section 2.
37 Loosen the clip and disconnect the top hose from the thermostat cover. Note that the end of the hose has a cut-out which locates with a lug on the cover. Release the wiring

harness from the clip on the thermostat cover.
38 Unscrew the two bolts and remove the cover from the thermostat housing **(see illustration)**.
39 Lift the thermostat from the housing **(see illustration)**. Remove the seal from the rim of the thermostat and discard it. Obtain a new one. Clean the contact surfaces of the cover and housing.

Testing

40 Refer to paragraphs 8 to 10 inclusive.

Refitting

41 Refitting is a reversal of removal, but fit a new seal and tighten the cover bolts to the specified torque. Refill the cooling system with reference to Section 2.

---

6 Electric cooling fan – testing, removal and refitting

⚠ *Warning: If the engine is hot, the cooling fan may start up at any time. Take extra precautions when working in the vicinity of the fan.*

Testing

1 The cooling fan is supplied with current via a fuse, the ignition switch, and a relay (see Chapter 12). The circuit is activated by the cooling module control unit, using an engine coolant temperature sensor. The cooling module control unit is located on the left-hand side of the front valance, behind the front bumper **(see illustration)**.
2 To test the electric fan, run the engine until normal operating temperature is reached, then allow it to idle. The fan should cut in within a few minutes, or at least before the temperature gauge indicates overheating. If it does not, check that battery voltage is available at the feed wire to the fan motor, and at the relay (refer to Chapter 12). No voltage

6.1 The cooling module control unit is located on the left-hand side of the front valance

6.26a Disconnect the wiring from the electric cooling fan assembly . . .

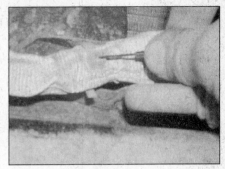

6.26b . . . and release the wiring from the cable tie

indicates a blown fuse, a faulty ignition switch, or a faulty relay or wiring.

3 If the switch, wiring and relay are in good working order, the fault must be in the motor itself.

Removal

Astras without air conditioning

4 Disconnect the battery negative terminal (refer to *Disconnecting the battery* in the Reference Chapter).

5 Disconnect the electric cooling fan wiring plug and release the wiring from the cable tie.

6 Unscrew the upper mounting bolts securing the fan assembly to the rear of the radiator.

7 Carefully lift the fan assembly from the bottom mounting brackets and withdraw it from the engine compartment.

8 With the assembly on the bench, undo the screw and detach the wiring plug and series resistor from the fan assembly frame. Undo the screws and remove the motor and fan from the frame, then undo the screws and remove the fan from the motor.

Zafiras without air conditioning

9 Remove the front bumper as described in Chapter 11.

10 Disconnect the electric cooling fan wiring plug and release the wiring from the cable tie.

11 Unscrew the side mounting bolts and carefully lower the fan assembly from the engine compartment.

12 With the assembly on the bench, unclip and remove the fan guard, then unscrew the three bolts and remove the fan. Undo the screw and detach the wiring plug and series resistor from the frame. Undo the screws and remove the motor.

Astras with air conditioning

13 Remove the battery and support tray as described in Chapter 5A.

14 Remove the air cleaner and air ducting as described in Chapter 4A.

15 Remove the front bumper as described in Chapter 11.

16 Drain the cooling system as described in Section 2.

17 Disconnect the electric cooling fan wiring plug, the air conditioning pressure sensor wiring plug, the compressor wiring plug and the rear wiring plug from the cooling module control unit located on the left-hand side of the front valance, then unscrew the nut and remove the earth cable from the inner wing panel.

18 Disconnect the upper and lower coolant hose from the radiator.

19 Unscrew the upper mounting bolts

securing the fan assembly to the rear of the radiator.

20 Carefully lift the fan assembly from the bottom mounting brackets and withdraw it from the engine compartment.

21 With the assembly on the bench, undo the screw and detach the wiring plug and series resistor from the fan assembly frame. Undo the screws and remove the motor and fan from the frame, then undo the screws and remove the fan from the motor.

Zafiras with air conditioning

22 Remove the air cleaner and air ducting, and disconnect the wiring from the air mass meter with reference to Chapter 4A.

23 Loosen the clip and disconnect the crankcase ventilation hose from the camshaft cover.

24 Remove the air intake resonator from the front crossmember by unscrewing the mounting bolts and releasing the clips.

25 Remove the front bumper as described in Chapter 11.

26 Disconnect the electric cooling fan wiring plug and release the wiring from the cable tie **(see illustrations)**.

27 Unscrew the mounting bolts and remove the fan assembly from the engine compartment **(see illustrations)**.

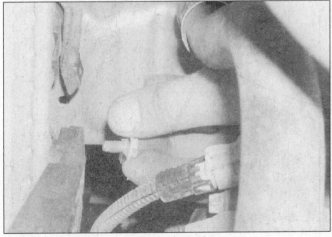

6.27a Unscrew the mounting bolts . . .

6.27b . . . and remove the fan assembly

6.28a Unscrew the bolts . . .

6.28b . . . and remove the fan . . .

6.28c . . . then remove the series resistor . . .

6.28d . . . unbolt the motor . . .

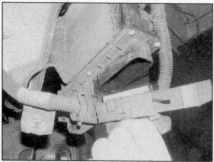

6.28e . . . and disconnect the wiring

28 With the assembly on the bench, unclip the protective grille, then undo the screws and remove the fan. Undo the screw and detach the wiring plug and series resistor, then undo the screws and remove the motor **(see illustrations)**.

Refitting

29 Refitting is a reversal of removal.

---

7 Cooling system electrical switches and sensors – testing, removal and refitting

---

Temperature sensor – testing

1 Testing of the coolant temperature sensor circuit is best entrusted to a Vauxhall dealer, who will have the necessary specialist diagnostic equipment.

7.21a The coolant control module is located on the left-hand side of the front valance

7.21b Disconnecting the wiring plugs from the coolant control module

Temperature sensor – removal

2 Drain the cooling system as described in Section 2.

1.6 litre SOHC engines

3 Remove the air cleaner and air ducts as described in Chapter 4A.
4 Disconnect the wiring from the sensor located on the inlet manifold behind the alternator.
5 Unscrew and remove the sensor from the inlet manifold. Remove the sealing ring and obtain a new one for refitting.

1.4 and 1.6 litre DOHC engines

6 Remove the air cleaner and air ducts as described in Chapter 4A.
7 Disconnect the wiring from the sensor located on the thermostat housing at the right-hand front of the engine.
8 Unscrew and remove the sensor from the thermostat housing.

1.8 litre DOHC engines

9 Remove the thermostat housing as described in Section 5.
10 With the housing removed, unscrew and remove the coolant temperature sensor.

2.0 and 2.2 litre DOHC engines

11 Remove the DIS ignition module with reference to Chapter 5B.
12 Disconnect the wiring from the coolant temperature sensor located on the thermostat housing/coolant flange at the left-hand end of the cylinder head.
13 Unscrew and remove the sensor.

Temperature sensor – refitting

14 Refitting is a reversal of removal, but tighten the sensor to the specified torque and refill the cooling system with reference to Section 2.

Coolant level warning switch

Removal

15 The switch is located in the expansion tank. With the engine cold, unscrew the expansion tank filler cap to dissipate any remaining pressure.
16 Partially drain the coolant from the expansion tank until the level is below the switch.
17 Disconnect the wiring, then unscrew the switch from the tank.

Refitting

18 Refitting is a reversal of removal.

Coolant control module

Removal

19 Disconnect the battery negative terminal (refer to *Disconnecting the battery* in the Reference Chapter).
20 Remove the front bumper as described in Chapter 11.
21 The coolant control module is located on the left-hand side of the front valance. Pull out the locking sliders and unhook the two wiring plugs from the coolant control module **(see illustrations)**.
22 Unscrew the mounting bolts and remove the module from the front valance.

Refitting

23 Refitting is a reversal of removal.

8 Coolant pump –
removal and refitting

1.4, 1.6 and 1.8 litre DOHC engines

Removal

1 Disconnect the battery negative terminal (refer to *Disconnecting the battery* in the Reference Chapter).
2 Drain the cooling system as described in Section 2.
3 Remove the timing belt, tensioner and timing belt rear cover as described in Chapter 2B.
4 Unscrew and remove the three coolant pump securing bolts **(see illustration)**.
5 Withdraw the coolant pump from the cylinder block, noting that it may be necessary to tap the pump lightly with a soft-faced mallet to free it from the cylinder block.
6 Recover the pump sealing ring, and discard it; a new one must be used on refitting.
7 Note that it is not possible to overhaul the pump. If it is faulty, the unit must be renewed complete.

Refitting

8 Ensure that the pump and cylinder block mating surfaces are clean and dry, and apply a smear of silicone grease to the pump mating surface in the cylinder block.
9 Fit a new sealing ring to the pump, and install the pump in the cylinder block. On 1.4 and 1.6 litre engines, align the mark on the edge of the coolant pump flange with the mark on the cylinder block. On 1.8 litre engines, make sure that the lugs on the pump and cylinder block are aligned with each other.
10 Insert the securing bolts and tighten to the specified torque.
11 Refit the timing belt rear cover, tensioner and timing belt as described in Chapter 2B.
12 Reconnect the battery negative terminal.
13 Refill the cooling system with reference to Section 2.

1.6 litre SOHC engines

Removal

14 Disconnect the battery negative terminal (refer to *Disconnecting the battery* in the Reference Chapter).
15 Drain the cooling system as described in Section 2.
16 Remove the timing belt and tensioner as described in Chapter 2A.
17 Unscrew and remove the three coolant pump securing bolts.
18 Withdraw the coolant pump from the cylinder block, noting that it may be necessary to tap the pump lightly with a soft-faced mallet to free it from the cylinder block.
19 Recover the pump sealing ring, and discard it; a new one must be used on

8.4 Removing the three coolant pump securing bolts – 1.4, 1.6 and 1.8 litre DOHC engines

refitting.
20 Note that it is not possible to overhaul the pump. If it is faulty, the unit must be renewed complete.

Refitting

21 Ensure that the pump and cylinder block mating surfaces are clean and dry, and apply a smear of silicone grease to the pump mating surface in the cylinder block.
22 Fit a new sealing ring to the pump, and install the pump in the cylinder block. Align the mark on the edge of the coolant pump flange with the mark on the cylinder block.
23 Insert the securing bolts and tighten to the specified torque.
24 Refit the timing belt rear cover and timing belt as described in Chapter 2A.
25 Reconnect the battery negative terminal.
26 Refill the cooling system with reference to Section 2.

2.0 litre DOHC engines

Removal

27 Disconnect the battery negative terminal (refer to *Disconnecting the battery* in the Reference Chapter).
28 Drain the cooling system as described in Section 2.
29 Remove the timing belt and tensioner as described in Chapter 2B.
30 Unscrew and remove the three coolant pump securing bolts.

8.46 Coolant pump drive sprocket access cover – 2.2 litre engines

31 Withdraw the coolant pump from the cylinder block, noting that it may be necessary to tap the pump lightly with a soft-faced mallet to free it from the cylinder block.
32 Recover the pump sealing ring, and discard it; a new one must be used on refitting.
33 Note that it is not possible to overhaul the pump. If it is faulty, the unit must be renewed complete.

Refitting

34 Ensure that the pump and cylinder block mating surfaces are clean and dry, and apply a smear of silicone grease to the pump mating surface in the cylinder block.
35 Fit a new sealing ring to the pump, and install the pump in the cylinder block. Make sure that the lugs on the pump and cylinder block are aligned with each other.
36 Insert the securing bolts and tighten to the specified torque.
37 Refit the timing belt and tensioner as described in Chapter 2B.
38 Reconnect the battery negative terminal.
39 Refill the cooling system with reference to Section 2.

2.2 litre DOHC engines

Removal

40 Apply the handbrake, then jack up the front of the vehicle and support it on axle stands (see *Jacking and vehicle support*). Remove the engine compartment undertray.
41 Disconnect the battery negative terminal (refer to *Disconnecting the battery* in the Reference Chapter).
42 Drain the cooling system as described in Section 2.
43 Unbolt the right-hand engine lifting eye from the cylinder head.
44 Unbolt the lower heat shield from the exhaust manifold, followed by the upper heat shield.
45 Unclip the oxygen sensor wiring from the thermostat housing, then remove the cable retainer from the stud bolts.
46 Unbolt the coolant pump drive sprocket access cover from the timing cover on the right-hand side of the engine **(see illustration)**.
47 Vauxhall technicians use a special tool (KM-J-43651) to hold the sprocket stationary while the coolant pump is being removed. The tool consists of a flanged tube which is bolted to the sprocket and also to the timing housing, with holes to allow removal of the coolant pump bolts. It is possible to fabricate a simple home-made tool from a length of flat metal bar using two threaded rods screwed into the sprocket. First unscrew one of the pump mounting bolts from the sprocket taking care not to drop it into the timing case, then bolt the tool into position to hold the sprocket. With the tool in position, unscrew the two remaining bolts from the sprocket

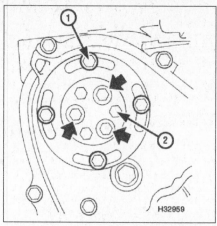

8.47a Home-made tool holding the coolant pump drive sprocket stationary – 2.2 litre engines

8.47b Unscrew the two remaining bolts securing the coolant pump to the sprocket – 2.2 litre engines

8.47c Vauxhall tool KM-J-43651 retaining the coolant pump sprocket while the pump is being removed – 2.2 litre engines

1 *Bolts holding the tool to the timing housing*
2 *Bolts holding the sprocket to the tool*
Arrows indicate pump mounting bolts

(see illustrations). To prevent losing any of the bolts, temporarily place a cloth rag beneath the sprocket in the timing case.

48 Loosen the clip and disconnect the hose from the thermostat housing cover. Also disconnect the heater hoses from the thermostat housing and heater matrix. Remove the hoses.

49 Unclip the coolant temperature sensor wiring from the thermostat housing cover, then disconnect the wiring from the sensor.

50 Unscrew and remove the coolant temperature sensor from the thermostat housing.

51 Unclip the oxygen sensor wiring plug from the loom bracket and disconnect.

52 Unscrew the bolts and remove the thermostat housing and coolant pipe from the cylinder block and coolant pump. Note the lower bolt is a stud bolt, and note the location of the O-ring seal in the pump housing (see illustrations).

53 Unscrew the pump mounting bolts noting that if you are using the Vauxhall tool, one of the bolts cannot be removed completely. There are two bolts at the front and two at the rear. Remove the pump from the timing housing and withdraw upwards from the engine (see illustrations).

54 Recover the pump sealing ring, and discard it; a new one must be used on refitting.

55 Note that it is not possible to overhaul the

pump. If it is faulty, the unit must be renewed complete.

Refitting

56 Ensure that the pump and timing housing mating surfaces are clean and dry, and apply

8.52a Thermostat housing retaining bolts – 2.2 litre engines

8.52b Removing the coolant pipe from the pump housing – 2.2 litre engines

8.53a Unscrew the rear bolts . . .

8.53b . . . and the front bolts . . .

8.53c . . . and withdraw the coolant pump from the timing housing – 2.2 litre engines

a smear of silicone grease to the pump mating surface.

57 Fit a new sealing ring to the groove in the pump, then locate the pump in the timing housing, making sure that the three bolt holes are aligned with the holes in the sprocket.

58 Insert the pump mounting bolts and two of the sprocket bolts hand-tight to start with, then tighten them to the specified torque.

59 Remove the holding tool and refit the final sprocket bolt, tightening it to the specified torque.

60 Refit the coolant pump drive sprocket access cover to the timing cover together with a new gasket, and tighten the bolts securely.

61 Refit the coolant pipe and thermostat housing together with new sealing rings, and tighten the bolts securely.

62 Reconnect the oxygen sensor wiring and refit the plug to the loom bracket.

63 Refit the coolant temperature sensor to the thermostat housing and tighten to the specified torque, then reconnect the wiring and secure.

64 Refit the hoses to the thermostat housing cover and tighten the clips.

65 Refit the cable retainer and secure the oxygen sensor wiring.

66 Refit the exhaust manifold heat shields and engine lifting eye.

67 Reconnect the battery negative terminal.

68 Refill the cooling system as described in Section 2.

69 Refit the engine compartment undertray and lower the vehicle to the ground.

9 Heating and ventilation system – general information

The heater/ventilation system consists of a four-speed blower motor (housed behind the facia), face-level vents in the centre and at each end of the facia, and air ducts to the front and rear footwells. Zafira models also have central vents at the rear of the centre console.

The heater controls are located in the centre of the facia, and the controls operate flap valves to deflect and mix the air flowing through the various parts of the heater/ventilation system. The flap valves are contained in the air distribution housing, which acts as a central distribution unit, passing air to the various ducts and vents.

Cold air enters the system through the grille at the rear of the engine compartment.

The air (boosted by the blower fan when required) then flows through the various ducts, according to the settings of the controls. Stale air is expelled through ducts at the rear corners of the vehicle. If warm air is required, the cold air is passed through the heater matrix, which is heated by the engine coolant.

A recirculation switch enables the outside air supply to be closed off, while the air inside the vehicle is recirculated. This can be useful to prevent unpleasant odours entering from outside the vehicle, but should only be used briefly, as the quality of the recirculated air inside the vehicle will soon deteriorate.

10 Heater/ventilation system components – removal and refitting

Note: *Note that there are two different types of heater supplied – either Delphi or Behr.*

Air vents

Astra models

1 To remove an air vent grille from the centre of the facia, insert a small screwdriver on each side and carefully lever it out. Removal of the air vent housing involves first removing the facia surround panel as described in Chapter 11, then removing the hazard warning switch and carefully prising out the vent housing.

2 To remove the vent from the driver's side of the facia, it will be necessary to remove the lighting switch assembly first (see Chapter 12), then turn the vent down past its stop position and undo the two upper and single lower retaining screws, using a screwdriver through the grille. The screws will drop inside the housing, but take care not to allow them to enter the rear vent tubing. Disconnect the wiring and remove the vent.

3 To remove the vent from the passenger's side of the facia, first open the glovebox, then turn the vent past its stop position and undo the two upper and single lower retaining screws, using a screwdriver through the grille. Withdraw the vent assembly from the facia.

4 Refitting of the centre air vent grille is a reversal of removal. To refit the side vents, first use a screwdriver to lever out the side clip, then turn the grille down so that the upper mounting holes are visible – this will enable the upper screws to be inserted without dropping them into the vent housing.

Zafira models

5 To remove the passenger's side vent, first remove the glovebox as described in Chapter 11. Pull out the upper grille from the air vent. Undo the upper and lower screws and remove the vent.

6 To remove the air vent from the rear of the centre console, first remove the cover beneath the handbrake lever, then release the lever gaiter. Insert the hand through the aperture in the console and push out the vent.

7 The centre vent is part of the surround.

8 Refitting of the air vents is a reversal of removal.

Blower motor resistor

9 Remove the passenger side glovebox with reference to Chapter 11.

10 Remove the lower trim panel from under the passenger side of the facia panel, then where applicable disconnect the fastener and withdraw the heater air duct.

11 Unclip the cover and remove the pollen filter. Note that there are two types of cover, one requiring sealant to seal it to the housing. Alternatively, remove the blower motor as described later in this Section.

12 Carefully push the resistor upwards, disconnect the wiring, and withdraw it from the housing **(see illustrations)**.

13 Refitting is a reversal of removal, but apply sealant to the pollen filter cover where applicable.

Heater blower motor

Delphi type

14 Remove the passenger side glovebox with reference to Chapter 11.

15 Remove the lower trim panel from under the passenger side of the facia panel, then disconnect the fastener and withdraw the heater air duct from the side of the heater housing **(see illustration)**.

10.12a Push the resistor upwards . . .

10.12b . . . and withdraw it from the housing

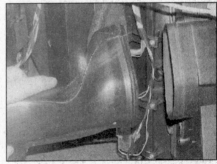

10.15 Disconnecting the heater air duct

10.16a Disconnect the recirculating flap servo motor linkage . . .

10.16b . . . and disconnect the servo wiring

10.16c Servo motor removed – Astra

10.17a Disconnect the wiring . . .

10.17b . . . then undo the bolts . . .

10.17c . . . and withdraw the motor from its housing

16 Temporarily switch on the ignition then set the heater controls to the 'air recirculating' position. Switch off the ignition, then disconnect the recirculating flap servo motor linkage and the servo wiring. Undo the screws and remove the servo motor (see illustrations).
17 Disconnect the blower motor wiring, then unscrew the three bolts and release the clips. Withdraw the motor from its housing (see illustrations).
18 Refitting is a reversal of removal.

Behr type

19 Temporarily switch on the ignition then set the heater controls to the 'air recirculating' position. Switch off the ignition, then disconnect the recirculating flap servo motor linkage and the servo wiring. Undo the screws and remove the servo motor. Note: New servo motors are supplied set to the 'recirculating' position.
20 Undo the five bolts and release the single clip, and withdraw the motor from its housing. Note that sealant is used in the housing groove – thoroughly clean out the groove.
21 Refitting is a reversal of removal, but apply new sealant to the housing groove. Make sure that the servo motor master gear aligns with the master gear on the flap.

Heater control panel

Astra Delphi type

22 Remove the ashtray as described in Chapter 11, then unclip and remove the storage compartment.
23 Remove the radio/cassette and the mounting box as described in Chapter 12.

Also, where applicable, remove the navigation system unit.
24 Carefully prise the surround from the facia.
25 Unclip the controls and press out the vents from the surround. Remove the multi-function display unit with reference to Chapter 12.
26 Set the temperature control knob vertical, then disconnect the control cable after noting its fitted position.
27 Disconnect the wiring from the controls.
28 Disconnect the remaining control cables after noting their fitted position, then remove the control panel from the surround.
29 Refitting is a reversal of removal, however, first make sure that the bulbs are correctly fitted. Note that the mixed air cable is correctly adjusted if the control knob does not spring back from either the maximum cold or hot positions.

Astra Behr type

30 Remove the glovebox as described in Chapter 11.
31 Remove the trim panel from under each side of the facia.
32 On LHD models, remove the air duct from the passenger's side. Also remove the instrument panel as described in Chapter 12.
33 Disconnect the control cables from the upper and lower air distribution flaps.
34 Release the cables from the support clips.
35 Remove the ashtray as described in Chapter 11, then unclip and remove the storage compartment.
36 Remove the radio/cassette and the

mounting box as described in Chapter 12. Also, where applicable, remove the navigation system unit.
37 Carefully prise the surround from the facia.
38 Disconnect the wiring from the control panel.
39 Note the location of the control cables, then disconnect them from the control panel.
40 Refitting is a reversal of removal, however, first make sure that the bulbs are correctly fitted.

Zafira

41 Remove the glovebox as described in Chapter 11.
42 Remove the trim panel from under each side of the facia.
43 Remove the front ashtray as described in Chapter 11.
44 Undo the lower screws and unhook the upper part of the control panel. Withdraw the panel from the facia (see illustrations).

10.44a Undo the lower screws . . .

10.44b . . . and unhook the upper part of the heater control panel

10.45a Remove the switches . . .

10.45b . . . then disconnect the wiring

45 Using a screwdriver, carefully prise out the hazard warning switch, traction control switch (where fitted), and seat heating switch (where fitted). Disconnect the wiring from the control panel **(see illustrations)**.

46 Unclip the heating and air conditioning controls from the rear of the control panel, and withdraw the panel **(see illustration)**.

47 Note the location of the control cables, then disconnect them **(see illustration)**.

48 Refitting is a reversal of removal.

Heater main housing

Note: *On models with air conditioning it is necessary to drain the refrigerant. This work **must** be carried out by qualified personnel.*

49 On models with air conditioning, have the refrigerant drained from the system by a qualified air conditioning engineer.

50 Remove the centre console and facia panel as described in Chapter 11. On automatic transmission models, also remove the transmission control unit.

51 Remove the rear footwell air duct from the heater main housing, then place cloth rags on the floor to absorb any spilt coolant from the heater matrix.

52 Remove the passenger's airbag as described in Chapter 12.

53 With both front doors open, unscrew the Torx bolts and remove the steering crossmember from the bulkhead.

54 On models with air conditioning, remove the condensation drain from the floor. To do this, apply the handbrake then jack up the front of the vehicle and support it on axle stands (see *Jacking and vehicle support*). Where necessary, remove the splash guard from the bottom of the engine compartment. Remove the rear engine mounting (see the relevant Part of Chapter 2), then unscrew the two bolts and remove the condensation drain. **Note:** *Access is possible without having to remove the rear engine mounting, however the work is much easier with the mounting removed.*

55 Drain the cooling system as described in Section 2.

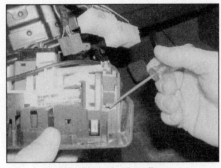

10.46a Release the clips . . .

10.46b . . . and withdraw the controls from the control panel

56 Remove the plastic insert from the windscreen scuttle, then unbolt and remove the lower cover panel.

57 Working in the engine compartment, disconnect the hoses from the heater matrix stubs. Identify each hose for position to ensure correct refitting. **Note:** *The original hoses have quick-release fittings.*

58 On models with air conditioning, remove the coolant line lock bolt connection on the expansion valve.

59 Unbolt the air distribution housings from the top of the bulkhead.

60 On models with air conditioning, disconnect the wiring from the coolant cut-off valve.

61 Inside the vehicle, disconnect the wiring for the recirculation flap servo motor and the blower motor. Also disconnect the control

cables from the heater housing **(see illustration)**.

62 With the help of an assistant, withdraw the heater main housing from the bulkhead and remove it from inside the vehicle.

63 Refitting is a reversal of removal, but refill the cooling system as described in Section 2. On models with air conditioning, have the system charged by the air conditioning engineer. When refitting the steering crossmember, make sure that the upper guides are located first before tightening the bolts.

Heater matrix

64 Drain the cooling system as described in Section 2.

65 Working in the engine compartment, disconnect the hoses from the heater matrix

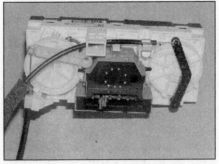

10.47 Cable connections on the rear of the heater control panel – Zafira

10.61 Control cable on the side of the heater housing

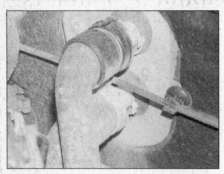

10.65 Hose connections to the heater matrix stubs in the engine compartment

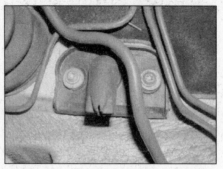

10.67a The air conditioning condensation drain is located at the rear of the engine compartment

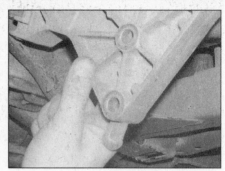

10.67b Removing the rear engine mounting

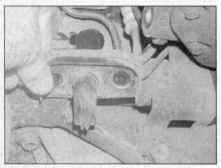

10.67c Removing the air conditioning condensation drain

10.67d Air conditioning condensation drain removed

10.68 Removing the rear footwell air distribution housing

stubs **(see illustration)**. Identify each hose for position to ensure correct refitting. **Note:** *The original hoses have quick-release fittings.*

66 At this stage, if an airline is available, it is possible to blow the remaining coolant from the matrix to prevent it spilling onto the interior carpet when the matrix is removed. Connect a drain tube to one of the matrix stubs with its free end in a suitable container, then blow through the other stub. If an airline is not available, plug the ends of the stubs.

67 On models with air conditioning, remove the condensation drain from the floor. To do this, apply the handbrake then jack up the

front of the vehicle and support it on axle stands (see *Jacking and vehicle support*). Where necessary, remove the splash guard from the bottom of the engine compartment. Remove the rear engine mounting (see the relevant Part of Chapter 2), then unscrew the two bolts and remove the condensation drain **(see illustrations)**. **Note:** *Access is possible without having to remove the rear engine mounting, however the work is much easier with the mounting removed.*

68 Remove the centre console as described in Chapter 11, then pull the rear footwell air distribution housing forwards and remove it **(see illustration)**. On Zafira models, unbolt

the stays before removing the rear footwell air housing.

69 On automatic transmission models, remove the transmission control unit with reference to Chapter 7B.

70 Release the 9 clips securing the cover to the heater main housing, and lower the cover **(see illustrations)**. Note on certain models, there are also two retaining bolts.

71 On models with air conditioning, disconnect the wiring from the coolant cut-off valve **(see illustration)**.

72 Pull out the clips and disconnect the coolant pipes (non-air conditioned) or cut-off valves (air conditioned) from the matrix.

10.70a Release the clips . . .

10.70b . . . and lower the cover

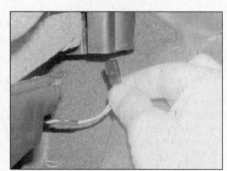

10.71 On models with air conditioning, disconnect the wiring from the coolant cut-off valve

Withdraw the matrix from the housing (see illustrations).

73 Recover the O-rings and discard them – new ones must be used on refitting. Check the quick-release fittings and if necessary renew the O-ring seals.

74 Refitting is a reversal of removal, but apply a little silicone grease to the new O-rings before fitting them. On Zafira models, support the connection pipes against the bulkhead with a suitable tool (eg, hammer handle), in order to ensure the matrix stubs engage correctly. On completion refill the cooling system as described in Section 2. Make sure that the quick-release hose fittings are correctly engaged by checking that the green lock-ring is released.

Heater switch

75 Remove the heater control panel as described earlier in this Section.

76 Position the temperature control knob vertical to the warm-air setting. Position the air distributor control knob to the head-space setting.

77 Carefully pull off the heater blower speed control knob.

78 Using a screwdriver, release the clips on the rear of the control panel, then remove the switch.

79 Refitting is a reversal of removal.

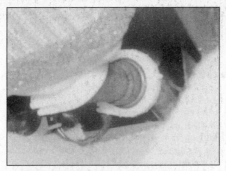

10.72a Cut-off valve connection to the heater matrix – air conditioned models

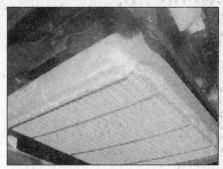

10.72b Removing the heater matrix

11 Air conditioning system – general information and precautions

General information

Air conditioning is fitted as standard on certain models, and optional on other models (see illustration). It enables the temperature of incoming air to be lowered, and also dehumidifies the air, which makes for rapid demisting and increased comfort.

The cooling side of the system works in the same way as a domestic refrigerator. Refrigerant gas is drawn into a belt-driven compressor, and passes into a condenser mounted in front of the radiator, where it loses heat and becomes liquid. The liquid passes through an expansion valve to an evaporator, where it changes from liquid under high pressure to gas under low pressure. This change is accompanied by a drop in temperature, which cools the evaporator. The refrigerant returns to the compressor, and the cycle begins again.

Air blown through the evaporator passes to the heater assembly, where it is mixed with hot air blown through the heater matrix, to

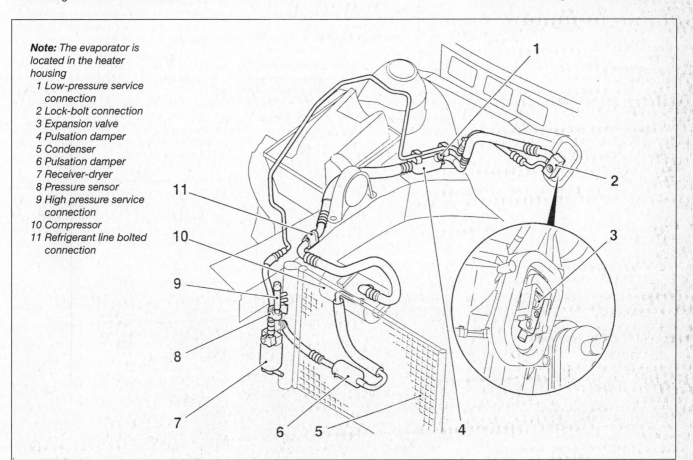

Note: The evaporator is located in the heater housing

1 Low-pressure service connection
2 Lock-bolt connection
3 Expansion valve
4 Pulsation damper
5 Condenser
6 Pulsation damper
7 Receiver-dryer
8 Pressure sensor
9 High pressure service connection
10 Compressor
11 Refrigerant line bolted connection

11.1 Air conditioning components – Zafira

achieve the desired temperature in the passenger compartment.

The heating side of the system works in the same way as on models without air conditioning (see Section 9).

The operation of the system is controlled electronically. Any problems with the system should be referred to a Vauxhall dealer or an air conditioning specialist.

Many car accessory shops sell one-shot air conditioning recharge aerosols. These generally contain refrigerant, compressor oil, leak sealer and system conditioner. Some also have a dye to help pinpoint leaks.

⚠ **Warning:** *These products must only be used as directed by the manufacturer, and do not remove the need for regular maintenance.*

Precautions

It is necessary to observe special precautions whenever dealing with any part of the system, its associated components, and any items which necessitate disconnection of the system.

⚠ **Warning:** *The refrigeration circuit contains a liquid refrigerant (R134a). This refrigerant is potentially dangerous, and should only be handled by qualified persons. If it is splashed onto the skin, it can cause frostbite. It is not itself poisonous, but in the presence of a naked flame it forms a poisonous gas; inhalation of the vapour through a lighted cigarette could prove fatal. Gaseous refrigerant is heavier than air and*

can therefore become concentrated in certain working conditions (for instance in a pit). Uncontrolled discharging of the refrigerant is dangerous, and potentially damaging to the environment. It is therefore dangerous to disconnect any part of the system without specialised knowledge and equipment. If for any reason the system must be disconnected, entrust this task to an authorised dealer or an air conditioning specialist. The system should be sealed by the specialist until just before recharging. It is recommended that the receiver-dryer is renewed whenever the refrigerant lines are depressurised, and it should be kept sealed until just before fitting it – it should be the last item fitted before recharging the system. All O-rings should be renewed, and they must be coated with genuine Vauxhall lubricant (part number 90001810/1949870) before fitting. Any spilt compressor lubricant must be topped-up with genuine Vauxhall lubricant (part number 90509933/1949873).

Caution: *Do not operate the air conditioning system if it is known to be short of refrigerant, as this may damage the compressor.*

12 Air conditioning system components – removal and refitting

⚠ **Warning:** *Read the precautions given in Section 11, and have the system discharged by a Vauxhall dealer or an air conditioning specialist. Do not carry out the following work unless the system has been discharged.*

Compressor

1 Have the air conditioning system discharged by a qualified engineer.
2 Apply the handbrake, then jack up the front of the vehicle and support it on axle stands (see *Jacking and vehicle support*). Where necessary, remove the splash guard from the bottom of the engine compartment.
3 Remove the auxiliary drivebelt as described in Chapter 1.
4 Unscrew the bolt and detach the combined line adapter from the compressor. Recover the seal. Tape over the apertures in the

compressor and adapter to prevent entry of dust and dirt.
5 Disconnect the wiring plug.
6 On Zafira models with the 1.6 and 1.8 litre DOHC engines, remove the exhaust downpipe from the exhaust manifold as described in Chapter 4A. On the 1.8 litre engine also remove the oxygen sensor with reference to Chapter 4B.
7 Unscrew the mounting bolts and remove the compressor downwards from the mounting bracket **(see illustrations)**. Withdraw it from under the engine compartment.
8 Refitting is a reversal of removal but tighten the bolts to the specified torque and tension the auxiliary drivebelt with reference to Chapter 1. On completion, have the refrigerant engineer charge the system and fit new O-rings to the line connections. If a new compressor is being fitted, make sure that the oil level is topped-up before fitting it. Note that a new compressor must be run-in as follows:
a) Open all vents on the facia, then run the engine at idle speed for 5 seconds.
b) Switch the blower to its maximum speed.
c) Switch on the air conditioning system for at least 2 minutes with the engine speed less than 1500 rpm.

Evaporator
Astra models
9 Have the air conditioning system discharged by a qualified refrigerant engineer.
10 On the 1.6 litre SOHC engine, remove the engine air inlet duct from the throttle body (see Chapter 4A, Section 12).
11 At the rear of the engine compartment, unbolt the refrigerant line lock-bolt connection for the thermostatically-controlled expansion valve, then insert a bolt and remove the expansion valve. Also remove the seal. Plug or seal the open apertures. **Note:** *Two guide rods must be inserted when refitting the valve, and Vauxhall technicians use a special tool (KM-6012) to press the connection onto the valve without damaging the pipes.*
12 Remove the glovebox and facia lower trim panels as described in Chapter 11.
13 Remove the heater blower motor as described in Section 10.
14 Remove the pollen filter (see Chapter 1), then disconnect the wiring for the defroster sensor **(see illustration)**.

12.7a Air conditioning compressor

12.7b Air conditioning compressor rear mounting

12.14 Removing the pollen filter

15 Undo the screws and remove the cover for the evaporator. Note if the cover has any sealant; if necessary obtain new sealant. **Note:** *On some models, it may be necessary to cut free the cover using a knife on the inner groove* **(see illustration).**

16 Note its fitted location, then remove the defroster sensor. Carefully pull the evaporator from the heater housing.

17 Refitting is a reversal of removal, but have the refrigerant engineer charge the system and fit new O-rings to the line connections. To ensure the pipes are not damaged, have the engineer refit the expansion valve as well. Where the evaporator cover was cut free, it will be necessary to obtain a sealing kit from a Vauxhall dealer.

Zafira models

Note: *Some models may also have a rear evaporator located behind the rear quarter trim panel.*

18 Have the air conditioning system discharged by a qualified refrigerant engineer.

19 At the rear of the engine compartment, unbolt the refrigerant line lock-bolt connection for the thermostatically-controlled expansion valve **(see illustration)**, then insert a bolt and remove the expansion valve. Also remove the clamp and seal, noting that the outer seal must be renewed on refitting. Plug or seal the open apertures. **Note:** *Two guide rods must be inserted when refitting the valve.*

20 Remove the pollen filter (see Chapter 1), then disconnect the wiring for the defroster sensor.

21 Unbolt the cover for the pollen filter and evaporator, and remove the filter **(see illustrations)**.

22 Note its fitted location, then remove the defroster sensor. Carefully pull the evaporator from the heater housing.

23 Refitting is a reversal of removal, but have the refrigerant engineer charge the system and fit new O-rings to the line connections.

Condenser

24 Have the air conditioning system discharged by a qualified refrigerant engineer.

25 With the bonnet open, reach down behind the front bumper and disconnect the wiring plug for the auxiliary cooling fan. Unscrew the upper mounting bolts and remove the auxiliary cooling fan.

26 Unscrew the bolts and disconnect the refrigerant lines from the condenser and receiver-dryer. Also disconnect the wiring from the system pressure sensor.

12.15 On some models it is necessary to cut free the evaporator cover

12.21a Removing the cover for the pollen filter and evaporator

27 Unscrew the mounting bolts for the receiver-dryer.

28 Unscrew the upper mounting bolts securing the condenser to the radiator, then lift it from the lower mounting clips and withdraw it, together with the receiver-dryer.

29 If necessary, detach the receiver-dryer from the condenser.

30 Refitting is a reversal of removal. On completion, have the refrigerant engineer charge the system and fit new O-rings to the line connections.

Receiver-dryer

31 Have the air conditioning system discharged by a qualified refrigerant engineer.

32 Where applicable, remove the auxiliary electric fan from the front of the condenser as described later in this Section.

33 On models without an auxiliary electric fan, remove the front bumper as described in Chapter 11.

34 Unscrew the bolt and disconnect the compressor refrigerant line from the receiver-dryer.

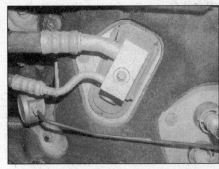

12.19 Air conditioning evaporator refrigerant line lock-bolt located at the rear of the engine compartment

12.21b Removing the pollen filter from the heater housing

35 Unscrew the receiver-dryer cap from the condenser.

36 Withdraw the receiver-dryer upwards, then disconnect the wiring plug and remove the air conditioning pressure sensor pick-up.

37 Remove the receiver-dryer.

38 Refitting is a reversal of removal. On completion, have the refrigerant engineer charge the system and fit new O-rings to the line connections.

Auxiliary fan and motor

39 Remove the front bumper as described in Chapter 11.

40 Disconnect the wiring plug for the auxiliary cooling fan.

41 Unscrew the upper mounting bolts from the crossmember and remove the auxiliary cooling fan assembly downwards.

42 To remove the motor, unclip the plastic grille, then unbolt the wiring plug connector and series resistor. Unscrew the three bolts and remove the fan from the motor, then unbolt the motor from the housing.

43 Refitting is a reversal of removal.

Notes

Chapter 4 Part A:
Fuel and exhaust systems

Contents

Accelerator cable – removal, refitting and adjustment 4
Accelerator pedal – removal and refitting 5
Air cleaner assembly and intake ducts – removal and refitting 2
Exhaust manifold – removal and refitting 19
Exhaust system – general information, removal and refitting 20
Fuel gauge sender unit – removal and refitting 10
Fuel injection system – depressurisation 8
Fuel injection system – testing and adjustment 13
Fuel injection systems – general information 7
Fuel pump – removal and refitting 9
Fuel tank – removal and refitting 11
General information and precautions 1
GMPT – E15 multi-point injection system components –
    removal and refitting 17
Inlet manifold – removal and refitting 18
Intake air temperature control system (single-point injection) 3
Multec S multi-point injection system components –
    removal and refitting 15
Multec single-point injection system components –
    removal and refitting 14
Simtec 70 and 71 multi-point injection system components –
    removal and refitting 16
Throttle body/housing – removal and refitting 12
Unleaded petrol – general information and usage 6

Degrees of difficulty

Easy, suitable for novice with little experience	Fairly easy, suitable for beginner with some experience	Fairly difficult, suitable for competent DIY mechanic	Difficult, suitable for experienced DIY mechanic	Very difficult, suitable for expert DIY or professional

Specifications

System type*

1.4 litre DOHC (X14XE and Z14XE) engines	Multec S multi-point injection
1.6 litre SOHC (X16SZR) engines	Multec single-point injection
1.6 litre SOHC (Z16SE) engines	Multec S multi-point injection
1.6 litre DOHC (X16XEL and Z16XE) engines	Multec S multi-point injection
1.8 litre DOHC (X18XE1) engines	Simtec 70 multi-point injection
1.8 litre DOHC (Z18XE and Z18XEL) engines	Simtec 71 multi-point injection
2.0 litre DOHC (X20XEV) engines	Simtec 70 multi-point injection
2.2 litre DOHC (Z22SE) engines	GMPT – E15 multi-point injection

See Section 7 for further information

Fuel system data

Fuel pump type	Electric, immersed in tank
Fuel pump regulated constant pressure (approximate):	
Single-point injection system	0.8 bar
Multi-point injection system	3.0 to 3.8 bar
Specified idle speed	Not adjustable – controlled by ECU
Idle mixture CO content	Not adjustable – controlled by ECU

Recommended fuel

Minimum octane rating	95 RON* unleaded (UK unleaded premium). Leaded fuel (4-star/LRP) must **not** be used

* 91 RON unleaded fuel can be used but a slight power loss maybe noticeable.

Live data/sensor values

The following values/data are included in the hope that they may be of assistance to anyone attempting fault diagnosis. The values were recorded using a Professional Fault Code Reader, from a vehicle running correctly with the engine at idle, and increased idle speed.

Engine type . . . . 1.6 litre DOHC

	Idle	Increased idle
Battery	14.2V	14.1V
Throttle position sensor	0.64V	0.86V
MAP sensor	0.25 bar 1.27V	0.16 bar 0.86V
Intake air temperature	24°C	21°C
Injector pulse	3.2 ms	1.8 ms
Spark advance angle (BTDC)	5° to 8°	18°
Knock retard:		
Cylinder No 1	0.0°	1.1°
Cylinder No 2	0.0°	0.0°
Cylinder No 3	0.0°	0.4°
Cylinder No 4	0.0°	0.0°
Engine speed	750 rpm	1980 rpm
Air:fuel ratio	14.6:1	14.6:1
Oxygen sensor	62 to 900 mV	58 to 940 mV
Desired idle	775 rpm	1900 rpm
Engine load	9%	14%
Coolant temperature	86°C 2.17V	89°C 2.05V

Torque wrench settings

	Nm	lbf ft
Accelerator pedal nuts	9	7
Braking system vacuum hose union nut	15	11
Camshaft sensor:		
1.4, 1.6, 1.8 and 2.2 litre DOHC engines	8	6
1.6 litre SOHC (Z16SE) engines	16	12
2.0 litre DOHC engines	6	4
Crankshaft sensor bolt:		
SOHC engines	10	7
DOHC engines	8	6
Exhaust front pipe-to-manifold:		
SOHC engines – nuts	45	33
SOHC engines – bolts	35	26
DOHC engines except 2.2 litre	20	15
2.2 litre DOHC engines	16	12
Exhaust manifold nuts:*		
All except 2.2 litre DOHC engines	22	16
2.2 litre DOHC engines	12	9
Exhaust manifold shroud bolts:		
All except 2.2 litre DOHC engines	8	6
2.2 litre DOHC engines:		
Upper shroud-to-cylinder head and manifold	25	18
Lower shroud-to-upper shroud	10	7
Fuel hose union nuts	15	11
Fuel pressure regulator clamp	5	4
Fuel rail bolts	8	6
Fuel tank retaining strap bolts	20	15
Inlet manifold nuts and bolts:		
SOHC engines*	22	16
1.4 and 1.6 litre DOHC engines:		
Manifold-to-manifold flange nuts and bolts	8	6
Manifold flange-to-cylinder head nuts and bolts	20	15
1.8 and 2.0 litre DOHC engines*	22	16
2.2 litre DOHC engines*	10	7
Inlet manifold support bracket-to-manifold bolt	20	15
Inlet manifold support bracket-to-cylinder block bolt	35	26
Knock sensor bolt	20	15
Spark plug heat shields – SOHC engines	30	22
Throttle body – SOHC (X16SZR) engines:		
Retaining nuts	22	16
Upper body-to-lower body screws	6	4
Throttle housing nuts/bolts	9	7
Transport shackle-to-cylinder head bolts	20	15

* Use new bolts/nuts

1 General information and precautions

The fuel system consists of a fuel tank (which is mounted under the rear of the car, with an electric fuel pump immersed in it), a fuel filter and the fuel feed and return lines. On single-point injection models the fuel is supplied by a throttle body assembly which incorporates the single fuel injector and the fuel pressure regulator. On multi-point injection models the fuel pump supplies fuel to the fuel rail, which acts as a reservoir for the four fuel injectors which inject fuel into the inlet tracts. In addition, there is an Electronic Control Unit (ECU) and various sensors, electrical components and related wiring.

Refer to Section 7 for further information on the operation of each fuel injection system, and to Section 20 for information on the exhaust system.

⚠ **Warning: Many of the procedures in this Chapter require the removal of fuel lines and connections, which may result in some fuel spillage. Before carrying out any operation on the fuel system, refer to the precautions given in 'Safety first!' at the beginning of this manual, and follow them implicitly. Petrol is a highly-dangerous and volatile liquid, and the precautions necessary when handling it cannot be overstressed.**

Note: *Residual pressure will remain in the fuel lines long after the vehicle was last used. Before disconnecting any fuel line, first depressurise the fuel system as described in Section 8.*

2 Air cleaner assembly and intake ducts – removal and refitting

Removal

Astra models

1 To remove the air cleaner housing, slacken the retaining clip securing the intake trunking to the throttle body/housing. Release the trunking from the air cleaner assembly by slackening the retaining clip or by levering up the edge of the clip as applicable. Unscrew the retaining screw/nut(s) and remove the housing from the engine compartment. Unclip the vapour hoses or canister purge valve from the bracket on the housing **(see illustrations)**. On single-point injection models, it will be necessary to disconnect the vacuum hose and the hot air intake hose from the housing as it is removed.

2 The various ducts can be disconnected and removed once the retaining clips have been slackened. In some cases it will be necessary to disconnect breather hoses and wiring connectors to allow the duct to be removed; the duct may also be bolted to a support bracket **(see illustration)**.

Zafira models

3 Remove the engine compartment seal and water deflector cover from in front of the windscreen.

4 Undo the retaining nuts and bolts, and remove the bulkhead cover plate to allow access to the air intake trunking.

5 Remove the air cleaner assembly and ducts as described in paragraphs 1 and 2.

Refitting

6 Refitting is the reverse of removal, making sure that the locating pin at the front lower edge of the housing engages correctly with the corresponding lug on the inner wing, and all the ducts are securely reconnected **(see illustration)**.

3 Intake air temperature control system (single-point injection)

General information

1 The system is controlled by a heat-sensitive vacuum switch, mounted in the throttle body cover. When the temperature of the air passing through the cover is cold (below approximately 35°C), the vacuum switch is open, allowing inlet manifold depression to act on the air temperature control valve diaphragm in the base of the air cleaner housing. This vacuum causes the diaphragm to rise, drawing a flap valve across the cold-air intake, allowing only warmed air from the exhaust manifold shroud to enter the air cleaner.

2 As the temperature of the exhaust-warmed air entering the throttle body rises, the wax capsule in the vacuum switch deforms and closes the switch, cutting off the vacuum supply to the air temperature control valve assembly. As the vacuum supply is cut, the flap is gradually lowered across the hot-air intake until, when the temperature of the air in the duct is fully warmed-up (approximately 40°C), the control valve closes, allowing only cold air from the front of the car to enter the air cleaner.

Testing

3 To check the system, allow the engine to cool down completely, then detach the intake

2.1a Use a small screwdriver to release the trunking retaining clip

2.1b Unclip the canister purge valve

2.1c Undo the air cleaner housing retaining screw

2.2 Disconnect any wiring connectors from the air intake trunking

2.6 Ensure that the air cleaner housing pin engages correctly with the rubber locating bush

duct from the front of the air cleaner housing; the control valve assembly flap valve in the housing duct should be securely seated across the hot-air intake. Start the engine: the flap should immediately rise to close off the cold-air intake, and should then lower steadily as the engine warms up, until it is eventually seated across the hot-air intake again.

4 To check the vacuum switch, disconnect the vacuum pipe from the control valve when the engine is running, and place a finger over the pipe end. When the engine is cold, full inlet manifold vacuum should be felt in the pipe, and when the engine is at normal operating temperature, there should be no vacuum in the pipe.

5 To check the air temperature control valve assembly, detach the intake duct from the air cleaner housing; the flap valve should be securely seated across the hot-air intake. Disconnect the vacuum pipe and, using a suitable length of hose, suck hard at the control valve stub; the flap should rise to shut off the cold-air intake.

6 If either component is faulty, it must be renewed. The vacuum switch is an integral part of the throttle body cover and the temperature control valve is an integral part of the air cleaner housing; neither component is available separately.

7 On completion of the check, ensure all disturbed items are securely reconnected.

---

4 Accelerator cable – removal, refitting and adjustment

Note: *On 1.4 litre (Z14XE), 1.6 litre (Z16SE and Z16XE), 1.8 litre (Z18XE) and 2.2 litre (Z22SE) engine models, an electronic accelerator system is fitted (no accelerator cable), this consists of an accelerator pedal module and a throttle valve module. The accelerator pedal module has two potentiometers (sensors) which determine the position of the pedal, and transmit a signal to the ECU. The throttle valve module consists of a throttle valve potentiometer and a throttle valve servo motor which actuates the throttle valve.*

4.1 Release the clip and slide the cable end fitting from the throttle lever

Removal

1 Working in the engine compartment, release the inner cable retaining clip then slide the clip out of the end fitting and release the cable from the throttle lever **(see illustration)**.

2 Free the accelerator outer cable from its mounting bracket, taking care not to lose the adjusting clip **(see illustration)**. Work back along the length of the cable, free it from any retaining clips or ties, noting its correct routing. On models with automatic transmission it will be necessary to disconnect the wiring from the kickdown switch which is built into the cable.

3 From inside the vehicle, unscrew the fasteners and remove the lower trim panel from underneath the driver's side of the facia to gain access to the accelerator pedal.

4 Reaching up behind the facia, unclip the accelerator inner cable grommet from the top of the accelerator pedal **(see illustration)**.

5 Return to the engine compartment then free the cable sealing grommet from the bulkhead and remove the cable and grommet from the vehicle.

6 Examine the cable for signs of wear or damage and renew if necessary. Check the rubber grommet for signs of damage or deterioration and renew it if necessary **(see illustration)**.

Refitting

7 Feed the cable into position from the engine compartment and seat the outer cable grommet in the bulkhead.

8 From inside the vehicle, clip the inner cable

4.2 Remove the adjustment clip

grommet into position in the pedal end and check to make sure the grommet is correctly located in the bulkhead. Check that the cable is securely retained, then refit the trim panel to the facia.

9 From within the engine compartment, ensure the outer cable is correctly seated in the bulkhead, then work along the cable, securing it in position with the retaining clips and ties, ensuring that the cable is correctly routed. On models with automatic transmission, reconnect the wiring connector to the kickdown switch.

10 Connect the inner cable to the throttle lever and secure it in position with the retaining clip. Clip the outer cable into its mounting bracket and adjust the cable as described below.

Adjustment

11 Working in the engine compartment, slide the adjustment clip from accelerator outer cable **(see illustration 4.2)**.

12 With the clip removed, ensure that the throttle cam is fully against its stop. Gently pull the cable out of its grommet until all free play is removed from the inner cable.

13 With the cable held in this position, refit the spring clip to the last exposed outer cable groove in front of the rubber grommet. When the clip is refitted and the outer cable is released, there should be only a small amount of free play in the inner cable.

14 Have an assistant depress the accelerator pedal, and check that the throttle cam opens fully and returns smoothly to its stop.

---

5 Accelerator pedal – removal and refitting

Note: *On 1.4 litre (Z14XE), 1.6 litre (Z16SE and Z16XE), 1.8 litre (Z18XE) and 2.2 litre (Z22SE) engine models, an electronic accelerator system is fitted (no accelerator cable), this consists of an accelerator pedal module and a throttle valve module. The accelerator pedal module has two potentiometers (sensors) which determine the position of the pedal, and transmit a signal to the ECU. The throttle valve module consists of*

4.4 Pull the cable grommet up and out from the end of the pedal

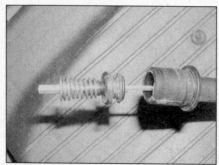

4.6 Accelerator cable grommet – pedal end

5.4 Undo the three pedal bracket retaining bolts

a throttle valve potentiometer and a throttle valve servo motor which actuates the throttle valve.

Removal

1 From inside the vehicle, unscrew the fasteners and remove the lower trim panel from underneath the driver's side of the facia to gain access to the accelerator pedal.
2 On models with an accelerator cable, reach up behind the facia and unclip the accelerator inner cable grommet from the top of the accelerator pedal **(see illustration 4.4)**.
3 On models with an electronic accelerator (no accelerator cable), disconnect the wiring connector from the pedal position sensor by sliding it towards the rear of the vehicle. Undo the retaining bolts and remove the pedal position sensor from the pedal assembly.
4 Unscrew the three retaining nuts and remove the pedal assembly from the bulkhead **(see illustration)**.
5 Inspect the pedal assembly for signs of wear, paying particular attention to the pedal bushes, and renew as necessary. To dismantle the assembly, unhook the return spring then slide off the retaining clip and separate the pedal, mounting bracket, return spring and pivot bushes.

Refitting

6 If the assembly has been dismantled, apply a smear of multi-purpose grease to the pedal pivot shaft and bushes. Fit the bushes and return spring to the mounting bracket and insert the pedal, making sure it passes through the return spring bore. Secure the pedal in position with the retaining clip and hook the return spring back behind the pedal.
7 Refit the pedal assembly and tighten its retaining nuts to the specified torque setting.
8 On models with an electronic accelerator (no accelerator cable), refit the pedal position sensor to the pedal assembly and reconnect the wiring connector.
9 On models with an accelerator cable, clip the accelerator cable into position on the pedal then refit the trim panel to the facia. On completion, adjust the accelerator cable as described in Section 4.

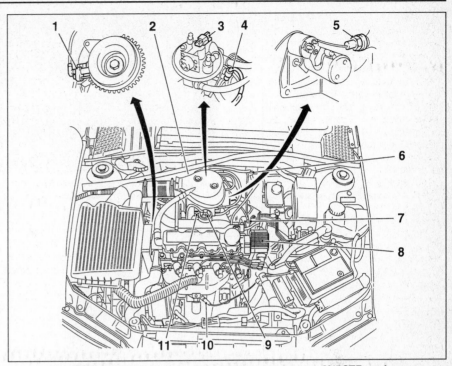

7.1 Multec single-point injection system components – X16SZR engines

1 Crankshaft sensor
2 Throttle body
3 Fuel injector
4 Throttle potentiometer
5 Knock sensor
6 Manifold absolute pressure (MAP) sensor
7 Evaporative emission system purge valve
8 Ignition module
9 Exhaust gas recirculation (EGR) valve
10 Oxygen sensor
11 Idle speed control stepper motor

6 Unleaded petrol – general information and usage

Note: *The information given in this Chapter is correct at the time of writing. If updated information is thought to be required, check with a Vauxhall dealer. If travelling abroad, consult one of the motoring organisations (or a similar authority) for advice on the fuel available.*
1 The fuel recommended by Vauxhall is given in the Specifications Section of this Chapter, followed by the equivalent petrol currently on sale in the UK.
2 All petrol models are designed to run on fuel with a minimum octane rating of 95 RON. Lower octane fuel, down to minimum of rating 91 RON, can be safely used since the engine management system automatically adjusts the ignition timing to suit (using the information supplied by the knock sensor). However, a slight power loss is likely if fuel with a octane rating of less than 95 RON is used.
3 All models have a catalytic converter, and so must be run on unleaded fuel only. Under no circumstances should leaded fuel (UK 4-star/LRP) be used, as this may damage the converter.
4 Super unleaded petrol (98 octane) can also be used in all models if wished, though there is no advantage in doing so.

7 Fuel injection systems – general information

Multec single-point injection

1 The Multec engine management (fuel injection/ignition) system **(see illustration)** incorporates a closed-loop catalytic converter, an evaporative emission control system and an exhaust gas recirculation (EGR) system, and complies with the latest emission control standards. The fuel injection side of the system operates as follows (refer to Chapter 5B for information on the ignition systems).
2 The fuel pump, immersed in the fuel tank, pumps fuel from the fuel tank to the fuel injector, via a filter mounted underneath the rear of the vehicle. Fuel supply pressure is controlled by the pressure regulator in the throttle body assembly. The regulator operates by allowing excess fuel to return to the tank.
3 The electrical control system consists of the ECU, along with the following sensors.
a) *Throttle potentiometer – informs the ECU of the throttle position, and the rate of throttle opening or closing.*
b) *Coolant temperature sensor – informs the ECU of engine coolant temperature.*
c) *Oxygen sensor – informs the ECU of the oxygen content of the exhaust gases*

(explained in greater detail in Part B of this Chapter).

d) *Crankshaft sensor – informs the ECU of engine speed and crankshaft position.*

e) *Knock sensor – informs the ECU when pre-ignition ('pinking') is occurring.*

f) *Manifold absolute pressure (MAP) sensor – informs the ECU of the engine load by monitoring the pressure in the inlet manifold.*

g) *ABS control unit – informs the ECU of the vehicle speed.*

h) *Air conditioning system compressor switch (where fitted) – informs ECU when the air conditioning system is switched on.*

4 All the above information is analysed by the ECU and, based on this, the ECU determines the appropriate ignition and fuelling requirements for the engine. The ECU controls the fuel injector by varying its pulse width – the length of time the injector is held open – to provide a richer or weaker mixture, as appropriate. The mixture is constantly varied by the ECU, to provide the best setting for cranking, starting (with either a hot or cold engine), warm-up, idle, cruising, and acceleration.

5 The ECU also has full control over the engine idle speed, via a stepper motor which is fitted to the throttle body. The motor

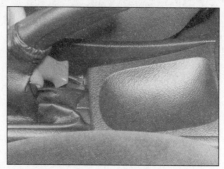

7.8a Unclip the trim panel from the top of the centre console . . .

pushrod controls the opening of an air passage which bypasses the throttle valve. When the throttle valve is closed (accelerator pedal released), the ECU uses the motor to vary the amount of air entering the engine and so controls the idle speed.

6 The ECU also controls the exhaust and evaporative emission control systems, which are described in detail in Part B of this Chapter.

7 If there is an abnormality in any of the readings obtained from any sensor, the ECU enters its back-up mode. In this event, the ECU ignores the abnormal sensor signal, and assumes a preprogrammed value which will allow the engine to continue running (albeit at

7.8b . . . to gain access to the diagnostic connector (arrowed)

reduced efficiency). If the ECU enters this back-up mode, the warning light on the instrument panel will come on, and the relevant fault code will be stored in the ECU memory.

8 If the warning light comes on, the vehicle should be taken to a Vauxhall dealer or specialist at the earliest opportunity. A complete test of the engine management system can then be carried out, using a special electronic diagnostic test unit which is simply plugged into the system's diagnostic connector. The connector is located under the trim beneath the handbrake lever handle; unclip the trim panel situated beneath the handbrake lever to gain access **(see illustrations)**.

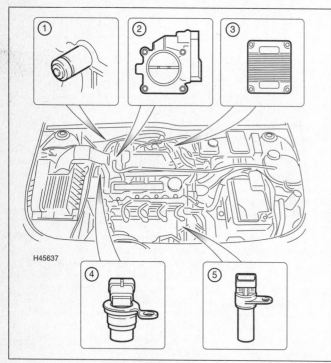

7.9a Multec S multi-point injection system components – Z16SE engines

1	Knock sensor	3	Engine electronic	4	Camshaft position
2	Throttle housing		control unit (ECU)		sensor
				5	Crankshaft sensor

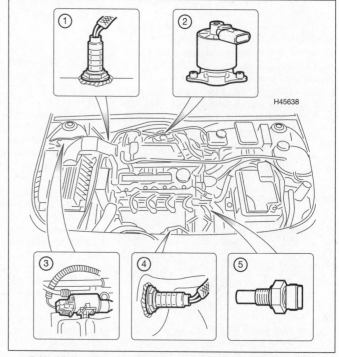

7.9b Multec S multi-point injection system components – Z16SE engines

1	Oxygen sensor – catalytic	3	Evaporative emission system
	converter control		purge valve
2	Exhaust gas recirculation (EGR) valve	4	Oxygen sensor – mixture regulation
		5	Coolant temperature sensor

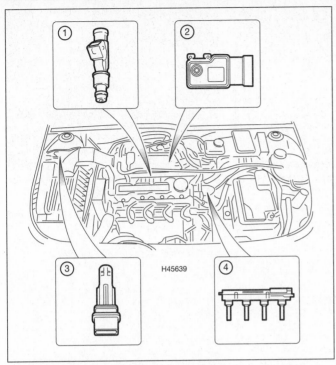

H45639

**7.9c Multec S multi-point injection system components –
Z16SE engines**

1   Injectors
2   Manifold absolute pressure
    (MAP) sensor
3   Intake air temperature
    sensor
4   Ignition module

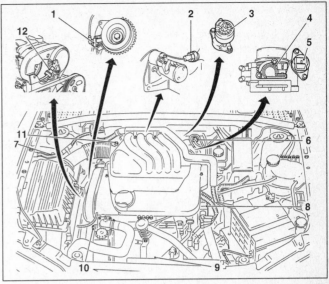

**7.9d Multec S multi-point injection system components – X14XE
and X16XEL engines**

1   Crankshaft sensor
2   Knock sensor
3   Exhaust gas recirculation
    (EGR) valve
4   Throttle potentiometer
5   Idle speed control stepper
    motor
6   Manifold absolute pressure
    (MAP) sensor
7   Evaporative emission system
    purge valve
8   Ignition module
9   Oxygen sensor
10 Coolant temperature
    sensor
11 Intake air temperature
    sensor
12 Camshaft position sensor

Multec S multi-point injection

9 The Multec S engine management (fuel
injection/ignition) system **(see illustrations)**
incorporates a closed-loop catalytic converter,
an evaporative emission control system, and
an exhaust gas recirculation (EGR) system, and
complies with the latest emission control
standards. The fuel injection side of the system
operates as follows (refer to Chapter 5B for
information on the ignition systems).

10 The fuel pump, immersed in the fuel tank,
pumps fuel from the fuel tank to the fuel rail,
via a filter mounted underneath the rear of the
vehicle. Fuel supply pressure is controlled by
the pressure regulator which allows excess
fuel to be returned to the tank.

11 The electrical control system consists of
the ECU, along with the following sensors.

a) Throttle potentiometer – informs the ECU
   of the throttle position, and the rate of
   throttle opening or closing.
b) Coolant temperature sensor – informs the
   ECU of engine temperature.
c) Intake air temperature sensor – informs
   the ECU of the temperature of the air
   entering the manifold.
d) Oxygen sensor(s) – informs the ECU of
   the oxygen content of the exhaust gases
   (explained in greater detail in Part B of
   this Chapter).
e) Crankshaft sensor – informs the ECU of
   engine speed and crankshaft position.

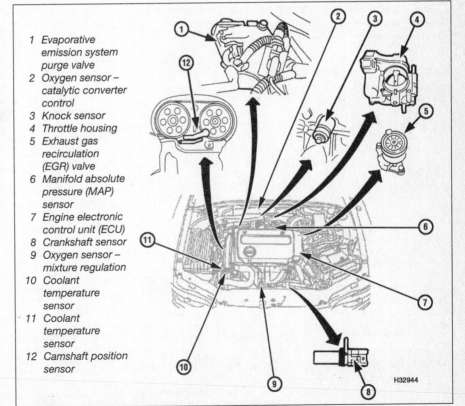

1   Evaporative
    emission system
    purge valve
2   Oxygen sensor –
    catalytic converter
    control
3   Knock sensor
4   Throttle housing
5   Exhaust gas
    recirculation
    (EGR) valve
6   Manifold absolute
    pressure (MAP)
    sensor
7   Engine electronic
    control unit (ECU)
8   Crankshaft sensor
9   Oxygen sensor –
    mixture regulation
10 Coolant
    temperature
    sensor
11 Coolant
    temperature
    sensor
12 Camshaft position
    sensor

H32944

7.9e Multec S multi-point injection system components – Z14XE and Z16XE engines

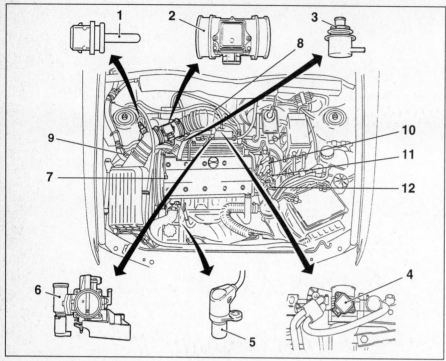

7.18a Simtec 70 multi-point fuel injection system components – X18XE1 and X20XEV engines

1 Intake air temperature sensor	6 Idle speed control stepper motor
2 Hot film mass airflow meter	7 Camshaft position sensor
3 Fuel pressure regulator	8 Knock sensor (on rear of the cylinder block)
4 Throttle potentiometer	
5 Crankshaft sensor	
9 Evaporative emission system purge valve	
10 Ignition module	
11 Coolant temperature sensor	
12 Exhaust gas recirculation (EGR) valve	

1 Camshaft position sensor
2 Hot film mass airflow meter
3 Ignition module
4 Oxygen sensor – catalytic converter control
5 Knock sensor
6 Throttle housing
7 Engine electronic control unit (ECU)
8 Crankshaft sensor
9 Oxygen sensor – mixture regulation
10 Coolant temperature sensor
11 Coolant temperature sensor
12 Evaporative emission system purge valve

H32943

7.18b Simtec 71 multi-point fuel injection system components – Z18XE and Z18XEL engines

f) Camshaft sensor – informs the ECU of speed and position of the camshaft.
g) Knock sensor – informs the ECU when pre-ignition (pinking) is occurring.
h) Manifold absolute pressure (MAP) sensor – informs the ECU of the engine load by monitoring the pressure in the inlet manifold.
i) ABS control unit – informs the ECU of the vehicle speed.
j) Air conditioning system compressor switch (where fitted) – informs ECU when the air conditioning system is switched on.

12 All the above information is analysed by the ECU and, based on this, the ECU determines the appropriate ignition and fuelling requirements for the engine. The ECU controls the fuel injectors by varying their pulse width – the length of time the injectors are held open – to provide a richer or weaker mixture, as appropriate. The mixture is constantly varied by the ECU, to provide the best setting for cranking, starting (with either a hot or cold engine), warm-up, idle, cruising, and acceleration. The Multec S system is a 'sequential' fuel injection system. This means that each of the four injectors is triggered individually just before the inlet valve of the relevant cylinder is about to open.

13 On early models, the ECU also has full control over the engine idle speed, via a stepper motor which is fitted to the throttle housing. The motor controls the opening of an air passage which bypasses the throttle valve. When the throttle valve is closed (accelerator pedal released), the ECU uses the motor to vary the amount of air entering the engine and so controls the idle speed.

14 On later models, the system has an electronic accelerator (no accelerator cable), which consists of an accelerator pedal module and a throttle valve module. The accelerator pedal module has two potentiometers (sensors) which determine the position of the pedal, and transmit a signal to the ECU. The throttle valve module consists of a throttle valve potentiometer and a throttle valve servo motor which actuates the throttle valve. Also the crankshaft sensor has been moved to the cylinder block, where it picks up the signal from an increment disc on number eight web on the crankshaft.

15 The ECU also controls the exhaust and evaporative emission control systems, which are described in detail in Part B of this Chapter.

16 If there is an abnormality in any of the readings obtained from any sensor, the ECU may enter its back-up mode. In this event, the ECU ignores the abnormal sensor signal, and assumes a preprogrammed value which will allow the engine to continue running (albeit at reduced efficiency). If the ECU enters this back-up mode, the warning light on the instrument panel will come on, and the relevant fault code will be stored in the ECU memory.

17 If the warning light comes on, the vehicle

should be taken to a Vauxhall dealer or specialist at the earliest opportunity. A complete test of the engine management system can then be carried out, using a special electronic diagnostic test unit which is simply plugged into the system's diagnostic connector. The connector is located under the trim beneath the handbrake lever handle; unclip the trim panel situated just in front of the handbrake lever to gain access **(see illustrations 7.8a and 7.8b).**

Simtec 70 and 71 multi-point injection systems

18 The Simtec 70 and 71 engine management (fuel injection/ignition) systems **(see illustrations)** are almost identical in operation to the Multec S system (see paragraphs 9 to 17). The only major change to the system is that a hot film mass airflow meter is fitted in place of the manifold pressure (MAP) sensor. The airflow meter informs the ECU of the amount of air entering the inlet manifold.

19 Another additional feature of the Simtec system is that it incorporates a variable tract inlet manifold to help increase torque output at low engine speeds. Each inlet manifold tract is fitted with a valve. The valve is controlled by the ECU via a solenoid valve and vacuum diaphragm unit.

20 At low engine speeds (below approximately 3600 rpm) the valves remain closed. The air entering the engine is then forced to take the long inlet path through the manifold which leads to an increase in the engine torque output.

21 At higher engine speeds, the ECU switches the solenoid valve which then allows vacuum to act on the diaphragm unit. The diaphragm unit is linked to the valve assemblies and opens up each of the four valves allowing the air passing through the manifold to take the shorter inlet path which is more suited to higher engine speeds.

GMPT – E15 multi-point injection system

22 The GMPT – E15 engine management (fuel injection/ignition) system **(see illustrations)** is very similar in operation to the Multec S system (see paragraphs 9 to 17).

23 The only major change to the system is that special sensors are incorporated in the ignition module to remove the need for a camshaft sensor. The sensors read the injection impulse so as to determine the cylinder position.

24 This system also has an electronic accelerator (no accelerator cable), which consists of an accelerator pedal module and a throttle valve module. The accelerator pedal module has two potentiometers (sensors) which determine the position of the pedal, and transmit a signal to the ECU. The throttle valve module consists of a throttle valve potentiometer and a throttle valve servo motor which actuates the throttle valve.

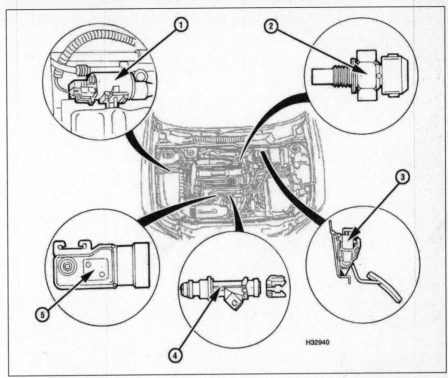

7.22a GMPT – E15 multi-point fuel injection system components – Z22SE engines

1 Evaporative emission system purge valve
2 Coolant temperature sensor
3 Accelerator pedal/accelerator pedal sensor
4 Injectors
5 Manifold absolute pressure (MAP) sensor

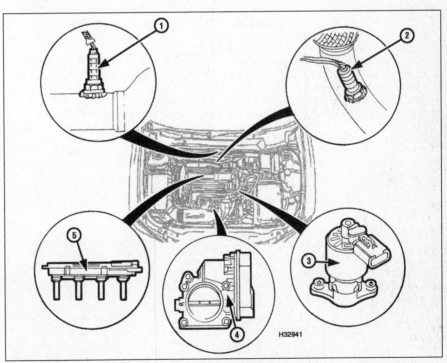

7.22b GMPT – E15 multi-point fuel injection system components – Z22SE engines

1 Oxygen sensor – mixture regulation
2 Oxygen sensor – catalytic converter control
3 Exhaust gas recirculation (EGR) valve
4 Throttle housing
5 Ignition module

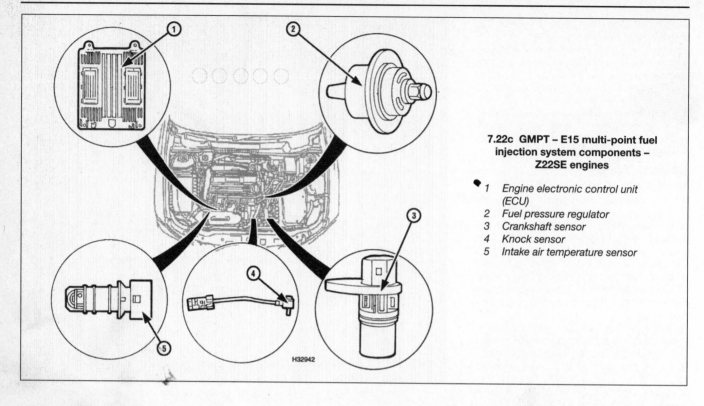

7.22c GMPT – E15 multi-point fuel injection system components – Z22SE engines

1 Engine electronic control unit (ECU)
2 Fuel pressure regulator
3 Crankshaft sensor
4 Knock sensor
5 Intake air temperature sensor

H32942

8 Fuel injection system – depressurisation

⚠ **Warning: Refer to the warning note in Section 1 before proceeding. The following procedure will merely relieve the pressure in the fuel system – remember that fuel will still be present in the system components, and take precautions accordingly before disconnecting any of them.**

1 The fuel system referred to in this Section is defined as the tank-mounted fuel pump, the fuel filter, the fuel injector(s) and the pressure regulator, and the metal pipes and flexible hoses of the fuel lines between these components. All these contain fuel which will be under pressure while the engine is running, and/or while the ignition is switched on. The pressure will remain for some time after the ignition has been switched off, and it must be relieved in a controlled fashion when any of these components are disturbed for servicing work.

SOHC (X16SZR) engines

2 Ensure the ignition is switched off then remove the cover from the engine compartment relay box, which is situated next to the left-hand suspension turret. Remove the fuel pump relay (the relay should be coloured purple) from the box **(see illustration)**.

3 Start the engine and allow it to idle until the engine starts to run roughly then switch the ignition off.

4 Disconnect the battery negative terminal (refer to *Disconnecting the battery* in the Reference Chapter) then refit the relay and cover to the relay box.

SOHC (Z16SE) and all DOHC engines

5 On these engines, the fuel system can either be depressurised as described above in paragraphs 2 to 4, or as follows.

6 Locate the valve assembly which is fitted to the fuel rail on the inlet manifold. On 1.4 and 1.6 litre (DOHC) engines the valve is on the right-hand end of the rail and on 1.6 litre (SOHC), 1.8, 2.0 and 2.2 litre (DOHC) engines it can be found on the top of the rail **(see illustrations)**.

7 Unscrew the cap from the valve and position a container beneath the valve. Hold a wad of rag over the valve and relieve the pressure in the fuel system by depressing the

8.2 Remove the fuel pump relay

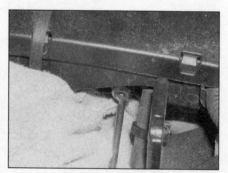

8.6a Fuel depressurisation valve – 1.4 and 1.6 litre (DOHC) engines

8.6b Fuel depressurisation valve – 1.8 and 2.0 litre engines

8.6c Fuel depressurisation valve –
2.2 litre engines

9.3 Fuel pump access cover

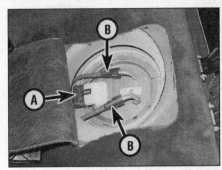

9.4 Fuel pump wiring connector (A) and
fuel hoses (B)

valve core with a suitable screwdriver. Be prepared for the squirt of fuel as the valve core is depressed and catch it with the rag. Hold the valve core down until no more fuel is expelled from the valve.

8 Once all pressure is relieved, securely refit the valve cap.

9 Fuel pump –
removal and refitting

 Warning: Refer to the warning note in Section 1 before proceeding.

Note 1: *A new fuel pump cover sealing ring will be required on refitting.*

Note 2: *On Z14XE, Z16SE, Z16XE, Z18XE, X18XE1 and Z22SE models the fuel pressure regulator is located in the fuel tank as part of the fuel tank sender unit/pump.*

Removal

Astra models

1 Depressurise the fuel system as described in Section 8 then disconnect the battery negative terminal (refer to *Disconnecting the battery* in the Reference Chapter).

2 Fold the rear seat cushion forwards and lift up the flap in the carpet to reveal the fuel pump access cover.

3 Using a screwdriver, carefully prise the plastic access cover from the floor to expose the fuel pump **(see illustration)**.

4 Disconnect the wiring connector from the

fuel pump, and tape the connector to the vehicle body, to prevent it disappearing behind the tank **(see illustration)**.

5 Mark the fuel hoses for identification purposes. The hoses are equipped with quick-release fittings to ease removal. To disconnect each hose, compress the clips located on each side of the fitting and ease the fitting off of its union. Disconnect both hoses from the top of the pump, noting the correct fitted position of the sealing rings and plug the hose ends to minimise fuel loss.

6 Unscrew the locking ring and remove it from the tank. This is best accomplished by using a screwdriver on the raised ribs of the locking ring. Carefully tap the screwdriver to turn the ring anti-clockwise until it can be unscrewed by hand **(see illustration)**.

7 Carefully lift the fuel pump cover away from tank until the wiring connector can be disconnected from its underside. Make alignment marks between the cover and hoses then release the retaining clips and remove the cover from the vehicle, along with its sealing ring. Discard the sealing ring; a new one must be used on refitting.

8 Release the three retaining clips by pressing them inwards then lift the fuel pump housing assembly out of the fuel tank, taking great care not to drop the fuel filter which is fitted to the pump base **(see illustration)**. Also try not to spill fuel onto the interior of the vehicle.

9 Inspect the fuel filter for signs of damage or deterioration and renew if necessary **(see illustration)**.

10 If necessary the pump housing assembly can be dismantled and the pump removed, noting the wiring connectors correct locations.

Zafira models

11 Remove the fuel tank as described in Section 11.

12 If not already done so, disconnect the wiring harness plug and fuel lines from the fuel pump access cover. Mark the fuel lines prior to removal to aid refitting, and plug the hose openings to minimise fuel loss.

13 Proceed as described in Paragraphs 6 to 10.

Refitting

Astra models

14 Where necessary, reassemble the pump and housing components ensuring the wiring connectors are correctly and securely reconnected.

15 Ensure the filter is securely fitted to the base of the pump then carefully manoeuvre the pump assembly into position, making sure it clips securely into position.

16 Fit a new sealing ring to the tank.

17 Reconnect the fuel hoses to the pump cover, using the marks made on removal, and securely tighten their retaining clips. Reconnect the wiring connector then seat the pump cover on the tank.

18 Refit the locking ring to the fuel tank and tighten it securely.

19 Reconnect the fuel hoses to the pump cover, ensuring each fitting clicks securely

9.6 Undo the locking ring

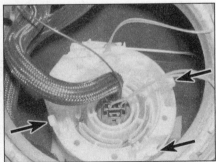

9.8 Press the retaining clips inwards, and lift the pump assembly from the tank

9.9 A fuel filter is fitted to the base of the pump assembly

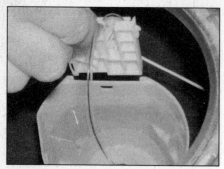

10.2 Release the clip and slide the sender unit upwards

into position, and reconnect the wiring connector.

20 Reconnect the battery then start the engine and check for fuel leaks. If all is well, refit the access cover and fold the seat back into position.

Zafira models

21 Proceed as described in Paragraphs 14 to 18.

22 Refit the fuel tank as described in Section 11.

10 Fuel gauge sender unit – removal and refitting

⚠️ *Warning: Refer to the warning note in Section 1 before proceeding.*

Note: *A new fuel pump cover sealing ring will be required on refitting.*

Removal

1 On Astra models, carry out the operations described in paragraphs 1 to 7 of Section 9 to remove the fuel pump cover. On Zafira models, carry out the operations described in paragraphs 11 to 13 of Section 9.

2 The fuel gauge sender unit is clipped to the side of the fuel pump mounting reservoir. Carefully release the retaining clip then slide the sender unit upwards to release it from its mounting **(see illustration)**.

3 Manoeuvre the sender unit through the fuel tank aperture, taking great care not damage the float arm.

Refitting

4 To refit, manoeuvre the sender unit carefully in through the tank aperture and slide it into position on the side of the fuel pump reservoir.

5 Ensure the sender unit is clipped securely in position then refit the fuel pump cover as described in paragraphs 14 to 20 (Astra models) or paragraphs 21 and 22 (Zafira models) of Section 9.

11 Fuel tank – removal and refitting

⚠️ *Warning: Refer to the warning note in Section 1 before proceeding.*

Removal

1 Depressurise the fuel system as described in Section 8, then disconnect the battery negative terminal (refer to *Disconnecting the battery* in the Reference Chapter).

2 Before removing the fuel tank, all fuel must be drained from the tank. Since a fuel tank drain plug is not provided, it is therefore preferable to carry out the removal operation when the tank is nearly empty. The remaining fuel can then be syphoned or hand-pumped from the tank.

3 Remove the exhaust system and relevant heat shield(s) as described in Section 18.

4 Chock the front wheels, and slacken the handbrake cable adjusting nut, with reference to Chapter 9.

5 On rear drum brake models, disconnect the handbrake cable at the connector just forward of the brake drum. On models with rear disc brakes, press the rear caliper handbrake lever downwards, detach the handbrake inner cable from the lever, remove the retaining clip and remove the outer cable from the retaining bracket on the caliper. Refer to Chapter 9 if necessary.

6 Release the handbrake cable from the retaining clips and brackets, and position clear of the fuel tank.

7 On Astra models, disconnect the wiring connector from the fuel pump as described in paragraphs 1 to 4 of Section 9. On Zafira

models, working under the vehicle, disconnect the wiring plug for the fuel pump **(see illustration)**.

8 Open up the fuel filler flap and remove the rubber cover from around the filler neck aperture. Slacken and remove the retaining bolt which secures the filler neck to the body **(see illustration)**.

9 Remove the right-hand rear wheel then undo the retaining screws and nuts and remove the plastic wheelarch liner.

10 Make alignment marks between the small hoses and the top of the filler neck assembly then release the retaining clips and disconnect both hoses.

11 Slacken the retaining clips and disconnect the main hoses from the base of the filler neck. Unscrew the filler neck lower retaining bolt and manoeuvre the assembly out from underneath the vehicle.

12 Trace the fuel feed and return hoses from the tank to their unions in front of the tank. Make alignment marks between the hoses then release the retaining clips and disconnect both hoses. If the hoses are equipped with quick-release fittings, disconnect each hose by depressing the clips on each side of the fitting and easing the fitting from the pipe.

13 Unclip/unscrew the fuel filter from the fuel tank retaining strap **(see illustration)**.

14 Place a trolley jack with an interposed block of wood beneath the tank, then raise the jack until it is supporting the weight of the tank.

15 Slacken and remove the retaining bolts and remove the retaining straps from underneath the fuel tank.

16 Slowly lower the fuel tank out of position, disconnecting any other relevant pipes as they become accessible (where necessary), and remove the tank from underneath the vehicle.

17 If the tank is contaminated with sediment or water, remove the fuel pump cover (Section 9), and swill the tank out with clean fuel. The tank is injection-moulded from a synthetic material – if seriously damaged, it should be renewed. However, in certain cases, it may be possible to have small leaks or minor damage repaired. Seek the advice of a specialist before attempting to repair the fuel tank.

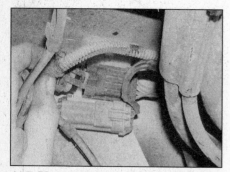

11.7 Disconnect the fuel pump wiring plug

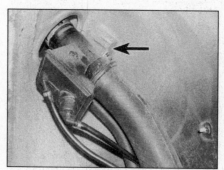

11.8 Remove the filler neck retaining bolt (arrowed)

11.13 The fuel filter is mounted on the tank retaining strap

12.2a Slacken and remove the retaining screws . . .

12.2b . . . and detach the intake duct from the throttle body

12.3 Disconnect the injector wiring connector and free it from the throttle body

Refitting

18 Refitting is the reverse of the removal procedure, noting the following points:
 a) When lifting the tank back into position, take care to ensure that none of the hoses become trapped between the tank and vehicle body. Refit the retaining straps and tighten the bolts to the specified torque.
 b) Ensure all pipes and hoses are correctly routed and all hoses unions are securely joined.
 c) Adjust the handbrake as described in Chapter 9.
 d) On completion, refill the tank with a small amount of fuel, and check for signs of leakage prior to taking the vehicle out on the road.

12 Throttle body/housing – removal and refitting

⚠ **Warning: Refer to the warning note in Section 1 before proceeding.**
Note: On 1.4 litre (Z14XE), 1.6 litre (Z16SE and Z16XE), 1.8 litre (Z18XE) and 2.2 litre (Z22SE) engine models, there is an electronic accelerator system fitted (no accelerator cable). The throttle valve potentiometer and servo motor are a combined part of the throttle housing. Individual parts for the housing are

not available separately and, if defective it must be renewed as a complete unit.

SOHC engines

X16SZR

1 Depressurise the fuel system as described in Section 8, then disconnect the battery negative terminal (refer to *Disconnecting the battery* in the Reference Chapter).
2 Slacken the retaining clip and disconnect the air intake duct from the throttle body cover. Disconnect the vacuum and breather hoses from the cover then undo the retaining screws and remove the cover and sealing ring from the top of the throttle body **(see illustrations)**.
3 Depress the retaining clips and disconnect the wiring connectors from the throttle potentiometer, the idle control stepper motor and the injector, and release the wiring from the throttle body **(see illustration)**.
4 Disconnect the fuel hoses from the side of the throttle body.
5 Unclip the accelerator linkage link rod from the balljoint on the throttle housing **(see illustration)**.
6 Disconnect the breather/vacuum hoses from the throttle body (as applicable).
7 Slacken and remove the nuts securing the throttle body assembly to the inlet manifold, then remove the assembly along with its gasket **(see illustration)**. Discard the gasket, a new one should be used on refitting.

8 If necessary, undo the retaining Torx screws and separate the upper and lower sections of the throttle body assembly **(see illustration)**. Remove the gasket and discard it, a new one should be used on refitting.
9 Where necessary, ensure the mating surfaces are clean and dry then fit a new gasket and rejoin the upper and lower sections of the throttle body. Apply locking compound to the retaining screw threads then fit the screws and tighten them evenly and progressively to the specified torque.
10 Ensure the throttle body and manifold mating surfaces are clean and dry and remove all traces of locking compound from the studs and nuts.
11 Fit the new gasket to the manifold then refit the throttle body. Apply a few drops of locking compound to the threads of each retaining nut then refit the nuts and tighten them evenly and progressively to the specified torque setting.
12 Reconnect the vacuum/breather hoses (as applicable) and clip the accelerator linkage back onto its balljoint.
13 Reconnect the fuel hoses to the throttle body, tightening the union nuts to the specified torque, and reconnect the wiring connectors.
14 Ensure the sealing ring is in position then refit the cover to the throttle body. Securely tighten the cover retaining screws then reconnect the intake duct and vacuum hoses.
15 Reconnect the battery then start the

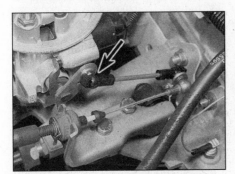

12.5 Unclip the accelerator link rod (arrowed) from the throttle housing balljoint

12.7 Remove the throttle body assembly

12.8 Undo the retaining screws and separate the upper and lower sections of the throttle body

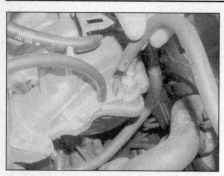

12.26 Disconnect the purge valve hose

12.34 Disconnect the hot film mass airflow meter

engine and check for signs of fuel leaks before taking the vehicle on the road.

Z16SE

16 Disconnect the battery negative terminal (refer to *Disconnecting the battery* in the Reference Chapter).

17 Remove the air cleaner assembly and intake ducts as described in Section 2.

18 Disconnect the evaporative emission system purge valve hose and engine breather hose from the throttle housing.

19 Clamp the coolant hoses, then release the retaining clips and disconnect both hoses from the throttle housing. Plug the hose ends to minimise coolant loss.

20 Disconnect the wiring block connector from the throttle housing electronic throttle valve module.

21 Slacken and remove the throttle housing retaining bolts and free the housing from the manifold. Recover the housing gasket and discard it, a new one should be used on refitting.

22 Refitting is the reverse of removal, bearing in mind the following points.

a) *Fit a new gasket and tighten the housing bolts to the specified torque.*
b) *Ensure all wiring connectors and coolant hoses are correctly and securely reconnected.*
c) *Refit the air cleaner assembly and intake ducts as described in Section 2.*
d) *On completion check, and if necessary top-up, the cooling system as described in Chapter 3.*

DOHC engines

1.4 and 1.6 litre

23 Disconnect the battery negative terminal (refer to *Disconnecting the battery* in the Reference Chapter).

24 Remove the engine oil filler cap then undo the retaining screws and lift off the engine cover. Refit the oil filler cap.

25 Disconnect the wiring plug from the intake air temperature sensor and detach the air intake manifold from the upper part of the air cleaner housing as well as the throttle housing. On Zafira models, it will be necessary to remove the engine compartment seal and water deflector cover from in front of the windscreen, then undo the retaining nuts

and bolts, and remove the bulkhead cover plate to allow access to the air intake trunking.

26 Disconnect the evaporative emission system purge valve hose from the left-hand end of the manifold **(see illustration)**.

27 On models with an accelerator cable, remove the retaining clip then free the cable end fitting from the throttle cam. Pull the outer cable grommet from the bracket, and position the cable clear of the housing.

28 Slacken and remove the throttle housing retaining bolts and free the housing from the manifold. Recover the housing gasket and discard it, a new one should be used on refitting.

29 Rotate the throttle housing until access can be gained to the housing coolant hoses. Make alignment marks between the hoses and housing then release the retaining clips and disconnect both from the housing. Plug the hose ends to minimise coolant loss.

30 On electronic accelerator pedal models, disconnect the wiring block connector from the electronic throttle valve module. On other models, disconnect the wiring connectors from the throttle potentiometer and the idle control stepper motor. Carefully manoeuvre the throttle housing assembly out from the engine compartment.

31 Refitting is the reverse of removal, bearing in mind the following points.

a) *Ensure the wiring connectors and coolant hoses are correctly and securely reconnected before bolting the housing to the manifold.*
b) *Fit a new gasket and tighten the housing bolts to the specified torque.*

12.39 Throttle housing coolant hoses

c) *Ensure all hoses are correctly and securely reconnected.*
d) *Adjust the accelerator cable as described in Section 4 (where applicable).*
e) *On completion check, and if necessary top-up, the cooling system as described in Chapter 3.*

1.8, 2.0 and 2.2 litre

32 Disconnect the battery negative terminal (refer to *Disconnecting the battery* in the Reference Chapter).

33 Remove the oil filler cap, undo the retaining screws, and remove the engine cover.

34 Disconnect the wiring connector from the hot film mass airflow meter **(see illustration)**.

35 Release the retaining clips and detach the air intake trunking, complete with hot film mass airflow meter from the air cleaner housing and the throttle housing. On Zafira models, it will be necessary to remove the engine compartment seal and water deflector cover from in front of the windscreen, then undo the retaining nuts and bolts, and remove the bulkhead cover plate to allow access to the air intake trunking.

36 On models with an accelerator cable, remove the retaining clip and detach the accelerator cable from the throttle lever balljoint and unclip the cable from its mounting bracket. On models with cruise control it will also be necessary to detach the cruise control cable. The end fitting of the cruise control cable is secured to the throttle lever balljoint by a circlip.

37 On models with an accelerator cable, undo the retaining bolts and free the cable mounting bracket from the throttle housing.

38 Release the retaining clips and remove the engine vent hose from the camshaft cover to the throttle housing.

39 On models with an accelerator cable, clamp the coolant hoses which are connected to the rear of the throttle housing then release the retaining clips and disconnect both hoses. Wipe away any spilt coolant **(see illustration)**.

40 Detach the fuel tank vent valve hose from the throttle housing.

41 On electronic accelerator pedal models, disconnect the wiring block connector from the electronic throttle valve module **(see illustrations)**. On other models, disconnect

12.41a Release the securing clip . . .

12.41b ... and disconnect the wiring connector from the throttle valve module

12.42a Remove the throttle housing ...

12.42b ... and renew the gasket

the wiring connectors from the throttle potentiometer and the idle control stepper motor.

42 Disconnect any remaining vacuum/breather hoses from the throttle housing, noting their correct fitted locations, then undo the retaining Torx screws and remove the housing from the manifold. Remove the gasket and discard it, a new one should be used on refitting **(see illustrations)**.

43 Refitting is the reverse of removal, bearing in mind the following points.
a) *Ensure the mating surfaces are clean and dry then fit a new gasket and tighten the housing screws to the specified torque.*
b) *Ensure all hoses are correctly and securely reconnected.*
c) *Adjust the accelerator cable as described in Section 4 (where applicable).*
d) *On completion check, and if necessary top-up, the cooling system as described in Chapter 3.*

Note: *If the throttle housing has been renewed, the 'adaption' values for the old unit, stored in the engine management ECU, must be deleted by the use of specialist diagnostic equipment. Refer to your local Vauxhall dealer or specialist.*

13 Fuel injection system – testing and adjustment

Testing

1 If a fault appears in the fuel injection system, first ensure that all the system wiring connectors are securely connected and free of corrosion. Ensure that the fault is not due to poor maintenance; ie, check that the air cleaner filter element is clean, the spark plugs are in good condition and correctly gapped (where applicable), the cylinder compression pressures are correct, and that the engine breather hoses are clear and undamaged.

2 If these checks fail to reveal the cause of the problem, the vehicle should be taken to a suitably-equipped Vauxhall dealer or specialist for testing. A wiring block connector is incorporated in the engine management circuit, into which a special electronic diagnostic tester

can be plugged (see Section 7). The tester will locate the fault quickly and simply, alleviating the need to test all the system components individually, which is a time-consuming operation that carries a risk of damaging the ECU.

Adjustment

3 Experienced home mechanics with a considerable amount of skill and equipment (including a tachometer and an accurately calibrated exhaust gas analyser) may be able to check the exhaust CO level and the idle speed. However, if these are found to be in need of adjustment, the car will have to be taken to a suitably-equipped Vauxhall dealer or specialist who has access to the necessary diagnostic equipment required to test and adjust the settings.

14 Multec single-point injection system components – removal and refitting

⚠ Warning: Refer to the warning note in Section 1 before proceeding.

Fuel injector

Note: *Before condemning an injector, it is worth trying the effect of one of the proprietary injector-cleaning treatments.*

1 Depressurise the fuel system as described in Section 8, then disconnect the battery negative terminal (refer to *Disconnecting the battery* in the Reference Chapter).

2 Slacken the retaining clip and disconnect the air intake duct from the throttle body cover. Disconnect the vacuum and breather hoses from the cover then undo the retaining screws and remove the cover and sealing ring from the top of the throttle body.

3 Release the retaining clips and disconnect the wiring connector from the injector **(see illustration)**.

4 Undo the retaining screw and remove the injector retaining plate **(see illustrations)**.

5 Ease the injector out from the throttle body along with its sealing rings **(see illustration)**. Discard the sealing rings, they must be renewed whenever the injector is disturbed.

6 Refitting is a reversal of the removal procedure using new injector sealing rings. When refitting the retaining clip, ensure it is correctly engaged with the injector and securely tighten its retaining screw.

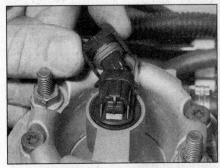

14.3 Disconnect the wiring connector from the fuel injector ...

14.4a ... then undo the retaining screw ...

14.4b ... and remove the injector retaining plate

14.5 Remove the injector from the throttle body, noting the sealing rings (arrowed)

14.9 Fuel pressure regulator retaining screws (arrowed)

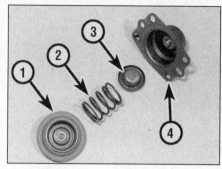

14.10 Fuel pressure regulator components

1 *Diaphragm*   3 *Spring seat*
2 *Spring*   4 *Cover*

Fuel pressure regulator

Note: *At the time of writing it appears that the regulator assembly is not available separately; if it is faulty the complete throttle body upper section must be renewed. Although the unit can be dismantled for cleaning, if required, it should not be disturbed unless absolutely necessary.*

7 Depressurise the fuel system as described in Section 8, then disconnect the battery negative terminal (refer to *Disconnecting the battery* in the Reference Chapter).

8 Slacken the retaining clip and disconnect the air intake duct from the throttle body cover. Disconnect the vacuum and breather hoses from the cover then undo the retaining screws and remove the cover and sealing ring from the top of the throttle body.

9 Using a marker pen, make alignment marks between the regulator cover and throttle body, then slacken and remove the cover retaining screws **(see illustration)**.

10 Lift off the cover, then remove the spring seat and spring then withdraw the diaphragm, noting its correct fitted orientation **(see illustration)**. Remove all traces of dirt, and examine the diaphragm for signs of splitting. If damage is found, it will probably be necessary to renew the throttle body assembly.

11 Refitting is a reverse of the removal procedure, ensuring that the diaphragm and cover are fitted the correct way round, and that the retaining screws are securely tightened.

Idle speed control stepper motor

12 Disconnect the battery negative terminal (refer to *Disconnecting the battery* in the Reference Chapter).

13 To improve access to the motor, slacken the retaining clip and disconnect the air intake duct from the throttle body cover. Disconnect the vacuum and breather hoses from the cover then undo the retaining screws and remove the cover and sealing ring from the top of the throttle body.

14 Release the retaining clip and disconnect the wiring connector from the motor which is fitted to the front of the throttle body assembly **(see illustration)**.

15 Undo the retaining screws and carefully manoeuvre the motor out of position, taking great care not to damage the motor plunger. Remove the sealing ring from the motor and discard it; a new one should be used on refitting **(see illustration)**.

16 Refitting is the reverse of removal, using a new sealing ring. To ensure the motor plunger is not damaged on refitting, prior to installation, check that the plunger tip does not extend more than 28 mm from the motor mating flange **(see illustration)**. If necessary, **gently** push the plunger into the body until it is correctly positioned.

Throttle potentiometer

17 Disconnect the battery negative terminal (refer to *Disconnecting the battery* in the Reference Chapter).

18 Release the retaining clip and disconnect the wiring connector from the throttle potentiometer which is fitted to the left-hand side of the throttle body. Slacken and remove the retaining screws and remove the potentiometer **(see illustrations)**.

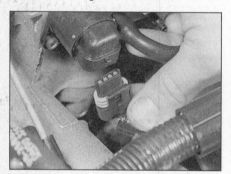

14.14 Disconnecting the idle speed control stepper motor

14.15 Remove the motor from the throttle body noting the sealing ring (arrowed)

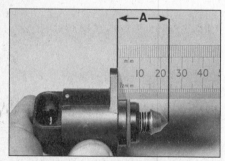

14.16 Ensure that the plunger does not extend more than the specified distance (A) from the mating flange (see text)

14.18a Disconnect the wiring connector . . .

14.18b . . . then undo the retaining screws and remove the potentiometer from the throttle body

19 Prior to refitting, clean the threads of the retaining bolts and apply a drop of fresh locking compound to each one. Ensure the potentiometer is correctly engaged with the throttle valve spindle then tighten its retaining bolts and reconnect the wiring connector.

Coolant temperature sensor

20 The coolant temperature sensor is screwed into the rear of the inlet manifold. Refer to Chapter 3 for removal and refitting details.

Manifold absolute pressure (MAP) sensor

21 The MAP sensor is mounted onto the engine compartment bulkhead, just to the left of the throttle body (see illustration). Ensure the ignition is switched off then disconnect the wiring connector and vacuum hose from the sensor. The MAP sensor can then be unclipped and removed from its mounting.
22 Refitting is the reverse of removal.

Crankshaft sensor

23 The sensor is mounted on the rear of the cylinder block and is accessible from underneath the vehicle. Firmly apply the handbrake, then jack up the front of the car and support it securely on axle stands (see *Jacking and vehicle support*).
24 Trace the wiring back from the sensor, releasing it from all the relevant clips and ties whilst noting its correct routing. Disconnect the wiring connector so the wiring is free to be removed with the sensor.
25 Unscrew the retaining bolt and remove the sensor from underneath the vehicle (see illustration).
26 Refitting is the reverse of removal, tightening the retaining bolt to the specified torque. Ensure the wiring is correctly routed and retained by all the necessary clips and ties.
27 On completion, using feeler gauges, check that the clearance between the sensor tip and the crankshaft pulley teeth is 1.0 ± 0.7 mm. If the clearance is not within the specified range, renew the sensor mounting bracket.

Knock sensor

28 The knock sensor is mounted on the rear of the cylinder block and is accessible from underneath the vehicle. Firmly apply the handbrake, then jack up the front of the car and support it securely on axle stands (see *Jacking and vehicle support*).
29 Trace the wiring back from the sensor, noting its correct routing, and disconnect it at the connector.
30 Slacken and remove the retaining bolt and remove the sensor from the engine.
31 On refitting ensure the mating surfaces are clean and dry then fit the sensor and tighten its retaining bolt to the specified torque. Ensure the wiring is correctly routed and securely reconnected then lower the vehicle to the ground.

14.21 Manifold absolute pressure (MAP) sensor

Electronic control unit (ECU)

32 The ECU is located beside the battery on the left-hand side of the engine compartment.
33 Disconnect the battery negative terminal (refer to *Disconnecting the battery* in the Reference Chapter).
34 Remove both windscreen wiper arms as described in Chapter 12.
35 Remove the protective cover from the ECU, then pull the unit upwards out of the retaining bracket. Disconnect the ECU wiring plugs. **Note:** *Prior to renewing an ECU, the security code must be reset using dedicated diagnostic equipment. Refer to your local Vauxhall dealer or specialist.*
36 Refitting is a reversal of removal.

Fuel pump relay

37 The fuel pump relay is located in the engine compartment main relay box.
38 Unclip the cover and remove it from the relay box. Identify the fuel pump relay which is coloured purple. Ensure the ignition is switched off then pull out the relay.
39 Refitting is the reverse of removal.

Air conditioning system switch

40 The air conditioning system switch is screwed into one of the refrigerant pipes and cannot be removed without first discharging the refrigerant (see Chapter 3). Renewal of the switch should therefore be entrusted to a suitably-equipped garage.

---

15 Multec S multi-point injection system components – removal and refitting

Warning: Refer to the warning note in Section 1 before proceeding.

SOHC engines
Fuel rail and injectors

Note: *If a faulty injector is suspected, it is worth trying the effect of one of the proprietary injector-cleaning treatments.*
1 Depressurise the fuel system as described in Section 8, then disconnect the battery negative terminal (refer to *Disconnecting the battery* in the Reference Chapter).

14.25 Crankshaft sensor retaining bolt (arrowed) – viewed from underneath the vehicle

2 Remove the air cleaner assembly and intake ducts as described in Section 2.
3 Disconnect the wiring connector at the oxygen sensor, camshaft sensor and throttle housing.
4 Disconnect the wiring connector at each fuel injector, then move the wiring harness to one side.
5 Disconnect the fuel supply pipe from the fuel rail and release it from its support bracket.
6 Unscrew the two retaining bolts and remove the fuel rail with the injectors from the inlet manifold.
7 If required, the injectors can be separated from the fuel rail by sliding off the relevant retaining clip and withdrawing the injector from the fuel rail. Remove the upper sealing ring from the injector and discard it; all disturbed sealing rings must be renewed.
8 Refitting is a reversal of the removal procedure, noting the following points.
   a) *Renew all disturbed sealing rings and apply a smear of engine oil to them to aid installation.*
   b) *Ease the injector(s) into the fuel rail, ensuring that the sealing ring(s) remain correctly seated, and secure in position with the retaining clips.*
   c) *On refitting the fuel rail, take care not to damage the injectors and ensure that all sealing rings remain in position. Once the fuel rail is correctly seated, tighten its retaining bolts to the specified torque.*
   d) *On completion start the engine and check for fuel leaks.*

Fuel pressure regulator

9 Fuel pressure regulation is a function of the fuel tank pump module. The regulator is located under the fuel pump access cover. The regulator does not appear to be available as a separate part – check with your Vauxhall dealer. To remove the regulator, follow the procedure for fuel pump renewal, as described in Section 9, and disconnect the regulator from the fuel pipes and wiring connector located on the underside of the fuel pump access cover.

Coolant temperature sensor

10 The coolant temperature sensor is screwed into the thermostat housing. Refer to Chapter 3 for removal and refitting details.

Intake air temperature sensor

11 The intake air temperature sensor is mounted in the intake duct which connects the air cleaner housing to the throttle housing.
12 Ensure the ignition is switched off, then disconnect the wiring connector from the sensor.
13 Carefully ease the sensor out of position and remove its sealing grommet from the intake duct. If the sealing grommet shows signs of damage or deterioration it should be renewed.
14 Refitting is the reverse of removal, ensuring the sensor and grommet are correctly located in the duct.

Manifold absolute pressure (MAP) sensor

15 The MAP sensor is located on the left-hand side of the inlet manifold.
16 Release the pressure sensor wiring harness from the bracket on the ECU, then disconnect the wiring connector from the sensor.
17 Turn the sensor 1/4 turn clockwise and carefully pull it out of the inlet manifold.
18 Refitting is the reverse of removal using a new sealing ring.

Crankshaft sensor

19 The sensor is mounted on the front of the cylinder block at the left-hand end and is accessible from underneath the vehicle. Firmly apply the handbrake, then jack up the front of the car and support it securely on axle stands (see *Jacking and vehicle support*).
20 Disconnect the wiring connector, then unscrew the retaining bolt and remove the sensor from underneath the vehicle.
21 Refitting is the reverse of removal using a new sealing ring. Tighten the sensor retaining bolt to the specified torque.

Camshaft sensor

22 Remove the air cleaner assembly and intake ducts as described in Section 2.
23 Disconnect the sensor wiring connector, unscrew the retaining bolt and remove the sensor from the end of the cylinder head.
24 Refitting is the reverse of removal tightening the sensor retaining bolt to the specified torque.

Knock sensor

25 The knock sensor is mounted on the rear of the cylinder block and is accessible from underneath the vehicle. Firmly apply the handbrake, then jack up the front of the car and support it securely on axle stands (see *Jacking and vehicle support*).
26 Trace the wiring back from the sensor, noting its correct routing, and disconnect it at the connector.
27 Slacken and remove the retaining bolt and remove the sensor from the engine.
28 On refitting ensure the mating surfaces are clean and dry then fit the sensor and tighten its retaining bolt to the specified torque. Ensure the wiring is correctly routed and securely reconnected then lower the vehicle to the ground.

Electronic control unit (ECU)

29 The ECU is located on the left-hand end of the inlet manifold.
30 Disconnect the battery negative terminal (refer to *Disconnecting the battery* in the Reference Chapter).
31 Release the locking catches, then disconnect the wiring connectors from the ECU.
32 Release the manifold absolute pressure sensor wiring harness from the bracket on the ECU.
33 Undo the retaining bolt and disconnect the ECU earth cable.
34 Detach the fuel pipe bracket then remove the ECU from the inlet manifold.
35 Refitting is the reverse of removal, ensuring the wiring connectors are securely reconnected. **Note:** *Prior to renewing an ECU, the security code must be reset using dedicated diagnostic equipment. Refer to your local Vauxhall dealer or specialist.*

Fuel pump relay

36 Refer to Section 14, paragraphs 37 to 39.

Air conditioning system switch

37 Refer to Section 14, paragraph 40.

DOHC engines

Fuel rail and injectors

Note: *If a faulty injector is suspected, it is worth trying the effect of one of the proprietary injector-cleaning treatments.*

38 Depressurise the fuel system as described in Section 8, then disconnect the battery negative terminal (refer to *Disconnecting the battery* in the Reference Chapter).
39 Remove the oil filler cap, undo the retaining screws, and remove the engine cover.
40 Disconnect the wiring plug from the intake air temperature sensor, and detach the intake trunking from the air cleaner housing and the throttle housing. On Zafira models, it will be necessary to remove the engine compartment seal and water deflector cover from in front of the windscreen, then undo the retaining nuts and bolts, and remove the bulkhead cover plate to allow access to the air intake trunking.
41 Disconnect the engine breather hoses from the camshaft cover.
42 Detach all of the wiring connectors which are associated with the wiring harness plastic tray which runs above the fuel rail. Note the cable routing **(see illustration)**. The items to disconnect are:
Evaporative canister purge valve.
Crankshaft position sensor.
Oil pressure switch.
Idle speed stepper motor.
Coolant temperature sensor.
Throttle position sensor.
Camshaft position sensor.
MAP sensor.
EGR valve.
Ignition module.
Oxygen sensor.
ECU (top connector).
Knock sensor.
Interference suppressor (on Ignition module).
Earth connections on manifold (two).
The grey connector in front of the engine compartment relay box.
43 On X14XE and X16XEL engines, detach the vacuum hose from the fuel pressure regulator on the left-hand end of the fuel rail.
44 Disconnect the supply pipe and, on X14XE and X16XEL engines, the return pipe from the fuel rail or fuel pressure regulator **(see illustration)**. Note that the unions are different sizes.
45 Unscrew the two retaining bolts and remove the fuel rail with the injectors complete with the plastic wiring tray **(see illustration)**.

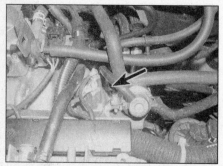

15.42 Earth connections on the inlet manifold (arrowed)

15.44 Fuel pressure regulator supply and return pipes

15.45 Fuel rail retaining bolt

15.50 Fuel pressure regulator clamp

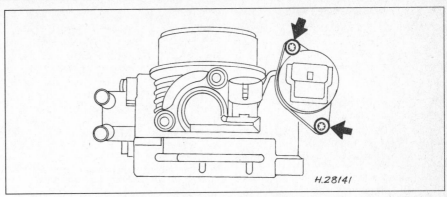

15.56 Idle speed control stepper motor retaining screws (arrowed) – shown with the throttle housing removed

46 If required, the injectors can be separated from the fuel rail by sliding off the relevant retaining clip and withdrawing the injector from the fuel rail. Remove the upper sealing ring from the injector and discard it; all disturbed sealing rings must be renewed.

47 Refitting is a reversal of the removal procedure, noting the following points.

  a) *Renew all disturbed sealing rings and apply a smear of engine oil to them to aid installation.*

  b) *Ease the injector(s) into the fuel rail, ensuring that the sealing ring(s) remain correctly seated, and secure in position with the retaining clips.*

  c) *On refitting the fuel rail, take care not to damage the injectors and ensure that all sealing rings remain in position. Once the fuel rail is correctly seated, tighten its retaining bolts to the specified torque.*

  d) *On completion start the engine and check for fuel leaks.*

Fuel pressure regulator

Note: On 1.4 litre (Z14XE) and 1.6 litre (Z16XE) engines, fuel pressure regulation is a function of the fuel tank pump module. The regulator is located under the fuel pump access cover. The regulator does not appear to be available as a separate part – check with your Vauxhall dealer. To remove the regulator, follow the procedure for fuel pump renewal, as described in Section 9, and disconnect the regulator from the fuel pipes and wiring connector located on the underside of the fuel pump access cover.

48 Undo the two retaining screws and the oil filler cap, and remove the engine cover. Depressurise the fuel system as described in Section 8, then disconnect the battery negative terminal (refer to *Disconnecting the battery* in the Reference Chapter).

49 Detach the vacuum hose from the regulator.

50 Undo the screw and remove the regulator retaining clamp **(see illustration)**.

51 Carefully pull the regulator from the fuel rail along with its sealing rings.

52 Refitting is the reverse of removal, using new sealing rings. On completion start the engine and check for fuel leaks.

Idle speed control stepper motor

Note: On 1.4 litre (Z14XE) and 1.6 litre (Z16XE) engines, there is an electronic accelerator system fitted (no accelerator cable). The throttle valve potentiometer and servo motor are a combined part of the throttle housing. Individual parts for the housing are not available separately and, if defective, it must be renewed as a complete unit. Refer to Section 12 for the throttle housing renewal procedure.

53 Undo the two retaining screws and the oil filler cap, and remove the engine cover.

54 Disconnect the intake air temperature sensor and remove the air intake trunking from the air cleaner housing and the throttle housing. On Zafira models, it will be

necessary to remove the engine compartment seal and water deflector cover from in front of the windscreen, then undo the retaining nuts and bolts, and remove the bulkhead cover plate to allow access to the air intake trunking.

55 Detach the wiring harness plug from the stepper motor.

56 Undo the two screws and remove the motor from the throttle housing **(see illustration)**.

57 Refitting is the reverse of removal, noting the following points.

  a) *Prior to installation, check that the plunger tip does not extend more than 33 mm from the motor mating flange (see illustration 14.16). If necessary, gently push the plunger into the body until it is correctly positioned. Failure to do this could lead to the motor being damaged.*

  b) *Apply locking compound to the motor screws.*

Throttle potentiometer

Note: On 1.4 litre (Z14XE) and 1.6 litre (Z16XE) engines, there is an electronic accelerator system fitted (no accelerator cable). The throttle valve potentiometer and servo motor are a combined part of the throttle housing. Individual parts for the housing are not available separately and, if defective, it must be renewed as a complete unit. Refer to Section 12 for the throttle housing renewal procedure.

58 Undo the two retaining screws and the oil filler cap, and remove the engine cover.

59 Disconnect the intake air temperature sensor and remove the air intake trunking from the air cleaner housing and the throttle housing. On Zafira models, it will be necessary to remove the engine compartment seal and water deflector cover from in front of the windscreen, then undo the retaining nuts and bolts, and remove the bulkhead cover plate to allow access to the air intake trunking.

60 Disconnect the wiring harness plug from the potentiometer.

61 Undo the two retaining screws and remove the potentiometer from the throttle housing **(see illustration)**.

62 On refitting, fit the potentiometer,

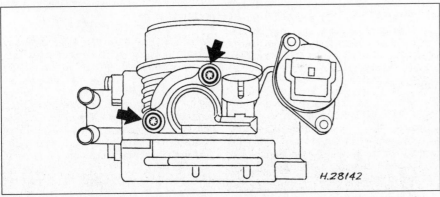

15.61 Throttle potentiometer retaining screws (arrowed) – shown with the throttle housing removed

15.62 Align the throttle potentiometer with the throttle spindle

ensuring it is correctly engaged with the throttle valve spindle. Apply locking compound to the retaining screws and tighten securely. Check the operation of the throttle valve then reconnect the wiring plug and refit the air intake trunking **(see illustration)**.

Coolant temperature sensor

63 The coolant temperature sensor is screwed into the thermostat housing. Refer to Chapter 3 for removal and refitting details.

Intake air temperature sensor

64 The intake air temperature sensor is mounted in the intake duct which connects the air cleaner housing to the inlet manifold.
65 Ensure the ignition is switched off, then disconnect the wiring connector from the sensor.
66 Carefully ease the sensor out of position and remove its sealing grommet from the intake duct. If the sealing grommet shows signs of damage or deterioration it should be renewed.
67 Refitting is the reverse of removal, ensuring the sensor and grommet are correctly located in the duct.

Manifold absolute pressure (MAP) sensor

68 On X14XE and X16XEL engines, the MAP sensor is mounted onto the engine compartment bulkhead, just to the left of the inlet manifold. On Z14XE and Z16XE engines, the MAP sensor is located on the left-hand side of the inlet manifold.
69 On X14XE and X16XEL engines, ensure the ignition is switched off then disconnect the wiring connector and vacuum hose from the sensor. The MAP sensor can then be unclipped and removed from its mounting. On Z14XE and Z16XE engines, undo the two retaining screws and the oil filler cap, and remove the engine cover. Ensure the ignition is switched off then disconnect the wiring connector from the sensor. The MAP sensor can then be unbolted and removed from the manifold.
70 Refitting is the reverse of removal.

Crankshaft sensor

71 On X14XE and X16XEL engines, the sensor is mounted on a bracket at the rear of the right-hand end of the cylinder block and is accessible from underneath the vehicle.

15.73 Crankshaft position sensor

Firmly apply the handbrake, then jack up the front of the car and support it securely on axle stands (see *Jacking and vehicle support*). On Z14XE and Z16XE engines, the sensor is mounted on the front of the cylinder block below the oil filter.
72 Trace the wiring back from the sensor, releasing it from all the relevant clips and ties whilst noting its correct routing. Disconnect the wiring connector so the wiring is free to be removed with the sensor.
73 Unscrew the retaining bolt and remove the sensor from underneath the vehicle **(see illustration)**.
74 Refitting is the reverse of removal, tightening the retaining bolt to the specified torque. Ensure the wiring is correctly routed and retained by all the necessary clips and ties.
75 On X14XE and X16XEL engines, using feeler gauges, check that the clearance between the sensor tip and the crankshaft pulley teeth is 1.0 ± 0.7 mm. If the clearance is not within the specified range, check that the bracket mounting surface is clean and flat with no corrosion.

Camshaft sensor

76 Remove the timing belt upper cover as described in Chapter 2B.
77 Trace the wiring back from the sensor, releasing it from all the relevant clips and ties whilst noting its correct routing. Disconnect the wiring connector so the wiring is free to be removed with the sensor.
78 Unscrew the retaining bolts and remove the sensor from the end of the cylinder head.
79 Refitting is the reverse of removal, apply a little locking compound, and tighten the retaining bolts to the specified torque. Ensure the wiring is correctly routed and retained by all the necessary clips and ties.

Knock sensor

80 The knock sensor is mounted onto the rear of the cylinder block, just to the right of the starter motor, and is accessible from underneath the vehicle. Firmly apply the handbrake, then jack up the front of the car and support it securely on axle stands (see *Jacking and vehicle support*).
81 Trace the wiring back from the sensor, noting its correct routing, and disconnect it at the connector.

82 Slacken and remove the retaining bolt and remove the sensor from the engine.
83 On refitting ensure the mating surfaces are clean and dry then fit the sensor and tighten its retaining bolt to the specified torque. Ensure the wiring is correctly routed and securely reconnected then lower the vehicle to the ground.

Electronic control unit (ECU)

84 Disconnect the battery negative terminal (refer to *Disconnecting the battery* in the Reference Chapter).
85 Undo the two retaining screws and the oil filler cap, and remove the engine cover.
86 Release the retaining clips then disconnect the wiring connectors from the ECU. Undo the three retaining bolts and remove the ECU from the vehicle.
87 Refitting is the reverse of removal, ensuring the wiring connectors are securely reconnected. **Note:** *Prior to renewing an ECU, the security code must be reset using dedicated diagnostic equipment. Refer to your local Vauxhall dealer or specialist.*

Fuel pump relay

88 Refer to Section 14, paragraphs 37 to 39.

Air conditioning system switch

89 Refer to Section 14, paragraph 40.

---

16 Simtec 70 and 71 multi-point injection system components – removal and refitting

⚠️ *Warning: Refer to the warning note in Section 1 before proceeding.*

Fuel rail and injectors

Note: *Before condemning an injector, it is worth trying the effect of one of the proprietary injector-cleaning treatments.*
1 Undo the retaining screws, remove the oil filler cap, and remove the engine cover.
2 Depressurise the fuel system as described in Section 8, then disconnect the battery negative terminal (refer to *Disconnecting the battery* in the Reference Chapter).
3 Disconnect the wiring connectors from the hot film mass airflow meter.
4 Release the retaining clips then disconnect the intake duct from the air cleaner and throttle housing and remove the duct assembly, complete with hot film mass airflow meter, from the engine compartment, freeing it from the wiring harness. On Zafira models, it will be necessary to remove the engine compartment seal and water deflector cover from in front of the windscreen, then undo the retaining nuts and bolts, and remove the bulkhead cover plate to allow access to the air intake trunking.
5 Release the retaining clips and disconnect the breather hoses from the rear of the camshaft cover and throttle housing.
6 Detach all wiring connectors which are

16.7a ECU location

16.7b Engine wiring loom plug strip retaining bolt

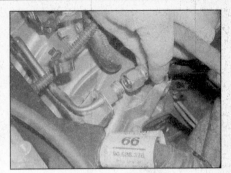

16.8 Fuel supply pipe

connected to the plug strip located on top of the injectors. Release all the plug strip wiring loom retaining clips.

7 Undo the bolts securing the plug strip earth connections on the right-hand end of the inlet manifold, and the engine ECU at the left-hand end of the manifold. Undo the plug strip retaining bolt **(see illustrations)**.

8 Unscrew the union nut(s) and disconnect the fuel hose(s) from the fuel rail. Whilst the unions are being slackened, retain the fuel rail adapters with an open-ended spanner **(see illustration)**.

9 Slacken and remove the two retaining bolts then carefully ease the fuel rail and injector assembly, complete with plug strip and loom, out of position and remove it from the manifold. Remove the lower sealing rings from the injectors and discard them; they must be renewed whenever they are disturbed **(see illustration)**.

10 Carefully release the retaining clips and lift the plug strip assembly away from the top of the injectors; the wiring connectors are an integral part of the plug strip **(see illustration)**.

11 Slide off the relevant retaining clip and withdraw the injector from the fuel rail. Remove the upper sealing ring from the injector and discard it; all disturbed sealing rings must be renewed.

12 Refitting is a reversal of the removal procedure, noting the following points.
  a) Renew all disturbed sealing rings and apply a smear of engine oil to them to aid installation.
  b) Ease the injector(s) into the fuel rail, ensuring that the sealing ring(s) remain correctly seated, and secure in position with the retaining clips.
  c) On refitting the fuel rail, take care not to damage the injectors and ensure that all sealing rings remain in position. Once the fuel rail is correctly seated, tighten its retaining bolts to the specified torque.
  d) Once the fuel rail has been refitted, the plug strip can be pressed onto the top of the injectors. Ensure that the plug strip connectors engage fully with the injectors **(see illustration)**.
  e) On completion start the engine and check for fuel leaks.

Fuel pressure regulator

Note: On all 1.8 litre engines, fuel pressure regulation is a function of the fuel tank pump module. The regulator is located under the fuel pump access cover. The regulator does not appear to be available as a separate part – check with your Vauxhall dealer. To remove the regulator, follow the procedure for fuel pump renewal, as described in Section 9, and disconnect the regulator from the fuel pipes and wiring connector located on the underside of the fuel pump access cover.

13 On 2.0 litre engines, remove the engine cover, depressurise the fuel system as described in Section 8, then disconnect the battery negative terminal (refer to *Disconnecting the battery* in the Reference Chapter).

14 Detach the vacuum hose from the regulator. Undo the screw and remove the regulator retaining clamp **(see illustration)**.

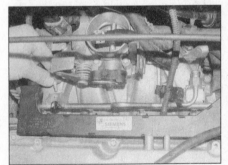

16.9 Undo the fuel rail bolts

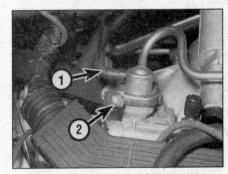

16.12 Ensure that the connectors engage fully onto the injectors

15 Carefully pull the regulator from the fuel rail along with its sealing rings.

16 Refitting is the reverse of removal, using new sealing rings. On completion start the engine and check for fuel leaks.

Throttle valve adjuster

1.8 litre engines

17 The engine idle speed (X18XE1 engines) and throttle valve position (Z18XE and Z18XEL engines) is controlled by the ECU by means of a throttle valve adjuster. The throttle potentiometer is integrated into the adjuster, which is part of the throttle housing. Individual parts for the housing are not available separately and, if defective, the throttle valve adjuster must be renewed as a complete assembly with the throttle housing. Refer to Section 12 for the throttle housing renewal procedure.

16.10 Lever out the spring clip and pull apart the connector

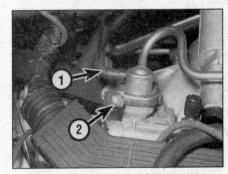

16.14 Fuel pressure regulator vacuum hose (1) and retaining clamp (2)

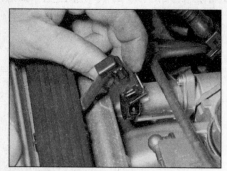

16.19a Disconnect the wiring connector . . .

16.19b . . . then undo the retaining screws (one hidden) and remove the idle speed control strpper motor from the throttle housing

16.26 Hot film mass airflow meter

Idle speed control stepper motor

2.0 litre engines

18 Disconnect the wiring connectors from the hot film mass airflow meter. Release the retaining clip and disconnect the breather hose from the rear of the camshaft cover then slacken the retaining clips and remove the intake duct assembly from the engine compartment. On Zafira models, it will be necessary to remove the engine compartment seal and water deflector cover from in front of the windscreen, then undo the retaining nuts and bolts, and remove the bulkhead cover plate to allow access to the air intake trunking.

19 Disconnect the wiring connector then undo the two retaining screws and remove the motor assembly from the side of the throttle housing (see illustrations). Remove the gasket and discard it; a new one should be used on refitting.

20 Refitting is the reverse of removal using a new gasket.

Throttle potentiometer

21 On 1.8 litre engines, the function of the throttle potentiometer is incorporated within the throttle valve adjuster. On 2.0 litre engines, remove the throttle housing as described in Section 12.

22 Slacken and remove the two retaining screws then remove the potentiometer from the housing.

23 Refitting is the reverse of removal, making sure the potentiometer is correctly engaged with the throttle valve spindle.

Coolant temperature sensor

24 The coolant temperature sensor is screwed into the housing on the left-hand end of the cylinder head. Refer to Chapter 3, for removal and refitting details.

Intake air temperature sensor

25 The function of the intake air temperature sensor is incorporated within the hot film mass airflow meter. Therefore, no removal or refitting procedure is applicable.

Hot film mass airflow meter

26 Ensure the ignition is switched off then disconnect the wiring connector from the hot film mass airflow meter (see illustration).

27 Slacken the retaining clips then disconnect the intake ducts and remove the airflow meter from the vehicle. On Zafira models, it will be necessary to remove the engine compartment seal and water deflector cover from in front of the windscreen, then undo the retaining nuts and bolts, and remove the bulkhead cover plate to allow access to the air intake trunking. Inspect the meter for signs of damage and renew if necessary.

28 Refitting is the reverse of removal, ensuring the intake ducts are correctly engaged with the meter recesses.

Crankshaft sensor

1.8 litre engines

29 On X18XE1 engines, the sensor is mounted on a bracket at the rear of the right-hand end of the cylinder block and is accessible from underneath the vehicle. Firmly apply the handbrake, then jack up the front of the car and support it securely on axle stands (see Jacking and vehicle support). On Z18XE and Z18XEL engines, the sensor is mounted on the front of the cylinder block below the oil filter.

30 Trace the wiring back from the sensor, releasing it from all the relevant clips and ties whilst noting its correct routing. Disconnect the wiring connector so the wiring is free to be removed with the sensor.

31 Unscrew the retaining bolt and remove the sensor from underneath the vehicle (see illustration).

32 Refitting is the reverse of removal, tightening the retaining bolt to the specified

torque. Ensure the wiring is correctly routed and retained by all the necessary clips and ties.

2.0 litre engines

33 Remove the air cleaner housing, with reference to Section 2.

34 On models with air conditioning, undo the retaining bolt and remove the engine oil dipstick guide tube from the front of the cylinder block.

35 Trace the wiring back from the sensor, releasing it from all the relevant clips and ties whilst noting its correct routing. At the rear of the cylinder head, disconnect the wiring connector so the wiring is free to be removed with the sensor.

36 Undo the single retaining screw and remove the sensor from the block. Discard the seal ring.

37 Refitting is a reversal of removal. Fit a new seal ring to the sensor and smear a little clean engine oil on the ring before the sensor is refitted to the block. Tighten the sensor retaining screw to the specified torque.

Camshaft sensor

38 On 1.8 litre engines, remove the oil filler cap, undo the retaining screws, and remove the engine cover. On 2.0 litre engines, undo the retaining screws and remove the spark plug cover from the top of the camshaft cover.

39 Ensure the ignition is switched off then disconnect the wiring connector from the camshaft sensor.

40 Remove the timing belt upper cover as described in Chapter 2B.

41 Unscrew the retaining bolts and remove the camshaft sensor from the top of the cylinder head (see illustration).

16.31 Crankshaft sensor – 1.8 litre engines

16.41 Remove the camshaft sensor – note the location dowel

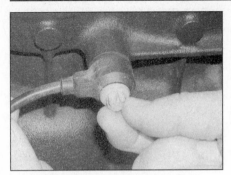

16.46 Knock sensor retaining bolt

16.51a ECU retaining bolts – 1.8 litre engines

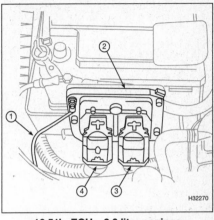

16.51b ECU – 2.0 litre engines

1	Earth connection	3	ECU connector
2	ECU	4	ECU connector

42 Refitting is the reverse of removal. Apply a little locking compound, tighten the sensor retaining bolts to the specified torque.

Knock sensor

43 The knock sensor is mounted on the rear of the cylinder block and is accessible from underneath the vehicle. Firmly apply the handbrake, then jack up the front of the car and support it securely on axle stands (see *Jacking and vehicle support*).
44 On 2.0 litre engines remove the starter motor as described in Chapter 5A.
45 Trace the wiring back from the sensor, releasing it from all the relevant clips and ties whilst noting its correct routing, and disconnect the wiring plug.
46 Slacken and remove the retaining bolt and remove the sensor from the engine **(see illustration)**.
47 On refitting, ensure the mating surfaces are clean and dry then fit the sensor and tighten its retaining bolt to the specified torque. Ensure the wiring is correctly routed and securely reconnected then clip the wiring cover assembly back into position. On 2.0 litre engines, refit the starter motor as described in Chapter 5A.

Electronic control unit (ECU)

48 Disconnect the battery negative terminal (refer to *Disconnecting the battery* in the Reference Chapter).
49 On 1.8 litre engines, the ECU is bolted directly onto the left-hand side of the inlet manifold. Whilst on 2.0 litre engines, the ECU is located next to the battery.
50 Release the retaining clips then disconnect the wiring connectors from the ECU. Detach the earth connection from the ECU frame. On 1.8 litre engines, release the knock sensor wiring harness plug from the bracket on the ECU frame, but do not disconnect it.
51 Undo the three retaining bolts and remove the ECU from the vehicle. Note that the lower retaining bolt also secures a wiring plug support bracket **(see illustrations)**.
52 Refitting is the reverse of removal, ensuring the wiring connectors are securely reconnected. **Note:** *Prior to renewing an ECU, the security code must be reset using*

dedicated diagnostic equipment. Refer to your local Vauxhall dealer or specialist.

Fuel pump relay

53 Refer to Section 14, paragraphs 37 to 39.

Air conditioning system switch

54 Refer to Section 14, paragraph 40.

Inlet manifold valve switching solenoid

55 The solenoid which operates the inlet manifold valve assemblies is mounted on the left-hand end of the manifold **(see illustration)**.
56 Ensure the ignition is switched off then disconnect the wiring connector from the solenoid.
57 Disconnect both vacuum hoses, undo the retaining screw, then remove the solenoid from the manifold.
58 Refitting is the reverse of removal.

Inlet manifold valve vacuum diaphragm unit

59 The inlet manifold valve vacuum diaphragm unit is fitted to the left-hand end of the manifold **(see illustration 16.55)**.
60 On 1.8 litre engines, remove the ECU as described in paragraphs 48 to 51. On 2.0 litre engines, remove the inlet manifold as described in Section 18.
61 On 1.8 litre engines, disconnect the vacuum hose, unclip the diaphragm rod from its balljoint, undo the two retaining bolts and remove the unit from the manifold. On 2.0 litre engines, undo the nut that secures the diaphragm rod to the valve

16.55 Inlet manifold valve switching solenoid and diaphragm

actuating arm, drift out the pin securing the diaphragm housing to the inlet manifold, and disconnect the vacuum hose.
62 Refitting is the reverse of removal.

17 GMPT – E15 multi-point injection system components – removal and refitting

⚠️ *Warning: Refer to the warning note in Section 1 before proceeding.*

Fuel rail and injectors

Note: *Before condemning an injector, it is worth trying the effect of one of the proprietary injector cleaning treatments.*
1 Unclip the engine cover, depressurise the fuel system as described in Section 8, then disconnect the battery negative terminal (refer to *Disconnecting the battery* in the Reference Chapter).
2 Disconnect the wiring connector from the air temperature sensor in the air intake pipe.
3 Release the retaining clip and disconnect the breather hose from the camshaft cover.
4 Release the retaining clips then disconnect the intake pipe from the air cleaner assembly and throttle housing and remove the pipe assembly from the engine compartment, detach the vacuum pipe(s) from the intake pipe on removal.
5 Unscrew the union nuts and disconnect the fuel pipes from the fuel rail, release the fuel pipes from the retaining clips and move to one side.
6 Release the wiring harness plugs and disconnect them from the injectors, the ignition module and the EGR valve.
7 Unclip the coolant hose from the top of the wiring trough, undo the two retaining nuts and carefully unclip the wiring trough and move it to one side.
8 Undo the wiring trough bracket retaining nut and bolt and move the bracket and wiring harness to one side.
9 Slacken and remove the two retaining bolts

17.10 Release the retaining clip to remove the injector from the fuel rail

17.14a Disconnect the vacuum pipe, undo the bolts . . .

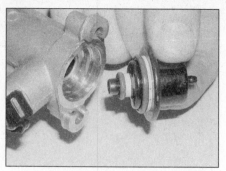

17.14b . . . and remove the pressure regulator from the fuel rail

then carefully ease the fuel rail and injector assembly out of position and remove it from the manifold. Remove the lower sealing rings from the injectors and discard them; they must be renewed whenever they are disturbed.

10 Slide off the relevant retaining clip and withdraw the injector from the fuel rail. Remove the upper sealing ring from the injector and discard it; all disturbed sealing rings must be renewed **(see illustration)**.

11 Refitting is a reversal of the removal procedure, noting the following points.

 a) Renew all disturbed sealing rings and apply a smear of engine oil to them to aid installation.

 b) Ease the injector(s) into the fuel rail, ensuring that the sealing ring(s) remain correctly seated, and secure in position with the retaining clips.

 c) On refitting the fuel rail, take care not to damage the injectors and ensure that all sealing rings remain in position. Once the fuel rail is correctly seated, tighten its retaining bolts to the specified torque.

 d) Ensure that all the wiring connectors engage fully to make a good connection.

 e) On completion start the engine and check for fuel leaks.

Fuel pressure regulator

12 Unclip the engine cover, depressurise the fuel system as described in Section 8, then disconnect the battery negative terminal (refer to *Disconnecting the battery* in the Reference Chapter).

13 Disconnect the vacuum line from the pressure regulator and from the inlet manifold.

14 Slacken and remove the two retaining bolts, then carefully ease the pressure regulator from the end of the fuel rail along with its sealing rings **(see illustrations)**.

15 Refitting is the reverse of removal, using new sealing rings. On completion start the engine and check for fuel leaks.

Accelerator pedal position sensor

16 From inside the vehicle, unscrew the fasteners and remove the lower trim panel from underneath the driver's side of the facia to gain access to the accelerator pedal.

17 Disconnect the wiring connector from the pedal position sensor by sliding it to the rear of the vehicle.

18 Undo the retaining bolts and remove the pedal position sensor from the pedal assembly.

Throttle valve servo motor

19 The servo motor is a combined part of the throttle housing. Individual parts for the housing are not available separately and, if defective, it must be renewed as a complete unit. Refer to Section 12 for the throttle housing renewal procedure.

Throttle valve potentiometer

20 The throttle valve potentiometer is a combined part of the throttle housing. Individual parts for the housing are not available separately and, if defective, it must be renewed as a complete unit. Refer to Section 12 for the throttle housing renewal procedure.

Coolant temperature sensor

21 The coolant temperature sensor is screwed into the thermostat housing. Refer to Chapter 3 for removal and refitting details.

Intake air temperature sensor

22 The intake air temperature sensor is mounted in the intake pipe which connects the air cleaner housing to the inlet manifold.

23 Ensure the ignition is switched off, then disconnect the wiring connector from the sensor.

24 Carefully ease the sensor out of position

17.31a Disconnect the wiring connector from the MAP sensor . . .

(note position for refitting) and remove its sealing grommet from the intake pipe. If the sealing grommet shows signs of damage or deterioration it should be renewed.

25 Refitting is the reverse of removal, ensuring the sensor and grommet are correctly located in the intake pipe.

Manifold absolute pressure (MAP) sensor

26 Unclip the engine cover, depressurise the fuel system as described in Section 8, then disconnect the battery negative terminal (refer to *Disconnecting the battery* in the Reference Chapter).

27 Disconnect the wiring connector from the air temperature sensor in the air intake pipe.

28 Release the retaining clip and disconnect the breather hose from the camshaft cover.

29 Release the retaining clips then disconnect the intake pipe from the air cleaner assembly and throttle housing and remove the pipe assembly from the engine compartment, detach the vacuum pipe(s) from the intake pipe on removal.

30 Disconnect the wiring connector from the throttle housing, then undo the securing bolts/stud and remove the throttle housing unit from the inlet manifold. Note the position of the cable retaining clip on the securing stud.

31 Disconnect the wiring connector from the MAP sensor, turn the sensor 1/4 of a turn clockwise and carefully pull out of the inlet manifold **(see illustrations)**.

32 Refitting is the reverse of removal, using a new sealing ring.

17.31b . . . and turn clockwise 1/4 of a turn, to release from the manifold

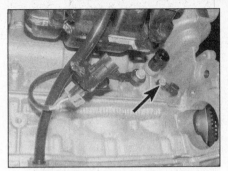

17.35 Unbolt the crankshaft sensor (arrowed) – starter removed

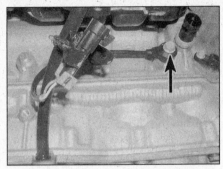

17.39 Unbolt the knock sensor (arrowed) – starter removed

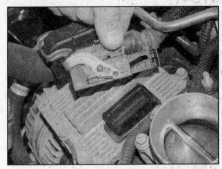

17.45 Releasing the wiring harness plugs from the engine ECU

Crankshaft sensor

33 The sensor is mounted on the front of the cylinder block above the starter motor. **Note:** *It may be necessary to remove the starter motor to gain better access to the sensor (see Chapter 5A).*

34 Trace the wiring back from the sensor, releasing it from all the relevant clips and ties whilst noting its correct routing. Disconnect the wiring connector from the sensor.

35 Unscrew the retaining bolt and remove the sensor from the cylinder block **(see illustration)**.

36 Refitting is the reverse of removal, tightening the retaining bolt to the specified torque. Ensure the wiring is correctly routed and retained by all the necessary clips and ties.

Knock sensor

37 The sensor is mounted on the front of the cylinder block above the starter motor. **Note:** *It may be necessary to remove the starter motor to gain better access to the sensor.*

38 Disconnect the wiring block connector at the bottom of the oil dipstick tube, so the wiring is free to be removed with the sensor.

39 Unscrew the retaining bolt and remove the sensor from the cylinder block **(see illustration)**.

40 On refitting ensure the mating surfaces are clean and dry then fit the sensor and tighten its retaining bolt to the specified torque. Ensure the wiring is correctly routed and retained by all the necessary clips and ties.

Electronic control unit (ECU)

41 Unclip the engine cover, depressurise the fuel system as described in Section 8, then disconnect the battery negative terminal (refer to *Disconnecting the battery* in the Reference Chapter).

42 Disconnect the wiring connector from the air temperature sensor in the air intake pipe.

43 Release the retaining clip and disconnect the breather hose from the camshaft cover.

44 Release the retaining clips then disconnect the intake pipe from the air cleaner assembly and throttle housing and remove the pipe assembly from the engine compartment, detach the vacuum pipe(s) from the intake pipe on removal.

45 Release the two wiring harness plugs from the ECU, then undo the securing bolts and remove the unit from the inlet manifold **(see illustration)**. Note the position of the earth cable on one of the securing bolts.

46 Refitting is the reverse of removal, ensuring the wiring connectors are securely reconnected. **Note:** *Prior to renewing an ECU, the security code must be reset using dedicated diagnostic equipment. Refer to your local Vauxhall dealer or specialist.*

Fuel pump relay

47 Refer to Section 14, paragraphs 37 to 39.

Air conditioning system switch

48 Refer to Section 14, paragraph 40.

---

18 Inlet manifold – removal and refitting

SOHC engines – X16SZR

Removal

Note: *New manifold nuts will be required on refitting.*

1 Depressurise the fuel system as described in Section 8, then disconnect the battery negative terminal (refer to *Disconnecting the battery* in the Reference Chapter).

2 Remove the auxiliary drivebelt then drain the cooling system as described in Chapters 1 and 3.

3 Remove the air cleaner assembly and intake duct as described in Section 2.

4 Disconnect the vacuum and breather hoses from the throttle body cover then undo the retaining screws and remove the cover and sealing ring from the top of the throttle body.

5 Disconnect the wiring connectors from the throttle potentiometer, the idle control stepper motor, the throttle body injector, the coolant temperature sender, the exhaust gas recirculation (EGR) valve, the fuel tank vent valve and the manifold absolute pressure (MAP) sensor. Note the correct routing of the wiring then free it from all the relevant clips and ties. Unclip the wiring duct from the camshaft cover and position it clear of the inlet manifold.

6 Undo and remove the bolts securing the alternator support bracket to the inlet manifold. Release the alternator from its shackle, and swing the alternator to the rear.

7 Slacken the unions nuts and disconnect the fuel hoses from the side of the throttle body. Whilst slackening the nuts, retain the throttle body adapters with an open-ended spanner.

8 Unclip the throttle linkage at the throttle spindle, and undo the two bolts and remove the accelerator cable support bracket from the manifold, complete with cable **(see illustration)**.

9 Disconnect the breather/vacuum hoses from the throttle body (as applicable) noting each hose's correct fitted location. Disconnect the vacuum hose from the fuel tank vent valve.

10 Slacken the retaining clip and disconnect the coolant hose from the rear of the manifold.

11 Depress the retaining clip and disconnect the braking system servo unit hose from the manifold **(see illustration)**.

18.8 Remove the accelerator cable bracket

18.11 Disconnect the brake servo hose

12 Check that all the necessary vacuum/ breather hoses have been disconnected then slacken and remove the manifold retaining nuts.

13 Remove the manifold from the engine and recover the manifold gasket, noting which way around it is fitted.

Refitting

14 Refitting is the reverse of removal bearing in mind the following points.

a) Prior to refitting, check the manifold studs and renew any that are worn or damaged. New manifold retaining nuts must be used.

b) Ensure the manifold and cylinder mating surfaces are clean and dry and fit the new gasket. Refit the manifold and tighten the retaining nuts evenly and progressively to the specified torque.

c) Ensure that all relevant hoses are reconnected to their original positions, and are securely held (where necessary) by their retaining clips.

d) Tighten the fuel hose and vacuum servo hose union nuts to their specified torque settings (where applicable).

e) Refit the auxiliary drivebelt and refill the cooling system as described in Chapters 1 and 3.

SOHC engines – Z16SE

Removal

Note: New manifold nuts will be required on refitting.

15 Depressurise the fuel system as described in Section 8, then disconnect the battery negative terminal (refer to *Disconnecting the battery* in the Reference Chapter).

16 Remove the auxiliary drivebelt then drain the cooling system as described in Chapters 1 and 3.

17 Remove the air cleaner assembly and intake duct as described in Section 2.

18 Disconnect the breather/vacuum hoses from the throttle housing (as applicable) noting each ones correct fitted location. Disconnect the vacuum hose from the fuel tank vent valve.

19 Slacken the retaining clips and disconnect the coolant hoses from the throttle housing.

20 Depress the retaining clip and disconnect the braking system servo unit hose from the manifold.

21 Release the locking catches, then disconnect the wiring connectors from the engine management ECU.

22 Release the manifold absolute pressure sensor wiring harness from the bracket on the ECU.

23 Undo the retaining bolt and disconnect the ECU earth cable.

24 Disconnect the wiring connectors from the exhaust gas recirculation (EGR) valve, manifold absolute pressure sensor, oxygen sensor, camshaft sensor, throttle housing and

18.35 Lower alternator mounting bolt

fuel injectors. Detach the wiring harness support bracket from the manifold and move the wiring harness to one side.

25 Undo and remove the bolts securing the alternator support bracket to the inlet manifold. Release the alternator from its shackle, and swing the alternator to the rear.

26 Slacken the retaining clips and disconnect the coolant hose from the inlet manifold.

27 Disconnect the fuel supply pipe from the fuel rail and release it from its support bracket.

28 Check that all the necessary vacuum/ breather hoses have been disconnected then slacken and remove the manifold retaining nuts.

29 Remove the manifold from the engine and recover the manifold gasket.

Refitting

30 Refitting is the reverse of removal bearing in mind the following points.

a) Prior to refitting, check the manifold studs and renew any that are worn or damaged. New manifold retaining nuts must be used.

b) Ensure the manifold and cylinder mating surfaces are clean and dry and fit the new gasket. Refit the manifold and tighten the retaining nuts evenly and progressively to the specified torque.

c) Ensure that all relevant hoses are reconnected to their original positions, and are securely held (where necessary) by their retaining clips.

d) Refit the auxiliary drivebelt and refill the cooling system as described in Chapters 1 and 3.

1.4 and 1.6 litre DOHC engines

Removal

Note: If only the upper section of the manifold is to be removed carry out the operations described in paragraphs 31 to 45.

31 Remove the oil filler cap then undo the retaining screws and lift off the cover from the top of the engine. Refit the oil filler cap. Drain the cooling system with reference to Chapter 3.

32 Remove the air cleaner assembly and intake ducting as described in Section 2.

18.36 Remove the manifold-to-cylinder block bracket

33 Using a spanner on the auxiliary drivebelt tensioner pulley central bolt, hold the tensioner against the spring pressure, and disengage the belt from the pulleys.

34 Undo the retaining bolts and remove the alternator mounting bracket from the right-hand end of the manifold.

35 Slacken the lower alternator fastening bolt and twist the alternator rearwards **(see illustration)**.

36 Remove the support bracket between the inlet manifold and the cylinder block **(see illustration)**.

37 Detach the engine vent hose from the camshaft cover.

38 Remove the fuel injectors and fuel rail assembly, as described in Section 15.

39 Where applicable, free the accelerator cable from the throttle housing and mounting bracket (see Section 4).

40 Disconnect the wiring connectors from the throttle valve adjuster, or idle speed stepper motor and throttle potentiometer, as applicable.

41 Release the retaining clip and disconnect the braking system vacuum servo hose from the manifold.

42 Disconnect the MAP sensor vacuum hose.

43 Disconnect the fuel tank vent hose from the throttle housing **(see illustration)**.

44 Release the retaining clips and disconnect the coolant pipes from the throttle housing.

45 Undo the five manifold-to-flange retaining bolts and remove the manifold **(see**

18.43 Fuel tank vent hose

18.45 Undo the five manifold-to-flange retaining bolts

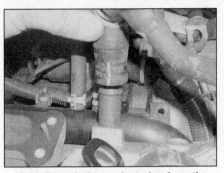

18.46 Detach the coolant pipe from the left-hand end of the manifold flange

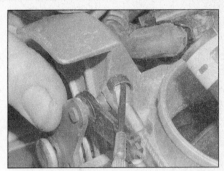

18.54a Accelerator cable retaining clip

illustration). No further dismantling of the manifold is recommended.

46 To remove the manifold flange, first detach the coolant hose from the left-hand end of the flange **(see illustration)**.

47 Slacken and remove the nine retaining nuts then manoeuvre the manifold flange away from the cylinder head and out of the engine compartment. It will be necessary to gently push the coolant pipe at the rear of the cylinder head downwards a little, to allow the manifold flange to clear the mounting studs.

Refitting

48 Refitting is the reverse of removal bearing in mind the following points.
   a) *Prior to refitting, check the manifold studs and renew any that are worn or damaged.*
   b) *Ensure the manifold flange and cylinder mating surfaces are clean and dry and fit the new gasket. Fit the manifold flange and tighten the retaining nuts and bolts evenly and progressively to the specified torque.*
   c) *Fit the rear section of the manifold using a new gasket and tighten its retaining bolts to the specified torque.*
   d) *Ensure that all relevant hoses are reconnected to their original positions, and are securely held (where necessary) by their retaining clips.*
   e) *Tighten the fuel hose union nuts to their specified torque settings.*
   f) *Refill the cooling system as described in Chapter 3.*
   g) *On completion, adjust the accelerator*

cable as described in Section 4 (where applicable).

1.8 and 2.0 litre DOHC engines

Removal

Note: *New manifold nuts will be required on refitting.*

49 Remove the auxiliary drivebelt and drain the coolant system as described in Chapters 1 and 3.

50 Depressurise the fuel system as described in Section 8, then disconnect the battery negative terminal (refer to *Disconnecting the battery* in the Reference Chapter).

51 Remove the oil filler cap, undo the retaining screws, and remove the engine cover.

52 Disconnect the wiring connector from the hot film mass airflow meter.

53 Release the retaining clips and detach the air intake trunking, complete with hot film mass airflow meter from the air cleaner housing and the throttle housing. On Zafira models, it will be necessary to remove the engine compartment seal and water deflector cover from in front of the windscreen, then undo the retaining nuts and bolts, and remove the bulkhead cover plate to allow access to the air intake trunking.

54 On models with an accelerator cable, remove the retaining clip, detach the cable from the throttle lever balljoint and unclip the cable from its mounting bracket. On models with cruise control it will also be necessary to

detach the cruise control cable. The cruise control cable end fitting is secured to the throttle lever balljoint by a circlip **(see illustrations)**.

55 Undo the retaining bolts and free the cable mounting bracket from the throttle housing.

56 Release the retaining clips and remove the engine vent hose from the camshaft cover to the throttle housing.

57 Disconnect the coolant hoses from the throttle housing **(see illustration)**. Detach the coolant pipe from the camshaft cover, and left-hand end of the manifold, and place to one side.

58 Detach the fuel tank vent valve hose from the throttle housing.

59 On 2.0 litre engines, disconnect the wiring connectors from the throttle potentiometer and the idle air control valve. On 1.8 litre engines, disconnect the throttle valve adjuster wiring plug.

60 Disconnect any remaining vacuum/breather hoses from the throttle housing, noting the fitted locations.

61 On 1.8 litre engines, slacken the lower alternator mounting bolt, and remove the upper mounting bolt. Unscrew the retaining bolts and remove the alternator support bracket from the inlet manifold and cylinder head **(see illustration)**. On 2.0 litre engines, remove the alternator support bracket from the inlet manifold, and the bracket from the alternator to the coolant flange and inlet manifold. Twist the alternator rearwards.

62 Undo the retaining bolts and remove the

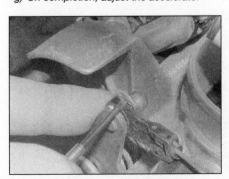

18.54b Cruise control cable circlip

18.57 Detach the coolant hoses from the throttle housing

18.61 Alternator support bracket – note the earth connection

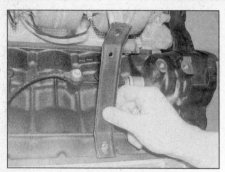

18.62 Unbolt the manifold support bracket

18.65 Remove the injectors complete with fuel rail and plug strip

18.66 Disconnect the brake servo vacuum hose

support bracket from the base of the manifold **(see illustration)**.

63 On 1.8 litre engines, slacken the union nut and disconnect the fuel hose from the fuel rail. Whilst slackening the nut, retain the fuel rail adapter with an open-ended spanner. On 2.0 litre engines, detach the fuel return pipe from the fuel pressure regulator, and the supply pipe from the fuel rail.

64 Disconnect the wiring connectors from the crankshaft sensor, manifold valve switchover solenoid, and all wiring plugs connected to the plug strip above the injectors. Undo the plug strip retaining bolt at its left-hand end. On 2.0 litre engines, remove the spark plug cover and disconnect the wiring harness plug from the camshaft sensor.

65 Unscrew the bolts securing the fuel rail to the inlet manifold, and remove the injectors, complete with fuel rail and plug strip **(see illustration)**.

66 Depress the retaining clip and disconnect the braking system servo unit hose from the manifold. Disconnect all remaining vacuum/breather hoses from the manifold, noting each ones correct fitted location **(see illustration)**.

67 Disconnect the heater hose from the inlet manifold.

68 Undo the retaining bolts and remove the rear engine transport shackle from the cylinder head **(see illustration)**.

69 Unscrew the Torx screws (1.8 litre engines) or nuts (2.0 litre engines), and

remove the throttle housing from the inlet manifold.

70 On 2.0 litre engines with manual transmission, release the retaining clip and disconnect the clutch pressure pipe from the master cylinder. On 1.8 litre engines, disconnect the remaining connector, undo the three retaining bolts, and lift the engine ECU from the inlet manifold **(see illustration 16.51a)**.

71 Slacken and remove the retaining nuts and bolts and manoeuvre the manifold assembly away from the engine. Remove the gasket and discard it **(see illustrations)**. **Note:** *The manifold assembly must be treated as a sealed unit; do not attempt to dismantle it, as no components, other than the switchover diaphragm and solenoid, are available separately.*

Refitting

72 Refitting is the reverse of removal noting the following.

a) *Prior to refitting, check the manifold studs and renew any that are worn or damaged. New manifold retaining bolts must be used.*

b) *Ensure the manifold and cylinder mating surfaces are clean and dry and fit the new gasket. Refit the manifold and tighten the retaining nuts and bolts evenly and progressively to the specified torque.*

c) *Ensure that all relevant hoses are*

reconnected to their original positions, and are securely held (where necessary) by their retaining clips.

d) *Check the clutch operation, and if necessary bleed the clutch hydraulic system as described in Chapter 6.*

e) *Tighten the fuel hose and vacuum servo hose union nuts to their specified torque settings (where applicable).*

f) *Refit the auxiliary drivebelt as described in Chapter 1.*

g) *On completion, adjust the accelerator cable as described in Section 4.*

2.2 litre DOHC engines

Removal

73 Remove the fuel rail and injectors as described in Section 17.

74 Release the two wiring harness plugs from the engine electronic control unit, then undo the securing bolts and remove the control unit from the inlet manifold. Note the position of the earth cable on one of the securing bolts.

75 Detach the fuel tank vent valve hose from the inlet manifold.

76 Disconnect the wiring connector from the throttle housing and the MAP sensor.

77 Remove the engine oil dipstick, then undo the bolt securing the dipstick guide tube to the manifold.

78 Release the retaining clip for the exhaust

18.68 Detach the engine transport shackle

18.71a Lift the inlet manifold away . . .

18.71b . . . and renew the gasket

18.78 Release the retaining clip and remove the EGR pipe from the inlet manifold

18.79 Remove the bracket and undo the studs (arrowed) to remove the EGR pipe from the engine

gas recirculation (EGR) pipe, and disconnect it from the inlet manifold **(see illustration)**.

79 Unclip the brake vacuum line and remove the securing nuts from the bracket on the EGR pipe to cylinder head retaining studs. Undo the two studs and remove the EGR pipe from the engine **(see illustration)**.

80 Firmly apply the handbrake, then jack up the front of the car and support it securely on axle stands (see *Jacking and vehicle support*). Remove the splash guard from the bottom of the engine compartment.

81 Suitably support the radiator, then unbolt the bottom mounting brackets from the subframe. Slide the brackets with rubbers from the extensions on the bottom of the radiator.

82 Release the adjacent wiring harness, then withdraw the engine oil dipstick guide tube from the sump.

83 Release the wiring harness from the lower part of the inlet manifold and the knock sensor wiring block connector from its retaining clip.

84 On models with air conditioning, using a spanner on the auxiliary drivebelt tensioner pulley central bolt, hold the tensioner against the spring pressure, and disengage the belt from the pulleys. Undo the three air conditioning compressor retaining bolts, and support the compressor clear of the manifold. Do not disconnect the refrigerant lines.

85 Unbolt the air intake resonator from the front crossmember and withdraw the resonator toward the timing chain end of the engine.

86 Slacken and remove the retaining nuts and bolts and manoeuvre the manifold assembly away from the engine.

Refitting

87 Refitting is the reverse of removal noting the following.
   a) Prior to refitting, check the manifold studs and renew any that are worn or damaged.
   b) Ensure the manifold and cylinder head mating surfaces are clean and dry and fit new gaskets. Refit the manifold and tighten the retaining nuts and bolts evenly and progressively to the specified torque.
   c) Refit the fuel rail and injectors as described in Section 17.
   d) Ensure that all relevant hoses are reconnected to their original positions,

and are securely held (where necessary) by their retaining clips.
   e) Tighten all fastenings to their specified torque settings, where given.
   f) Refit the auxiliary drivebelt (where removed) as described in Chapter 1.

19 Exhaust manifold –
removal and refitting

Note: *New manifold nuts will be required on refitting.*

SOHC engines

Removal

1 Trace the wiring back from the oxygen sensor and disconnect its wiring connector. Free the wiring from all the necessary clips and ties so the sensor is free to be removed with the manifold.

2 Remove the exhaust system front pipe as described in Section 20.

3 Pull the plug caps off spark plugs, release the HT cable guide from the camshaft cover and position the leads to one side. Unscrew the centre spark plug heat shields and remove them from the manifold (a special socket, number KM-834, is available to ease removal of the heat shields).

4 Disconnect the hot air hose (where fitted) from the exhaust manifold shroud then undo the retaining bolts and remove the shroud from the manifold.

5 Undo the retaining nuts securing the manifold to the head. Manoeuvre the manifold out of the engine compartment, complete with the gasket.

Refitting

6 Examine all the exhaust manifold studs for signs of damage and corrosion; remove all traces of corrosion, and repair or renew any damaged studs.

7 Ensure that the manifold and cylinder head sealing faces are clean and flat, and fit the new gasket.

8 Refit the manifold then fit the new retaining nuts and tighten them to the specified torque.

9 Refit the shroud to the manifold, tightening its retaining bolts to the specified torque, and reconnect the hot air hose (where fitted).

10 Apply a smear of high-temperature grease to the threads of the spark plug heat shields then refit the shields and tighten them to the specified torque. Reconnect the plug caps and cable guide.

11 Reconnect the oxygen sensor wiring connector making sure the wiring is correctly routed and retained by all the necessary clips.

12 Refit the front pipe as described in Section 20.

1.4 and 1.6 litre DOHC engines

Removal

13 Remove the oil filler cap, undo the retaining screws, and remove the engine cover. Trace the wiring back from the oxygen sensor and disconnect its wiring connector. Free the wiring from all the necessary clips and ties so the sensor is free to be removed with the manifold.

14 Slacken and remove the bolts securing the front pipe to the manifold and recover the gasket. Undo the three bolts and remove the exhaust manifold heat shield.

15 Undo the retaining nuts securing the manifold to the head. Manoeuvre the manifold out of the engine compartment, complete with the gasket.

Refitting

16 Refit the manifold as described in paragraphs 6 to 8.

17 Fit a new gasket between the manifold and front pipe then refit the front pipe bolts and tighten them to the specified torque.

18 Reconnect the oxygen sensor wiring connector making sure the wiring is correctly routed and retained by all the necessary clips.

1.8 litre DOHC engines

Removal

19 Undo the retaining screws, remove the oil filler cap, and remove the engine cover. Slacken and remove the bolts securing the front pipe to the manifold and recover the gasket.

20 Drain the cooling system as described in Chapter 3.

21 Release the retaining clip and disconnect the large coolant hose from the thermostat housing.

22 Undo the three bolts and remove the heat shield from the manifold **(see illustration)**.

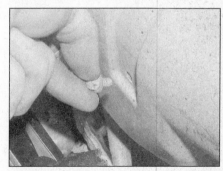

19.22 Undo the exhaust heat shield bolts

19.24 Removing the exhaust manifold

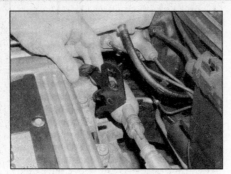

19.40 Unbolt the engine lifting shackle

23 Undo the engine oil dipstick guide bracket retaining bolt, and twist the dipstick guide tube to one side.

24 Slacken and remove the manifold retaining nuts, remove the manifold and recover the gasket **(see illustration)**.

Refitting

25 Refit the manifold as described in paragraphs 6 to 8.

26 Realign the dipstick guide tube, and tighten the mounting bracket bolt securely.

27 Refit the heat shield to the manifold (noting that the lower bolt is the shorter of the three), and reconnect the coolant hose to the thermostat. Refill the cooling system as described in Chapter 3.

28 Reconnect the front exhaust pipe to the manifold, using a new gasket.

29 Refit the engine cover.

2.0 litre DOHC engines

Removal

30 Remove the two engine transport brackets from the cylinder head.

31 Loosen the front coolant hose from the cylinder head, but do not disconnect the pipe.

32 Undo the retaining screws and remove the heat shield from the manifold.

33 Remove the manifold-to-front pipe bolts and recover the gasket. Slacken and remove the retaining nuts, and manoeuvre the manifold out of the engine compartment. Recover the gasket.

Refitting

34 Refit the manifold as described in paragraphs 6 to 8.

19.41 Removing the upper heat shield

35 Reconnect the front exhaust pipe, using a new gasket. Tighten the bolts to the specified torque.

36 Align the heat shield with the manifold, and tighten the screws to the specified torque.

37 Fasten the front coolant pipe to the cylinder head.

38 Re-attach the transport shackles to the cylinder head. Tighten the bolts securely.

2.2 litre DOHC engines

Removal

39 On Zafira models, remove the engine compartment seal and water deflector cover from in front of the windscreen, then undo the retaining nuts and bolts, and remove the bulkhead cover plate.

40 Remove the engine transport shackle from the cylinder head **(see illustration)**.

41 Undo the retaining screws and remove the lower and upper heat shield from the manifold **(see illustration)**.

42 Trace the wiring back from the oxygen sensor and free the wiring from the rear engine mounting assembly.

43 Slacken and remove the nuts securing the front pipe to the manifold and recover the gasket.

44 Slacken and remove the retaining nuts, and manoeuvre the manifold out of the engine compartment **(see illustration)**. Recover the gasket.

Refitting

45 Refit the manifold as described in paragraphs 6 to 8.

19.44 Manoeuvre the manifold out from the engine

46 Reconnect the front exhaust pipe, using a new gasket. Tighten the nuts to the specified torque.

47 Align the heat shields with the manifold, and tighten the screws to the specified torque.

48 Make sure the oxygen sensor wiring is correctly routed and retained by all the necessary clips.

49 On Zafira models, refit the bulkhead cover plate, water deflector cover and engine compartment seal.

20 Exhaust system – general information, removal and refitting

General information

1 On all models, the exhaust system consists of three sections: the front pipe, the intermediate pipe and centre silencer, and the tailpipe and main silencer box. According to engine type, the catalytic converter will either be incorporated in the front pipe, or will be integral with the exhaust manifold.

2 All exhaust sections are joined by flanged joints which are secured by bolts. Some of the joints are of the spring-loaded ball type, to allow for movement in the exhaust system. The system is suspended throughout its entire length by rubber mountings.

3 Each exhaust section can be removed individually, or alternatively, the complete system can be removed as a unit. Even if only one part of the system needs attention, it is often easier to remove the whole system and separate the sections on the bench.

4 To remove the system or part of the system, first jack up the front or rear of the car and support it securely on axle stands (see *Jacking and vehicle support*). Alternatively, position the car over an inspection pit or on car ramps.

Front pipe removal

SOHC engines

5 Where applicable, trace the wiring back from the oxygen sensor, noting the correct routing, and disconnect the wiring connector. Free the wiring from any clips so the sensor is free to be removed with the front pipe.

6 Slacken and remove the bolts and springs, or the three nuts, securing the front pipe flange joint to the manifold.

7 Undo the bolts securing the front pipe to the intermediate pipe and remove the pipe from underneath the vehicle. Recover the gasket from the pipe-to-manifold joint.

1.4 and 1.6 litre DOHC engines

8 Where applicable, trace the wiring back from the oxygen sensor, noting the correct routing, and disconnect the wiring connector. Free the wiring from any clips so the sensor is free to be removed with the front pipe.

9 Slacken and remove the bolts securing the

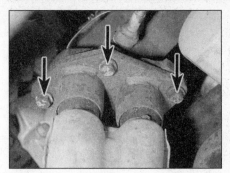

20.9 Exhaust front pipe-to-manifold bolts (arrowed) . . .

front pipe flange joint to the manifold **(see illustration)**.

10 Unscrew the nut securing the front pipe to its mounting bracket and remove the washer, spacer and mounting rubber **(see illustration)**. Slacken and remove the bolts securing the front pipe to the intermediate pipe and remove the front pipe from the vehicle. Recover the gasket from the front pipe-to-manifold joint.

1.8, 2.0 and 2.2 litre DOHC engines

11 Trace the wiring back from the oxygen sensor(s), noting the correct routing, and disconnect the wiring connector(s). Free the wiring from any clips so the sensor(s) are free to be removed with the front pipe.
12 Slacken and remove the bolts/nuts securing the front pipe flange joint to the manifold.
13 Where applicable, unscrew the nuts securing the front pipe to its mounting bracket and remove the retaining plate.
14 Slacken and remove the bolts securing the front pipe to the intermediate pipe and remove the front pipe from the vehicle. Recover the gasket from the front pipe-to-manifold joint.

Intermediate pipe removal

SOHC engines

15 Slacken and remove the bolts securing the intermediate pipe to the front pipe and slacken the clamp securing the pipe to the tailpipe.

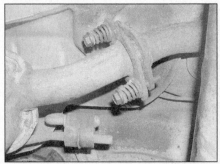

20.17 Intermediate pipe-to-tail pipe joint

20.10 . . . and front pipe mounting nut – 1.4 and 1.6 litre DOHC engines

16 Free the intermediate pipe from its mounting rubbers and manoeuvre it out from underneath the vehicle.

DOHC engines

17 Slacken and remove the bolts securing the intermediate pipe to the front pipe and the bolts and springs securing it to the tailpipe **(see illustration)**.
18 Free the intermediate pipe from its mounting rubbers and manoeuvre it out from underneath the vehicle. Recover the gasket from the rear tailpipe joint **(see illustration)**.

Tailpipe removal

19 Slacken and remove the bolts and springs securing the tailpipe joint to the intermediate pipe.
20 Free the tailpipe from its mounting rubbers and remove it along with its gasket.

Complete system removal

SOHC engines

21 Where applicable, trace the wiring back from the oxygen sensor, noting the correct routing, and disconnect the wiring connector. Free the wiring from any clips so the sensor is free to be removed with the front pipe.
22 Slacken and remove the bolts and springs, or the three nuts, securing the front pipe flange joint to the manifold.
23 Free the system from all its mounting rubbers and lower it from under the vehicle. Recover the gasket from the front pipe joint.

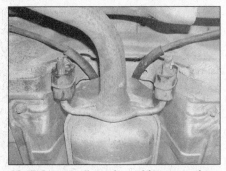

20.18 Intermediate pipe rubber mountings

1.4 and 1.6 litre DOHC engines

24 Where applicable, trace the wiring back from the oxygen sensor, noting the correct routing, and disconnect the wiring connector. Free the wiring from any clips so the sensor is free to be removed with the front pipe.
25 Undo the nut(s) securing the front pipe to its mounting bracket and remove the retaining plate or washer spacer and mounting rubber (as applicable)
26 Undo the bolts securing the front pipe to the manifold then separate the flange joint and recover the gasket.
27 Free the exhaust system from all its mounting rubbers and lower it from underneath the vehicle.

1.8, 2.0 and 2.2 litre engines

28 Trace the wiring back from the oxygen sensor(s), noting the correct routing, and disconnect the wiring connector(s). Free the wiring from any clips so the sensor(s) are free to be removed with the front pipe.
29 Slacken and remove the bolts/nuts securing the front pipe flange joint to the manifold and recover the gasket.
30 Where applicable, unscrew the nuts securing the front pipe to its mounting bracket and remove the retaining plate.
31 Free the exhaust system from all its mounting rubbers and lower it from underneath the vehicle.

Heat shield(s) removal

32 The heat shields are secured to the underside of the body by various nuts and bolts. Each shield can be removed once the relevant exhaust section has been removed. If a shield is being removed to gain access to a component located behind it, it may prove sufficient in some cases to remove the retaining nuts and/or bolts, and simply lower the shield, without disturbing the exhaust system.

Refitting

33 Each section is refitted by reversing the removal sequence, noting the following points:
  a) *Ensure that all traces of corrosion have been removed from the flanges and renew all necessary gaskets.*
  b) *Inspect the rubber mountings for signs of damage or deterioration, and renew as necessary.*
  c) *Where no gasket is fitted to a joint, apply a smear of exhaust system jointing paste to ensure a gas-tight seal.*
  d) *Prior to tightening the exhaust system fasteners, ensure that all rubber mountings are correctly located, and that there is adequate clearance between the exhaust system and vehicle underbody.*

Chapter 4 Part B:
Emission control systems

Contents

Catalytic converter – general information and precautions 3
Engine emission control systems – testing and component renewal   2

General information 1

Degrees of difficulty

Easy, suitable for novice with little experience		Fairly easy, suitable for beginner with some experience		Fairly difficult, suitable for competent DIY mechanic		Difficult, suitable for experienced DIY mechanic		Very difficult, suitable for expert DIY or professional	

Specifications

Torque wrench settings	Nm	lbf ft
Exhaust gas recirculation (EGR) valve bolts	20	15
Oxygen sensor	40	30

1 General information

1 All models use unleaded petrol and also have various other features built into the fuel system to help minimise harmful emissions. All models are equipped with a crankcase emission control system, a catalytic converter, an exhaust gas recirculation (EGR) system, and an evaporative emission control system to keep fuel vapour/exhaust gas emissions down to a minimum.
2 The emission control systems function as follows.

Crankcase emission control

3 To reduce the emission of unburned hydrocarbons from the crankcase into the atmosphere, the engine is sealed and the blow-by gases and oil vapour are drawn from inside the crankcase, through a wire mesh oil separator, into the inlet tract to be burned by the engine during normal combustion.
4 Under all conditions the gases are forced out of the crankcase by the (relatively) higher crankcase pressure; if the engine is worn, the raised crankcase pressure (due to increased blow-by) will cause some of the flow to return under all manifold conditions.

Exhaust emission control

5 To minimise the amount of pollutants which escape into the atmosphere, all models are fitted with a catalytic converter in the exhaust system. The system is of the closed-loop type, in which an oxygen sensor(s) in the exhaust system provides the fuel injection/ignition system ECU with constant feedback, enabling the ECU to adjust the mixture to provide the best possible conditions for the converter to operate.
6 On Z14XE, Z16SE, Z16XE, Z18XE and Z22SE engines there are two heated oxygen sensors fitted to the exhaust system (see illustrations). The sensor nearest the engine (before the catalytic converter) determines the residual oxygen content of the exhaust gases for mixture correction. The sensor in the exhaust front pipe (after the catalytic converter) monitors the function of the catalytic converter to give the driver a warning signal if there is a fault.
7 The oxygen sensor's tip is sensitive to oxygen and sends the ECU a varying voltage depending on the amount of oxygen in the exhaust gases; if the intake air/fuel mixture is too rich, the exhaust gases are low in oxygen so the sensor sends a low-voltage signal, the voltage rising as the mixture weakens and the amount of oxygen rises in the exhaust gases. Peak conversion efficiency of all major pollutants occurs if the intake air/fuel mixture is maintained at the chemically-correct ratio for the complete combustion of petrol of 14.7 parts (by weight) of air to 1 part of fuel (the 'stoichiometric' ratio). The sensor output voltage alters in a large step at this point, the ECU using the signal change as a

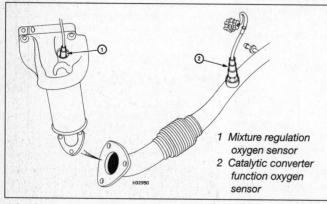

1.6a Oxygen sensor location (typical) – Z14XE, Z16SE, Z16XE and Z18XE engines

1 Mixture regulation oxygen sensor
2 Catalytic converter function oxygen sensor

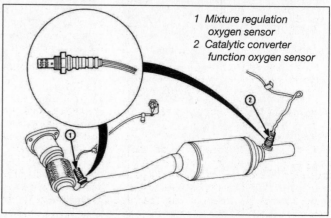

1.6b Oxygen sensor location – Z22SE engines

1 Mixture regulation oxygen sensor
2 Catalytic converter function oxygen sensor

reference point and correcting the intake air/fuel mixture accordingly by altering the fuel injector pulse width.

Evaporative emission control

8 To minimise the escape into the atmosphere of unburned hydrocarbons, an evaporative emissions control system is also fitted to all models. The fuel tank filler cap is sealed and a charcoal canister is mounted behind the right-hand front wing. The canister collects the petrol vapours generated in the tank when the car is parked and stores them until they can be cleared from the canister (under the control of the fuel-injection/ignition system ECU) via the purge valve into the inlet tract to be burned by the engine during normal combustion.

9 To ensure that the engine runs correctly when it is cold and/or idling and to protect the catalytic converter from the effects of an over-rich mixture, the purge control valve is not opened by the ECU until the engine has warmed-up, and the engine is under load; the valve solenoid is then modulated on and off to allow the stored vapour to pass into the inlet tract.

Exhaust gas recirculation (EGR)

10 This system is designed to recirculate small quantities of exhaust gas into the inlet tract, and therefore into the combustion process. This process reduces the level of unburnt hydrocarbons present in the exhaust gas before it reaches the catalytic converter. The system is controlled by the fuel-injection/ignition ECU, using the information from its various sensors, via the EGR valve.

11 On 1.4, 1.6 and early 1.8 litre engines the EGR valve is an electrically-operated valve mounted on the inlet manifold or at the left-hand end of the cylinder head.

12 On later 1.8 litre, and all 2.0 and 2.2 litre engines, the EGR valve assembly is mounted on the left-hand end of the cylinder head. The valve assembly contains the vacuum-operated valve and the electrical solenoid valve which is used to switch the valve on and off.

---

2 Engine emission control systems – testing and component renewal

---

Crankcase emission control

1 The components of this system require no attention other than to check that the hoses are clear and undamaged at regular intervals.

Evaporative emission control

Testing

2 If the system is thought to be faulty, disconnect the hoses from the charcoal canister and purge control valve and check that they are clear by blowing through them. Full testing of the system can only be carried out using specialist electronic equipment which is connected to the engine management system diagnostic wiring

2.6 Undo the retaining nut, and lift the canister from the bracket

connector (see Chapter 4A, Section 7. If the purge control valve or charcoal canister are thought to be faulty, they must be renewed.

Charcoal canister renewal

3 The charcoal canister is located behind the right-hand front wing. To gain access to the canister, firmly apply the handbrake then jack up the front of the vehicle and support it on axle stands.

4 Remove the retaining screws and fasteners and remove the wheelarch liner to gain access to the canister.

5 Disconnect the right-hand side turn signal repeater lamp wiring connector, and remove the side repeater. Refer to Chapter 12, Section 7.

6 Slacken and remove the canister retaining nut. Working in the engine compartment, mark the hoses for identification purposes then disconnect them and remove the canister from the vehicle (see illustration).

7 Refitting is a reverse of the removal procedure, ensuring the hoses are correctly and securely reconnected.

Purge valve renewal

8 The purge valve is mounted on the right-hand side of the engine compartment, behind the air cleaner housing.

9 To renew the valve, ensure the ignition is switched off then depress the retaining clip and disconnect the wiring connector from the valve.

10 Disconnect the hoses from the valve, noting their correct fitted locations then unclip the valve from the air cleaner housing and remove it from the engine (see illustration).

11 Refitting is a reversal of the removal procedure, ensuring the valve is fitted the correct way around and the hoses are securely connected.

Exhaust emission control

Testing

12 The performance of the catalytic converter can be checked only by measuring the exhaust gases using a good-quality, carefully-calibrated exhaust gas analyser.

13 If the CO level at the tailpipe is too high, the vehicle should be taken to a Vauxhall dealer or specialist so that the complete fuel-injection and ignition systems, including the oxygen sensor(s), can be thoroughly checked using the special diagnostic equipment. Once these have been checked and are known to

2.10 Unclip the purge valve

be free from faults, the fault must be in the catalytic converter, which must be renewed.

Catalytic converter renewal

14 Refer to Chapter 4A, Section 20.

Oxygen sensor renewal

Note 1: *On Z14XE, Z16SE, Z16XE, Z18XE and Z22SE engines there are two heated oxygen sensors fitted to the exhaust system. The sensor nearest the engine is for mixture regulation and the sensor furthest from the engine is to check the operation of the catalytic converter (see Section 1).*

Note 2: *The oxygen sensor is delicate and will not work if it is dropped or knocked, if its power supply is disrupted, or if any cleaning materials are used on it.*

15 Warm the engine up to normal operating temperature then stop the engine and disconnect the battery negative terminal (refer to *Disconnecting the battery* in the Reference Chapter).

16 For sensors fitted in the exhaust front pipe, firmly apply the handbrake, then jack up the front of the car and support it securely on axle stands (see *Jacking and vehicle support*).

17 Trace the wiring back from the oxygen sensor which is to be renewed, and disconnect its wiring connector, freeing the wiring from any relevant retaining clips or ties and noting its correct routing (see illustrations).

Caution: Take great care not burn yourself on the hot manifold/sensor.

18 Unscrew the sensor and remove it from the exhaust system front pipe/manifold. Where applicable recover the sealing washer and discard it; a new one should be used on refitting.

2.17a Oxygen sensor (arrowed) – X16XEL engines

2.17b Oxygen sensor – X18XE and X20XEV engines

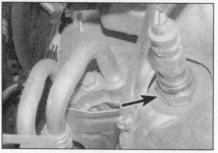

2.17c Mixture regulation sensor (arrowed) fitted to the top of the manifold – Z16XE and Z18XE engines

2.21 On 1.6 litre SOHC engines, disconnect the wiring connector . . .

19 Refitting is a reverse of the removal procedure, using a new sealing washer (where applicable). Prior to installing the sensor, apply a smear of high temperature grease to the sensor threads (Vauxhall recommend the use of special grease 19 48 602, part no 90 295 397 – available from your Vauxhall dealer). Tighten the sensor to the specified torque and ensure that the wiring is correctly routed and in no danger of contacting either the exhaust system or engine.

Exhaust gas recirculation

Testing

20 Comprehensive testing of the system can only be carried out using specialist electronic equipment which is connected to the engine management system diagnostic wiring connector (see Chapter 4A, Section 7). If the EGR valve is thought to be faulty, it must be renewed.

Valve renewal – 1.4 and 1.6 litre engines

21 Ensure the ignition is switched off, then disconnect the wiring connector from the valve. On SOHC engines the valve is fitted to the centre of the inlet manifold and on DOHC engines it is mounted on the left-hand end of the manifold **(see illustration)**.
22 Undo the retaining screws and remove the valve and its gasket from the manifold **(see illustration)**.
23 Refitting is the reverse of removal, using a new gasket and tightening the valve bolts to the specified torque.

Valve renewal – 1.8, 2.0 and 2.2 litre engines

24 Ensure the ignition is switched off then disconnect the wiring connector and vacuum

hose from the EGR valve which is mounted on the left-hand end of the cylinder head **(see illustrations)**.
25 Undo the retaining screws and remove the valve and its gasket from the end of the cylinder head.
26 Refitting is the reverse of removal using a new gasket and tightening the valve bolts to the specified torque **(see illustration)**.

---

3 Catalytic converter – general information and precautions

1 The catalytic converter is a reliable and simple device which needs no maintenance in itself, but there are some facts of which an owner should be aware if the converter is to function properly for its full service life.

a) DO NOT use leaded petrol or LRP in a car equipped with a catalytic converter – the lead will coat the precious metals, reducing their converting efficiency and will eventually destroy the converter.
b) Always keep the ignition and fuel systems well-maintained in accordance with the manufacturer's schedule.
c) If the engine develops a misfire, do not drive the car at all (or at least as little as possible) until the fault is cured.
d) DO NOT push- or tow-start the car – this will soak the catalytic converter in unburned fuel, causing it to overheat when the engine does start.
e) DO NOT switch off the ignition at high engine speeds.
f) DO NOT use fuel or engine oil additives –

these may contain substances harmful to the catalytic converter.
g) DO NOT continue to use the car if the engine burns oil to the extent of leaving a visible trail of blue smoke.
h) Remember that the catalytic converter operates at very high temperatures. DO NOT, therefore, park the car in dry undergrowth, over long grass or piles of dead leaves after a long run.
i) Remember that the catalytic converter is FRAGILE – do not strike it with tools during servicing work.
j) In some cases a sulphurous smell (like that of rotten eggs) may be noticed from the exhaust. This is common to many catalytic converter-equipped cars and once the car has covered a few thousand miles the problem should disappear.
k) The catalytic converter, used on a well-maintained and well-driven car, should last for between 50 000 and 100 000 miles – if the converter is no longer effective it must be renewed.

2.22 . . . then undo the retaining screws (arrowed) and remove the EGR valve from the inlet manifold

2.24a EGR valve location (arrowed) – X18XE engines

2.24b Disconnecting the wiring connector from the EGR valve – Z22SE engines

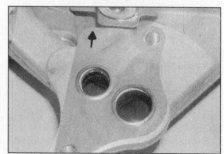

2.26 Fit a new metal gasket – note position of arrow for refitting

Chapter 5 Part A:
Starting and charging systems

Contents

Alternator – removal and refitting 8
Alternator – brush renewal 9
Alternator drivebelt – removal, refitting and tensioning 6
Alternator drivebelt tensioner – removal and refitting 7
Battery – removal and refitting 4
Battery – testing and charging 3
Battery check . . . . .See *Weekly checks*
Charging system – testing 5
Electrical fault finding – general information 2

Electrical system check . . . . .See Chapter 1
General information and precautions 1
Ignition switch – removal and refitting 13
Oil level sensor – removal and refitting 15
Oil pressure warning light switch – removal and refitting 14
Starter motor – removal and refitting 11
Starter motor – testing and overhaul 12
Starting system – testing 10

Degrees of difficulty

Easy, suitable for novice with little experience		Fairly easy, suitable for beginner with some experience		Fairly difficult, suitable for competent DIY mechanic		Difficult, suitable for experienced DIY mechanic		Very difficult, suitable for expert DIY or professional	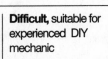

Specifications

System type . . . . 12 volt, negative earth

Battery
Charge condition:
Poor	12.5 volts
Normal	12.6 volts
Good	12.7 volts

Torque wrench settings	Nm	lbf ft
Alternator fixings:		
Alternator-to-bracket bolts:		
Except 2.2 litre engines	35	26
2.2 litre engines	20	15
Alternator bracket-to-cylinder block bolts:		
Except 2.2 litre engines	35	26
2.2 litre engines	20	15
Support bracket bolts	20	15
Alternator drivebelt tensioner mounting bolt(s):		
Models with one mounting bolt:		
SOHC engines	25	18
DOHC engines	35	26
Models with two mounting bolts	25	18
Knock sensor retaining bolt (2.2 litre engines)	20	15
Oil level sensor-to-sump bolts	8	6
Oil pressure switch:		
1.4, 1.6 and 1.8 litre engines	30	22
2.0 litre engines	40	30
2.2 litre engines	18	13
Starter motor bolts:		
1.4, 1.6 and 1.8 litre engines:		
Upper starter bolt	40	30
Lower starter bolt	25	18
2.0 litre engines	60	44
2.2 litre engines	40	30

1 General information and precautions

General information

1 The engine electrical system consists mainly of the charging and starting systems. Because of their engine-related functions, these components are covered separately from the body electrical devices such as the lights, instruments, etc (which are covered in Chapter 12). Refer to Part B for information on the ignition system.

2 The electrical system is of the 12 volt negative earth type.

3 The battery is of the low maintenance or 'maintenance-free' (sealed for life) type and is charged by the alternator, which is belt-driven from the crankshaft pulley.

4 The starter motor is of the pre-engaged type incorporating an integral solenoid. On starting, the solenoid moves the drive pinion into engagement with the flywheel ring gear before the starter motor is energised. Once the engine has started, a one-way clutch prevents the motor armature being driven by the engine until the pinion disengages from the flywheel.

Precautions

5 Further details of the various systems are given in the relevant Sections of this Chapter. While some repair procedures are given, the usual course of action is to renew the component concerned. The owner whose interest extends beyond mere component renewal should obtain a copy of the *Automotive Electrical & Electronic Systems Manual*, available from the publishers of this manual.

6 It is necessary to take extra care when working on the electrical system to avoid damage to semi-conductor devices (diodes and transistors), and to avoid the risk of personal injury. In addition to the precautions given in *Safety first!* at the beginning of this manual, observe the following when working on the system:

• *Always remove rings, watches, etc, before working on the electrical system.* Even with the battery disconnected, capacitive discharge could occur if a component's live terminal is earthed through a metal object. This could cause a shock or nasty burn.

• *Do not reverse the battery connections.* Components such as the alternator, electronic control units, or any other components having semi-conductor circuitry could be irreparably damaged.

• If the engine is being started using jump leads and a slave battery, connect the batteries *positive-to-positive* and *negative-to-negative* (see *Jump starting*). This also applies when connecting a battery charger.

• Never disconnect the battery terminals, the alternator, any electrical wiring or any test instruments when the engine is running.

• Do not allow the engine to turn the alternator when the alternator is not connected.

• Never 'test' for alternator output by 'flashing' the output lead to earth.

• Never use an ohmmeter of the type incorporating a hand-cranked generator for circuit or continuity testing.

• Always ensure that the battery negative lead is disconnected when working on the electrical system.

• Before using electric-arc welding equipment on the car, disconnect the battery, alternator and components such as the fuel injection/ignition electronic control unit to protect them from the risk of damage.

• Several systems fitted to the vehicle require battery power to be available at all times, either to ensure their continued operation (such as the clock) or to maintain control unit memories or security codes which would be wiped if the battery were to be disconnected. To ensure that there are no unforeseen consequences of this action, refer to *Disconnecting the battery* in the Reference Chapter for further information.

2 Electrical fault finding – general information

Refer to Chapter 12.

3 Battery – testing and charging

Testing

Traditional-style and low maintenance battery

1 If the vehicle covers a small annual mileage, it is worthwhile checking the specific gravity of the electrolyte every three months to determine the state of charge of the battery. Use a hydrometer to make the check and compare the results with the following table. Note that the specific gravity readings assume an electrolyte temperature of 15°C (60°F); for every 10°C (18°F) below 15°C (60°F) subtract 0.007. For every 10°C (18°F) above 15°C (60°F) add 0.007.

	Ambient temperature	
	above	below
	25°C (77°F)	**25°C (77°F)**
Fully-charged	*1.210 to 1.230*	*1.270 to 1.290*
70% charged	*1.170 to 1.190*	*1.230 to 1.250*
Discharged	*1.050 to 1.070*	*1.110 to 1.130*

2 If the battery condition is suspect, first check the specific gravity of electrolyte in each cell. A variation of 0.040 or more between any cells indicates loss of electrolyte or deterioration of the internal plates.

3 If the specific gravity variation is 0.040 or more, the battery should be renewed. If the cell variation is satisfactory but the battery is discharged, it should be charged as described later in this Section.

Maintenance-free battery

4 In cases where a 'sealed for life' maintenance-free battery is fitted, topping-up and testing of the electrolyte in each cell is not possible. The condition of the battery can therefore only be tested using a battery condition indicator or a voltmeter.

5 Certain models may be fitted with a 'Delco' type maintenance-free battery, with a built-in charge condition indicator. The indicator is located in the top of the battery casing, and indicates the condition of the battery from its colour **(see illustration)**. If the indicator shows green, then the battery is in a good state of charge. If the indicator turns darker, eventually to black, then the battery requires charging, as described later in this Section. If the indicator shows clear/yellow, then the electrolyte level in the battery is too low to allow further use, and the battery should be renewed. **Do not** attempt to charge, load or jump start a battery when the indicator shows clear/yellow.

All battery types

6 If testing the battery using a voltmeter, connect the voltmeter across the battery and compare the result with those given in the Specifications under 'charge condition'. The test is only accurate if the battery has not been subjected to any kind of charge for the previous six hours. If this is not the case, switch on the headlights for 30 seconds, then wait four to five minutes before testing the battery after switching off the headlights. All other electrical circuits must be switched off, so check that the doors and tailgate are fully shut when making the test.

7 If the voltage reading is less than 12.2 volts, then the battery is discharged, whilst a reading of 12.2 to 12.4 volts indicates a partially-discharged condition.

8 If the battery is to be charged, remove it from the vehicle (Section 4) and charge it as described later in this Section.

Charging

Note: *The following is intended as a guide only. Always refer to the manufacturer's recommendations (often printed on a label*

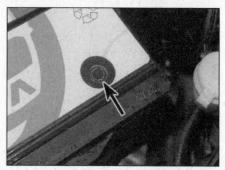

3.5 Battery charge indicator

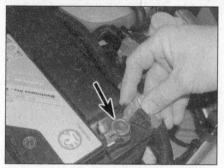

4.2 Disconnect the battery negative terminal (arrowed)

4.4 Battery clamp (arrowed)

4.5 Remove the battery tray bolts

attached to the battery) before charging a battery.

Traditional-style and low maintenance battery

9 Charge the battery at a rate of 3.5 to 4 amps and continue to charge the battery at this rate until no further rise in specific gravity is noted over a four hour period.
10 Alternatively, a trickle charger charging at the rate of 1.5 amps can safely be used overnight.
11 Specially rapid 'boost' charges which are claimed to restore the power of the battery in 1 to 2 hours are not recommended, as they can cause serious damage to the battery plates through overheating.
12 While charging the battery, note that the temperature of the electrolyte should never exceed 37.8°C (100°F).

Maintenance-free battery

13 This battery type takes considerably longer to fully recharge than the standard type, the time taken being dependent on the extent of discharge, but it can take anything up to three days.
14 A constant voltage type charger is required, to be set, when connected, to 13.9 to 14.9 volts with a charger current below 25 amps. Using this method, the battery should be usable within three hours, giving a voltage reading of 12.5 volts, but this is for a partially-discharged battery and, as mentioned, full charging can take considerably longer.
15 If the battery is to be charged from a fully-discharged state (condition reading less than 12.2 volts), have it recharged by your Vauxhall dealer or local automotive electrician, as the charge rate is higher and constant supervision during charging is necessary.

4 Battery – removal and refitting

Note: *Refer to 'Disconnecting the battery' in the Reference Chapter before proceeding.*

Removal

1 The battery is located on the left-hand side of the engine compartment. On some models

the battery will be housed in a protective casing.
2 Unclip the cover (where fitted) then slacken the clamp nut and disconnect the clamp from the battery negative (earth) terminal **(see illustration)**. **Note:** *The battery must be disconnected within 15 seconds of the ignition switch being turned off, otherwise the alarm system will activate.*
3 Lift the insulation cover and disconnect the positive terminal lead in the same way.
4 Unscrew the bolt and remove the battery retaining clamp and lift the battery out of the engine compartment **(see illustration)**.
5 If necessary, unbolt the mounting plate and remove it from the engine compartment, freeing all the relevant wiring from its retaining clips **(see illustration)**.

Refitting

6 Refitting is a reversal of removal, but smear petroleum jelly on the terminals after reconnecting the leads, and always reconnect the positive lead first, and the negative lead last.

5 Charging system – testing

Note: *Refer to the warnings given in 'Safety first!' and in Section 1 of this Chapter before starting work.*

1 If the ignition warning light fails to illuminate when the ignition is switched on, first check the alternator wiring connections for security. If satisfactory, check that the warning light bulb has not blown, and that the bulbholder is secure in its location in the instrument panel. If the light still fails to illuminate, check the continuity of the warning light feed wire from the alternator to the bulbholder. If all is satisfactory, the alternator is at fault and should be renewed or taken to an auto-electrician for testing and repair.
2 If the ignition warning light illuminates when the engine is running, stop the engine and check that the drivebelt is correctly tensioned (see Chapter 1) and that the alternator connections are secure. If all is so far

satisfactory, have the alternator checked by an auto-electrician for testing and repair.
3 If the alternator output is suspect even though the warning light functions correctly, the regulated voltage may be checked as follows.
4 Connect a voltmeter across the battery terminals and start the engine.
5 Increase the engine speed until the voltmeter reading remains steady; the reading should be approximately 12 to 13 volts, and no more than 14 volts.
6 Switch on as many electrical accessories (eg, the headlights, heated rear window and heater blower) as possible, and check that the alternator maintains the regulated voltage at around 13 to 14 volts.
7 If the regulated voltage is not as stated, the fault may be due to worn brushes, weak brush springs, a faulty voltage regulator, a faulty diode, a severed phase winding, or worn or damaged slip-rings. The brushes may be renewed, otherwise the alternator should be renewed or taken to an auto-electrician for testing and repair.

6 Alternator drivebelt – removal, refitting and tensioning

1 Refer to the procedure given for the auxiliary drivebelt in Chapter 1.

7 Alternator drivebelt tensioner – removal and refitting

Removal

1 Firmly apply the handbrake, then jack up the front of the car and support it securely on axle stands (see *Jacking and vehicle support*). Remove the right-hand front roadwheel and the lower wheelarch panel. If necessary, refer to Chapter 11.
2 With reference to Chapter 4A, remove the air cleaner assembly.
3 Hold the tensioner arm against the spring pressure, and lift the drivebelt from the pulleys. Refer to Chapter 1 if necessary.

7.5 Ensure the tensioner locating pins engage with the corresponding holes in the bracket

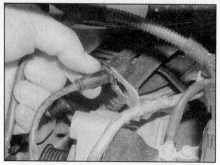

8.12 Remove the camshaft sensor wiring plug from the bracket

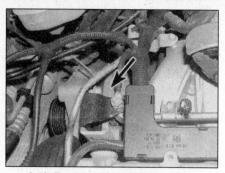

8.13 Remove the alternator upper mounting bolt

4 Undo the central mounting bolt, and remove the tensioner assembly from the alternator support bracket. On some models, the tensioner assembly is secured by two bolts.

Refitting

5 Align the tensioner assembly with the alternator support bracket. Ensure that the locating pins on the tensioner mounting surface engage correctly with the corresponding holes in the support bracket. Tighten the tensioner central mounting bolt to the specified torque **(see illustration)**. On models where the tensioner is secured by two bolts, there are no locating pins to align.

6 Hold the tensioner against the spring pressure, and refit the drivebelt around the pulleys (refer to Chapter 1 if necessary).

7 Refit the wheelarch panel and the roadwheel. Lower the vehicle to the ground, and refit the air cleaner housing.

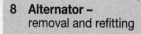

8 Alternator –
removal and refitting

Removal

1 Firmly apply the handbrake, then jack up the front of the car and support it securely on axle stands (see *Jacking and vehicle support*). Undo the retaining bolts and remove the

undercover from beneath the engine/transmission unit.

2 Disconnect the battery negative terminal (refer to *Disconnecting the battery* in the Reference Chapter), and proceed as described under the relevant sub-heading.

1.6 litre SOHC engines

3 Remove the air cleaner assembly and intake duct (see Chapter 4A).

4 Release the auxiliary drivebelt as described in Chapter 1 and disengage it from the alternator pulley.

5 Slacken and remove the mounting bolts and remove the support bracket from the alternator to the inlet manifold.

6 Undo the bolts and remove the support bracket securing the alternator to the cylinder head. Swing the alternator to the rear.

7 Unclip the wiring harness from the bracket, and remove the bracket.

8 Remove the rubber covers (where fitted) from the alternator terminals, then unscrew the retaining nuts and disconnect the wiring from the rear of the alternator.

9 Slacken and remove the lower alternator mounting bolt, and manoeuvre the alternator out of position.

1.4, 1.6 and 1.8 litre DOHC engines

10 Remove the air cleaner assembly (see Chapter 4A).

11 Push the auxiliary drivebelt tensioner against the spring pressure, and disengage the belt from the pulleys (refer to Chapter 1 if necessary).

12 On 1.8 litre models, disconnect the camshaft sensor wiring plug and unclip it from the mounting bracket **(see illustration)**.

13 Remove the upper alternator mounting bolt **(see illustration)**.

14 Slacken the lower alternator bolt, and swing the alternator to the rear.

15 Undo the bolt(s) and remove the alternator drivebelt tensioner, as described in Section 7.

16 On 1.8 litre models, disconnect the wiring plugs for the crankshaft sensor and oil pressure switch. Place the cables out of the way.

17 Remove the rubber covers (where fitted) from the alternator terminals, then unscrew the retaining nuts and disconnect the wiring from the rear of the alternator **(see illustration)**.

18 Slacken and remove the bolts securing the alternator mounting bracket to the cylinder block, then manoeuvre the alternator and bracket assembly upwards and out of position. On models fitted with air conditioning, manoeuvre the alternator and bracket assembly downwards and out of position **(see illustration)**.

19 Slacken and remove the bolts securing the alternator to its mounting bracket and separate the two components **(see illustration)**.

2.0 litre DOHC engines

20 Remove the air cleaner assembly (see Chapter 4A).

21 Push the auxiliary drivebelt tensioner

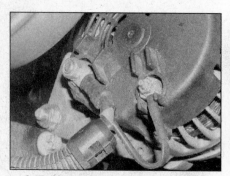

8.17 Alternator connections – rubber covers removed

8.18 Alternator mounting bracket bolts

8.19 Withdraw the alternator lower mounting bolt

8.32a Undo the retaining nut . . .

8.32b . . . and disconnect the wiring terminal – 2.2 litre engines

8.33 Alternator mounting bracket bolts (arrowed) – 2.2 litre engines

against the spring pressure, and disengage the belt from the pulleys (refer to Chapter 1 if necessary).

22 On models without air conditioning, remove the alternator drivebelt tensioner as described in Section 7.

23 Undo the retaining bolts and remove the alternator support brackets from the alternator to the inlet manifold and cylinder had.

24 Remove the rubber covers (where fitted) from the alternator terminals, then unscrew the retaining nuts and disconnect the wiring from the rear of the alternator.

25 Remove the three bolts securing the alternator mounting bracket to the cylinder block, and manoeuvre the alternator and bracket assembly downwards and out of the engine compartment.

26 Slacken and remove the bolts securing the alternator to its mounting bracket and separate the two components.

2.2 litre DOHC engines

27 Remove the air cleaner assembly and intake duct (see Chapter 4A).

28 Push the auxiliary drivebelt tensioner against the spring pressure, and disengage the belt from the pulleys (refer to Chapter 1 if necessary).

29 Drain the cooling system as described in Chapter 3, then disconnect the bottom hose from the radiator.

30 Release the two wiring harness plugs from the engine electronic control unit, then undo the securing bolts and remove the control unit from the inlet manifold. Note the position of the earth cable on one of the securing bolts.

31 Undo the bolt and remove the transport shackle from above the alternator.

32 Unscrew the retaining nut and disconnect the wiring terminal **(see illustrations)**, then unplug the wiring block connector from the rear of the alternator.

33 Slacken and remove the four alternator mounting bolts, and manoeuvre the alternator out of position **(see illustration)**.

Refitting

34 Refitting is the reverse of removal, tightening all mounting bolts to their specified

torque settings (where given). Ensure the drivebelt is correctly refitted and tensioned as described in Chapter 1.

9 Alternator – brush renewal

Note: If the alternator is thought to be suspect, it can be removed from the vehicle and taken to an auto-electrician for testing. Most auto-electricians will be able to supply and fit brushes at a reasonable cost. However, check on the cost of repairs and availability of parts before proceeding as it may prove more economical to obtain a new or exchange alternator.

Note: *This is the procedure for a typical alternator*

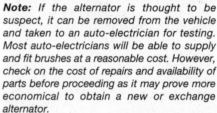

9.3 Undo the screws and lift away the plastic cover

9.4b . . . and ease the connector apart

1 Remove the alternator, as described in Section 8.

2 Place the alternator on a clean work surface, with the pulley facing down.

3 Undo the retaining screws, and lift away the outer plastic cover **(see illustration)**.

4 Unscrew the two retaining screws and ease the wire from the connector **(see illustrations)**.

5 If the brushes are damaged or excessively worn, the brush pack must be renewed.

6 Clean and inspect the surfaces of the slip-rings, at the end of the alternator shaft. If they are excessively worn, or damaged, the alternator must be renewed.

7 Reassemble the alternator by following the dismantling procedure in reverse, taking care to ease the brushes over the end of the slip-rings **(see illustration)**. On completion, refer to Section 8 and refit the alternator.

9.4a Unscrew the brush pack screws . . .

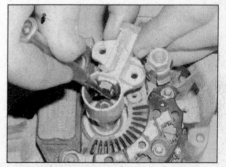

9.7 Compress the brushes and refit the brush pack

10 Starting system – testing

11.7 Disconnect the starter motor solenoid

11.9 Starter motor removal

Note: *Refer to the precautions given in 'Safety first!' and in Section 1 of this Chapter before starting work.*

1 If the starter motor fails to operate when the ignition key is turned to the appropriate position, the following possible causes may be to blame.
 a) *The battery is faulty.*
 b) *The electrical connections between the switch, solenoid, battery and starter motor are somewhere failing to pass the necessary current from the battery through the starter to earth.*
 c) *The solenoid is faulty.*
 d) *The starter motor is mechanically or electrically defective.*

2 To check the battery, switch on the headlights. If they dim after a few seconds, this indicates that the battery is discharged – recharge (see Section 3) or renew the battery. If the headlights glow brightly, operate the ignition switch and observe the lights. If they dim, then this indicates that current is reaching the starter motor, therefore the fault must lie in the starter motor. If the lights continue to glow brightly (and no clicking sound can be heard from the starter motor solenoid), this indicates that there is a fault in the circuit or solenoid – see following paragraphs. If the starter motor turns slowly when operated, but the battery is in good condition, then this indicates that either the starter motor is faulty, or there is considerable resistance somewhere in the circuit.

3 If a fault in the circuit is suspected, disconnect the battery leads (including the earth connection to the body), the starter/solenoid wiring and the engine/transmission earth strap. Thoroughly clean the connections, and reconnect the leads and wiring, then use a voltmeter or test lamp to check that full battery voltage is available at the battery positive lead connection to the solenoid, and that the earth is sound. Smear petroleum jelly around the battery terminals to prevent corrosion – corroded connections are amongst the most frequent causes of electrical system faults.

4 If the battery and all connections are in good condition, check the circuit by disconnecting the wire from the solenoid blade terminal. Connect a voltmeter or test lamp between the wire end and a good earth (such as the battery negative terminal), and check that the wire is live when the ignition switch is turned to the 'start' position. If it is, then the circuit is sound – if not the circuit wiring can be checked as described in Chapter 12, Section 2.

5 The solenoid contacts can be checked by connecting a voltmeter or test lamp between the battery positive feed connection on the starter side of the solenoid, and earth. When the ignition switch is turned to the 'start' position, there should be a reading or lighted bulb, as applicable. If there is no reading or lighted bulb, the solenoid is faulty and should be renewed.

6 If the circuit and solenoid are proved sound, the fault must lie in the starter motor. In this event, it may be possible to have the starter motor overhauled by a specialist, but check on the cost of spares before proceeding, as it may prove more economical to obtain a new or exchange motor.

11 Starter motor – removal and refitting

Removal

1 Disconnect the battery negative terminal (refer to *Disconnecting the battery* in the Reference Chapter).

2 Firmly apply the handbrake, then jack up the front of the car and support it securely on axle stands (see *Jacking and vehicle support*). Where necessary, undo the retaining bolts and remove the undercover from beneath the engine/transmission unit. Proceed as described under the relevant sub-heading.

SOHC engines

3 Slacken and remove the two retaining nuts and disconnect the wiring from the starter motor solenoid. Recover the washers under the nuts.

4 Unscrew the retaining nut and disconnect the earth lead from the starter motor upper bolt.

5 Slacken and remove the retaining bolt and nut, then manoeuvre the starter motor out from underneath the engine.

DOHC engines

6 Undo the retaining bolts and remove the support bracket from the underside of the inlet manifold.

7 Slacken and remove the two retaining nuts and disconnect the wiring from the starter motor solenoid. Recover the washers under the nuts **(see illustration)**.

8 Unscrew the retaining nut and disconnect the earth lead from the starter motor upper bolt.

9 Slacken and remove the retaining bolt and nut, then manoeuvre the starter motor out from underneath the engine. Note the dissimilar lengths of the securing bolts – the upper bolt is the longer **(see illustration)**.

Refitting

10 Refitting is a reversal of removal, tightening the retaining bolts to the specified torque. Ensure all wiring is correctly routed and its retaining nuts are securely tightened.

12 Starter motor – testing and overhaul

1 If the starter motor is thought to be suspect, it should be removed from the vehicle and taken to an auto-electrician for testing. Most auto-electricians will be able to supply and fit brushes at a reasonable cost. However, check on the cost of repairs before proceeding as it may prove more economical to obtain a new or exchange motor.

13 Ignition switch – removal and refitting

1 The ignition switch is integral with the steering column lock, and can be removed as described in Chapter 12, Section 4.

14 Oil pressure warning light switch – removal and refitting

Removal

All engines except 2.2 litre

1 The switch is screwed into the rear of the oil pump housing which is located on the right-hand end of the engine, on the end of the crankshaft. To improve access to the switch, firmly apply the handbrake then jack up the front of the vehicle and support it on axle stands (see *Jacking and vehicle support*). Where necessary, undo the retaining bolts

14.2 Oil pressure switch

15.5 Remove the oil level sensor and renew the seal

and remove the undercover from beneath the engine/transmission unit.

2 Disconnect the wiring connector then unscrew the switch and recover the sealing washer. Be prepared for oil spillage, and if the switch is to be left removed from the engine for any length of time, plug the switch aperture **(see illustration).**

2.2 litre engines

3 The switch is screwed into the front of the cylinder block, behind the starter motor. To gain access to the switch, it may be necessary to remove the starter motor as described in Section 11.

4 If a spanner (and not a deep socket) is to be used to remove the oil pressure switch, it may be necessary to undo the retaining bolt and remove the knock sensor from the cylinder block.

5 Disconnect the wiring connector then unscrew the switch and recover the sealing washer. Be prepared for oil spillage, and if the switch is to be left removed from the engine for any length of time, plug the switch aperture.

Refitting

6 Examine the sealing washer for signs of

damage or deterioration and if necessary renew.

7 Refit the switch and washer, tightening it to the specified torque, and reconnect the wiring connector.

8 Lower the vehicle to the ground (where necessary) then check and, if necessary, top up the engine oil as described in *Weekly checks.*

15 Oil level sensor – removal and refitting

1.4, 1.6 and 1.8 litre engines

Removal

1 The oil level sensor is located on the front face of the engine sump.

2 To gain access to the sensor, firmly apply the handbrake then jack up the front of the vehicle and support it on axle stands (see *Jacking and vehicle support*). Where necessary, undo the retaining bolts and remove the undercover from beneath the engine/transmission unit.

3 Drain the engine oil into a clean container

then refit the drain plug and tighten it to the specified torque setting (see Chapter 1).

4 Disconnect the wiring connector(s) from the sensor.

5 Undo the retaining bolts then ease the sensor out from the sump and remove it along with its sealing ring. Discard the sealing ring, a new one should be used on refitting **(see illustration).**

Refitting

6 Refitting is the reverse of removal, ensuring the wiring is correctly routed and securely reconnected. On completion refill the engine with oil (see Chapter 1).

2.0 and 2.2 litre engines

Removal

7 The oil level sensor (where fitted) is located inside the sump. Remove the lower part of the sump (as described in the relevant Part of Chapter 2).

8 Note the correct routing of the wiring then undo the retaining screws and remove the sensor assembly from the sump. Check the wiring connector seal for signs or damage and renew if necessary.

Refitting

9 Prior to refitting remove all traces of locking compound from the sensor retaining screw threads. Apply a drop of fresh locking compound to the screw threads and lubricate the wiring connector seal with a smear of engine oil.

10 Fit the sensor, making sure the wiring is correctly routed, and securely tighten its retaining screws. Ease the wiring connector through the sump, taking care not to damage its seal, and secure it in position with the retaining clip.

11 Ensure the sensor is correctly refitted then fit the sump as described in the relevant Part of Chapter 2.

Notes

Chapter 5 Part B:
Ignition system

Contents

Ignition module – removal and refitting 3
Ignition system – general information 1
Ignition system – testing 2
Ignition timing – checking and adjustment 4
Knock sensor – removal and refitting . . . . See Chapter 4A
Spark plug renewal . . . . See Chapter 1

Degrees of difficulty

Easy, suitable for novice with little experience	**Fairly easy,** suitable for beginner with some experience	**Fairly difficult,** suitable for competent DIY mechanic	**Difficult,** suitable for experienced DIY mechanic	**Very difficult,** suitable for expert DIY or professional

Specifications

System type	Distributorless ignition system controlled by engine management ECU	
Firing order	1-3-4-2 (No 1 cylinder at timing belt/chain end)	
Torque wrench setting	**Nm**	**lbf ft**
Ignition module screws	8	6

1 Ignition system – general information

1 The ignition system is integrated with the fuel injection system to form a combined engine management system under the control of one ECU (See Chapter 4A for further information). The ignition side of the system is of the distributorless type, and consists of the ignition module and the knock sensor.

2 On 1.6 litre SOHC and 2.0 litre DOHC engines, the ignition module is actually a four output ignition coil. The module consists of two separate HT coils which supply two cylinders each (one coil supplies cylinders 1 and 4, and the other cylinders 2 and 3). Under the control of the ECU, the module operates on the 'wasted spark' principle, ie, each spark plug sparks twice for every cycle of the engine, once on the compression stroke and once on the exhaust stroke. On 1.4, 1.6, 1.8 and 2.2 litre DOHC engines, the ignition module consists of four ignition coils, one per cylinder, in one casing mounted longitudinally

directly above the spark plugs. This module eliminates the need for any HT leads as the coils locate directly onto the relevant spark plug. The ECU uses its inputs from the various sensors to calculate the required ignition advance setting and coil charging time.

3 The knock sensor is mounted onto the cylinder block and informs the ECU when the engine is 'pinking' under load. The sensor is sensitive to vibration and detects the knocking which occurs when the engine starts to 'pink' (pre-ignite). The knock sensor sends an electrical signal to the ECU which in turn retards the ignition advance setting until the 'pinking' ceases.

 Warning: Voltages produced by an electronic ignition system are considerably higher than those produced by conventional ignition systems. Extreme care must be taken when working on the system with the ignition switched on. Persons with surgically-implanted cardiac pacemaker devices should keep well clear of the ignition circuits, components and test equipment.

2 Ignition system – testing

1 If a fault appears in the engine management (fuel injection/ignition) system first ensure that the fault is not due to a poor electrical connection or poor maintenance: ie, check that the air cleaner filter element is clean, the spark plugs are in good condition and correctly gapped (where applicable), and that the engine breather hoses are clear and undamaged. Also, where applicable, check that the accelerator cable is correctly adjusted (where applicable) as described in Chapter 4A. If the engine is running very roughly, check the compression pressures as described in the relevant Part of Chapter 2.

2 If these checks fail to reveal the cause of the problem the vehicle should be taken to a suitably-equipped Vauxhall dealer or specialist for testing. A wiring block connector is incorporated in the engine management circuit into which a special electronic diagnostic tester can be plugged. The tester will locate the fault quickly and simply alleviating the need to test all the system components individually which is a time consuming operation that carries a high risk of damaging the ECU.

3 The only ignition system checks which can be carried out by the home mechanic are those described in Chapter 1, relating to the spark plugs. If necessary, the system wiring and wiring connectors can be checked as described in Chapter 12, Section 2, ensuring that the ECU wiring connector(s) have first been disconnected.

3 Ignition module – removal and refitting

Removal

SOHC and 2.0 litre DOHC engines

1 Disconnect the battery negative terminal (refer to *Disconnecting the battery* in the Reference Chapter).

2 Disconnect the wiring connector and HT leads from the ignition module **(see illustrations)**. The module HT lead terminals are numbered (the leads should also be numbered) with their respective cylinder number to avoid confusion on refitting.

3 Slacken and remove the retaining screws and remove the ignition module from the end of the cylinder head.

3.5 Ignition module wiring plug – 1.4, 1.6, 1.8 and 2.2 litre DOHC engines

3.2a Ignition module – 1.6 litre SOHC engines

1.4, 1.6, 1.8 and 2.2 litre DOHC engines

4 Disconnect the battery negative terminal (refer to *Disconnecting the battery* in the Reference Chapter). Undo the retaining bolts (where applicable), unscrew the oil filler cap, and remove the engine cover.

5 The ignition module is mounted at the top of the engine, between the inlet and exhaust camshaft casings. Disconnect the wiring plug at the left-hand end of the module **(see illustration)**.

6 Undo the retaining screws, and lift the module up and out of position **(see illustration)**. Note that on certain 1.4 and 1.6 litre engines, an interference suppressor is mounted on the left-hand retaining bolt. If the module proves reluctant to separate from the spark plugs, insert two long 8 mm bolts into

3.6 Pull the ignition module up and off from the top of the spark plugs

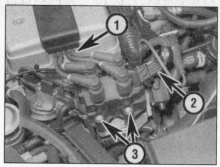

3.2b Ignition module – 2.0 litre DOHC engines

1 HT leads   3 Retaining screws
2 Wiring connector

the threaded holes in the top of the module, and pull up on the bolts to free the module from the plugs.

Refitting

7 Refit the module to the cylinder head and tighten its retaining screws to the specified torque setting.

8 On SOHC and 2.0 litre DOHC engines, reconnect each HT lead to its corresponding terminal on the ignition module using the numbers on the leads and modules.

9 Connect the wiring connector to the ignition module then reconnect the battery.

4 Ignition timing – checking and adjustment

1 There are no timing marks on the flywheel or crankshaft pulley. The timing is constantly being monitored and adjusted by the engine management ECU, and nominal values cannot be given. Therefore, it is not possible for the home mechanic to check the ignition timing.

2 The only way in which the ignition timing can be checked and (where possible) adjusted is by using special electronic test equipment, connected to the engine management system diagnostic connector (refer to Chapter 4A). Refer to your Vauxhall dealer for further information.

Chapter 6
Clutch

Contents

Clutch assembly – removal, inspection and refitting 6
Clutch hydraulic system – bleeding 2
Clutch pedal – removal and refitting 5
Fluid level check . . . . .See *Weekly checks*

General information 1
Master cylinder – removal and refitting 3
Release cylinder – removal and refitting 4

Degrees of difficulty

Easy, suitable for novice with little experience	**Fairly easy,** suitable for beginner with some experience	**Fairly difficult,** suitable for competent DIY mechanic	**Difficult,** suitable for experienced DIY mechanic	**Very difficult,** suitable for expert DIY or professional

Specifications

Type . . . . Single dry plate with diaphragm spring, hydraulically-operated

Friction plate

Diameter:
  1.4 and 1.6 litre engines . . . . 200 mm
  1.8 litre engines . . . . 205 mm
  2.0 litre engines . . . . 216 mm
  2.2 litre engines . . . . 228 mm
New lining thickness . . . . 7.65 mm

Torque wrench settings	**Nm**	**lbf ft**
Hydraulic pipe union nut	14	10
Master cylinder retaining nuts*	20	15
Pedal mounting bracket nuts*	20	15
Pedal mounting bracket-to-steering crossmember bolts/nut	20	15
Pressure plate retaining bolts*	15	11
Release cylinder mounting bolts	5	4

* *Use new bolts/nuts*

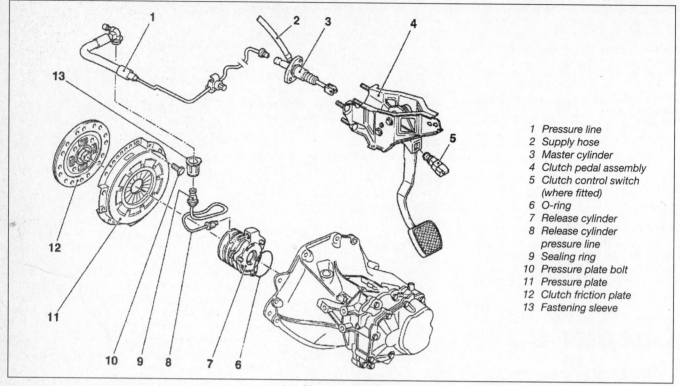

1 Pressure line
2 Supply hose
3 Master cylinder
4 Clutch pedal assembly
5 Clutch control switch
   (where fitted)
6 O-ring
7 Release cylinder
8 Release cylinder
   pressure line
9 Sealing ring
10 Pressure plate bolt
11 Pressure plate
12 Clutch friction plate
13 Fastening sleeve

1.1 Clutch components

1 General information

1 The clutch consists of a friction plate, a pressure plate assembly, and the hydraulic release cylinder (which incorporates the release bearing); all of these components are contained in the large cast-aluminium alloy bellhousing, sandwiched between the engine and the transmission (see illustration).
2 The friction plate is fitted between the engine flywheel and the clutch pressure plate, and is allowed to slide on the transmission input shaft splines.
3 The pressure plate assembly is bolted to the engine flywheel. When the engine is running, drive is transmitted from the crankshaft, via the flywheel, to the friction plate (these components being clamped securely together by the pressure plate assembly) and from the friction plate to the transmission input shaft.
4 To interrupt the drive, the spring pressure must be relaxed. This is achieved using a hydraulic release mechanism which consists of the master cylinder, the release cylinder and the pipe/hose linking the two components. Depressing the pedal pushes on the master cylinder pushrod which hydraulically forces the release cylinder piston against the pressure plate spring fingers. This causes the springs to deform and releases the clamping force on the friction plate.

5 The clutch is self-adjusting and requires no manual adjustment.

2 Clutch hydraulic system – bleeding

 Warning: Hydraulic fluid is poisonous; wash off immediately and thoroughly in the case of skin contact, and seek immediate medical advice if any fluid is swallowed or gets into the eyes. Certain types of hydraulic fluid are flammable, and may ignite when allowed into contact with hot components; when servicing any hydraulic system, it is safest to assume that the fluid is flammable, and to take precautions against the risk of fire as though it is petrol that is being handled. Hydraulic fluid is also an effective paint stripper, and will attack plastics; if any is spilt, it should be washed off immediately, using copious quantities of fresh water. Finally, it is hygroscopic (it absorbs moisture from the air) – old fluid may be contaminated and unfit for further use. When topping-up or renewing the fluid, always use the recommended type, and ensure that it comes from a freshly-opened sealed container.

1 The correct operation of any hydraulic system is only possible after removing all air from the components and circuit; this is achieved by bleeding the system.

2 During the bleeding procedure, add only clean, unused hydraulic fluid of the recommended type; never re-use fluid that has already been bled from the system. Ensure that sufficient fluid is available before starting work.
3 If there is any possibility of incorrect fluid being already in the system, the hydraulic circuit must be flushed completely with uncontaminated, correct fluid.
4 If hydraulic fluid has been lost from the system, or air has entered because of a leak, ensure that the fault is cured before continuing further.
5 A bleed screw is screwed into the hose end fitting which is situated on the top of the transmission housing. On some models access to the bleed screw is limited and it may be necessary to jack up the front of the vehicle and support it on axle stands so that the screw can be reached from below (see *Jacking and vehicle support*).
6 Check that all pipes and hoses are secure, unions tight and the bleed screw is closed. Clean any dirt from around the bleed screw.
7 Unscrew the master cylinder fluid reservoir cap (the clutch shares the same fluid reservoir as the braking system), and top the master cylinder reservoir up to the upper (MAX) level line. Refit the cap loosely, and remember to maintain the fluid level at least above the lower (MIN) level line throughout the procedure, or there is a risk of further air entering the system.
8 There are a number of one-man, do-it-

yourself bleeding kits currently available from motor accessory shops. It is recommended that one of these kits is used whenever possible, as they greatly simplify the bleeding operation, and reduce the risk of expelled air and fluid being drawn back into the system. If such a kit is not available, the basic (two-man) method must be used, which is described in detail below.

9 If a kit is to be used, prepare the vehicle as described previously, and follow the kit manufacturer's instructions, as the procedure may vary slightly according to the type being used; generally, they are as outlined below in the relevant sub-section.

Bleeding

Basic (two-man) method

10 Collect a clean glass jar, a suitable length of plastic or rubber tubing which is a tight fit over the bleed screw, and a ring spanner to fit the screw. The help of an assistant will also be required.

11 Remove the dust cap from the bleed screw. Fit the spanner and tube to the screw, place the other end of the tube in the jar, and pour in sufficient fluid to cover the end of the tube.

12 Ensure that the fluid level is maintained at least above the lower level line in the reservoir throughout the procedure.

13 Have the assistant fully depress the clutch pedal several times to build-up pressure, then maintain it on the final downstroke.

14 While pedal pressure is maintained, unscrew the bleed screw (approximately one turn) and allow the compressed fluid and air to flow into the jar. The assistant should maintain pedal pressure and should not release it until instructed to do so. When the flow stops, tighten the bleed screw again, have the assistant release the pedal slowly, and recheck the reservoir fluid level.

15 Repeat the steps given in paragraphs 13 and 14 until the fluid emerging from the bleed screw is free from air bubbles. If the master cylinder has been drained and refilled allow approximately five seconds between cycles for the master cylinder passages to refill.

16 When no more air bubbles appear, tighten the bleed screw securely, remove the tube and spanner, and refit the dust cap. Do not overtighten the bleed screw.

Using a one-way valve kit

17 As their name implies, these kits consist of a length of tubing with a one-way valve fitted, to prevent expelled air and fluid being drawn back into the system; some kits include a translucent container, which can be positioned so that the air bubbles can be more easily seen flowing from the end of the tube.

18 The kit is connected to the bleed screw, which is then opened. The user returns to the driver's seat, depresses the clutch pedal with a smooth, steady stroke, and slowly releases it; this is repeated until the expelled fluid is clear of air bubbles.

19 Note that these kits simplify work so much that it is easy to forget the clutch fluid reservoir level; ensure that this is maintained at least above the lower level line at all times.

Using a pressure-bleeding kit

20 These kits are usually operated by the reservoir of pressurised air contained in the spare tyre. However, note that it will probably be necessary to reduce the pressure to a lower level than normal; refer to the instructions supplied with the kit.

21 By connecting a pressurised, fluid-filled container to the clutch fluid reservoir, bleeding can be carried out simply by opening the bleed screw and allowing the fluid to flow out until no more air bubbles can be seen in the expelled fluid.

22 This method has the advantage that the large reservoir of fluid provides an additional safeguard against air being drawn into the system during bleeding.

All methods

23 When bleeding is complete, and correct pedal feel is restored, tighten the bleed screw securely and wash off any spilt fluid. Refit the dust cap to the bleed screw.

24 Check the hydraulic fluid level in the master cylinder reservoir, and top-up if necessary (see *Weekly Checks*).

25 Discard any hydraulic fluid that has been bled from the system; it will not be fit for re-use.

26 Check the operation of the clutch pedal. If the clutch is still not operating correctly, air must still be present in the system, and further bleeding is required. Failure to bleed satisfactorily after a reasonable repetition of the bleeding procedure may be due to worn master cylinder/release cylinder seals.

---

3 Master cylinder – removal and refitting

Note: *A new hydraulic pipe union sealing ring will be required on refitting.*

Removal

Right-hand drive models

1 Working in the engine compartment, remove all traces of dirt from the outside of the master cylinder and position some cloth beneath the cylinder to catch any spilt fluid.

2 Detach the fluid supply hose from the brake and clutch fluid reservoir. Plug the apertures to minimise fluid loss.

3 Slide out the retaining clip, and free the hydraulic pipe from the connector in the end of the master cylinder at the engine compartment bulkhead. Plug the pipe end and master cylinder port to minimise fluid loss and prevent the entry of dirt. Recover the sealing ring from the union and discard it; a new one must be used on refitting **(see illustration)**.

4 From inside the vehicle, remove the

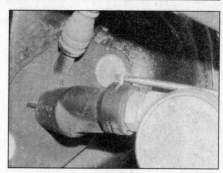
3.3 Lever out the retaining clip and disconnect the pipe

driver's side footwell trim below the facia (see Chapter 11), release the pedal return spring, slide off the retaining clip and remove the clevis pin securing the master cylinder pushrod to the pedal.

5 Still inside the vehicle, undo the two retaining nuts securing the master cylinder to the bulkhead/pedal bracket. Return to the engine compartment and manoeuvre the master cylinder from its position.

Left-hand drive models

6 To gain access to the master cylinder, unclip the relay box from the top of the ABS hydraulic modulator unit. Remove the relay holder bracket and position it clear.

7 Remove all traces of dirt from the outside of the master cylinder and position some cloth beneath the cylinder to catch any spilt fluid.

8 Detach the fluid supply hose from the brake fluid reservoir. Plug the apertures to minimise fluid loss.

9 Detach the return spring from the pedal. Slide out the retaining clip and free the hydraulic pipe from the connector in the pipe to the release cylinder. Plug the pipe end and master cylinder port to minimise fluid loss and prevent the entry of dirt. Recover the sealing ring from the union and discard it; a new one must be used on refitting.

10 From inside the vehicle, remove the driver's side footwell trim below the facia (see Chapter 11), and slide off the retaining clip and remove the clevis pin securing the master cylinder pushrod to the pedal.

11 Still inside the vehicle, undo the two retaining nuts securing the master cylinder to the bulkhead/pedal bracket. Return to the engine compartment and manoeuvre the master cylinder from its position.

Refitting

Right-hand drive models

12 Ensure the cylinder and bulkhead mating surfaces are clean and dry and the gasket is in position.

13 Manoeuvre the master cylinder into position whilst ensuring that the pushrod clevis engages correctly with the pedal. Ensure the pushrod is correctly engaged then tighten the new master cylinder retaining nuts to the specified torque.

14 Apply a smear of multi-purpose grease to the clevis pin then align the clevis and pedal and insert the pin. Secure the clevis pin in position with the retaining clip, making sure it is correctly located in the pin groove. Reconnect the pedal return spring, and refit the lower trim panel.

15 Fit a new sealing ring to the hydraulic pipe union. Reconnect the pipe to the release cylinder, pushing the connectors together until a distinct 'click' can be heard.

16 Reconnect the fluid supply hose to the brake master cylinder reservoir.

17 Bleed the clutch hydraulic system as described in Section 2.

Left-hand drive models

18 Carry out the operations described in paragraphs 12 to 17.

19 Refit the relay holder bracket, and the relay box.

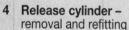
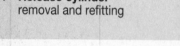

4 Release cylinder –
removal and refitting

Note: *Refer to the warning concerning the dangers of asbestos dust at the beginning of Section 6.*

Removal

1 Unless the complete engine/transmission unit is to be removed from the car and separated for major overhaul (see Chapter 2D), the clutch release cylinder can be reached by removing the transmission only, as described in Chapter 7A.

2 Wipe clean the outside of the release cylinder then slacken the union nut and disconnect the hydraulic pipe **(see illustration)**. Wipe up any spilt fluid with a clean cloth.

3 Unscrew the three retaining bolts and slide the release cylinder off from the transmission input shaft. Remove the sealing ring which is fitted between the cylinder and transmission housing and discard it; a new one must be used on refitting. Whilst the cylinder is removed, take care not to allow any debris to enter the transmission unit.

4 The release cylinder is a sealed unit and cannot be overhauled. If the cylinder seals are leaking or the release bearing is noisy or rough in operation, then the complete unit must be renewed.

5 To remove the hydraulic pipe, unclip the fastening sleeve from the bellhousing and release it from the hydraulic pipe **(see illustration)**. Check the sealing ring on the bellhousing end of the hydraulic pipe.

Refitting

6 Ensure the release cylinder and transmission mating surfaces are clean and dry and fit the new sealing ring to the transmission recess.

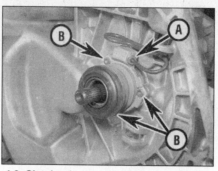

4.2 Clutch release cylinder hydraulic pipe union nut (A) and retaining bolts (B)

7 Lubricate the release cylinder seal with a smear of transmission oil then carefully ease the cylinder along the input shaft and into position. Ensure the sealing ring is still correctly seated in its groove then refit the release cylinder retaining bolts and tighten them to the specified torque.

8 Reconnect the hydraulic pipe to the release cylinder, tightening its union nut to the specified torque.

9 Refit the fastening sleeve to the bellhousing and locate the hydraulic pipe, making sure the lug on the fastening sleeve locates correctly in the bellhousing **(see illustration)**. Fit new sealing ring to the bellhousing end of the hydraulic pipe.

10 Refit the transmission unit as described in Chapter 7A.

5 Clutch pedal –
removal and refitting

Removal

1 From inside the passenger compartment, remove the driver's side footwell lower trim panel from under the facia (see Chapter 11).

2 Detach the return spring from the clutch pedal. Slide off the retaining clip and remove the clevis pin securing the master cylinder pushrod to the clutch pedal **(see illustration)**.

3 Slacken and remove the two bolts (LHD) or nut (RHD) securing the pedal bracket to the steering crossmember.

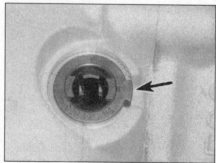

4.9 Make sure the lug (arrowed) on the fastening sleeve is located correctly in the bellhousing

4.5 The fastening sleeve which locates the end of the hydraulic pipe in the bellhousing

4 On models with cruise control, disconnect the wiring connector from the clutch switch then remove the switch from the pedal bracket.

5 Slacken and remove the two nuts securing the pedal bracket to the master cylinder/bulkhead.

6 Carefully push the master cylinder studs back until they no longer protrude into the footwell.

7 Carefully manoeuvre the pedal and mounting bracket assembly out from the footwell.

8 Check the pedal mounting brackets for signs of damage or deformation (the brackets are designed to bend easily as a safety feature in the event of a collision) and check the pedal mounting bushes for signs of wear. If any component is worn or damaged it should be renewed; the pedal and brackets can be separated once the bracket bolts have been unscrewed.

Refitting

9 If the pedal and bracket assembly has been dismantled, apply a smear of multi-purpose grease to the pedal pivot shaft and bushes prior to reassembly. Reassemble all components, making sure the pedal return spring is correctly engaged with the bracket, then securely tighten the bracket bolts. Check that the pedal pivots smoothly before refitting the assembly to the vehicle.

10 Manoeuvre the pedal and bracket assembly into position, engaging the pedal with the master cylinder pushrod, then loosely refit the bolts or nut securing the bracket to the steering crossmember.

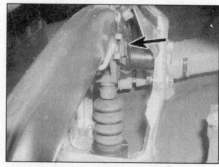

5.2 Slide off the clevis pin retaining clip (arrowed)

11 Pull the master cylinder pushrod so that the mounting studs protrude once again into the footwell and through the corresponding holes in the pedal bracket. Fit the new retaining nuts and tighten them to the specified torque.

12 From inside the vehicle, apply a smear of multi-purpose grease to the clevis pin then align the pushrod with the clutch pedal hole and insert the pin. Secure the pin in position with the retaining clip, making sure it is correctly located in the groove.

13 Tighten the bolts or nut securing the pedal bracket to the steering crossmember to the specified torque setting.

14 Hook the return spring into position behind the clutch pedal **(see illustration 5.2)**.

15 On models with cruise control, ensure the switch plunger is fully depressed then refit the switch to the bracket and connect the wiring connector. Fully depress the clutch pedal and extend the switch plunger then release the pedal to set the switch adjustment.

16 Refit the lower cover to the facia and check the operation of the clutch before using the vehicle on the road.

---

6 Clutch assembly – removal, inspection and refitting

⚠ *Warning: Dust created by clutch wear and deposited on the clutch components may contain asbestos, which is a health hazard. DO NOT blow it out with compressed air, or inhale any of it. DO NOT use petrol or petroleum-based solvents to clean off the dust. Brake system cleaner or methylated spirit should be used to flush the dust into a suitable receptacle. After the clutch components are wiped clean with rags, dispose of the contaminated rags and cleaner in a sealed, marked container.*

Note: *Although some friction materials may no longer contain asbestos, it is safest to assume that they do, and to take precautions accordingly.*

Removal

1 Unless the complete engine/transmission unit is to be removed from the car and separated for major overhaul (see Chapter 2D), the clutch can be reached by removing the transmission as described in Chapter 7A.

2 Before disturbing the clutch, use chalk or a marker pen to mark the relationship of the pressure plate assembly to the flywheel.

3 Working in a diagonal sequence, slacken the pressure plate bolts by half a turn at a time, until spring pressure is released and the bolts can be unscrewed by hand.

4 Remove the pressure plate assembly and collect the friction plate, noting which way round the friction plate is fitted.

Inspection

Note: *Due to the amount of work necessary to remove and refit clutch components, it is usually considered good practice to renew the clutch friction plate, pressure plate assembly and release bearing as a matched set, even if only one of these is actually worn enough to require renewal. It is also worth considering the renewal of the clutch components on a preventative basis if the engine and/or transmission have been removed for some other reason.*

5 Remove the clutch assembly.

6 When cleaning clutch components, read first the warning at the beginning of this Section; remove dust using a clean, dry cloth, and working in a well-ventilated atmosphere.

7 Check the friction plate facings for signs of wear, damage or oil contamination. If the friction material is cracked, burnt, scored or damaged, or if it is contaminated with oil or grease (shown by shiny black patches), the friction plate must be renewed.

8 If the friction material is still serviceable, check that the centre boss splines are unworn, that the torsion springs are in good condition and securely fastened, and that all the rivets are tight. If any wear or damage is found, the friction plate must be renewed.

9 If the friction material is fouled with oil, this must be due to an oil leak from the crankshaft oil seal, from the sump-to-cylinder block joint, or from the release cylinder assembly (either the main seal or the sealing ring). Renew the crankshaft oil seal or repair the sump joint as described in the relevant Part of Chapter 2, before installing the new friction plate. The clutch release cylinder is covered in Section 4.

10 Check the pressure plate assembly for obvious signs of wear or damage; shake it to check for loose rivets, or worn or damaged fulcrum rings, and check that the drive straps securing the pressure plate to the cover do not show signs of overheating (such as a deep yellow or blue discoloration). If the diaphragm spring is worn or damaged, or if its pressure is in any way suspect, the pressure plate assembly should be renewed.

11 Examine the machined bearing surfaces of the pressure plate and of the flywheel; they should be clean, completely flat, and free from scratches or scoring. If either is discoloured from excessive heat, or shows signs of cracks, it should be renewed – although minor damage of this nature can sometimes be polished away using emery paper.

12 Check that the release cylinder bearing rotates smoothly and easily, with no sign of noise or roughness. Also check that the surface itself is smooth and unworn, with no signs of cracks, pitting or scoring. If there is any doubt about its condition, the clutch release cylinder should be renewed (it is not possible to renew the bearing separately).

Refitting

13 On reassembly, ensure that the bearing surfaces of the flywheel and pressure plate are completely clean, smooth, and free from oil or grease. Use solvent to remove any protective grease from new components.

14 Fit the friction plate so that its spring hub assembly faces away from the flywheel; there may also be a marking showing which way round the plate is to be refitted. For example: 'Getriebeseite', meaning 'Gearbox side' **(see illustration)**.

15 Refit the pressure plate assembly, aligning the marks made on dismantling (if the original pressure plate is re-used). Fit new pressure plate bolts, but tighten them only finger-tight so that the friction plate can still be moved **(see illustration)**.

16 The friction plate must now be centralised so that, when the transmission is refitted, its input shaft will pass through the splines at the centre of the friction plate.

17 Centralisation can be achieved by passing a screwdriver or other long bar through the friction plate and into the hole in the crankshaft; the friction plate can then be moved around until it is centred on the crankshaft hole. Alternatively, a clutch-aligning tool can be used to eliminate the guesswork; these can be obtained from most accessory shops. A home-made aligning tool can be fabricated from a length of metal rod or wooden dowel which fits closely inside the crankshaft hole, and has insulating tape wound around it to match the diameter of the friction plate splined hole.

18 When the friction plate is centralised, tighten the pressure plate bolts evenly and in a diagonal sequence to the specified torque setting.

19 Refit the transmission as described in Chapter 7A.

6.14 The friction plate spring hub assembly faces away from the flywheel

6.15 Fit the pressure plate, and centralise the friction plate

Notes

Chapter 7 Part A:
Manual transmission

Contents

Gearchange mechanism – adjustment 3
Gearchange mechanism – removal and refitting 4
General information 1
Oil seals – renewal 5
Reversing light switch – testing, removal and refitting 6

Transmission – removal and refitting 7
Transmission oil – draining and refilling 2
Transmission oil level check 9
Transmission overhaul – general information 8

Degrees of difficulty

Easy, suitable for novice with little experience	Fairly easy, suitable for beginner with some experience	Fairly difficult, suitable for competent DIY mechanic	Difficult, suitable for experienced DIY mechanic	Very difficult, suitable for expert DIY or professional 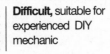

Specifications

General

Type	Manual, five forward speeds and reverse. Synchromesh on all forward speeds
Identification code*:	
1.4 litre engines	F13 or F17
1.6 litre engines:	
SOHC	F13
DOHC	F17
1.8 litre engines	F17
2.0 litre engines	F18
2.2 litre engines	F23

The transmission identification code is cast onto the top of the transmission housing, next to the selector mechanism cover

Lubrication

Oil type	See *Lubricants and fluids*
Oil capacity	See Specifications, Chapter 1

Torque wrench settings

	Nm	lbf ft
Differential lower cover plate bolts:		
F18 transmissions	40	30
F13 and F17 transmissions:		
Models with an alloy cover plate	18	12
Models with a steel cover plate	30	22
Engine-to-transmission bolts	60	44
Flywheel cover plate	8	6
Gearchange mechanism (F13, F17 and F18 transmissions):		
Selector rod clamp bolt:		
Stage 1	12	9
Stage 2	Angle-tighten a further 180°	
Housing mounting bolts	6	4
Oil drain plug (F23 transmissions)	35	26
Oil filler plug (F23 transmissions)	35	26
Oil level plug:		
F13, F17 and F18 transmissions:		
Stage 1	4	3
Stage 2	Angle-tighten a further 45° to 180°	
F23 transmissions	35	26
Oil sump-to-transmission bolts	40	30
Reversing light switch	20	15
Roadwheel bolts	110	81
Shift assembly to transmission (F23 transmissions)	25	18
Shift Bowden cable bracket to transmission (F23 transmissions)	20	15

1 General information

1 The transmission is contained in a cast-aluminium alloy casing bolted to the engine's left-hand end, and consists of the gearbox and final drive differential – often called a transaxle.

2 Drive is transmitted from the crankshaft via the clutch to the input shaft, which has a splined extension to accept the clutch friction plate, and rotates in sealed ball-bearings. From the input shaft, drive is transmitted to the output shaft, which rotates in a roller bearing at its right-hand end, and a sealed ball-bearing at its left-hand end. From the output shaft, the drive is transmitted to the differential crownwheel, which rotates with the differential case and planetary gears, thus driving the sun gears and driveshafts. The rotation of the planetary gears on their shaft allows the inner roadwheel to rotate at a slower speed than the outer roadwheel when the car is cornering.

3 The input and output shafts are arranged side-by-side, parallel to the crankshaft and driveshafts, so that their gear pinion teeth are in constant mesh. In the neutral position, the output shaft gear pinions rotate freely, so that drive cannot be transmitted to the crownwheel.

4 Gear selection is via a floor-mounted lever and selector linkage mechanism. The selector linkage causes the appropriate selector fork to move its respective synchro-sleeve along the shaft, to lock the gear pinion to the synchro-hub. Since the synchro-hubs are splined to the output shaft, this locks the pinion to the shaft, so that drive can be transmitted. To ensure that gearchanging can be made quickly and quietly, a synchromesh system is fitted to all forward gears, consisting of baulk rings and spring-loaded fingers, as well as the gear pinions and synchro-hubs. The synchromesh cones are formed on the mating faces of the baulk rings and gear pinions.

2 Transmission oil – draining and refilling

1 This operation is much more efficient if the car is first taken on a journey of sufficient length to warm the engine/transmission up to normal operating temperature.

Caution: If the procedure is to be carried out on a hot transmission unit, take care not to burn yourself on the hot exhaust or the transmission/engine unit.

2 Park the car on level ground, switch off the ignition. Firmly apply the handbrake, then jack up the front of the car and support it securely on axle stands (see *Jacking and vehicle support*). Where necessary, undo the retaining bolts/clip and remove the engine undertray.

F13, F17 and F18 transmissions

Note: *A new differential lower cover plate gasket will be required for this operation.*

3 Since the transmission oil is not renewed as part of the manufacturer's maintenance schedule, no drain plug is fitted to the transmission. If for any reason the transmission needs to be drained, the only way of doing so is to remove the differential lower cover plate.

4 Wipe clean the area around the differential cover plate and position a suitable container underneath the cover.

5 Evenly and progressively slacken and remove the retaining bolts then withdraw the cover plate and allow the transmission oil to drain in to the container. If the oil is hot, take precautions against scalding. Remove the gasket and discard it; a new one should be used on refitting **(see illustration)**.

6 Remove all traces of dirt and oil from the cover and transmission mating surfaces and wipe clean the inside of the cover plate.

7 Once the oil has finished draining, ensure the mating surfaces are clean and dry then refit the cover plate to the transmission unit, complete with a new gasket. Refit the retaining bolts and evenly and progressively tighten them to the specified torque setting. Lower the vehicle to the ground.

8 The transmission is refilled via the reversing light switch aperture until oil begins to trickle out of the level plug aperture. Wipe clean the area around the reversing light switch and level plug, and remove the switch and plug as described in Section 9. Refill the transmission with the specified type and amount of oil given in the Specifications, using the procedure described in Section 9. On completion, refit the reversing light switch and level plug and tighten both to the specified torque **(see illustration)**.

9 Take the vehicle on a short journey so that the new oil is distributed fully around the transmission components.

10 On your return, park the vehicle on level ground and check the transmission oil level again as described in Section 9.

F23 transmissions

11 As with the F13, F17 and F18 transmissions, the transmission oil is not renewed as part of the manufacturer's maintenance schedule and no drain plug is fitted to the transmission. On the F23 transmission, the only way to drain the transmission completely is by extensive dismantling.

12 Refer to Section 9 for oil level checking and topping-up procedures.

3 Gearchange mechanism – adjustment

F13, F17 and F18 transmissions

Note: *A 5 mm drill or punch will be required to carry out this procedure.*

1 Adjustment of the gearchange mechanism

2.5 Undo the transmission cover plate bolts and allow the oil to drain

2.8 Refill the transmission through the reversing light aperture

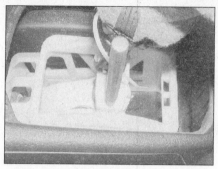

3.4 Insert a 5 mm drill or a punch through the lever base

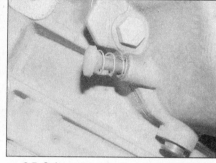

3.5 Selector mechanism locking pin

3.6 Selector rod clamp

is not a routine operation and should only be needed if the mechanism has been removed. If the gearchange action is stiff or imprecise, check that it is correctly adjusted as follows.

2 The mechanism is adjusted via the clamp bolt which secures the selector rod to the transmission linkage (see Section 4). The bolt is located at the rear of the engine/ transmission unit, just in front of the engine compartment bulkhead and, on most models, access to the bolt can be gained from above. If the bolt can not be reached from above, firmly apply the handbrake then jack up the front of the vehicle and support it securely on axle stands. Limited access can then be gained from underneath the vehicle.

3 Slacken the gearchange selector rod clamp bolt which is situated at the front of the rod. Do not remove the bolt completely.

4 From inside the vehicle, unclip the gearchange lever gaiter from the console and fold it back. Lock the gearchange lever in position by inserting a 5 mm drill or a punch through the clamp on the left-hand side of the lever base and into its locating hole **(see illustration)**.

5 With the selector mechanism in the neutral position, turn the selector shaft against the spring pressure, and lock the transmission selector mechanism in position by pressing in the spring-loaded locking pin on the selector mechanism cover, which is located on the top of the transmission unit **(see illustration)**.

6 With both the lever and transmission locked in position, tighten the selector rod clamp bolt

to the specified torque Stage 1 setting then tighten it through the specified Stage 2 angle **(see illustration)**.

7 Remove the locking rod from the gearchange lever and check the operation of the gearchange mechanism; the transmission locking pin will automatically release when the lever is moved into the reverse position.

8 Ensure the transmission locking pin has released then (where necessary) lower the vehicle to the ground.

F23 transmissions

9 Remove the centre console central cover from under the handbrake lever, then undo the two screws and remove the gear lever cover from the console. If improved access is required, remove the centre console completely as described in Chapter 11.

10 Using a small screwdriver, release both gearshift cable clamping pieces **(see illustration)**.

11 In the engine compartment, set the gearchange selector on the transmission to 'neutral' position.

12 Working back inside the vehicle, position the gear lever in the 'neutral' position, and lock it there by pushing in the clamp **(see illustration)**.

13 Lock both cable clamping pieces by pushing down **(see illustration)**.

14 Pull out the clamp locking the gear lever, and refit the gear lever gaiter and centre console central cover. Check the gear selector mechanism for correct operation.

4 Gearchange mechanism – removal and refitting

F13, F17 and F18 transmissions

1 The gearchange mechanism consists of the gearchange lever, the selector rod and the linkage assembly on the transmission. The lever and selector rod and the linkage assembly can be removed separately.

Gearchange lever and selector rod

2 Firmly apply the handbrake, then jack up the front of the car and support it securely on axle stands (see *Jacking and vehicle support*). Where necessary, undo the retaining bolts and remove the undercover from beneath the engine/transmission unit.

3 Using paint or a suitable marker pen, make alignment marks between the selector rod and the clamp on the front end of the rod. Loosen the clamp bolt by a couple of turns but do not remove it completely. Move the gearchange lever into the 4th gear position then free the selector rod from the clamp and slide off the rubber gaiter.

4 Remove the centre console as described in Chapter 11.

5 Undo the retaining screws and remove the switch panel from around the gearchange lever, disconnecting the wiring connectors as they become accessible.

6 Slacken and remove the four nuts securing

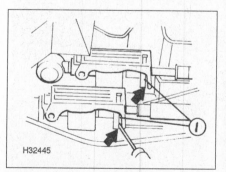

3.10 Use a small screwdriver to release the cable clamping pieces (1)

3.12 Lock the gear lever in 'neutral' by pushing in the clamp with a screwdriver

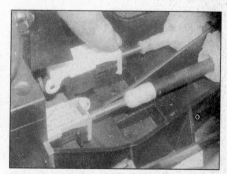

3.13 Locking the cables by pushing down on the clamping pieces

4.15 Remove the linkage pivot pin

4.17 Examine the linkage assembly for wear and damage

4.19 Locate the linkage bracket on the mountings

the gearchange lever to the floor then manoeuvre the lever and selector rod assembly out of position.

7 To dismantle the lever and rod assembly, carefully release the retaining clip from the base of the lever then separate the rod and lever and remove them from the housing. Examine all components for signs of wear or damage, paying particular attention to the selector rod and lever locating pivot bushes, and renew as necessary.

8 If necessary, reassemble the lever and rod, making sure the lever base is correctly located in the housing pivot, and secure them in position with the retaining clip.

9 Lubricate all pivot points and bearing surfaces with silicone grease then manoeuvre the assembly into position. Refit the housing retaining bolts and tighten them to the specified torque setting.

10 Refit the switch panel, making sure its wiring is correctly routed, then refit the centre console as described in Chapter 11.

11 From underneath the vehicle, slide the rubber gaiter onto the end of the selector rod and locate it securely in the bulkhead.

12 Engage the selector rod end with its linkage clamp. Align the marks made prior to removal and tighten the clamp bolt to the specified Stage 1 torque then tighten it through the specified Stage 2 angle.

13 Check the gearchange mechanism operation before lowering the vehicle to the ground. If the mechanism seems notchy or imprecise, adjust it as described in Section 3.

Transmission linkage assembly

Note: *A new linkage-to-transmission lever pivot pin should be used on refitting.*

14 Separate the selector rod from its clamp as described in paragraph 3. The bolt is located at the rear of the engine/transmission unit, just in front of the engine compartment bulkhead and on most models access to the bolt can be gained from above. If the bolt cannot be reached from above, firmly apply the handbrake then jack up the front of the vehicle and support it securely on axle stands. Limited access can then be gained from underneath the vehicle.

15 Depress the detent mechanism and remove the pivot pin connecting the linkage to the selector lever on the top of the transmission unit **(see illustration)**. Discard the pivot pin, a new one should be used on refitting.

16 Slide off the retaining clips securing the linkage bracket to its mountings then manoeuvre the assembly upwards and out of position. If necessary, the mounting brackets can then be unbolted and removed.

17 Examine the linkage assembly closely for signs of wear or damage, renewing worn components as necessary **(see illustration)**.

18 Prior to refitting, lubricate the balljoints and pivot points with silicone grease.

19 Manoeuvre the assembly into position and locate the linkage bracket on its mountings. Secure the assembly in position with the retaining clips, ensuring they are

correctly located in the mounting bracket pin grooves **(see illustration)**.

20 Align the linkage with the transmission selector lever and insert the new pivot pin. Ensure the pin is securely retained by its detent mechanism **(see illustration)**.

21 Engage the selector rod end with its linkage clamp. Align the marks made prior to removal and tighten the clamp bolt to the specified Stage 1 torque then tighten it through the specified Stage 2 angle.

22 Check the gearchange mechanism operation before lowering the vehicle to the ground. If the mechanism seems notchy or imprecise, adjust it as described in Section 3.

F23 transmission

23 The gearchange mechanism consists of the gear lever, selector cables and linkage assembly on the transmission.

Gear lever

24 Remove the centre console as described in Chapter 11.

25 Using a small screwdriver, open the selector cables clamping pieces as far as the notch. Opening them any further may damage the clamping pieces **(see illustration)**.

26 Note the fitted locations of the cables, then prise the ends of the cables from the gear lever assembly **(see illustration)**.

27 Slide the inner cables from the cable clamping pieces at the front of the gearchange assembly.

28 Undo the four retaining bolts and lift the gear lever assembly from the floor.

4.20 Insert a new pivot pin

4.25 Clamping piece unclipped to the first notch to remove the inner cable

4.26 Unclip the outer cable from the gear lever assembly

4.29 The clamping pieces are attached to the bottom of the gear lever assembly by a ball and socket arrangement

4.42 Prise the gear linkage cables off the selector on the transmission

4.43 Unclip the outer cables from the bracket on the transmission casing

29 If required, the cable clamping pieces attached to the gear lever can be prised from their position. No further dismantling of the assembly is recommended **(see illustration)**.

30 If previously removed, attached the cable end fittings to the base of the lever using a pair of pliers.

31 Position the gear lever assembly on the floor, insert the securing bolts and tighten securely.

32 Refit the cable clamping pieces into the front of the gear lever housing. Do not lock the clamping pieces at this stage.

33 Reconnect the ends of the cables to the cable end fittings attached to the base of the gear lever.

34 Carry out the gearchange mechanism adjustment procedure, as described in the previous Section.

35 Refit the centre console as described in Chapter 11.

Selector cables

36 Remove the centre console as described in Chapter 11.

37 Using a small screwdriver, open the selector cables clamping pieces as far as the notch. Opening them any further may damage the clamping pieces **(see illustrations 3.10 and 4.25)**.

38 Note the fitted locations of the cables, then prise the ends of the cables from the gear lever assembly **(see illustrations 4.26)**.

39 Slide the inner cables from the cable clamping pieces at the front of the gearchange assembly.

40 Disconnect the battery negative terminal (refer to *Disconnecting the battery* in the Reference Chapter).

41 Support the engine/transmission and remove the rear engine/transmission mounting as described in Chapter 2C.

42 Note the fitted locations of the cables, then prise the ends of the cables from the selector linkage assembly above/behind the transmission **(see illustration)**.

43 Release the outer cables from the linkage assembly bracket **(see illustration)**.

44 Pull the cables (complete with grommet) out of the bulkhead and into the engine compartment.

45 Push the selector cables through the bulkhead passage from the engine compartment.

46 Refit the outer cables to the retaining bracket at the transmission end.

47 Engage the cable end fittings with the selector linkage assembly, squeezing them together with pliers if necessary.

48 Check the cables are routed as noted during removal, and refit the outer cable clamping pieces with corresponding cut-outs in the front of the gear lever housing. Do not lock the clamping pieces at this stage.

49 Reconnect the cables to the end fittings attached to the base of the gear lever.

50 Carry out the gearchange mechanism adjustment procedure, as described in the previous Section.

51 Refit the centre console as described in Chapter 11.

5 Oil seals – renewal

Driveshaft oil seals

1 Firmly apply the handbrake, then jack up the front of the car and support it securely on axle stands (see *Jacking and vehicle support*). Remove the appropriate front roadwheel.

2 Where possible, drain the transmission oil as described in Section 2 or be prepared for oil loss as the seal is changed.

3 Remove the driveshaft as described in Chapter 8.

4 Carefully prise the oil seal out of position using a large flat-bladed screwdriver **(see illustration)**.

5 Remove all traces of dirt from the area around the oil seal aperture, then apply a smear of grease to the outer lip of the new oil seal. Ensure the seal is correctly positioned, with its sealing lip and spring facing inwards, and tap it squarely into position, using a suitable tubular drift (such as a socket) which bears only on the hard outer edge of the seal **(see illustration)**. Ensure the seal is fitted flush with the seal housing.

6 Refit the driveshaft as described in Chapter 8.

7 If the transmission was drained, refill the transmission with the specified type and amount of oil, as described in Section 2. If the oil was not drained top-up the transmission oil level and check as described in Section 9.

Input shaft oil seal

8 The input shaft oil seal is an integral part of the clutch release cylinder; if the seal is leaking the complete release cylinder assembly must be renewed. Before condemning the release cylinder, check that the leak is not coming from the sealing ring which is fitted between the cylinder and the transmission housing; the sealing ring can be renewed once the release cylinder assembly has been removed. Refer to Chapter 6 for removal and refitting details.

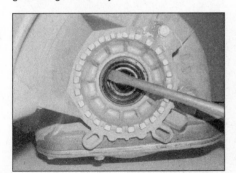

5.4 Prise out the driveshaft oil seal

5.5 Fit the new oil seal using a socket as a tubular drift

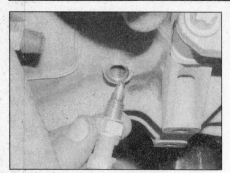

**6.6 Unscrew the reversing light switch –
F13/17/18 transmission**

Selector rod oil seal

9 Renewal of the selector rod oil seal requires the selector mechanism cover to be unbolted from the transmission and dismantled. This task is considered to be beyond the scope of the DIY mechanic, and should therefore be entrusted to a Vauxhall dealer or specialist.

6 Reversing light switch – testing, removal and refitting

Testing

F13, F17 and F18 transmissions

1 The reversing light circuit is controlled by a plunger-type switch that is screwed into the top of the transmission, towards the front of the housing. If a fault develops in the circuit, first ensure that the circuit fuse has not blown.
2 To test the switch, disconnect the wiring connector. Use a multimeter (set to the resistance function) or a battery-and-bulb test circuit to check that there is continuity between the switch terminals only when reverse gear is selected. If this is not the case, and there are no obvious breaks or other damage to the wires, the switch is faulty, and must be renewed.

F23 transmissions

3 The reversing light circuit is controlled by a plunger-type switch that is screwed into the rear of the transmission. If a fault develops in

7.5a Prise out the retaining clip and lift the union from the release cylinder pipe

6.8 The reversing light switch is positioned above the left-hand driveshaft – F23 transmission

the circuit, first check that the circuit fuse has not blown.
4 To test the switch, disconnect the wiring connector. Use a multimeter (set to the resistance function) or a battery-and-bulb test circuit to check that there is continuity between the switch terminals only when the reverse gear is selected. If this is not the case, and there are no obvious breaks or other damage to the wires, the switch is faulty, and must be renewed.

Removal

F13, F17 and F18 transmissions

5 To improve access to the switch, remove the battery and mounting plate (see Chapter 5A).
6 Disconnect the wiring connector, then unscrew the switch and remove it from the transmission casing along with its sealing washer **(see illustration)**.

F23 transmissions

7 Firmly apply the handbrake, then jack up the front of the car and support it securely on axle stands (see *Jacking and vehicle support*). Where necessary, undo the retaining bolts/clip and remove the undertray from beneath the engine/transmission unit.
8 Disconnect the wiring connector, then unscrew the switch and remove it from the transmission casing along with its sealing washer **(see illustration)**.

Refitting

F13, F17 and F18 transmissions

9 Fit a new sealing washer to the switch, then

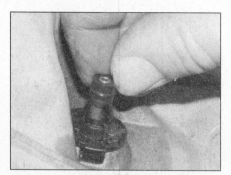

7.5b The release cylinder pipe seal must be renewed

screw it back into position in the top of the transmission housing and tighten it to the specified torque. Reconnect the wiring connector, then refit the battery (where removed) and test the operation of the circuit.

F23 transmissions

10 Fit a new sealing washer to the switch, then screw it back into position in the rear of the transmission housing and tighten it to the specified torque. Reconnect the wiring connector, then refit the engine undertray and lower the vehicle to the ground.

7 Transmission – removal and refitting

Removal

1 Firmly apply the handbrake, then jack up the front of the car and support it securely on axle stands (see *Jacking and vehicle support*). Remove both front roadwheels then, where necessary, undo the retaining bolts and remove the undercover from beneath the engine/transmission unit. Remove the air cleaner housing and intake trunking (see Chapter 4A).
2 Where possible, drain the transmission oil as described in Section 2 or be prepared for oil loss as the transmission is removed.
3 Remove the battery and mounting plate and the starter motor (see Chapter 5A).
4 Disconnect the wiring connector from the reversing light switch and free the wiring from the transmission unit and retaining brackets.
5 Minimise clutch fluid loss by clamping the flexible hose next to the connection on the transmission housing. Prise out the retaining clip securing the clutch hydraulic pipe/hose end fitting to the top of the transmission bellhousing and detach the end fitting from the transmission. Fix the retaining clip back into position in the end fitting and discard the sealing ring from the pipe end; a new sealing ring must be used on refitting **(see illustrations)**. Plug/cover both the union and pipe ends to minimise fluid loss and prevent the entry of dirt into the hydraulic system. **Note:** *Whilst the hose/pipe is disconnected, do not depress the clutch pedal.*
6 Remove the front exhaust downpipe, catalytic converter and intermediate pipe, as described in Chapter 4A.
7 On models fitted with F13, F17 or F18 transmissions, detach the gearchange mechanism linkage assembly from the top of the transmission unit as described in Section 4. On models equipped with F23 transmissions, prise the ends of the gearchange cables from the linkage on the top of the transmission, and unclip the outer cables from the retaining bracket as described in Section 4.
8 Referring to Chapter 8, remove both

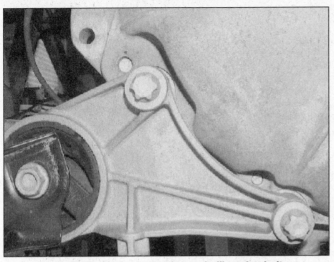

7.11 Transmission mounting-to-bellhousing bolts

7.12 Undo the six transmission mounting bolts

driveshafts. If the transmission has not been drained, be prepared for fluid loss.

9 Remove the front suspension subframe assembly as described in Chapter 10, ensuring that the engine unit is securely supported by connecting a hoist to the engine assembly. If available, the type of support bar which locates in the engine compartment side channels is to be preferred.

10 Place a jack with a block of wood beneath the transmission, and raise the jack to take the weight of the transmission.

11 Unscrew the retaining bolts, and remove the front engine mounting bracket from the transmission bellhousing **(see illustration)**.

12 Slacken and remove the six bolts securing the left-hand mounting block to the mounting bracket on the transmission casing, and remove the bracket **(see illustration)**. Using the hoist or support bar, lower the transmission end of the assembly approximately 50mm. Ensure that the various coolant hoses and wiring harnesses are not stretched.

13 On models where a pressed-steel sump is fitted to the engine, unbolt the flywheel cover plate and remove it from the base of the transmission unit.

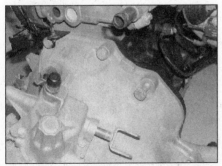

7.14 Upper transmission-to-cylinder block bolts

14 Slacken and remove the upper and lower bolts securing the transmission housing to the engine. Note the correct fitted positions of each bolt, and the necessary brackets, as they are removed, to use as a reference on refitting. Make a final check that all components have been disconnected, and are positioned clear of the transmission so that they will not hinder the removal procedure **(see illustration)**.

15 With the bolts removed, move the trolley jack and transmission to free it from its locating dowels. Once the transmission is free, lower the jack and manoeuvre the unit out from under the car. Remove the locating dowels from the transmission or engine if they are loose, and keep them in a safe place.

Refitting

16 The transmission is refitted by a reversal of the removal procedure, bearing in mind the following points.

a) Ensure the locating dowels are correctly positioned prior to installation.
b) Tighten all nuts and bolts to the specified torque (where given).
c) Renew the driveshaft oil seals (see Section 5) before refitting the driveshafts.
d) Refit the front suspension subframe assembly as described in Chapter 10.
e) Fit a new sealing ring to the transmission clutch hydraulic pipe before clipping the hose/pipe end fitting into position. Ensure the end fitting is securely retained by its clip then bleed the hydraulic system as described in Chapter 6.
f) If the transmission was drained, refill the transmission with the specified type and amount of oil, as described in Section 2. If the oil was not drained, top-up the transmission oil and check the level as described in Section 9.
g) On completion, adjust the gearchange mechanism as described in Section 3.

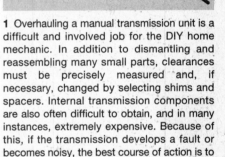

8 Transmission overhaul – general information

1 Overhauling a manual transmission unit is a difficult and involved job for the DIY home mechanic. In addition to dismantling and reassembling many small parts, clearances must be precisely measured and, if necessary, changed by selecting shims and spacers. Internal transmission components are also often difficult to obtain, and in many instances, extremely expensive. Because of this, if the transmission develops a fault or becomes noisy, the best course of action is to have the unit overhauled by a specialist repairer, or to obtain an exchange reconditioned unit.

2 Nevertheless, it is not impossible for the more experienced mechanic to overhaul the transmission, provided the special tools are available, and the job is done in a deliberate step-by-step manner, so that nothing is overlooked.

3 The tools necessary for an overhaul include internal and external circlip pliers, bearing pullers, a slide hammer, a set of pin punches, a dial test indicator, and possibly a hydraulic press. In addition, a large, sturdy workbench and a vice will be required.

4 During dismantling of the transmission, make careful notes of how each component is fitted, to make reassembly easier and more accurate.

5 Before dismantling the transmission, it will help if you have some idea what area is malfunctioning. Certain problems can be closely related to specific areas in the transmission, which can make component examination and replacement easier. Refer to the *Fault finding* Section of this manual for more information.

9.2a F13/17/18 transmission oil level aperture (arrowed)

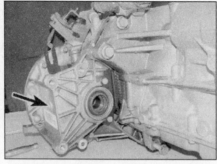

9.2b F23 transmission oil level checking plug (arrowed)

9.4 F23 transmission oil filler plug (arrowed)

9 Transmission oil level check

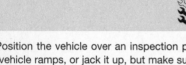

1 Position the vehicle over an inspection pit, on vehicle ramps, or jack it up, but make sure that it is level. The oil must be checked before the car is driven, or at least 5 minutes after the engine has been switched off. If the oil is checked immediately after driving the car, some of the oil will remain distributed around the transmission components, resulting in an inaccurate level reading.

2 Wipe clean the area around the level plug. The level plug is located behind the driveshaft inner joint on the left-hand side of the transmission (F13, F17 and F18 transmissions), or the rear of the differential housing (F23 transmissions) **(see illustrations)**. Unscrew the plug and clean it.

3 The oil level should reach the lower edge of the level plug hole. **Note:** *For some models fitted with the F23 transmission, the transmission is overfilled as part of a modification (see your local Vauxhall dealer). These transmissions have a yellow mark on the oil filler plug. On these vehicles, after filling up to the bottom of the level plug, fit and tighten the plug and add a further 0.5 litres of oil to the transmission.*

4 If topping-up is necessary, unscrew the reversing light switch (F13, F17 and F18 transmissions) or filler plug (F23 transmissions) and add the specified type of oil through the hole until oil begins to trickle out from the level plug hole **(see illustration)**.

5 Allow the excess oil to drain out from the level plug hole then refit the plug, tightening it to the specified torque.

6 Refit the switch/filler plug, tightening it securely, and wash off any spilt oil.

7 If necessary (see paragraph 3) add the additional oil.

Chapter 7 Part B:
Automatic transmission

Contents

Automatic transmission – removal and refitting 9
Automatic transmission fluid – draining and refilling 2
Automatic transmission fluid level check ....See Chapter 1
Automatic transmission overhaul – general information 10
Fluid cooler – general information 7
General information 1
Oil seals – renewal 6
Selector cable – adjustment 3
Selector cable – removal and refitting 4
Selector lever assembly – removal and refitting 5
Selector lever position indicator LEDs –
   removal and refitting ....See Chapter 12
Transmission control system electrical components –
   removal and refitting 8

Degrees of difficulty

Easy, suitable for novice with little experience	**Fairly easy,** suitable for beginner with some experience	**Fairly difficult,** suitable for competent DIY mechanic	**Difficult,** suitable for experienced DIY mechanic	**Very difficult,** suitable for expert DIY or professional

Specifications

General

Type	Four forward and 1 reverse speed electronically-controlled automatic with three driving modes (economy, sport and winter)

Identification code*:
1.4 and 1.6 litre models	AF13
1.8 litre models	AF17
2.0 litre models	AF20
2.2 litre models	AF22

* The identification code is marked on the identification plate which is attached to the top of the transmission unit

Lubrication

Fluid type	See *Lubricants and fluids*
Fluid capacity	See Specifications, Chapter 1

Torque wrench settings

	Nm	lbf ft
Drain plug	35	26
Driveplate cover plate	8	6
Engine-to-transmission unit bolts	60	44
Fluid temperature sensor	10	7
Input shaft speed sensor bolt	5	4
Oil sump to transmission	40	30
Output shaft speed sensor bolt	5	4
Selector lever:		
Pivot crank nut	28	21
Lever-to-vehicle body bolts	5	4
Starter inhibitor/reversing light switch bolt	25	18
Torque converter-to-driveplate bolts*:		
Stage 1	20	15
Stage 2	45	33
Stage 3	Angle-tighten a further 30°	
Transmission selector shaft nuts:		
Main (starter/reversing light switch) nut	8	6
Selector lever nut	16	12

* Use new bolts

1 General information

1 Most models covered in this manual were offered with the option of a four-speed, electronically-controlled automatic transmission, consisting of a torque converter, an epicyclic geartrain, and hydraulically-operated clutches and brakes. The unit is controlled by the electronic control unit (ECU) via four electrically-operated solenoid valves. The transmission unit has three driving modes; economy, sport and winter modes.

2 The economy mode is the standard mode for driving in which the transmission shifts up at relatively low engine speeds to combine reasonable performance with economy. If the transmission unit is switched into sport mode, using the button on the selector lever, the transmission shifts up only at high engine speeds, giving improved acceleration and overtaking performance. When the transmission is in sport mode, the indicator light in the instrument panel is illuminated. If the transmission is switched into winter mode, using the button on the selector lever indicator panel, the transmission will select third gear as the vehicle pulls away from a standing start; this helps to maintain traction on very slippery surfaces.

3 The torque converter provides a fluid coupling between engine and transmission, which acts as an automatic clutch, and also provides a degree of torque multiplication when accelerating.

4 The epicyclic geartrain provides either of the four forward or one reverse gear ratios, according to which of its component parts are held stationary or allowed to turn. The components of the geartrain are held or released by brakes and clutches which are activated by the control unit. A fluid pump within the transmission provides the necessary hydraulic pressure to operate the brakes and clutches.

5 Driver control of the transmission is by a seven-position selector lever. The drive D position, allows automatic changing throughout the range of all four gear ratios. An automatic kickdown facility shifts the transmission down a gear if the accelerator pedal is fully depressed. The transmission also has three hold positions, 1 means only the first gear ratio can be selected, 2 allows both the first and second gear ratios position to be automatically selected and 3 allows automatic changing between the first three gear ratios. These hold positions are useful for providing engine braking when travelling down steep gradients. Note, however, that the transmission should *never* be shifted down a position at high engine speeds.

6 Due to the complexity of the automatic transmission, any repair or overhaul work must be left to a Vauxhall dealer with the necessary special equipment for fault diagnosis and repair. The contents of the following Sections

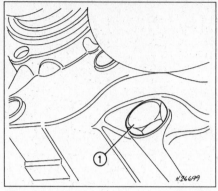

2.3 Automatic transmission drain plug (1)

are therefore confined to supplying general information, and any service information and instructions that can be used by the owner.

2 Automatic transmission fluid – draining and refilling

Draining

1 This operation is much quicker and more efficient if the vehicle is first taken on a journey of sufficient length to warm the engine /transmission up to normal operating temperature.

2 Park the vehicle on level ground, switch off the ignition, and apply the handbrake firmly. For improved access, jack up the front of the car and support it securely on axle stands (see *Jacking and vehicle support*).

3 Withdraw the dipstick, then position a container under the drain plug at the rear right-hand side of the transmission, below the driveshaft. Unscrew the plug and remove it along with its sealing washer **(see illustration)**.

4 Allow the fluid to drain completely into the container. If the fluid is hot, take precautions against scalding.

5 When the fluid has finished draining, clean the drain plug threads and those of the transmission casing, fit a new sealing washer

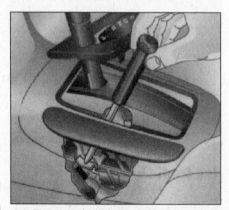

3.0 To move the selector lever from the P position with the battery disconnected, manually release the detent lever

and refit the drain plug, tightening it to the specified torque wrench setting. Where applicable, lower the vehicle to the ground.

Refilling

6 Refilling the transmission is an awkward operation, adding the specified type and amount of fluid to the transmission a little at a time via the dipstick tube. Use a funnel with a fine mesh gauze, to avoid spillage, and to ensure that no foreign matter enters the transmission. Allow plenty of time for the fluid level to settle properly.

7 Start the engine, and allow it to idle for a few minutes whilst moving the selector lever through its various positions. Switch off the engine and add sufficient fluid to bring the level up to the lower mark on the dipstick. Take the car on a short run to fully distribute the new fluid around the transmission, then recheck the fluid level as described in Chapter 1 with the transmission at normal operating temperature.

3 Selector cable – adjustment

Note: *If the battery is disconnected with the selector lever in the P position, the lever will be locked in position. To manually release the lever, carefully prise out the selector lever surround from the top of the centre console then, using a flat-bladed screwdriver, depress the detent lever on the left-hand side of the selector lever (see illustration).*

1 Operate the selector lever throughout its entire range and check that the transmission engages the correct gear indicated on the selector lever position indicator. If adjustment is necessary, continue as follows.

2 Position the selector lever in the P (Park) position.

3 Working in the engine compartment, to gain access to the transmission end of the selector cable, remove the battery and mounting plate (see Chapter 5A).

4 Locate the selector cable mounting bracket on the top of the transmission unit and release the inner cable by carefully lifting the locking clip in the cable end fitting **(see illustration)**.

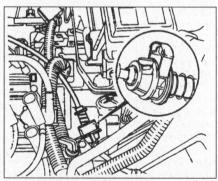

3.4 Release the selector cable inner cable by lifting the locking clip (inset)

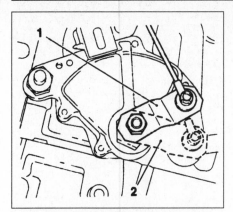

3.5 Move the transmission selector (1) fully forwards so that it is in the P position (2)

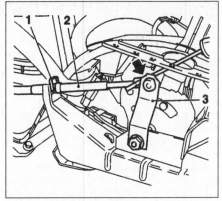

4.2 Remove the retaining clip (1) then lever the selector cable (2) off from the selector lever balljoint (3)

5 Ensure that the selector lever is locked in the P position and move the lever on the transmission selector mechanism fully forwards so that the transmission is also positioned in the Park position **(see illustration)**. With both the selector lever and transmission correctly positioned, lock the cable adjuster in position by pushing the locking clip firmly down until it clicks in position.

6 Refit the battery then check the operation of the selector lever and, if necessary, repeat the adjustment procedure.

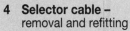

4 Selector cable – removal and refitting

Removal

1 Remove the centre console as described in Chapter 11 then position the selector lever in the P (Park) position.

2 Using a flat-bladed screwdriver, carefully lever the selector cable end fitting off from the balljoint from the base of the lever. Slide out the retaining clip and release the cable from the front of the lever mounting plate **(see illustration)**.

3 Working in the engine compartment, to gain access to the transmission end of the selector cable, remove the battery and mounting plate (see Chapter 5A).

4 Slide off the retaining clip (where fitted) then carefully unclip the selector cable end fitting from the transmission lever. Unclip the outer cable from its mounting bracket.

5 Work back along the cable, noting its correct routing, and free it from all the relevant retaining clips. Ensure that the rubber cable grommet stays in the bulkhead.

6 Examine the cable, looking for worn end fittings or a damaged outer casing, and for signs of fraying of the inner cable. Check the cable's operation; the inner cable should move smoothly and easily through the outer casing. Remember that a cable that appears

serviceable when tested off the car may well be much heavier in operation when curved into its working position. Renew the cable if it shows any signs of excessive wear or any damage.

Refitting

7 Manoeuvre the cable into position, ensuring it is correctly routed and pass it through the bulkhead. Ensure the cable passes through the selector lever mounting plate. In order to allow the cable to pass easily through the bulkhead, lubricate the grommet with a little soap solution.

8 Pass the transmission end of the cable through its mounting bracket and clip the outer cable securely in position. Align the inner cable end fitting with the transmission lever then clip it on the lever and (where necessary) secure it in position with the retaining clip.

9 From inside the vehicle, secure the outer cable in position with the retaining clip, and clip the inner cable end fitting securely onto the selector lever balljoint.

10 Adjust the selector cable as described in Section 3.

11 Refit the centre console, as described in Chapter 11, and refit all components removed to gain access to the transmission end of the cable.

5 Selector lever assembly – removal and refitting

Note: *Renewal of the sport and winter mode switches is covered in Section 8*

Removal

1 Remove the centre console, as described in Chapter 11, then position the selector lever in the P (Park) position.

2 Disconnect the wiring connectors from the selector lever mode switches and free the bulbholder from the indicator panel.

3 Using a flat-bladed screwdriver, carefully lever the selector cable end fitting off from the balljoint from the base of the lever. Slide out the retaining clip and release the cable from the front of the lever mounting plate.

4 Slacken and remove the four mounting bolts then manoeuvre the lever assembly out of position.

5 Inspect the selector lever mechanism for signs of wear or damage. To dismantle, slacken and remove the nut and washer then withdraw the pivot crank assembly. Unclip the indicator panel then separate the lever assembly and mounting plate. No further dismantling is possible.

Refitting

6 Where necessary, reassemble the lever and mounting plate and insert the pivot crank. Ensure the crank is correctly engaged with the selector lever then refit the washer and tighten its retaining nut to the specified torque. Clip the indicator panel onto the mounting plate then check the operation of the lever before refitting it to the car.

7 Manoeuvre the lever assembly into position, engage it with the selector cable. Refit the retaining bolts and tighten them to the specified torque setting.

8 Secure the outer cable in position with the retaining clip and securely clip the cable end fitting onto the selector lever crank balljoint.

9 Ensuring the wiring is correctly routed, refit the bulbholder to the indicator panel and reconnect the switch wiring connectors.

10 Adjust the selector cable, as described in Section 3, then refit the centre console as described in Chapter 11.

6 Oil seals – renewal

Driveshaft oil seals

1 Refer to Chapter 7A, Section 5.

Torque converter oil seal

2 Remove the transmission as described in Section 9.

3 Carefully slide the torque converter off of the transmission shaft whilst being prepared for fluid spillage.

4 Note the correct fitted position of the seal in the oil pump housing then carefully lever the seal out of position taking care not to mark the housing or input shaft.

5 Remove all traces of dirt from the area around the oil seal aperture then press the new seal into position, ensuring its sealing lip is facing inwards.

6 Lubricate the seal with clean transmission fluid then carefully ease the torque converter into position.

7 Refit the transmission (see Section 9).

7 Fluid cooler – general information

1 The transmission fluid cooler is an integral part of the radiator assembly. Refer to Chapter 3 for removal and refitting details, if the cooler is damaged the complete radiator assembly must be renewed.

8 Transmission control system electrical components – removal and refitting

Starter inhibitor/reversing light switch

1 The switch is a dual-function switch, performing the reversing light and starter inhibitor switch functions. The switch operates the reversing lights when reverse gear is selected and prevents the engine being started when the transmission is in gear. If at any time the reversing light operation becomes faulty, or it is noted that the engine can be started with the selector lever in any position other than P (Park) or N (Neutral), then it is likely that the switch is faulty. If adjustment fails to correct the fault then the complete switch must be renewed as a unit.

Removal

2 Position the selector lever in the N (Neutral) position.
3 To gain access to the switch, remove the battery and mounting plate as described in Chapter 5A.
4 Slide off the retaining clip (where fitted) then carefully unclip the selector cable end fitting from the transmission lever. Unscrew the retaining nut and remove the lever from the transmission selector shaft.
5 Trace the wiring back from the switch and

disconnect it at the wiring connector. Unlock the wiring plug by pulling the lock clip away from the main body of the plug.
6 On 2.0 and 2.2 litre models, withdraw the transmission fluid dipstick then undo the retaining nut and ease the dipstick out from the transmission. Remove the dipstick seal and discard it; a new one should be used on refitting.
7 Bend back the lockwasher (where fitted) then slacken and remove the main nut and washer(s) from the transmission selector shaft.
8 Slacken and remove the switch and wiring retaining plate bolts, and manoeuvre the switch assembly upwards and away from the transmission unit.

Refitting

9 Prior to refitting, first make sure that the transmission selector shaft is still in the N (Neutral) position. If there is any doubt, engage the selector lever with the transmission shaft and move the lever fully forwards (to the P position) then move it two notches backwards.
10 Locate the switch on the transmission shaft then refit the wiring retaining plate. Refit the retaining bolts, tightening them by hand only at this stage.
11 Refit the washer(s) and main nut to the selector shaft. Tighten the nut to the specified torque setting and secure it in position by bending up the locking washer against one of its flats.
12 Adjust the switch as described in paragraph 18.
13 Once the switch is correctly adjusted, reconnect the wiring connector, ensuring that the wiring is correctly routed.
14 On 2.0 and 2.2 litre models, fit a new seal to the transmission aperture then ease the dipstick tube into position. Securely tighten the dipstick retaining nut then refit the dipstick.
15 Refit the selector lever to the shaft and tighten its retaining nut to the specified

torque. Clip the selector cable end fitting securely onto the lever balljoint.
16 Refit the battery and check the operation of the switch. If necessary, adjust the selector cable as described in Section 3.

Adjustment

Note: *Before adjusting the switch first ensure the selector cable is correctly adjusted (see Section 3).*

17 Carry out the operations described in paragraphs 2 to 4.
18 With the transmission in Neutral, the flats on the selector shaft should be parallel to the marking on the switch assembly **(see illustration)**. If adjustment is necessary, slacken the switch retaining bolts and rotate the switch assembly as necessary before retightening the bolts to the specified torque setting.
19 Refit the selector lever to the shaft and tighten its retaining nut to the specified torque. Refit the selector cable end fitting securely onto the lever and (where necessary) secure it in position with the retaining clip.
20 Refit the battery and check the operation of the switch. If adjustment of the switch has not been successful, then the switch must be faulty and should be renewed.

Sport mode switch

Note: *A soldering iron and solder will be required to renew the switch.*

Removal

21 Remove the selector lever assembly as described in Section 5.
22 Push the switch out of the top of the selector lever by inserting a length of welding rod up through the selector lever bore **(see illustration)**.
23 Make identification marks between the switch and wires then carefully unsolder the wires from the switch terminals and remove the switch. The wiring can then be withdrawn from the base of the lever.

Refitting

24 Feed the wiring up through the selector lever bore until it appears at the top. Solder the wires to the terminals of the switch, using the marks made prior to removal to ensure they are correctly connected.
25 Push the switch securely into position then refit the selector lever as described in Section 5.

Winter mode switch

Removal

26 Remove the centre console, as described in Chapter 11, to gain access to the selector lever trim cover screws. Slacken and remove the two screws from the rear of the cover and lift the cover off of the lever.
27 Release the retaining clips and free the selector lever position indicator panel from the lever mounting plate.
28 Trace the wiring back from the switch and disconnect it at the wiring connector. Unclip

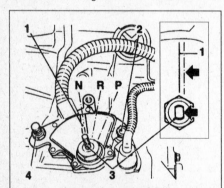

8.18 Starter inhibitor/reversing light switch adjustment details

1 *Switch assembly marking*
2 *Retaining bolt*
3 *Selector shaft*
4 *Retaining bolt*

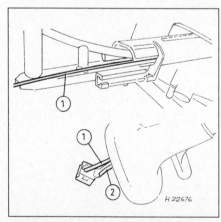

8.22 Insert a welding rod (1) in through the base of the selector lever and push the sport mode switch out of position. The switch wires (2) can then be unsoldered

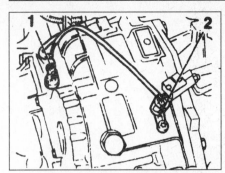

8.35 Transmission input shaft sensor (1) and output shaft speed sensor (2) locations – 2.0 and 2.2 litre models

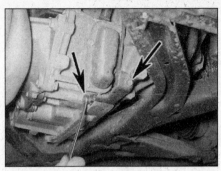

8.45 Undo the retaining bolts (arrowed) and remove the cover plate . . .

8.46 . . . to gain access to the fluid temperature sensor (arrowed)

the switch from the indicator panel and remove it from the vehicle.

Refitting

29 Refitting is the reverse of removal, ensuring the wiring is correctly routed.

Kickdown switch

30 The kickdown switch is an integral part of the accelerator cable and cannot be renewed separately. Refer to Chapter 4A for details of accelerator cable removal and refitting. **Note:** *On models with electronic throttle body and pedal sensor, the kickdown is controlled by the ECU.*

Electronic control unit (ECU)

Removal

31 The ECU is located in front of the centre console, and clipped into a bracket on the heater distribution housing. Prior to removal, disconnect the battery negative terminal (refer to *Disconnecting the battery* in the Reference Chapter).
32 Remove the centre console as described in Chapter 11, and the left-hand central air distribution duct (see Chapter 3, Section 10).
33 Unclip the ECU bracket from the heater distribution housing, and pull out to one side. If the wiring harness prevents the ECU from being moved to one side, cut the cable tie securing the harness in place. Disconnect the ECU wiring plug, and if necessary, unclip the ECU from the bracket.

Refitting

34 Refitting is the reverse of removal, ensuring that the wiring is securely reconnected.

Input and output shaft speed sensors

Removal

35 On 2.0 and 2.2 litre models, the speed sensors are fitted to the top of the transmission unit. The input shaft speed sensor is the front of the two sensors and is nearest to the left-hand end of the transmission. The output shaft sensor is the rear of the two **(see illustration)**. On 1.4, 1.6 and 1.8 litre models, the sensors are fitted to the top-rear of the transmission unit. The

output shaft speed sensor is the uppermost of the two sensors.
36 On 1.4, 1.6 and 1.8 litre models, firmly apply the handbrake, jack up the front of the car and support it securely on axle stands (see *Jacking and vehicle support*). Remove the left-front roadwheel and lower wheelarch liner (where fitted – see Chapter 11). On 2.0 and 2.2 litre models, to gain access to the sensors, remove the battery and mounting plate as described in Chapter 5A.
37 Disconnect the wiring connector and wipe clean the area around the relevant sensor.
38 Undo the retaining bolt and remove the sensor from the transmission. Remove the sealing ring from the sensor and discard it, a new one should be used on refitting.

Refitting

39 Fit the new sealing ring to the sensor groove and lubricate it with a smear of transmission fluid.
40 Ease the sensor into position then refit the retaining bolt and tighten it to the specified torque setting. Reconnect the wiring connector.
41 On 2.0 and 2.2 litre models, refit the battery. On 1.4, 1.6 and 1.8 litre models, refit the lower wheelarch liner (where removed) and the left-front roadwheel, and lower the vehicle to the ground.

Fluid temperature sensor

Note: *On 1.4, 1.6 and 1.8 litre models, the temperature sensor is not available separately from the transmission wiring harness. Also, in order to remove the sensor, it is necessary to remove the transmission side cover and expose the various shift valves and solenoids. This is a difficult task requiring the highest standards of cleanliness. For these reasons, the task of renewing the temperature sensor should be entrusted to a Vauxhall dealer or specialist. The procedure described below is applicable only to the AF20/22 transmission unit as fitted to 2.0 and 2.2 litre models.*

Removal

42 The fluid temperature sensor is screwed into the base of the transmission unit, at the front. Before removing the sensor, disconnect the battery negative terminal.

43 Firmly apply the handbrake then jack up the front of the vehicle and support it on axle stands.
44 Trace the wiring back from the sensor, noting its correct routing. Disconnect the wiring connector and free the wiring from its retaining clips.
45 Undo the retaining bolts and remove the cover plate from the sensor **(see illustration)**.
46 Wipe clean the area around the sensor and have a suitable plug ready to minimise fluid loss as the sensor is removed **(see illustration)**.
47 Unscrew the sensor and remove it from the transmission unit along with its sealing washer. Quickly plug the transmission aperture and wipe up any spilt fluid.

Refitting

48 Fit a new sealing washer to the sensor then remove the plug and quickly screw the sensor into the transmission unit. Tighten the sensor to the specified torque and wipe up any spilt fluid. Refit the cover plate and securely tighten its retaining bolts.
49 Ensure the wiring is correctly routed and retained by all the necessary clips then securely reconnect the wiring connector.
50 Lower the vehicle to the floor and reconnect the battery. Check the transmission fluid level as described in Chapter 1.

9 Automatic transmission – removal and refitting

Note: *New torque converter-to-driveplate bolts and fluid cooler union sealing rings will be required on refitting.*

Removal

1 Chock the rear wheels, apply the handbrake, and place the selector lever in the N (Neutral) position. Jack up the front of the vehicle, and securely support it on axle stands. Remove both front roadwheels then remove the retaining screws and fasteners and (where necessary) remove the undercover from beneath the engine/transmission unit.

9.14 Remove the three bolts securing the right-hand engine mounting

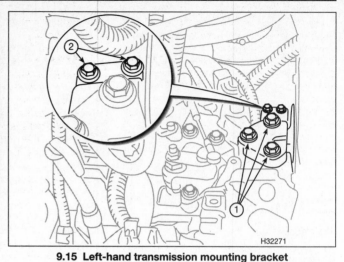

9.15 Left-hand transmission mounting bracket

1 Bracket-to-mounting bolts   2 Bracket-to-transmission bolts

2 Drain the transmission fluid as described in Section 2, then refit the drain plug and tighten it to the specified torque.

3 Remove the battery and mounting plate as described in Chapter 5A.

4 With reference to Chapter 4A, remove the front exhaust pipe, catalytic converter and intermediate pipe.

5 Referring to Chapter 8, remove both driveshafts. If the transmission has not been drained, be prepared for fluid loss.

6 Remove the front suspension subframe assembly as described in Chapter 10, ensuring that the engine unit is securely supported by connecting a hoist to the engine assembly. If available, the type of support bar which locates in the engine compartment side channels is to be preferred.

7 Slide off the retaining clip (where fitted) then carefully unclip the selector cable end fitting from the transmission lever. Unclip the outer cable from its mounting bracket and position the cable clear of the transmission unit.

8 Undo the retaining bolt and remove the automatic transmission fluid filler pipe/dipstick tube – recover the sealing ring.

9 Trace the wiring back from the transmission switches and sensors and disconnect the various connectors by lifting their retaining clips. Release the main wiring harness from any clips or ties securing it to the transmission unit.

10 Remove the fastening bolts for the selector outer cable retaining bracket/wiring harness bracket, and withdraw the bracket.

11 Disconnect the breather hose (where fitted) from the top of the transmission unit.

12 Remove the air cleaner housing and intake hose (see Chapter 4A).

13 Place a jack with a block of wood beneath the transmission, and raise the jack to take the weight of the transmission.

14 Slacken and remove the three bolts securing the right-hand engine mounting to the bracket bolted to the end of the cylinder block **(see illustration)**.

15 Unscrew the bolts securing the left-hand engine/transmission mounting and

bracket to the transmission casing **(see illustration)**.

16 Make identification marks between the oil cooler hoses and their unions on the front of the transmission housing. Using a flat-bladed screwdriver, prise out the retaining clips from each hose end fitting and detach both hoses from the transmission. There are two types of fitting depending on model **(see illustrations)**. Clip the retaining clips back into position in the end fittings and discard the sealing rings; new sealing rings must be used on refitting. Plug/cover both the union and hose ends to prevent the entry of dirt.

17 Undo the two retaining bolts and remove the front engine/transmission mounting assembly from the front of the transmission housing.

18 By manipulating the engine hoist and the jack under the transmission, lower the engine/transmission approximately 50mm. Ensure that the various coolant hoses and wiring harnesses are not stretched.

19 Remove the rubber cover(s) from the cylinder block/sump flange to gain access to the torque converter retaining bolts. Slacken and remove the visible bolt(s) then, using a socket and extension bar to rotate the crankshaft pulley, undo the remaining bolts securing the torque converter to the driveplate as they become accessible. On 1.4, 1.6, 1.8 and 2.2 litre models there are three bolts in total and on 2.0 litre models there are six. Discard the bolts, new ones must be used on refitting.

20 To ensure that the torque converter does not fall out as the transmission is removed, slide the converter along the shaft and fully into the transmission housing.

21 With the jack positioned beneath the transmission taking the weight, slacken and remove the upper and lower bolts securing the transmission housing to the engine. Note the correct fitted positions of each bolt, and the necessary brackets, as they are removed, to use as a reference on refitting. On 1.4, 1.6,

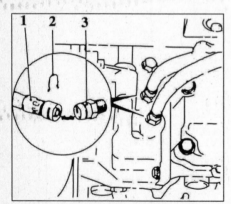

9.16a Transmission fluid cooler hose connections – type 1

1 Hose end fitting   3 Transmission
2 Retaining clip   union

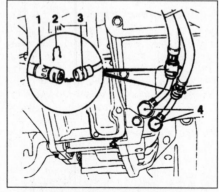

9.16b Transmission fluid cooler hose connections – type 2

1 Hose end fitting   4 Transmission
2 Retaining clip   unions
3 Pipe end fitting

1.8 and 2.2 litre models, do not overlook the two bolts securing the engine oil sump to the transmission casing. Make a final check that all components have been disconnected, and are positioned clear of the transmission so that they will not hinder the removal procedure.

22 With all the bolts removed, move the trolley jack and transmission to free it from its locating dowels. Once the transmission is free, lower the jack and manoeuvre the unit out from under the car, taking care to ensure that the torque converter does not fall off. Remove the locating dowels from the transmission or engine if they are loose, and keep them in a safe place.

Refitting

23 The transmission is refitted by a reversal of the removal procedure, bearing in mind the following points.

a) *Prior to refitting, remove all traces of old locking compound from the torque converter threads by running a tap of the correct thread diameter and pitch down the holes. In the absence of a suitable*

tap, use one of the old bolts with slots cut in its threads.

b) *Prior to refitting, ensure the engine/transmission locating dowels are correctly positioned and apply a smear of molybdenum disulphide grease to the torque converter locating pin and its centring bush in the crankshaft end.*

c) *Once the transmission and engine are correctly joined, refit the securing bolts, tightening them to the specified torque setting.*

d) *Fit the new torque converter-to-driveplate bolts and tighten them lightly only to start then go around and tighten them to the specified torque setting in a diagonal sequence.*

e) *Tighten all nuts and bolts to the specified torque (where given).*

f) *Renew the driveshaft oil seals (see Chapter 7A) and refit the driveshafts to the transmission as described in Chapter 8.*

g) *Fit new sealing rings to the fluid cooler hose unions and ensure both unions are*

securely retained by their clips.

h) *Fit a new sealing ring to the fluid filler pipe/dipstick guide tube.*

i) *On completion, refill the transmission with the specified type and quantity of fluid as described in Section 2 and adjust the selector cable as described in Section 3.*

10 Automatic transmission overhaul – general information

1 In the event of a fault occurring with the transmission, it is first necessary to determine whether it is of a mechanical or hydraulic nature, and to do this, special test equipment is required. It is therefore essential to have the work carried out by a Vauxhall dealer or specialist if a transmission fault is suspected.

2 Do not remove the transmission from the car for possible repair before professional fault diagnosis has been carried out, since most tests require the transmission to be in the vehicle.

Notes

Chapter 8
Driveshafts

Contents

Description – general 1
Driveshaft – removal and refitting 2
Driveshaft gaiter check . . . . .See Chapter 1
Driveshaft joint – checking and renewal 3
Driveshaft joint gaiter – renewal 4

Degrees of difficulty

Easy, suitable for novice with little experience	Fairly easy, suitable for beginner with some experience	Fairly difficult, suitable for competent DIY mechanic	Difficult, suitable for experienced DIY mechanic	Very difficult, suitable for expert DIY or professional

Specifications

Type . . . . Unequal-length open shafts, with constant velocity joint at each end. All models have a vibration damper fitted to the right-hand driveshaft

Driveshaft vibration damper
Dimension from outer joint:
  1.4 and 1.6 litre models . . . . 332.0 mm
  1.8, 2.0 and 2.2 litre models . . . . 310.0 mm

Driveshaft joint grease specification . . . . Special Grease (Vauxhall P/N 90094176)

Torque wrench settings

	Nm	lbf ft
Front anti-roll bar to suspension strut	65	48
Front hub nut (refer to text):		
Stage 1	120	89
Stage 2	Loosen nut fully	
Stage 3	20	15
Stage 4	Angle-tighten by a further 80° (plus to next split pin hole as necessary)	
Front suspension lower balljoint clamp bolt	100	74
Roadwheel	110	81
Track rod end balljoint to knuckle	60	44
Vibration damper	10	7

1 Description – general

Drive is transmitted from the differential to the front wheels by means of two, unequal-length driveshafts.

Each driveshaft is fitted with an inner and outer constant velocity (CV) joint. From model year 2000, the inner joints on 1.8 litre Astra and Zafira models are of tripod type. Each outer joint is splined to engage with the wheel hub, and is retained by a large nut. The inner joint is also splined to engage with the differential sunwheel and is held in place by an internal circlip. A vibration damper is attached to the right-hand driveshaft.

2 Driveshaft – removal and refitting

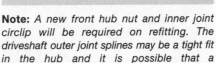

Note: *A new front hub nut and inner joint circlip will be required on refitting. The driveshaft outer joint splines may be a tight fit in the hub and it is possible that a puller/extractor will be required to draw the hub assembly off the driveshaft during removal.*

Removal

1 Apply the handbrake, then jack up the front of the vehicle and support it on axle stands (see *Jacking and vehicle support*). Remove the roadwheel. It is an advantage to only jack up one side of the vehicle as this will reduce loss of oil from the transmission when the driveshaft is withdrawn **(see illustration)**.

2.1 The right-hand driveshaft viewed from under the vehicle

2.2 Use a cold chisel to tap off the hub nut cap

2.3 Removing the split pin from the castellated hub nut

2.4 Removing the front hub nut and washer

2.7 Anti-roll bar link attachment to the front strut

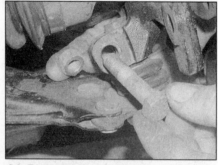

2.8 Removing the clamp bolt securing the front lower suspension arm to the hub carrier

2.9 Using a cold chisel to expand the balljoint clamp at the bottom of the hub carrier

2 Using a cold chisel or screwdriver, tap off the hub nut cap **(see illustration)**.
3 Extract the split pin from the castellated hub nut on the end of the driveshaft **(see illustration)**.
4 The hub nut must now be loosened. The nut is extremely tight, and an extension bar will be required to loosen it. To prevent the driveshaft from turning, insert two roadwheel bolts, and insert a metal bar between them to counterhold the hub. Remove the hub nut and washer from the driveshaft **(see illustration)**.
5 Unscrew the nut securing the track rod end to the steering arm on the hub carrier, then use a balljoint separator tool to remove the track rod end.
6 Unbolt the hydraulic brake hose support bracket from the front suspension strut, and release the hose from it.
7 Unscrew and remove the nut securing the

anti-roll bar link to the strut, while holding the joint stub on the flats provided with a further spanner **(see illustration)**. Release the link from the strut and move it to one side.
8 Unscrew and remove the clamp bolt securing the front lower suspension arm to the hub carrier. Note that the bolt head faces the front of the vehicle **(see illustration)**.
9 Using a chisel or screwdriver as a wedge, expand the balljoint clamp at the bottom of the hub carrier **(see illustration)**.
10 Using a lever, push down on the suspension lower arm to free the balljoint from the hub carrier **(see illustration)**, then move the hub carrier to one side and release the arm, taking care not to damage the balljoint rubber boot.
11 The hub must now be freed from the end of the driveshaft. It should be possible to pull the hub off the driveshaft, but if the end of the

driveshaft is tight in the hub, temporarily refit the hub nut to protect the driveshaft threads, then tap the end of the driveshaft with a soft-faced hammer while pulling outwards on the hub carrier **(see illustrations)**. Alternatively, use a suitable puller to press the driveshaft through the hub.
12 With the driveshaft detached from the hub carrier, tie the suspension strut to one side and support the driveshaft on an axle stand.
13 Where fitted, remove the splash guard from the bottom of the engine compartment. Position a suitable container beneath the transmission to catch any spilt oil.
14 A lever will now be required to release the inner end of the driveshaft from the differential. Carefully lever between the driveshaft and differential housing to release the driveshaft circlip **(see illustration)**. **Note:** *Model year 2000 1.8 litre models have an*

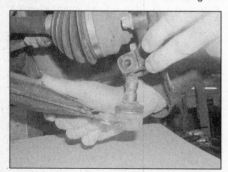

2.10 Push down the suspension lower arm to free the balljoint from the hub carrier

2.11a Use a soft-faced hammer to drive the driveshaft from the hub splines . . .

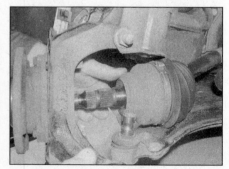

2.11b . . . then pull the hub carrier outwards

2.14 Carefully lever between the driveshaft and differential housing to release the driveshaft

2.16 Vibration damper fitted to the right-hand driveshaft

2.17 Examine the oil seal in the transmission before refitting the driveshaft

indentation in the joint housing to facilitate removal.

15 Withdraw the driveshaft from the transmission, ensuring that the constant velocity joints are not placed under excessive strain, and remove the driveshaft from beneath the vehicle. Whilst the driveshaft is removed, plug or tape over the differential aperture to prevent dirt entry.

Caution: Do not allow the vehicle to rest on its wheels with one or both driveshafts removed, as damage to the wheel bearings(s) may result. If the vehicle must be moved on its wheels, clamp the wheel bearings using spacers and a long threaded rod to take the place of the driveshaft.

16 All models have a vibration damper fitted to the right-hand driveshaft. If the damper is transferred to a new driveshaft, measure its fitted position before removing and locate it in the same position on the new driveshaft **(see illustration)**. The correct dimension from the outer gaiter is given in the Specifications.

Refitting

17 Before refitting the driveshaft, examine the oil seal in the transmission housing and renew it if necessary as described in Chapter 7A or 7B **(see illustration)**.

18 Remove the circlip from the end of the driveshaft inner joint splines and discard it. Fit a new circlip, making sure it is correctly located in the groove.

19 Thoroughly clean the driveshaft splines, and the apertures in the transmission and hub assembly. Apply a thin film of grease to the oil seal lips, and to the driveshaft splines and shoulders. Check that all gaiter clips are securely fastened.

20 Offer up the driveshaft, and engage the inner joint splines with those of the differential sun gear, taking care not to damage the oil seal. Push the joint fully into position, then check that the circlip is correctly located and securely holds the joint in position. If necessary, use a soft-faced mallet or drift to drive the driveshaft inner joint fully into position.

21 Align the outer constant velocity joint splines with those of the hub, and slide the joint back into position in the hub.

22 Using the lever, push down on the lower suspension arm, then re-locate the balljoint and release the arm. Make sure that the balljoint stub is fully entered in the hub carrier.

23 Insert the clamp bolt with its head facing the front of the vehicle, and tighten it to the specified torque.

24 Refit the anti-roll bar link to the strut, and tighten the nut to the specified torque while holding the joint stub on the flats provided with a further spanner.

25 Locate the support bracket on the brake hose, then refit the bracket to the strut and tighten the bolt.

26 Refit the track rod end to the steering arm on the hub carrier and tighten the nut to the specified torque.

27 Refit the washer to the end of the driveshaft, then screw on a new nut and tighten moderately at this stage.

28 Refit the splash guard (where fitted), then refit the roadwheel and lower the vehicle to the ground. Tighten the wheel bolts to the specified torque.

29 Tighten the hub nut in the stages given in the Specifications, and fit a new split pin. Bend the outer leg of the split pin over the end of the driveshaft, then cut the inner leg as necessary and bend it inwards **(see illustrations)**.

30 Tap the hub nut cap into position then refit the wheel trim.

31 Check and if necessary top-up the oil level in the transmission as described in Chapter 7A (manual transmission) or Chapter 1 (automatic transmission).

2.29a Insert the new split pin . . .

3 Driveshaft joint – checking and renewal

Checking

1 Road test the vehicle, and listen for a metallic clicking noise from the front as the vehicle is driven slowly in a circle on full-lock. If evident, this indicates wear in the outer constant velocity joint which must be renewed.

2 To check for wear on the inner joint, apply the handbrake then jack up the front of the vehicle and support it on axle stands (see *Jacking and vehicle support*). Where necessary, remove the splash guard from the bottom of the engine compartment. Attempt to move the inner end of the driveshaft up and down, then hold the joint with one hand and attempt to rotate the driveshaft with the other. If excessive wear is evident, the joint must be renewed.

Renewal

Note: *It is not possible to renew the tripod-type inner joint on later models, as it is integral with the driveshaft.*

3 With the driveshaft removed, as described in Section 2, release the securing clips and slide back the rubber gaiter from the worn joint.

4 Using a screwdriver or circlip pliers, expand the circlip that secures the joint to the driveshaft **(see illustrations)**.

2.29b . . . and bend the legs to secure

3.4a Driveshaft joint retaining circlip

3.4b Expanding the driveshaft joint retaining circlip

3.7 Packing the joint with grease

4.2 Cutting the gaiter free

5 Using a soft-faced mallet, tap the joint from the driveshaft.

6 Ensure that a new circlip is fitted to the new joint, then tap the new joint onto the driveshaft until the circlip engages in its groove.

7 Pack the joint with the specified type of grease (see illustration).

8 Refit the rubber gaiter to the new joint, referring to Section 4.

9 Refit the driveshaft to the vehicle, as described in Section 2.

4 Driveshaft joint gaiter – renewal

Note: Where a tripod-type inner joint is fitted, access to the inner gaiter is gained by first removing the outer gaiter.

1 With the driveshaft removed as described in Section 2, remove the relevant joint as described in Section 3. Note that if both gaiters on a driveshaft are to be renewed it is only necessary to remove one joint, although on the right-hand driveshaft it will also be necessary to remove the vibration damper after noting its location.

2 Remove the gaiter from the driveshaft – if necessary, cut the gaiter free (see illustration).

3 Clean the old grease from the joint. If excessively worn or damaged, the driveshaft joint should be renewed as described in Section 3.

4 Slide the new gaiter and new inner securing clip onto the driveshaft so that the smaller diameter opening is located in the groove in the driveshaft (see illustrations). Note: The inner end of the inner gaiter must be 135 mm from the end of the driveshaft on 1.4 and 1.6 litre engine models, and 128 mm from the end of the driveshaft on 1.8 and 2.0 litre engine models.

5 Pack the joint with the specified type of grease (see illustration).

6 Refit the joint, using a new inner securing circlip. Tap the joint onto the driveshaft until the circlip engages in its groove.

7 Slide the gaiter onto the joint, then release any excess air by lifting the gaiter from the joint with a screwdriver.

8 Secure the gaiter using new clips. To fit a loop-type clip, locate it over the gaiter then squeeze the raised loop using pincers – note that Vauxhall technicians use a special tool to do this, however careful use of pincers or a

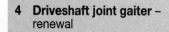

4.4a Locate the new inner securing clip on the driveshaft . . .

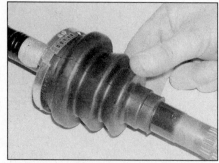

4.4b . . . followed by the new gaiter

4.5 Pack the joint with the specified type of grease

4.8a Fitting the outer securing clip

4.8b . . . and tightening using a pair of pincers

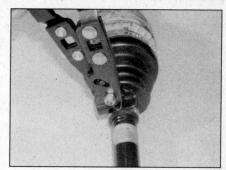

4.8c Tightening the outer securing clip using the special tool

similar tool will be sufficient **(see illustrations)**. To fit a lug-and-slot type clip, wrap it around the gaiter and while pulling on the clip as tight as possible, engage the lug on the end of the clip with one of the slots. Use a screwdriver if necessary to push the clip as tight as possible before engaging the lug and slot. Finally tighten the clip by compressing the raised square portion of the clip with pliers, taking care not to cut the gaiter.

9 Refit the driveshaft to the vehicle, as described in Section 2.

Chapter 9
Braking system

Contents

Anti-lock Braking and Traction Control system components –
  removal and refitting 22
Anti-lock Braking and Traction Control systems – general
  information 21
Brake disc – inspection, removal and refitting 7
Brake fluid renewal . . . . .See Chapter 1
Brake pad and disc wear check . . . . See Chapter 1
Brake pedal – removal and refitting 13
Brake proportioning valve – removal and refitting 23
Front brake caliper – removal, overhaul and refitting 9
Front brake pads – renewal 4
General information 1
Handbrake – adjustment 16
Handbrake cables – removal and refitting 18
Handbrake lever – removal and refitting 17

Handbrake 'on' warning light switch – removal and refitting 20
Hydraulic fluid level check .See Weekly checks
Hydraulic pipes and hoses – renewal 3
Hydraulic system – bleeding 2
Master cylinder – removal, overhaul and refitting 12
Rear brake caliper – removal, overhaul and refitting 10
Rear brake drum – removal, inspection and refitting 8
Rear brake pads – renewal 5
Rear brake shoe and drum check . . . . .See Chapter 1
Rear brake shoes – renewal 6
Rear wheel cylinder – removal, overhaul and refitting 11
Stop-light switch – removal, refitting and adjustment 19
Vacuum servo unit – testing, removal and refitting 14
Vacuum servo unit check valve and hose – removal, testing
  and refitting 15

Degrees of difficulty

| Easy, suitable for novice with little experience | | Fairly easy, suitable for beginner with some experience | | Fairly difficult, suitable for competent DIY mechanic | | Difficult, suitable for experienced DIY mechanic | | Very difficult, suitable for expert DIY or professional | |

Specifications

System type

All models . . . . Front discs with rear drums or discs (depending on model), all having vacuum servo assistance. ABS is fitted as standard to most models and is available as an option on others. Dual hydraulic circuit split diagonally. Cable-operated handbrake on rear wheels

Front discs

Type . . . . Ventilated
Diameter:
   1.4, 1.6 and 1.8 (without ABS) litre models . . . . 256 mm
   1.8 (with ABS), 2.0 and 2.2 litre models . . . . 280 mm
Maximum disc run-out . . . . 0.11 mm
Minimum pad friction material thickness . . . . 2.0 mm
Minimum disc thickness after machining*:
   Hub carrier with integrated caliper bracket . . . . 21 mm
   Hub carrier without integrated caliper bracket . . . . 22 mm
* When this dimension is reached, only one further new set of brake pads is permissible, then renew the discs

Rear discs

Type . . . . Solid
Diameter:
   1.4, 1.6 and 1.8 (without ABS) litre models . . . . 240 mm
   1.8 (with ABS), 2.0 and 2.2 litre models . . . . 264 mm
Maximum disc run-out . . . . 0.13 mm
Minimum pad friction material thickness . . . . 2.0 mm
Minimum disc thickness after machining* . . . . 8.0 mm
* When this dimension is reached, only one further new set of disc pads is permissible, then renew the discs

Rear drums

Internal diameter . . . . 230 mm
Maximum internal diameter . . . . 231 mm
Minimum shoe friction material thickness . . . . 1.00 mm

ABS system type
1.4 litre and 1.6 litre engine models . . . . ABS 5.3
1.8, 2.0 and 2.2 litre models . . . . ABS 5.3/TC

Torque wrench settings

	Nm	lbf ft
ABS control unit to hydraulic modulator body:		
Stage 1	6	4
Stage 2	7	5
Brake disc securing screw	4	3
Brake fluid line unions	16	12
Brake hydraulic line to wheel cylinder	16	12
Brake pedal bracket side mounting nuts	20	15
Brake pedal bracket to vacuum servo	20	15
Caliper bleed screw	9	7
Flexible brake hose to caliper	40	30
Front caliper mounting bracket to hub carrier	95	70
Front caliper-to-mounting bracket guide pin bolts	28	21
Handbrake lever mounting	10	7
Hydraulic line branch bracket (LHD models without ABS)	20	15
Hydraulic line relay carrier bracket (LHD models without ABS)	20	15
Hydraulic lines union nuts	16	12
Hydraulic modulator (ABS)	8	6
Master cylinder	25	18
Rear brake drum	4	3
Rear brake proportioning valve	20	15
Rear caliper damping weight	11	8
Rear caliper mounting bolt	25	18
Rear caliper mounting bracket to trailing arm	100	74
Rear wheel cylinder	9	7
Roadwheel bolts	110	81
Wheel speed sensor	8	6

1 General information

The braking system is of servo-assisted, dual-circuit hydraulic type split diagonally. The arrangement of the hydraulic system is such that each circuit operates one front and one rear brake from a tandem master cylinder. Under normal circumstances, both circuits operate in unison. However, in the event of hydraulic failure in one circuit, full braking force will still be available at two wheels.

All models are fitted with front disc brakes, with rear drum brakes or disc brakes, depending on model. The disc brakes are actuated by single-piston sliding type calipers, which ensure that equal pressure is applied to each disc pad. The rear drum brakes incorporate leading and trailing shoes, which are actuated by twin-piston wheel cylinders. A self-adjust mechanism is incorporated, to automatically compensate for brake shoe wear. As the brake shoe linings wear, the footbrake operation automatically operates the adjuster mechanism, which effectively lengthens the shoe strut and repositions the brake shoes, to reduce the lining-to-drum clearance.

Zafira models not fitted with ABS are equipped with a rear brake proportioning valve. The valve senses the load in the rear of the vehicle, and controls the effort transferred to the rear brakes. With a heavy load, more effort can be applied to the rear brakes before skidding occurs.

ABS (Anti-lock Braking System) is available on most models. When the ignition is switched on, an 'ABS' symbol illuminates in the instrument panel for a short time while the system performs a self-test. The system comprises an electronic control unit, roadwheel sensors, hydraulic modulator, and the necessary valves and relays. The purpose of the system is to stop the wheel(s) locking during heavy brake applications. This is achieved by automatic release of the brake on the locked wheel, followed by re-application of the brake. This procedure is carried out several times a second by the hydraulic modulator. The modulator is controlled by the electronic control unit, which itself receives signals from the wheel sensors, which monitor the locked or unlocked state of the wheels. The ABS unit is fitted between the brake master cylinder and the brakes. If the 'ABS' symbol, in the instrument panel stays lit, or if it comes on whilst driving, there is a fault in the system and the vehicle must be taken to a Vauxhall dealer for assessment using specialist diagnostic equipment.

TC (Traction Control) is available as standard or optional equipment on various models. TC is a refinement of ABS; if the system ECU senses that a front driving wheel is about to lose traction, it prevents this by momentarily applying the relevant front brake. The master cylinder fitted to models with traction control is different to that fitted to models without traction control.

ESP (Electronic Stability Program) is also optionally available on certain later models. ESP is a further refinement of the ABS and TC systems, and takes into consideration centrifugal force and the centre of gravity during understeer and oversteer situations.

The handbrake is cable-operated on the rear brakes by a lever mounted between the front seats.

Warning: When servicing any part of the system, work carefully and methodically; also observe scrupulous cleanliness when overhauling any part of the hydraulic system. Always renew components (in axle sets, where applicable) if in doubt about their condition, and use only genuine Vauxhall replacement parts, or at least those of known good quality. Note the warnings given in 'Safety first!' and at relevant points in this Chapter concerning the dangers of asbestos dust and hydraulic fluid.

2 Hydraulic system – bleeding

⚠️ **Warning: Hydraulic fluid is poisonous; wash off immediately and thoroughly in the case of skin contact, and seek immediate medical advice if any fluid is swallowed or gets into the eyes. Certain types of hydraulic fluid are inflammable, and may ignite when allowed into contact with hot components; when servicing any hydraulic system, it is safest to assume that the fluid is inflammable, and to take precautions against the risk of fire as though it is petrol that is being handled. Hydraulic fluid is also an effective paint stripper, and will attack plastics; if any is spilt, it should be washed off immediately, using copious quantities of fresh water. Finally, it is hygroscopic (it absorbs moisture from the air) – old fluid may be contaminated and unfit for further use. When topping-up or renewing the fluid, always use the recommended type, and ensure that it comes from a freshly-opened sealed container.**

General

1 The correct operation of any hydraulic system is only possible after removing all air from the components and circuit; this is achieved by bleeding the system.

2 During the bleeding procedure, add only clean, unused hydraulic fluid of the recommended type; never re-use fluid that has already been bled from the system. Ensure that sufficient fluid is available before starting work.

3 If there is any possibility of incorrect fluid being already in the system, the brake components and circuit must be flushed completely with uncontaminated, correct fluid, and new seals should be fitted to the various components.

4 If hydraulic fluid has been lost from the system, or air has entered because of a leak, ensure that the fault is cured before proceeding further.

5 Park the vehicle over an inspection pit or on car ramps. Alternatively, apply the handbrake then jack up the front and rear of the vehicle and support it on axle stands (see *Jacking and vehicle support*). Where necessary, remove the splash guard from the bottom of the engine compartment. For improved access with the vehicle jacked up, remove the roadwheels.

6 Check that all pipes and hoses are secure, unions tight and bleed screws closed. Clean any dirt from around the bleed screws.

7 Unscrew the master cylinder reservoir cap, and top-up the master cylinder reservoir to the MAX level line; refit the cap loosely, and remember to maintain the fluid level at least above the MIN level line throughout the procedure, otherwise there is a risk of further air entering the system.

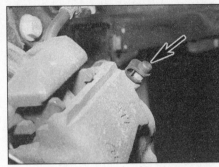

2.14 Dust cap on a bleed screw (arrowed)

8 There are many one-man, do-it-yourself brake bleeding kits currently available from motor accessory shops. It is recommended that one of these kits is used whenever possible, as they greatly simplify the bleeding operation, and also reduce the risk of expelled air and fluid being drawn back into the system. If such a kit is not available, the basic (two-man) method must be used, which is described in detail below.

9 If a kit is to be used, prepare the vehicle as described previously, and follow the kit manufacturer's instructions, as the procedure may vary slightly according to the type being used; generally, they are as outlined below in the relevant sub-section.

10 Whichever method is used, the same sequence must be followed (paragraphs 11 and 12) to ensure the removal of all air from the system.

Bleeding sequence

11 If the system has been only partially disconnected, and suitable precautions were taken to minimise fluid loss, it should be necessary only to bleed that part of the system (ie, the primary or secondary circuit).

12 If the complete system is to be bled, then it should be done working in the following sequence:

Right-hand drive models

 a) *Left-hand rear brake.*
 b) *Right-hand rear brake.*
 c) *Left-hand front brake.*
 d) *Right-hand front brake.*

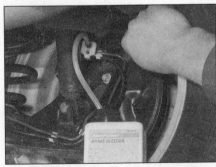

2.22 Using a one-way valve kit to bleed the rear brake

Left-hand drive models

 a) *Right-hand rear brake.*
 b) *Left-hand rear brake.*
 c) *Right-hand front brake.*
 d) *Left-hand front brake.*

Bleeding – basic (two-man) method

13 Collect together a clean glass jar, a suitable length of plastic or rubber tubing which is a tight fit over the bleed screw, and a ring spanner to fit the screw. The help of an assistant will also be required.

14 Remove the dust cap from the first bleed screw in the sequence (see illustration). Fit the spanner and tube to the screw, place the other end of the tube in the jar, and pour in sufficient fluid to cover the end of the tube.

15 Ensure that the master cylinder reservoir fluid level is maintained above the MIN level line throughout the procedure.

16 Unscrew the first bleed screw approximately half a turn, then have the assistant fully depress and release the brake pedal slowly several times. On the final stroke, have the assistant hold the pedal firmly to the floor, then tighten the bleed screw. If only a small amount or fluid flows from the bleed screw, have the assistant depress the pedal vigorously for several strokes in order to force any trapped air along the hydraulic lines.

17 Have the assistant release the pedal slowly, then top-up the reservoir fluid level as necessary.

18 Repeat the steps given in paragraphs 16 and 17 until the fluid emerging from the bleed screw is free from air bubbles.

19 When no more air bubbles appear, securely tighten the bleed screw, remove the tube and spanner, and refit the dust cap. Do not overtighten the bleed screw.

20 Repeat the procedure on the remaining screws in the sequence, until all air is removed from the system and the brake pedal feels firm again.

Bleeding – using a one-way valve kit

21 As the name implies, these kits consist of a length of tubing with a one-way valve fitted, to prevent expelled air and fluid being drawn back into the system; some kits include a translucent container, which can be positioned so that the air bubbles can be more easily seen flowing from the end of the tube.

22 The kit is connected to the bleed screw, which is then opened (see illustration). The user returns to the driver's seat, depresses the brake pedal with a smooth, steady stroke, and slowly releases it; this is repeated until the expelled fluid is clear of air bubbles.

23 Note that these kits simplify work so much that it is easy to forget the master cylinder reservoir fluid level; ensure that this is maintained above the MIN level line at all times.

Bleeding –
using a pressure-bleeding kit

24 These kits are usually operated by a reservoir of pressurised air contained in the spare tyre. However, note that it will probably be necessary to reduce the pressure to a lower level than normal; refer to the instructions supplied with the kit.

25 By connecting a pressurised, fluid-filled container to the master cylinder reservoir, bleeding can be carried out simply by opening each screw in turn (in the specified sequence), and allowing the fluid to flow out until no more air bubbles can be seen in the expelled fluid.

26 This method has the advantage that the large reservoir of fluid provides an additional safeguard against air being drawn into the system during bleeding.

27 Pressure-bleeding is particularly effective when bleeding 'difficult' systems, or when bleeding the complete system at the time of routine fluid renewal.

All methods

28 When bleeding is complete, and firm pedal feel is restored, wash off any spilt fluid, securely tighten the bleed screws, and refit the dust caps.

29 Check the hydraulic fluid level in the master cylinder reservoir, and top-up if necessary (see *Weekly checks*).

30 Discard any hydraulic fluid that has been bled from the system; it will not be fit for re-use.

31 Check the feel of the brake pedal. If it feels at all spongy, air must still be present in the system, and further bleeding is required. Failure to bleed satisfactorily after a reasonable repetition of the bleeding procedure may be due to worn master cylinder seals.

3 Hydraulic pipes and hoses – renewal

Note: *Before starting work, refer to the note at the beginning of Section 2 concerning the dangers of hydraulic fluid.*

1 If any pipe or hose is to be renewed, minimise fluid loss by first removing the master cylinder reservoir cap, then tightening it down onto a piece of polythene to obtain an

3.2 The front brake flexible hoses are supported in rubber grommets and retained with spring clips on the front suspension struts

airtight seal. Alternatively, hose clamps can be fitted to flexible hoses to isolate sections of the circuit; metal brake pipe unions can be plugged (if care is taken not to allow dirt into the system) or capped immediately they are disconnected. Place a wad of rag under any union that is to be disconnected, to catch any spilt fluid.

2 If a flexible hose is to be disconnected, unscrew the brake pipe union nut before removing the spring clip which secures the hose to its mounting bracket. Where applicable, unscrew the banjo union bolt securing the hose to the caliper and recover the copper washers. When removing the front flexible hose, pull out the spring clip and pull the rubber grommet from the bracket on the front suspension strut **(see illustration)**.

3 To unscrew union nuts, it is preferable to obtain a brake pipe spanner of the correct size; these are available from most motor accessory shops. Failing this, a close-fitting open-ended spanner will be required, though if the nuts are tight or corroded, their flats may be rounded-off if the spanner slips. In such a case, a self-locking wrench is often the only way to unscrew a stubborn union, but it follows that the pipe and the damaged nuts must be renewed on reassembly. Always clean a union and surrounding area before disconnecting it. If disconnecting a component with more than one union, make a careful note of the connections before disturbing any of them.

4 If a brake pipe is to be renewed, it can be obtained, cut to length and with the union

nuts and end flares in place, from Vauxhall dealers. All that is then necessary is to bend it to shape, following the line of the original, before fitting it to the car. Alternatively, most motor accessory shops will make up brake pipes from kits, but this requires very careful measurement of the original, to ensure that the replacement is of the correct length. The safest answer is usually to take the original to the shop as a pattern.

5 On refitting, securely tighten the union nuts but do not overtighten.

6 When refitting hoses to the calipers, always use new copper washers and tighten the banjo union bolts to the specified torque. Make sure that the hoses are positioned so that they will not touch surrounding bodywork or the roadwheels.

7 Ensure that the pipes and hoses are correctly routed, with no kinks, and that they are secured in the clips or brackets provided. After fitting, remove the polythene from the reservoir, and bleed the hydraulic system as described in Section 2. Wash off any spilt fluid, and check carefully for fluid leaks.

4 Front brake pads – renewal

⚠ *Warning: Renew BOTH sets of front brake pads at the same time – NEVER renew the pads on only one wheel, as uneven braking may result. Note that the dust created by wear of the pads may contain asbestos, which is a health hazard. Never blow it out with compressed air, and do not inhale any of it. An approved filtering mask should be worn when working on the brakes. Use brake cleaner or methylated spirit to clean brake components.*

1 Apply the handbrake, then jack up the front of the vehicle and support it on axle stands (see *Jacking and vehicle support*). Remove both front roadwheels.

2 Where applicable, use a screwdriver to lever out the brake pad warning sensor and unclip it from the retainer **(see illustrations)**.

3 Prise the retaining spring from the outer edge of the caliper, noting its correct fitted position **(see illustrations)**.

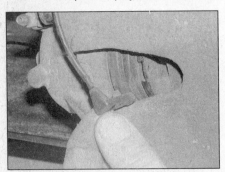

4.2a Removing the front brake pad warning sensor . . .

4.2b . . . and unclipping the wire from the retainer

4.3a Removing the retaining spring from the front caliper (Zafira)

4.3b Removing the retaining spring from the front caliper (Astra)

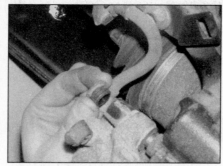

4.4 Remove the dust caps . . .

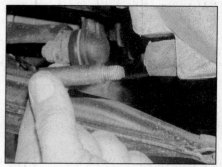

4.5a . . . then unscrew the guide bolts . . .

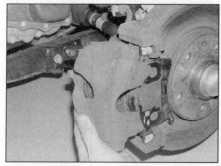

4.5b . . . and lift the caliper away from the mounting bracket (Zafira)

4.5c Removing the caliper from the hub carrier (Astra)

4.6a Removing the outer pad from the mounting bracket . . .

4 Remove the dust caps from the inner ends of the guide bolts **(see illustration)**.

5 Unscrew the guide bolts from the caliper, and lift the caliper and pads away from the mounting bracket or hub carrier (as applicable) **(see illustrations)**. Tie the caliper to the suspension strut using a suitable piece of wire. Do not allow the caliper to hang unsupported on the flexible brake hose.

6 Remove the outer pad, then remove the inner pad, noting that it is retained by a spring clip attached to the pad backing plate **(see illustrations)**.

7 Brush the dirt and dust from the caliper and piston, but take care not to inhale it. Scrape any rust from the edge of the brake disc.

8 Measure the thickness of the friction lining on each brake pad **(see illustration)**. If either pad is worn at any point to the specified

minimum thickness or less, all four pads must be renewed. The pads should also be renewed if any are contaminated with oil or grease, since there is no satisfactory way of degreasing friction material, once contaminated. If any of the brake pads are worn unevenly, or contaminate with oil or grease, trace and rectify the cause before reassembly.

9 If the brake pads are still serviceable, carefully clean them using a clean, fine wire brush or similar, paying particular attention to the sides and back of the metal backing. Clean out the grooves in the friction material, and pick out any large embedded particles of dirt or debris. Carefully clean the pad locations in the caliper body/mounting bracket.

10 Prior to fitting the pads, check that the

guide bolts are a snug fit in the caliper bushes. Apply a little copper brake grease to the areas on the pad backing plates which contact the caliper and piston **(see illustration)**. Inspect the dust seal around the piston for damage, and the piston for evidence of fluid leaks, corrosion or damage. If attention to any of these components is necessary, refer to Section 9.

11 If new brake pads are to be fitted, the caliper piston must be pushed back into the caliper to make room for them. Vauxhall technicians use a special tool, and a similar tool may be obtained from a car accessory shop **(see illustrations)**. Alternatively, a G-clamp or similar tool may be used, or suitable pieces of wood may be used as levers. Provided that the master cylinder reservoir has not been overfilled with

4.6b . . . and the inner pad from the caliper

4.8 Using a rule to measure the thickness of the front brake pad lining

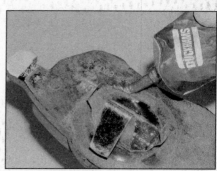

4.10 Apply a little copper grease to the contact areas of the pad backing plates

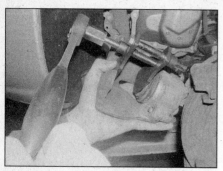

4.11a Using a clamp tool to force the piston into the front brake caliper

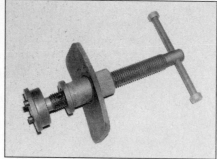

4.11b Clamping tool used to retract the caliper piston

18 Refit the brake pad warning sensor.
19 Depress the brake pedal repeatedly, until normal pedal pressure is restored.
20 Repeat the above procedure on the remaining front brake caliper.
21 Refit the roadwheels, then lower the vehicle to the ground and tighten the road-wheel bolts to the specified torque setting.
22 Check the hydraulic fluid level as described in *Weekly checks*.
Caution: New pads will not give full braking efficiency until they have bedded-in. Be prepared for this, and avoid hard braking as far as possible for the first hundred miles or so after pad renewal.

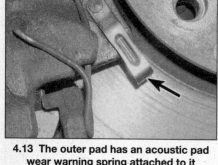

4.13 The outer pad has an acoustic pad wear warning spring attached to it

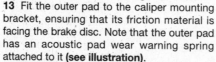

4.15 Tightening the caliper guide bolts with a torque wrench

hydraulic fluid, there should be no spillage, but keep a watch on the fluid level while retracting the piston. If the fluid level rises above the MAX level line at any time, the surplus should be syphoned off or ejected via a plastic tube connected to the bleed screw.

There have been some instances of damage being caused to the master cylinder seals when pushing the piston back into the caliper, and we therefore recommend that a hose clamp is fitted to the brake hose leading to the caliper and hydraulic fluid drained through the bleed nipple. Using this method will also remove any deteriorated hydraulic fluid which may have accumulated near the caliper.

12 Fit the inner pad to the caliper, ensuring that its clip is correctly located in the caliper piston. **Note:** *The pads are 'handed' for each side – make sure that the arrow on the backing plate points in the direction of rotation of the brake disc when the vehicle is travelling forwards.*
13 Fit the outer pad to the caliper mounting bracket, ensuring that its friction material is facing the brake disc. Note that the outer pad has an acoustic pad wear warning spring attached to it **(see illustration)**.
14 Slide the caliper and inner pad into position over the outer pad, and locate it in the mounting bracket.
15 Insert the caliper guide bolts, and tighten them to the specified torque setting **(see illustration)**.
16 Refit the guide bolt dust caps.
17 Refit the retaining spring to the caliper, ensuring that its ends are correctly located in the caliper holes.

5 Rear brake pads – renewal

⚠ *Warning: Renew BOTH sets of rear brake pads at the same time – NEVER renew the pads on only one wheel, as uneven braking may result. Note that the dust created by wear of the pads may contain asbestos, which is a health hazard. Never blow it out with compressed air, and do not inhale any of it. An approved filtering mask should be worn when working on the brakes. Use brake cleaner or methylated spirit to clean brake components.*

1 Chock the front wheels, then jack up the rear of the vehicle and support it on axle stands (see *Jacking and vehicle support*). Remove both rear roadwheels.
2 Fully release the handbrake lever, then back off the adjustment nut to provide slack in the handbrake cable (see Section 16).
3 Using a screwdriver, press down the handbrake lever on the back of the rear caliper, then disconnect the inner cable. Disconnect the cable from the support bracket by first removing the retaining clip **(see illustrations)**.
4 Unscrew and remove the brake caliper lower mounting bolt, noting that the guide pin is held stationary by the special clip. Recover the special clip **(see illustrations)**.
5 Swivel the caliper upwards around the upper guide pin and withdraw the brake pads

5.3a Disconnecting the handbrake inner cable from the lever on the rear caliper

5.3b Remove the retaining clip and disconnect the handbrake cable from the support bracket

5.4a Unscrew the rear brake caliper lower mounting bolt . . .

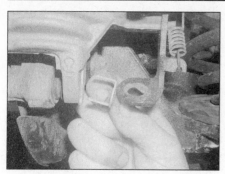

5.4b . . . and recover the special clip

5.5a Removing the outer brake pad . . .

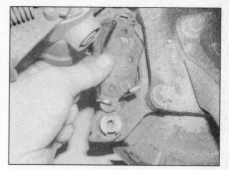

5.5b . . . and inner brake pad from the rear caliper

from their location in the mounting bracket **(see illustrations)**.

6 Brush the dirt and dust from the caliper and piston, but take care not to inhale it. Scrape any rust from the edge of the brake disc.

7 Measure the thickness of the friction lining on each brake pad **(see illustration)**. If either pad is worn at any point to the specified minimum thickness or less, all four pads must be renewed. The pads should also be renewed if any are contaminated with oil or grease; there is no satisfactory way of degreasing friction material, once contaminated. If any of the brake pads are worn unevenly, or contaminated with oil or grease, trace and rectify the cause before reassembly.

8 If the brake pads are still serviceable, clean them using a clean, fine wire brush or similar, paying particular attention to the sides and back of the metal backing. Clean the pad locations in the caliper body/mounting bracket.

9 Apply a little copper brake grease to the areas on the pad backing plates which contact the caliper and piston. Inspect the dust seal around the piston for damage, and the piston for evidence of fluid leaks, corrosion or damage. If attention to any of these components is necessary, refer to Section 10.

10 If new brake pads are to be fitted, the caliper piston must be pushed back into the cylinder to make room for them. First, however, note the alignment marks on the piston and caliper – the piston cut-out must be aligned with the raised nib on the caliper. Vauxhall technicians use a special tool which engages the cut-outs in the piston, and a similar tool may be obtained from a car accessory shop **(see illustrations)**. Alternatively, a G-clamp or similar tool may be used, but note that the piston must be turned as it is being forced into its bore. Provided

that the master cylinder reservoir has not been overfilled with hydraulic fluid, there should be no spillage, but keep a careful watch on the fluid level while retracting the piston. If the fluid level rises above the MAX level line at any time, the surplus should be syphoned off or ejected via a plastic tube connected to the bleed screw.

> **HAYNES HINT** *There have been some instances of damage being caused to the master cylinder seals when pushing the piston back into the caliper, and we therefore recommend that a hose clamp is fitted to the brake hose leading to the caliper and hydraulic fluid drained through the bleed nipple. Using this method will also remove any deteriorated hydraulic fluid which may have accumulated near the caliper.*

11 Turn the piston as necessary to align the mark with the nib on the caliper.

12 Swivel the caliper upwards, then locate the new pads in the mounting bracket, making sure that the friction material faces the disc, and the audio wear sensor is on the inner pad **(see illustration)**.

13 Swivel the caliper down and make sure that the pads are correctly seated. Use a wire brush to clean the threads of the caliper lower mounting bolt, then apply a little locking fluid to the threads and insert the bolt **(see illustration)**. Tighten the bolt to the specified torque while holding the guide pin with a further spanner.

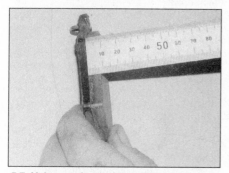

5.7 Using a rule to measure the thickness of the brake pad friction lining

5.10a The cut-out in the piston must be aligned with the raised nib on the caliper

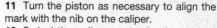

5.10b Using the special tool to force the piston into the caliper

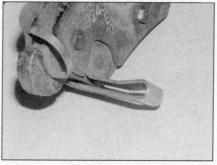

5.12 The audio wear sensor is located on the inner brake pad

5.13 Apply locking fluid to the threads of the caliper mounting bolt before refitting it

6.3 Checking the wear of the rear brake shoe friction material

6.5 Prior to disturbing the shoes, note the correct fitted locations of all components, paying particular attention to the adjuster strut components

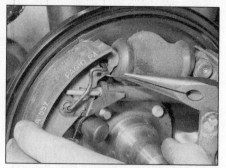

6.6 Unhook the upper return spring, and remove it from the brake shoes

14 Refit the handbrake cable to the support bracket and secure with the retaining clip.
15 Press down the handbrake lever and reconnect the end of the cable to it.
16 Depress the brake pedal several times to restore normal pedal feel.
17 Repeat the above procedure on the remaining rear brake caliper.
18 Adjust the handbrake cable as described in Section 16.
19 Refit the roadwheels, then lower the vehicle to the ground and tighten the roadwheel bolts to the specified torque.
20 Check the brake hydraulic fluid level as described in *Weekly checks*.
Caution: New pads will not give full braking efficiency until they have bedded-in. Be prepared for this, and avoid hard braking as far as possible for the first hundred miles or so after pad renewal.

6.7 Remove the retaining spring, followed by the lever and return spring (arrowed)

6 Rear brake shoes – renewal

> ⚠ *Warning: Brake shoes must be renewed on both rear wheels at the same time – never renew the shoes on only one wheel, as uneven braking may result. Also, the dust created by wear of the shoes may contain asbestos, which is a health hazard. Never blow it out with compressed air, and do not inhale any of it. An approved filtering mask should be worn when working on the brakes. DO NOT use petrol or petroleum-based solvents to clean brake parts; use brake cleaner or methylated spirit only.*

1 Remove the rear brake drum as described in Section 8.
2 Taking precautions to avoid inhalation of dust, remove the brake dust from the brake drum, shoes and backplate.
3 Measure the thickness of the friction material of each brake shoe at several points; if either shoe is worn at any point to the specified minimum thickness or less, **all four** shoes must be renewed as a set **(see illustration)**. The shoes should also be renewed if any are contaminated with oil or grease, since there is no satisfactory way of degreasing the friction material.
4 If any of the brake shoes are worn excessively, or contaminated with oil or

grease, trace and rectify the cause before reassembly.
5 Note the location and orientation of all components before dismantling, as an aid to reassembly **(see illustration)**.
6 Using a pair of pliers, carefully unhook the upper shoe return spring, and remove it from the brake shoes **(see illustration)**.
7 Prise the adjusting lever retaining spring out of the front shoe, and remove the retaining spring, lever and return spring from the brake shoe, noting each component's correct fitted position **(see illustration)**.
8 Prise the upper ends of the brake shoes apart, and withdraw the adjuster strut from between the shoes.
9 Using a pair of pliers, remove the front shoe retainer spring cup by depressing and turning it through 90°. With the cup removed, lift off the spring and withdraw the retainer pin **(see illustrations)**.
10 Detach the front shoe from the lower return spring, and remove both the shoe and return spring.
11 Remove the rear shoe retainer spring cup, spring and retainer pin as described in paragraph 9, then remove the shoe, detaching it from the handbrake cable.
12 Do not depress the brake pedal with the shoes removed. As a precaution, fit a strong elastic band or plastic cable tie around the wheel cylinder pistons to retain them **(see illustration)**.
13 If both brake assemblies are dismantled at the same time, take care not to mix them

6.9a Using pliers, remove the spring cup . . .

6.9b . . . then lift off the spring and retainer pin

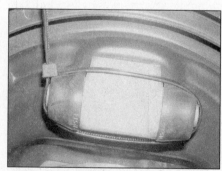

6.12 Plastic cable tie retaining the wheel cylinder pistons

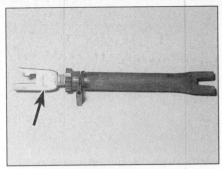

6.13 The left-hand adjuster strut assembly is marked L (arrow)

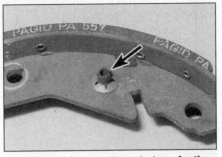

6.16 It may be necessary to transfer the adjusting lever pivot pin and clip (arrowed) from the original shoes to the new ones

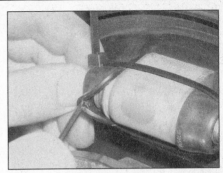

6.17 Checking the wheel cylinder for hydraulic fluid leaks

up. Note that the left-hand and right-hand adjuster components are marked: the threaded rod is marked L or R, and the other 'handed' components are colour-coded black for the left-hand side, and silver for the right-hand side **(see illustration)**.

14 Dismantle and clean the adjuster strut. Apply a smear of silicone-based grease to the adjuster threads.

15 Examine the return springs. If they are distorted, or if they have seen extensive service, renewal is advisable. Weak springs may cause the brakes to bind.

16 If a new handbrake operating lever was not supplied with the new shoes (where applicable), transfer the lever from the old shoes. The lever may be secured with a pin and circlip, or by a rivet, which will have to be drilled out. It may also be necessary to transfer the adjusting lever pivot pin and clip from the original front shoe to the new shoe **(see illustration)**.

6.18 Apply a smear of anti-seize compound to the shoe contact surfaces of the backplate

17 Peel back the rubber protective caps, and check the wheel cylinder for fluid leaks or other damage **(see illustration)**. Ensure that both cylinder pistons are free to move easily. Refer to Section 11, if necessary, for information on wheel cylinder overhaul.

6.19 Engage the rear brake shoe with the handbrake cable, and locate the shoe on the backplate

18 Prior to installation, clean the backplate thoroughly. Apply a thin smear of high-temperature copper-based brake grease or anti-seize compound to the shoe contact surfaces on the backplate and wheel cylinder pistons **(see illustration)**. Do not allow the grease to foul the friction lining material.

19 Ensure that the handbrake cable is correctly retained by the clip on the lower brake shoe pivot point, then engage the rear shoe with the cable. Locate the shoe on the backplate **(see illustration)**.

20 Install the rear shoe retainer pin and spring, and secure it in position with the spring cup **(see illustrations)**.

21 Hook the lower return spring onto the rear shoe, then engage the front shoe with the return spring. Locate the front shoe on the backplate, and secure it in position with its retainer pin, spring and spring cup **(see illustrations)**.

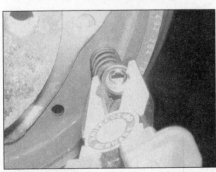

6.20a Fit the rear shoe retainer pin . . .

6.20b . . . and spring . . .

6.20c . . . then secure with the spring cup

6.21a Fit the lower return spring . . .

6.21b . . . then secure the front shoe by fitting the shoe retainer pin . . .

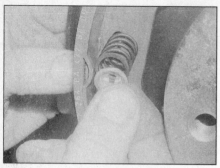

6.21c ... followed by the spring and spring cup

6.22 Screw in the adjuster strut to its shortest length

6.23 Fit the adjuster strut between the brake shoes, making sure that the longer fork is located to the rear of the shoe

22 Screw the adjuster strut wheel fully onto the forked end of the adjuster, so that the adjuster strut is set to its shortest possible length. Back the wheel off a half a turn, and check that it is free to rotate easily **(see illustration)**.

23 Manoeuvre the adjuster strut assembly into position between the brake shoes. Make sure that both ends of the strut are correctly engaged with the shoes, noting that the forked end of the strut must be positioned so that its longer, straight fork is to the rear of the shoe **(see illustration)**.

24 Engage the adjusting lever plate with the front shoe and strut ratchet, and locate the plate on its pivot pin. Check that the plate is correctly located, and secure in position with the retaining spring, making sure the spring ends are securely located in the retaining pin and shoe **(see illustrations)**.

25 Remove the rubber band or plastic cable

tie from the wheel cylinder. Make sure that both shoes are correctly positioned on the wheel cylinder pistons, then fit the upper return spring **(see illustrations)**.

26 Fit the tension spring to the adjusting lever plate and leading shoe **(see illustration)**.

27 Ensure that the handbrake operating lever stop peg is correctly positioned against the edge of the shoe web, then refit the brake drum as described in Section 8.

28 Repeat the operation on the remaining brake.

29 Once both sets of rear shoes have been renewed, with the handbrake fully released, adjust the lining-to-drum clearance by repeatedly depressing the brake pedal at least 20 to 25 times. Whilst depressing the pedal, have an assistant listen to the rear drums, to check that the adjuster strut is functioning correctly; if so, a clicking sound will be emitted by the strut as the pedal is depressed.

30 Check and, if necessary, adjust the handbrake as described in Section 16.

31 On completion, check the hydraulic fluid level as described in *Weekly checks*.

Caution: New shoes will not give full braking efficiency until they have bedded-in. Be prepared for this, and avoid hard braking as far as possible for the first hundred miles or so after shoe renewal.

7 Brake disc – inspection, removal and refitting

⚠ *Warning: Before starting work, refer to the warning at the beginning of Section 4 or 5 concerning the dangers of asbestos dust. If either disc requires renewal, both should be renewed at the same time together with new pads, to ensure even and consistent braking.*

Inspection

1 Remove the wheel trim, then loosen the roadwheel bolts. If checking a front disc, apply the handbrake, and if checking a rear disc, chock the front wheels, then jack up the relevant end of the vehicle and support on axle stands (see *Jacking and vehicle support*). Remove the roadwheel.

2 Check that the brake disc securing screw is tight, then fit spacers approximately 10.0 mm thick to the roadwheel bolts, and tighten them into the hub **(see illustration)**.

3 Rotate the brake disc, and examine it for deep scoring or grooving. Light scoring is

6.24a Fit the adjusting lever plate ...

6.24b ... and secure with the retaining spring

6.25a Hook the rear end of the upper return spring in the trailing shoe ...

6.25b ... then pull the front end of the spring onto the leading shoe

6.26 Fitting the adjusting lever tension spring

7.2 Tighten the roadwheel bolts onto spacers before checking the brake disc for wear

7.3 Checking the brake disc thickness with a micrometer

7.4 Using a dial gauge to check the brake disc for run-out

7.10a Unscrew the mounting bolts . . .

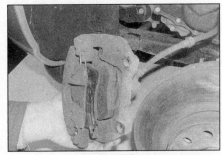

7.10b . . . and remove the front brake caliper, complete with disc pads and mounting bracket

7.11a Remove the securing screw . . .

normal, but if excessive, the disc should be removed and either renewed or machined (within the specified limits) by an engineering works. Check the thickness of the disc using a micrometer. The minimum thickness is stamped on the outer face of the rear disc **(see illustration)**.

4 Using a dial gauge, or a flat metal block and feeler blades, check that the disc run-out does not exceed the figure given in the Specifications **(see illustration)**. Measure the run-out 10.0 mm (0.4 in) in from the outer edge of the disc.

5 If the rear disc run-out is excessive, check the rear wheel bearing adjustment, as described in Chapter 10.

6 If the front disc run-out is excessive, remove the disc as described later, and check that the disc-to-hub surfaces are perfectly clean. Refit the disc and check the run-out again.

7 If the run-out is still excessive, the disc should be renewed.

8 To remove a disc, proceed as follows.

Front disc

Removal

9 Remove the roadwheel bolts and spacers used when checking the disc.

10 Unbolt and remove the front brake caliper complete with disc pads and mounting bracket and tie it to one side **(see illustrations)**. On 1.8 litre models with ABS, and all 2.0 and 2.2 litre models, remove the mounting bracket with reference to Section 9, and also release the flexible brake hose from the support on the strut.

11 Remove the securing screw and withdraw the disc from the hub **(see illustrations)**.

Refitting

12 Refitting is a reversal of removal, but make sure that the mating faces of the disc and hub are perfectly clean, and apply a little locking fluid to the threads of the securing screw.

13 Refit the disc pads with reference to Section 4.

Rear disc

Removal

14 Remove the roadwheel bolts and spacers used when checking the disc.

15 Remove the rear brake pads, as described in Section 5, then slide the caliper from its upper swivel bearing. Move the caliper to one side, and suspend it using wire or string to avoid straining the pipe.

16 Unbolt the caliper mounting bracket from the trailing arm.

17 Undo the securing screw and withdraw the disc from the hub **(see illustrations)**.

7.11b . . . and remove the front brake disc

7.17a Remove the securing screw . . .

7.17b . . . and remove the rear brake disc

8.3a Undo the screw . . .

8.3b . . . and remove the brake drum

Refitting

18 Refitting is a reversal of removal, but make sure that the mating faces of the disc and hub are perfectly clean, and apply a little locking fluid to the threads of the securing screw. Refit the caliper mounting bracket and tighten the mounting bolts to the specified torque. Clean the caliper upper pin, then apply silicone grease to it. Slide the caliper into its upper swivel bearing and refit the brake pads as described in Section 5.

8 Rear brake drum –
removal, inspection and refitting

 Warning: Before starting work, refer to the warning at the beginning of Section 6 concerning the dangers of asbestos dust.

Removal

1 Remove the relevant wheel trim, then loosen the rear roadwheel bolts and chock the front wheels. Jack up the rear of the vehicle, and support on axle stands (see *Jacking and vehicle support*) positioned under the body side-members. Remove the roadwheel.
2 Fully release the handbrake.
3 Extract the drum securing screw and remove the drum **(see illustrations)**. If the drum is tight, remove the plug from the inspection hole in the brake backplate, and

push the handbrake operating lever away from the brake shoe to allow the shoes to move away from the drums. If necessary, slacken the handbrake cable adjuster on the lever inside the vehicle (see Section 16).

Inspection

4 Brush the dirt and dust from the drum, taking care not to inhale it.
5 Examine the internal friction surface of the drum. If deeply scored, or so worn that the drum has become ridged to the width of the shoes, then both drums must be renewed.
6 Regrinding of the friction surface may be possible, provided the maximum diameter given in the Specifications is not exceeded, but note that both rear drums should be reground to the identical diameter.

Refitting

7 Before refitting the drum, make sure that the handbrake operating lever is returned to its normal position on the brake shoe.
8 Refit the brake drum and tighten the securing screw. If necessary, back off the adjuster wheel on the strut until the drum will pass over the shoes.
9 Adjust the brakes by operating the footbrake a number of times. A clicking noise will be heard at the drum as the automatic adjuster operates. When the clicking stops, adjustment is complete.
10 Refit the roadwheel and lower the vehicle to the ground.

9 Front brake caliper –
removal, overhaul and refitting

 Warning: Before starting work, refer to the note at the beginning of Section 2 concerning the dangers of hydraulic fluid, and to the warning at the beginning of Section 4 concerning the dangers of asbestos dust.

Removal

1 Apply the handbrake, then jack up the front of the vehicle and support it on axle stands (see *Jacking and vehicle support*). Remove the roadwheel.

2 Minimise fluid loss by first removing the master cylinder reservoir cap, then tightening it down onto a piece of polythene to obtain an airtight seal. Alternatively, use a brake hose clamp, a G-clamp or a similar tool to clamp the flexible hose leading to the brake caliper.
3 Clean the area around the caliper brake hose union. Unscrew and remove the union bolt, and recover the sealing washer from each side of the hose union. Discard the washers; new ones must be used on refitting. Plug the hose end and caliper hole, to minimise fluid loss and prevent the ingress of dirt into the hydraulic system.
4 Remove the brake pads as described in Section 4, then remove the caliper from the vehicle.
5 If necessary on 1.8 litre models with ABS, and all 2.0 and 2.2 litre models, unbolt the caliper mounting bracket from the hub carrier. On all other models, the bracket is incorporated in the hub carrier casting **(see illustration)**.

Overhaul

Note: *Check that spare parts are available before deciding to overhaul the caliper.*
6 With the caliper on the bench, wipe it clean with a clean rag.
7 Withdraw the partially-ejected piston from the caliper body, and remove the dust seal. The piston can be withdrawn by hand, or if necessary pushed out by applying compressed air to the brake hose union hole. Only low pressure should be required, such as is generated by a foot pump, and as a precaution a block of wood should be positioned to prevent any damage to the piston.
8 Using a small screwdriver, carefully remove the piston seal from the caliper, taking care not to mark the bore **(see illustration)**.
9 Carefully press the guide bushes out of the caliper body.
10 Thoroughly clean all components, using only methylated spirit or clean hydraulic fluid. Never use mineral-based solvents such as petrol or paraffin, which will attack the rubber components of the hydraulic system. Dry the components using compressed air or a clean, lint-free cloth. If available, use compressed air to blow clear the fluid passages.

9.5 Type of hub carrier incorporating an integral caliper mounting bracket

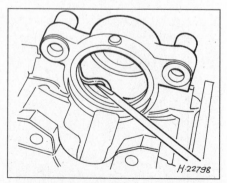

9.8 Removing the piston seal from the caliper body

Warning: Wear eye protection when using compressed air.

11 Check all components, and renew any that are worn or damaged. If the piston and/or cylinder bore are scratched excessively, renew the complete caliper body. Similarly check the condition of the guide bushes and bolts; both bushes and bolts should be undamaged and (when cleaned) a reasonably tight sliding fit. If there is any doubt about the condition of any component, renew it.

12 If the caliper is fit for further use, obtain the necessary components from your Vauxhall dealer. Renew the caliper seals and dust covers as a matter of course, as these should never be re-used.

13 On reassembly, first ensure that all components are absolutely clean and dry.

14 Dip the piston and the new piston seal in clean hydraulic fluid, and smear clean fluid on the cylinder bore surface.

15 Locate the new seal in the cylinder bore groove, using only the fingers to manipulate it into position.

16 Fit the new dust seal to the piston, then insert the piston into the cylinder bore using a twisting motion to ensure it enters the seal correctly. Make sure the piston enters squarely into the bore. Locate the dust seal in the body groove, and push the piston fully into the caliper bore.

17 Insert the guide bushes into position in the caliper body.

Refitting

18 On 1.8 litre models with ABS, and all 2.0 and 2.2 litre models, locate the caliper mounting bracket on the hub carrier, then insert and tighten the bolts (with locking fluid applied to their threads) to the specified torque.

19 Refit the brake pads as described in Section 4, together with the caliper which at this stage will not have the hose attached.

20 Position a new copper sealing washer on each side of the hose union, and connect the brake hose to the caliper. Ensure that the hose is correctly positioned against the caliper body lug, then insert the union bolt and tighten it to the specified torque.

21 Remove the brake hose clamp or the polythene, where fitted, and bleed the

10.6 Sliding the rear brake caliper from the mounting bracket

hydraulic system as described in Section 2. Note that, providing the precautions described were taken to minimise brake fluid loss, it should only be necessary to bleed the relevant front brake circuit.

22 Refit the roadwheel, then lower the vehicle to the ground and tighten the roadwheel bolts to the specified torque.

10 Rear brake caliper – removal, overhaul and refitting

Warning: Before starting work, refer to the note at the beginning of Section 2 concerning the dangers of hydraulic fluid, and to the warning at the beginning of Section 5 concerning the dangers of asbestos dust.

Removal

1 Chock the front wheels, then jack up the rear of the vehicle and support it on axle stands (see *Jacking and vehicle support*). Remove the rear roadwheels.

2 Fully release the handbrake lever, then unscrew the adjustment nut to provide slack in the handbrake cable.

3 Using a screwdriver, press down the handbrake lever on the back of the rear caliper, then disconnect the inner cable. Disconnect the outer cable from the support bracket by first removing the retaining clip.

4 Minimise fluid loss by first removing the master cylinder reservoir cap, then tightening it down onto a piece of polythene to obtain an

10.7 Removing the rear brake caliper mounting bracket

airtight seal. Alternatively, use a brake hose clamp, a G-clamp or a similar tool to clamp the flexible hose leading to the brake caliper.

5 Clean the area around the caliper brake hose union. Unscrew and remove the union bolt, and recover the sealing washer from each side of the hose union. Discard the washers; new ones must be used on refitting. Plug the hose end and caliper hole, to minimise fluid loss and prevent the ingress of dirt into the hydraulic system.

6 Remove the brake pads as described in Section 5, then slide the caliper from its upper swivel bearing **(see illustration)**.

7 If necessary, unbolt the caliper mounting bracket from the trailing arm **(see illustration)**.

Overhaul

8 Check if spare parts are available before deciding to overhaul the caliper. The procedure is similar to that in Section 9 for the front caliper.

9 Remove the caliper lower guide pin from the mounting bracket and wipe it clean. Check the pin for excessive wear and renew it if necessary. Smear some silicone grease on the guide pin inner and outer surfaces, then refit it.

10 Where the caliper incorporates a damping weight/absorber, disconnect the spring and unbolt the handbrake cable bracket. Transfer the parts to the new caliper, and tighten the bolt to the specified torque. The bolt threads should have locking fluid applied to them.

Refitting

11 Where removed, refit the caliper mounting bracket to the trailing arm. Apply locking fluid to the threads of the mounting bolts, then insert them and tighten to the specified torque **(see illustrations)**.

12 Clean the caliper upper swivel pin, then apply silicone grease to it. Slide the caliper into its upper guide bearing and refit the brake pads as described in Section 5.

13 Position a new copper sealing washer on each side of the hose union, and connect the brake hose to the caliper. Ensure that the hose is correctly positioned, then insert the union bolt and tighten it to the specified torque.

14 Remove the brake hose clamp or the polythene, where fitted, and bleed the hydraulic system as described in Section 2.

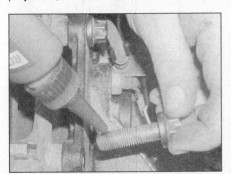

10.11a Apply locking fluid to the threads . . .

10.11b . . . before inserting and tightening the rear caliper mounting bracket bolts

Note that, providing the precautions described were taken to minimise brake fluid loss, it should only be necessary to bleed the relevant rear brake circuit.

15 Refit the handbrake cable to the support bracket and secure with the retaining clip.

16 Press down the handbrake lever and reconnect the end of the cable to it.

17 Depress the brake pedal several times to ensure the brake pads are set to their normal position.

18 Adjust the handbrake cable as described in Section 16, then refit the lever gaiter.

19 Refit the roadwheels, then lower the vehicle to the ground and tighten the roadwheel bolts to the specified torque.

20 Check the brake hydraulic fluid level as described in *Weekly checks*.

21 Refit the roadwheel, then lower the vehicle to the ground and tighten the roadwheel bolts to the specified torque.

11 Rear wheel cylinder – removal, overhaul and refitting

⚠ **Warning: Before starting work, refer to the note at the beginning of Section 2 concerning the dangers of hydraulic fluid, and to the warning at the beginning of Section 6 concerning the dangers of asbestos dust.**
Note: *Check that an overhaul kit of rubbers is available.*

Removal

1 Remove the brake drum (see Section 8).

2 Minimise fluid loss by first removing the master cylinder reservoir cap, and then tightening it down onto a piece of polythene, to obtain an airtight seal. Alternatively, use a brake hose clamp, a G-clamp or a similar tool to clamp the flexible hose at the nearest convenient point to the wheel cylinder.

3 Carefully unhook the brake shoe upper

return spring, and remove it from both brake shoes. Pull the upper ends of the shoes away from the wheel cylinder to disengage them from the pistons.

4 Wipe away all traces of dirt around the brake pipe union nut at the rear of the wheel cylinder, and unscrew the nut. Carefully ease the pipe out of the wheel cylinder, and plug or tape over its end to prevent dirt entry. Wipe off any spilt fluid immediately.

5 Unscrew the retaining bolt from the rear of the backplate, and remove the wheel cylinder, taking care not to allow surplus hydraulic fluid to contaminate the brake shoe linings.

Overhaul

6 Brush the dirt and dust from the wheel cylinder, but take care not to inhale it.

7 Pull the rubber dust seals from the ends of the cylinder body **(see illustration).**

8 The pistons will normally be ejected by the pressure of the coil spring, but if they are not, tap the end of the cylinder body on a piece of wood, or apply low air pressure (eg, from a foot pump) to the hydraulic fluid union hole to eject the pistons from their bores.

9 Inspect the surfaces of the pistons and their bores in the cylinder body for scoring, or evidence of metal-to-metal contact. If evident, renew the complete wheel cylinder assembly.

10 If the pistons and bores are in good condition, discard the seals and obtain a repair kit, which will contain all the necessary renewable items.

11 Lubricate the piston seals with clean brake fluid, and insert them into the cylinder bores, with the spring between them, using finger pressure only.

12 Dip the pistons in clean brake fluid, and insert them into the cylinder bores.

13 Fit the dust seals, and check that the pistons can move freely in their bores.

Refitting

14 Ensure that the backplate and wheel cylinder mating surfaces are clean, then

spread the brake shoes and manoeuvre the wheel cylinder into position.

15 Insert the brake pipe, and screw in the union nut two or three turns to ensure that the thread has started.

16 Insert the wheel cylinder retaining bolt, and tighten to the specified torque setting. Now tighten the brake pipe union nut to the specified torque.

17 Remove the clamp from the flexible brake hose, or the polythene from the master cylinder reservoir (as applicable).

18 Ensure that the brake shoes are correctly located in the cylinder pistons, then refit the brake shoe upper return spring.

19 Refit the brake drum as described in Section 8.

20 Bleed the brake hydraulic system as described in Section 2. Providing suitable precautions were taken to minimise loss of fluid, it should only be necessary to bleed the relevant rear brake.

21 Adjust the handbrake cable as described in Section 16, then refit the lever gaiter.

12 Master cylinder – removal, overhaul and refitting

⚠ **Warning: Before starting work, refer to the note at the beginning of Section 2 concerning the dangers of hydraulic fluid.**

Removal

1 Dissipate the vacuum present in the brake servo unit by repeatedly depressing the brake pedal. On Zafira models, remove the windscreen plastic deflector from the rear of the engine compartment.

2 Remove the master cylinder reservoir cap and syphon the hydraulic fluid from the reservoir **(see illustration).** Alternatively, open any convenient bleed screw in the system,

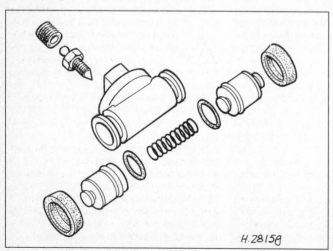

11.7 Exploded view of the rear brake wheel cylinder

H.2815B

12.2 Brake master cylinder and fluid reservoir (Zafira)

and pump the brake pedal to expel the fluid through a plastic tube connected to the bleed screw (see Section 2).

 Warning: Do not syphon the fluid by mouth, as it is poisonous; use a syringe or an old poultry baster.

3 Disconnect the wiring connector from the brake fluid level sender unit, and unclip the wiring from the top of the reservoir.

4 Place cloth rags beneath the master cylinder, then unscrew the union nuts and disconnect the hydraulic fluid lines. Carefully pull back the lines so that they are just clear of the master cylinder. Identify the lines to ensure correct refitting.

5 On manual transmission models, disconnect the clutch hydraulic fluid line from the reservoir. Plug the end of the line.

6 Unscrew the mounting nuts and withdraw the master cylinder from the front of the vacuum servo. Recover the seal. Take care not to spill fluid on the vehicle paintwork.

7 Using a screwdriver, carefully lever out the reservoir retaining shackle, then prise the reservoir from the top of the master cylinder. Prise the two seals from the master cylinder apertures.

Overhaul

8 At the time of writing, master cylinder overhaul is not possible as no spares are available.

9 The only parts available individually are the fluid reservoir, its mounting seals, the filler cap and the master cylinder mounting seal.

10 If the master cylinder is worn excessively, it must be renewed.

Refitting

11 Ensure that the mating surfaces are clean and dry then fit the new seal to the rear of the master cylinder.

12 Fit the master cylinder to the servo unit, ensuring that the servo unit pushrod enters the master cylinder piston centrally. Fit the retaining nuts and tighten them to the specified torque setting.

13 Refit the brake lines and tighten the union nuts securely.

14 Smear a little brake fluid on the rubber seals and locate them in the top of the master cylinder, then press the fluid reservoir firmly into the seals.

15 On manual transmission models, reconnect the clutch hydraulic pipe and tighten the clip.

16 Reconnect the wiring connector to the brake fluid level sender unit, and fit the wiring in the clips on top of the reservoir.

17 Top-up the reservoir with fresh hydraulic fluid to the MAX mark (see *Weekly checks*).

18 Bleed the hydraulic system as described in Section 2 then refit the filler cap. Thoroughly check the operation of the braking and clutch systems before using the vehicle on the road.

13 Brake pedal – removal and refitting

Removal

1 Disconnect the battery negative (earth) lead and position it away from the terminal.

2 Remove the instrument panel as described in Chapter 12.

3 Unbolt the side nuts securing the pedal support to the steering crossmember.

4 Undo the screws and remove the side panels from the driver's footwell.

5 Turn the fasteners and remove the facia lower panels for access to the stop-light switch. Remove the footwell air duct, then disconnect the wiring from the switch. Turn the switch to remove it from the pedal support bracket.

6 Disconnect the wiring loom from the fusebox carrier.

7 Unhook and remove the brake pedal return spring.

8 Use a screwdriver to prise the retaining plate and remove the pin attaching the vacuum servo pushrod to the pedal. Recover the washer.

9 Unscrew the nuts securing the vacuum servo to the pedal bracket, and withdraw the bracket, together with the pedal, from inside the vehicle. There is little working room to do this; first release the bracket from the steering crossmember studs, then tilt it upwards and turn it as necessary to remove it. Take care not to damage the wiring loom and surrounding components.

10 Note the fitted position of the pedal, then unscrew the nuts and push out the pivot shaft. Recover the pedal, bushes and return spring.

11 Inspect the pedal for signs of wear or damage, paying particular attention to the pivot bushes, and renew worn components as necessary.

Refitting

12 Apply some multi-purpose grease to the bearing surfaces of the pedal, pivot shaft and bushes. Fit the pedal and components to the bracket then refit the nuts and tighten securely.

13 Carefully locate the pedal and bracket on the bulkhead and onto the vacuum servo studs. Refit the nuts and tighten to the specified torque.

14 Refit the vacuum servo pushrod onto the brake pedal, then insert the pin and washer and retain with the plate.

15 Refit the brake pedal return spring.

16 Reconnect the wiring loom to the fusebox carrier.

17 Before refitting the stop-light switch to the pedal bracket, first push the actuator pin fully into the switch. Insert the switch in the bracket and turn to secure. Reconnect the wiring to the switch. Depress the pedal and pull out the actuator pin from the switch. Now release the pedal, and the pin will be adjusted to its correct position.

18 Refit the side panels to the driver's footwell.

19 Refit and tighten the side nuts securing the pedal support to the steering crossmember.

20 Refit the instrument panel as described in Chapter 12.

21 Reconnect the battery negative (earth) lead.

22 Check the operation of the brake pedal and stop-light switch before using the vehicle on the road.

14 Vacuum servo unit – testing, removal and refitting

Testing

1 To test the operation of the servo unit, with the engine off, depress the footbrake several times to exhaust the vacuum. Now start the engine, keeping the pedal firmly depressed. As the engine starts, there should be a noticeable 'give' in the brake pedal as the vacuum builds up. Allow the engine to run for at least two minutes, then switch it off. The brake pedal should now feel normal, and further applications should result in the pedal feeling firmer, the pedal stroke decreasing with each application.

2 If the servo does not operate as described, first inspect the servo unit check valve as described in Section 15.

3 If the servo unit still fails to operate satisfactorily, the fault lies within the unit itself. Repairs to the unit are not possible, and, if faulty, the servo unit must be renewed.

Removal

Right-hand drive models

4 On models equipped with air conditioning, have the refrigerant evacuated from the system. This is necessary in order to disconnect the refrigerant lines later.

 Warning: Have the system discharged by a Vauxhall dealer or an air conditioning specialist.

5 Remove the air cleaner housing and inlet duct as described in Chapter 4A.

6 Remove the windscreen wiper motor as described in Chapter 12.

7 Remove the alternator as described in Chapter 5A.

8 Unbolt the alternator mounting bracket from the inlet manifold and cylinder head.

9 Remove the brake master cylinder as described in Section 12.

10 Disconnect the vacuum line from the vacuum servo unit, or alternatively remove the non-return valve from the unit.

11 On models with air conditioning, unscrew the refrigerant line lock bolt (located on the bulkhead behind the inlet manifold), then

14.14a Vacuum servo left-hand side mounting nuts . . .

14.14b . . . and right-hand side mounting nuts viewed from the driver's footwell

15 Vacuum servo unit check valve and hose – removal, testing and refitting

Removal

1 Using a screwdriver, carefully ease the vacuum hose end adapter from the front of the servo unit.
2 At the inlet manifold end of the hose, depress the quick-release fitting and disconnect the hose. Withdraw the complete hose from the engine.
3 The hose sections can be renewed separate to the check valve and adapters. Cut the hose with a sharp knife and disconnect it from the relevant part. Cut the new hose to the same length and press it firmly onto the part. Note that the check valve must be fitted so that the arrow points towards the inlet manifold.

Testing

4 Examine the check valve, hoses and adapters for signs of damage, and renew if necessary. The check valve may be tested by blowing through it in both directions. Air should flow through the valve in one direction only – when blown through from the servo unit end. Renew the parts and hoses as necessary.

Refitting

5 Refitting is a reversal of removal, but make sure that the arrow on the non-return check valve points towards the inlet manifold.
6 On completion, start the engine and check the hose for air leaks. Check the vacuum servo operation as described in Section 14.

remove the expansion valve and inner sealing frame. **Note:** *If necessary, have this work carried out by a specialist refrigeration engineer, noting that, if the system will be left open for a long period, it must be sealed until recharged.*
12 Remove the side panels from the driver's footwell, then disconnect the pedal return spring.
13 Use a screwdriver to prise the retaining plate and remove the pin attaching the vacuum servo pushrod to the pedal. Recover the washer.
14 Unscrew and remove the upper left and lower right nuts securing the pedal bracket to the vacuum servo unit **(see illustrations)**.
15 Working in the engine compartment, withdraw the vacuum servo unit from the bulkhead, taking care not to damage the hydraulic brake lines or surrounding components. Recover the gasket.

Left-hand drive models with ABS

16 Remove the hydraulic modulator with reference to Section 22.
17 Remove the brake master cylinder as described in Section 12.
18 Unbolt the hydraulic modulator mounting bracket.
19 Disconnect the vacuum line from the vacuum servo unit, or alternatively remove the non-return valve from the unit.
20 Remove the side panels from the driver's footwell, then disconnect the pedal return spring.
21 Use a screwdriver to prise the retaining

plate and remove the pin attaching the vacuum servo pushrod to the pedal. Recover the washer.
22 Unscrew and remove the upper left and lower right nuts securing the pedal bracket to the vacuum servo unit.
23 Working in the engine compartment, withdraw the vacuum servo unit from the bulkhead, taking care not to damage the hydraulic brake lines or surrounding components. Recover the gasket.

Left-hand drive models without ABS

24 Remove the brake master cylinder as described in Section 12.
25 Disconnect the vacuum line from the vacuum servo unit, or alternatively remove the non-return valve from the unit.
26 Detach the relay carrier from its mounting bracket, and position to one side, then disconnect the wiring multi-plugs from the bracket.
27 Unscrew the union nuts and remove the hydraulic brake lines from between the master cylinder and the branch.
28 Place cloth rags beneath the branch bracket, then unbolt it.
29 Remove the side panels from the driver's footwell, then disconnect the pedal return spring.
30 Use a screwdriver to prise the retaining plate and remove the pin attaching the vacuum servo pushrod to the pedal. Recover the washer.
31 Unscrew and remove the upper left and lower right nuts securing the pedal bracket to the vacuum servo unit.
32 Working in the engine compartment, withdraw the vacuum servo unit from the bulkhead, taking care not to damage the hydraulic brake lines or surrounding components. Recover the gasket.

Refitting

33 Refitting is a reversal of removal, using a new gasket between the vacuum servo unit and bulkhead, and tightening all nuts and bolts to the specified torque, where given. On completion, bleed the brake hydraulic system as described in Section 2. Start the engine and check for air leaks at the vacuum hose-to-servo unit connection.

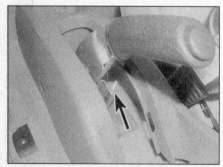

16.3 Handbrake cable adjustment nut on the front of the handbrake lever

16 Handbrake – adjustment

1 Adjust the handbrake at the specified intervals (see Chapter 1), and also after renewing or dismantling the rear brake shoes, or renewing the drum/disc.
2 Chock the front wheels, then jack up the rear of the vehicle and support on axle stands (see *Jacking and vehicle support*).
3 Prise out the console central cover then unclip the gaiter from the centre console and lift it up for access to the adjustment nut on the front of the handbrake lever **(see illustration)**.
4 Fully release the handbrake lever, then back off the adjustment nut to provide some slack in the cable.
5 Depress the brake pedal a minimum of 5 times. On drum brake models, have an assistant listen for the automatic self-adjustment mechanism to operate on the rear brakes – operate the brake pedal until this stops.
6 Fully apply and release the handbrake lever a minimum of 5 times.
7 Apply the handbrake lever to the 3rd notch, then tighten the adjustment nut until the rear wheels are binding, but it is still just possible

to turn them. Each rear wheel brake should have identical resistance – if not, check for seized cables.

8 Fully apply the handbrake lever and check that both rear wheels are locked. Fully release the lever and check that both wheels turn freely.

9 Refit the gaiter to the centre console, and refit the console central cover.

10 Apply the handbrake, then lower the vehicle to the ground.

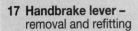

17 Handbrake lever – removal and refitting

Removal

1 Prise out the central cover from the console, then unclip and remove the handbrake lever gaiter.

2 Completely unscrew the handbrake adjustment nut from the front of the lever.

3 Remove the centre console, as described in Chapter 11.

4 Remove the 'handbrake-on' warning switch from the lever as described in Section 20.

5 Unscrew and remove the lever mounting nuts **(see illustration)**.

6 Prise out the plastic clips from the mounting plate, then withdraw the lever and remove from inside the vehicle.

7 Withdraw the mounting plate from the front of the cable, and recover the gasket.

Refitting

8 Refitting is a reversal of removal, but adjust the handbrake as described in Section 16.

18 Handbrake cables – removal and refitting

Removal

1 On rear-drum brake models, the handbrake cable consists of four sections, a short front (primary) section which connects the lever to the compensator plate, the main cable (secondary) section which links the compensator plate to the rear brakes, and two short rear cables which connect each main cable to the rear brake shoes. On rear-disc models, the secondary cable sections connect directly to the rear brake calipers, and there are no short rear sections. Each section can be removed individually as follows.

Primary (front) cable

2 Firmly chock the front wheels, then jack up the rear of the vehicle and support it on axle stands (see *Jacking and vehicle support*). Fully release the handbrake lever.

3 Inside the vehicle, remove the centre console as described in Chapter 11.

4 Unscrew and remove the adjustment nut from the front of the handbrake lever.

17.5 Handbrake lever and mounting bolts

5 Release the cable from the guide on the mounting plate where necessary.

6 Working beneath the vehicle, disconnect the oxygen sensor wiring.

7 Remove the exhaust front pipe and intermediate section with reference to Chapter 4A. Also disconnect the rubber mountings for the central exhaust silencer on the underbody.

8 Unscrew the nuts and remove the exhaust heatshield from the underbody.

9 Detach the front cable from the compensator plate by twisting it through 90°.

10 Release the grommet from the lever mounting plate, and withdraw the front cable from inside the vehicle. Remove the grommet from the cable.

Secondary (main) cable

Note: *The secondary cables are supplied as one part together with the compensator plate.*

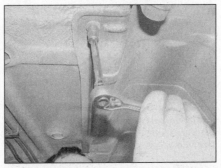

18.17 Removing the exhaust heat shield from the underbody

18.19a Handbrake cable support on the rear suspension trailing arm

11 Firmly chock the front wheels, then jack up the rear of the vehicle and support it on axle stands (see *Jacking and vehicle support*). Remove both rear roadwheels, then fully release the handbrake lever.

12 Prise out the console central cover then unclip the gaiter from the centre console and lift it up for access to the adjustment nut on the front of the handbrake lever.

13 Back off the adjustment nut to provide some slack in the cable.

14 Working on each side in turn, on rear-drum models unclip the rear of each main cable from the connector to the short rear cables. On rear-disc models, use a screwdriver to push down the lever on the calipers in order to disconnect the inner cables, the pull out the clips and disconnect the outer cables from the support bracket.

15 Working beneath the vehicle, disconnect the oxygen sensor wiring.

16 Remove the exhaust front pipe and intermediate section with reference to Chapter 4A. Also disconnect the rubber mountings for the central exhaust silencer on the underbody.

17 Unscrew the nuts and remove the exhaust heatshield from the underbody **(see illustration)**.

18 Detach the front cable from the compensator plate by twisting it through 90° **(see illustration)**.

19 Release the main cable sections from the supports on the rear axle and fuel tank, and withdraw from under the vehicle **(see illustrations)**.

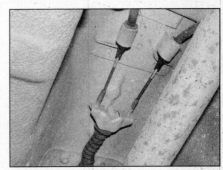

18.18 Handbrake cable compensator plate

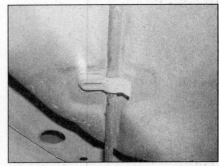

18.19b Handbrake cable support on the underbody

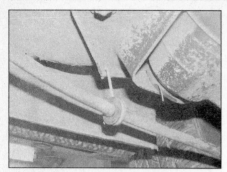

18.19c Handbrake cable support on the rear torsion beam mounting bracket

18.22 Handbrake cable on the rear brake backplate

18.23 Rear cable to main cable connector

Rear cable (rear-drum models)

20 Firmly chock the front wheels, then jack up the rear of the vehicle and support it on axle stands (see *Jacking and vehicle support*). Remove the relevant rear roadwheel, then fully release the handbrake lever.

21 Remove the rear brake shoes as described in Section 6.

22 Pull out the cable retaining clip from the backplate, and release the cable forwards **(see illustration)**.

23 Disconnect the rear cable from the main cable at the connector **(see illustration)**.

Refitting

24 Refitting is a reversal of the removal procedure, but adjust the handbrake as described in Section 16. Where applicable, make sure that the fitting on the rear of the front cable locates correctly in the compensator plate. Also make sure that the protective sleeve on the front cable is firmly located over the bead next to the compensator plate.

19 Stop-light switch – removal, refitting and adjustment

Removal

1 The stop-light switch is located on the pedal bracket in the driver's footwell.

2 To remove the switch, first remove the lower facia trim panel (see Chapter 11,

Section 44), then disconnect the heating duct for access to the switch.

3 Disconnect the wiring plug from the top of the switch, then twist the switch and remove it from the pedal bracket **(see illustrations)**.

Refitting and adjustment

4 Before refitting the switch, push the actuation pin fully in.

5 Refit the switch to the pedal bracket and twist fully to secure.

6 Depress the brake pedal then pull the actuation pin fully out of the switch so that it contacts the pedal. Now release the pedal to set the pin.

7 Refit the heating duct and the lower facia trim panel. Check the operation of the stop-light.

20 Handbrake 'on' warning light switch – removal and refitting

Removal

1 Remove the centre console as described in Chapter 11.

2 Disconnect the wiring from the warning switch located on the front of the handbrake lever **(see illustration)**.

3 Unscrew the bolt and remove the switch from the handbrake lever bracket.

Refitting

4 Refitting is a reversal of removal.

21 Anti-lock Braking and Traction Control systems – general information

The ABS system comprises a hydraulic modulator and electronic control unit together with four roadwheel sensors. The hydraulic modulator contains the electronic control unit (ECU), the hydraulic solenoid valves (one set for each brake) and the electrically-driven pump. The purpose of the system is to prevent the wheel(s) locking during heavy braking. This is achieved by automatic release of the brake on the relevant wheel, followed by re-application of the brake.

The solenoid valves are controlled by the ECU, which itself receives signals from the four wheel sensors which monitor the speed of rotation of each wheel. By comparing these signals, the ECU can determine the speed at which the vehicle is travelling. It can then use this speed to determine when a wheel is decelerating at an abnormal rate, compared to the speed of the vehicle, and therefore predicts when a wheel is about to lock. During normal operation, the system functions in the same way as a non-ABS braking system.

If the ECU senses that a wheel is about to lock, it operates the relevant solenoid valve(s) in the hydraulic unit, which then isolates from the master cylinder the relevant brake on the wheel which is about to lock, effectively sealing-in the hydraulic pressure.

If the speed of rotation of the wheel

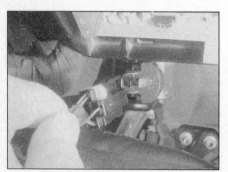

19.3a Disconnect the wiring . . .

19.3b . . . then twist the switch and remove it from the pedal bracket

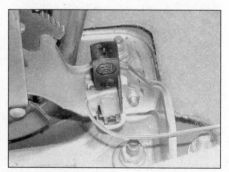

20.2 Handbrake 'on' warning light switch

continues to decrease at an abnormal rate, the ECU operates the electrically-driven pump which pumps the hydraulic fluid back into the master cylinder, releasing the brake. Once the speed of rotation of the wheel returns to an acceptable rate, the pump stops, and the solenoid valves switch again, allowing the hydraulic master cylinder pressure to return to the caliper/wheel cylinder (as applicable), which then re-applies the brake. This cycle can be carried out many times a second.

The action of the solenoid valves and return pump creates pulses in the hydraulic circuit. When the ABS system is functioning, these pulses can be felt through the brake pedal.

On models with traction control, the ABS hydraulic unit incorporates an additional set of solenoid valves which operate the traction control system. The system operates at speeds up to approximately 30 mph (60 km/h) using the signals supplied by the wheel sensors. If the ECU senses that a driving wheel is about to lose traction, it prevents this by momentarily applying the relevant front brake.

The operation of the ABS and the traction control system is entirely dependent on electrical signals. To prevent the system responding to any inaccurate signals, a built-in safety circuit monitors all signals received by the ECU. If an inaccurate signal or low battery voltage is detected, the system is automatically shut down, and the warning light on the instrument panel is illuminated, to inform the driver that the system is not operational. Normal braking is still available, however.

If a fault develops in the ABS/traction control system, the vehicle must be taken to a Vauxhall dealer for fault diagnosis and repair.

22 Anti-lock Braking and Traction Control system components – removal and refitting

Hydraulic modulator and electronic control unit

Removal

1 Remove the battery as described in Chapter 5A.
2 Disconnect the two wiring multi-plugs from the relay carrier bracket.
3 Remove the relay carrier cover, then detach the relay box from the bracket and position to one side.
4 Disconnect the wiring looms from the carrier bracket.
5 Unscrew the three nuts and remove the relay carrier bracket.
6 Remove the holder from the brake fluid hydraulic pipes.
7 Unscrew and remove the filler cap from the brake fluid reservoir, then draw out all of the hydraulic fluid using a poultry baster or old battery hydrometer.

8 Identify the hydraulic pipes for location then unscrew the union nuts and disconnect them from the modulator. Ideally, a special split ring spanner should be used to unscrew the nuts as they may be tight. Be prepared for some loss of fluid by placing cloth rags beneath the lines. On LHD models, it will also be necessary to disconnect the hydraulic pipes from the master cylinder which is located on the left-hand side of the engine compartment. Plug or tape over the apertures in the modulator to prevent entry of dust and dirt.
9 Disconnect the special wiring multi-plug from the top of the hydraulic modulator by lifting the clip and unhooking the multi-plug **(see illustration)**.
10 Unscrew the mounting nuts/bolts and withdraw the modulator and ABS control unit from the bracket. Remove from the engine compartment taking care not to spill any hydraulic fluid on the vehicle's paintwork.
Caution: Keep the modulator upright while it is removed from the vehicle, so that no fluid is allowed to leak out.

Refitting

11 Refitting is a reversal of removal, but finally bleed the hydraulic system as described in Section 2.

Wheel sensor

Renewal

12 Both the front and rear wheel sensors are integral with their hubs. If the sensor is faulty, the wheel hub must be renewed complete as described in Chapter 10.

Traction Control switch

Removal

13 Carefully prise the switch from the facia panel, using a small screwdriver. Use card or cloth to prevent damage to the facia.

Refitting

14 Refitting is a reversal of removal.

ABS Control Unit

Removal

15 Remove the hydraulic modulator and electronic control unit as previously described in this Section.
16 Disconnect the wiring then unscrew the mounting bolts and carefully remove the ABS control unit from the hydraulic body taking care not to damage the coil carrier.
17 Recover the seal from between the coil carrier and control unit.

Refitting

18 Insert the new seal, then carefully position the ABS control unit on the hydraulic modulator and tighten the bolts (new) to the specified torque in the stages given. **Do not** tilt the control unit when positioning it on the modulator. If the bolts become difficult to move during the tightening procedure, the unit is faulty and must be renewed complete.

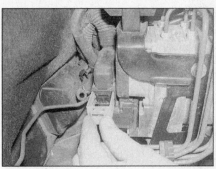

22.9 Lift the clip to disconnect the wiring multi-plug from the top of the hydraulic modulator

Note: *If a spring plate was positioned between the control unit and modulator on removal, leave this out when reassembling the unit.*
19 The remaining procedure is a reversal of the removal procedure.

23 Brake proportioning valve – removal and refitting

Removal

1 Chock the front roadwheels, then jack up the rear of the vehicle and support on axle stands (see *Jacking and vehicle support*).
2 Minimise fluid loss by first removing the master cylinder reservoir cap, then tightening it down onto a piece of polythene to obtain an airtight seal.
3 Unscrew the bolt and remove the bearing for the tension spring from the underbody bracket **(see illustration)**.
4 Note the fitted position of the clamp on the spring, then unscrew the clamp bolt and remove the stop. Remove the spring from the lever on the valve.
5 Clean the area around the hydraulic union nuts on the brake proportioning valve, then unscrew them and disconnect the hydraulic lines.
6 Unscrew the mounting bolts and remove the proportioning valve from the underbody bracket. Take care not to damage the brake pipes.

23.3 Brake proportioning valve viewed from under the rear of the vehicle

7 Note that three different valves are fitted, and it is important to fit the correct type.

Refitting and adjustment

8 Refitting is a reversal of removal, but tighten the bolts to the specified torque and bleed the brake hydraulic system as described in Section 2. Finally, adjust the proportioning valve as follows.

9 The vehicle should be empty with a maximum of half a tank of fuel, and with the correct tyre pressures. On models with ride height control, a minimum pressure of 0.8 bar should be in the system. The rear wheels of the vehicle must be on the ground so that the weight of the vehicle is on the rear suspension. Alternatively, the rear wheels can be lowered onto car ramps.

10 Have an assistant fully depress the brake pedal and quickly release it. The lever on the proportioning valve should move indicating that the unit is working correctly. If the lever does not move, renew the valve.

11 With the adjustment stop free of the valve lever, push the lever fully forwards onto the stop, then release it. Now locate the stop on the spring so that all free play is removed and tighten the clamp bolt in this position.

12 Lower the vehicle to the ground.

Chapter 10
Suspension and steering

Contents

Auxiliary drivebelt check and renewal . . . . .See Chapter 1
Electro-hydraulic power steering pump – removal and refitting 22
Front hub carrier – removal and refitting 2
Front subframe – removal and refitting 4
Front suspension anti-roll bar and links – removal and refitting 6
Front suspension lower arm – removal, overhaul and refitting 7
Front suspension lower balljoint – renewal 8
Front suspension strut – removal, overhaul and refitting 5
Front wheel hub and bearings – checking and renewal 3
General information and precautions 1
Power steering hydraulic system – bleeding 23
Rear hub and bracket – removal and refitting 9
Rear shock absorber – removal, inspection and refitting 11
Rear suspension coil spring – removal and refitting 12
Rear suspension level control air valve and lines – removal and
    refitting 16
Rear suspension level control system – general 15
Rear suspension torsion beam and trailing arms – removal and
    refitting 13
Rear suspension torsion beam mounting bushes – renewal 14
Rear wheel bearings – checking and renewal 10
Steering and suspension check . . . . .See Chapter 1
Steering column – removal and refitting 18
Steering column intermediate shaft – removal and refitting 19
Steering gear – removal and refitting 21
Steering gear rubber gaiters – renewal 20
Steering wheel – removal and refitting 17
Track rod – removal and refitting 25
Track rod end – removal and refitting 24
Wheel alignment and steering angles – general information 26

Degrees of difficulty

Easy, suitable for novice with little experience	**Fairly easy,** suitable for beginner with some experience	**Fairly difficult,** suitable for competent DIY mechanic	**Difficult,** suitable for experienced DIY mechanic	**Very difficult,** suitable for expert DIY or professional

Specifications

General

Front suspension type	Independent, with MacPherson struts, gas-filled shock absorbers and anti-roll bar
Rear suspension type	Semi-independent torsion beam, with trailing arms, coil springs and telescopic shock absorbers. Level control system optional on Estate models.
Steering type	Rack and pinion. Power steering standard on all models

Front wheel alignment

Models up to and including 1999:
Camber	−1°10' ± 45'
Castor:	
Astra Hatchback/Saloon	4° ± 1°
Astra Estate	3°25' ± 1°
Zafira	3°00' +1°/−50'
Max. difference between sides	1°
Toe-in	+0°00' ± 10'
Toe-out on turns (inner wheel turned in 20°)	1°20' ± 45'

Front wheel alignment (continued)

Models from 2000:

Camber:

Astra:

Standard suspension	−1°00' ± 30'
Lowered suspension	−1°10' ± 30'
'Bad road surface' equipment	−0°50' ± 30'
Zafira	−0°20' ± 30'
Max. difference between sides	1°

Castor:

Astra Hatchback/Saloon:

Standard or lowered suspension	4°00' ± 30'
'Bad road surface' equipment	4°15' ± 30'

Astra Estate:

Standard or lowered suspension	3°30' ± 30'
'Bad road surface' equipment	3°45' ± 30'
Zafira	3°10' ± 30'
Max. difference between sides	1°
Toe-in	+0°00' ± 20'

Toe-out on turns (inner wheel turned in 20°):

Astra	1°20' ± 45'
Zafira	1°09' ± 45'

Rear wheel alignment

Models up to and including 1999:

Camber:

Astra	−1°40' ± 30'
Zafira	−1°45' ± 30'
Max. difference between sides	35'
Toe-in	+0°10' +30'/−20'

Models from 2000:

Camber:

Astra Hatchback/Saloon	−1°40' ± 30'
Astra Estate	−1°45' ± 30'
Zafira	−1°45' ± 30'
Max. difference between sides	35'

Toe-in:

Astra Hatchback/Saloon:

Standard suspension	+0°20' +30'/−20'
Lowered suspension	+0°25' +30'/−20'
'Bad road surface' equipment	+0°15' +30'/−20'

Astra Estate:

Standard suspension	+0°12' +30'/−20'
Lowered suspension	+0°17' +30'/−20'
'Bad road surface' equipment	+0°07' +30'/−20'
Zafira	+0°10' +30'/−20'
Max. difference between sides	15'

Steering

Ratio	17 : 1
Electro-hydraulic power steering fluid type	See *Lubricants and fluids*

Fluid capacity:

TRW type (round reservoir)	0.7 litre
Delphi/Saginaw type (angular reservoir)	1.1 litre

Rear wheel bearings

Bearing lateral run-out	0.05 mm max
Bearing radial run-out	0.04 mm max
Bearing tilt	0.1 mm max

Wheels and tyres

Wheel size:

1.4 and 1.6 (SOHC) models	5 1/2 J x 14 (standard), 6J x 15 and 6J x 16 (optional)
1.6 (DOHC), 1.8, 2.0 and 2.2 models	6J x 15 (standard), 5 1/2 J x 14 and 6J x 16 (optional)

Tyre size:

5 1/2 J x 14 wheels	175/70 R14-84T, 185/70 R14-88T, 185/70 R14-88H, 185/65 R14-86T, 185/65 R14-86H
6J x 15 wheels	195/60 R15-88H, 195/60 R15-88V, 195/65 R15-91H
6J x 16 wheels	205/50 R16-87V

Torque wrench settings

	Nm	lbf ft
Front suspension		
Anti-roll bar link:		
To strut	65	48
To anti-roll bar	65	48
Anti-roll bar to subframe	20	15
Front engine mounting through-bolt	55	41
Hub carrier to strut:		
Stage 1	50	37
Stage 2	90	66
Stage 3	Angle-tighten 45°	
Stage 4	Angle-tighten 15°	
Hub nut:		
Stage 1	120	89
Stage 2	Loosen nut fully (until it can be turned by hand)	
Stage 3	20	15
Stage 4	Angle-tighten by a further 80° (plus to next split pin hole as necessary)	
Lower arm to subframe:		
Stage 1	90	66
Stage 2	Angle-tighten 75°	
Stage 3	Angle-tighten 15°	
Lower balljoint-to-hub carrier clamp bolt	100	74
Lower balljoint to lower arm	35	26
Rear engine mounting bracket to transmission	80	59
Strut upper mounting	55	41
Subframe mounting bolts:		
Stage 1	90	66
Stage 2	Angle-tighten 45°	
Stage 3	Angle-tighten 15°	
Wheel bearing hub to carrier:		
Stage 1	90	66
Stage 2	Angle-tighten 30°	
Stage 3	Angle-tighten 15°	
Rear suspension		
Brake hydraulic line union nuts	16	12
Hub bracket to trailing arm:		
Stage 1	50	37
Stage 2	Angle-tighten 30°	
Stage 3	Angle-tighten 15°	
Shock absorber:		
To body	90	66
To trailing arm	110	81
Torsion beam front mounting bracket:		
Centre bolt:		
Stage 1	90	66
Stage 2	Angle-tighten 60°	
Stage 3	Angle-tighten 15°	
Bracket-to-underbody bolts:		
Stage 1	90	66
Stage 2	Angle-tighten 30°	
Stage 3	Angle-tighten 15°	
Steering		
Airbag unit to steering wheel	8	6
Electric hydraulic pump to steering gear and subframe	22	16
Hydraulic pressure and return line union nuts ...	27	20
Pressure and return line bracket to steering gear	4	3
Rear engine mounting bracket to subframe (LHD models)	55	41
Steering column intermediate shaft to steering gear pinion	22	16
Steering column to bulkhead crossmember	22	16
Steering gear to subframe:		
Stage 1	45	33
Stage 2	Angle-tighten 45°	
Stage 3	Angle-tighten 15°	
Steering wheel	22	16
Track rod end locking nut	60	44
Track rod end to steering arm on hub carrier	60	44
Track rod to steering rack	90	66
Wheels		
All models	110	81

1 General information and precautions

General information

The front suspension is of independent type, with a subframe, MacPherson struts, lower arms, and an anti-roll bar. The struts, which incorporate coil springs and integral gas-filled shock absorbers, are attached at their upper ends to the reinforced strut mountings on the body shell. The lower end of each strut is bolted to the top of a cast hub carrier, which carries the hub, and the brake disc and caliper. The hubs run within non-adjustable bearings in the hub carriers. The lower end of each hub carrier is attached, via a balljoint, to a pressed-steel lower arm assembly. The balljoints are bolted to the lower arms and attached to the hub carriers by a clamp bolt. Each lower arm is attached at its inboard end to the subframe with flexible rubber bushes, and controls both lateral and fore-and-aft movement of the front wheels. An anti-roll bar is fitted to all models; the anti-roll bar is mounted on the subframe, and is connected to the suspension struts by vertical drop links.

The rear suspension is of semi-independent type, consisting of a torsion beam and trailing arms, with double-conical coil springs and telescopic shock absorbers. The front ends of the trailing arms are attached to the vehicle underbody by horizontal bushes, and the rear ends are located by the shock absorbers, which are bolted to the underbody at their upper ends. The coil springs are mounted independently of the shock absorbers, and act directly between the trailing arms and the underbody. Each rear wheel bearing, hub and stub axle assembly is manufactured as a sealed unit, and cannot be dismantled.

The steering is of conventional rack-and-pinion type, incorporating a collapsible safety column. The column is joined to the steering gear by an intermediate shaft incorporating two universal joints. The upper section of the column includes an outer slip coupling into which the steering lock engages. With the steering lock engaged, the coupling allows the column to turn at torques above 200 Nm only, so making it impossible to break the steering lock shear pin. However, at this torque it is not possible to control the vehicle. The steering gear is mounted on the front suspension subframe. The steering gear track rods are attached to the steering arms on the hub carriers by track rod ends.

All models are fitted with power-assisted steering. The electro-hydraulic power steering pump is located directly on the steering gear and is non-serviceable. The pump incorporates a hydraulic fluid reservoir.

Precautions

An airbag is fitted to the steering wheel. To ensure it operates correctly in the event of an accident, and to avoid the risk of personal injury from it being accidentally triggered, the following precautions must be observed. Also refer to Chapter 12 for more information:

a) *Before carrying out any operations on the airbag system, disconnect the battery negative terminal, and wait at least 1 minute to ensure that the system capacitor has been discharged.*

b) *Note that the airbag must not be subjected to temperatures in excess of 90°C (194°F). When the airbag is removed, ensure that it is stored with the pad facing upwards.*

c) *Do not allow any solvents or cleaning agents to contact the airbag assembly. The unit must be cleaned using only a damp cloth.*

d) *The airbag and control unit are both sensitive to impact. If either is dropped from a height of more than 500 mm, they must be renewed.*

e) *Disconnect the airbag control unit wiring plug prior to using arc-welding equipment on the vehicle.*

f) *On vehicles fitted with a passenger's airbag, do not fit accessories in the airbag zone. Items like telephones, cassette storage boxes, additional mirrors, etc, can be ripped off and cause serious injury, if the airbag inflates.*

2 Front hub carrier – removal and refitting

Note: *It is recommended that all mounting nuts and bolts are renewed. A balljoint separator tool will be required for this operation.*

Caution: The front wheel camber setting is controlled by the bolts securing the hub carrier to the front suspension strut. Before removing the bolts, mark the hub carrier in relation to the strut accurately. On completion, the camber setting must be checked and adjusted by a suitably-equipped garage.

Removal

1 Apply the handbrake, then jack up the front of the vehicle and support it on axle stands (see *Jacking and vehicle support*). Remove the relevant front wheel.

2 Unscrew the nut securing the track rod end to the steering arm on the hub carrier. Using a balljoint separator, separate the track rod end from the steering arm.

3 Remove the front wheel hub complete as described in Section 3.

4 Mark the position of the front hub carrier on the front suspension strut (see *Caution* at beginning of the Section), then unscrew and remove the two nuts and bolts, noting that their heads face the front of the vehicle. Remove the carrier from the strut. Discard the nuts and bolts and obtain new ones.

Refitting

5 Locate the hub carrier on the strut and fit the new bolts. Position the carrier as previously noted, then tighten the bolts to the specified torque and angle in the specified stages.

6 Refit the front wheel hub with reference to Section 3.

7 Refit the track rod end to the steering arm on the hub carrier and tighten the nut to the specified torque.

8 Refit the front wheel and lower the vehicle to the ground.

9 Check and if necessary adjust the steering toe-in setting at the earliest opportunity.

3 Front wheel hub and bearings – checking and renewal

Checking

1 To check the front wheel bearings for wear, apply the handbrake then jack up the front of the vehicle and support it on axle stands (see *Jacking and vehicle support*). Spin the wheel by hand and check for a noisy or rough bearing. Grip the wheel and rock it to check for excessive play in the bearing, however be careful not to confuse wear in the suspension or steering joints with wear in the bearing. Refer to Chapter 1 for more information.

Renewal

2 With the front of the vehicle supported on axle stands, remove the relevant front wheel.

3 Remove the brake disc as described in Chapter 9. This procedure involves removing the brake caliper and tying it to one side, leaving the hydraulic hose attached; pull out the spring clip and disconnect the flexible hose from the support bracket **(see illustration)**.

4 Carefully tap the protective cap from the centre of the hub, then extract the split pin and unscrew the driveshaft retaining nut while holding the hub stationary with a bar positioned between two wheel bolts temporarily refitted to the hub. Note: *The nut is tightened to a high torque.* Remove the nut and spacer.

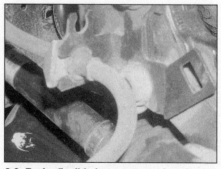

3.3 Brake flexible hose support bracket on the hub carrier

3.8 Separating the suspension lower arm balljoint from the hub carrier

3.9 Disconnecting the ABS front wheel sensor wiring

3.12 The front hub carrier mounting bolts, showing the ABS sensor wiring

5 Extract the split pin where necessary, then unscrew the nut securing the track rod end to the steering arm on the hub carrier. Using a balljoint separator, separate the track rod end from the steering arm. Also unscrew the nut and disconnect the anti-roll bar link from the strut.

6 Unscrew and remove the clamp bolt securing the front suspension lower arm balljoint to the hub carrier, noting which way round it is fitted. It is recommended that the clamp bolt and nut are renewed.

7 Using a chisel or screwdriver as a wedge, expand the balljoint clamp at the bottom of the hub carrier.

8 Using a lever, push down on the suspension lower arm to free the balljoint from the hub carrier, then move the hub carrier to one side and release the arm, taking care not to damage the balljoint rubber boot **(see illustration)**.

9 On models with ABS, disconnect the wiring from the front wheel sensor at the connector **(see illustration)**.

10 Pull the hub carrier out while pressing the driveshaft through the hub. If it is tight use a suitable puller to push the driveshaft from the hub.

11 Mark the hub, hub carrier and backplate in relation to each other.

12 From the rear of the hub carrier, unscrew and remove the three hub mounting bolts **(see illustration)**. Discard the bolts as new ones must be fitted.

13 Withdraw the hub from the hub carrier, and recover the backplate. Take care not to damage the ABS sensor wiring, where fitted.

14 It is not possible to obtain the drive flange or bearings separately from the hub housing. If the bearings are worn excessively, the complete hub assembly must be renewed.

15 Clean the hub and hub carrier, then locate the backplate on the carrier and insert the hub with the previously-made marks and bolt holes aligned. Apply locking fluid to the threads of the new mounting bolts then insert them and tighten to the specified torque and angle in the stages given in the Specifications.

16 Pull out the hub carrier then insert the driveshaft into the hub. Fit the spacer and new nut, and tighten the nut moderately to draw the driveshaft into the hub. Leave final tightening of the nut until later (see paragraph 20).

17 On models with ABS, reconnect the wiring for the front wheel sensor at the connector.

18 Push down on the suspension lower arm and locate the balljoint stub in the bottom of the hub carrier. Remove the wedge from the balljoint clamp and insert the new bolt. Tighten the nut to the specified torque.

19 Refit the track rod end to the steering arm, then refit the new nut and tighten to the specified torque. Where necessary, fit a new split pin. Also refit the anti-roll bar link to the strut and tighten the nut.

20 With the hub held stationary, tighten the hub nut to the specified torque and angle in the stages given in the Specifications, and fit a new split pin. Bend the outer leg of the split pin over the end of the driveshaft, then cut the inner leg as necessary and bend it inwards.

21 Tap the protective cap into position in the centre of the hub.

22 Refit the brake disc and caliper with reference to Chapter 9.

23 Refit the front wheel and lower the vehicle to the ground.

---

4 Front subframe – removal and refitting

Note: *Vauxhall technicians use special jigs to ensure that the engine/transmission is correctly aligned. Without the use of these tools it is important to note the position of the engine/transmission accurately before removal.*

4.3 Battery positive terminal and cable

Removal

1 Turn the steering to the straight-ahead position, then remove the ignition key and allow the steering lock to engage.

2 In the driver's footwell, unscrew the bolt securing the bottom of the steering column intermediate shaft to the steering gear pinion. Pull the shaft from the pinion and position to one side.

3 Remove the battery and battery tray as described in Chapter 5A **(see illustration)**.

4 Disconnect the oxygen sensor wiring and position to one side.

5 On Zafira models, at the rear of the engine compartment, remove the rubber weatherseal and plastic access cover. Also unscrew the nuts and remove the main cover from the bulkhead.

6 Secure the radiator to the front panel using two bolts inserted through the side mountings. This is necessary as the radiator bottom mounting rubbers are located in the subframe.

7 Detach the cover from the fusebox on the left-hand side of the engine compartment, and remove the fuse for the electric power steering system. Release the clips and detach the fuse carrier from the retainer, then slide out the power steering pump fuseholder and wire.

8 Unscrew the nut and remove the earth lead for the steering wiring harness from the body. Note the cable routing then feed the wiring harness down through the engine compartment and onto the steering gear.

9 Connect a hoist to the engine/transmission assembly and support its weight **(see illustration)**. If available, the type of support bar which locates in the engine compartment side

4.9 Supporting the engine/transmission with a hoist

4.15 Unbolting the exhaust front pipe from the exhaust manifold

4.17 The engine rear mounting

4.22a Unscrew the subframe front mounting bolts . . .

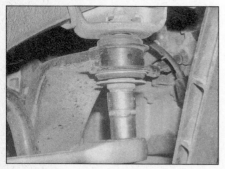

4.22b . . . side mounting bolts . . .

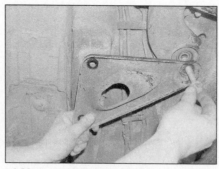

4.22c . . . and rear support bracket bolts

4.23a Lowering the front suspension subframe from the vehicle underbody

channels is to be preferred, as this will ensure correct repositioning during refitting. Connect the hoist chains to the two eyes located at the left-hand end of the cylinder head, and also connect another chain to the eye located on the rear right-hand end of the cylinder head.

10 Apply the handbrake, then jack up the front of the vehicle and support it on axle stands (see *Jacking and vehicle support*). Where necessary, remove the splash guard from the bottom of the engine compartment. Remove both front wheels.

11 Remove the front bumper as described in Chapter 11.

12 Remove the lower liner from the right-hand wheelarch.

13 Working on each side in turn, unscrew the nuts and disconnect the anti-roll bar links from the front suspension struts.

14 Disconnect the steering track rod ends from the steering arms on the hub carriers

with reference to Section 24. Unscrew the clamp bolts and lever the lower balljoints from the bottom of each hub carrier.

15 Remove the exhaust front pipe **(see illustration)**, catalytic converter and intermediate pipe as described in Chapter 4A.

16 On manual transmission models, note the position of the gearchange linkage located above the engine rear mounting, then disconnect it from the support bracket on the subframe (refer to Chapter 7A if necessary).

17 Unbolt the rear mounting from the transmission **(see illustration)**.

18 At the front of the engine, unscrew and remove the centre bolt from the front mounting.

19 On models with air conditioning, unclip the A/C resonator from the front right-hand side of the subframe.

20 Support the subframe with a length of wood on a trolley jack. Ideally, a purpose-

made cradle should be used. Enlist the help of an assistant.

21 Accurately mark the position of the subframe and mounting bolts to ensure correct refitting. Note that Vauxhall technicians use a special jig with guide pins located through the alignment holes in the subframe and underbody.

22 Unscrew and remove the subframe mounting bolts, noting the position of each bolt, as they are of different lengths **(see illustrations)**. There are two bolts at the front, two bolts located above the lower suspension arms, and six bolts located on the triangular rear support brackets.

23 With the help of an assistant, carefully lower the subframe taking care not to damage the wiring harness for the power-assisted steering. As it is being lowered, guide the steering gear pinion through the rubber grommet in the floor **(see illustrations)**.

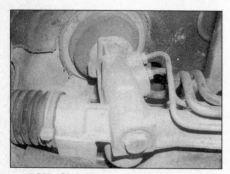

4.23b Steering gear showing rubber grommet in the floor

4.23c Guide the steering gear pinion through the rubber grommet when lowering the subframe

4.23d Front suspension subframe removed from the vehicle

4.24 Gearchange bracket on the front subframe

4.25a Steering gear location for the rubber grommet

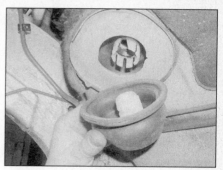

4.25b Fit the lower half of the rubber grommet while an assistant holds the upper half inside the vehicle

24 Remove the steering gear, front suspension lower arms and anti-roll bar with reference to Sections 21, 7 and 6. If necessary, the subframe mounting rubbers may be renewed, however, they must be renewed in pairs only (ie, left and right together). Use a metal tube, a long threaded bar, and two nuts and washers to force out the rubbers. If necessary, unbolt and remove the gearchange bracket **(see illustration)**.

Refitting

25 Refitting is a reversal of removal, but tighten all nuts and bolts to the specified torque where necessary in the stages given. Make sure that the previously-made marks are correctly aligned, and make sure that the holes in the subframe and underbody are correctly aligned before fully tightening the mounting bolts. Make sure that the rubber

grommet is correctly located on the steering gear and in the underbody – if the grommet has become displaced, have an assistant hold the upper half inside the vehicle while you press up the lower half from underneath until the two sections snap together **(see illustrations)**.

5 Front suspension strut – removal, overhaul and refitting

Note: *A balljoint separator tool will be required for this operation. Both front suspension struts should be renewed at the same time in order to maintain good steering and suspension characteristics. It is recommended that all mounting nuts and bolts are renewed.*

Removal

1 Apply the handbrake, then jack up the front of the vehicle and support it on axle stands (see *Jacking and vehicle support*). Remove the front wheel.

2 Unscrew the nut and disconnect the anti-roll bar link from the strut **(see illustration)**. Use a spanner on the special flats to hold the link while the nut is being loosened.

3 Pull out the clip and disconnect the brake hose from the bracket on the strut.

4 Unclip the brake pad wiring harness from the strut. On models with ABS, disconnect the wheel sensor wiring **(see illustration)**.

5 Mark the position of the strut on the hub carrier to ensure the camber setting is maintained **(see illustration)**.

6 Unscrew and remove the two bolts securing the hub carrier to the strut, noting which way round they are fitted. With the two bolts removed, pull the hub carrier away from the strut and support on an axle stand **(see illustrations)**.

7 Support the strut beneath the front wing. In the engine compartment, remove the cap then unscrew the strut upper mounting nut while counterholding the piston rod with a further spanner. Recover the upper mounting from the suspension tower **(see illustrations)**. On Zafira models it will be necessary to remove the plastic water deflectors from in front of the windscreen for access to the nut.

8 Lower the strut and withdraw from under the front wing **(see illustration)**.

5.2 Removing the nut securing the anti-roll bar link to the strut

5.4 Disconnecting the wiring for the front wheel ABS sensor

5.5 Mark the position of the strut on the hub carrier to maintain the camber setting

5.6a Unscrew the nuts . . .

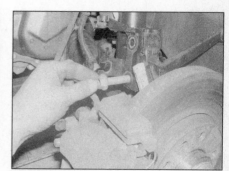

5.6b . . . and bolts securing the strut to the hub carrier

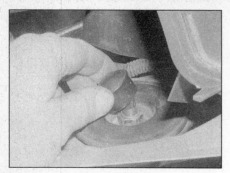

5.7a Remove the cap . . .

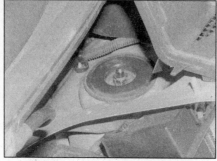

5.7b . . . for access to the front suspension strut upper mounting nut

5.7c Recover the upper mounting from the suspension tower

Overhaul

Note: *A spring compressor tool will be required for this operation.*

9 With the suspension strut resting on a bench, or clamped in a vice, fit a spring compressor tool, and compress the coil spring to relieve the pressure on the spring seats. Ensure that the compressor tool is securely located on the spring, in accordance with the tool manufacturer's instructions **(see illustration)**.

10 Counterhold the strut piston rod with a spanner, and unscrew the piston rod nut **(see illustrations)**.

11 Remove the upper damping ring with support bearing, upper spring seat, and (where fitted) the buffer **(see illustrations)**.

12 Remove the coil spring from the strut **(see illustration)**.

13 With the strut assembly now completely dismantled **(see illustration)**, examine all the components for wear, damage or deformation, and check the support bearing for smoothness of operation. Renew any of the components as necessary.

14 Examine the strut for signs of fluid leakage. Check the strut piston for signs of pitting along its entire length, and check the strut body for signs of damage. While holding it in an upright position, test the operation of the strut by moving the piston through a full

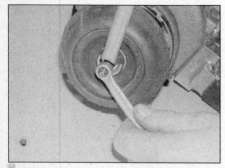

5.8 Lowering the strut from under the front wing

5.9 Fitting a spring compressor tool to the front suspension strut coil spring

5.10a Hold the strut piston rod with a spanner when loosening the nut . . .

5.10b . . . then remove the nut . . .

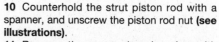

5.11a . . . the upper damping ring and support bearing . . .

5.11b . . . the upper spring seat . . .

5.12 . . . and the coil spring

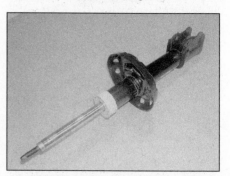

5.13 Front suspension strut completely dismantled

stroke, and then through short strokes of 50 to 100 mm. In both cases, the resistance felt should be smooth and continuous. If the resistance is jerky or uneven or if there is any visible sign of wear or damage to the strut, renewal is necessary.

15 If any doubt exists as to the condition of the coil spring, carefully remove the spring compressors and check the spring for distortion and signs of cracking. Renew the spring if it is damaged or distorted, or if there is any doubt as to its condition.

16 Inspect all other components for damage or deterioration, and renew any that are suspect.

17 With the spring compressed with the compressor tool, locate the spring on the strut, making sure that it is correctly seated with its lower end against the stop.

18 Refit the buffer, upper spring seat, and upper damping ring.

19 Refit the piston rod nut and tighten it securely while counterholding the piston rod with a spanner.

20 Slowly slacken the spring compressor tool to relieve the tension in the spring. Check that the ends of the spring locate correctly against the stops on the spring seats. If necessary, turn the spring and the upper seat so that the components locate correctly before the compressor tool is removed. Remove the compressor tool when the spring is fully seated.

Refitting

21 Refitting is a reversal of removal, bearing in mind the following points.
  a) *Renew the two bolts securing the hub carrier to the strut, also the piston rod upper nuts.*
  b) *Tighten all nuts and bolts to the specified torque, where given.*
  c) *On completion have the front wheel alignment setting checked by a suitably-equipped garage.*

6 Front suspension anti-roll bar and links – removal and refitting

Note: *It is recommended that all mounting nuts and bolts are renewed.*

Removal

1 Remove the front subframe as described in Section 4.

2 Identify the links side-for-side to ensure correct refitting, then unscrew the nuts and remove the links from the anti-roll bar **(see illustration)**. Use a spanner on the special flats to hold the links while the nuts are being loosened.

3 Unbolt the clamps securing the anti-roll bar to the subframe **(see illustration)**. **Note:** *If the bolts are rusted in position, they can be cut off and drilled out and new inserts fitted. Consult a Vauxhall dealer for more information.*

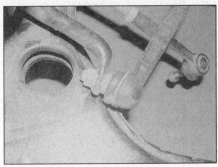

6.2 Side link connection to the anti-roll bar

4 Lift the anti-roll bar from the subframe.

5 Note the position of the rubber bushes, then prise them from the anti-roll bar.

6 Examine the anti-roll bar, links, and rubber bushes for wear and damage and renew them if necessary.

Refitting

7 Refitting is a reversal of removal, but note the following points.
  a) *The slits of the rubber bushes must face forwards when fitted to the anti-roll bar.*
  b) *Renew all nuts and bolts and tighten them to the specified torque.*
  c) *Refit the front subframe with reference to Section 4.*

7 Front suspension lower arm – removal, overhaul and refitting

Note: *The lower arm inner pivot bolts must be renewed when refitting.*

Removal

1 Apply the handbrake, then jack up the front of the vehicle and support it on axle stands (see *Jacking and vehicle support*). Remove the front wheel.

2 Unscrew and remove the clamp bolt securing the front suspension lower arm balljoint to the bottom of the hub carrier, noting which way round it is fitted.

3 Using a suitable lever, push down the lower arm and separate it from the hub carrier. When releasing the lower arm, take care not

7.4 Front suspension lower arm inner mounting located on the subframe

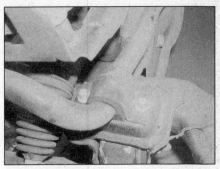

6.3 One of the clamps securing the anti-roll bar to the front suspension subframe

to damage the balljoint rubber boot on the bottom of the hub carrier; if necessary protect it with a piece of card or plastic. **Note:** *If the balljoint stub is tight in the hub carrier, use a screwdriver or cold chisel as a wedge to force the clamp apart.*

4 Note that the lower arm inner retaining bolt heads are facing the front of the vehicle. Unscrew and remove the bolts and withdraw the lower arm from the subframe **(see illustration)**. It will be necessary to slightly press the arms to release the rubber mountings.

Overhaul

5 The lower balljoint may be renewed as described in Section 8. The rubber bushes are a tight fit in the arm and must be pressed out. If a press is not available, the bushes can be drawn out using a long bolt, nut, washers and a socket or length of metal tubing.

6 Prior to fitting the new bushes, coat them with silicone grease or soapy water. Press both bushes fully into the lower arm; when fitting the rear bush, make sure that one of the recesses in the bush is aligned with the seam in the lower arm **(see illustration)**.

Refitting

7 Locate the lower arm on the subframe and fit the retaining bolts from the front of the vehicle. Hand tighten the bolts at this stage.

8 Locate the lower balljoint stub fully in the bottom of the hub carrier, then refit the clamp bolt and tighten to the specified torque. Make sure the bolt head is facing the front.

9 Refit the front wheel and lower the vehicle to the ground.

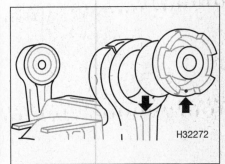

7.6 Alignment of the recess in the bush with the seam in the lower arm

8.2 Front suspension lower balljoint showing rivets securing it to the lower arm

10 With the weight of the vehicle on the suspension, tighten the lower arm inner pivot bolts to the specified torque and in the stages given.

11 Have the front wheel alignment settings checked by a suitably-equipped garage.

8 Front suspension lower balljoint – renewal

Note: *The original balljoint is riveted to the lower arm; service replacements are bolted in position.*

1 Remove the front suspension lower arm as described in Section 7. **Note:** *If the fitted balljoint is a service replacement, it is not necessary to completely remove the arm but only to disconnect the balljoint from the bottom of the hub carrier then unbolt the old balljoint.*

2 Mount the lower arm in a vice, then drill the heads from the three rivets that secure the balljoint to the lower arm, using a 12.0 mm diameter drill **(see illustration)**.

3 If necessary, tap the rivets from the lower arm, then remove the balljoint.

4 Clean any rust from the rivet holes, and apply rust inhibitor.

5 The new balljoint must be fitted using three special bolts, spring washers and nuts, available from a Vauxhall parts centre.

6 Ensure that the balljoint is fitted the correct way up, noting that the securing nuts are positioned on the underside of the lower arm. Tighten the nuts to the specified torque.

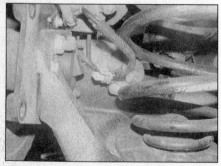

9.2 Disconnecting the ABS wiring from the inside of the rear hub

7 Refit the front suspension lower arm as described in Section 7.

9 Rear hub and bracket – removal and refitting

Note: *New nuts will be required when refitting the rear hub bracket to the trailing arm.*

Removal

1 Remove the rear brake drum or disc, as applicable, as described in Chapter 9.

2 On models with ABS, disconnect the wiring for the wheel speed sensor located on the inside of the rear hub **(see illustration)**.

3 On rear drum models, support the rear brake backplate and shoes on an axle stand. On rear disc models, attach the brake caliper carrier plate to the rear coil spring with a plastic cable tie to prevent straining the hydraulic brake line.

4 Support the rear hub and unscrew the mounting nuts on the inside of the trailing arm. Withdraw the hub and bracket from the rear trailing arm. Note that the locating studs are spaced so that the hub bracket will only fit in one position. On rear disc models, remove the backplate.

Refitting

5 Locate the backplate or caliper carrier plate on the trailing arm and align the mounting bolt holes.

6 Locate the hub and bracket on the trailing arm and fit new nuts to secure. Tighten the nuts to the specified torque and angles in the stages given.

7 Reconnect the wiring for the wheel speed sensor on models with ABS.

8 Refit the rear brake drum or disc, as applicable, as described in Chapter 9. Check and adjust the handbrake as described in Chapter 9.

10 Rear wheel bearings – checking and renewal

1 Chock the front wheels, then jack up the rear of the vehicle and support on axle stands (see *Jacking and vehicle support*). Remove the rear wheels.

2 Remove the brake drums or brake disc (as applicable) as described in Chapter 9.

3 A dial test indicator (DTI) or datum bar and feeler blades will be required to measure the amount of radial and lateral run-out in the bearing. Zero the indicator on the outer edge of the hub flange. Alternatively, position the datum bar against the surface and use a feeler blade to measure the clearance.

4 To measure lateral run-out, locate the probe on the surface of the hub which contacts the drum or disc. To measure radial run-out, locate the probe on the outer

perimeter of the hub so that it is pointing towards the centre of the hub.

5 Slowly turn the hub and note the maximum amount of run-out. If the run-out exceeds the amounts given in the Specifications, renew the hub bearing and bracket as described in Section 9.

6 Finally, check the amount of tilt in the bearing. To do this, use two wheel bolts to attach a metal bar to the outer face of the hub, then attempt to tilt the hub by pressing the bar in and out. The indicator probe must also be located on the outer face of the hub. If the tilt exceeds the maximum amount given in the Specifications, renew the hub bearing and bracket.

7 Remove the indicator and refit the brake drums or brake disc with reference to Chapter 9.

8 Refit the rear wheels and lower the vehicle to the ground.

11 Rear shock absorber – removal, inspection and refitting

Note: *Always renew shock absorbers in pairs to maintain good road handling.*

Removal

1 Chock the front roadwheels, then jack up the rear of the vehicle and support on axle stands positioned under the rear jacking points (see *Jacking and vehicle support*). Remove the rear roadwheels.

2 On Estate models with a rear suspension level control system, remove the cover for the right-hand rear light cluster in the rear luggage compartment, and vent the air pressure from the system Schrader valve. At the shock absorber, release the clip and detach the pressure line.

3 Using a trolley jack, slightly raise the trailing arm on the relevant side.

4 Unscrew and remove the shock absorber lower mounting bolt from the trailing arm **(see illustration)**.

5 Support the shock absorber, then unscrew and remove the upper mounting bolt and withdraw the shock absorber from the underbody bracket **(see illustration)**.

11.4 Rear shock absorber lower mounting bolt on the trailing arm

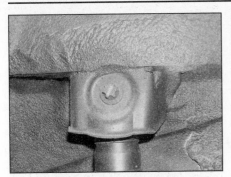

11.5 Rear shock absorber upper mounting bolt on the underbody bracket

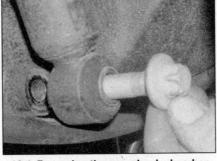

12.4 Removing the rear shock absorber lower mounting bolt

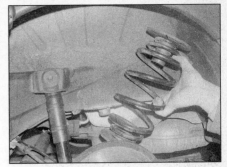

12.6a Remove the rear coil spring, together with the spring seats . . .

Inspection

6 The shock absorber can be tested by clamping the lower mounting eye in a vice, then fully extending and compressing the shock absorber several times. Any evidence of jerky movement or lack of resistance indicates the need for renewal.

7 Examine the mounting rubbers in the shock absorber for excessive wear.

8 If the shock absorber or its mounting rubbers are worn excessively, renew the complete shock absorber.

Refitting

9 Refitting is a reversal of removal, but tighten the mounting bolts to the specified torque. On models with rear suspension level control, pre-charge the system with 0.8 bar pressure, then adjust the pressure according to the load being carried.

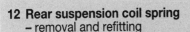

12 Rear suspension coil spring – removal and refitting

Note: *Due to the design of the rear suspension, it is important to note that only one coil spring should be removed at a time. Note that the rear springs should be renewed in pairs.*

Removal

1 Chock the front roadwheels, then jack up the rear of the vehicle and support on axle stands positioned under the rear jacking points (see *Jacking and vehicle support*). Remove the rear roadwheels.

2 On Estate models with a rear suspension level control system, remove the cover for the right-hand rear light cluster in the rear luggage compartment, and vent the air pressure from the system Schrader valve.

3 Using a trolley jack, slightly raise the trailing arm on the relevant side.

4 Unscrew and remove the shock absorber lower mounting bolt from the trailing arm **(see illustration)**.

5 Carefully lower the trailing arm as far as possible without straining the brake flexible hoses leading to the rear brakes.

6 Remove the coil spring and spring seats

12.6b . . . then remove the upper spring seat . . .

from the underbody and trailing arm, and withdraw from under the vehicle. Note that the upper spring seat incorporates a damper buffer **(see illustrations)**.

Refitting

7 Refitting is a reversal of removal, but note the following points.

a) *Ensure that the spring locates correctly on the upper and lower seats, as well as on the trailing arm and underbody.*

b) *Tighten the shock absorber lower mounting bolt to the specified torque.*

c) *If both springs are being renewed, repeat the procedure on the remaining side of the vehicle.*

d) *On models with rear suspension level control, pre-charge the system with 0.8 bar pressure, then adjust the pressure according to the load being carried.*

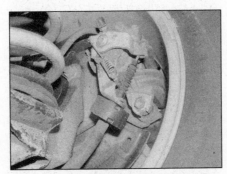

13.4 Handbrake cable connection to the rear disc caliper

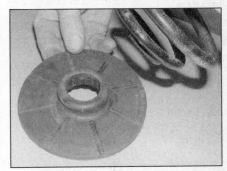

12.6c . . . and lower spring seat

13 Rear suspension torsion beam and trailing arms – removal and refitting

Removal

1 Chock the front roadwheels, then jack up the rear of the vehicle and support on axle stands positioned under the rear jacking points (see *Jacking and vehicle support*). Remove the rear roadwheels.

2 On Estate models with a rear suspension level control system, remove the access cover for the right-hand rear light cluster in the rear luggage compartment, and vent the air pressure from the system Schrader valve.

3 Fully release the handbrake lever, then unclip the gaiter and pull it up the lever. Fully unscrew the adjustment nut on the front of the handbrake primary cable.

4 On rear disc brake models, working on each side in turn, use a screwdriver to press down the lever on the caliper, then disconnect the cable from the lever **(see illustration)**. Remove the clips and disconnect the outer cables from the support brackets on the trailing arms. Also release the handbrake cables from the supports on the torsion beam.

5 On rear drum brake models, disconnect the short rear cables at the connectors located each side just in front of the drums.

6 On models with ABS, disconnect the rear wheel sensor wiring from the rear hubs, and unclip the wiring from the torsion beam.

7 On models with a rear brake load proportioning valve, unbolt the retainer from the underbody bracket and disconnect the tension spring.

8 Remove the filler cap from the brake hydraulic fluid reservoir in the engine compartment, then tighten the cap down onto a piece of polythene sheeting. This will help prevent the fluid from draining from the system when the rear brake flexible hoses are disconnected.

9 Unscrew the union nuts and disconnect the rear brake hydraulic lines from the flexible hoses at the support brackets on the trailing arms on each side. Recover the retaining plates. Be prepared for some loss of brake fluid, and plug or tape over the ends of the lines and hoses to prevent entry of dust and dirt.

10 Support the weight of the torsion beam and trailing arms using two trolley jacks. Alternatively, one trolley jack and a length of wood may be used, but the help of an assistant will be required.

11 Unscrew the lower mounting bolts and detach both shock absorbers from the torsion beam.

12 Carefully lower the torsion beam until it is possible to remove the coil springs and spring seats. Note that the upper spring seats incorporate buffers.

13 Make sure that the torsion beam is supported, then unscrew and remove the front mounting bracket bolts from the underbody **(see illustration)**.

14 Lower the torsion beam to the ground and remove it from under the vehicle.

15 The brake components can be removed from the trailing arms, referring to the relevant Sections of Chapter 9. The hub units can be removed with reference to Section 9.

16 If necessary, the front mounting bushes can be renewed as described in Section 14.

Refitting

17 Refit any components that were removed from the torsion beam, referring to the relevant Sections of this Chapter and Chapter 9, as applicable.

18 Check the condition of the threads in the front mounting bracket captive nuts on the underbody. If necessary, use a tap to clean out the threads.

19 Support the torsion beam on the trolley jacks, and position the assembly under the rear of the vehicle.

13.13 Rear suspension torsion beam front mounting bracket

20 Raise the jacks, and fit the mounting bracket bolts. Do not fully tighten the bolts at this stage.

21 Position the torsion beam so that the distance between the coil spring contact surfaces on the trailing arms and underbody is 168.0 ± 10.0 mm on Saloon and Hatchback models, and 198.0 ± 10.0 mm on Estate and Zafira models. With the torsion beam in this position, loosen then tighten the front mounting bracket centre bolts on each side to the specified torque.

22 Fully tighten the front mounting bracket-to-underbody bolts to the specified torque in the stages given.

23 Locate the upper and lower seats on the coil springs, then refit the springs on the torsion beam.

24 Raise the torsion beam until the shock absorber lower mounting bolts can be inserted. Tighten the bolts to the specified torque.

25 Refit the brake hydraulic lines and flexible hoses together with the retaining plates and tighten the union nuts to the specified torque.

26 On models with a rear brake load proportioning valve, refit the retainer and spring and tighten the bolt to the torque given in Chapter 9.

27 On models with ABS, clip the wiring to the torsion beam and reconnect it to the rear wheel sensors.

28 On rear drum models, reconnect the short rear cables at the connectors.

29 On rear disc models, reconnect the handbrake cables to the caliper levers and fit the cables in the supports.

30 Bleed the complete brake hydraulic system, as described in Chapter 9.

31 Adjust the handbrake cable as described in Chapter 9, then refit the handbrake lever gaiter.

32 On Estate models with a rear suspension level control system, pressurise the system to 0.8 bars then adjust the pressure according to the load being carried. Refit the access cover for the right-hand rear light cluster.

33 Refit the roadwheels and lower the vehicle to the ground.

14 Rear suspension torsion beam mounting bushes – renewal

Note: *Trailing arm bushes should always be renewed in pairs – ie, on both sides of the vehicle.*

Removal

1 Remove the torsion beam and trailing arms as described in Section 13.

2 Before removing the bushes, use a cold chisel to tap the spacers from the inner faces of the trailing arms.

3 A special Vauxhall tool is available for removal and refitting of the bushes, but an alternative can be improvised using a long

bolt, nut, washers, and a length of metal tubing or a socket. Note the fitted position of the bushes, then draw them out from the arms.

Refitting

4 Lubricate the new bushes with silicone grease or soapy water, then draw them into position in the trailing arms.

5 Refit the torsion beam and trailing arms as described in Section 13.

15 Rear suspension level control system – general

1 Where fitted on Estate models, the rear suspension level control system is adjusted by altering the air pressure in the rear shock absorbers, through a valve located on the right-hand side of the luggage compartment.

2 For safety reasons, the level control system must not be fully pressurised when the vehicle is being driven in an unladen condition.

3 To adjust the system, continue as follows.

4 With the vehicle unladen, use a tyre pressure gauge on the air valve to check that the system pressure is 0.8 bar unladen. Adjust if necessary. The system pressure must never be allowed to fall below 0.8 bar.

5 With the vehicle standing on a level surface, measure the distance from the bottom of the rear bumper to the ground. Subtract 40.0 mm from the distance measured, and note the new value.

6 Load the vehicle, and if necessary increase the pressure in the system until the noted value for the bumper height is reached. Do not exceed a pressure of 5.0 bars.

7 After unloading the vehicle, depressurise the system to the minimum pressure of 0.8 bar.

16 Rear suspension level control air valve and lines – removal and refitting

Removal

1 With the tailgate open, turn the two fasteners through 90° and swivel open the cover for access to the right-hand rear light cluster. Remove the cap then release the pressure from the level system by depressing the centre core of the Schrader valve.

2 Unscrew the mounting nut and detach the air valve from the mounting bracket, then squeeze together the lugs and disconnect the air line.

3 Twist the retaining clip and disconnect the air valve line from the right-hand pressure line on the underbody.

4 Twist the retaining clips and disconnect the right and left-hand pressure lines from the tee-piece. Release the pressure lines from the underbody clips and remove.

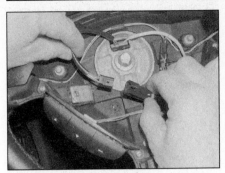

17.4 Disconnect the wiring for the radio control switches

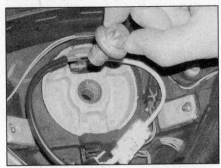

17.5 Removing the Torx retaining bolt securing the steering wheel to the column

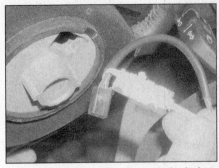

17.7 Guide the wiring through the hole when removing the steering wheel

Refitting

5 Refitting is a reversal of removal, but on completion, pressurise the system and check for air leaks.

17 Steering wheel – removal and refitting

> ⚠ **Warning: Before removing the steering wheel, observe the safety precautions for air bags given in Chapter 12 and in Section 1 of this Chapter.**

Removal

1 Disconnect the battery negative (earth) lead (see Chapter 5A).
Caution: Wait at least one minute before proceeding. This is necessary to allow the airbag condenser to fully discharge.

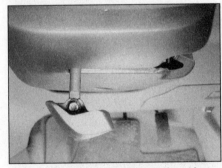

18.3 Removing the knob from the column adjuster lever

2 Set the front wheels in the straight-ahead position, then lock the column in position after removing the ignition key.
3 Remove the airbag/horn-push from the steering wheel as described in Chapter 12, Section 24. Position the airbag in a safe place where it cannot be tampered with, making sure that the padded side is facing upwards.
4 Where fitted, disconnect the wiring from the radio control switches **(see illustration)**.
5 Unscrew the Torx retaining bolt securing the steering wheel to the column **(see illustration)**.
6 Make alignment marks between the steering wheel and steering column shaft.
7 Grip the steering wheel with both hands and carefully rock it from side-to-side to release it from the splines on the steering column. As it is being removed, guide the wiring for the contact unit (and radio control if fitted) through the hole **(see illustration)**.
8 With the steering wheel removed, do not disturb the contact unit. If necessary hold it in its central position with tape.

Refitting

9 Check that the contact unit is positioned with the arrows aligned with each other. If it has been disturbed, return it to its central position by depressing the detent and rotating it fully anti-clockwise then clockwise to determine the central position – instructions are given on the unit.
10 Position the steering wheel over the column splines and guide the wiring for the contact unit (and radio control if fitted) through the hole.

11 Ensure that the indicator switch stalk is in its central (off) position, then locate the steering wheel on the column splines, aligning the marks made prior to removal. When locating the steering wheel on the splines, make sure that the contact unit is correctly engaged with both the steering column and indicator switch.
12 Fit the retaining bolt and tighten to the specified torque while holding the steering wheel stationary.
13 Reconnect the wiring for the radio control switches where fitted.
14 Refit the airbag/horn-push and reconnect the wiring. Insert the two screws and tighten to the specified torque.
15 Release the steering lock, then reconnect the battery negative lead.

18 Steering column – removal and refitting

Removal

1 Remove the steering wheel as described in Section 17.
2 Adjust the steering column to its maximum reach and lowest position, and lock it in this position.
3 Undo the screw and remove the knob from the column adjuster lever **(see illustration)**.
4 Prise out the covers, then undo the two screws and remove the upper steering column shroud **(see illustrations)**.

18.4a Prise out the covers . . .

18.4b . . . then undo the screws . . .

18.4c . . . and remove the upper steering column shroud

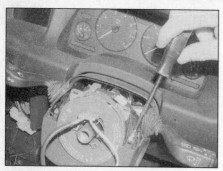

18.5a Undo the upper screws . . .

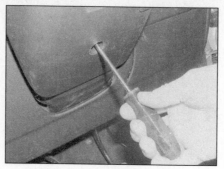

18.5b . . . and one lower screw . . .

18.5c . . . and remove the lower steering column shroud

5 Undo the two upper and one lower screw and remove the lower steering column shroud **(see illustrations)**.
6 Using a screwdriver, carefully lever the wiring plug from the top of the airbag contact unit.
7 Release the clips and withdraw the contact unit from the steering column. **Note:** *All later units have a locking device which holds it in its central position.* **Do not** *release this device with the contact unit removed.*
8 Release and remove the indicator and wiper switches from the housing on the column with reference to Chapter 12, Section 4.
9 Remove the ignition key and prise out the circular trim for the immobiliser/transponder.
10 With the ignition key inserted and positioned in the 'Accessories' position, insert a screwdriver in the hole in the ignition switch and depress the locking tab, then carefully pull the switch from the steering lock housing **(see illustration)**.
11 Where fitted, remove the immobiliser/transponder unit from the steering column as follows. On models with an immobiliser/transponder **without** catch lugs, disconnect the wiring, then unclip the unit from the ignition lock housing. Remove the ignition lock cylinder as described in Chapter 12, Section 4. On models with an immobiliser/transponder **with** catch lugs, remove the ignition lock cylinder as described in Chapter 12, then unclip the unit from the ignition lock housing. Where necessary, remove the protective cap, then disconnect the wiring.

12 Carefully remove the column cover and tension springs **(see illustration)**.
13 Unclip the wiring loom channel from the steering column, then, on the driver's side, remove the footwell panels and air vent duct.
14 Mark the steering column intermediate shaft upper joint in relation to the steering column to aid refitting, then unscrew the remove the clamp bolt. Push the joint from the splines on the bottom of the steering column, noting that the intermediate shaft is telescopic.
15 On models with ESP (Electronic Stabilisation System), disconnect the wiring from the steering angle sensor, then use a screwdriver to depress the tab and release the sensor from the adapter. Move the sensor down slightly.
16 Support the steering column, then unscrew the steering column lower clamp and upper mounting bolts **(see illustration)**. Where applicable, release the lower mounting catch, taking care not to bend the catch. On models with ESP, pull the column upwards slightly and release the sensor from the bottom of the column. Note the location of any shims located behind the lower mounting clamp upper mounting bracket.
17 Withdraw the column from the bulkhead bracket and remove from inside the vehicle.

Refitting

18 Before refitting the steering column, loosely fit the lower mounting clamp and screw on the bolt several turns; do not fit the upper mounting bolts at this stage. Carefully locate the steering column through the lower

mounting clamp, making sure that the wiring is not damaged. On models with ESP, locate the steering angle sensor on the bottom of the column, making sure that the retaining tab is correctly engaged.
19 On models manufactured from 2000, refit the upper mounting bolts and tighten them to the specified torque.
20 On models manufactured up to and including 1999 where shims were fitted, insert them between the lower mounting bracket and crossmember, then insert the lower clamp and upper mounting bolts and tighten to the specified torque.
21 On models manufactured up to and including 1999 where no shims were fitted, obtain 4 shims (each 1.0 mm thick) from a Vauxhall dealer, and fit them as a 4.0 mm thick pack between the lower mounting bracket and crossmember. Tighten the clamp bolt to the specified torque, then grip the lower end of the inner column and attempt to push it upwards (ie, towards the steering wheel position). The grey guide sleeve on the lower mounting should not move. If it does, remove one of the shims and make the check again. If necessary, repeat the procedure until the guide sleeve is held firmly, then insert the upper mounting bolts and tighten to the specified torque. Where applicable, make sure that the detent is positioned in front of the lower bearing sleeve.
22 On models with ESP, reconnect the wiring to the steering angle sensor.
23 Engage the intermediate shaft with the splines on the bottom of the column, making sure that the previously-made marks are

18.10 Removing the ignition switch

18.12 Removing the column cover and tension springs

18.16 Steering column upper mounting bolt (left-hand side)

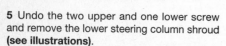

correctly aligned with each other. Note that if the shaft and column are not aligned correctly, it will be impossible to insert the clamp bolt. Insert the clamp bolt and tighten securely.

24 Refit the air vent duct and footwell panels, and clip the wiring loom channel to the steering column.

25 Refit the immobiliser/transponder unit to the steering column using a reversal of the removal procedure. On models with an immobiliser/transponder **without** catch lugs, refit the ignition lock cylinder as described in Chapter 12, Section 4, then clip the unit onto the ignition lock housing. On models with an immobiliser/transponder **with** catch lugs, clip the unit onto the ignition lock housing, then refit the ignition lock cylinder as described in Chapter 12. Where necessary, reconnect the wiring then refit the protective cap.

26 Refit the column cover and tension springs.

27 With the ignition key inserted in the 'Accessories' position, refit the ignition switch to the steering lock housing, making sure that the clip engages correctly.

28 Remove the ignition key then refit the circular trim for the immobiliser/transponder.

29 Refit the indicator and wiper switches to the housing on the column with reference to Chapter 12, Section 4.

30 Refit the airbag contact unit to the steering column making sure that the guide pins enter their holes correctly and the retaining clips are engaged correctly. **Note:** *It is important that the retaining clips are fully engaged. If they are damaged in any way, the complete contact unit must be renewed.*

31 Carefully refit the wiring plug to the top of the contact unit.

32 Refit the lower steering column shroud followed by the upper shroud, and secure with the retaining screws.

33 Refit the knob to the column adjuster lever and tighten the screw.

34 Refit the steering wheel with reference to Section 17.

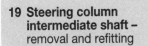

19 Steering column intermediate shaft – removal and refitting

Removal

1 Set the front wheels in the straight-ahead position. Remove the ignition key and allow the steering lock to engage.

2 Remove the footwell panels and air vent duct from the driver's footwell.

3 Mark the steering column intermediate shaft upper and lower joints in relation to the steering column and steering gear pinion as an aid to refitting, then unscrew both clamp bolts **(see illustrations)**.

4 Compress the telescopic intermediate shaft and slide the joints from the column and

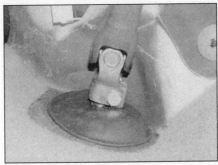

19.3a Intermediate shaft joint connection to the steering gear pinion

pinion **(see illustration)**. Withdraw the intermediate shaft from inside the vehicle.

Inspection

5 Inspect the intermediate shaft universal joints for excessive wear or damage. If either joint is worn or damaged, the complete shaft assembly must be renewed.

Refitting

6 Check that the front wheels and steering wheel are still in the straight-ahead position, and that the steering wheel is still locked.

7 Slide the intermediate shaft lower joint onto the steering gear pinion, aligning the previously-made marks. Note that it will not be possible to insert the clamp bolt if the splines are not correctly aligned. Apply a little locking fluid to the threads of the clamp bolt, then insert it and tighten to the specified torque.

8 Slide the upper end of the intermediate shaft onto the column splines, aligning the previously-made marks. Insert the clamp bolt and tighten securely.

9 Refit the air vent duct and footwell panels to the driver's footwell.

---

20 Steering gear rubber gaiters – renewal

1 Remove the relevant track rod end as described in Section 24.

2 Remove the inner and outer securing clips

20.2 Outer clip for the steering gear rubber gaiter

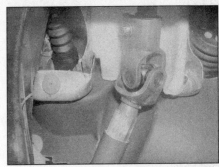

19.3b Intermediate shaft joint connection to the steering column

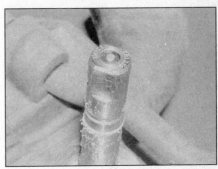

19.4 View of the pinion (steering gear removed from the vehicle)

(see illustration), then slide the gaiter off the end of the track rod.

3 Thoroughly clean the track rod, then slide the new gaiter into position. Note that a groove is provided in the track rod for the outer end of the gaiter to locate in.

4 Fit the gaiter securing clips, using new clips if necessary, making sure that the gaiter is not twisted.

5 Refit the track rod end as described in Section 24.

6 Have the front wheel toe-setting checked and adjusted at the earliest opportunity.

---

21 Steering gear – removal and refitting

Removal

1 Set the front wheels in the straight-ahead position. Remove the ignition key and allow the steering lock to engage.

2 Remove the front subframe as described in Section 4.

3 On LHD models, unbolt the rear engine mounting bracket from the subframe.

4 Where fitted, unbolt the support bracket for the pressure and return lines from the subframe.

5 Position a suitable container beneath the steering gear fluid unions to catch spilt hydraulic fluid.

6 Unscrew the union nuts and disconnect the fluid pressure and return lines from the steering gear **(see illustration)**.

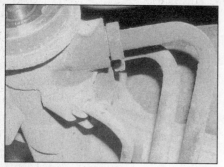

21.6 Hydraulic fluid lines on the steering gear

7 Note the routing of the wiring loom then disconnect it from the electric hydraulic pump and remove it from the subframe.

8 Unscrew the mounting nuts and withdraw the electric hydraulic pump together with the fluid reservoir and pressure/return lines from the subframe and steering gear. Note whether a round (TRW) or angular (Delphi) hydraulic fluid reservoir is fitted.

9 Unscrew the mounting bolts and remove the steering gear from the subframe (see illustration). If necessary, remove the anti-roll bar first with reference to Section 6. The manufacturers recommend that the mounting bolts are renewed whenever removed.

10 If necessary, remove the track rod ends and track rods with reference to Sections 24 and 25. **Note:** *New steering gears are available from Vauxhall either with or without the track rods fitted. Also remove the rubber grommets from the pinion.*

Refitting

11 Refit the track rods and track rod ends with reference to Sections 24 and 25. Also refit the rubber grommets to the pinion.

12 Clean any dirt from the steering gear and subframe, then locate the steering gear in position. Insert the mounting bolts and tighten to the specified torque.

13 Where removed, refit the anti-roll bar with reference to Section 6.

14 Refit the electric hydraulic pump, together with the fluid reservoir and pressure/return lines to the subframe and steering gear, and tighten the mounting nuts to the specified torque.

22.5a Power steering electric hydraulic pump

21.9 A steering gear mounting bolt

15 Reconnect the wiring loom to the electric hydraulic pump and attach it to the subframe.

16 Fit new rubber sealing rings to the pressure and return lines, then refit the lines to the steering gear and tighten the union nuts to the specified torque.

17 Where fitted, refit the support bracket for the pressure and return lines to the subframe and tighten the mounting bolts to the specified torque.

18 On LHD models, refit the rear engine mounting bracket to the subframe and tighten to the specified torque.

19 Refit the front subframe as described in Section 4.

20 Bleed the power steering hydraulic system as described in Section 23.

21 Have the front wheel toe-setting checked and adjusted at the earliest opportunity.

22 Electro-hydraulic power steering pump – removal and refitting

Removal

1 Remove the front subframe as described in Section 4.

2 Position a suitable container beneath the power steering pump fluid unions to catch spilt hydraulic fluid.

3 Disconnect the pressure and return lines from the power steering pump. Use a spanner to unscrew the pressure line union nut. If necessary, cut free the return line clip and replace it with a screw-type clip.

4 Note the routing of the wiring loom then disconnect it at the connector and body earthing point. **Note:** *The wiring loom is supplied together with the pump and cannot be separated.*

5 Unscrew the mounting nuts and withdraw the electric hydraulic pump, together with the bracket, wiring and fluid reservoir from the subframe and steering gear (see illustrations). Note that either a round (TRW) or angular (Delphi) hydraulic fluid reservoir is fitted. Also note that the wiring connector is 2-pin before model year 2000, but 3-pin thereafter, and an adapter is available from Vauxhall in the event of a new pump being fitted to a pre-2000 model.

6 Unscrew the mounting nuts and remove the electric hydraulic pump and mounting bushes from the bracket. Check the rubber mounting bushes for wear and damage and renew them if necessary.

Refitting

7 Refit the pump and bushes to the bracket and tighten the mounting nuts.

8 Refit the electric hydraulic pump and bracket on the subframe and steering gear and tighten the mounting nuts to the specified torque.

9 Reconnect the wiring loom and attach the cable to the earthing point. Make sure that the loom is routed as noted during removal.

10 Fit a new rubber sealing ring to the pressure line, then reconnect the pressure and return lines to the power steering pump. Tighten the pressure line union nut securely, and fit a new clip to the return line.

11 Unscrew the cap from the fluid reservoir and remove the filter. Clean the filter and refit it, then fill the reservoir with the specified fluid and tighten the cap. Fluid level marks are provided on the reservoir, but note that on the TRW system, the fluid level marks are on the dipstick integral with the cap, whereas on the Delphi system, the level dipstick is attached to the bottom of the filter. **Note:** *Do not re-use drained hydraulic fluid.*

12 Refit the front subframe as described in Section 4.

13 Bleed the power steering hydraulic system as described in Section 23.

23 Power steering hydraulic system – bleeding

Note: *The system must be bled at room temperature – do not bleed the system immediately after using the vehicle on the road.*

1 Check and top-up the power steering fluid level in the reservoir to the MAX mark as described in *Weekly checks*. If the system regularly requires more fluid, check the hoses for leaks.

TRW system

2 Start the engine, then slowly turn the steering wheel fully from left to right three times with the engine still running.

22.5b Mounting nuts for the hydraulic pump

3 Switch off the engine and check the level of the fluid. If necessary, top up the level to the MAX mark **(see illustrations)**.

4 Start the engine and turn the steering wheel from left to right several times while checking for excessive noise. Repeat the bleeding procedure if the power steering operation is noisy, as this indicates there is still some air in the system.

Delphi system

5 Start the engine, then slowly turn the steering wheel fully from left to right twice with the engine still running.

6 Switch off the engine and check the level of the fluid. If necessary, top up the level to the MAX mark.

7 Start the engine and turn the steering wheel from left to right several times while checking for excessive noise. Repeat the bleeding procedure if the power steering operation is noisy, as this indicates there is still some air in the system.

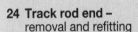

24 Track rod end –
removed and refitting

Note: *A balljoint separator tool will be required for this operation.*

Removal

1 Apply the handbrake, then jack up the front of the vehicle, and support securely on axle stands (see *Jacking and vehicle support*). Remove the relevant roadwheel.

2 Loosen the track rod end securing locknut on the track rod a quarter turn, while holding the track rod stationary with a second spanner on the flats provided **(see illustration)**. If necessary, use a wire brush to remove rust from the nut and threads and lubricate the threads with penetrating oil before unscrewing the nut. As an additional check, measure the visible amount of threads on the track rod using vernier calipers. This will ensure the track rod end is refitted in the same position.

3 Where necessary, extract the split pin, then unscrew and remove the balljoint nut securing the track rod end to the steering arm on the hub carrier **(see illustration)**.

4 Disconnect the track rod end balljoint from the steering arm on the hub carrier using a balljoint separator tool, taking care not to damage the balljoint boot **(see illustrations)**.

5 Unscrew the track rod end from the track rod, counting the number of turns necessary to remove it and taking care not to disturb the locknut. **Note:** *The track rod ends are handed side-for-side. The right-hand track rod end is marked with an R and has a right-hand thread, whereas the left-hand one is marked with an L and has a left-hand thread.*

Refitting

6 Screw the track rod end onto the track rod

23.3a Power steering fluid reservoir (Zafira model)

the number of turns noted during removal. Check that the visible amount of threads on the track rod is as previously noted.

7 Insert the track rod end balljoint in the steering arm on the hub carrier, then fit the nut and tighten to the specified torque. If the balljoint stud turns as the nut is being tightened, press down on the track rod end to force the stud into the arm. Where necessary, fit a new split pin.

8 Tighten the track rod end securing locknut on the track rod while holding the track rod stationary with a second spanner on the flats provided. If possible, tighten the nut to the specified torque using a special crow's-foot adapter for the torque wrench.

9 Refit the roadwheel, then lower the vehicle to the ground, and tighten the wheelbolts.

10 Have the front wheel alignment checked and adjusted at the earliest opportunity.

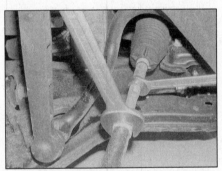

24.2 Hold the track rod stationary while loosening the track rod end securing locknut

24.4a Using a balljoint separator tool . . .

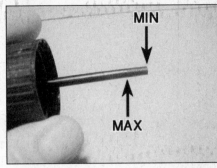

23.3b The hydraulic fluid level is marked on the integral dipstick on the TRW system

25 Track rod –
removal and refitting

Removal

1 Remove the track rod end from the relevant track rod as described in Section 24. Note, however, that on RHD models it is necessary to remove both track rod ends and bellows when removing the left-hand track rod. Conversely, on LHD models it is necessary to remove both track rod ends and bellows when removing the right-hand track rod.

2 Where necessary, remove the wheelarch liner or trim from under the wheelarch by removing the fasteners (see Chapter 11).

3 Release the clips and slide the rubber bellows from the steering gear and track rod.

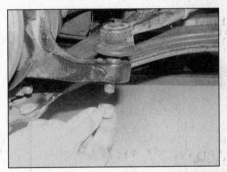

24.3 Unscrewing the balljoint nut securing the track rod end to the steering arm on the hub carrier

24.4b . . . to disconnect the track rod end balljoint from the steering arm

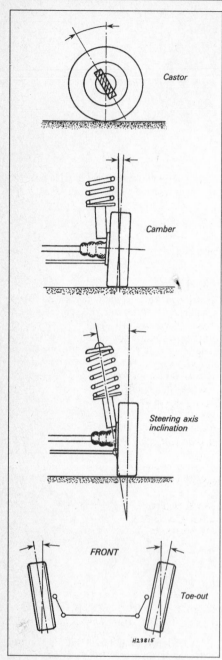

26.2 Wheel alignment and steering angles

5 Hold the rack stationary with a spanner on the flats provided, then unscrew and remove the track rod inner joint housing. Use either a large adjustable spanner or grips.

Refitting

6 Clean the threads and apply a little locking fluid to them, then screw the track rod inner joint housing into the rack and tighten to the specified torque. Because of its size and design, using a torque wrench may be difficult, in which case the joint housing should be tightened until the previously-made marks are aligned with each other.

7 Refit the bellows making sure that the inner end is pushed fully onto the steering gear and the outer end is seated in the groove on the track rod. Use new clips if necessary.

8 Where necessary, refit the wheelarch liner or trim.

9 Refit the track rod end(s) as described in Section 24.

10 Have the front wheel alignment checked and adjusted at the earliest opportunity.

26 Wheel alignment and steering angles – general information

Front wheel alignment

1 Accurate front wheel alignment is essential to good steering and for even tyre wear. Before considering the steering angles, check that the tyres are correctly inflated, that the front wheels are not buckled, the hub bearings are not worn and that the steering linkage is in good order without slackness or wear at the joints. The fuel tank must be half full and each front seat must be loaded with 70 kg.

2 Wheel alignment consists of four factors **(see illustration):**

Camber, is the angle at which the roadwheels are set from the vertical when viewed from the front or rear of the vehicle. Positive camber is the angle (in degrees) that the wheels are tilted outwards at the top from the vertical. Negative camber is the angle that the wheels are tilted inwards at the top from the vertical. The camber angle is set during production and cannot be adjusted.

Castor, is the angle between the steering axis and a vertical line when viewed from each side of the vehicle. Positive castor is indicated when the steering axis is inclined towards the rear of the vehicle at its upper end. This angle is not adjustable.

Steering axis inclination (kingpin inclination), is the angle, when viewed from the front or rear of the vehicle, between the vertical and an imaginary line drawn between the upper and lower front suspension strut mountings. This angle is not adjustable.

Toe, is the amount by which the distance between the front inside edges of the roadwheel rim differs from that between the rear inside edges. If the distance between the front edges is less than that at the rear, the wheels are said to toe-in. If the distance between the front inside edges is greater than that at the rear, the wheels are toe-out.

3 Owing to the need for precision gauges to measure the small angles of the steering and suspension settings, it is preferable that checking of camber and castor is left to a service station having the necessary equipment. Castor is set during production of the vehicle, and any deviation from the specified angle will be due to accident damage or gross wear in the suspension mountings.

4 To check the front wheel alignment, first make sure that the lengths of both track rods are equal when the steering is in the straight-ahead position. The track rod lengths can be adjusted if necessary by releasing the locknuts from the track rod ends and rotating the track rods. If necessary, self-locking grips can be used to rotate the track rods.

5 Obtain a tracking gauge. These are available in various forms from accessory stores, or one can be fabricated from a length of steel tubing suitably cranked to clear the sump and transmission, and having a setscrew and locknut at one end.

6 The vehicle must be on level ground. With the gauge, measure the distances between the two wheel inner rims (at hub height) at the rear of the wheel. Push the vehicle forward to rotate the wheel through 180° (half a turn) and measure the distance between the wheel inner rims, again at hub height, at the front of the wheel. This last measurement should differ from the first by the appropriate toe-in which is given in the Specifications.

7 If the toe-in is found to be incorrect, release the track rod end locknuts and turn both track rods equally. Only turn them a quarter-of-a-turn at a time before re-checking the alignment. If necessary use self-locking grips to turn the track rods. It is important not to allow the track rods to become unequal in length during adjustment, otherwise the alignment of the steering wheel will become incorrect and tyre scrubbing will occur on turns.

8 On completion tighten the locknuts without disturbing the setting. Check that the balljoints are at the centre of their arcs of travel.

Rear wheel alignment

9 The rear wheel toe and camber setting is given for reference only since no adjustment is possible.

Remove the bellows from both sides where necessary (see paragraph 1). Where metal clips are fitted, either prise them free with a screwdriver, or carefully cut them off with a hacksaw.

4 Turn the steering on full lock so that the rack protrudes from the steering gear on the relevant side. Mark the inner joint housing and rack in relation to each other to indicate how tight it is (see paragraph 6).

Chapter 11
Bodywork and fittings

Contents

Bonnet – removal, refitting and adjustment 9
Bonnet hinge – removal and refitting 10
Bonnet lock components – removal and refitting 11
Bonnet release cable – removal and refitting 12
Boot lid – removal and refitting 21
Boot lid components – removal and refitting 23
Boot lid hinge – removal and refitting 22
Central locking components – removal and refitting 27
Centre console – removal and refitting 45
Door exterior handle – removal and refitting 15
Door interior handle – removal and refitting 14
Door lock cylinder – removal and refitting 17
Door locks – removal and refitting 16
Door window glass – removal and refitting 19
Doors – removal, refitting and adjustment 13
Electric mirror components – removal and refitting 31
Electric window components – removal and refitting 28
Exterior body components – removal and refitting 38
Exterior door mirror – removal and refitting 29
Exterior door mirror glass – removal and refitting 30
Facia panel – removal and refitting 47
Front and rear bumpers – removal and refitting 6
Front seat belt tensioner – removal and refitting 41
Front seats – removal and refitting 39

Fuel filler flap – removal and refitting 37
General information 1
Glovebox – removal and refitting 46
Inner trim panels – removal and refitting 44
Interior mirror – removal and refitting 32
Lock striker – removal and refitting 18
Maintenance of bodywork and underframe – general 2
Maintenance of upholstery and carpets – general 3
Major body damage repair – general 5
Minor body damage repair – general 4
Radiator grille – removal and refitting 7
Rear seats – removal and refitting 40
Seat belt height adjuster – removal and refitting 43
Seat belts – removal and refitting 42
Sunroof components – removal and refitting 35
Sunroof glass panel – removal and refitting 34
Tailgate – removal and refitting 24
Tailgate components – removal and refitting 26
Tailgate hinge – removal and refitting 25
Wheelarch liners – general 36
Window regulator – removal and refitting 20
Windscreen cowl panel – removal and refitting 8
Windscreen, rear window and quarter window glass – general 33

Degrees of difficulty

Easy, suitable for novice with little experience	Fairly easy, suitable for beginner with some experience	Fairly difficult, suitable for competent DIY mechanic	Difficult, suitable for experienced DIY mechanic	Very difficult, suitable for expert DIY or professional

Specifications

Torque wrench settings

	Nm	lbf ft
Bonnet striker	22	16
Front seat backrest to cushion	35	26
Front seat belt	20	15
Front seat	20	15
Rear seat belt lock to floor	35	26
Seat belt height adjuster securing bolts	20	15
Seat belt reel to B-pillar	35	26
Seat belt reel to C-pillar	35	26
Seat belt reel to rear seat backrest	35	26
Seat belt tensioner to front seat	35	26
Seat belt to front seat	20	15
Seat belt to height adjuster	35	26

1 General information

The bodyshell and floorpan are manufactured from pressed-steel, and together make up the vehicle's structure. The Astra is available in 4-door Saloon, 3- and 5-door Hatchback and 5-door Estate. The Zafira is the 7-seater MPV version of the Astra.

Various areas of the structure are strengthened to provide for suspension, steering and engine mounting points, and load distribution. One notable feature is the use of tubular reinforcing bars in the doors, to provide the occupants with additional protection in the event of a side impact.

Extensive corrosion protection is applied to all new vehicles. Various anti-corrosion preparations are used, including galvanising, zinc phosphatisation, and PVC underseal. Protective wax is injected into the box sections and other hollow cavities.

Extensive use is made of plastic for peripheral components, such as the radiator grille, bumpers and wheel trims, and for much of the interior trim.

Interior fittings are to a high standard on all models, and a wide range of optional equipment is available throughout the range.

2 Maintenance of bodywork and underframe – general

Cleaning the vehicle's exterior

The general condition of a vehicle's bodywork is the one thing that significantly affects its value. Maintenance is easy but needs to be regular. Neglect, particularly after minor damage, can lead quickly to further deterioration and costly repair bills. It is important also to keep watch on those parts of the vehicle not immediately visible, for instance the underbody, inside all the wheelarches and the lower part of the engine compartment.

The basic maintenance routine for the bodywork is washing preferably with a lot of water, from a hose. This will remove all the loose solids that may have stuck to the vehicle. It is important to flush these off in such a way as to prevent grit from scratching the finish. The wheelarches and underbody need washing in the same way to remove any accumulated mud, which will retain moisture and tend to encourage rust, particularly in Winter, when it is essential that any salt (from that put down on the roads) is washed off. Paradoxically enough, the best time to clean the underbody and wheelarches is in wet weather, when the mud is thoroughly wet and soft. In very wet weather, the underbody is usually cleaned automatically of large accumulations; this is therefore a good time for inspection.

If the vehicle is very dirty, especially underneath or in the engine compartment, it is tempting to use one of the pressure-washers or steam-cleaners available on garage forecourts, while these are quick and effective, especially for the removal of the accumulation of oily grime which sometimes is allowed to become thick in certain areas, their usage does have some disadvantages. If caked-on dirt is simply blasted off the paintwork, its finish soon becomes scratched and dull, and the pressure can allow water to penetrate door and window seals and the lock mechanisms; if the full force of such a jet is directed at the vehicle's underbody, the wax-based protective coating can easily be damaged, and water (with whatever cleaning solvent is used) could be forced into crevices or components that it would not normally reach. Similarly, if such equipment is used to clean the engine compartment, water can be forced into the components of the fuel and electrical systems, and the protective coating can be removed that is applied to many small components during manufacture; this may therefore actually promote corrosion (especially inside electrical connectors) and initiate engine problems or other electrical faults. Also, if the jet is pointed directly at any of the oil seals, water can be forced past the seal lips and into the engine or transmission. Great care is required, therefore, if such equipment is used and, in general, regular cleaning by such methods should be avoided.

A much better solution in the long term is just to flush away as much loose dirt as possible using a hose alone, even if this leaves the engine compartment looking 'dirty'. If an oil leak has developed, or if any other accumulation of oil or grease is to be removed, there are one or two excellent grease solvents available that can be brush-applied. The dirt can then be simply hosed off. Take care to replace the wax-based protective coat, if this was affected by the solvent.

Normal washing of the vehicle's bodywork is best carried out using cold or warm water, with a proprietary vehicle shampoo, tar spots can be removed by using white spirit, followed by soapy water to remove all traces of spirit. Try to keep water out of the bonnet air inlets, and check afterwards that the heater air inlet box drain tube is clear, so that any water has drained out of the box.

After washing the paintwork, wipe off with a chamois leather to give an unspotted clear finish. A coat of clear protective wax polish will give added protection against chemical pollutants in the air. If the paintwork sheen has dulled or oxidised, use a cleaner/polisher combination to restore the brilliance of the shine. This requires a little effort, but such dulling is usually caused because regular washing has been neglected. Care needs to be taken with metallic paintwork, as special non-abrasive cleaner/polisher is required to avoid damage to the finish.

Any polished metals should be treated in the same way as paintwork.

Windscreens and windows can be kept clear of the smeary film that often appears with proprietary glass cleaner. Never use any form of wax, or other body or chromium polish on glass.

Exterior paintwork and body panels check

Once the vehicle has been washed, and all tar spots and other surface blemishes have been cleaned off, check carefully all paintwork, looking closely for chips or scratches; check with particular care vulnerable areas such as the front (bonnet and spoiler) and around the wheelarches. Any damage to the paintwork must be rectified as soon as possible, to comply with the terms of the manufacturer's cosmetic and anti-corrosion warranties; check with a Vauxhall dealer for details.

If a chip or (light) scratch is found that is recent and still free from rust, it can be touched-up using the appropriate touch-up pencil; these can be obtained from Vauxhall dealers. Any more serious damage, or rusted stone chips, can be repaired as described in Section 4, but if damage or corrosion is so severe that a panel must be renewed, seek professional advice as soon as possible.

Always check that the door and ventilator opening drain holes and pipes are completely clear, so that water can drain out.

Underbody sealer check

The wax-based underbody protective coating should be inspected annually, preferably just before Winter. Wash the underbody down as thoroughly but gently as possible (see the above concerning steam cleaners, etc) and any damage to the coating repaired. If any of the body panels are disturbed for repair or renewed, do not forget to replace the coating and to inject wax into door panels, sills, box sections, etc, to maintain the level of protection provided by the vehicle manufacturer.

3 Maintenance of upholstery and carpets – general

Mats and carpets should be brushed or vacuum-cleaned regularly, to keep them free of grit. If they are badly stained, remove them from the vehicle for scrubbing or sponging, and make quite sure they are dry before refitting. Seats and interior trim panels can be kept clean by wiping with a damp cloth. If they do become stained (which can be more apparent on light-coloured upholstery), use a little liquid detergent and a soft nail brush to scour the grime out of the grain of the material. Do not forget to keep the headlining clean in the same way as the upholstery. When using liquid cleaners inside the vehicle, do not over-wet the surfaces being cleaned. Excessive damp could get into the seams and padded interior, causing stains, offensive odours or even rot. If the inside of the vehicle gets wet accidentally, it is worthwhile taking some trouble to dry it out properly, particularly where carpets are involved. *Do not leave oil or electric heaters inside the vehicle for this purpose.*

4 Minor body damage repair – general

Repairs of minor scratches in bodywork

If the scratch is very superficial, and does not penetrate to the metal of the bodywork, repair is very simple. Lightly rub the area of the scratch with a paintwork renovator, or a very fine cutting paste, to remove loose paint from the scratch, and to clear the surrounding bodywork of wax polish. Rinse the area with clean water.

Apply touch-up paint to the scratch using a fine paint brush; continue to apply fine layers of paint until the surface of the paint in the scratch is level with the surrounding paintwork. Allow the new paint at least two weeks to harden, then blend it into the surrounding paintwork by rubbing the scratch area with a paintwork renovator or a very fine cutting paste. Finally, apply wax polish.

Where the scratch has penetrated right through to the metal of the bodywork, causing the metal to rust, a different repair technique is required. Remove any loose rust from the bottom of the scratch with a penknife, then apply rust-inhibiting paint to prevent the formation of rust in the future. Using a rubber or nylon applicator, fill the scratch with bodystopper paste. If required, this paste can be mixed with cellulose thinners to provide a very thin paste that is ideal for filling narrow scratches. Before the stopper-paste in the scratch hardens, wrap a piece of smooth cotton rag around the top of a finger. Dip the finger in cellulose thinners, and quickly sweep it across the surface of the stopper-paste in the scratch; this will ensure that the surface of the stopper-paste is slightly hollowed. The scratch can now be painted over as described earlier in this Section.

Repairs of dents in bodywork

When deep denting of the vehicle's bodywork has taken place, the first task is to pull the dent out, until the affected bodywork almost attains its original shape. There is little point in trying to restore the original shape completely, as the metal in the damaged area will have stretched on impact, and cannot be reshaped fully to its original contour. It is better to bring the level of the dent up to a point that is about 3 mm below the level of the surrounding bodywork. In cases where the dent is very shallow anyway, it is not worth trying to pull it out at all. If the underside of the dent is accessible, it can be hammered out gently from behind, using a mallet with a wooden or plastic head. Whilst doing this, hold a block of wood firmly against the outside of the panel, to absorb the impact from the hammer blows and thus prevent a large area of the bodywork from being 'belled-out'.

Should the dent be in a section of the bodywork that has a double skin, or some other factor making it inaccessible from behind, a different technique is called for. Drill several small holes through the metal inside the area – particularly in the deeper section. Then screw long self-tapping screws into the holes, just sufficiently for them to gain a good purchase in the metal. Now the dent can be pulled out by pulling on the protruding heads of the screws with a pair of pliers.

The next stage of the repair is the removal of the paint from the damaged area, and from an inch or so of the surrounding 'sound' bodywork. This is accomplished most easily by using a wire brush or abrasive pad on a power drill, although it can be done just as effectively by hand, using sheets of abrasive paper. To complete the preparation for filling, score the surface of the bare metal with a screwdriver or the tang of a file, or alternatively, drill small holes in the affected area. This will provide a good 'key' for the filler paste.

To complete the repair, see the Section on filling and respraying.

Repairs of rust holes or gashes in bodywork

Remove all paint from the affected area, and from an inch or so of the surrounding 'sound' bodywork, using an abrasive pad or a wire brush on a power drill. If these are not available, a few sheets of abrasive paper will do the job most effectively. With the paint removed, you will be able to judge the severity of the corrosion, and therefore decide whether to renew the whole panel (if this is possible) or to repair the affected area. New body panels are not as expensive as most people think, and it is often quicker and more satisfactory to fit a new panel than to attempt to repair large areas of corrosion.

Remove all fittings from the affected area, except those which will act as a guide to the original shape of the damaged bodywork (eg, headlight shells, etc.). Then, using tin snips or a hacksaw blade, remove all loose metal and any other metal badly affected by corrosion. Hammer the edges of the hole inwards, to create a slight depression for the filler paste.

Wire-brush the affected area to remove the powdery rust from the surface of the remaining metal. Paint the affected area with rust-inhibiting paint, if the back of the rusted area is accessible, treat this also.

Before filling can take place, it will be necessary to block the hole in some way. This can be achieved with aluminium or plastic mesh, or aluminium tape.

Aluminium or plastic mesh, or glass-fibre matting, is probably the best material to use for a large hole. Cut a piece to the approximate size and shape of the hole to be filled, then position it in the hole so that its edges are below the level of the surrounding bodywork. It can be retained in position by several blobs of filler paste around its periphery.

Aluminium tape should be used for small or very narrow holes. Pull a piece off the roll, trim it to the approximate size and shape required, then pull off the backing paper (if used) and stick the tape over the hole. It can be overlapped if the thickness of one piece is insufficient. Burnish down the edges of the tape with the handle of a screwdriver or similar, to ensure that the tape is securely attached to the metal underneath.

Bodywork repairs – filling and respraying

Before using this Section, see the Sections on dent, deep scratch, rust holes and gash repairs.

Many types of bodyfiller are available, but generally speaking, those proprietary kits that contain a tin of filler paste and a tube of resin hardener are best for this type of repair. A wide, flexible plastic or nylon applicator will be found invaluable for imparting a smooth and well-contoured finish to the surface of the filler.

Mix up a little filler on a clean piece of card or board – measure the hardener carefully (follow the maker's instructions on the pack), otherwise the filler will set too rapidly or too slowly. Using the applicator, apply the filler paste to the prepared area; draw the applicator across the surface of the filler to achieve the correct contour and to level the surface. When a contour that follows the original is achieved, stop working the paste. If you carry on too long, the paste will become sticky and begin to 'pick-up' on the applicator. Continue to add thin layers of filler paste at 20-minute intervals, until the level of the filler is just proud of the surrounding bodywork.

Once the filler has hardened, the excess can be removed using a metal plane or file. From then on, progressively-finer grades of abrasive paper should be used, starting with a 40-grade production paper, and finishing with a 400-grade wet-and-dry paper. Always wrap the abrasive paper around a flat rubber, cork, or wooden block – otherwise the surface of the filler will not be completely flat. During the smoothing of the filler surface, the wet-and-dry paper should be periodically rinsed in water. This will ensure that a very smooth finish is imparted to the filler at the final stage.

At this stage, the 'dent' should be surrounded by a ring of bare metal, which in turn should be encircled by the finely 'feathered' edge of the good paintwork. Rinse the repair area with clean water, until all of the dust produced by the rubbing-down operation has gone.

Spray the whole area with a light coat of primer – this will show up any imperfections in the surface of the filler. Repair these imperfections with fresh filler paste or bodystopper, and again smooth the surface with abrasive paper. If bodystopper is used, it can be mixed with cellulose thinners, to form a thin paste that is ideal for filling small holes.

Repeat this spray-and-repair procedure until you are satisfied that the surface of the filler, and the feathered edge of the paintwork, are perfect. Clean the repair area with clean water, and allow to dry fully.

The repair area is now ready for final spraying. Paint spraying must be carried out in a warm, dry, windless and dust-free atmosphere. This condition can be created artificially if you have access to a large indoor working area, but if you are forced to work in the open, you will have to pick your day very carefully. If you are working indoors, dousing the floor in the work area with water will help to settle the dust that would otherwise be in the atmosphere. If the repair area is confined to one body panel, mask off the surrounding panels; this will help to minimise the effects of a slight mis-match in paint colours. Bodywork fittings (eg, chrome strips, door handles, etc.), will also need to be masked off. Use genuine masking tape, and several thicknesses of newspaper, for the masking operations.

Before starting to spray, agitate the aerosol can thoroughly, then spray a test area (an old tin, or similar) until the technique is mastered. Cover the repair area with a thick coat of primer; the thickness should be built up using several thin layers of paint, rather than one thick one. Using 400-grade wet-and-dry paper, rub down the surface of the primer until it is smooth. While doing this, the work area should be thoroughly doused with water, and the wet-and-dry paper periodically rinsed in water. Allow to dry before spraying on more paint.

Spray on the top coat, again building up the thickness by using several thin layers of paint. Start spraying at one edge of the repair area, and then, using a side-to-side motion, work until the whole repair area and about 2 inches of the surrounding original paintwork is covered. Remove all masking material 10 to 15 minutes after spraying on the final coat of paint.

Allow the new paint at least two weeks to harden, then, using a paintwork renovator, or a very fine cutting paste, blend the edges of the paint into the existing paintwork. Finally, apply wax polish.

Plastic components

With the use of more and more plastic body components by the vehicle manufacturers (eg, bumpers. spoilers, and in some cases major

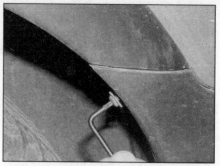

6.2 Removing the upper screws securing the front bumper to the wheelarch liners

body panels), rectification of more serious damage to such items has become a matter of either entrusting repair work to a specialist in this field, or renewing complete components. Repair of such damage by the DIY owner is not feasible, owing to the cost of the equipment and materials required for effecting such repairs. The basic technique involves making a groove along the line of the crack in the plastic, using a rotary burr in a power drill. The damaged part is then welded back together, using a hot-air gun to heat up and fuse a plastic filler rod into the groove. Any excess plastic is then removed, and the area rubbed down to a smooth finish. It is important that a filler rod of the correct plastic is used, as body components can be made of a variety of different types (eg, polycarbonate, ABS, polypropylene).

Damage of a less serious nature (abrasions, minor cracks, etc.), can be repaired by the DIY owner using a two-part epoxy filler repair material. Once mixed in equal proportions, this is used in similar fashion to the bodywork filler used on metal panels. The filler is usually cured in twenty to thirty minutes, ready for sanding and painting.

If the owner is renewing a complete component himself, or if he has repaired it with epoxy filler, he will be left with the problem of finding a paint for finishing which is compatible with the type of plastic used. At one time, the use of a universal paint was not possible, owing to the complex range of plastics encountered in body component applications. Standard paints, generally

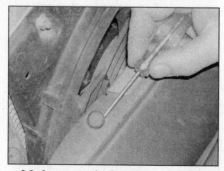

6.3 Access to the front bumper upper screws is gained by removing the plastic covers

speaking, will not bond to plastic or rubber satisfactorily. However, it is now possible to obtain a plastic body parts finishing kit that consists of a pre-primer treatment, a primer and coloured top coat. Full instructions are normally supplied with a kit, but basically, the method of use is to first apply the pre-primer to the component concerned, and allow it to dry for up to 30 minutes. Then the primer is applied, and left to dry for about an hour before finally applying the special-coloured top coat. The result is a correctly coloured component, where the paint will flex with the plastic or rubber, a property that standard paint does not normally possess.

5 Major body damage repair – general

Where serious damage has occurred, or large areas need renewal due to neglect, it means that complete new panels will need welding-in; this is best left to professionals. If the damage is due to impact, it will also be necessary to check the alignment of the bodyshell; this can only be carried out accurately by a Vauxhall dealer using special jigs. If the body is left misaligned, it is primarily dangerous (as the car will not handle properly) and secondly, uneven stresses will be imposed on the steering, suspension and possibly transmission, causing abnormal wear or complete failure, particularly to items such as the tyres.

6 Front and rear bumpers – removal and refitting

Front bumper

Removal

1 Working under the front of the vehicle, remove the three plastic clips securing the front bumper to the splash guard. To do this, depress the central pins.
2 On each side of the vehicle, unscrew the upper screws and remove the lower clips securing the wheelarch liners to the front bumper **(see illustration)**.
3 Have an assistant support the front bumper, then prise out the plastic covers and undo the three upper screws from the front body panel **(see illustration)**.
4 Carefully pull the sides of the front bumper out from the wing panels and withdraw it from the front of the vehicle. On models with front foglights or headlight washers, disconnect the wiring as it is being removed. Where applicable, disconnect the wiring from the exterior temperature sensor **(see illustrations)**.

Refitting

5 Refitting is a reversal of removal. Check the

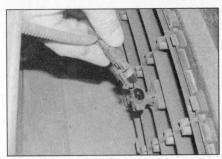

6.4a Disconnecting the wiring from the exterior temperature sensor on the front bumper

6.4b Removing the front bumper (Astra)

6.5 Polystyrene packing for the front bumper

condition of the bumper polystyrene packing on the front valance, and renew it if necessary **(see illustration)**.

Rear bumper

Removal

6 Open the rear tailgate.
7 Working under the rear of the vehicle, undo the screws securing the bottom of the rear bumper to the rear panel **(see illustration)**.
8 At the rear of each wheelarch, undo the two securing screws **(see illustration)**.
9 Have an assistant support the rear bumper, then undo the upper securing screws **(see illustration)**.
10 Carefully pull the sides of the rear bumper out from the guides on the wing panels and withdraw it from the rear of the vehicle **(see illustrations)**. On Zafira models fitted with a tow bar, access to the hitch is made by

moving the sliders inwards and releasing the cover.

Refitting

11 Refitting is a reversal of removal.

7 Radiator grille – removal and refitting

Removal

1 Open the bonnet.
2 The radiator grille is secured to the bonnet by six screws. Undo the screws and withdraw the grille.

Refitting

3 Refitting is a reversal of removal, but clean the surface of the bonnet first.

8 Windscreen cowl panel – removal and refitting

Removal

1 Open the bonnet.
2 Pull the weatherstrip from the firewall panel at the rear of the engine compartment.
3 Unclip and remove the water deflector panel located in front of the windscreen. Disconnect the tubing from the windscreen washer jets.
4 Remove the windscreen wiper arms, as described in Chapter 12.
5 Unscrew the two large nuts from the windscreen wiper arm spindles.
6 Note how the cowl panel engages with the weatherstrip at the base of the windscreen,

6.7 Undo the rear bumper lower mounting screws . . .

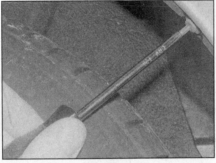

6.8 . . . the mounting screws located in the rear wheelarches . . .

6.9 . . . and the upper mounting screws . . .

6.10a . . . then remove the rear bumper (Zafira)

6.10b Removing the rear bumper (Astra)

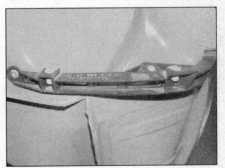

6.10c Rear bumper support guides (Astra)

9.2 Bonnet-to-hinge mounting bolts

9.6 Bonnet striker

11.1 Bonnet lock safety hook

then carefully release the ends of the cowl panel from the scuttle and withdraw from the vehicle.

Refitting

7 Refitting is a reversal of removal.

9 Bonnet – removal, refitting and adjustment

Removal

1 Open the bonnet and support it in the fully open position with the stay.
2 Mark the position of the mounting bolts on the hinges, to aid alignment on refitting (see illustration).
3 With the help of an assistant, support the weight of the bonnet and lower the stay.
4 Unscrew the mounting bolts and lift the bonnet from the hinges. Rest it carefully on

rags or cardboard, to avoid damaging the paint.
5 If necessary, remove the hinges as described in Section 10. If a new bonnet is to be fitted, transfer all the serviceable fixings to it with reference to Sections 7 and 11.

Refitting and adjustment

6 Refitting is a reversal of removal. Position the hinge bolts as previously noted and tighten them securely. Lower the bonnet slowly and check that the striker enters the centre of the lock. With the bonnet shut, check that the gap between it and the front wings is equal on both sides. Also check that the height of the bonnet matches the height of the front wings. Adjustment of the bonnet in its aperture is made on the bonnet-to-hinge bolts, and adjustment of the height is made at the hinge-to-body panel bolts (see Section 10) and the bonnet striker (see illustration). If necessary, adjust the front rubber buffers to obtain sufficient support.

10 Bonnet hinge – removal and refitting

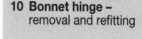

Removal

1 Remove the bonnet, (see Section 9).
2 Remove the windscreen cowl panel, as described in Section 8.
3 Mark the position of the hinges on the body panels, then unbolt them and remove the hinges.

Refitting

4 Refitting is a reversal of removal. Adjust the height of the bonnet as described in Section 9.

11 Bonnet lock components – removal and refitting

Bonnet lock safety hook

Removal

1 The bonnet lock hook is riveted to the bonnet, and removal involves drilling out the rivet (see illustration).

Refitting

2 Refitting is a reversal of removal, using a new rivet.

Lock striker

Removal

3 To remove the lock striker from the bonnet, loosen the locknut, then unscrew the striker, and recover the washer and spring.

Refitting

4 Refitting is a reversal of removal, but adjust the striker dimension as shown (see illustration), before tightening the locknut.

Locking spring

Removal

5 Disconnect the end of the bonnet release cable from the spring, then unhook the end of the spring from the slot in the front body panel, taking care not to damage the paint.

Refitting

6 Refitting is a reversal of removal.

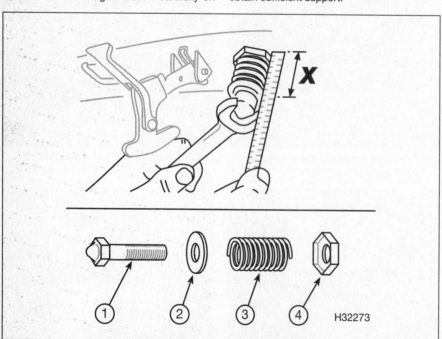

11.4 Bonnet lock striker adjustment

1 Striker   2 Washer   3 Coil spring   4 Locknut   X = 40 to 45 mm

12.4a Removing the bonnet release lever from its mounting

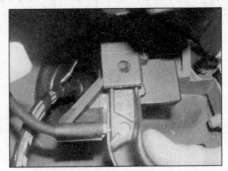

12.4b Bonnet release lever and cable

12 Bonnet release cable – removal and refitting

Removal

1 Open the bonnet, and support it in the fully open position.
2 Unscrew the release cable clip from the front body cross panel.
3 Disconnect the end of the release cable from the locking spring under the cross panel.
4 Disconnect the release cable from the release lever in the driver's footwell. If necessary, remove the release lever from its mounting for access to the cable end **(see illustrations)**.
5 Pull the cable assembly through the grommet in the engine compartment bulkhead and into the engine compartment.

6 Note the routing of the cable, then release the cable from any remaining clips and cable-ties, and withdraw it from the engine compartment.

Refitting

7 Refitting is a reversal of removal, but ensure that the cable is correctly routed, and on completion, check the release mechanism for satisfactory operation.

13 Doors – removal, refitting and adjustment

Front door

Removal

1 To remove a door, open it fully and support it under its lower edge on blocks or axle stands covered with pads of rag.

2 Disconnect the wiring connector from the front edge of the door. To release the connector, pull out the locking clip, then twist the collar and pull the connector from the socket in the door **(see illustrations)**.
3 Unscrew the Torx bolt securing the door check arm pivot to the A-pillar **(see illustration)**.
4 Where applicable, remove the plastic covers from the hinge pins **(see illustration)**, then drive out the pins using a punch. Have an assistant support the door as the pins are driven out, then withdraw the door from the vehicle. If renewing a door, transfer all the serviceable fixings to the new door. **Note:** *On models without side airbags, the packing piece must be fitted inside the door.*

Refitting

5 Refitting is a reversal of removal.

Adjustment

6 The door hinges are welded onto the door frame and the body pillar, so that there is no provision for adjustment or alignment.
7 If the door can be moved up and down on its hinges due to wear in the hinge pins or their holes, it may be possible to drill out the holes and fit slightly oversize pins. Consult a Vauxhall dealer for further advice.
8 Door closure may be adjusted by altering the position of the lock striker on the body pillar, using an Allen key or a hexagon bit **(see illustration)**.

Rear door

Removal

9 Disconnect the wiring connector from the front edge of the door **(see illustration)**. To

13.2a Pull out the locking clip . . .

13.2b . . . then twist the collar and pull the connector from the socket

13.3 The front door check arm pivot is attached to the A-pillar with a Torx bolt

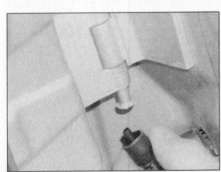

13.4 Removing the plastic covers from the front door hinge pins

13.8 Front door lock striker on the B-pillar

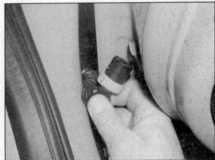

13.9 Disconnecting the wiring from the front edge of the rear door

13.10 Rear door check arm

13.11 Removing the plastic covers from the rear door hinge pins

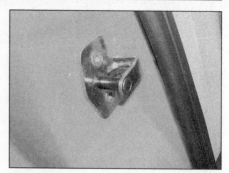

13.15 Rear door lock striker on the C-pillar

release the connector, twist the locking collar, then pull the connector from the socket in the door.

10 Unscrew the Torx bolt securing the door check arm pivot to the A-pillar **(see illustration)**.

11 Where applicable, remove the plastic covers from the hinge pins **(see illustration)**, then drive out the pins using a punch. Have an assistant support the door as the pins are driven out, then withdraw the door from the vehicle. If renewing a door, transfer all the serviceable fixings to the new door.

Refitting

12 Refitting is a reversal of removal.

Adjustment

13 The door hinges are welded onto the door frame and the body pillar, so that there is no provision for adjustment or alignment.

14 If the door can be moved up and down on

its hinges due to wear in the hinge pins or their holes, it may be possible to drill out the holes and fit slightly oversize pins. Consult a Vauxhall dealer for further advice.

15 Door closure may be adjusted by altering the position of the lock striker on the body pillar, using an Allen key or a hexagon bit **(see illustration)**.

<hr>

14 Door interior handle – removal and refitting

Removal

1 Remove the door inner trim panel, as described in Section 44.

2 Release the spring clip and push out the interior handle from the inside of the trim panel.

Refitting

3 Refitting is a reversal of removal.

<hr>

15 Door exterior handle – removal and refitting

Front door handle

Removal

1 Remove the door inner trim panel, and peel back the plastic insulating sheet for access to the handle, as described in Section 44. Also remove the window glass rear channel with reference to Section 19 **(see illustration)**.

2 Reach through the hole in the inner door panel, and disconnect the private lock and exterior handle operating rods. The rods are retained with plastic clips **(see illustration)**.

3 Unscrew the two nuts and withdraw the housing plate from inside the door **(see illustrations)**.

4 Carefully remove the exterior handle from the outside of the door **(see illustration)**.

Refitting

5 Refitting is a reversal of removal, but check the operation of the mechanism before refitting the door inner trim panel with reference to Section 44. If necessary, adjust the operating rod to eliminate play by turning the knurled plastic adjuster wheel.

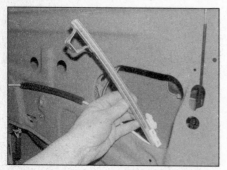

15.1 Removing the window glass rear channel

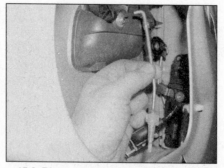

15.2 Disconnecting the operating rods from the exterior door handle

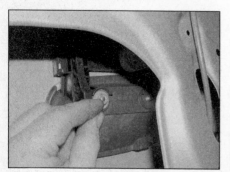

15.3a Unscrew the nuts . . .

15.3b . . . and remove the housing plate from inside the door

15.4 Removing the exterior handle from the front door

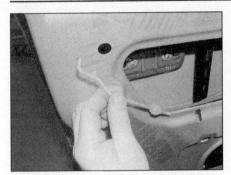

15.7a Disconnecting the rear door exterior handle operating rod

15.7b Rear door exterior handle viewed from inside the door

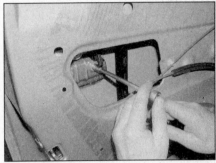

15.8a Unscrew the two nuts . . .

Rear door handle

Removal

6 Remove the door inner trim panel, and peel back the plastic insulating sheet for access to the handle, as described in Section 44.

7 Reach through the hole in the inner door panel, and disconnect the exterior handle operating rod **(see illustrations)**. The rod is retained with a plastic clip.

8 Unscrew the two nuts and withdraw the housing plate from inside the door **(see illustrations)**.

9 Carefully remove the exterior handle from the outside of the door **(see illustration)**.

Refitting

10 Refitting is a reversal of removal, but check the operation of the mechanism before refitting the door inner trim panel with reference to Section 44.

 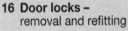

16 Door locks –
removal and refitting

Front

Removal

1 Remove the door inner trim panel, and peel back the plastic insulating sheet from the rear edge of the door, with reference to Section 44.

2 With the window closed, drill out the pop-rivets securing the rear window glass channel to the inner door panel, then withdraw the channel through the aperture in the door. Working through the aperture in the door, disconnect the central locking wiring plug by pulling out the red button **(see illustration)**.

3 Reach through the aperture in the door and disconnect the exterior door handle and private lock cylinder operating rods from the lock. The rods are retained with plastic clips. Alternatively, the exterior door handle can be removed, together with the door lock, by referring to Section 15.

4 On the rear edge of the door, unscrew and remove the three screws securing the lock to the door panel **(see illustration)**.

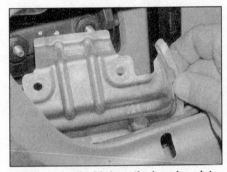

15.8b . . . and withdraw the housing plate from inside the door

16.2 Disconnecting the central locking wiring plug from the front door lock

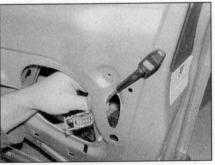

16.5 Removing the front door lock from the door

5 Lower the lock and withdraw it from inside the door, at the same time release the locking knob and guide it through the hole in the door panel **(see illustration)**.

15.9 Removing the rear door exterior handle

16.4 Removing the front door lock retaining screws

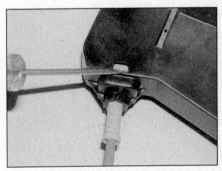

16.6a Release the clips . . .

6 Release the outer cable end fittings for the inner door handle and locking knob, and disconnect the cables from the lock **(see illustrations)**.

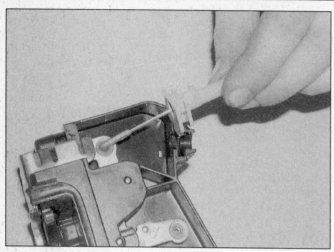

16.6b . . . and disconnect the cables from the lock

16.6c Front door lock with cables disconnected

Refitting

7 Refitting is a reversal of removal. Check the operation of the door lock by inserting a screwdriver in the lock mechanism to simulate the striker entry. Check that the door locks and unlocks correctly. If the lock operation is not satisfactory, note that the exterior handle operating rod can be adjusted by turning the knurled plastic adjuster wheel at the end of the rod.

Rear door

Removal

8 Fully lower the window, then remove the door inner trim panel and the plastic insulating sheet, as described in Section 44.
9 Undo the screws and release the locking knob outer cable from the door panel, then unhook the inner cable from the intermediate lever.
10 Disconnect the exterior handle operating rod by releasing the plastic clip.
11 On the rear edge of the door, unscrew and remove the three screws securing the lock to the door panel **(see illustration)**.
12 Reach through the aperture in the door and move the lock forwards until the wiring harness can be disconnected. Pull out the red button to do this **(see illustration)**.

13 Release the locking cable from the clip, then withdraw the lock together with handle and locking knob cables from inside the door and at the same time release the locking knob **(see illustrations)**.
14 Release the outer cable end fittings for the inner door handle and locking knob, and disconnect the cables from the lock.

Refitting

15 Refitting is a reversal of removal. Check the operation of the door lock by inserting a screwdriver in the lock mechanism to simulate the striker entry. Check that the door locks and unlocks correctly.

---

17 Door lock cylinder –
removal and refitting

Removal

1 Remove the door exterior handle and housing plate, as described in Section 15.
2 Insert the key into the lock, then remove the retaining ring from the inner end of the lock cylinder **(see illustration)**.
3 Note how it is fitted, then remove the carrier and arm from the inner end of the lock

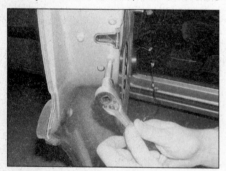

16.11 Unscrewing the rear door lock retaining screws

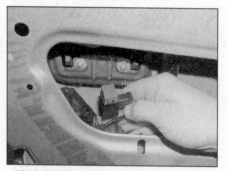

16.12 Disconnecting the wiring from the rear door lock

16.13a Release the locking cable from the clip . . .

16.13b . . . then remove the lock from inside the rear door

16.13c Rear door lock removed from the door

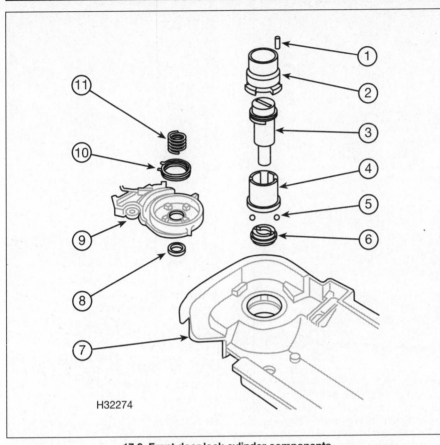

H32274

17.2 Front door lock cylinder components

1 Roll pin	5 Ball
2 Housing	6 Clutch
3 Lock cylinder	7 Housing plate
4 Sleeve	8 Retaining ring

9 Carrier with lever (central locking version)
10 Torsion spring
11 Pressure spring

cylinder. Remove the torsion and pressure springs, noting how they are fitted.

4 Mark the lock cylinder housing and plate in relation to each other. Using a 2.5 mm diameter punch, drive out the retaining spring roll pin, taking care not to damage the hole.

5 Remove the lock cylinder, channel sleeve, balls and clutch. **Note:** *The lock cylinder and clutch must be renewed together.*

Refitting

6 Refitting is a reversal of removal, but use a

centre punch to secure the bottom of the roll pin to the housing.

18 Lock striker – removal and refitting

Removal

1 The lock striker is screwed into the door pillar on the body.

2 Before removing the striker, mark its position, so that it can be refitted in exactly the same position.

3 To remove the striker, simply unscrew the securing screws using an Allen key or hexagon bit.

Refitting

4 Refitting is a reversal of removal, but if necessary, adjust the position of the striker to achieve satisfactory closing of the door.

19 Door window glass – removal and refitting

Front

Removal

1 Remove the door inner trim panel and the plastic insulating sheet, as described in Section 44. Make sure the window is fully raised.

2 On models with side airbags, make sure that the battery negative lead has been disconnected for at least 1 minute, then remove the sensor bracket and sensor. To do this, unbolt the bracket, then disconnect the wiring and remove the sensor. **Note:** *The sensors for each side of the vehicle are different – make sure the correct one is refitted.*

3 Drill out the pop-rivets securing the rear window glass channel to the inner door panel, then withdraw the channel through the aperture in the door **(see illustrations)**.

4 On models with electric front windows, temporarily reconnect the electric window switch to the wiring and reconnect the battery negative lead. On manual front windows, temporarily refit the regulator handle to the regulator. Position the window so that the regulator-to-window channel bolts are visible through the access holes in the door, then unscrew and remove them **(see illustrations)**.

5 Tilt the window forwards as necessary then release the regulator roller from the rear channel and lift the glass upwards, withdrawing it from the outside of the door **(see illustrations)**. It may be necessary to reposition the window height before being

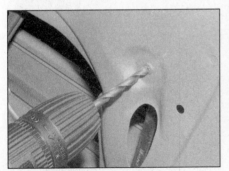
19.3a Drill out the pop-rivets . . .

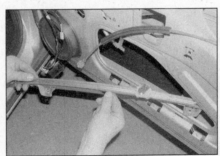
19.3b . . . and withdraw the rear window glass channel through the inner door aperture

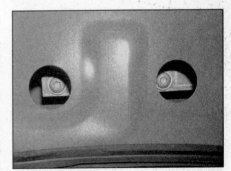
19.4a The regulator-to-window channel bolts are visible through the access holes

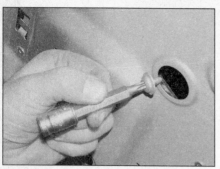

19.4b Unscrewing the front door regulator-to-window channel bolts

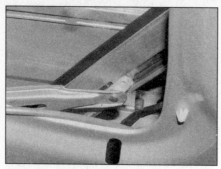

19.5a Release the regulator roller from the rear channel . . .

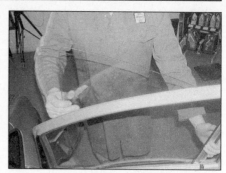

19.5b . . . then withdraw the window from the outside of the door

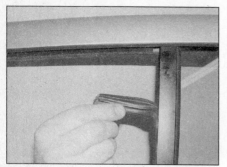

19.9a Pull the rubber weatherstrip away from the top of the window rear guide channel . . .

19.9b . . . then unscrew the upper guide retaining screw . . .

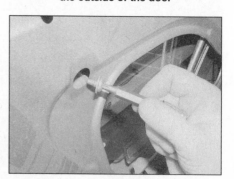

19.9c . . . and lower guide retaining screw . . .

able to release the regulator from the channel, since the working room is restricted.

Refitting

6 Refitting is a reversal of removal, but use

19.10 . . . and withdraw the window guide channel

19.11 Removing the fixed window glass from the rear door

new pop-rivets to secure the window channel. The regulator-to-window channel bolts should first be hand-tightened, then the window raised and lowered before fully tightening the bolts.

Rear (including fixed window)

Removal

7 Remove the door inner trim panel and the plastic insulating sheet, as described in Section 44.
8 On models with electric rear windows, temporarily reconnect the electric window switch to the wiring and reconnect the battery negative lead. On manual rear windows, temporarily refit the regulator handle to the regulator. Fully lower the window.
9 Carefully pull the rubber weatherstrip away from the top of the window rear guide channel, then undo and remove the upper guide retaining screw. Unscrew and remove

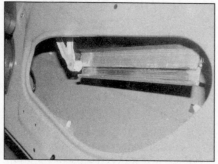

19.12a Release the window from the regulator channel . . .

the guide lower retaining screws using a Torx key through the holes in the inner door panel **(see illustrations)**.
10 Carefully ease the window guide channel away from the fixed window and withdraw it upwards from the door **(see illustration)**. The seal for the fixed window should remain in the channel.
11 Ease the fixed window glass forwards and withdraw it from the door **(see illustration)**.
12 Slightly tilt the window glass while releasing it from the regulator channel, and withdraw it upwards from the rear door **(see illustrations)**. **Note:** *It may be necessary to partially remove the weatherstrip, and also reposition the window by turning the regulator handle.*

Refitting

13 Refitting is a reversal of removal.

19.12b . . . and remove the window glass from the rear door

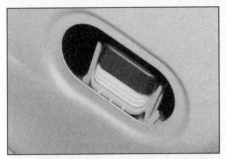

20.2a The wiring connector for the electric front window regulator is hooked onto the inner panel

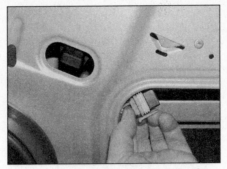

20.2b Disconnecting the wiring for the electric front window regulator

20.3a Drill out the rivets . . .

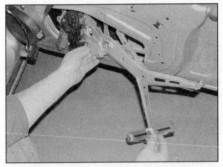

20.3b . . . and withdraw the window regulator from the door

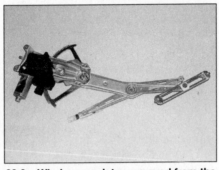

20.3c Window regulator removed from the front door

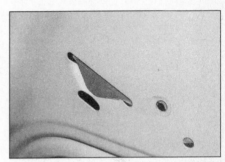

20.3d Note the bottom of the window regulator locates in a slot in the inner door panel

20 Window regulator – removal and refitting

Front door

Removal

1 Remove the front door window glass as described in Section 19.
2 On models with electric front windows, make sure the battery negative lead is disconnected then reach inside the door and disconnect the wiring from the regulator. Unhook the connector from the door **(see illustrations)**.
3 Drill out the rivets securing the regulator to the door inner panel, and withdraw the regulator through the lower aperture. Note that the bottom of the regulator is located in a slot **(see illustrations)**.

Refitting

4 Refitting is a reversal of removal, but use new pop-rivets to secure the regulator **(see illustration)**. On models with electric windows programme the closed position of the glass in the control unit as follows. Sit in the driver's seat with all the doors closed. Switch on the ignition and slightly open the window. Close the window and hold the rocker switch depressed for a further 2 seconds.

Rear door

Removal

5 Remove the rear door window glass as described in Section 19.
6 On models with electric rear windows, make sure the battery negative lead is disconnected then reach inside the door and disconnect the wiring from the regulator.
7 Drill out the four rivets securing the

regulator to the door inner panel, and withdraw the regulator through the upper aperture **(see illustration)**.

Refitting

8 Refitting is a reversal of removal, but use new pop-rivets to secure the regulator. On models with electric rear windows programme the closed position of the glass as described in paragraph 4.

21 Boot lid – removal and refitting

Removal

1 Open the boot lid fully.
2 On models with central locking, disconnect the battery negative lead, then disconnect the wiring from the lock motor. If the original boot lid is to be refitted, first tie a length of string to the end of the wiring. Feed the wiring through the boot lid, then untie the string, leaving it in position in the boot lid to assist refitting.
3 Mark the position of the hinges on the boot lid.
4 With the help of an assistant, support the weight of the boot lid, then unscrew the securing bolts from the hinges, and lift the boot lid from the vehicle.

Refitting

5 If a new boot lid is to be fitted, transfer all the serviceable fittings (rubber buffers, lock mechanism, etc) to it.

20.4 Securing the window regulator with new pop-rivets

20.7 Drilling out the rivets securing the window regulator to the rear door inner panel

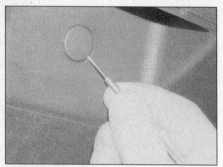

24.1a Prise out the plastic covers . . .

24.1b . . . then undo the screws . . .

24.1c . . . and remove the lower trim panel

6 Refitting is a reversal of removal, but check that the boot lid closes correctly and is located centrally within the body aperture. If necessary, adjust the hinge bolts, rubber buffers and lock striker.

22 Boot lid hinge –
removal and refitting

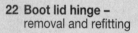

Removal

1 Remove the boot lid, (see Section 21).
2 Remove the rear quarter trim panel, as described in Section 44.
3 Note the position of the hinge counter-balance spring in the bracket on the body, so that it can be refitted in its original position, then unhook the spring from the body. Use a lever to release the spring if necessary.
4 Unscrew the securing bolt, and remove the hinge from the body.

Refitting

5 Refitting is a reversal of removal.

23 Boot lid components –
removal and refitting

Handle

Removal

1 Open the boot lid and remove the lock cylinder as described later in this Section.

2 Unscrew the two securing nuts, then withdraw the handle from outside the boot lid. Note that the securing nuts also secure the lock cylinder assembly to the boot lid.

Refitting

3 Refitting is a reversal of removal.

Lock

Removal

4 Proceed as described in paragraph 1.
5 Unscrew the two securing bolts, and withdraw the lock from the boot lid.

Refitting

6 Refitting is a reversal of removal, but if necessary, adjust the position of the lock striker on the body, to achieve satisfactory lock operation.

Lock cylinder

Removal

7 Open the boot lid fully.
8 Remove the four securing screws, and withdraw the lock cylinder assembly cover panel.
9 Unscrew the two securing nuts, and withdraw the lock cylinder assembly, unhooking the lock operating rod(s) as the assembly is withdrawn. Note that the securing nuts also secure the boot lid handle.
10 No spare parts are available for the lock cylinder assembly, and if faulty, the complete assembly must be renewed.

Refitting

11 Refitting is a reversal of removal.

Lock striker

Removal

12 The lock striker is screwed into the lower body panel.
13 Remove the securing screws, then unclip the rear boot trim panel to expose the lock striker securing bolt.
14 Before removing the striker, mark its position, so that it can be refitted in exactly the same position.
15 To remove the striker, simply unscrew the securing screw.

Refitting

16 Refitting is a reversal of removal, but if necessary, adjust the position of the striker to achieve satisfactory closing of the boot lid.

24 Tailgate –
removal and refitting

Removal

1 With the tailgate open, prise out the plastic covers, undo the screws, and remove the lower and upper trim panels from the inside of the tailgate. Note that the lower panel has extensions which slot into the upper panels **(see illustrations)**.
2 Undo the screws, then release the clips and remove the high-level stop-light.
3 Inside the tailgate, disconnect the earth cable then tie a length of string to the wiring harness. Release the rubber grommet and pull the wiring from the top of the tailgate **(see illustration)**.

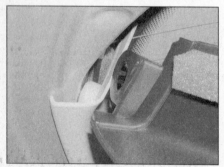

24.1d Note how the lower trim panel locates in the upper side trim panels

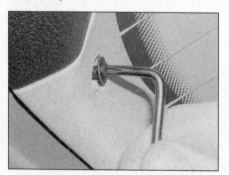

24.1e Removing the upper trim panel retaining screws

24.3 Release the rubber grommet and pull the wiring from the top of the tailgate

Untie the string and leave it in position to aid refitting the wiring harness.

4 Using a screwdriver through the hole, depress the tabs of the washer jet and pull out the jet. Disconnect the washer tube and tie a length of string to it, then draw out the tube from the tailgate and untie the string.

5 Have an assistant support the tailgate, then use a screwdriver to prise out the spring clips from the support struts. Release the struts from the socket balls and lower them onto the body.

6 Extract the clips and carefully drive out the hinge pins, using a small drift **(see illustrations)**.

7 Lift the tailgate away from the body.

Refitting

8 If a new tailgate is to be fitted, transfer all serviceable components (rubber buffers, lock mechanism, etc) to it.

9 Refitting is a reversal of removal, but smear a little grease on the hinge pins before inserting them, and make sure that the tailgate closes correctly and that the gap between it and the surrounding bodywork is equal all the way around. If necessary, loosen the hinge bolts after removing the trim at the rear of the headlining and reposition the hinges as required. Check that the tailgate striker enters the lock centrally, and if necessary adjust the position of the striker. When closed, the tailgate should be firmly supported by the rubber buffers – if necessary, adjust the buffers **(see illustrations)**.

---

25 Tailgate hinge –
removal and refitting

Removal

1 Remove the tailgate as described in Section 24.

2 Carefully pull down the rubber weatherstrip from the upper edge of the tailgate aperture.

3 Remove the trim panels from the C-pillar on both sides of the rear luggage compartment as described in Section 44.

4 Remove the moulded trim panel from the rear of the headlining.

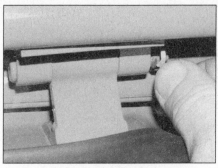
24.6a Extract the clips . . .

24.9a Removing the trim at the rear of the headlining

5 Mark the position of the hinges on the body to ensure correct refitting, then unbolt and remove them.

Refitting

6 Refitting is a reversal of removal, but align the hinges with the previously made marks on the body.

---

26 Tailgate components –
removal and refitting

Support strut

Removal

1 Open the tailgate fully, and have an assistant support it.

2 Release the strut from its mounting ball-

24.6b . . . then drive out the hinge pins

24.9b Tailgate support rubber buffer (adjustable)

joints by prising the spring clips out a little way, and pulling the strut off the balljoints **(see illustrations)**.

Refitting

3 Refitting is a reversal of removal.

Lock

Removal

4 With the tailgate open, remove the lower trim panel as described in Section 44.

5 Reach through the tailgate aperture and disconnect the private lock and lock operating rods by releasing the plastic clips **(see illustration)**.

6 Undo the securing screws and withdraw the lock **(see illustrations)**.

Refitting

7 Refitting is a reversal of removal, but if necessary, adjust the position of the lock

26.2a Prise out the spring clip to release the strut from the balljoint

26.2b Tailgate strut lower balljoint and bracket on the body

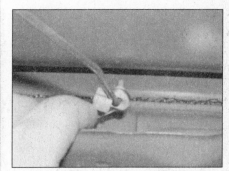
26.5 Disconnecting the operating rods

26.6a On Astra models, undo the screws . . .

26.6b . . . and withdraw the lock from the tailgate

26.6c On Zafira models, undo the screws . . .

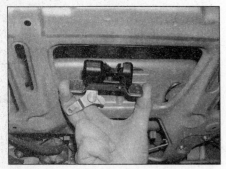

26.6d . . . and withdraw the lock from the tailgate

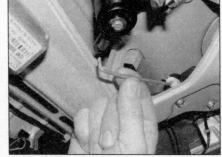

26.9 Disconnect the operating rod . . .

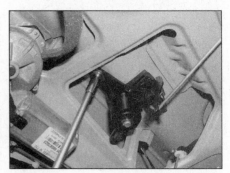

26.10a . . . then unscrew the mounting nuts . . .

striker on the body, to achieve satisfactory lock operation.

Lock cylinder

Removal

8 With the tailgate open, remove the lower trim panel as described in Section 44.

9 Reach through the tailgate aperture and disconnect the operating rod by releasing the plastic clip (see illustration).

10 Unscrew the mounting nuts and withdraw the lock cylinder from the tailgate (see illustrations).

Refitting

11 Refitting is a reversal of removal.

Lock striker

Removal

12 The lock striker is screwed into the lower

body panel (see illustration).

13 Where applicable, extract the securing screws, and remove the luggage compartment rear trim panel for access to the lock striker securing bolts.

14 Before removing the striker, mark its position, so that it can be refitted in exactly the same position.

15 Undo the screws and remove the striker.

Refitting

16 Refitting is a reversal of removal, but if necessary, adjust the position of the striker to achieve satisfactory closing of the tailgate.

Handle

Removal

17 Open the tailgate and remove the lower trim panel as described in Section 44.

18 Unscrew the two nuts and withdraw the handle from the tailgate.

Refitting

19 Refitting is a reversal of removal.

27 Central locking components – removal and refitting

Electronic control unit

Note: *If the electronic control unit is renewed, the new unit must be programmed by a Vauxhall dealer using specialist equipment. The unit also incorporates a crash sensor.*

Removal

1 The control unit is located behind the right-hand footwell side/sill trim panel.

2 Disconnect the battery negative lead as described in Chapter 5A.

3 Remove the footwell side/sill trim panel, as described in Section 44.

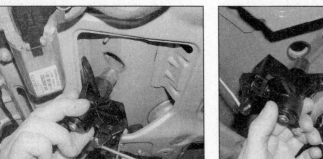

26.10b . . . and withdraw the lock cylinder from the tailgate (Zafira)

26.10c Removing the lock cylinder from the tailgate (Astra Hatchback)

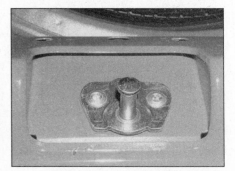

26.12 Tailgate lock striker

27.4 Central locking electronic control unit

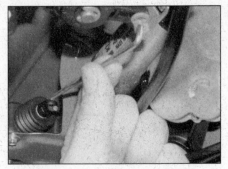

27.10 Disconnect the operating rod . . .

27.11 . . . then disconnect the wiring . . .

4 Disconnect the two wiring harness plugs **(see illustration)**.
5 Undo the two securing screws and lift the control unit from its location.

Refitting

6 Refitting is a reversal of removal.

Front and rear door servo units

Removal and refitting

7 The servo units are incorporated in the door locks and their removal and refitting is described in Section 16.

Tailgate/boot lid servo units

Removal

8 Remove the trim panel from the inside of the tailgate/boot lid.
9 On Saloon models remove the lock cylinder cover.
10 Release the plastic clip and disconnect the servo unit operating rod from the lock **(see illustration)**.
11 Disconnect the servo unit wiring **(see illustration)**.
12 Undo the screws and withdraw the servo unit from the tailgate/boot lid **(see illustrations)**.

Refitting

13 Refitting is a reversal of removal.

Fuel filler flap servo unit (Hatchbach/Saloon models)

Removal

14 Remove the carpet from the rear luggage compartment.
15 Remove the rear quarter trim panel as described in Section 44.
16 Disconnect the wiring plug from the servo unit.
17 Open the fuel filler flap then undo the mounting screws and withdraw the servo unit from inside the vehicle.

Refitting

18 Refitting is a reversal of removal.

Fuel filler flap servo unit (Estate/Zafira models)

Removal

19 In the rear luggage compartment, turn the

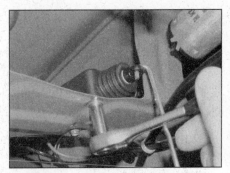

27.12a . . . and unbolt the servo unit

fasteners and open the access cover to the filler flap servo unit.
20 Disconnect the wiring plug from the servo unit.
21 Open the fuel filler flap then undo the mounting screws and withdraw the servo unit from inside the vehicle.

Refitting

22 Refitting is a reversal of removal.

28 Electric window components – removal and refitting

Switches

Removal

1 The switches are located in the driver's and passenger's doors.
2 Using a small screwdriver, carefully prise the switch from the door inner trim panel.
3 Disconnect the wiring and remove the switch.

Refitting

4 Refitting is a reversal of removal.

Window motors

Removal

5 Remove the door window regulator, as described in Section 20.
6 To remove the motor assembly from the regulator, unscrew the three securing screws.

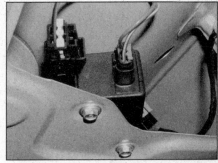

27.12b Central locking servo unit in the tailgate (Zafira)

Refitting

7 Refitting is a reversal of removal. On completion, programme the closed position of the windows as follows. Sit in the driver's seat with all the doors closed. Switch on the ignition and slightly open the window. Close the window and hold the rocker switch depressed for a further 2 seconds.

29 Exterior door mirror – removal and refitting

Removal

1 Remove the door inner trim panel as described in Section 44.
2 Disconnect the wiring for the exterior door mirror, and prise out the rubber grommet from the inner panel **(see illustration)**.

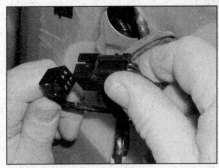

29.2 Disconnecting the wiring for the exterior door mirror

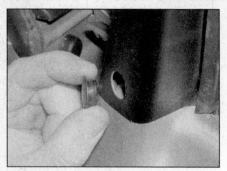

29.3 Prise out the rubber plugs for access to the exterior mirror retaining bolts

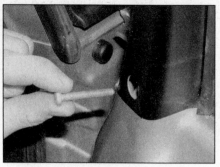

29.4a Unscrew the mounting bolts . . .

29.4b . . . and withdraw the exterior mirror from the outside of the door

3 Prise out the rubber plugs as necessary for access to the mirror retaining bolts **(see illustration)**. To prevent the mirror mounting bolts dropping inside the inner trim panel, it is suggested that a rag is put over the hole.
4 Support the mirror, then unscrew and remove the mounting bolts and withdraw the mirror from the outside of the door **(see illustrations)**.

Refitting

5 Refitting is a reversal of removal.

30 Exterior door mirror glass – removal and refitting

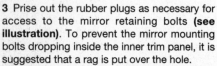

Removal

1 The mirror glass can be removed for renewal without removing the mirror. Using protective gloves, carefully push in the upper, inner (nearest the door) corner of the glass in order to release the lower, outer corner from the door mirror. If necessary, assist the removal of the glass by using a small screwdriver under the lower, outer corner of the glass. The upper internal clip may be released using a small screwdriver inserted through the hole in the mirror cover **(see illustration)**.
2 Where applicable, disconnect the two wires from the heating element while holding the riveted tags to avoid damage **(see illustration)**.

Refitting

3 Reconnect the wiring to the heating element where applicable, then locate the glass in the mirror making sure that the plastic retaining clips are correctly aligned with each other. Depress carefully until the retaining clips engage.

31 Electric mirror components – removal and refitting

Switches

Removal

1 The switches are located in the driver's and passenger's doors.
2 Using a small screwdriver, carefully prise the switch from the door inner trim panel.
3 Disconnect the wiring and remove the switch.

Refitting

4 Refitting is a reversal of removal.

Motor

Removal

5 Remove the exterior mirror as described in Section 29, and the mirror glass as described in Section 30.
6 Undo the three screws and remove the servo motor from the mirror body, then disconnect the wiring.

Refitting

7 Refitting is a reversal of removal, but ensure that the wiring is routed behind the motor, to avoid interfering with the adjustment mechanism.

32 Interior mirror – removal and refitting

Removal

1 Depress the plastic tabs and slide the interior mirror from the mounting plate **(see illustration)**.
2 The mounting plate is fixed to the windscreen using a special adhesive, and should not normally be disturbed. Note that there is a risk of cracking the windscreen if an attempt is made to remove a securely bonded mounting plate.

Refitting

3 If necessary, the special adhesive required to fix the mounting plate to the windscreen can be obtained from a Vauxhall dealer or hardware store. The top of the mounting plate should be located 15.0 mm from the headlining, and the plate should be held in position with masking tape until the adhesive has cured.
4 Slide the interior mirror into the mounting plate until the plastic tabs engage.

30.1 Use a screwdriver to assist removing the glass from the exterior mirror

30.2 Disconnecting the wiring from the exterior mirror heating element

32.1 Removing the interior mirror from the mounting plate

33 Windscreen, rear window and quarter window glass – general

1 The windscreen, rear window, and quarter window glass is bonded in position, using a special adhesive.
2 Special tools, adhesives and expertise are required for successful removal and refitting of glass fixed by this method. Such work must therefore be entrusted to a Vauxhall dealer, a windscreen specialist, or other competent professional.

34 Sunroof glass panel – removal and refitting

Removal

1 Push the sunshade fully rearwards, and open the glass panel halfway.
2 Unscrew the four bolts from the front edge of the glass panel and remove the cover.
3 Unscrew the guide bolts at each side of the glass panel.
4 Carefully lift the glass panel from the roof aperture, taking care not to damage the vehicle paintwork. Check the weatherstrip for wear and damage and renew it if necessary.

Refitting

5 Refitting is a reversal of removal, but if necessary adjust the front height of the glass panel so that it is level with or a maximum of 1.0 mm below the roof panel. The rear height of the panel should be level with or a maximum of 1.0 mm above the roof panel.

35 Sunroof components – removal and refitting

Note: *The sunroof is a complex piece of equipment, consisting of a large number of components. It is strongly recommended that the sunroof mechanism is not disturbed unless necessary. If the sunroof mechanism is faulty, or requires overhaul, consult a Vauxhall dealer for advice. In an emergency the sunroof can be operated manually by removing the cover from the front interior light panel, and using a screwdriver to turn the motor (see illustrations).*

Wind deflector

Removal

1 Open the glass roof panel, then undo the bolts for the swing-out arm on both sides.
2 Disconnect the spring from the pin and lift out the wind deflector.
3 Press the swing-out spring from the guide by turning it.

Refitting

4 Refitting is a reversal of removal.

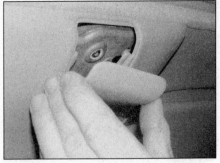

35.0a In an emergency, remove the cover . . .

Electric drive

Removal

5 The electric drive unit is located on the roof above the headlining. Removal of the headlining involves removal of the front interior light, sun visors and handgrips and is a difficult job. It is recommended that a qualified upholsterer carries out this work.
6 With the headlining removed, disconnect the wiring plug from the drive unit (see illustration).
7 Unscrew the retaining screws and withdraw the electric drive unit from the roof panel.

Refitting

8 Before refitting the electric drive, set the switch in its basic position. To do this, the bore just inside the serrated centre drive must be located between the two outer extensions. The remaining refitting procedure is a reversal of removal.

Actuation cable adjustment

9 Remove the electric drive as described previously in this Section.
10 Loosen the front and rear guide screws, then align the front and rear guide pins with the marks on the guides.
11 Insert a 4.0 mm diameter drill bit or similar tool through the rear guide and bracket, then tighten the screws.
12 Refit the electric drive with reference to paragraph 8.

Actuation switch

Removal

13 Remove the front interior light as described in Chapter 12, Section 6.
14 Carefully unclip the actuation switch from the headlining and through the hole in the front interior light.
15 Disconnect the wiring and remove the switch.

Refitting

16 Refitting is a reversal of removal.

Crank drive

Removal

17 Fully open the sunroof.
18 On the manually-operated roof, undo the

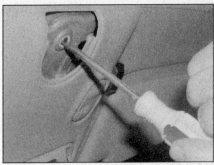

35.0b . . . and turn the motor with a screwdriver

screw and remove the crank handle from the splines.
19 On the electrically-operated roof, use a small screwdriver to carefully prise out the emergency cover on the rear of the front interior light housing.
20 Prise out the interior light lens and disconnect the wiring.
21 Undo the screws and lower the sun roof trim panel from the headlining.
22 Undo the two screws and lower the crank drive from the roof.

Refitting

23 Refitting is a reversal of removal, but first carry out the following adjustment. Turn the drive fully clockwise making sure that the locking pin does not engage. If the pin does engage, it will not be possible to turn the drive fully clockwise, in which case pull the pin outwards.

36 Wheelarch liners – general

1 The plastic wheelarch liners are secured by a combination of self-tapping screws and plastic bolts and plastic clips. Removal and refitting is self-evident, remembering the following points.
2 Some of the securing clips may be held in place using a central pin, which must be tapped out to release the clip.
3 The clips are easily broken during removal, and it is advisable to obtain a few spare clips for possible use when refitting.

35.6 View of the sunroof electric drive unit with the front interior light panel removed

4 Certain models may have additional under-body shields and splashguards fitted, which may be attached to the wheelarch liners.

37 Fuel filler flap –
removal and refitting

Removal

1 Open the flap for access to the two securing screws.
2 Remove the securing screws and withdraw the flap.

Refitting

3 Refitting is a reversal of removal.

38 Exterior body components –
removal and refitting

Door side strip

Removal

1 Remove the door inner trim panel as described in Section 44, then unscrew the side strip retaining screw using a screwdriver through the inner panel aperture **(see illustration)**.
2 The front door side protective trim strip is removed by carefully pulling it backwards. Slightly open the door before removing the strip.

39.2 Removing the oddments box from the sill panel (Zafira)

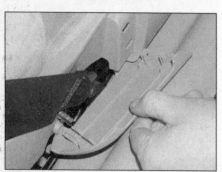

39.3a Unclip the cover from the outside of the front seat . . .

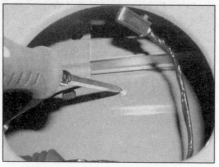

38.1 Undo the retaining screw . . .

3 The rear door side protective trim strip is removed by carefully pulling it forwards **(see illustration)**. Open the front door but leave the rear door closed before removing the strip.

Refitting

4 Refitting is a reversal of removal.

Rear quarter side strip

Removal

5 The side strip is held to the rear quarter panel by clips. Carefully release the strip from the clips.

Refitting

6 Check the condition of the clips and if necessary renew them.
7 Press the side strip onto the clips making sure that they are correctly engaged.

Roof trim strip

Removal

8 With the door open, release the upper rubber weatherstrip from the roof.
9 Undo the screws securing the trim strip to the roof above the door.
10 Release the strip from the rear clips and withdraw it to the rear.

Refitting

11 Refitting is a reversal of removal.

39.3b . . . then undo the screw and detach the seat belt

38.3 . . . and slide the strip from the slots in the door

39 Front seats –
removal and refitting

⚠ *Warning: The seat belt tensioners fitted to the front seat assemblies may cause injury if triggered inadvertently. Before carrying out any work on the front seats, refer to the precautions for airbag systems given in Chapter 12.*

Removal

1 Disconnect the battery negative lead and wait a minimum of 1 minute to allow the airbag system capacitor to discharge (refer to Chapter 12 if necessary).
2 Where necessary to provide additional working room, remove the oddments box from the sill panel by lifting out the padding and unscrewing the retaining screws **(see illustration)**.
3 Carefully unclip the plastic cover from the outside of the seat, then undo the screw and detach the seat belt from the front seat **(see illustrations)**.
4 Adjust the seat fully to the rear, then disconnect the wiring as applicable for the seat belt tensioner, side airbag, heating, and passenger detection as follows. Pull out the red locking pin and release the wiring plug from the seat base. Depress the tab and separate the wiring plug **(see illustration)**.

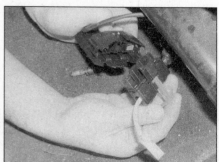

39.4 Disconnecting the seat wiring

5 Unscrew the front mounting bolts securing the seat to the base. The bolts are located on the front of each sliding channel **(see illustration)**.

6 Adjust the seat fully to the front and unscrew the rear mounting bolts securing the seat to the base **(see illustration)**.

7 With the help of an assistant, carefully lift the seat and remove it from inside the vehicle.

8 If necessary, unbolt the seat base from the floor **(see illustrations)**.

Refitting

9 Refitting is a reversal of removal, but apply a little locking fluid to the threads of the bolts before inserting them, and tighten them to the specified torque.

40 Rear seats –
removal and refitting

Cushion

Removal

1 On the split-type rear seat, press in the spring-tensioned pins located at the front of the seat, and release the seat from the pivot brackets. Recover the pins and springs. Lift the seat from the floor and remove from the vehicle.

2 On the non-split-type rear seat, first raise the rear of the cushion, then release the front hooks from the hinge brackets by pressing the cushion down directly over the brackets.

39.5 Unscrewing the front seat front mounting bolts

39.8a Unscrew the mounting bolts . . .

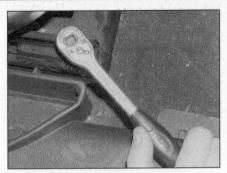

39.6 Unscrewing the front seat rear mounting bolts

39.8b . . . and remove the seat base

Lift the seat from the floor and remove from the vehicle **(see illustrations)**.

Refitting

3 Refitting is a reversal of removal, but make

sure that the seat belt stalks are located on top of the cushion.

Backrest (Astra models)

Removal

4 Remove the rear seat cushion as previously described in this Section.

5 Fold the backrest forwards, then prise out the plastic fasteners and lift the felt flaps from the outer corners of the backrest **(see illustrations)**.

6 Using a Torx key, unscrew and remove the bolts securing the outer hinge brackets to the backrest, then remove the brackets from the body slots **(see illustration)**. If necessary, use a screwdriver to prise the spring tensioned collars from the slots.

7 Unscrew the centre hinge bracket bolts, including the bolts securing the split seats together **(see illustrations)**.

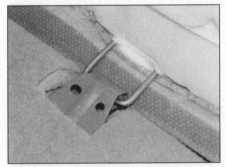

40.2a The non-split rear seat cushion is secured with metal loops . . .

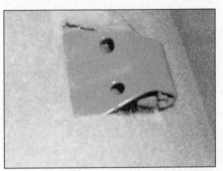

40.2b . . . to hooks

40.5a Prise out the plastic fasteners . . .

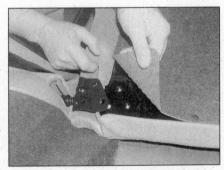

40.5b . . . and lift the felt flaps from the outer corners of the backrest

40.6 Removing the outer hinge brackets from the body slots

40.7a Unscrew the centre hinge bracket bolts . . .

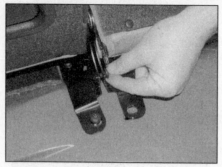

40.7b . . . and the bolts securing the split seats together

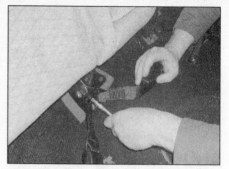

40.8 Unscrewing the front hinge bracket and seat belt stalk bolts

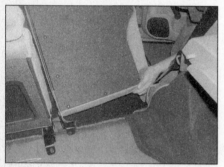

40.9 Removing the backrest from inside the vehicle

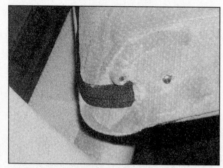

40.10 Removing the armrest from the rear seat backrest

8 Lift the front of the backrest and unscrew the front hinge bracket and seat belt stalk bolts (see illustration).
9 Lift the backrest and withdraw it from inside the vehicle (see illustration).
10 If necessary, the armrest in the backrest may be removed by carefully releasing each side from the housing (see illustration).

Refitting

11 When refitting the backrest, it is easier to assemble the split sections and outer hinge brackets outside of the vehicle. First, fit the brackets to the outer lower corners of the backrest, and tighten the bolts.
12 Assemble the split sections together, then refit the bolts and tighten securely.
13 With the help of an assistant, locate the backrest inside the vehicle with the outer bracket hinge pins resting over the mounting slots in the floor. Press down the backrest

ends so that the spring-tensioned collars engage with the cut-outs in the slots.
14 Refit the seat belt stalk and centre bracket bolts and tighten securely.
15 Secure the felt flaps with the plastic fasteners.
16 Refit the rear seat cushion as previously described in this Section.

Backrest (Zafira models)
Removal

17 Remove the floor covering from the rear luggage compartment.
18 Undo the screws and remove the seat belt lock bracket from the floor.
19 Undo the screws from the centre hinge bracket.
20 Release the rear catch and lift the rear seat backrest from inside the vehicle.

Refitting

21 Refitting is a reversal of removal.

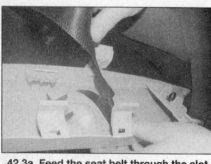

42.3a Feed the seat belt through the slot in the upper trim panel as it is being removed

42.3b Removing the lower trim panel from the B-pillar

41 Front seat belt tensioner – removal and refitting

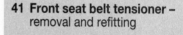

⚠ **Warning:** *The seat belt tensioners fitted to the front seat assemblies may cause injury if triggered inadvertently. Before carrying out any work on the front seats, refer to the precautions for airbag systems given in Chapter 12.*

Removal

1 Disconnect the battery negative lead and wait a minimum of 1 minute to allow the airbag system capacitor to discharge (refer to Chapter 12 if necessary).
2 Remove the front seat as described in Section 39.
3 Release the seat belt tensioner wiring from the base of the seat.
4 Undo the single screw and remove the seat belt tensioner from the front seat.

Refitting

5 Refitting is a reversal of removal, but apply a little locking fluid to the threads before inserting the mounting screw. Tighten the screw to the specified torque.

42 Seat belts – removal and refitting

Front seat belt and reel
Removal

1 Remove the front seat as described in Section 39.
2 Unbolt and remove the belt lower guide rail from the bottom of the B-pillar. Slide the end of the seat belt from the rail.
3 Pull the rubber weatherstrip away from the B-pillar, then ease out the upper and lower trim panels. The panels are retained with clips, and a wide-bladed screwdriver will be necessary to release them, but first make a careful note of how the panels clip into place as it is important they are refitted correctly. Feed the seat belt through the slot in the upper panel as it is being removed (see illustrations).

4 Unscrew the bolt and remove the seat belt upper anchor from the height adjuster **(see illustration)**.

5 If necessary, unclip the outer trim, then undo the screws and remove the height adjuster from the B-pillar **(see illustration)**.

6 Release the belt, then if necessary undo the screw and remove the belt guide from the B-pillar **(see illustration)**.

7 Remove the sill inner trim panels for access to the bottom of the B-pillar **(see illustration)**.

8 On the outside of the B-pillar, prise out the plug for access to the reel mounting nut. A deep socket will be necessary to unscrew the nut as it is located at the end of a pin welded to the pillar. The pin is fitted to prevent loss of the nut, as otherwise it would fall inside the sill panel. Unscrew the nut, then withdraw the reel unit from inside and withdraw it, together with the seat belt **(see illustrations)**.

9 The stalk is attached to the inner side of the seat and is removed by unscrewing the mounting bolt which also secures the tensioner.

Refitting

10 Refitting is a reversal of removal, but apply a little locking fluid to the threads of the mounting bolts/nuts before inserting them and tightening them to the specified torque.

Rear seat belt and reel

Removal

11 Remove the rear quarter inner trim panel (Section 44). This procedure includes unbolting the seat belt lower anchor **(see illustration)**.

42.4 Front seat belt upper anchor and height adjuster

42.5 Unclipping the trim from the outside of the B-pillar

42.6 The belt guide on the B-pillar

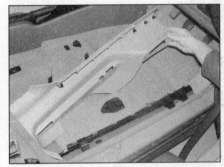
42.7 Removing the sill inner trim panels

12 Unscrew the bolt and remove the upper anchor. On Zafira models it is attached to the height adjuster **(see illustrations)**.

13 On Zafira models, remove the trim and unscrew the bolt securing the seat belt to the lower side panel.

14 On Zafira models, unbolt the guide from the C-pillar and remove it from the seat belt.

42.8a View of the front seat belt reel from inside the vehicle

42.8b Prise out the plug . . .

42.8c . . . for access to the reel retaining nut which is located on a pin

42.8d Unscrewing the front seat belt reel retaining nut

42.11 Unbolting the rear seat belt lower anchor from the body

42.12a Rear seat belt upper anchor and height adjuster (Zafira)

42.12b Rear seat belt upper anchor
(Astra)

42.15a Rear seat belt reel unit
(Zafira)

42.15b Rear seat belt reel unit
(Astra)

42.17 Removing the rear seat belt stalk
(Zafira)

42.18a Apply locking fluid to the threads
of the seat belt mounting bolts before
fitting them . . .

42.18b . . . and tighten the bolts to the
specified torque

15 Unscrew the bolt and remove the reel from the body **(see illustrations)**.

16 On Zafira models, undo the screws and remove the height adjuster from the C-pillar.

17 The stalk can be unbolted after removing the rear seat cushion **(see illustration)**.

Refitting

18 Refitting is a reversal of removal, but apply a little locking fluid to the threads of the mounting bolts/nuts before inserting them and tightening them to the specified torque **(see illustrations)**.

3rd row rear seat belt and reel (Zafira)

Removal

19 Remove the floor covering from the rear luggage compartment.

20 Remove the upper trim panel from the side of the luggage compartment.

21 Prise off the cap and undo the screw securing the anchor to the C-pillar. Also remove the lower anchor **(see illustrations)**.

22 Undo the screws and remove the belt guide from the C-pillar.

23 Remove the lower trim panel from the side of the luggage compartment.

24 Unscrew the mounting bolt and remove the seat belt reel unit from the side panel **(see illustration)**.

25 The stalk can be removed after removing the centre trim **(see illustration)**.

42.18c Refitting the central seat belt stalk

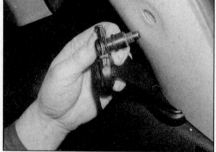

42.21a Removing the 3rd row seat belt
upper anchor

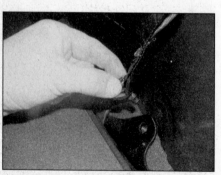

42.21b Removing the 3rd row seat belt
lower anchor

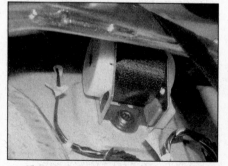

42.24 3rd row rear seat belt reel unit

42.25 Removing the 3rd row rear seat belt
stalk

Refitting

26 Refitting is a reversal of removal, but apply a little locking fluid to the threads of the mounting bolt before inserting it and tightening it to the specified torque.

3rd row rear centre seat belt (Zafira)

Removal

27 Remove the rear seat cushion and backrest as described in Section 40.
28 Undo the screws and remove the cover for access to the centre seat belt stalks.
29 Undo the bolts and remove the stalks from the floor.
30 Disconnect the cable from the reel, then unbolt the reel from the backrest.

Refitting

31 Refitting is a reversal of removal, but tighten the mounting bolts to the specified torque.

43 Seat belt height adjuster – removal and refitting

Front

Removal

1 Remove the B-pillar upper trim panel, as described in Section 44.
2 Remove the two Torx type securing bolts, and withdraw the height adjuster assembly from the B-pillar.

Refitting

3 Refitting is a reversal of removal, but ensure that the height adjuster is fitted the correct way up. The top of the adjuster is marked with two arrows, which should point towards the vehicle roof.

Rear

General

4 The procedure is as described for the front seat belt height adjuster, but for access to the height adjuster, remove the rear quarter trim panel (see Section 44) instead of the B-pillar trim panel.

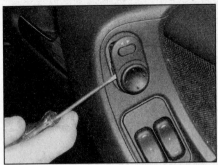

44.2a Ease the electric exterior mirror switch from the door interior trim panel . . .

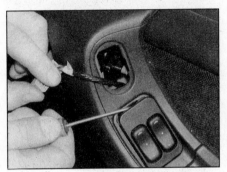

44.2c Ease out the electric window switch . . .

44 Inner trim panels – removal and refitting

> **Warning: Before carrying out any work in the vicinity of the front seats, refer to the precautions for airbag systems given in Chapter 12.**

Front door

Removal

1 Disconnect the battery negative lead and wait a minimum of 1 minute before proceeding. This will allow time for the airbag system capacitor to discharge.
2 On models with electrical exterior mirrors, carefully prise out the control switch from the trim panel and disconnect the wiring. Similarly, on models with electric front

44.2b . . . then disconnect the wiring plug

44.2d . . . and disconnect the wiring plug

window winders, remove the window control switch (see illustrations).
3 On models with manually-operated windows, release the securing clip, and remove the window regulator handle. To release the securing clip, insert a length of wire with a hooked end between the handle and the trim bezel on the door trim panel, and manipulate it to free the securing clip from the handle. Take care not to damage the door trim panel. Recover the trim bezel.
4 Pull off the knob rubber gaiter, then carefully prise the trim panel for the exterior door mirror from the inside of the door. Where the 'tweeter' loudspeaker is located in the mirror trim panel, disconnect the wiring. Where the 'tweeter' loudspeaker is located in the door inner trim panel, prise it out and disconnect the wiring (see illustrations).
5 On Astra models, carefully prise the cover from the inner door handle (see illustrations).

44.4a Pull off the rubber gaiter . . .

44.4b . . . then prise off the cover . . .

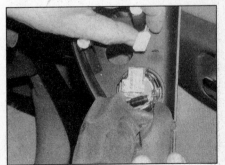

44.4c . . . and disconnect the wiring from the 'tweeter'

44.4d Where the 'tweeter' loudspeaker is located in the door inner trim panel, prise it out . . .

44.4e . . . and disconnect the wiring

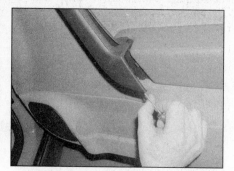

44.5a Use a screwdriver to carefully release the inner door handle cover . . .

44.5b . . . then remove it from the panel

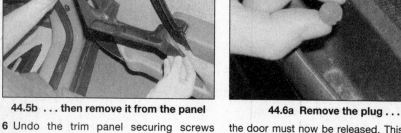

44.6a Remove the plug . . .

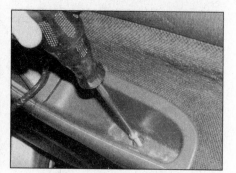

44.6b . . . undo the screw . . .

6 Undo the trim panel securing screws located on the lower edge of the panel. On some models one of the screws is located behind the grip, which can be removed by prising out the plug and unscrewing the retaining screw (see illustrations).

7 The plastic clips securing the trim panel to

the door must now be released. This can be done using a screwdriver, but it is preferable to use a forked tool, to minimise the possibility of damage to the trim panel and the clips. The clips are located around the outer edge of the trim panel and if necessary a piece of card or cloth may be used to protect

the door paintwork (see illustrations).

8 With the clips released, disconnect the cable from the inner door handle located in the trim panel. Unhook the top of the panel and withdraw it from the vehicle (see illustrations).

9 The plastic insulating sheet can be peeled

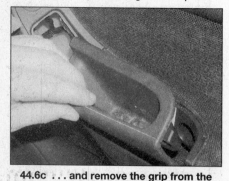

44.6c . . . and remove the grip from the door inner trim panel

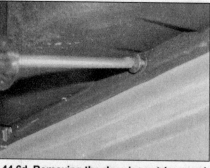

44.6d Removing the door inner trim panel retaining screws

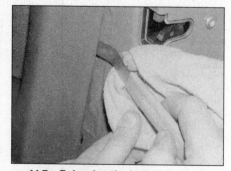

44.7a Releasing the inner trim panel retaining clips

44.7b Removing the trim panel from the door

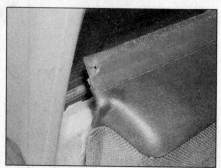

44.8a Unhook the top of the trim panel . . .

44.8b . . . and disconnect the cable from the inner door handle located in the trim panel

44.9 Peeling the plastic insulating sheet from the front door

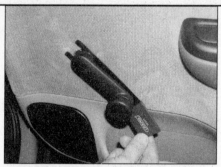

44.13a Using a special forked tool to release the window regulator handle securing clip

44.13b Removing the window regulator handle and trim bezel

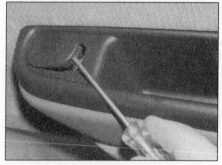

44.14a Prise out the cover . . .

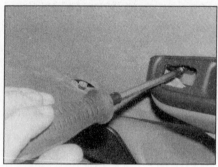

44.14b . . . then undo the front screw . . .

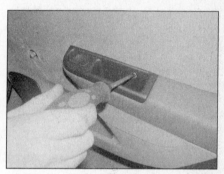

44.14c . . . and rear screw securing the pocket in the trim panel

from the door. Peel the sheet back slowly to prevent damage to the sealant, and take care not to damage the sheet **(see illustration)**.

Refitting

10 Refitting is a reversal of removal, but if necessary renew any broken plastic retaining clips. If the plastic insulating sheet has been removed from the door, make sure that it is refitted intact, and securely fixed to the door.

Rear door

Removal

11 Disconnect the battery negative lead and wait a minimum of 1 minute before proceeding. This will allow time for the airbag system capacitor to discharge.

12 On models with electric rear window winders, remove the window control switch by prising it out of the panel with a screwdriver and disconnecting the wiring. Note that on certain models the switch is retained with screws.

13 On models with manually-operated windows, release the securing clip, and remove the window regulator handle. To release the securing clip, either use a special forked tool, or insert a length of wire with a hooked end between the handle and the trim bezel on the door trim panel, and manipulate it to free the securing clip from the handle. Take care not to damage the door trim panel. Recover the trim bezel **(see illustrations)**.

14 Where applicable, prise out the plastic cover, then undo the screws and remove the pocket from the trim panel **(see illustrations)**.

15 Unclip and remove the ashtray, then, where necessary, unclip and remove the tweeter grille **(see illustration)**.

16 Undo the trim panel securing screws located on the lower edge of the panel **(see illustration)**.

17 The plastic clips securing the trim panel to the door must now be released. This can be done using a screwdriver, but it is preferable to use a forked tool, to minimise the possibility of damage to the trim panel and the clips. The clips are located around the outer edge of the trim panel.

18 With the clips released, disconnect the inner door handle cables and the tweeter wiring and withdraw the panel from the vehicle **(see illustrations)**.

19 The plastic insulating sheet can be peeled from the door, but remove the operating cable and locking knob link. Peel the sheet back slowly to prevent damage to the sealant, and take care not to damage the sheet **(see illustrations)**.

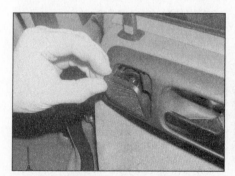

44.15 Removing the tweeter grille

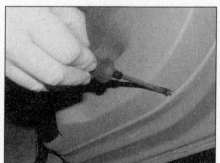

44.16 Removing the door inner trim panel securing screws

44.18a Release the rear door handle outer cable . . .

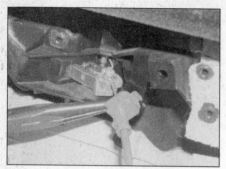

44.18b . . . and inner cable

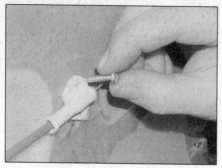

44.19a Undo the screws . . .

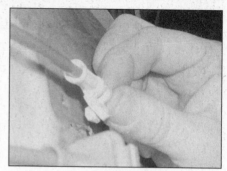

44.19b . . . and remove the operating cable . . .

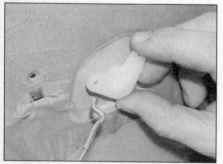

44.19c . . . and locking knob link . . .

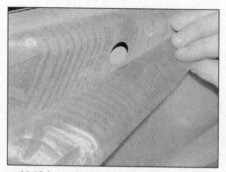

44.19d . . . then slowly peel the plastic insulating sheet from the door inner panel

44.27 Removing the rubber weatherstrips from the body aperture

Refitting

20 Refitting is a reversal of removal, but if necessary renew any broken plastic retaining clips. If the plastic insulating sheet has been removed from the door, make sure that it is refitted intact, and securely fixed to the door.

Tailgate

Removal

21 With the tailgate open, prise out the plastic covers, undo the screws, and remove the lower and upper trim panels from the inside of the tailgate. Note that the lower panel has extensions which slot into the upper panels.
22 Release the clips and remove the high-level stop-light.

Refitting

23 Refitting is a reversal of removal.

Rear quarter panel (Coupe models)

Removal

24 Remove the rear seat backrest as described in Section 40.
25 Using a wide-blade screwdriver, carefully prise the rear quarter panel from the body. Take care not to break the plastic clips.

Refitting

26 Refitting is a reversal of removal.

Rear quarter panel (Hatchback models)

Removal

27 With the tailgate and rear door open, prise the rubber weatherstrips from the body aperture in the vicinity of the rear quarter

panel and rear valance panel **(see illustration)**. Also remove the rear shelf.
28 Remove the rear door inner sill trim on the relevant side **(see illustration)**.
29 Remove the rear seat cushion (Section 40), then fold the rear seat backrest forwards.
30 Undo the screws and remove the plastic trim from the rear valance **(see illustration)**.
31 Prise out the plastic covers and undo the screws securing the upper rear quarter trim to the body **(see illustrations)**.
32 Unscrew the rear seat belt lower anchor bolt and remove the seat belt from the floor.
33 Unclip the upper rear quarter trim and feed the rear seat belt through the hole in the trim **(see illustrations)**.
34 Remove the rear seat backrest rubber buffer, then unclip and remove the lower rear quarter trim **(see illustrations)**.

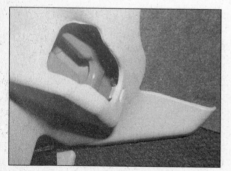

44.28 Rear door inner sill trim

44.30 Removing the plastic trim from the rear valance

44.31a Prise out the plastic covers . . .

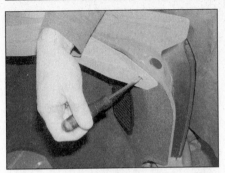

44.31b . . . and undo the screws securing the upper rear quarter trim

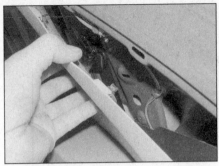

44.33a Unclip the upper rear quarter trim . . .

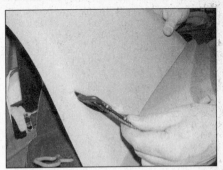

44.33b . . . and feed the rear seat belt through the hole in the trim

44.34a Remove the rear seat backrest rubber buffer . . .

44.34b . . . release the clips . . .

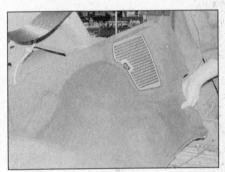

44.34c . . . and remove the lower rear quarter trim

Refitting

35 Refitting is a reversal of removal. Use a block of wood and a mallet to tap the rubber weatherstrip fully onto the body flange.

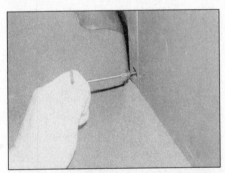

44.40 Undo the screws securing the lower trim panel to the side of the heater

C-pillar (Coupe models)

Removal

36 Remove the rear quarter panel as described above.
37 Undo the retaining screws.
38 Using a wide-blade screwdriver, carefully prise the panel from the body. Take care not to break the plastic clips.

Refitting

39 Refitting is a reversal of removal.

Facia lower trim panels

Removal

40 The facia lower trim panels are fitted to the driver and passenger footwells. To remove

either, first undo the screws securing the panel to the side of the heater (see illustration).
41 Undo the outer screws and withdraw the lower trim panel from under the facia (see illustrations).

Refitting

42 Refitting is a reversal of removal.

Other inner trim panels

Removal and refitting

43 Most small trim panels are secured with plastic clips which can easily be broken on removal. Always try to lever out the clips by inserting a forked tool directly beneath them, rather than levering out the panel.

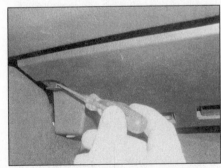

44.41a Undo the lower trim panel outer screws

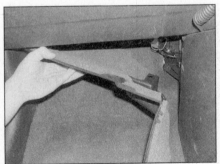

44.41b Removing the lower trim panel from the passenger's side footwell

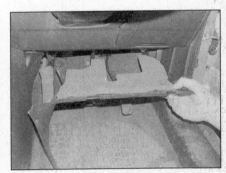

44.41c Removing the lower trim panel from the driver's side footwell

45.2 Removing the central cover from under the handbrake lever

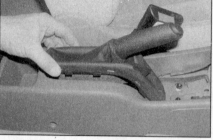

45.3 Removing the handbrake lever gaiter from the centre console

45.4 Removing the gear lever gaiter from the centre console

45 Centre console –
removal and refitting

Removal

1 Disconnect the battery negative lead with reference to Chapter 5A.
2 Prise out the central cover from under the handbrake lever **(see illustration)**.
3 Prise the handbrake lever gaiter from the centre console. Make sure that the handbrake is applied **(see illustration)**.
4 Prise the gear lever gaiter from the centre console **(see illustration)**.
5 On automatic transmission models, remove the selector lever cover (see Chapter 7B).
6 At the front of the console, carefully lever out the seat heating switch panel using a screwdriver.

7 On models with a TC (Traction Control) switch, prise out the switch.
8 Unclip the panel then undo the screws and remove the ashtray from the front of the console. Disconnect the wiring for the cigarette lighter **(see illustrations)**.

9 Prise out the covers where necessary then undo the mounting screws. There are two screws on each side of the console, one screw located beneath the handbrake lever, and one screw located at the front of the console **(see illustrations)**.

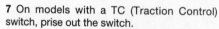
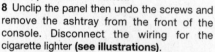
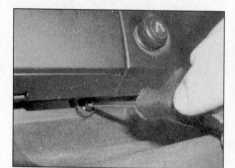

45.8a Undo the screw . . .

45.8b . . . remove the ashtray . . .

45.8c . . . and disconnect the wiring for the cigarette lighter (Zafira)

45.8d Removing the ashtray . . .

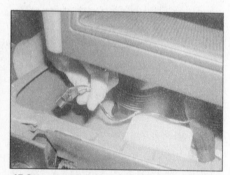

45.8e . . . and disconnecting the wiring for the cigarette lighter (Astra)

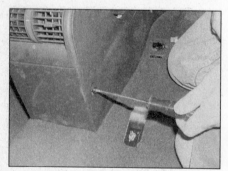

45.9a Undo the rear screws . . .

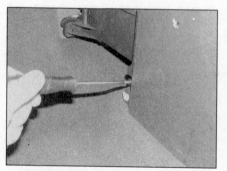

45.9b . . . front screws . . .

45.9c . . . central screw . . .

45.9d ... and front screw

45.10 Removing the central console

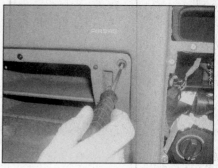

46.1a Remove the glovebox upper mounting screws ...

10 Lift the central console from the floor and withdraw it through a door aperture **(see illustration)**.

Refitting

11 Refitting is a reversal of removal.

46 Glovebox – removal and refitting

Removal

1 With the glovebox open, unscrew the three upper and three lower screws securing it to the facia panel **(see illustrations)**.
2 Pull out the glovebox a little way and disconnect the wiring from the illumination light **(see illustration)**. On models with a CD changer or navigation control, disconnect the wiring/aerial from the respective unit.
3 Withdraw the glovebox from the facia and remove from inside the vehicle.
4 If necessary, remove the lid from the glovebox by driving out the hinge pins.
5 Where applicable, remove the CD changer or navigation control unit from the glovebox with reference to Chapter 12.

Refitting

6 Refitting is a reversal of removal. If a new glovebox is being fitted, transfer the self-adhesive cushions and interior light/CD changer/navigation control unit from the old unit.

46.1b ... and lower mounting screws ...

47 Facia panel – removal and refitting

⚠ *Warning: Working in the vicinity of airbags is potentially dangerous. Refer to the precautions for airbag systems given in Chapter 12.*

Astra models

Removal

1 Disconnect the battery negative lead and wait a minimum of 1 minute to allow the airbag system capacitor to discharge (refer to Chapter 12 if necessary).
2 Remove the centre console and ashtray, as described in Section 45.

46.2 ... then disconnect the wiring from the illumination light

3 Remove the storage compartment from the facia. To do this, remove the mat then use a screwdriver to release the upper and lower clips, and withdraw the compartment **(see illustrations)**.
4 Remove the radio and mounting box as described in Chapter 12. On models with a navigation system, remove the system unit with reference to Chapter 12.
5 Working through the apertures in the surround panel, release the clips securing the heater controls and separate the control panel **(see illustration)**.
6 Undo the lower screws and carefully prise the surround panel from the facia, then reach up and disconnect the wiring from the multi-function display unit. Remove the hazard warning switch (Chapter 12, Section 4) then disconnect the wiring socket by sliding it

47.3a Remove the mat ...

47.3b ... then release the clips with a screwdriver ...

47.3c ... and remove the storage compartment

47.5 Releasing the heater controls from the rear of the surround panel

47.6a Undo the lower screws . . .

47.6b . . . release the surround panel from the facia clips . . .

down from the surround panel. If necessary, undo the screws and remove the multi-function display unit from the panel **(see illustrations)**.

7 Remove the light switch located on the driver's side of the facia with reference to Chapter 12, Section 4, then undo the screws and remove the side vent and switch surround from the facia. The screws are accessed by pressing down the vent past its stop until the screws are visible through the grille. If the vent is tight, access the screws through the vent grille for removal, then release the side clips and turn the vent before refitting **(see illustrations)**. Withdraw the vent from the facia and recover the screws.

8 Disconnect the wiring socket from the light switch surround and remove downwards **(see illustrations)**.

9 Remove the glovebox as described in Section 46.

10 Press down the passenger vent past its stop, until the vent securing screws are visible through the grille. Undo the screws, then unscrew the lower mounting bolt and withdraw the vent from the facia **(see illustrations)**.

11 Reach through the glovebox location and disconnect the wiring from the passenger airbag. Take care not to damage the wiring or terminals.

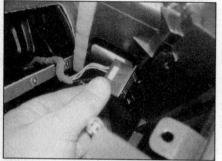

47.6c . . . slide the hazard warning switch wiring socket from the panel . . .

47.6d . . . and disconnect the wiring from the multi-info display unit

47.7a Undo the lower screw . . .

47.7b . . . and upper screws, to remove the switch surround

47.7c Turning the vent past its stop . . .

47.7d . . . before refitting

47.8a Release the clip . . .

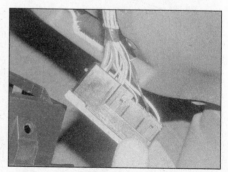

47.8b . . . and withdraw the socket from the surround

47.10a Undo the screws . . .

47.10b . . . and remove the passenger vent

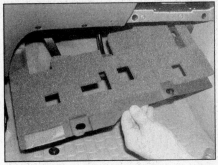

47.12 Removing the trim panel from under the facia on the driver's side

12 Remove the steering wheel as described in Chapter 10, then remove the trim panel from under the facia on the driver's side **(see illustration)**.

13 Undo the screws and remove the upper and lower shrouds from the steering column.

14 Remove the indicator switch and wiper switch as described in Chapter 12, Section 4.

15 Remove the instrument panel as described in Chapter 12.

16 Remove driver's side storage compartment, then undo the four fasteners and remove the compartment **(see illustrations)**.

17 For improved working room, remove both front seats as described in Section 39.

18 Carefully prise the inner trim panels from the sills, then undo the screws and release the footwell side trim panels **(see illustrations)**.

19 Note the location of the wiring loom on the rear of the facia panel, then disconnect it **(see illustration)**.

20 On the passenger side of the facia, remove the trim from under the facia, then remove the fasteners and remove the footwell air duct **(see illustrations)**.

21 Unclip the windscreen air duct panel from

the facia **(see illustration)**.

22 At the front of the facia below the windscreen, undo and remove the three screws securing the facia to the bulkhead, then unscrew the remaining screws at the

47.16a Remove the driver's side storage compartment . . .

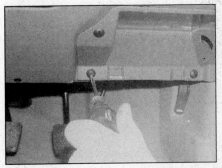

47.16b . . . then undo the screws . . .

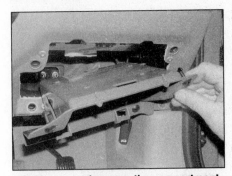

47.16c . . . and remove the compartment from the facia

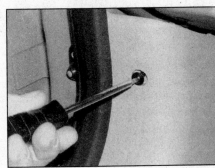

47.18a Undo the screws . . .

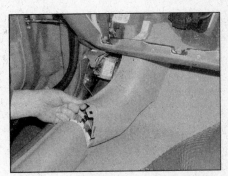

47.18b . . . and remove the footwell side trim panels

47.19 Disconnecting the wiring from the rear of the facia

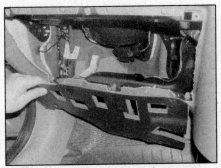

47.20a Remove the facia lower trim panel . . .

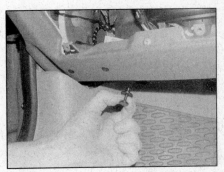

47.20b . . . then remove the fasteners . . .

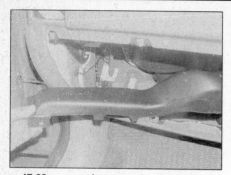

47.20c . . . and remove the footwell air duct

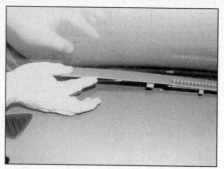

47.21 Removing the windscreen air duct panel

47.22a Front facia securing screws

sides and on the bulkhead. The side screws are beneath plastic covers **(see illustrations)**.
23 Check that all wiring has been disconnected from the facia components. Note the routing of the wiring to aid refitting.
24 With the help of an assistant, carefully ease the facia from the bulkhead and remove it from inside the vehicle. Take particular care not to damage the facia in the area around the steering column.

Refitting

25 Refitting is a reversal of removal, but make sure that the wiring is routed correctly and connected to the various components as noted during removal. Refer to Chapter 3, Section 10, for information on refitting the side vents.

Zafira models

Removal

26 Disconnect the battery negative lead and wait a minimum of 1 minute to allow the airbag system capacitor to discharge (refer to Chapter 12 if necessary).
27 Remove the centre console and ashtray, as described in Section 45.
28 Remove the heater control panel as described in Chapter 3, Section 10.
29 Remove the steering wheel as described in Chapter 10.
30 Remove the indicator and wiper switches as described in Chapter 12, Section 4.
31 Remove the ignition switch as described in Chapter 12, Section 4.
32 Remove the radio and mounting box as

described in Chapter 12. On models with a navigation system, remove the system unit with reference to Chapter 12.
33 Using a small screwdriver, release the clip and remove the control knob from the light switch. Insert the screwdriver through the hole in the bottom of the knob **(see illustration)**.
34 Insert two small screwdrivers in the holes located on the edge of the control knob aperture in order to release the clips, then withdraw the light switch from the facia **(see illustration)**. Note that the wiring plug remains in the facia.
35 Unclip and remove the fusebox cover.
36 Unclip the upper air vent grille from the outer end of the facia, then unscrew the instrument panel surround securing screws **(see illustrations)**. There are three screws

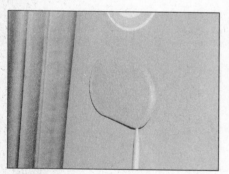

47.22b Prise off the plastic covers . . .

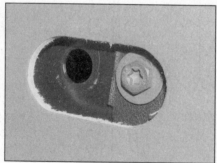

47.22c . . . for access to the side screws

47.33 Use a small screwdriver to release the control knob from the light switch

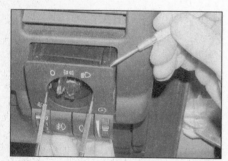

47.34 Using two small screwdrivers to release the clips when removing the light switch from the facia

47.36a Unclip and remove the upper air vent . . .

47.36b . . . then undo the surround mounting screws

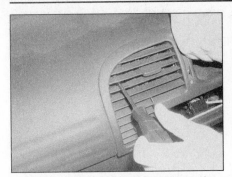

47.36c The inner screw is accessed through the air vent grille

47.36d Unscrewing the surround upper retaining screws

47.37a Withdraw the surround . . .

located above the instrument panel, one screw in the upper outer corner, one screw inside the grille of the upper inner corner, and four screws on the lower edge.

37 Withdraw the surround from the facia and disconnect the wiring **(see illustrations)**.

38 Remove the instrument panel with reference to Chapter 12. Also detach the wiring plug **(see illustration)**.

39 Unscrew the nut and screw securing the fusebox, then release the wiring plug from the retainer inside the instrument panel aperture, and release the plastic tie. Withdraw the fusebox and position it to one side **(see illustrations)**.

40 Using a wide-bladed screwdriver, carefully prise the windscreen trim panel from the front of the facia **(see illustrations)**.

41 Prise out the plastic plugs, then undo the screws and remove the vertical trim panels

47.37b . . . and disconnect the wiring

from the A-pillars. Also remove the outer panels from each side of the facia **(see illustrations)**.

42 Remove the front sill panels from each

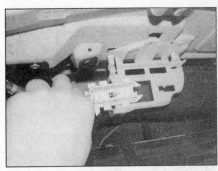

47.38 Releasing the wiring plug from the facia

side, then remove the lower trim panels from the A-pillars **(see illustration)**.

43 Remove the glovebox as described in Section 46.

47.39a Unscrew the nut and screw . . .

47.39b . . . and withdraw the fusebox from the facia

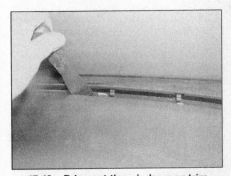

47.40a Prise out the windscreen trim panel . . .

47.40b . . . and remove it from the front of the facia

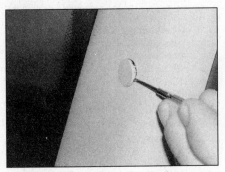

47.41a Prise out the plastic plugs . . .

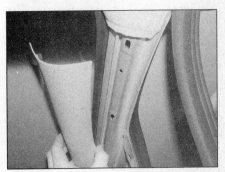

47.41b . . . and remove the vertical trim panels from the A-pillars . . .

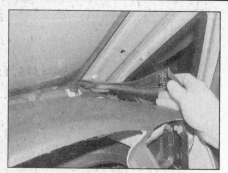

47.41c ... then prise out and remove the facia outer panels

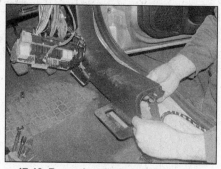

47.42 Removing the lower trim panels from the A-pillars

47.44a Pull out the passenger's side air vent ...

44 Pull out the air vent from the passenger's side of the facia, then undo the screws and withdraw the air vent **(see illustrations)**.

45 Remove the trim panels from under facia by releasing the fasteners, then remove the heater air ducts from both sides **(see illustration)**.

46 Note the routing and location of the wiring plugs on the facia, then disconnect them.

47 Unscrew the facia mounting screws, noting that access to the end screws is gained by prising out the covers **(see illustrations)**. Also pull out the rubber weatherstrip from the A-pillars on both sides in the area by the facia.

48 With the help of an assistant, carefully ease the facia from the bulkhead and remove it from inside the vehicle **(see illustration)**.

Take particular care not to damage the facia in the area around the steering column.

Refitting

49 Refitting is a reversal of removal, but make sure that the wiring is routed correctly and connected to the various components as noted during removal.

47.44b ... then undo the screws ...

47.44c ... and withdraw the air vent

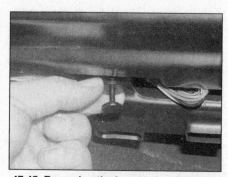

47.45 Removing the heater air ducts from under the facia

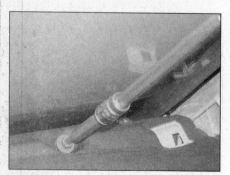

47.47a Unscrewing the facia front mounting screws

47.47b Prise out the side covers for access to the side mounting screws

47.48 Removing the facia from inside the vehicle

Chapter 12
Body electrical systems

Contents

Airbag system – general information, precautions and system de-
activation 23
Airbag system components – removal and refitting 24
Anti-theft alarm system and engine immobiliser – general
information 21
Bulbs (exterior lights) – renewal 5
Bulbs (interior lights) – renewal 6
Cigarette lighter – removal and refitting 11
Electrical fault finding – general information 2
Exterior light units – removal and refitting 7
Fuses and relays – general information 3
General information and precautions 1
Handbrake warning switch .... Refer to Chapter 9
Headlight beam alignment – general information 8
Heater blower switch .... Refer to Chapter 3

Horn – removal and refitting 12
Instrument panel – removal and refitting 9
Loudspeakers – removal and refitting 19
Multi-function display unit and components – removal and refitting 10
Radio aerial – removal and refitting 20
Radio remote control switches – removal and refitting 18
Radio/cassette/CD player/navigation units – removal and refitting . 17
Reversing light switch .... Refer to Chapter 7A
Speedometer sensor – general information 22
Switches – removal and refitting 4
Tailgate wiper motor – removal and refitting 15
Windscreen wiper motor and linkage – removal and refitting 14
Windscreen/tailgate/headlight washer system components –
removal and refitting 16
Wiper arm – removal and refitting 13

Degrees of difficulty

Easy, suitable for novice with little experience	**Fairly easy,** suitable for beginner with some experience	**Fairly difficult,** suitable for competent DIY mechanic	**Difficult,** suitable for experienced DIY mechanic 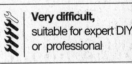	**Very difficult,** suitable for expert DIY or professional

Specifications

System type .... 12-volt, negative earth

Fuses .... See *Wiring diagrams*

Bulbs   **Wattage**
Headlights:
  Main beam H4 60
  Dipped beam H4 55
Sidelights 5
Front and rear direction indicators 21
Direction indicator side repeaters 5
Tail/stop-lights 21/4
Reversing lights 21
Rear foglights 21
Number plate light 10
Interior light and map-reading lights 10
Glovebox lighting 10
Cigar lighter illumination 0.5
Instrument panel warning lights:
  Headlight High Beam 1.1
  Foglight 1.1
  Instrument illumination 1.5
  LCD illumination 1.5
  Trailer direction indicators 1.1
  Charge warning light 3
Switch illumination 1.2

Note: *Actual electrical equipment fitted will vary according to the vehicle model and trim level. Refer to the vehicle's owner's handbook or check with the spares department of an authorised Vauxhall dealer for details of the bulbs used.*

Torque wrench settings

	Nm	lbf ft
Airbag control unit	10	7
Airbag unit to steering wheel	8	6
Oil level sensor to sump	8	6
Passenger airbag brackets	22	16
Passenger airbag to bracket	5	4
Radio aerial to roof	7	5
Side airbag to seat backrest	5	4
Steering wheel to column	25	18
Tailgate wiper motor	9	7
Windscreen wiper motor linkage	14	10

1 General information and precautions

⚠ **Warning: Before carrying out any work on the electrical system, read through the precautions given in 'Safety first!' at the beginning of this manual, and in Chapter 5A.**

1 The electrical system is of 12-volt negative earth type. Power for the lights and all electrical accessories is supplied by a lead-acid type battery, which is charged by the alternator.

2 This Chapter covers repair and service procedures for the various electrical components not associated with the engine. Information on the battery, alternator and starter motor can be found in Chapter 5A.

3 It should be noted that, before working on any component in the electrical system, the battery negative terminal should first be disconnected, to prevent the possibility of electrical short-circuits and/or fires. On models fitted with an alarm system, the battery must be disconnected within 15 seconds of switching off the ignition, otherwise the alarm will be activated (the alarm has a temporary independent electrical supply).

4 At regular intervals, carefully check the routing of the wiring harness, ensuring that it is correctly secured by the clips or ties provided so that it cannot chafe against other components. If evidence is found of the harness having chafed against other components, repair the damage and ensure that the harness is secured or protected so that the problem cannot occur again.

Caution: If the radio/cassette player fitted to the vehicle is one with an anti-theft security code, refer to 'Disconnecting the battery' in the Reference Section of this manual before disconnecting the battery.

2 Electrical fault finding – general information

Note: *Refer to the precautions given in 'Safety first!' (at the beginning of this manual) and to Section 1 of this Chapter before starting work. The following tests relate to testing of the main electrical circuits, and should not be used to test delicate electronic circuits (such as anti-lock braking systems), particularly where an electronic control module is used.*

General

1 A typical electrical circuit consists of an electrical component, any switches, relays, motors, fuses, fusible links or circuit breakers related to that component, and the wiring and connectors that link the component to both the battery and the chassis. To help to pinpoint a problem in an electrical circuit, wiring diagrams are included at the end of this chapter.

2 Before attempting to diagnose an electrical fault, first study the appropriate wiring diagram to obtain a complete understanding of the components included in the particular circuit concerned. The possible sources of a fault can be narrowed down by noting whether other components related to the circuit are operating properly. If several components or circuits fail at one time, the problem is likely to be related to a shared fuse or earth connection.

3 Electrical problems usually stem from simple causes, such as loose or corroded connections, a faulty earth connection, a blown fuse, a melted fusible link, or a faulty relay (refer to Section 3 for details of testing relays). Visually inspect the condition of all fuses, wires and connections in a problem circuit before testing the components. Use the wiring diagrams to determine which terminal connections will need to be checked, to pinpoint the trouble-spot.

4 The basic tools required for electrical fault-finding include the following:

a) a circuit tester or voltmeter (a 12-volt bulb with a set of test leads can also be used for certain tests).

b) a self-powered test light (sometimes known as a continuity tester).

c) an ohmmeter (to measure resistance).

d) a battery.

e) a set of test leads.

f) a jumper wire, preferably with a circuit breaker or fuse incorporated, which can be used to bypass suspect wires or electrical components.

Before attempting to locate a problem with test instruments, use the wiring diagram to determine where to make the connections.

5 To find the source of an intermittent wiring fault (usually due to a poor or dirty connection, or damaged wiring insulation), a 'wiggle' test can be performed on the wiring. This involves wiggling the wiring by hand, to see if the fault occurs as the wiring is moved. It should be possible to narrow down the source of the fault to a particular section of wiring. This method of testing can be used in conjunction with any of the tests described in the following sub-Sections.

6 Apart from problems due to poor connections, two basic types of fault can occur in an electrical circuit – open-circuit and short-circuit.

7 Open-circuit faults are caused by a break somewhere in the circuit, which prevents current from flowing. An open-circuit fault will prevent a component from working, but will not cause the relevant circuit fuse to blow.

8 Short-circuit faults are caused by a 'short' somewhere in the circuit, which allows the current flowing in the circuit to 'escape' along an alternative route, usually to earth. Short-circuit faults are normally caused by a breakdown in wiring insulation, which allows a feed wire to touch either another wire, or an earthed component such as the bodyshell. A short-circuit fault will normally cause the relevant circuit fuse to blow.

Finding an open-circuit

9 To check for an open-circuit, connect one lead of a circuit tester or voltmeter to either the negative battery terminal or a known good earth.

10 Connect the other lead to a connector in the circuit being tested, preferably nearest to the battery or fuse.

11 Switch on the circuit, remembering that some circuits are live only when the ignition switch is moved to a particular position.

12 If voltage is present (indicated either by the tester bulb lighting or a voltmeter reading, as applicable), this means that the section of the circuit between the relevant connector and the battery is problem-free.

13 Continue to check the remainder of the circuit in the same fashion.

14 When a point is reached at which no voltage is present, the problem must lie between that point and the previous test point with voltage. Most problems can be traced to a broken, corroded or loose connection.

Finding a short-circuit

15 To check for a short-circuit, first disconnect the load(s) from the circuit (loads are the components that draw current from a circuit, such as bulbs, motors, heating elements, etc).

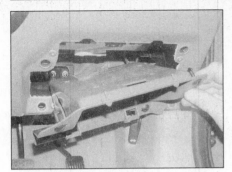

3.2a Remove the storage compartment and frame . . .

3.2b . . . then pull out the bottom of the fusebox

3.3 The fuse positions are marked on the back of the storage compartment

16 Remove the relevant fuse from the circuit, and connect a circuit tester or voltmeter to the fuse connections.

17 Switch on the circuit, remembering that some circuits are live only when the ignition switch is moved to a particular position.

18 If voltage is present (indicated either by the tester bulb lighting or a voltmeter reading, as applicable), this means that there is a short-circuit.

19 If no voltage is present, but the fuse still blows with the load(s) connected, this indicates an internal fault in the load(s).

Finding an earth fault

20 The battery negative terminal is connected to 'earth' (the metal of the engine/transmission and the car body), and most systems are wired so that they only receive a positive feed. The current returning through the metal of the car body. This means that the component mounting and the body form part of that circuit. Loose or corroded mountings can therefore cause a range of electrical faults, ranging from total failure of a circuit, to a puzzling partial fault. In particular, lights may shine dimly (especially when another circuit sharing the same earth point is in operation). Motors (eg, wiper motors or the radiator cooling fan motor) may run slowly, and the operation of one circuit may have an affect on another. Note that on many vehicles, earth straps are used between certain components, such as the engine/transmission and the body, usually where there is no metal-to-metal contact between components, due to flexible rubber mountings, etc.

21 To check whether a component is properly earthed, disconnect the battery, and connect one lead of an ohmmeter to a known good earth point. Connect the other lead to the wire or earth connection being tested. The resistance reading should be zero; if not, check the connection as follows.

22 If an earth connection is thought to be faulty, dismantle the connection, and clean back to bare metal both the bodyshell and the wire terminal or the component earth connection mating surface. Be careful to remove all traces of dirt and corrosion, then use a knife to trim away any paint, so that a clean metal-to-metal joint is made. On

reassembly, tighten the joint fasteners securely; if a wire terminal is being refitted, use serrated washers between the terminal and the bodyshell, to ensure a clean and secure connection. When the connection is remade, prevent the onset of corrosion in the future by applying a coat of petroleum jelly or silicone-based grease.

3 Fuses and relays – general information

Fuses

1 Fuses are designed to break a circuit when a predetermined current is reached, to protect the components and wiring which could be damaged by excessive current flow. Any excessive current flow will be due to a fault in the circuit, usually a short-circuit (see Section 2).

2 The main fuses and relays are located on the driver's end of the facia. On Astra models they are behind the storage compartment, and access is gained by opening the compartment and pressing in the sides of the tray in order to remove it from the compartment housing, then undoing the screws and withdrawing the housing and pulling out the bottom of the fusebox **(see illustrations)**. On Zafira models access is gained by pulling out the bottom of the cover, then lowering it from the facia. Additional

engine-related fuses are located in the left-hand side of the engine compartment.

3 The circuits protected by the various fuses and relays are marked on the inside of the compartment housing on Astra models **(see illustration)**, or on the inside of the cover on Zafira models.

4 A blown fuse can be recognised from its melted or broken wire.

5 To remove a fuse, first ensure that the relevant circuit is switched off. Then pull the relevant fuse from the panel using the tweezers supplied **(see illustrations)**.

6 Before renewing a blown fuse, trace and rectify the cause, and always use a fuse of the correct rating. Never substitute a fuse of a higher rating, or make temporary repairs using wire or metal foil, as more serious damage or even fire could result.

7 Spare fuses are generally provided in the blank terminal positions in the fusebox.

8 Note that the fuses are colour-coded.

Relays

9 A relay is an electrically-operated switch, which is used for the following reasons:

a) A relay can switch a heavy current remotely from the circuit in which the control current is flowing, allowing the use of lighter-gauge wiring and control switch contacts.

b) A relay can receive more than one control input, unlike a mechanical switch.

c) A relay can have a timer function.

10 The main relays are located on the main fusebox, although some engine-related relays

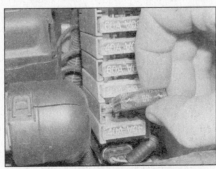

3.5a Removing a fuse from the fusebox located in the left-hand side of the engine compartment (Zafira)

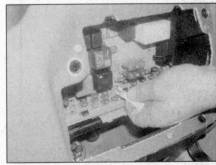

3.5b Removing a fuse from the fusebox (Astra)

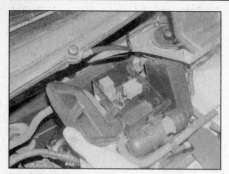

3.10 Engine-related relays located on the left-hand side of the engine compartment (Zafira)

3.12 Removing a relay from the fusebox

are located in a box on the left-hand side of the engine compartment **(see illustration)**.

11 If a circuit or system controlled by a relay develops a fault, and the relay is suspect, operate the system. If the relay is functioning, it should be possible to hear it 'click' as it is energised. If this is the case, the fault lies with the components or wiring of the system. If the relay is not being energised, then either the relay is not receiving a main supply or a switching voltage, or the relay itself is faulty. Testing is by the substitution of a known good unit, but be careful – while some relays are identical in appearance and in operation, others look similar but perform different functions.

12 To remove a relay, first ensure that the relevant circuit is switched off. The relay can then simply be pulled out from the socket, and pushed back into position **(see illustration)**.

13 Incorporated in the main fusebox is a multi-timer which combines the components and relays that were previously separate units. The timer slides into the side of the fusebox as a separate module.

4 Switches – removal and refitting

Ignition switch/steering column lock cylinder

Steering column lock cylinder

1 Remove the steering wheel as described in Chapter 10. Note that this procedure includes disconnecting the battery.

2 Undo the screws and remove the steering column shrouds and tilt lever knob.

3 Unclip the windscreen wiper switch from its position on the steering column. If necessary, also remove the anti-theft immobiliser transceiver unit from the steering lock and disconnect the wiring.

4 Insert the ignition key and turn to position I.

5 Using a small screwdriver or pin punch, depress the locking pin through the hole in the top of the column, then withdraw the lock cylinder using the key **(see illustrations)**.

6 To refit the lock cylinder, push the assembly into the lock housing, until the locking pin engages, then turn the ignition key to position 0 and withdraw the key. If the steering lock pin engages with the steering column as the cylinder is removed, it will not be possible to insert the cylinder so that the locking pin engages. In this case, use a screwdriver in the housing to press the steering lock pin down before inserting the lock cylinder **(see illustration)**.

Ignition switch

7 To remove the ignition switch, remove the lock cylinder as previously described in this Section, or insert the ignition key and turn it to position 0.

8 Insert a small screwdriver through the hole in the bottom of the switch and depress the internal lug, then use another screwdriver to lever off the wiring harness plug **(see illustration)**.

9 With the plug removed, unclip and remove the ignition switch.

10 Refitting is a reversal of removal.

Direction indicator /wiper switch assembly

11 The direction indicator and wiper switch assemblies are removed identically.

12 Remove the steering wheel as described in Chapter 10. Note that this procedure includes disconnecting the battery.

13 Undo the screws and remove the steering column shrouds and tilt lever knob.

14 Depress the clips and slide the direction indicator/wiper switch from the steering column **(see illustration)**.

15 Disconnect the wiring and withdraw the switch **(see illustration)**. Where applicable, also disconnect the wiring from the cruise control.

4.5a Depress the locking pin . . .

4.5b and withdraw the lock cylinder using the key

4.6 Pressing the steering lock pin down with a screwdriver before inserting the lock cylinder

4.8 Use a screwdriver to depress the internal lug, and withdraw the ignition switch

4.14 Remove the wiper switch from the steering column . . .

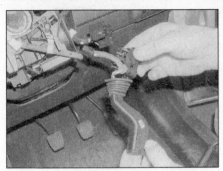

4.15 . . . and disconnect the wiring

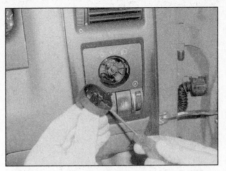

4.17 Removing the knob from the lighting and foglight switch

4.18 Insert two small screwdrivers as shown, and prise the switch from the facia

16 Refitting is a reversal of removal, but make sure that the switch clips engage correctly.

Lighting and foglight switch

17 Using a small screwdriver inserted through the hole in the bottom of the switch knob, carefully remove the knob from the switch **(see illustration)**.
18 Insert two small screwdrivers on each side of the central hole to release the retaining lugs, then prise the switch from the socket in the facia **(see illustration)**.
19 If necessary, the illumination bulb may be renewed, with reference to Section 6.
20 Refitting is a reversal of removal.

Hazard warning switch

21 Using a screwdriver, carefully prise the cover from the switch **(see illustration)**.

22 Insert the screwdriver at the top and bottom of the switch, and carefully prise the switch from the facia/surround **(see illustration)**.
23 Refitting is a reversal of removal.

Heater blower motor switch

24 Remove the heater control panel as described in Chapter 3.
25 Carefully pull off the knob from the blower motor switch.
26 Press the switch from the rear of the control panel, while releasing the clips located at the top, sides and bottom.
27 Refitting is a reversal of removal.

Stop-light switch and handbrake 'on' warning light switch

28 Refer to Chapter 9.

Courtesy light switch and rear luggage compartment switch

29 Undo the retaining screw and withdraw the switch **(see illustrations)**.
30 Disconnect the wiring and tape it to the panel to prevent it dropping out of reach. Note that, when removing the tailgate switch, it may be easier to remove the inner trim panels and disconnect the wiring from inside the tailgate **(see illustration)**.
31 Make sure that the retaining screw makes good contact with the body and switch. If necessary clean the contact points.
32 Refitting is a reversal of removal.

Electric sunroof switch

33 Remove the front interior light as described in Section 6.
34 Undo the screws securing the switch panel to the headlining **(see illustration)**.

4.21 Prise off the cover . . .

4.22 . . . then remove the hazard switch from the facia/surround

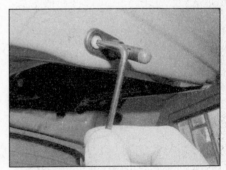

4.29a Use a Torx key to unscrew the courtesy light switch retaining screw . . .

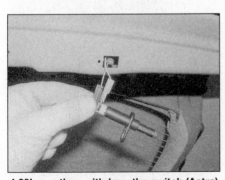

4.29b . . . then withdraw the switch (Astra)

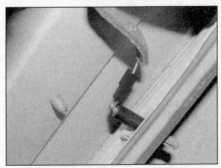

4.30 Wiring connected to the rear of the tailgate courtesy light switch (Zafira)

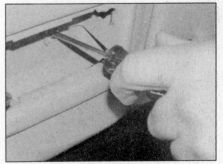

4.34 Remove the screws securing the switch panel to the headlining . . .

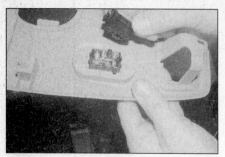

4.35 . . . disconnect the wiring from the switch . . .

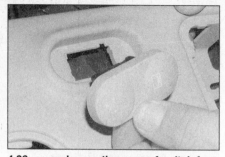

4.36 . . . and press the sunroof switch from the panel

remove it from the bulbholder, using the fingers on the metal base **(see illustration)**. Note the location tang on the top of the base.

4 When handling the new bulb, use a tissue or clean cloth, to avoid touching the glass with the fingers; moisture and grease from the skin can cause blackening of the bulb. If the glass is accidentally touched, wipe it clean using methylated spirit.

5 Fit the new bulb using a reversal of the removal procedure, using the fingers only to press the metal base into the bulbholder. Make sure that the bulb location tang is located in the top of the bulbholder.

35 Withdraw the panel from the headlining and disconnect the wiring from the switch **(see illustration)**.

36 Press the switch from the panel **(see illustration)**.

37 Refitting is a reversal of removal.

Reversing light switch

38 Refer to Chapter 7A (manual transmission) or Chapter 7B (automatic transmission).

5 Bulbs (exterior lights) – renewal

⚠️ **Warning: Certain later models may be equipped with a Xenon headlight system. All the bulbs in the headlight unit operate at very high voltages and there is a high risk of personal injury if any of the associated wiring is touched with the ignition switched on. For safety reasons it is recommended**

that bulb renewal on the Xenon system is entrusted to a Vauxhall dealer.

1 Whenever a bulb is renewed, note the following points.

a) *Remember that, if the light has just been in use, the bulb may be extremely hot.*

b) *Do not touch the bulb glass with the fingers, as this can result in early failure or a dull reflector.*

c) *Always check the bulb contacts and holder, ensuring that there is clean metal-to-metal contact between the bulb and its live(s) and earth. Clean off any corrosion or dirt before fitting a new bulb.*

d) *Ensure that the new bulb is of the correct rating.*

Headlight dipped beam

2 With the bonnet open, twist anti-clockwise the brown bulbholder from the rear, outer end of the headlight **(see illustration)**. Note that the inner bulb is for the main beam.

3 Note the orientation of the bulb, then

Headlight main beam

6 With the bonnet open, twist anti-clockwise the black bulbholder from the rear, inner end of the headlight **(see illustration)**. Note that the outer bulb is for the dipped beam.

7 Release the clip and disconnect the wiring from the bulbholder. The bulb is integral with the bulbholder.

8 When handling the new bulb, use a tissue or clean cloth, to avoid touching the glass with the fingers; moisture and grease from the skin can cause blackening of the bulb. If the glass is accidentally touched, wipe it clean using methylated spirit.

9 Fit the new bulb using a reversal of the removal procedure. Twist the bulbholder fully clockwise into the rear of the headlight.

Sidelight

10 Open the bonnet. The sidelight bulb is located under the rear of the headlight.

11 Twist the bulbholder anti-clockwise and withdraw it from the headlight **(see illustration)**.

5.2 Removing the headlight dipped beam bulbholder

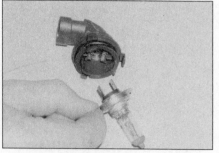

5.3 Removing the bulb from the dipped beam bulbholder

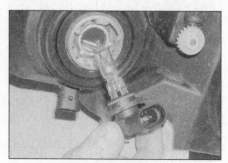

5.6 Removing the headlight main beam bulbholder

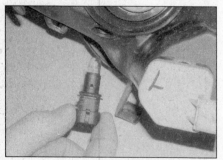

5.11 Removing the sidelight bulbholder from the headlight

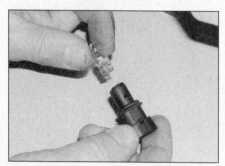

5.12 Removing the sidelight bulb from the bulbholder

5.14 Remove the front direction indicator bulbholder from the headlight . . .

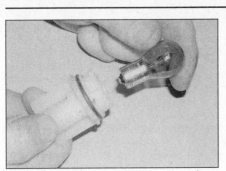

5.15 ... then depress and twist the bulb to remove it

5.18 Twist the rear cover from the foglight ...

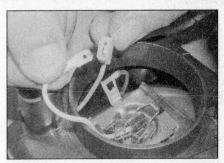

5.19 ... disconnect the wiring at the connector ...

12 Remove the bulb from the holder **(see illustration)**.
13 Fit the new bulb using a reversal of the removal procedure.

Front direction indicator

14 With the bonnet open, twist anticlockwise the white bulbholder from the direction

5.20a ... then unhook the spring clips ...

5.20b ... and remove the bulb

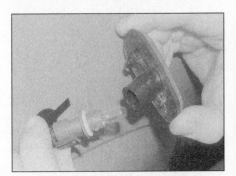

5.23 Twist the bulbholder from the light ...

indicator section of the headlight **(see illustration)**.
15 Depress and twist the bulb to remove it **(see illustration)**.
16 Refitting is a reversal of removal.

Front foglight

17 Remove the front bumper as described in Chapter 11.
18 Twist the cover from the rear of the foglight **(see illustration)**.
19 Disconnect the wiring at the connector **(see illustration)**.
20 Unhook the spring clips and remove the bulb from the foglight **(see illustrations)**. Note how the bulb is located in the reflector. The bulb is only available together with the fly-lead wire.
21 Refitting is a reversal of removal.

Front direction indicator side repeater

22 Carefully press the side repeater light

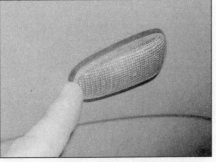

5.22a Carefully press the side repeater light rearwards ...

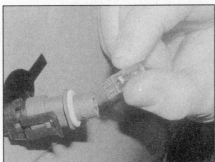

5.24 ... then pull out the wedge-type bulb

rearwards in order to release the front of the light from the front wing **(see illustrations)**.
23 Twist the bulbholder from the light **(see illustration)**.
24 Pull out the wedge-type bulb **(see illustration)**.
25 Fit the new bulb using a reversal of the removal procedure. Locate the front of the light in the front wing, then press in the rear until it clips in position.

Rear light cluster (Hatchback and Saloon models)

26 In the luggage compartment, release the clip and remove the access cover for the rear light cluster **(see illustration)**.
27 Disconnect the wiring plug **(see illustration)**.
28 Support the rear light cluster from the outside, then unscrew the two knurled nuts from inside **(see illustration)**.

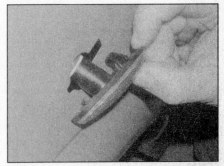

5.22b ... to release the front of the light from the front wing

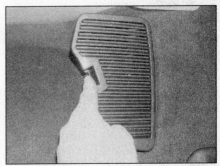

5.26 Removing the access cover for the rear light cluster (Astra)

5.27 Disconnect the wiring . . .

5.28 . . . then unscrew the two knurled nuts . . .

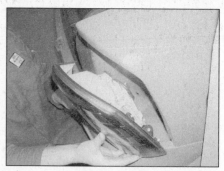

5.29 . . . and withdraw the rear light cluster (Astra)

29 Withdraw the rear light cluster from the rear of the vehicle (see illustration).
30 Press in the retaining lugs and remove the bulbholder from the light (see illustration).
31 Depress and twist the relevant bulb to remove it (see illustration).
32 Refitting is a reversal of removal.

Rear light cluster (Estate models)

33 In the luggage compartment, turn the fasteners and release the access cover from the side trim.
34 Support the rear light cluster from the outside, then unscrew the two knurled nuts from inside.
35 Withdraw the rear light cluster from the rear of the vehicle.
36 Press in the retaining lug and remove the bulbholder from the light.
37 Depress and twist the relevant bulb to remove it.

38 Refitting is a reversal of removal.

Rear light cluster (Zafira models)

39 In the luggage compartment, remove the access cover from the side trim.
40 Support the rear light cluster from the outside, then unscrew the two knurled nuts from inside.
41 Withdraw the rear light cluster from the rear of the vehicle.
42 Release the retaining lug and remove the bulbholder from the light.
43 Depress and twist the relevant bulb to remove it (see illustration).
44 Refitting is a reversal of removal.

Rear number plate light (Hatchback and Saloon models)

45 Open the tailgate or boot lid for improved

access to the number plate light located on the top of the rear bumper.
46 Insert a screwdriver vertically into the hole in the light lens and press in to release the clip (see illustration).
47 Press down the right-hand end of the light and lift up the left-hand end to release it from the bumper.
48 Depress the clip and release the lens from the light (see illustration).
49 Depress and twist the bulb to remove it from the bulbholder (see illustration).
50 Refitting is a reversal of removal.

Rear number plate light (Estate and Zafira models)

51 Open the tailgate and support at waist height for access to the number plate light located in the tailgate.
52 Undo the screws and withdraw the light unit.

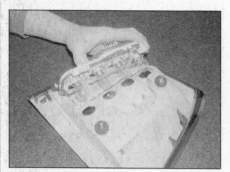

5.30 Remove the bulbholder . . .

5.31 . . . then depress and twist the relevant bulb to remove it (Astra)

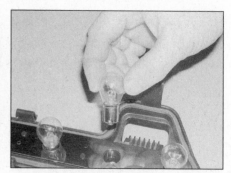

5.43 Removing a rear light cluster bulb (Zafira)

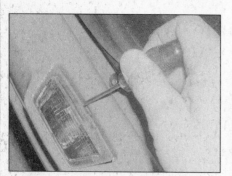

5.46 Use a screwdriver to release the rear number plate light retaining clip

5.48 Releasing the lens from the rear number plate light

5.49 Depress and twist the bulb to remove it

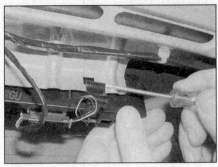

5.56a Unclip the high-level stop-light . . .

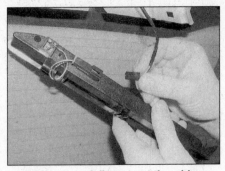

5.56b . . . and disconnect the wiring

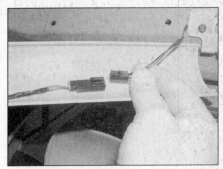

5.60 Disconnect the wiring . . .

5.61a . . . then undo the screws . . .

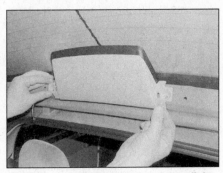

5.61b . . . unclip the high-level stop-light unit . . .

5.61c . . . and remove it from the tailgate

53 Ease the festoon-type bulb from the spring contacts.
54 Refitting is a reversal of removal, but make sure that the spring contacts are tensioned sufficiently to hold the festoon-type bulb firmly.

High-level stop-light (Saloon and Hatchback models)

55 With the tailgate open, prise out the plastic covers, undo the screws, and remove the lower and upper trim panels from the inside of the tailgate. Note that the lower panel has extensions which slot into the upper panels.
56 Undo the two screws then unclip and remove the high-level stop-light. Disconnect the wiring (see illustrations).

57 The stop-light is a complete unit and it is not possible to remove individual bulbs.
58 Fit the new light using a reversal of removal procedure.

High-level stop-light (Estate and Zafira models)

59 With the tailgate open, prise out the plastic covers, undo the screws, and remove the lower and upper trim panels from the inside of the tailgate. Note that the lower panel has extensions which slot into the upper panels.
60 Disconnect the wiring from the high-level stop-light (see illustration).
61 Undo the screws then unclip and remove the light (see illustrations).
62 The stop-light is a complete unit and it is not possible to remove individual bulbs.
63 Refitting is a reversal of removal.

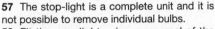

6 Bulbs (interior lights) – renewal

1 Whenever a bulb is renewed, note the following points.
 a) *Remember that, if the light has just been in use, the bulb may be extremely hot.*
 b) *Do not touch the bulb glass with the fingers, as this can result in early failure or a dull reflector.*
 c) *Always check the bulb contacts and holder, ensuring that there is clean metal-to-metal contact between the bulb and its live(s) and earth. Clean off any corrosion or dirt before fitting a new bulb.*
 d) *Ensure that the new bulb is of the correct rating.*

Front interior light

2 On Astra models carefully prise the interior light from the headlining using a screwdriver, then remove the festoon-type bulb from the spring contacts (see illustrations).
3 On Zafira models carefully prise the interior light from the headlining (or electric sunroof motor cover) using a screwdriver inserted beneath the front of the light. Disconnect the wiring then twist free the bulbholder and remove the wedge-type type bulb (see illustrations).
4 Fit the new bulb using a reversal of the removal procedure.

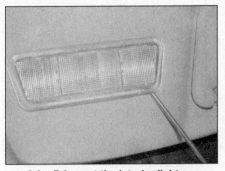

6.2a Prise out the interior light . . .

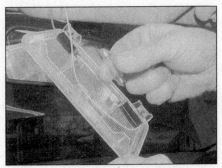

6.2b . . . then remove the festoon-type bulb (Astra)

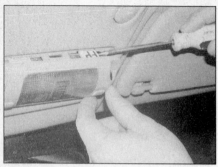

6.3a Prise out the front interior light . . .

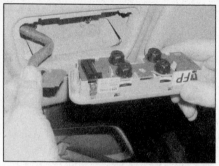

6.3b . . . disconnect the wiring . . .

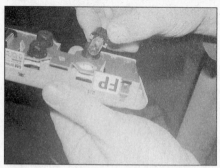

6.3c . . . then twist free the bulbholder . . .

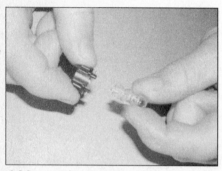

6.3d . . . and remove the wedge-type bulb (Zafira)

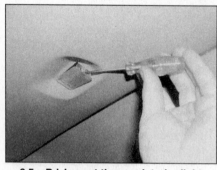

6.5a Prising out the rear interior light (Zafira)

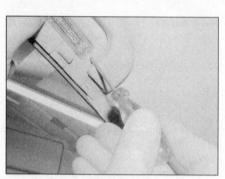

6.5b Prising out the rear interior light (Astra)

Rear interior light

5 Carefully prise the interior light from the headlining (see illustrations).
6 Remove the festoon type bulb from the spring contacts (see illustrations).

7 Fit the new bulb using a reversal of the removal procedure. Make sure that the bulb is held firmly between the spring contacts. If necessary, pre-tension the contacts before fitting the bulb.

Luggage compartment interior light

8 Carefully prise the light from the side trim (see illustration).
9 Remove the festoon-type bulb from the spring contacts (see illustration).
10 Fit the new bulb using a reversal of the removal procedure. Make sure that the bulb is held firmly between the spring contacts. If necessary, pre-tension the contacts before fitting the bulb.

Glovebox light

11 With the glovebox open, carefully prise out the light unit (see illustration).
12 Remove the festoon-type bulb from the spring contacts. To remove the light completely, disconnect the wiring (see illustrations).
13 Fit the new bulb using a reversal of the removal procedure. Make sure that the bulb is

6.6a Removing the festoon type bulb from the spring contacts (Zafira)

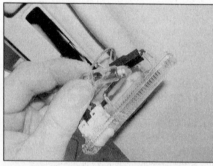

6.6b Removing the festoon type bulb from the spring contacts (Astra)

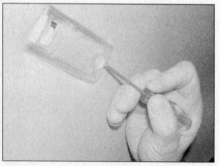

6.8 Prise out the luggage compartment interior light . . .

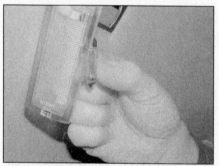

6.9 . . . and remove the festoon-type bulb from the spring contacts

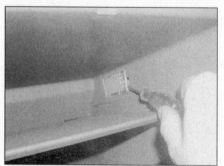

6.11 Prise the light from the glovebox . . .

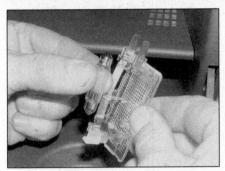

6.12a ... then remove the festoon-type bulb from the spring contacts

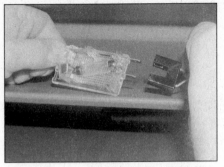

6.12b Disconnecting the wiring from the glovebox light

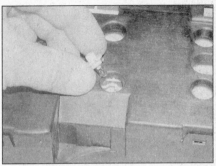

6.23 Removing a bulb from the instrument panel

held firmly between the spring contacts. If necessary, pre-tension the contacts before fitting the bulb.

Rear reading light

14 Carefully prise the light unit from the handle grip, using a screwdriver.
15 Remove the festoon-type bulb from the spring contacts.
16 Fit the new bulb using a reversal of the removal procedure. Make sure that the bulb is held firmly between the spring contacts. If necessary, pre-tension the contacts before fitting the bulb.

Cigarette lighter illumination

17 Unclip the panel located below the ashtray.
18 With the ashtray open, undo the screws and withdraw it from the centre console. Disconnect the wiring from the cigarette lighter.

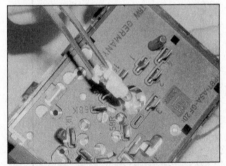

6.26 Removing the bulb from the rear of the light switch

19 Remove the heater coil, then use a screwdriver through the small hole to release the illumination light ring.
20 Remove the bulbholder and pull out the bulb.
21 Fit the new bulb using a reversal of removal procedure.

Instrument panel illumination and warning lights

22 Remove the instrument panel as described in Section 9.
23 To remove the bulbs, twist and turn the bulbholder and remove from the instrument panel **(see illustration)**, then where possible remove the bulb from the bulbholder. Note that some bulbs cannot be removed from their bulbholders.
24 Fit the new bulb using a reversal of removal procedure.

Light switch illumination

25 Remove the light switch as described in Section 4.
26 Using a screwdriver, twist the bulbholder from the rear of the switch **(see illustration)**.
27 Fit the new bulb using a reversal of the removal procedure.

Clock/multi-function display unit illumination

28 Remove the clock/display unit as described in Section 10.
29 Twist the relevant bulbholder from the rear of the display unit **(see illustrations)**.
30 Fit the new bulb using a reversal of removal procedure.

Heater control illumination

31 Remove the heater control assembly as described in Chapter 3.
32 Pull out the relevant wedge-type bulb from the assembly **(see illustration)**.
33 Fit the new bulb using a reversal of the removal procedure.

7 Exterior light units – removal and refitting

Headlight/front direction indicator

⚠ *Warning: The Xenon headlight system (where fitted) operates at very high voltages. Do not touch the associated wiring when the headlights or ignition are switched on. If in doubt about the type of system fitted, consult a Vauxhall dealer.*

Removal

1 Remove the front bumper as described in Chapter 11.
2 Unscrew and remove the two upper and one lower mounting bolts, then withdraw the headlight/front direction indicator unit sufficiently to disconnect the wiring. Withdraw the unit from the vehicle, then undo the screws and remove the bumper trim from the bottom of the headlight **(see illustrations)**.
3 If necessary, the headlight range control servo may be removed by twisting it through 90° **(see illustration)**.

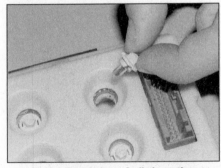

6.29a Removing a bulb from the clock/multi-function display unit (Zafira)

6.29b Removing a bulb from the multi-function display unit (Astra)

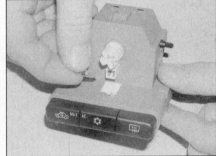

6.32 Removing a wedge-type bulb from the heater control panel

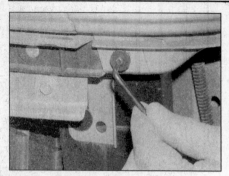

7.2a Unscrewing the headlight lower mounting bolt . . .

7.2b . . . withdraw the unit from the vehicle . . .

7.2c . . . and disconnect the wiring

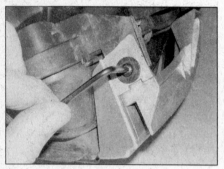

7.2d Undo the screws . . .

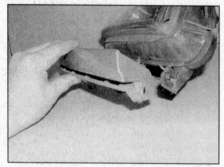

7.2e . . . and remove the bumper trim

7.3 Removing the headlight range control servo

Refitting

4 Refitting is a reversal of removal, and have the headlight beam alignment checked at the earliest opportunity.

7.6a Unscrew the mounting bolts . . .

Front foglight

Removal

5 Remove the front bumper as described in Chapter 11.
6 Unscrew the three mounting bolts and remove the foglight from the bumper, then disconnect the wiring **(see illustrations)**.

Refitting

7 Refitting is a reversal of removal, but on completion have the beam alignment checked at the earliest opportunity.

Front direction indicator side repeater

Removal

8 Carefully press the side repeater rearwards in order to release the front of the light from the front wing.

9 Remove the light and disconnect the wiring. If necessary remove the bulb with reference to Section 5.

Refitting

10 Refitting is a reversal of removal. Locate the front of the light in the front wing, then press in the rear until the rear clip engages.

Rear light cluster

Removal

11 In the luggage compartment, remove the side trim cover for access to the rear light cluster **(see illustration)**.
12 Disconnect the wiring plug **(see illustration)**.
13 Support the rear light cluster from the outside, then unscrew the two knurled nuts from inside **(see illustration)**.

7.11 Remove the side trim cover for access to the rear light cluster

7.12 Disconnecting the wiring from the rear light cluster

7.6b . . . and remove the foglight from the front bumper

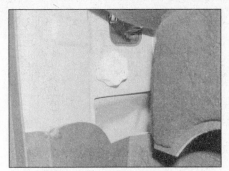

7.13 One of the plastic knurled nuts securing the rear light cluster to the body

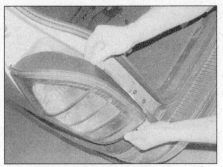

7.14 Withdrawing the rear light cluster from the rear of the vehicle

7.15 Removing the bulbholder from the rear light cluster

14 Withdraw the rear light cluster from the rear of the vehicle **(see illustration)**.

15 Press in the retaining lugs and remove the bulbholder from the light **(see illustration)**.

Refitting

16 Refitting is a reversal of removal.

Rear number plate light (Hatchback and Saloon models)

Removal

17 Open the tailgate or bootlid for improved access to the number plate light located on the top of the rear bumper.

18 Insert a screwdriver vertically into the hole in the light lens and press to release the clip.

19 Press down the right-hand end of the light and lift up the left-hand end to release it from the bumper.

20 Disconnect the wiring **(see illustration)**. If necessary, remove the bulb with reference to Section 5.

Refitting

21 Refitting is a reversal of removal.

Rear number plate light (Estate and Zafira models)

Removal

22 Open the tailgate and support at waist height for access to the number plate light located in the tailgate.

23 Undo the screws and withdraw the light unit.

24 Disconnect the wiring. If necessary, remove the bulb with reference to Section 5.

Refitting

25 Refitting is a reversal of removal.

High-level stop-light

26 The procedure is described in Section 5.

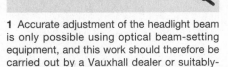

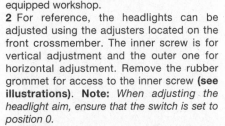

---

8 Headlight beam alignment – general information

1 Accurate adjustment of the headlight beam is only possible using optical beam-setting equipment, and this work should therefore be carried out by a Vauxhall dealer or suitably-equipped workshop.

2 For reference, the headlights can be adjusted using the adjusters located on the front crossmember. The inner screw is for vertical adjustment and the outer one for horizontal adjustment. Remove the rubber grommet for access to the inner screw **(see illustrations)**. **Note:** *When adjusting the headlight aim, ensure that the switch is set to position 0.*

3 All models have an electrically-operated headlight beam adjustment range system, controlled via a switch in the facia. The recommended settings are as follows.

Models without automatic level control

0 *Front seat(s) occupied*
1 *All seats occupied*
2 *All seats occupied, and load in luggage compartment*

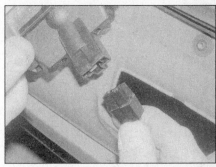

7.20 Disconnecting the wiring from the rear number plate light

3 *Driver's seat occupied and load in the luggage compartment*

Models with automatic level control

0 *All other load states*
1 *All seats occupied and full load in load compartment*

---

9 Instrument panel – removal and refitting

Removal

1 Remove the steering wheel as described in Chapter 10.

2 Undo the screws and remove the upper steering column shroud. The screws are accessed by removing the plastic covers.

3 Undo the screw and remove the knob from the tilt steering lever.

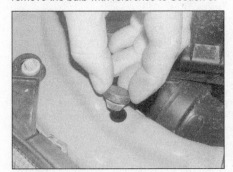

8.2a Remove the rubber grommet . . .

8.2b . . . for access to the vertical beam adjustment screw

8.2c The horizontal beam adjustment screw

9.5a **Prise out the covers . . .**

9.5b **. . . then undo the screws . . .**

9.5c **. . . and remove the instrument panel surround**

9.7a **Undo the lower mounting screws (Astra models only) . . .**

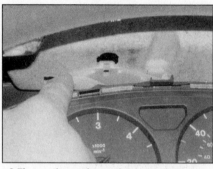

9.7b **. . . then release the upper lever . . .**

9.7c **. . . and withdraw the instrument panel**

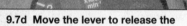

9.7d **Move the lever to release the instrument panel upper clips on Zafira models**

9.7e **Instrument panel removed from the vehicle (Zafira)**

4 Undo the screws and remove the lower steering column shroud.
5 On Astra models, prise out the covers, then undo the screws and remove the instrument panel surround from the facia **(see illustrations)**.
6 On Zafira models, remove the instrument panel surround as follows.
   a) *Remove the lighting and foglight switch (Section 4 of this Chapter).*
   b) *Remove the radio (Section 17 of this Chapter).*
   c) *Carefully remove the outer vent from the facia.*
   d) *Undo the retaining screws and remove the instrument panel surround panel, and disconnect the wiring as necessary. Note that the innermost screw is accessed through the grille of the inner vent.*
7 Undo the lower mounting screws on Astra

models. Release the upper clip by moving the lever, then withdraw the instrument panel from the facia and disconnect the wiring **(see illustrations)**.

10.8a **Undo the screws . . .**

Refitting

8 Refitting is a reversal of removal. Check the operation of all the warning and illumination bulbs on completion.

10 Multi-function display unit and components – removal and refitting

Note: *New multi-function display units must be programmed by a Vauxhall dealer after fitting. This is not necessary when removing and refitting an existing unit.*

Multi-function display unit (Astra models)

Removal

1 Remove the front ashtray.
2 Unclip the storage compartment cover from the facia.
3 Remove the radio and mounting box as described in Section 17.
4 Where fitted, remove the navigation system unit.
5 Unclip the heater control panel from the rear of the surround panel.
6 Press the central air vents rearwards out of the surround panel.
7 Pull out the surround panel and disconnect the wiring from the multi-function display unit. Also slide the wiring plug from the rear of the hazard switch socket.
8 On the rear of the panel, undo the screws and remove the multi-function display unit **(see illustrations)**.

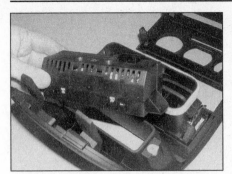

10.8b . . . and remove the multi-function display unit from the surround panel

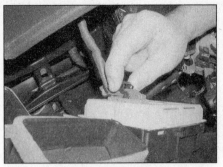

10.22 Disconnecting the wiring from the multi-function display unit

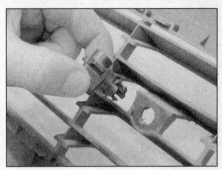

10.26 Removing the outside temperature sensor from the front bumper

Refitting

9 Refitting is a reversal of removal.

Multi-function display unit (Zafira models)

Removal

10 Remove the front ashtray.

11 Undo the two lower mounting screws, and unclip the heater/air conditioning control panel from the facia.

12 Unclip the hazard warning switch, TC (Traction Control) switch, and seat heating switch from the control panel and disconnect the wiring.

13 Unclip the heater/air conditioning unit from the panel.

14 Remove the steering wheel as described in Chapter 10. Note that this procedure includes disconnecting the battery.

15 Undo the screws and remove the steering column shrouds and tilt lever knob.

16 Release the clips and slide the wiper and indicator switches from the steering column.

17 Remove the radio as described in Section 17.

18 Remove the lighting and foglight switch as described in Section 4.

19 Unclip the fusebox cover from the facia.

20 Using a screwdriver through the grille slots, undo the outer vent securing screw and remove the vent.

21 Undo the screws securing the instrument panel surround to the facia. There are three located directly above the instrument panel, one either side of the steering column, and one at each lower corner of the surround.

22 Withdraw the surround from the facia, and at the same time slide the lighting switch from its guide. Disconnect the wiring from the multi-function display unit **(see illustration)**, then release the remaining wiring from the rear of the surround.

23 Unclip the multi-function display unit from the surround.

Refitting

24 Refitting is a reversal of removal.

Outside temperature sensor

Removal

25 With the bonnet open, reach down behind the front bumper and disconnect the wiring from the sensor located inside the front bumper.

26 Twist the sensor and unclip it from the front bumper **(see illustration)**.

Refitting

27 Refitting is a reversal of removal.

Coolant temperature sensor

Removal and refitting

28 Refer to Chapter 3, Section 7.

Coolant residue sensor

Removal

29 The coolant residue sensor is located on the base of the coolant expansion tank. Refer to Chapter 3 and partially drain coolant from the system until the coolant level is below the sensor, then remove the expansion tank and disconnect the wiring from the sensor.

30 With the expansion tank inverted, use a screwdriver to release the sensor.

Refitting

31 Refitting is a reversal of removal.

Windscreen washer fluid level sensor

Removal

32 The sensor is located beneath the left-hand end of the front bumper. First remove the bumper as described in Chapter 11.

33 Disconnect the wiring from the sensor located on the reservoir.

34 Carefully prise the sensor from the reservoir.

Refitting

35 Refitting is a reversal of removal.

Engine oil level sensor

Removal

36 Remove the sump as described in the relevant Part of Chapter 2.

37 Prise the retaining ring from the sump.

38 Press the sensor connection out of the sump.

39 Unbolt the sensor from the sump and remove the sealing ring.

Refitting

40 Refitting is a reversal of removal, but use a new sealing ring. Refit the sump with reference to Chapter 2.

11 Cigarette lighter – removal and refitting

Removal

1 Unclip the panel located below the ashtray.

2 With the ashtray open, undo the screws and withdraw it from the centre console. Disconnect the wiring from the cigarette lighter **(see illustrations)**.

3 Remove the heater coil, then remove the bulbholder and cover from the rear of the unit **(see illustrations)**.

11.2a Undo the screws . . .

11.2b . . . remove the ashtray and disconnect the wiring

11.3a Remove the heater coil . . .

11.3b . . . then remove the bulbholder . . .

11.3c . . . and cover from the rear of the unit

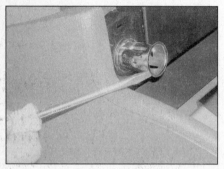

11.4a Prise out the body . . .

11.4b . . . then remove the light ring

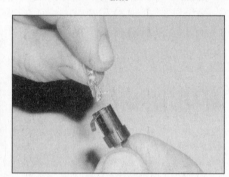

11.5 Removing the bulb from the bulbholder

4 Use a screwdriver to prise out the body, then remove the light ring **(see illustrations)**.

5 Pull the bulb from the bulbholder **(see illustration)**.

Refitting

6 Refitting is a reversal of removal.

12 Horn – removal and refitting

Removal

1 The horn or horns are located behind the right-hand end of the front bumper **(see illustration)**. If necessary for improved access, remove the front bumper as described in Chapter 11.

2 Disconnect the wiring from the horn(s).

3 Unscrew the nut(s) and remove the horn(s) from the mounting bracket. If necessary, unbolt the bracket from the body.

Refitting

4 Refitting is a reversal of removal.

13 Wiper arm – removal and refitting

Windscreen wiper arm

Removal

1 Operate the wiper motor, then switch it off so that the wiper arm returns to the at-rest position (see Haynes Hint).

2 Using a screwdriver prise the cover from the spindle end of the wiper arm **(see illustration)**.

3 Unscrew the spindle nut and recover the small washer **(see illustration)**.

12.1 The horns are located behind the right-hand end of the front bumper

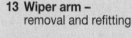

HAYNES
HiNT

Stick a piece of masking tape on the window, along the edge of the wiper blade, to use as an alignment aid on refitting.

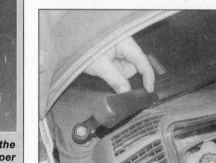

13.2 Prise up the cover . . .

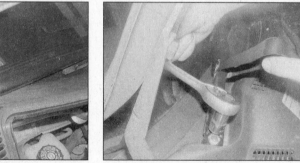

13.3 . . . unscrew the nut . . .

13.4 . . . and pull the wiper arm off its spindle splines

13.10a Lift the cover from the base of the wiper arm . . .

13.10b . . . then unscrew the retaining nut

4 Lift the blade off the glass, and pull the wiper arm off its spindle splines **(see illustration)**. Note that the wiper arms may be very tight on the spindle splines – if necessary, lever the arm off the spindle, using a flat-bladed screwdriver (take care not to damage the scuttle cover panel).
5 If necessary, remove the blade from the arm with reference to *Weekly checks*.

Refitting

6 If removed, refit the wiper blade to the arm at this stage. This will prevent any damage to the windscreen from the upper end of the arm.
7 Ensure that the wiper arm and spindle splines are clean and dry, then refit the arm to the spindle and align the blade with the previously noted rest position.
8 Refit the washer and spindle nut, and tighten it securely. Refit the cover.

Tailgate wiper arm

Removal

9 Operate the wiper motor, then switch it off so that the wiper arm returns to the at-rest position.

 Stick a piece of masking tape on the window, along the edge of the wiper blade, to use as an alignment aid on refitting.

10 Lift the cover from the base of the wiper arm and unscrew the retaining nut **(see illustrations)**.
11 Lift the blade off the glass, and pull the wiper arm off its spindle. If the arm is tight, use a suitable puller to release it from the spindle **(see illustration)**.
12 If necessary, remove the blade from the arm with reference to *Weekly checks*.

Refitting

13 If removed, refit the wiper blade to the arm at this stage. This will prevent any damage to the rear window from the upper end of the arm.
14 Ensure that the wiper arm and spindle splines are clean and dry, then refit the arm to the spindle and align the blade with the previously noted rest position.

15 Refit the spindle nut, and tighten it securely. Close the cover on the base of the arm.

---

14 Windscreen wiper motor and linkage – removal and refitting

Removal

1 Remove both wiper arms as described in Section 13.
2 Pull the rubber weatherstrip from the rear of the engine compartment, then unclip the plastic grille from the water deflector at the front of the windscreen **(see illustrations)**.
3 Disconnect the tubing from the windscreen washer jets on the water deflector **(see illustration)**.
4 Unscrew the nuts and unclip the water

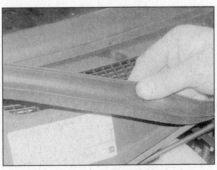

14.2a Pull up the rubber weatherstrip . . .

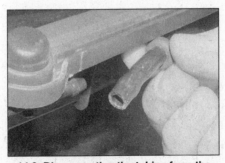

14.3 Disconnecting the tubing from the windscreen washer jets on the water deflector

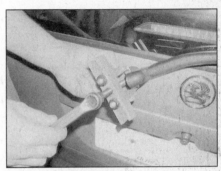

13.11 Using a small puller to release the wiper arm from the spindle

deflector from the bulkhead **(see illustrations)**.
5 Disconnect the wiring from the windscreen wiper motor **(see illustration)**.
6 Unscrew the mounting bolts and withdraw

14.2b . . . then unclip the plastic grille from the water deflector (Zafira)

14.4a Unscrew the nuts (Zafira models only) . . .

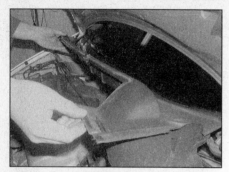

14.4b ... and unclip the water deflector from the bulkhead

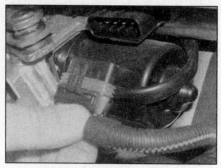

14.5 Disconnect the wiring ...

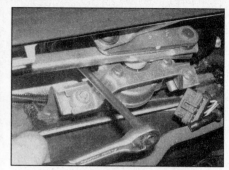

14.6a ... then unscrew the central mounting bolts ...

14.6b ... and outer mounting bolts ...

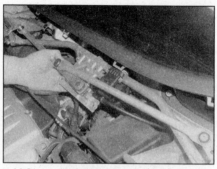

14.6c ... and withdraw the windscreen wiper motor and linkage

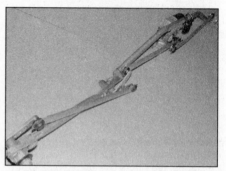

14.6d Windscreen wiper motor and linkage removed from the vehicle (Zafira)

the wiper motor and linkage **(see illustrations)**.

7 The motor can be removed from the linkage assembly by prising free the rod from the crank and unbolting the motor **(see**

illustration). The remaining linkage rods can also be dismantled if necessary.

8 Clean the assembly and examine the spindles and joints for wear and damage. Renew the components as required.

Refitting

9 Refitting is a reversal of removal, but lubricate the joints with a little grease before assembling them. Refit the wiper arms with reference to Section 13.

---

15 Tailgate wiper motor – removal and refitting

Removal

1 Remove the wiper arm from the tailgate as described in Section 13, then remove the trim panelling from the inside of the tailgate with reference to Chapter 11, Section 44.

2 On Astra models only, remove the tailgate lock cylinder as described in Chapter 11, Section 26.

3 Disconnect the wiring at the plug **(see illustration)**.

4 Unscrew the mounting bolts and withdraw the wiper motor while sliding the spindle housing through the rubber grommet **(see illustrations)**.

5 If necessary remove the rubber grommet from the tailgate **(see illustration)**. Examine the grommet for wear and damage and renew it if necessary.

Refitting

6 Refitting is a reversal of removal, but tighten the mounting bolts to the specified torque. Refit the wiper arm with reference to Section 13.

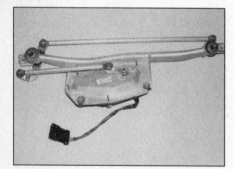

14.6e Windscreen wiper motor and linkage removed from the vehicle (Astra)

14.7 Windscreen wiper motor crank and mounting bolts

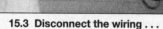

15.3 Disconnect the wiring ...

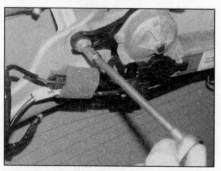

15.4a ... then unscrew the mounting bolts ...

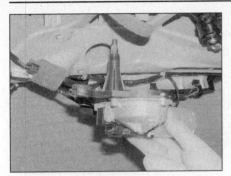

15.4b . . . and withdraw the wiper motor from the tailgate (Zafira)

15.4c Removing the wiper motor from the tailgate (Astra)

15.5 Check the rubber grommet in the tailgate before refitting the wiper motor

16 Windscreen/tailgate/headlight washer system components – removal and refitting

Washer fluid reservoir

Removal

1 Remove the front bumper as described in Chapter 11.
2 Remove the left-hand front wheelarch liner as described in Chapter 11.
3 Position a container beneath the washer fluid pump and reservoir to collect the fluid.
4 Disconnect the wiring from the pump and position to one side.
5 Disconnect the hose from the pump and allow the fluid to drain into the container.
6 On models with a multi-function display unit, disconnect the wiring from the level sensor on the fluid reservoir.
7 On models with a headlight washer system, disconnect the wiring and hose from the additional pump on the reservoir.
8 Disconnect the filler neck(s) from the reservoir.
9 Release the wiring from the clips on top of the reservoir.
10 Unscrew the mounting bolts and withdraw the reservoir from the front valance.

Refitting

11 Refitting is a reversal of removal. Fill the reservoir with washer fluid with reference to *Weekly checks*.

Washer fluid pump

Removal

12 Remove the front bumper as described in Chapter 11.
13 Remove the left-hand front wheelarch liner as described in Chapter 11.
14 Position a suitable container beneath the washer fluid pump and reservoir to collect the fluid.
15 Disconnect the wiring from the top of the pump and position to one side **(see illustration)**.
16 Disconnect the hose from the pump and allow the fluid to drain into the container.
17 Pull the pump to the side and extract it from the reservoir.

18 If necessary, remove the grommet from the reservoir.

Refitting

19 Refitting is a reversal of removal. Fill the reservoir with washer fluid with reference to *Weekly checks*.

Windscreen washer nozzle

Removal

20 Pull the rubber weatherstrip from the rear of the engine compartment, then unclip the plastic grille from the water deflector at the front of the windscreen.
21 Disconnect the tubing from the windscreen washer jets located on the water deflector.
22 Using a screwdriver, carefully release the plastic retaining tabs and remove the nozzle downwards from the water deflector **(see illustration)**.

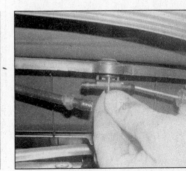

16.15 Washer fluid pump and wiring

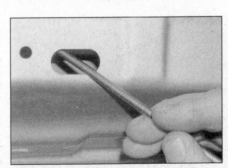

16.26a On Zafira models, release the nozzle from the tailgate using a screwdriver inserted through inner panel . . .

Refitting

23 Refitting is a reversal of removal.

Tailgate washer nozzle

Removal

24 On Hatchback models, carefully lever the nozzle out of the aerial base with a small screwdriver.
25 On Estate models, carefully insert a small screwdriver between the nozzle and the rubber seal. Depress the lugs and remove the nozzle from the tailgate.
26 On Zafira models, remove the top trim panel from inside the tailgate, then use a screwdriver to press the nozzle out of its location hole **(see illustrations)**.
27 Disconnect the nozzle from the hose.

Refitting

28 Refitting is a reversal of removal.

16.22 Prise out the windscreen washer nozzle with a screwdriver

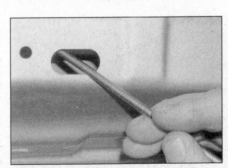

16.26b . . . then remove the tailgate washer nozzle

17.1 Using an Allen key to unscrew the grub screws

17.2 Insert the two DIN removal tools . . .

17.3a . . . and carefully withdraw the radio/CD player from the mounting box (Zafira)

17.3b Removing the radio/cassette player (Astra)

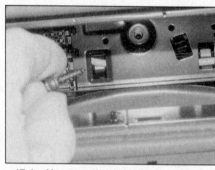

17.4a Unscrew the mounting screw . . .

17.4b . . . then release the side clips, withdraw the mounting box . . .

Headlight washer nozzle

Removal

29 Remove the front bumper and disconnect the washer tubing as described in Chapter 11.
30 Pull out the clip and remove the nozzle from the front bumper.
31 If necessary, remove the adapter from the nozzle.

Refitting

32 Refitting is a reversal of removal.

---

17 Radio/cassette/CD player/navigation units – removal and refitting

Note: *On models with a security-coded radio/cassette player, once the battery has been disconnected, the unit cannot be re-*activated until the appropriate security code has been entered. Do not remove the unit unless the appropriate code is known. The following information applies to radio/cassette players having standard DIN fixings. Two DIN removal tools will be required for this operation.

Radio/cassette/CD player

Removal

1 Using an Allen key, undo the grub screws from the four holes in each corner of the radio front face **(see illustration)**.
2 Insert the two DIN removal tools into the holes on each side of the radio until they are felt to engage with the retaining strips **(see illustration)**.
3 Carefully withdraw the radio/cassette player from the mounting box in the facia **(see illustrations)**.

4 Undo the mounting screw then release the side clips and withdraw the box from the facia. Disconnect the wiring and aerial from the rear of the box **(see illustrations)**.

Refitting

5 Refitting is a reversal of removal, but make sure that the retaining clips are correctly engaged. On completion, enter the security code.

Navigation unit (not NCDR 3000)

Removal and refitting

6 The procedure is identical to that for the radio/cassette player described earlier.

Navigation unit (NCDR 3000)

Removal

7 Depress the release button and remove the control panel from the front of the unit.

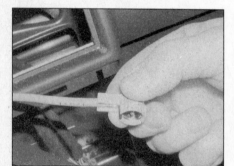

17.4c . . . and disconnect the aerial . . .

17.4d . . . and wiring plug (Zafira)

17.4e Removing the radio/cassette mounting box (Astra)

19.2 Low frequency loudspeaker in the front door

19.3 Disconnecting the wiring from the low frequency loudspeaker

19.9 Removing the low frequency loudspeaker from the rear door

8 Insert the two DIN removal tools into the holes on each side of the unit until they are felt to engage with the retaining strips.

9 Carefully withdraw the unit from the mounting box in the facia.

10 Undo the mounting screw then release the side clips and withdraw the box from the facia. Disconnect the wiring and aerial from the rear of the box.

Refitting

11 Refitting is a reversal of removal.

CD player

Removal

12 Remove the glovebox as described in Chapter 11.

13 Unclip the CD player and mounting bracket from inside the glovebox and withdraw the wiring.

14 Undo the screws and remove the player from the mounting bracket.

Refitting

15 Refitting is a reversal of removal.

Navigation control unit

Removal

16 Remove the glovebox as described in Chapter 11.

17 Unclip the navigation control unit and mounting bracket from inside the glovebox and withdraw the wiring.

18 Undo the screws and remove the navigation control unit from the mounting bracket.

Refitting

19 Refitting is a reversal of removal.

18 Radio remote control switches – removal and refitting

Removal

1 Remove the driver's airbag from the steering wheel as described in Section 24.

2 Disconnect the two wiring plugs.

3 Undo the screws and remove the two remote control switches from the steering wheel.

Refitting

4 Refitting is a reversal of removal.

19 Loudspeakers – removal and refitting

Front door-mounted low frequency loudspeaker

Removal

1 Remove the front door inner trim panel, as described in Chapter 11, Section 44.

2 Undo the mounting screws and withdraw the loudspeaker from the door inner panel **(see illustration)**.

3 Disconnect the wiring from the loudspeaker **(see illustration)**.

Refitting

4 Refitting is a reversal of removal.

Front door-mounted high-frequency ('tweeter') loudspeaker

Removal

5 On Astra models, carefully prise the exterior door mirror inner trim panel from the inside of the door, and remove the foam rubber insert. Disconnect the wiring, then carefully prise out the loudspeaker.

6 On Zafira models, it may be possible to remove the loudspeaker leaving the door inner trim panel *in situ*, however there may be only a short length of wire under the panel, making it difficult to disconnect and reconnect the wiring. Use a small screwdriver to carefully prise out the loudspeaker, then disconnect the wiring. If there is insufficient wiring, completely remove the inner trim panel as described in Chapter 11, Section 44.

Refitting

7 Refitting is a reversal of removal.

Rear door-mounted low frequency loudspeaker

Removal

8 Remove the rear door inner trim panel, as described in Chapter 11, Section 44.

9 Undo the mounting screws and withdraw the loudspeaker from the door inner panel **(see illustration)**.

10 Disconnect the wiring from the loudspeaker.

Refitting

11 Refitting is a reversal of removal.

Rear door-mounted high-frequency ('tweeter') loudspeaker

Removal

12 Remove the rear door inner trim panel, as described in Chapter 11, Section 44.

13 Release the retaining clips and remove the loudspeaker from the trim panel **(see illustration)**.

Refitting

14 Refitting is a reversal of removal.

Rear quarter panel low frequency loudspeaker (3-door Hatchback models)

Removal

15 Remove the inner trim panel from the rear quarter panel.

16 Undo the mounting screws, withdraw the loudspeaker, and disconnect the wiring.

Refitting

17 Refitting is a reversal of removal.

19.13 Removing the high frequency ('tweeter') loudspeaker from the rear door

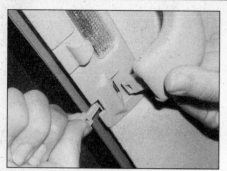

20.1 Remove the rear passenger grab handles by pulling out the plastic retainers

20 Radio aerial – removal and refitting

Removal

1 On Hatchback models, open the tailgate then pull the rubber weatherstrip away from the headlining. Remove the rear quarter trim panels with reference to Chapter 11, Section 44, then remove both rear passenger grab handles by pulling out the plastic retainers **(see illustration)**. The headlining is retained to the roof by Velcro – carefully pull

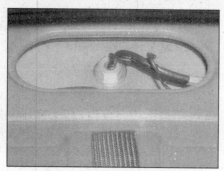

20.5 Aerial retaining nut on the roof

down the rear of the headlining.
2 On Saloon models, remove the headlining.
3 On Estate and Zafira models, open the tailgate and remove the rubber weatherstrip in the vicinity of the headlining rear trim panel. Remove the interior light from the panel as described in Section 6, then release the clips using a wide-bladed screwdriver and withdraw the panel from the roof.
4 Disconnect the cable from the aerial. Where applicable, also disconnect the GPS cable, telephone cable, and power supply wiring.
5 Unscrew the nut and remove the aerial from the roof **(see illustration)**.
6 If the aerial cable between the aerial and

radio/cassette is to be removed, it will be necessary to remove the centre console and side trim panels with reference to Chapter 11, Sections 44 and 45.

Refitting

7 Refitting is a reversal of removal, but tighten the nut to the specified torque.

21 Anti-theft alarm system and engine immobiliser – general information

1 All models have an engine immobiliser which effectively prevents the engine from being started except when using the original electronically-encoded ignition key. The system consists of the ignition key with integral transponder, and an electronic sensor mounted on the steering lock.
2 The anti-theft alarm system, where fitted, monitors the doors, bootlid or tailgate, bonnet, the passenger compartment, vehicle tilt, and the ignition system **(see illustration)**. Movement within the passenger compartment is monitored by an ultrasonic sensor located at the top of each B-pillar. Vehicle tilt is monitored so that the alarm is set off if the vehicle is raised (for example to remove the

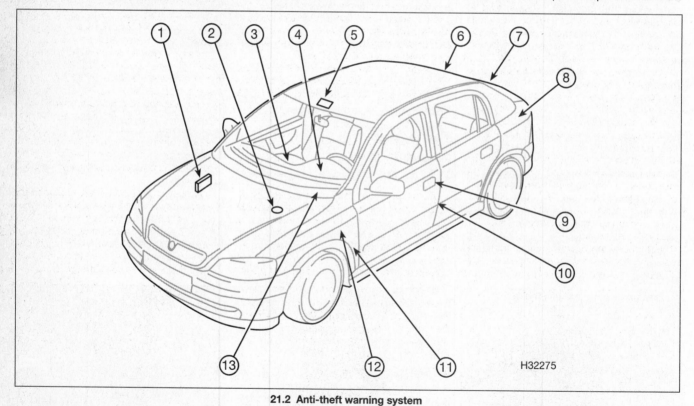

21.2 Anti-theft warning system

1 ATWS control unit including central door
 locking system (CDLS)
2 Bonnet contact
3 LED in hazard warning switch
4 Ignition lock

5 Ultrasonic sensor interior light
6 ATWS rear screen heating – glass
 breakage detector
7 Luggage compartment lid/tailgate switch
8 Load/luggage compartment light

9 Driver's door lock cylinder
10 Rear left-hand door courtesy light switch
11 Front left-hand door courtesy light switch
12 Power sounder
13 ATWS Horn

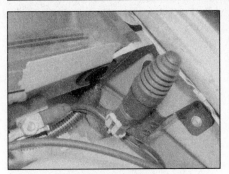

21.5 Anti-theft warning alarm system bonnet contact

21.9 The ATWS (anti-theft warning system)/ Central locking control unit is located at the bottom of the right-hand A-pillar

roadwheels). The anti-theft alarm system horn is located on the left-hand side of the bulkhead, and additionally a power-sounder horn is fitted beneath the liner at the rear of the left-hand wheelarch (LHD models) or right-hand wheelarch (RHD models). On Estate and Zafira models, a glass breakage detector is fitted to the luggage compartment rear side windows.

3 Before removing any component of the anti-theft or immobiliser systems, disconnect the battery as described in Chapter 5A.

4 To remove the immobiliser/transponder unit, remove the steering wheel and column shrouds as described in Chapter 10, then proceed as follows. On models with an immobiliser/transponder **without** catch lugs, disconnect the wiring, then unclip the unit from the ignition lock housing. On models with an immobiliser/transponder **with** catch lugs, remove the ignition lock cylinder as described in Section 4 of this Chapter, then unclip the unit from the ignition lock housing and disconnect the wiring. **Note:** *Note that if the immobiliser/transponder unit is renewed, it must be programmed by a Vauxhall dealer using specialist equipment.*

5 To remove the bonnet contact, undo the two mounting screws then lift the contact and disconnect the wiring **(see illustration)**.

6 To remove the system warning horn, remove the water deflector from the bulkhead, then unscrew the mounting nut and disconnect the wiring.

7 To remove the power-sounder horn, first remove the relevant front wheelarch liner (Chapter 11), then disconnect the wiring and

unbolt the horn, together with its bracket from the inner wing panel.

8 To remove a door contact (courtesy light) switch, refer to Section 4.

9 To remove the ATWS (anti-theft warning system)/Central locking control unit, undo the single screw and remove the trim panel from the bottom of the right-hand A-pillar, then remove the footwell side trim panel. Disconnect the wiring, then unscrew the two mounting nuts and remove the control unit **(see illustration)**.

10 Refer to Chapter 11 for the removal and refitting of central locking components.

11 To renew the remote control battery in the key fob, use a small screwdriver to release the plastic catch, then slide the fob directly from the key. Use the screwdriver to separate the two halves, then note how the battery is fitted and remove it **(see illustrations)**.

12 Refitting of the components is a reversal of the removal procedure. Any faults with the system should be referred to a Vauxhall dealer.

22 Speedometer sensor – general information

All models are fitted with an electronic speedometer sensor. This device measures the rotational speed of the transmission final drive or ABS wheel sensor (according to model) and converts the information into an electronic signal, which is then sent to the speedometer module in the instrument panel.

23 Airbag system – general information, precautions and system de-activation

General information

A driver's airbag, located on the steering wheel centre pad, is fitted as standard equipment on all models. A passenger's front airbag, front seat side airbags, and side curtain airbags (driver and passenger) may be fitted as an option. The passenger's airbag is located on the crossbar beneath the facia. The side airbags are located in the outer edge of the front seat backrests, and in the roof headlining.

The system is armed only when the ignition is switched on, however, a reserve power source maintains a power supply to the system in the event of a break in the main electrical supply. The system is activated by a 'g' sensor (deceleration sensor), incorporated in the electronic control unit. Note that the electronic control unit also controls the front seat belt tensioners. The airbags are inflated by gas generators, which force the bags out from their locations. The front airbags are only deployed in the event of a frontal impact at speeds in excess of 20 mph which occur within 30° each side of the vehicle centre line, and the side airbags are only deployed in the event of an impact on their respective sides. The front seat belt tensioners are deployed in the event of both front and rear impacts.

In the event of an accident which triggers the front airbags located in the steering wheel and facia, both the driver's and passenger's airbags must be renewed, however, the seat side airbags and seat belt tensioners can be deployed a maximum of three times before it is necessary to renew them. The airbag system control unit stores the number of deployments in its memory, and this can be read by Vauxhall technicians using specialist equipment.

On models fitted with a passenger airbag, the passenger seat incorporates a sensor mat. The passenger airbag is deactivated when the passenger seat is unoccupied. The system is also deactivated if a Vauxhall child seat is being used on the passenger seat, because transponders in the child seat are

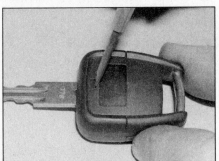

21.11a Use a small screwdriver to release the plastic catch . . .

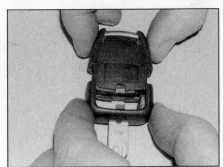

21.11b . . . then slide the fob directly from the key . . .

21.11c . . . for access to the battery

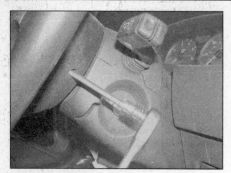

24.3a Remove the two screws . . .

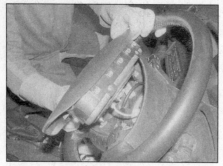

24.3b . . . and carefully lift the airbag/horn-push from the steering wheel

24.4 Disconnecting the wiring from the airbag

recognised by an antenna system in the passenger seat. The system can also detect if the child seat is fitted incorrectly (eg, the wrong way round), and a flashing warning light is illuminated in the front interior light.

In the event of a fault occurring in the airbag system, the warning light will illuminate on the instrument panel, and the system will need to be checked by a Vauxhall dealer.

Precautions

⚠️ **Warning: The following precautions must be observed when working on vehicles equipped with an airbag system, to prevent the possibility of personal injury.**

General precautions

The following precautions **must** be observed when carrying out work on a vehicle equipped with an airbag.

a) Do not disconnect the battery with the engine running.

b) Before carrying out any work in the vicinity of the airbag, removing of any of the airbag components, or welding any part of the vehicle, de-activate the system as described in the following sub-Section.

c) Do not attempt to test any of the airbag system circuits using test meters or any other test equipment.

d) If the airbag warning light comes on, or any fault in the system is suspected, consult a Vauxhall dealer without delay. **Do not** attempt to carry out fault diagnosis, or any dismantling of the components.

Precautions to be taken when handling an airbag

a) Transport the airbag by itself, bag upward.

b) Do not put your arms around the airbag.

c) Carry the airbag close to the body, bag outward.

d) Do not drop the airbag or expose it to impacts.

e) Do not attempt to dismantle the airbag unit.

f) Do not connect any form of electrical equipment to any part of the airbag circuit.

g) Do not allow any solvents or cleaning agents to contact the airbag assembly. The unit must be cleaned using only a damp cloth.

Precautions to be taken when storing an airbag unit

a) Store the unit in a cupboard with the airbag upward.

b) Do not expose the airbag to temperatures above 90ºC.

c) Do not expose the airbag to flames.

d) Do not attempt to dispose of the airbag – consult a Vauxhall dealer.

e) Never refit an airbag which is known to be faulty or damaged.

De-activation of airbag system

The system must be de-activated as follows, before carrying out any work on the airbag components or surrounding area.

a) Switch off the ignition.

b) Remove the ignition key.

c) Switch off all electrical equipment.

d) Disconnect the battery negative lead (see Chapter 5A).

e) Insulate the battery negative terminal and the end of the battery negative lead to prevent any possibility of contact.

f) Wait for at least one minute before carrying out any further work. This will allow the system capacitor to discharge.

24 Airbag system components – removal and refitting

⚠️ **Warning: Refer to the precautions given in Section 23 before attempting to carry out work on the airbag components.**

Driver's airbag unit

Removal

1 The driver's airbag unit is an integral part of the steering wheel centre pad. First de-activate the airbag system as described in Section 22.

2 Set the front wheels in the straight-ahead position, then lock the column in position after removing the ignition key.

3 Unscrew and remove the two screws from the rear of the steering wheel and carefully lift the airbag/horn-push from the steering wheel **(see illustrations)**.

4 Disconnect the wiring and remove the airbag **(see illustration)**. Position the airbag in a safe place where it cannot be tampered with, making sure that the padded side is facing upwards.

Refitting

5 Refitting is a reversal of removal, but make sure that the wiring connector is securely reconnected and tighten the retaining screws to the specified torque.

Passenger's airbag unit

Removal

6 The passenger's airbag unit is located on the crossbar beneath the facia panel. First de-activate the airbag system as described in Section 22.

7 Remove the glovebox as described in Chapter 11.

8 Using a Torx key, unscrew the mounting bolts and remove the airbag unit from the bracket on the crossbar **(see illustrations)**.

9 Disconnect the wiring and remove the airbag

24.8a Top view of the passenger side airbag (facia panel removed)

24.8b Bottom view of the passenger side airbag, showing mounting bolts

24.9 Passenger side airbag wiring

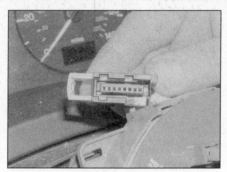

24.19 Disconnecting the wiring from the airbag contact unit

24.20 Removing the airbag contact unit from the top of the steering column

unit from inside the vehicle **(see illustration)**. Note that the bottom of the unit is shaped to locate in the mounting bracket holes.

Refitting

10 Refitting is a reversal of removal, but make sure that the wiring connector is securely reconnected and tighten the retaining screws to the specified torque.

Side airbag unit

Warning: Removal and refitting of the side curtain airbags, located in the vehicle headlining should be entrusted to a Vauxhall dealer.

Removal

11 The side airbag is located in the front seat backrest. First de-activate the airbag system as described in Section 22.
12 Unclip and remove the upholstery from the back of the seat.
13 Disconnect the wiring from the airbag.
14 Unscrew the three securing nuts and remove the airbag from the seat backrest. **Note:** *The manufacturers recommend that the nuts are renewed whenever removed as the integral washers are self-locking.*

Refitting

15 Refitting is a reversal of removal, but make sure that the wiring connector is securely reconnected and tighten the retaining nuts to the specified torque.

Airbag contact unit

Removal

16 Remove the driver's airbag unit as described earlier in this Section.
17 Remove the steering wheel as described in Chapter 10. Make sure that the front wheels are pointing straight-ahead, and that the steering is locked with the ignition key removed.
18 Remove the steering column shrouds with reference to Chapter 10. Recover the ignition key position indicator.
19 Pull out the locking plate, then disconnect the wiring plug from the rear of the contact unit **(see illustration)**.
20 Release the four rear clips and remove the contact unit from the top of the column **(see illustration)**. **Note:** *Make sure that the contact unit halves remain in their central position with the arrows aligned at the bottom. The unit*

automatically locks in its central position, however, if necessary apply tape to the halves to hold them.

Refitting

21 Before refitting the contact unit, if the centre position has been lost or if a new unit is being fitted, determine the centre position as follows. Depress the detent on top of the unit and carefully turn the centre part of the unit anti-clockwise until resistance is felt. Now turn it 2.5 turns clockwise and align the arrows on the centre part and outer edge.
22 If a new unit is fitted, first remove the transport clip.
23 Locate the contact unit on the top of the steering column making sure that the guide pins locate in the holes provided. Press the unit in until the clips engage. **Note:** *The clips must not be damaged in any way. If they are, the unit must be renewed.*
24 Reconnect the wiring and push in the locking plate.
25 Refit the ignition key position indicator, then refit the steering column shrouds and tighten the securing screws (see Chapter 10).
26 Refit the steering wheel (see Chapter 10).
27 Refit the driver's airbag unit as described earlier.

Electronic control unit (airbag module)

Removal

28 De-activate the airbag system as described in Section 22.
29 Remove the centre console as described in Chapter 11. On Zafira models, also remove the gearchange lever assembly with reference to

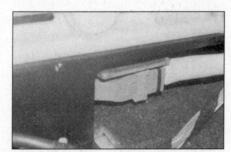

24.29 The airbag control unit is located beneath the gearchange lever assembly on Zafira models

Chapter 7A (the electronic control unit is located beneath the assembly) **(see illustration)**.
30 Disconnect the wiring from the control unit **(see illustration)**, then unscrew the mounting nuts and remove the unit from inside the vehicle. Note that the arrow on top of the unit points towards the front of the vehicle, however the three mounting nuts are arranged so that it is impossible to fit it incorrectly.

Refitting

31 Refitting is a reversal of removal but tighten the mounting nuts to the specified torque. **Note:** *Note that if the electronic control unit is renewed, it must be programmed by a Vauxhall dealer using specialist equipment.*

Side airbag sensor

Removal

32 The side airbag sensors are located inside the front doors. First, de-activate the airbag system as described in Section 22.
33 Remove the front door inner trim panel as described in Chapter 11, Section 44.
34 Pull back the water membrane for access to the sensor.
35 Disconnect the wiring, then unscrew the mounting bolts and remove the sensor.

Refitting

36 Refitting is a reversal of removal, but tighten the mounting bolts securely.

Front passenger seat sensor mat

Removal and refitting

37 It is recommended that a Vauxhall dealer carry out this work, as the upholstery has to be removed, and the position of the mat is critical.

24.30 On Astra models the airbag control unit is located beneath the rear of the centre console

VAUXHALL ASTRA 1998 on

Diagram 1

Key to symbols

Bulb

Switch

Multiple contact switch (ganged)

Fuse/fusible link

F24

Resistor

Variable resistor

Item no.

15

Pump/motor

M

Earth and location (via lead)

E1

Gauge/meter

Diode

Light emitting diode (LED)

Internal connection (connecting wires)

Wire splice or soldered joint

Solenoid actuator

Plug and socket connector

Connections to other circuits. Direction of arrow denotes current flow.

A

Diagram 3, Arrow A
High beam warning light

Wire colour (Red wire/white tracer)

Ro/Ws

Box shape denotes part of a larger component. Terminal identified by either standard termination (bold *italic*) or by connector number (plain text).

30 4

30 Terminal identification (i.e. battery +ve)
4 Connector pin number

Earth locations

E1	Battery ground strap	E7	Engine (electronic)
E2	Engine ground strap	E8	Engine distribution
E3	Ignition coil earth	E9	Rear panel
E4	"A" pillar	E10	Tailgate
E5	Steering column	E11	Heater blower
E6	Transmission tunnel		

Key to circuits

Diagram 1   Information for wiring diagrams
Diagram 2   Starting, charging, airbag and typical radio/CD
Diagram 3   X14XE & X16XEL engine management system
Diagram 4   X14XE & X16XEL engine management system cont. and electric windows
Diagram 5   X16SZR engine management system
Diagram 6   X18XE-1 engine management system
Diagram 7   X18XE-1 engine management system continued, ABS with traction control and speed sensor (non ABS models)
Diagram 8   X20XEV engine management system
Diagram 9   X20XEV engine management system cont. and wash/wipe
Diagram 10 Engine cooling and triple info display
Diagram 11 Front lights
Diagram 12 Fog, tail, reversing and direction indicator lights
Diagram 13 Number plate, stop, interior lights, heated rear window and cigarette lighter
Diagram 14 Multi-timer
Diagram 15 Glovebox light, horn, sunroof and central locking
Diagram 16 Power steering, exterior door mirrors, cruise control and heating
Diagram 17 Typical air conditioning and automatic transmission
Diagram 18 Automatic transmission continued
Diagram 19 Multi info display
Diagram 20 Instrument display

Engine fuse box

Fuse	Rating					
F1	60A	F5	60A		F8	40A (X20XEV or AC only)
F2	60A	F6	20A		F9	25A
F3	60A	F7	80A			
F4	40A	F8	20A (not X20XEV or AC)			

Main fuse box

Fuse	Rating	Circuit protected	Fuse	Rating	Circuit protected
F2	30A	Fans			
F3	40A	Heated rear window	F23	10A	ABS and power steering
F6	10A	RH dipped beam, headlight adjustment	F24	10A	LH dipped beam, headlight adjustment
F7	10A	RH parking, tail and number plate lights	F25	10A	LH parking, tail and number plate lights
F8	10A	RH main beam	F26	10A	LH main beam
F9	30A	Headlamp wash	F28	7.5A	Interior light
F10	15A	Horn	F29	10A	Hazard warning, interior light and automatic transmission
F11	20A	Central locking			
F12	15A	Front fog lights	F30	30A	Sunroof
F13	7.5A	Information display	F33	20A	Trailer connection
F14	30A	Windscreen wipers	F34	20A	CD player, radio, information display and GPS
F15	15A	Electric windows, sunroof and mirrors			
F16	10A	Rear fog lights	F35	10A	Automatic transmission, engine cooling, air con.
F17	30A	Electric windows	F36	20A	Cigarette lighter
F18	7.5A	Number plate lights and headlight range adjustment	F38	10A	Stop lights, auto. transmission info. display and cruise control
F20	30A	Electric windows	F39	7.5A	Auto. transmission, air con. and engine cooling
F21	7.5A	Radio			
F22	15A	Hazard warning, info. display, indicators and trip computer	F40	7.5A	Engine cooling and air con.
			F41	10A	Heated mirrors

MTS
H31931

Wire colours

Bl	Blue	Pu	Purple
Br	Brown	Ro	Red
Ge	Yellow	Sw	Black
Gr	Grey	Vi	Violet
Gn	Green	Ws	White
Or	Orange		

Key to items

1 Battery
2 Ignition switch
3 Engine fuse box
4 Alternator
5 Starter motor
6 Main fuse box
7 Radio
8 Diagnostic connector
9 Telephone connection
10 CD player
11 Aerial amplifier
12 LH front speaker
13 LH front tweeter
14 RH front tweeter
15 RH front speaker
16 LH rear speaker
17 LH rear tweeter
18 RH rear tweeter
19 RH rear speaker
20 Airbag module
21 LH seatbelt pretensioner
22 RH seatbelt pretensioner
23 Driver's airbag
24 Airbag contact unit
25 Passenger's airbag
26 Passenger's side airbag
27 Driver's side airbag
28 Passenger's side airbag sensor
29 Driver's side airbag sensor

Astra 1998 on - Diagram 2

MTS
H31932

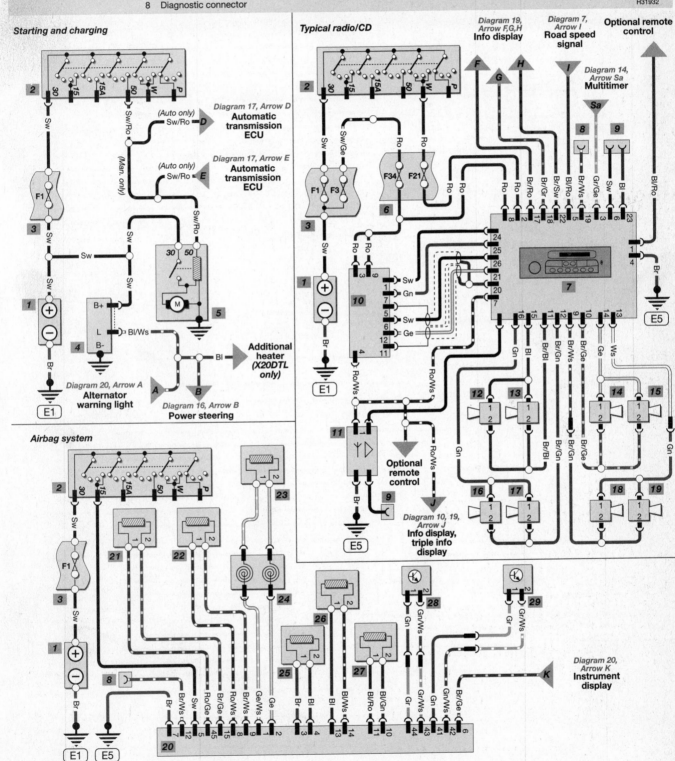

Starting and charging

Diagram 17, Arrow D
Automatic transmission ECU

Diagram 17, Arrow E
Automatic transmission ECU

Additional heater (X20DTL only)

Diagram 20, Arrow A
Alternator warning light

Diagram 16, Arrow B
Power steering

Typical radio/CD

Diagram 19, Arrow F,G,H
Info display

Diagram 7, Arrow I
Road speed signal

Optional remote control

Diagram 14, Arrow Sa
Multitimer

Optional remote control

Diagram 10, 19, Arrow J
Info display, triple info display

Airbag system

Diagram 20, Arrow K
Instrument display

Wire colours

Bl	Blue	**Pu**	Purple
Br	Brown	**Ro**	Red
Ge	Yellow	**Sw**	Black
Gr	Grey	**Vi**	Violet
Gn	Green	**Ws**	White
Or	Orange		

Key to items

1 Battery
2 Ignition switch
3 Engine fuse box
8 Diagnostic connector
30 Multec control unit
31 Camshaft position sensor

32 Fuel pump relay
33 Fuel pump
34 Fuel injector cylinder 1
35 Fuel injector cylinder 2
36 Fuel injector cylinder 3
37 Fuel injector cylinder 4

38 Ignition coil
39 Spark plugs
40 Canister purge soleniod valve
41 Oxygen sensor
42 EGR solenoid valve
43 MAP sensor

44 Throttle position sensor
45 Coolant temperature sensor
46 Intake air temperature sensor
47 Knock sensor
48 Idle speed stepper motor
49 Crankshaft sensor

Astra 1998 on - Diagram 3

Note: prefix 1/ = X53 multi plug
prefix 2/ = X54 multi plug

MTS
H31933

Engine management system X14XE & X16XEL engines

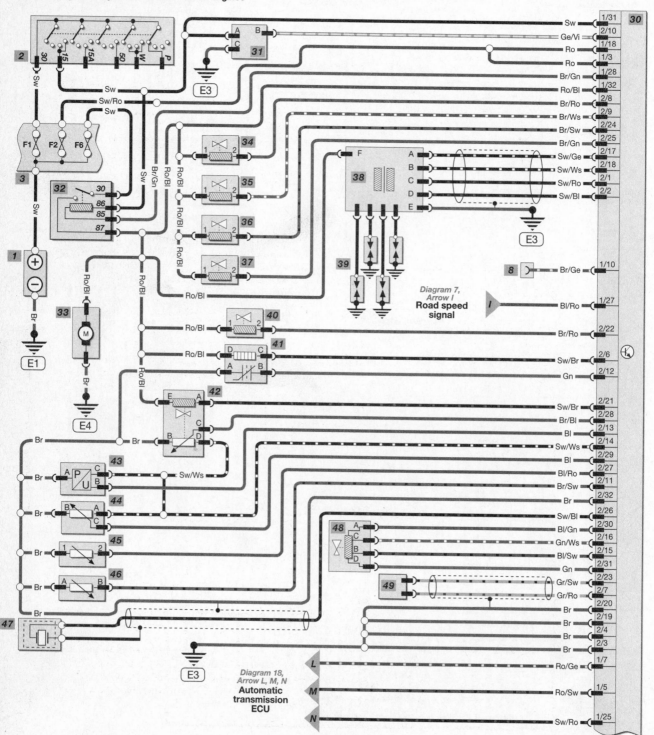

Diagram 7,
Arrow I
Road speed signal

Diagram 18,
Arrow L, M, N
Automatic transmission ECU

Wire colours

Bl	Blue	**Pu**	Purple
Br	Brown	**Ro**	Red
Ge	Yellow	**Sw**	Black
Gr	Grey	**Vi**	Violet
Gn	Green	**Ws**	White
Or	Orange		

Key to items

1 Battery
2 Ignition switch
3 Engine fuse box
6 Main fuse box
30 Multec control unit
50 Drivers electric window switch unit
51 Passenger electric window switch

52 LH rear electric window switch
53 RH rear electric window switch
54 Drivers electric window motor
55 Passenger electric window motor
56 LH rear electric window motor
57 RH rear electric window motor

Astra 1998 on - Diagram 4

Note: prefix 1/ = X53 multi plug
prefix 2/ = X54 multi plug

MTS
H31934

Engine management system X14XE & X16XEL engines continued

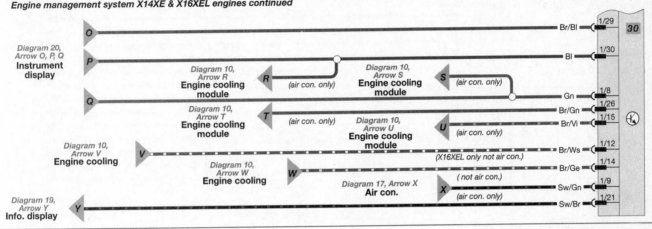

Electric windows

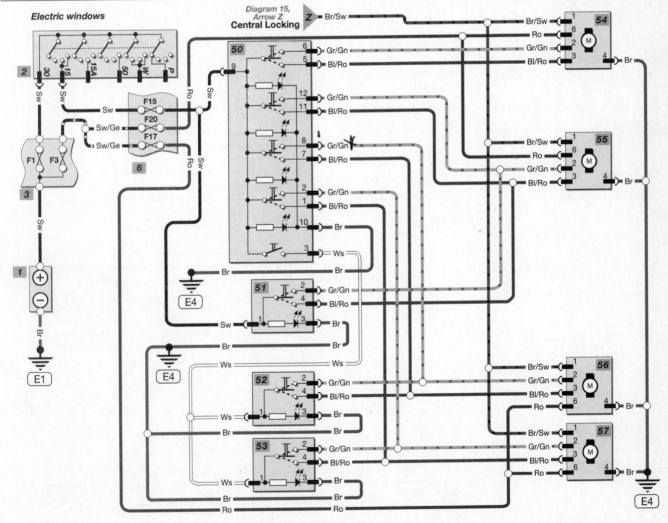

Wire colours

Bl	Blue	Pu	Purple
Br	Brown	Ro	Red
Ge	Yellow	Sw	Black
Gr	Grey	Vi	Violet
Gn	Green	Ws	White
Or	Orange		

Key to items

1 Battery
2 Ignition switch
3 Engine fuse box
8 Diagnostic connector
30 Multec control unit
32 Fuel pump relay
33 Fuel pump
38 Ignition coil
39 Spark plugs
40 Canister purge solenoid valve
41 Exhaust sensor
42 EGR solenoid valve
43 Intake pressure sensor
44 Throttle position sensor
45 Coolant temperature sensor
47 Knock sensor
48 Idle speed stepper motor
49 Crankshaft sensor
58 Single point fuel injector

Astra 1998 on - Diagram 5

Note: prefix 1/ = X55 multi plug
prefix 2/ = X56 multi plug

MTS
H31935

Ignition and injection X16SZR engine

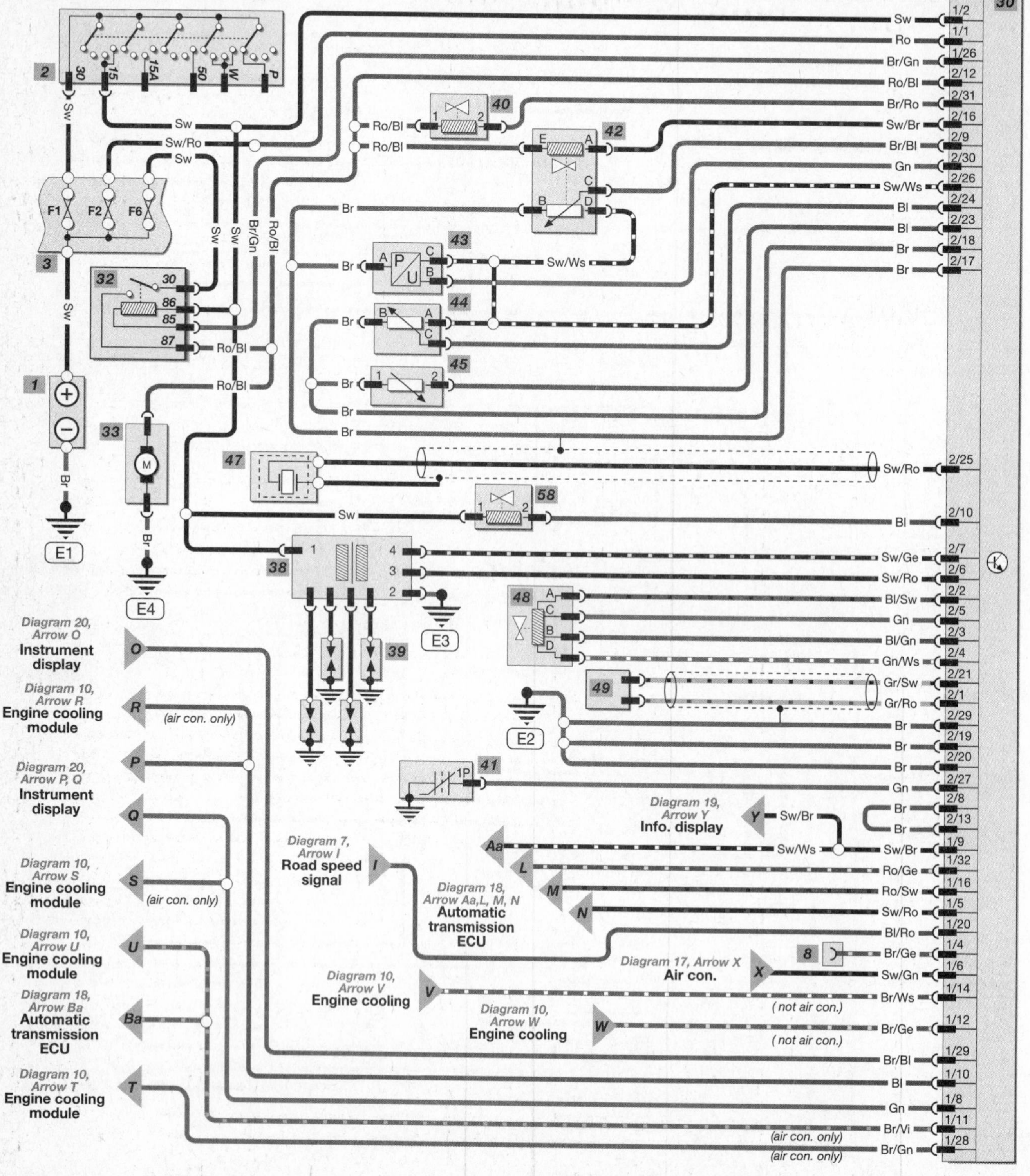

Sw 1/2
Ro 1/1
Br/Gn 1/26
Ro/Bl 2/12
Br/Ro 2/31
Sw/Br 2/16
Br/Bl 2/9
Gn 2/30
Sw/Ws 2/26
Bl 2/24
Bl 2/23
Br 2/18
Br 2/17

40

42

43

44

45

Ro/Bl
Ro/Bl
Br
Br
Br
Br
Br
Sw/Ws

30

F1 F2 F6

32 30
86
85
87

Ro/Bl
Ro/Bl

1
+
−

33
M

E1

E4

47
Sw/Ro 2/25

58
Sw
Bl 2/10

38
Sw/Ge 2/7
Sw/Ro 2/6
Bl/Sw 2/2
Gn 2/5
Bl/Gn 2/3
Gn/Ws 2/4
Gr/Sw 2/21
Gr/Ro 2/1
Br 2/29
Br 2/19
Br 2/20
Gn 2/27
Br 2/8
Br 2/13

48 A
C
B
D

49

E2

39

E3

41

Diagram 20, Arrow O
Instrument display
O

Diagram 10, Arrow R
Engine cooling module
R (air con. only)

Diagram 20, Arrow P, Q
Instrument display
P

Q

Diagram 10, Arrow S
Engine cooling module
S (air con. only)

Diagram 10, Arrow U
Engine cooling module
U

Diagram 18, Arrow Ba
Automatic transmission ECU
Ba

Diagram 10, Arrow T
Engine cooling module
T

Diagram 7, Arrow I
Road speed signal
I

Diagram 18, Arrow Aa, L, M, N
Automatic transmission ECU
Aa
L
M
N

Diagram 19, Arrow Y
Info. display
Y Sw/Br

Diagram 17, Arrow X
Air con.
X 8

Diagram 10, Arrow V
Engine cooling
V

Diagram 10, Arrow W
Engine cooling
W

Sw/Br 1/9
Ro/Ge 1/32
Ro/Sw 1/16
Sw/Ro 1/5
Bl/Ro 1/20
Br/Ge 1/4
Sw/Gn 1/6
Br/Ws 1/14 (not air con.)
Br/Ge 1/12 (not air con.)
Br/Bl 1/29
Bl 1/10
Gn 1/8
Br/Vi 1/11 (air con. only)
Br/Gn 1/28 (air con. only)

Sw/Ws

30

Wire colours

Bl	Blue	**Pu**	Purple
Br	Brown	**Ro**	Red
Ge	Yellow	**Sw**	Black
Gr	Grey	**Vi**	Violet
Gn	Green	**Ws**	White
Or	Orange		

Key to items

1 Battery
2 Ignition switch
3 Engine fuse box
8 Diagnostic connector
31 Camshaft position sensor
32 Fuel pump relay
33 Fuel pump
34 Fuel injector cylinder 1
35 Fuel injector cylinder 2
36 Fuel injector cylinder 3
37 Fuel injector cylinder 4
38 Ignition coil
39 Spark plugs
40 Canister purge solenoid valve
41 Oxygen sensor
42 EGR solenoid valve
44 Throttle position sensor
45 Coolant temperature sensor
47 Knock sensor
49 Crankshaft sensor
59 Simtec control unit
60 Intake manifold change-over valve
61 Air mass meter

Astra 1998 on - Diagram 6

Note: prefix 1/ = X57 multi plug
      prefix 2/ = X58 multi plug

MTS
H31936

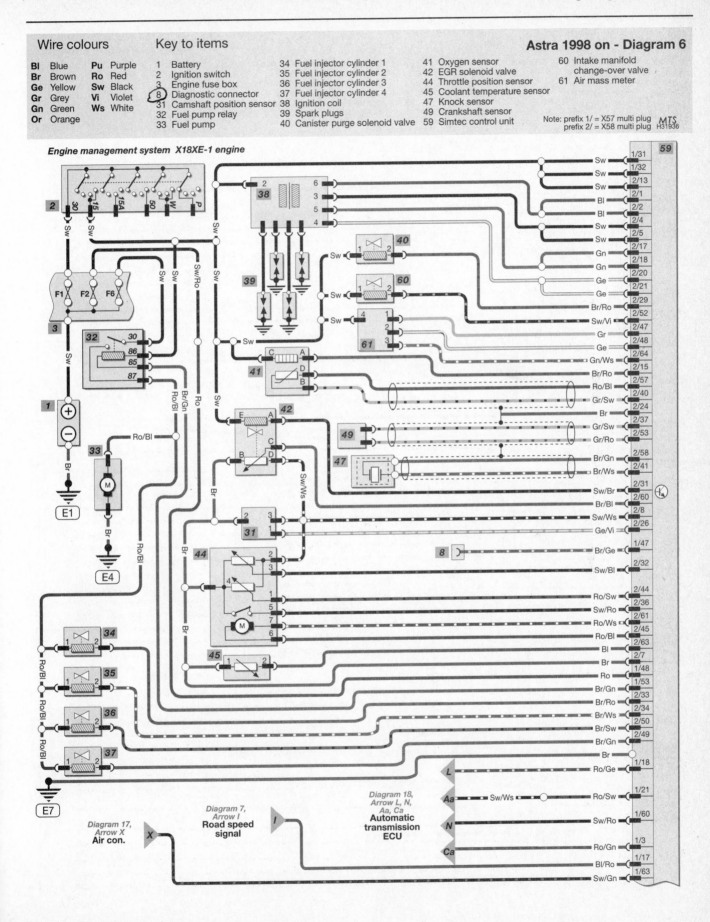

Engine management system **X18XE-1** engine

Diagram 17, Arrow X
Air con.

Diagram 7, Arrow I
Road speed signal

Diagram 18, Arrow L, N, Aa, Ca
Automatic transmission ECU

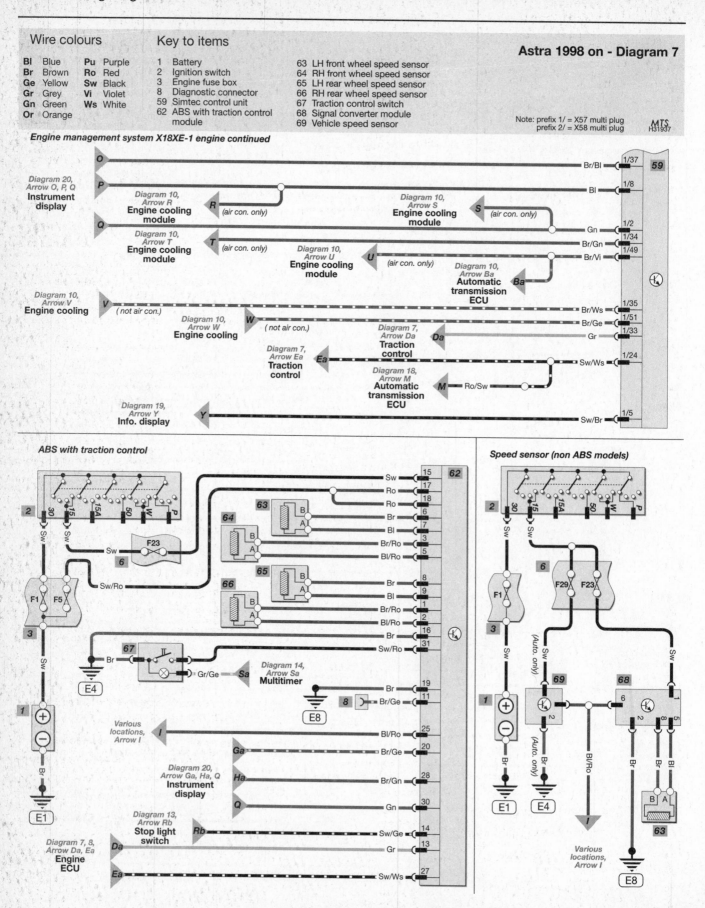

Wire colours

Bl Blue
Br Brown
Ge Yellow
Gr Grey
Gn Green
Or Orange
Pu Purple
Ro Red
Sw Black
Vi Violet
Ws White

Key to items

1 Battery
2 Ignition switch
3 Engine fuse box
8 Diagnostic connector
59 Simtec control unit
62 ABS with traction control module
63 LH front wheel speed sensor
64 RH front wheel speed sensor
65 LH rear wheel speed sensor
66 RH rear wheel speed sensor
67 Traction control switch
68 Signal converter module
69 Vehicle speed sensor

Astra 1998 on - Diagram 7

Note: prefix 1/ = X57 multi plug
prefix 2/ = X58 multi plug

MTS
H31937

Engine management system X18XE-1 engine continued

Diagram 20, Arrow O, P, Q **Instrument display**

Diagram 10, Arrow R **Engine cooling module** (air con. only)

Diagram 10, Arrow S **Engine cooling module** (air con. only)

Diagram 10, Arrow T **Engine cooling module** (air con. only)

Diagram 10, Arrow U **Engine cooling module** (air con. only)

Diagram 10, Arrow Ba **Automatic transmission ECU**

Diagram 10, Arrow V **Engine cooling** (not air con.)

Diagram 10, Arrow W **Engine cooling** (not air con.)

Diagram 7, Arrow Da **Traction control**

Diagram 7, Arrow Ea **Traction control**

Diagram 18, Arrow M **Automatic transmission ECU**

Diagram 19, Arrow Y **Info. display**

Br/Bl 1/37 | 59
Bl 1/8
Gn 1/2
Br/Gn 1/34
Br/Vi 1/49
Br/Ws 1/35
Br/Ge 1/51
Gr 1/33
Sw/Ws 1/24
Ro/Sw
Sw/Br 1/5

ABS with traction control

Sw 15 | 62
Ro 17
Ro 18
Br 6
Bl 7
Br/Ro 3
Bl/Ro 5
Br 8
Bl 9
Br/Ro 1
Bl/Ro 2
Br 16
Sw/Ro 31

F23

Sw
Sw/Ro

63
64
65
66

30 15 15A 50 W P

F1 F5

Sw
E4

67

Br

Gr/Ge *Sa*
Diagram 14, Arrow Sa **Multitimer**

Br 19
Br/Ge 11
8 E8

Various locations, Arrow I *I* Bl/Ro 25
Ga Br/Ge 20
Diagram 20, Arrow Ga, Ha, Q **Instrument display** *Ha* Br/Gn 28
Q Gn 30
Diagram 13, Arrow Rb **Stop light switch** *Rb* Sw/Ge 14
Gr 13
Diagram 7, 8, Arrow Da, Ea **Engine ECU** *Da*
Ea Sw/Ws 27

1 + - Br E1

3

Sw

Speed sensor (non ABS models)

2 30 15 15A 50 W P

F1 F29 F23

3 Sw Sw Sw
(Auto. only) (Auto. only)

69 68
6
2 2 8 5

1 + -

E1 E4

Br Br Bl/Ro Br Br Bl

B A
63

Various locations, Arrow I *I*

E8

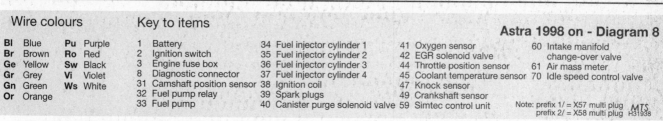

Wire colours

Bl	Blue	Pu	Purple
Br	Brown	Ro	Red
Ge	Yellow	Sw	Black
Gr	Grey	Vi	Violet
Gn	Green	Ws	White
Or	Orange		

Key to items

1 Battery
2 Ignition switch
3 Engine fuse box
8 Diagnostic connector
31 Camshaft position sensor
32 Fuel pump relay
33 Fuel pump

34 Fuel injector cylinder 1
35 Fuel injector cylinder 2
36 Fuel injector cylinder 3
37 Fuel injector cylinder 4
38 Ignition coil
39 Spark plugs
40 Canister purge solenoid valve

41 Oxygen sensor
42 EGR solenoid valve
44 Throttle position sensor
45 Coolant temperature sensor
47 Knock sensor
49 Crankshaft sensor
59 Simtec control unit

60 Intake manifold change-over valve
61 Air mass meter
70 Idle speed control valve

Astra 1998 on - Diagram 8

Note: prefix 1/ = X57 multi plug
prefix 2/ = X58 multi plug

MTS
H31938

Engine management system X20XEV engine

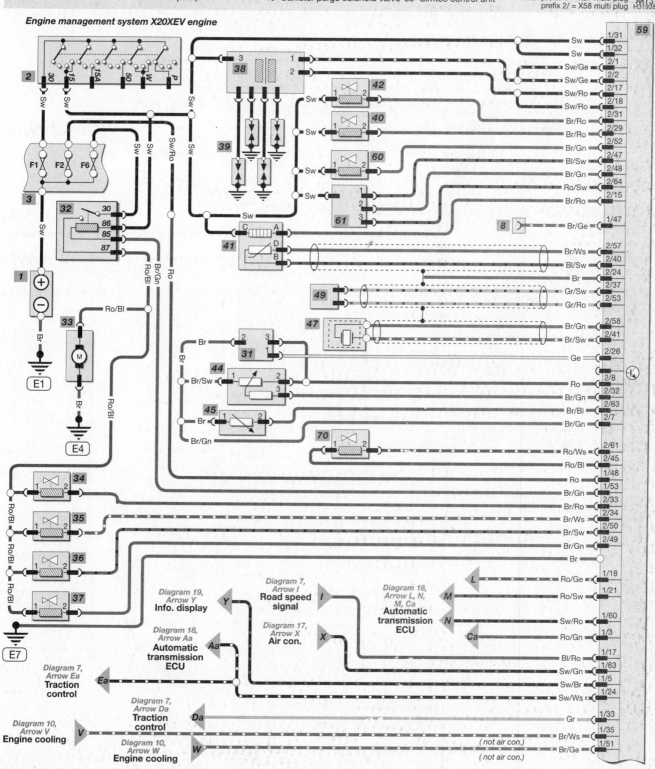

Wire colours

Bl Blue	**Pu** Purple
Br Brown	**Ro** Red
Ge Yellow	**Sw** Black
Gr Grey	**Vi** Violet
Gn Green	**Ws** White
Or Orange	

Key to items

1 Battery
2 Ignition switch
3 Engine fuse box
59 Simtec control unit
71 Headlight washer relay
72 Headlight washer pump

73 Wash/wipe switch
74 Windscreen washer pump
75 Windscreen wiper relay
76 Windscreen wiper motor
77 Rear wiper relay
78 Rear wiper motor

Astra 1998 on - Diagram 9

Note: prefix 1/ = X57 multi plug
prefix 2/ = X58 multi plug

MTS
H31939

Engine management system X20XEV engine continued

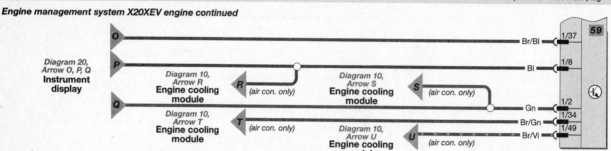

Wash/Wipe

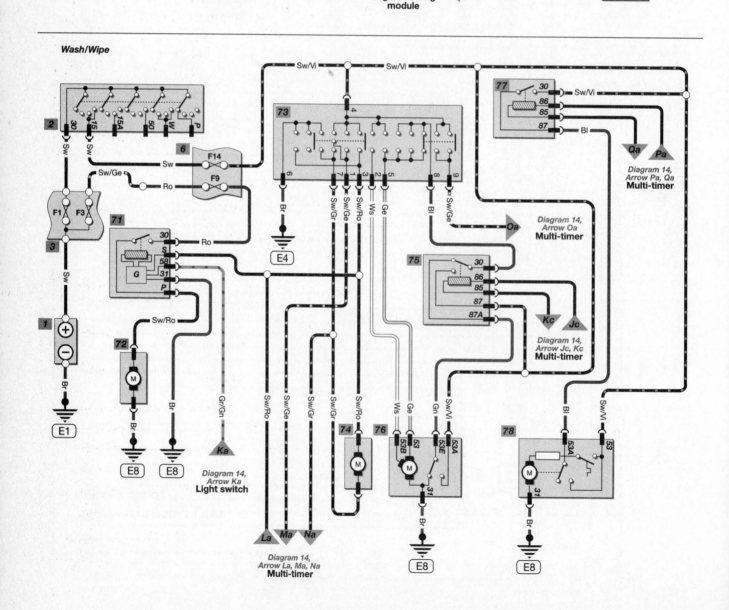

Wire colours

Bl	Blue	Pu	Purple
Br	Brown	Ro	Red
Ge	Yellow	Sw	Black
Gr	Grey	Vi	Violet
Gn	Green	Ws	White
Or	Orange		

Key to items

1 Battery
2 Ignition switch
3 Engine fuse box
8 Diagnostic connector
79 Engine cooling control unit
80 Air con. pressure sensor
81 Radiator blower motor
82 Air con. compressor clutch
83 Radiator blower motor relay
84 Triple info display
85 Outside temperature sensor

Astra 1998 on - Diagram 10

Note: prefix 1/ = X63 multi plug
prefix 2/ = X64 multi plug

MTS
H31940

Typical engine cooling (air con.)

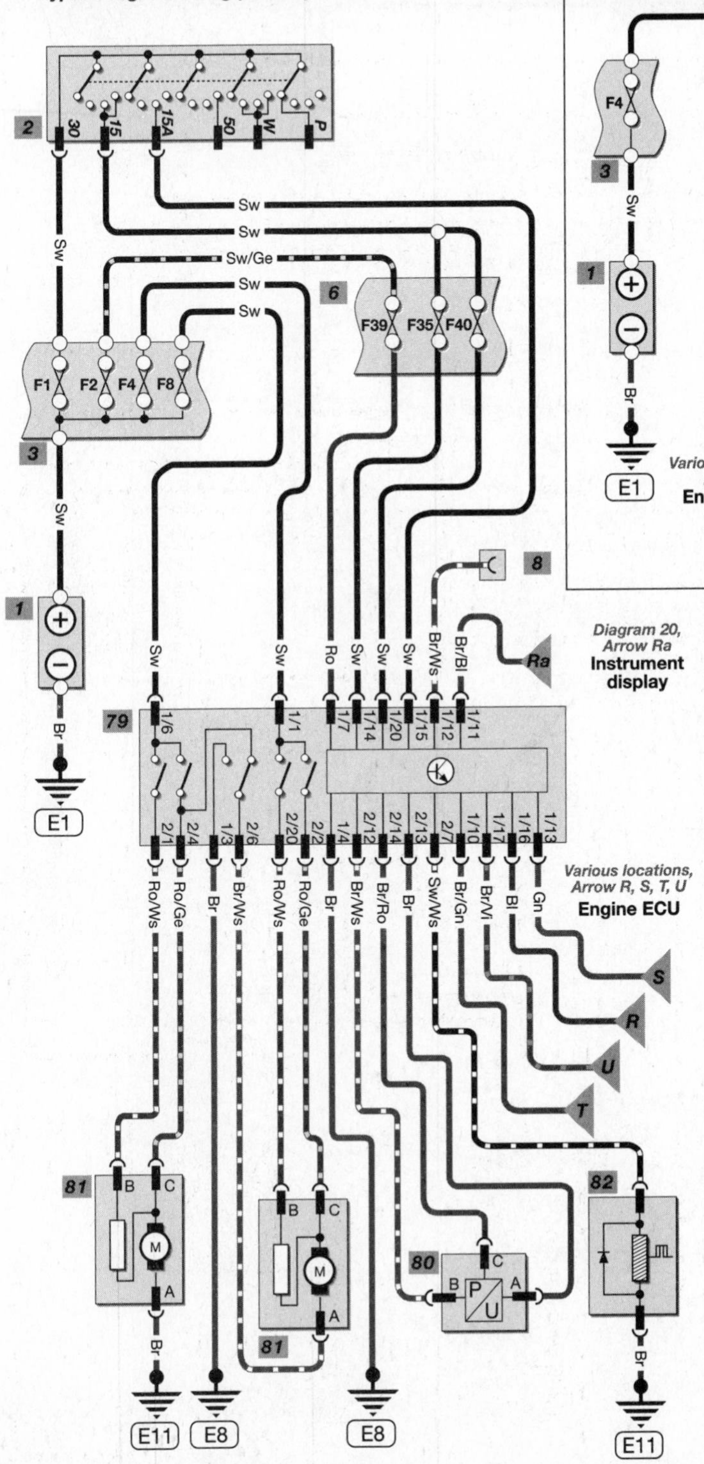

Engine cooling (not air con.)

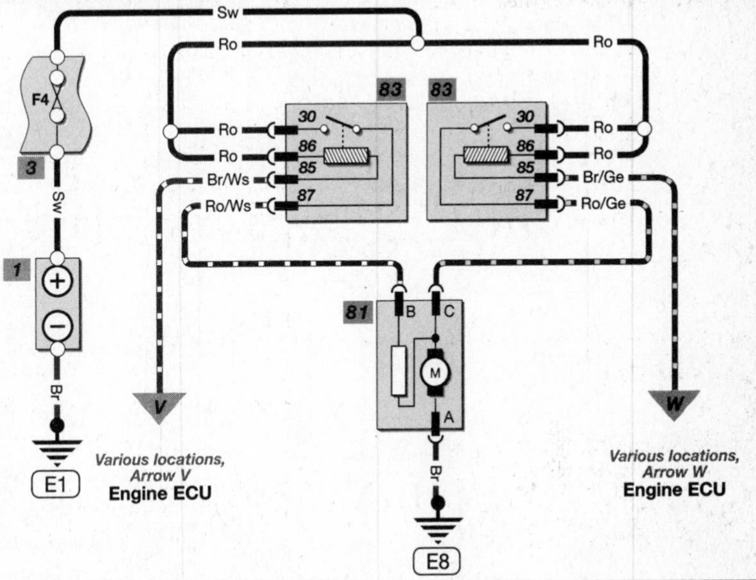

Various locations, Arrow V
Engine ECU

Various locations, Arrow W
Engine ECU

Diagram 20, Arrow Ra
Instrument display

Various locations, Arrow R, S, T, U
Engine ECU

Triple info. display

Diagram 14, Arrow Sa
Multi-timer

Diagram 7, Arrow I
Road speed signal

Diagram 2, Arrow F, G, H, J
Radio

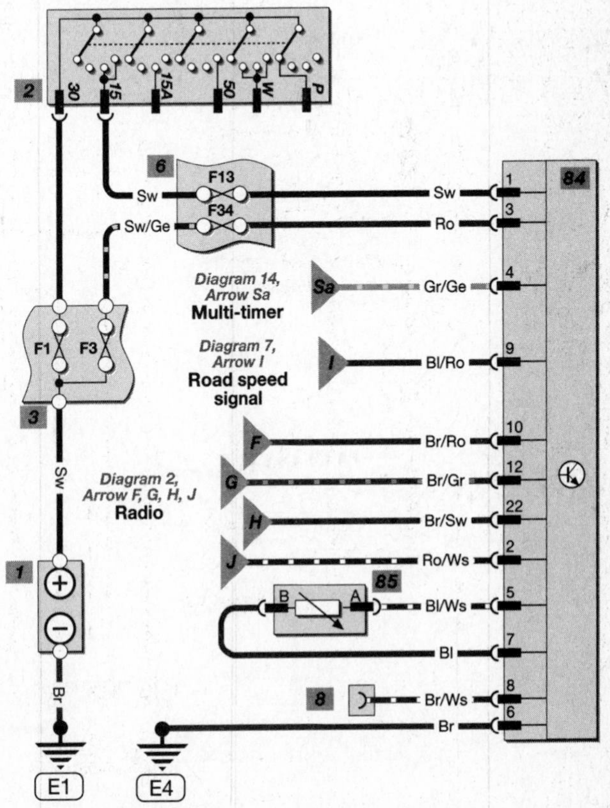

Wire colours

Bl	Blue	**Pu**	Purple
Br	Brown	**Ro**	Red
Ge	Yellow	**Sw**	Black
Gr	Grey	**Vi**	Violet
Gn	Green	**Ws**	White
Or	Orange		

Key to items

1 Battery
2 Ignition switch
3 Engine fuse box
6 Main fuse box
86 Main beam switch
87 Main beam relay
88 Light switch
89 LH headlight leveller

90 RH headlight leveller
91 LH front lights
  a) direction indicator
  b) main beam
  c) dipped beam
  d) side lights
  e) fog lights

92 RH front lights (as 91)
93 Trailer connection

Astra 1998 on - Diagram 11

MTS
H31941

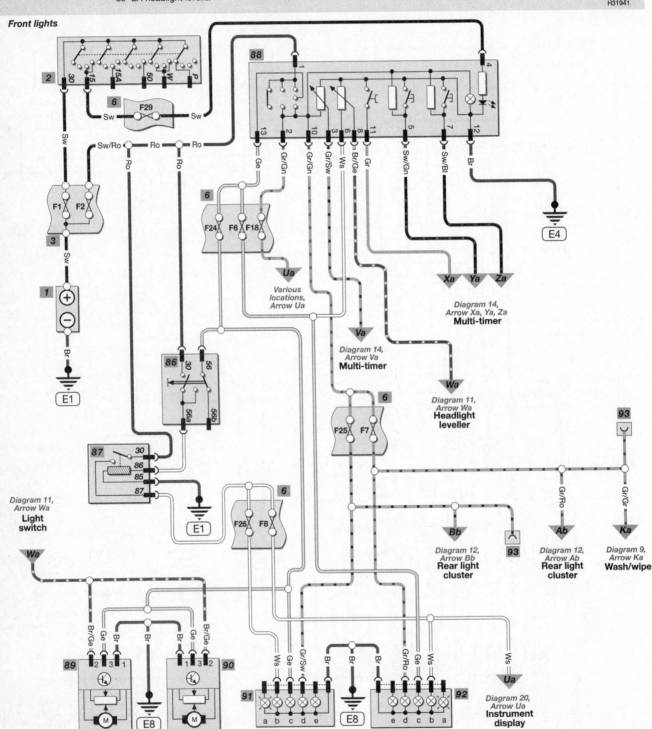

Front lights

Diagram 11,
Arrow Wa
Light switch

Diagram 14,
Arrow Va
Multi-timer

Various
locations,
Arrow Ua

Diagram 14,
Arrow Xa, Ya, Za
Multi-timer

Diagram 11,
Arrow Wa
Headlight leveller

Diagram 12,
Arrow Bb
Rear light cluster

Diagram 12,
Arrow Ab
Rear light cluster

Diagram 9,
Arrow Ka
Wash/wipe

Diagram 20,
Arrow Ua
Instrument display

Wire colours

Bl	Blue	Pu	Purple
Br	Brown	Ro	Red
Ge	Yellow	Sw	Black
Gr	Grey	Vi	Violet
Gn	Green	Ws	White
Or	Orange		

Key to items

1 Battery
2 Ignition switch
3 Engine fuse box
6 Main fuse box
91 LH front lights
  a) direction indicator
  b) main beam

  c) dipped beam
  d) side lights
  e) fog lights
92 RH front lights (as 91)
93 Trailer connection
94 Front fog light relay
95 Rear fog light relay

96 LH rear light cluster
  a) direction indicator
  b) stop light
  c) tail light
  d) reversing light
  e) fog light
97 RH rear light cluster (as 96)

98 Trailer socket switch
99 LH direction indicator relay
100 RH direction indicator relay
101 LH indicator side repeater
102 RH indicator side repeater
103 Reversing light switch

Astra 1998 on - Diagram 12

MTS
H31942

Fog lights, tail lights

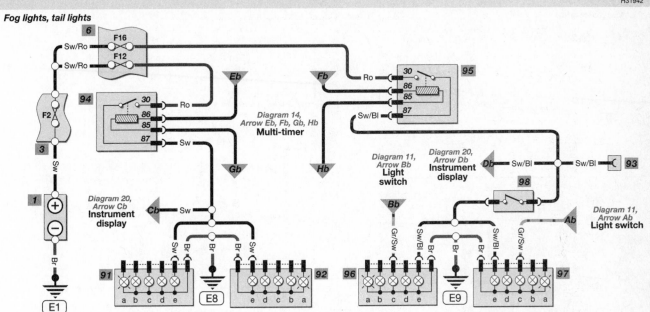

Direction indicators

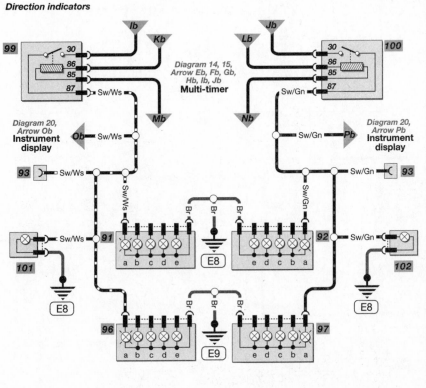

Reversing lights

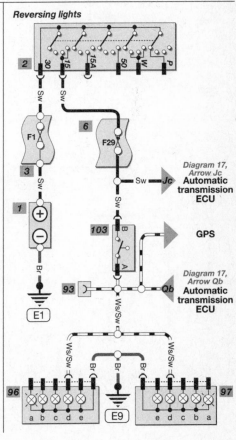

Astra 1998 on - Diagram 13

Wire colours

Bl	Blue	**Pu**	Purple
Br	Brown	**Ro**	Red
Ge	Yellow	**Sw**	Black
Gr	Grey	**Vi**	Violet
Gn	Green	**Ws**	White
Or	Orange		

Key to items

1 Battery
2 Ignition switch
3 Engine fuse box
6 Main fuse box
93 Trailer connection
96 LH rear light cluster
  a) direction indicator
  b) stop light
  c) tail light
  d) reversing light
  e) fog light
97 RH rear light cluster (as 96)
104 Single number plate light
105 LH number plate light
106 RH number plate light
107 Clutch pedal switch
108 Brake pedal/stop light switch
109 Stop light switch
110 High level stop light
111 Heated rear window relay
112 Heated rear window
113 Drivers door switch
114 Passenger door switch
115 LH rear door switch
116 RH rear door switch
117 Passenger compartment light, with time delay
118 LH rear reading light
119 RH rear reading light
120 Luggage compartment light
121 Tailgate switch
122 Cigarette lighter

MTS H31943

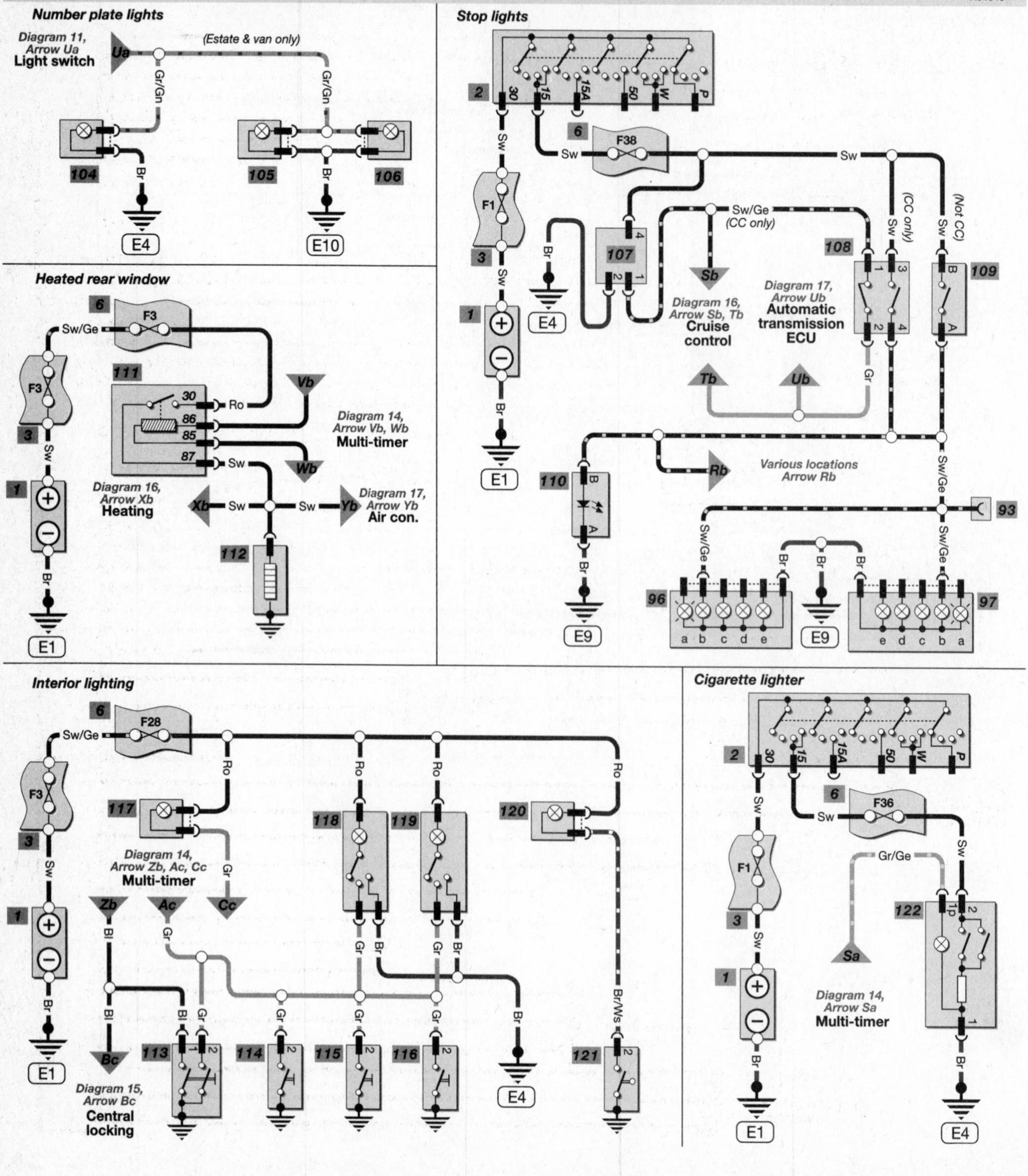
Number plate lights
Diagram 11, Arrow Ua
Light switch
Ua
(Estate & van only)
Gr/Gn
104
105
106
Br
E4
E10
Stop lights
30
15
15A
50
W
P
F38
F1
Sw
Sw/Ge
(CC only)
(Not CC)
107
108
109
110
Sb
Diagram 16, Arrow Sb, Tb
Cruise control
Diagram 17, Arrow Ub
Automatic transmission ECU
Tb
Ub
Rb
Various locations
Arrow Rb
93
96
97
a b c d e
e d c b a
E1
E4
E9
Heated rear window
F3
111
Ro
Vb
Wb
Diagram 14, Arrow Vb, Wb
Multi-timer
Diagram 16, Arrow Xb
Heating
Xb
Yb
Diagram 17, Arrow Yb
Air con.
112
Interior lighting
F28
117
118
119
120
Diagram 14, Arrow Zb, Ac, Cc
Multi-timer
Zb
Ac
Cc
Bl
Gr
Br/Ws
113
114
115
116
121
Bc
Diagram 15, Arrow Bc
Central locking
Cigarette lighter
F36
Gr/Ge
Sa
Diagram 14, Arrow Sa
Multi-timer
122

Wire colours

Bl	Blue	Pu	Purple
Br	Brown	Ro	Red
Ge	Yellow	Sw	Black
Gr	Grey	Vi	Violet
Gn	Green	Ws	White
Or	Orange		

Key to items

1 Battery
2 Ignition switch
3 Engine fuse box
6 Main fuse box

123 Multi-timer
124 Hazard warning light switch
125 Direction indicator switch

Astra 1998 on - Diagram 14

MTS
H31944

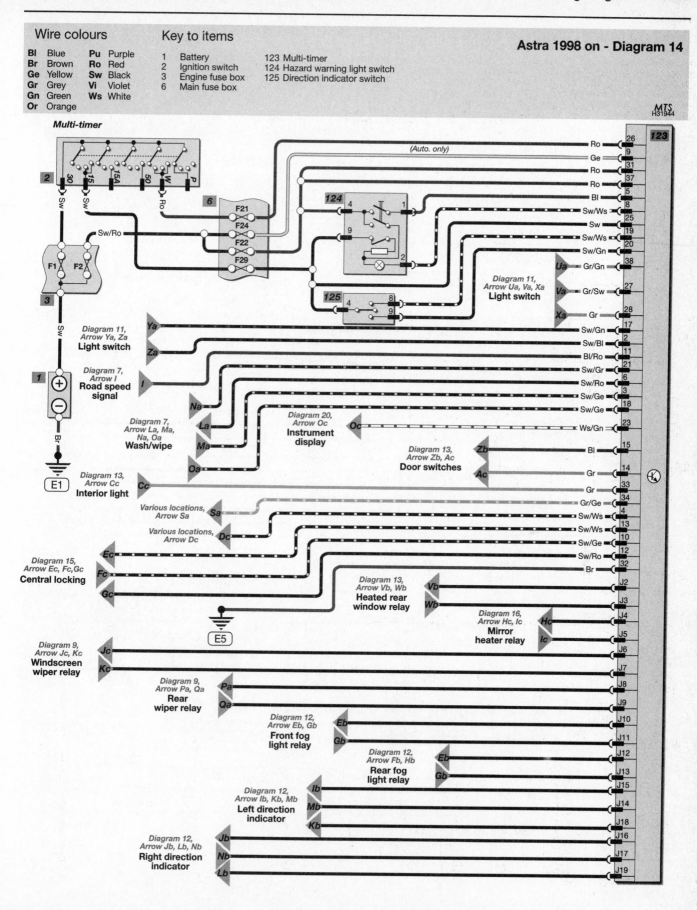

Wire colours

Bl	Blue	Pu	Purple
Br	Brown	Ro	Red
Ge	Yellow	Sw	Black
Gr	Grey	Vi	Violet
Gn	Green	Ws	White
Or	Orange		

Key to items

1 Battery
2 Ignition switch
3 Engine fuse box
6 Fuse box
8 Diagnostic connector
24 Steering wheel clock spring
124 Horn switch
125 Horn relay
126 Horn
127 Glovebox light/switch
128 Central locking module
129 Driver's door lock motor
130 Passenger door lock motor
131 LH rear door lock motor
132 RH rear door lock motor
133 Tailgate lock motor
134 Filler flap lock motor
135 Sunroof motor
136 Sunroof switch

Astra 1998 on - Diagram 15

Note: prefix 1/ = X61 multi plug
prefix 2/ = X62 multi plug

MTS
H31945

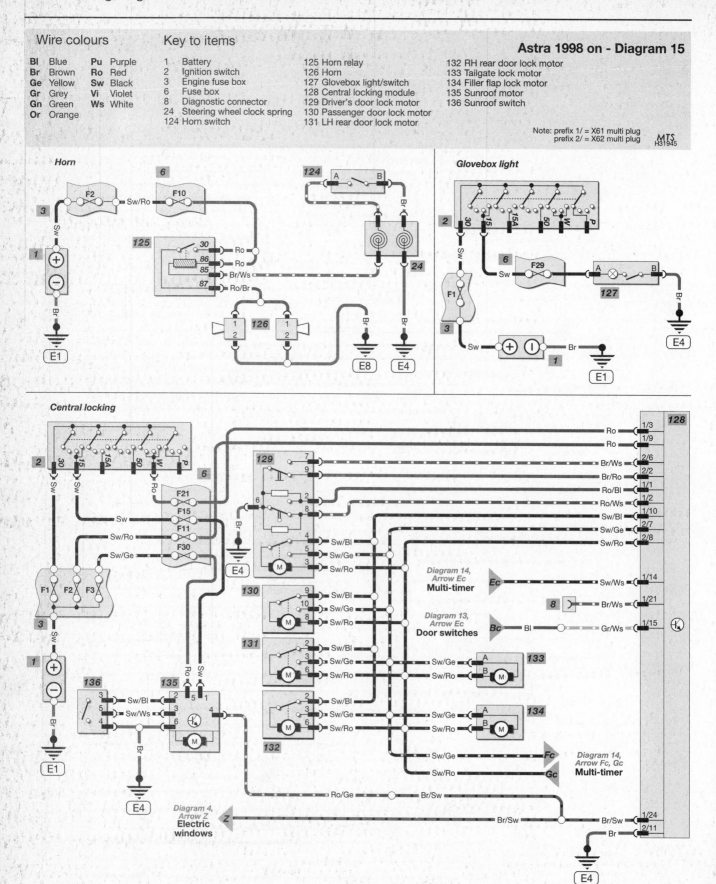

Wire colours

Bl	Blue	**Pu**	Purple
Br	Brown	**Ro**	Red
Ge	Yellow	**Sw**	Black
Gr	Grey	**Vi**	Violet
Gn	Green	**Ws**	White
Or	Orange		

Key to items

1 Battery
2 Ignition switch
3 Engine fuse box
6 Main fuse box
8 Diagnostic connector
137 Power steering motor
138 Heated mirror relay
139 Electric mirror switch
140 Driver's exterior door mirror
141 Passenger's exterior door mirror
142 Cruise control switch
143 Cruise control module
144 Heater control module
145 Circulation flap motor
146 Heater blower motor resistor
147 Heater blower motor

MTS
H31946

Power steering

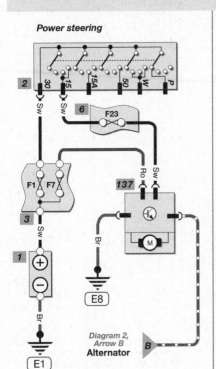

Exterior door mirrors

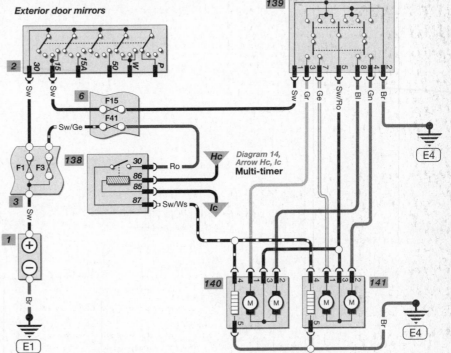

Diagram 14,
Arrow Hc, Ic
Multi-timer

Diagram 2,
Arrow B
Alternator

Cruise control

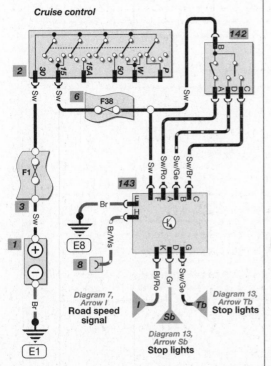

Diagram 7,
Arrow I
**Road speed
signal**

Diagram 13,
Arrow Tb
Stop lights

Diagram 13,
Arrow Sb
Stop lights

Heating

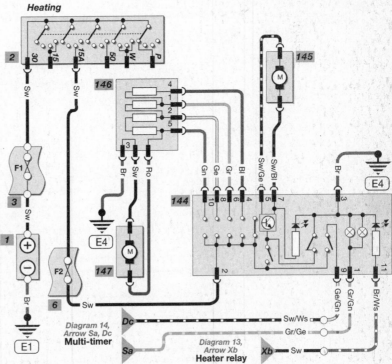

Diagram 14,
Arrow Sa, Dc
Multi-timer

Diagram 13,
Arrow Xb
Heater relay

Wire colours

Bl	Blue	**Pu**	Purple
Br	Brown	**Ro**	Red
Ge	Yellow	**Sw**	Black
Gr	Grey	**Vi**	Violet
Gn	Green	**Ws**	White
Or	Orange		

Key to items

1 Battery
2 Ignition switch
3 Engine fuse box
6 Main fuse box
8 Diagnostic connector
145 Circulation flap motor
146 Heater blower motor resistor
147 Heater blower motor

148 Air conditioning module
149 Coolant actuator
150 Anti freeze protection switch
151 Automatic transmission gear selector
152 Automatic transmission control unit
153 Selector display
154 Start assist switch

Astra 1998 on - Diagram 17

Note: prefix 1/ = X65 multi plug
       prefix 2/ = X66 multi plug

MTS
H31947

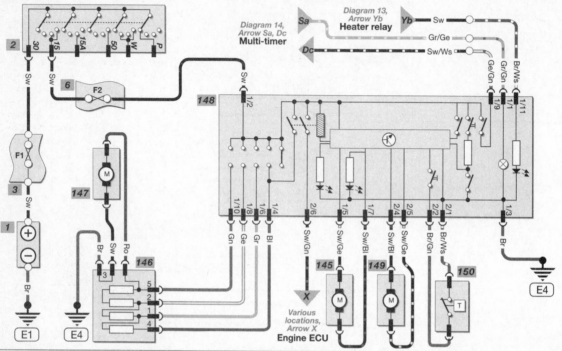

Typical air conditioning

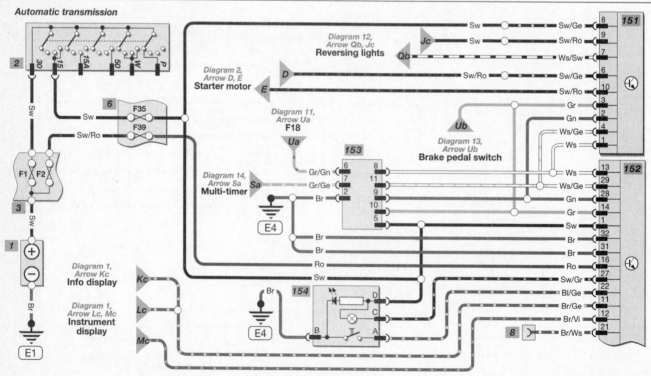

Automatic transmission

Wire colours

Bl	Blue	**Pu**	Purple
Br	Brown	**Ro**	Red
Ge	Yellow	**Sw**	Black
Gr	Grey	**Vi**	Violet
Gn	Green	**Ws**	White
Or	Orange		

Key to items

1 Battery
2 Ignition switch
3 Engine fuse box
6 Main fuse box
152 Automatic transmission control unit
155 Ignition key locking magnet
156 Ignition key locking magnet switch

157 Transmission mode button
158 Selector lever magnet switch
159 Kickdown switch
160 Neutral control solenoid valve
161 Transmission solenoid valve block
162 Transmission input sensor
163 Transmission output sensor
164 Transmission oil temperature sensor

Astra 1998 on - Diagram 18

MTS
H31948

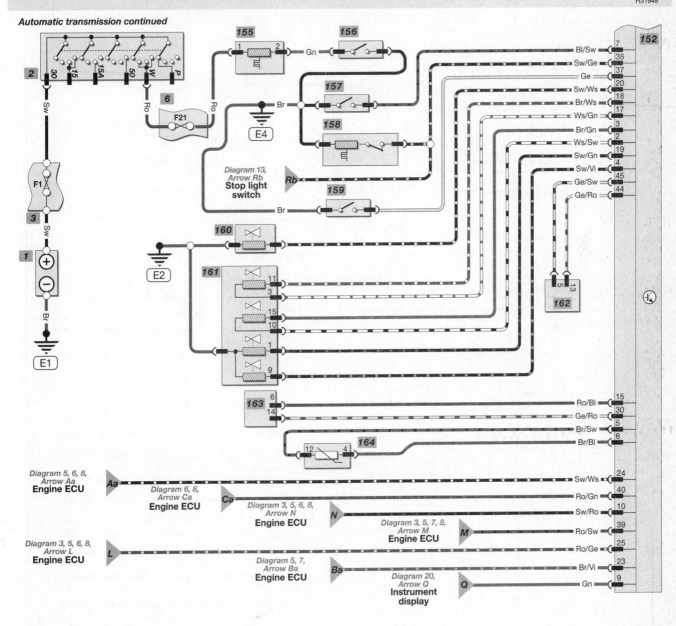

Automatic transmission continued

Wire colours

Bl	Blue	**Pu**	Purple
Br	Brown	**Ro**	Red
Ge	Yellow	**Sw**	Black
Gr	Grey	**Vi**	Violet
Gn	Green	**Ws**	White
Or	Orange		

Key to items

1 Battery
2 Ignition switch
3 Engine fuse box
6 Main fuse box
8 Diagnostic connector
165 Multi info display
166 LH front brake pad
warning sensor
167 RH front brake pad
warning sensor
168 Low washer fluid level switch
169 Low coolant level switch
170 Low oil level switch
171 Outside temperature sensor
172 Info display switch

Astra 1998 on - Diagram 19

MTS
H31949

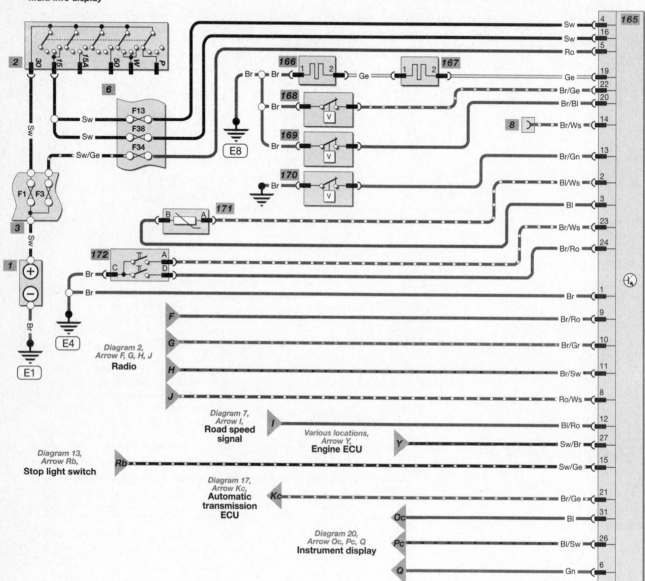

Wire colours

Bl	Blue	Pu	Purple
Br	Brown	Ro	Red
Ge	Yellow	Sw	Black
Gr	Grey	Vi	Violet
Gn	Green	Ws	White
Or	Orange		

Key to items

1 Battery
2 Ignition switch
3 Engine fuse box
6 Main fuse box
8 Diagnostic connector
173 Instrument panel
  a) charge warning
  b) oil pressure warning
  c) airbag warning
  d) ABS warning

173 Instrument panel cont.
  e) engine warning
  f) automatic program power
  g) traction control warning
  h) automatic transmission
  i) air conditioning
  j) brake system warning
  k) trailer turning signal
  l) coolant temp. gauge
  m) fuel reserve warning

173 Instrument panel cont.
  n) fuel gauge
  o) tachometer
  p) speedometer
  q) coolant temp warning
  r) instrument illumination
  s) rear fog light warning
  t*) high beam warning
  t) high beam warning
    (tachometer only)

173 Instrument panel cont.
  u*) front fog light warning
  u) front fog light warning
    (tachometer only)
  v) LH indicator
  w) RH indicator
174 Oil pressure switch
175 Brake fluid switch
176 Parking brake switch
177 Fuel tank sender

Astra 1998 on - Diagram 20

MTS
H31950

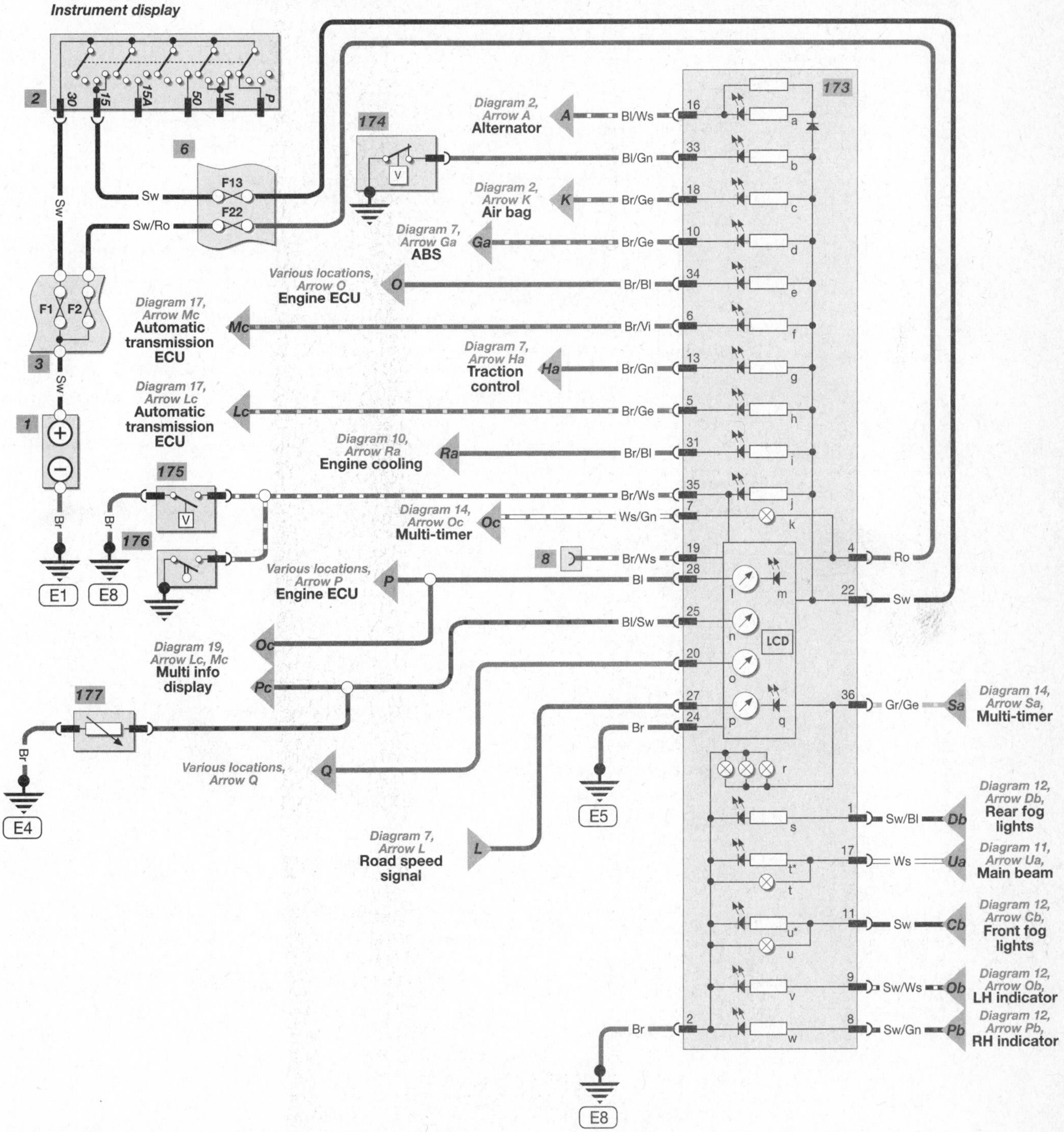

VAUXHALL ZAFIRA 1998 on

Diagram 1

Key to symbols

Bulb	⊗
Switch	
Multiple contact switch (ganged)	
Fuse/fusible link	F24
Resistor	
Variable resistor	
Item no.	15
Pump/motor	(M)
Earth and location (via lead)	E1
Gauge/meter	
Diode	
Light emitting diode (LED)	
Internal connection (connecting wires)	
Wire splice or soldered joint	
Solenoid actuator	
Plug and socket connector	

Connections to other circuits. Direction of arrow denotes current flow.

Diagram 3, Arrow A
A **High beam warning light**

Wire colour
(Red wire/white tracer)   Ro/Ws

Box shape denotes part of a larger component. Terminal identified by either standard termination (bold *italic*) or by connector number (plain text).

30   4

30 Terminal identification (i.e. battery +ve)
4 Connector pin number

Earth locations

E1	Battery ground strap	**E7**	Engine (electronic)
E2	Engine ground strap	**E8**	Engine distribution
E3	Ignition coil earth	**E9**	Rear panel
E4	"A" pillar	**E10**	Tailgate
E5	Steering column	**E11**	Heater blower
E6	Transmission tunnel		

Key to circuits

Diagram 1	Information for wiring diagrams
Diagram 2	Starting, charging, airbag and typical radio/CD
Diagram 3	X16XEL engine management system
Diagram 4	X16XEL engine management system cont. and electric windows
Diagram 5	X18XE1 engine management system
Diagram 6	X18XE1 engine management system continued, ABS with traction control and speed sensor (non ABS models)
Diagram 7	Wash/wipe and auxiliary heating
Diagram 8	Engine cooling and triple info display
Diagram 9	Front lights
Diagram 10	Fog, tail, reversing and direction indicator lights
Diagram 11	Number plate, brake, interior lights, heated rear window and cigarette lighter
Diagram 12	Multi-timer
Diagram 13	Glovebox light, horn, sunroof and central locking
Diagram 14	Power steering, exterior door mirrors, cruise control and heating
Diagram 15	Typical air con. and automatic transmission
Diagram 16	Automatic transmission continued
Diagram 17	Multi info display
Diagram 18	Instrument display

Engine fuse box

Fuse Rating

F1	60A	F5	60A	F60	110A
F2	60A	F6	20A		
F3	60A	F7	80A		
F4	40A	F8	20A		

Main fuse box

Fuse	Rating	Circuit protected	Fuse	Rating	Circuit protected
F2	30A	Fans	F23	10A	ABS and power steering
F3	40A	Heated rear window	F24	10A	LH dipped beam, headlight adjustment
F6	10A	RH dipped beam, headlight adjustment	F25	10A	LH parking, tail and number plate lights
F7	10A	RH parking, tail and number plate lights	F26	10A	LH main beam
F8	10A	RH main beam	F28	7.5A	Interior light
F9	30A	Headlamp wash	F29	10A	Hazard warning, interior light and automatic transmission
F10	15A	Horn			
F11	20A	Central locking	F30	30A	Sunroof
F12	15A	Front fog lights	F33	20A	Trailer
F13	7.5A	Information display	F34	20A	CD player, radio, information display and GPS
F14	30A	Windscreen wipers			
F15	7.5A	Electric windows, sunroof and mirrors	F35	10A	Automatic transmission, engine cooling, air con.
F16	10A	Rear fog lights	F36	20A	Cigarette lighter
F17	30A	Electric windows	F38	10A	Stop lights, auto. transmission info. display and cruise control
F18	7.5A	Number plate lights and headlight range adjustment	F39	7.5A	Auto. transmission, air con. and engine cooling
F20	30A	Electric windows	F40	7.5A	Engine cooling and air con.
F21	7.5A	Radio	F41	10A	Heated mirrors
F22	15A	Hazard warning, info. display, indicators and trip computer			

MTS
H31951

Wire colours

Bl	Blue	**Pu**	Purple
Br	Brown	**Ro**	Red
Ge	Yellow	**Sw**	Black
Gr	Grey	**Vi**	Violet
Gn	Green	**Ws**	White
Or	Orange		

Key to items

1 Battery
2 Ignition switch
3 Engine fuse box
4 Alternator
5 Starter motor
6 Main fuse box
7 Radio
8 Diagnostic connector
9 Telephone connection
10 CD player
11 Aerial amplifier
12 LH front speaker
13 LH front tweeter
14 RH front tweeter
15 RH front speaker
16 LH rear speaker
17 LH rear tweeter
18 RH rear tweeter
19 RH rear speaker
20 Airbag module
21 LH seatbelt pretensioner
22 RH seatbelt pretensioner
23 Driver's airbag
24 Airbag contact unit
25 Passenger's airbag
26 Passenger's side airbag
27 Driver's side airbag
28 Passenger's airbag sensor
29 Driver's airbag sensor

Zafira 1998 on - Diagram 2

MTS H31952

Starting and charging

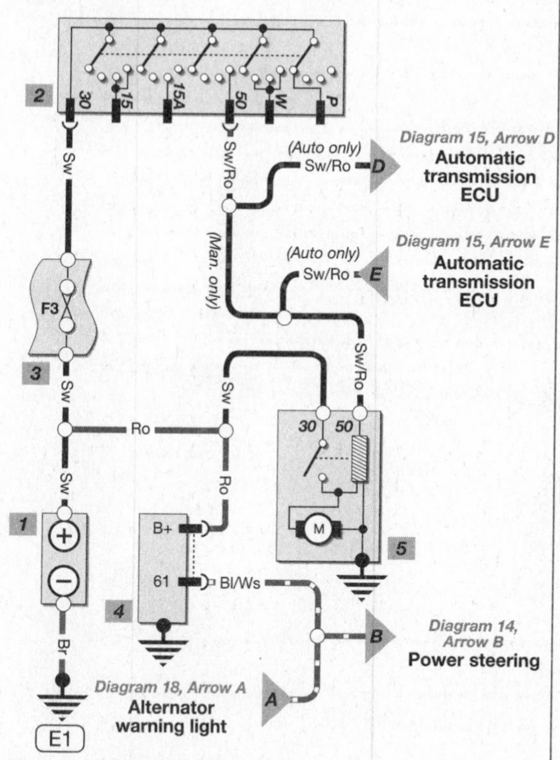
30
15
15A
50
W
P
Sw
Sw/Ro
(Auto only)
Sw/Ro
D
Diagram 15, Arrow D
Automatic transmission ECU
(Man. only)
(Auto only)
Sw/Ro
E
Diagram 15, Arrow E
Automatic transmission ECU
F3
Sw
Ro
Sw/Ro
30
50
M
B+
61
Bl/Ws
B
Diagram 14, Arrow B
Power steering
Br
Diagram 18, Arrow A
Alternator warning light
A
E1

Typical radio/CD

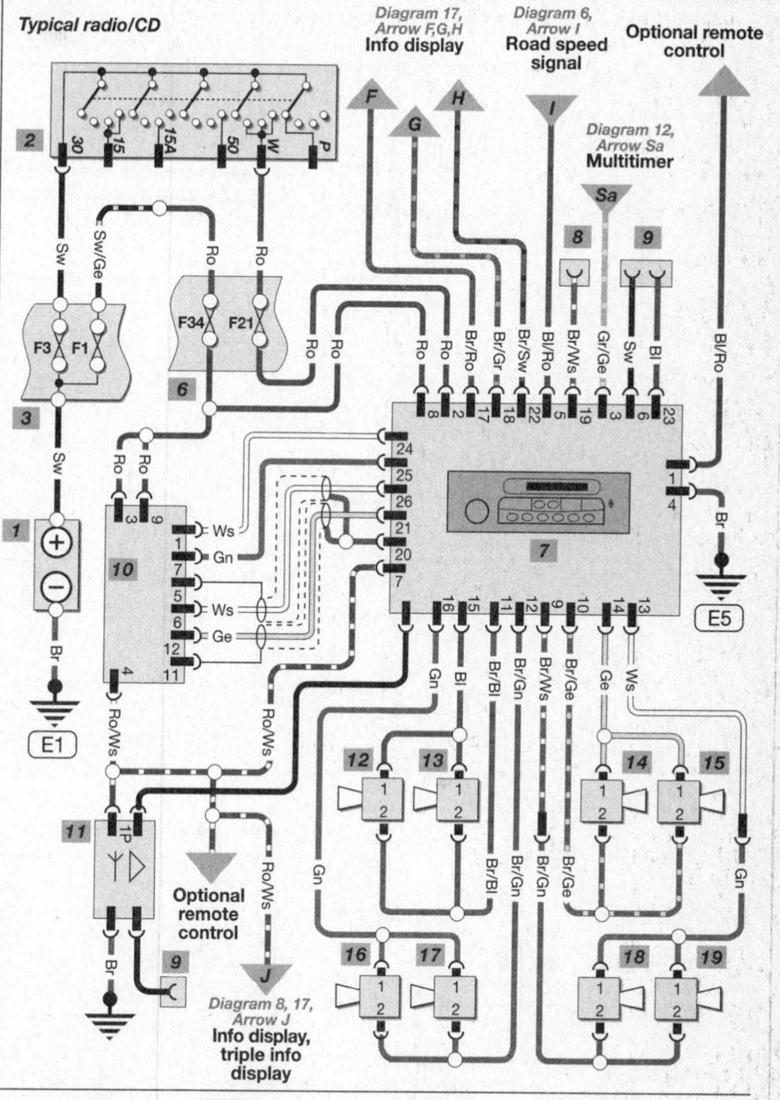
Diagram 17, Arrow F,G,H
Info display
Diagram 6, Arrow I
Road speed signal
Optional remote control
Diagram 12, Arrow Sa
Multitimer
Sa
F
G
H
I
Sw/Ge
Ro
F3
F1
F34
F21
Br/Ro
Br/Gr
Br/Sw
Bl/Ro
Br/Ws
Gr/Ge
Bl
Ws
Gn
Ge
Ro/Ws
Gn
Br/Bl
Br/Gn
Br/Ge
Optional remote control
J
Diagram 8, 17, Arrow J
Info display, triple info display
E1
E5

Airbag system

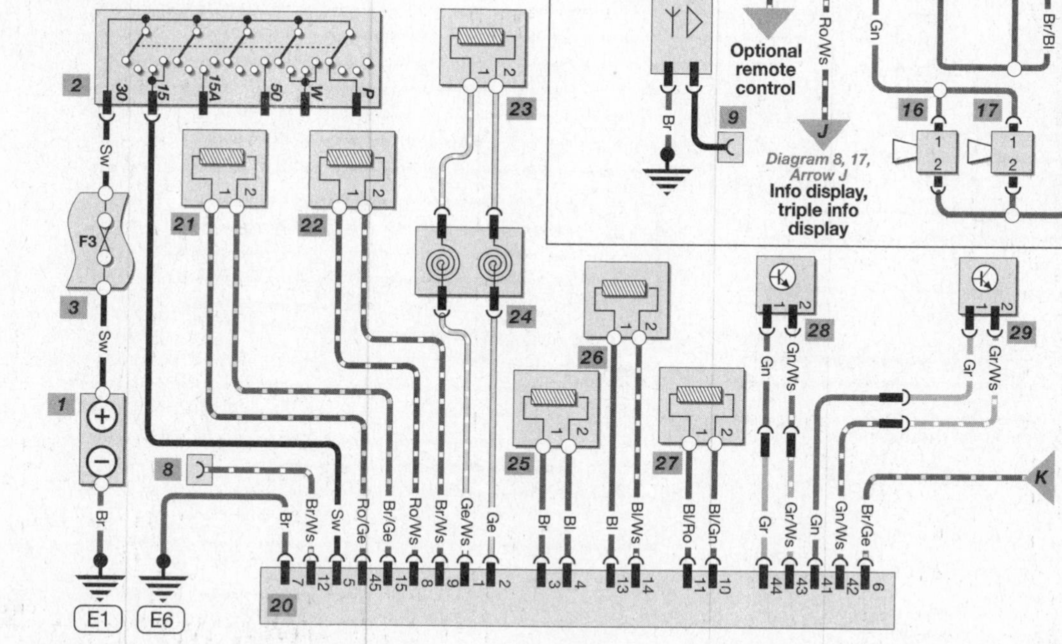
30
15
15A
50
W
P
Sw
F3
Br
E1
E6
Br/Ws
Ro/Ge
Br/Ge
Ro/Ws
Ge/Ws
Ge
Bl
Bl/Ws
Bl/Ro
Bl/Gn
Gr
Gr/Ws
Gn
Gn/Ws
Br/Ge
Diagram 18, Arrow K
Instrument display
K

Wire colours

Bl	Blue	**Pu**	Purple
Br	Brown	**Ro**	Red
Ge	Yellow	**Sw**	Black
Gr	Grey	**Vi**	Violet
Gn	Green	**Ws**	White
Or	Orange		

Key to items

1 Battery
2 Ignition switch
3 Engine fuse box
8 Diagnostic connector
30 Multec control unit
31 Camshaft position sensor
32 Fuel pump relay
33 Fuel pump
34 Fuel injector cylinder 1
35 Fuel injector cylinder 2
36 Fuel injector cylinder 3
37 Fuel injector cylinder 4
38 Ignition coil
39 Spark plugs
40 Canister purge solenoid valve
41 Oxygen sensor
42 EGR solenoid valve
43 MAP sensor
44 Throttle position sensor
45 Coolant temperature sensor
46 Air intake temperature sensor
47 Knock sensor
48 Idle speed stepper motor
49 Crankshaft sensor

Zafira 1998 on - Diagram 3

Note: prefix 1/ = X53 multi plug
prefix 2/ = X54 multi plug

MTS
H31953

Engine management system X16XEL engine

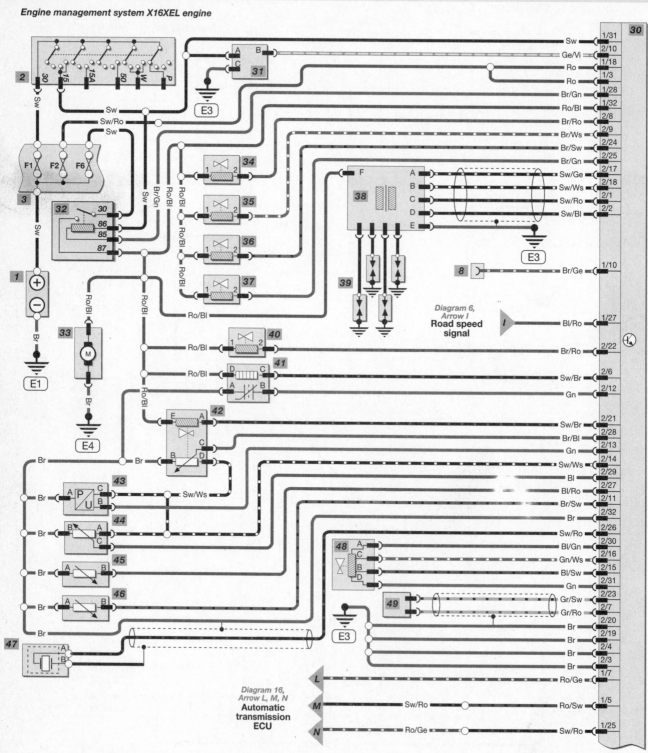

Diagram 6,
Arrow I
Road speed signal

Diagram 16,
Arrow L, M, N
Automatic transmission ECU

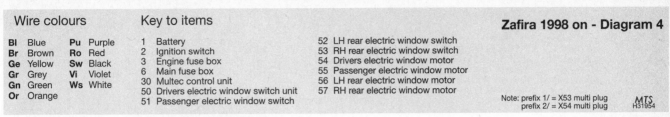

Wire colours

Bl	Blue	Pu	Purple
Br	Brown	Ro	Red
Ge	Yellow	Sw	Black
Gr	Grey	Vi	Violet
Gn	Green	Ws	White
Or	Orange		

Key to items

1 Battery
2 Ignition switch
3 Engine fuse box
6 Main fuse box
30 Multec control unit
50 Drivers electric window switch unit
51 Passenger electric window switch

52 LH rear electric window switch
53 RH rear electric window switch
54 Drivers electric window motor
55 Passenger electric window motor
56 LH rear electric window motor
57 RH rear electric window motor

Zafira 1998 on - Diagram 4

Note: prefix 1/ = X53 multi plug
prefix 2/ = X54 multi plug

MTS
H31954

Engine management system X16XEL engine continued

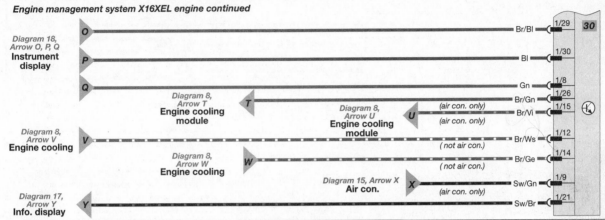

Diagram 18,
Arrow O, P, Q
Instrument display

Diagram 8,
Arrow T
Engine cooling module

Diagram 8,
Arrow U
Engine cooling module
(air con. only)

Diagram 8,
Arrow V
Engine cooling

Diagram 8,
Arrow W
Engine cooling
(not air con.)

Diagram 15, Arrow X
Air con.
(air con. only)

Diagram 17,
Arrow Y
Info. display

Br/Bl 1/29 30
Bl 1/30
Gn 1/8
Br/Gn 1/26
Br/Vi 1/15
Br/Ws 1/12
Br/Ge 1/14
Sw/Gn 1/9
Sw/Br 1/21

Electric windows

Diagram 13,
Arrow Z
Central Locking

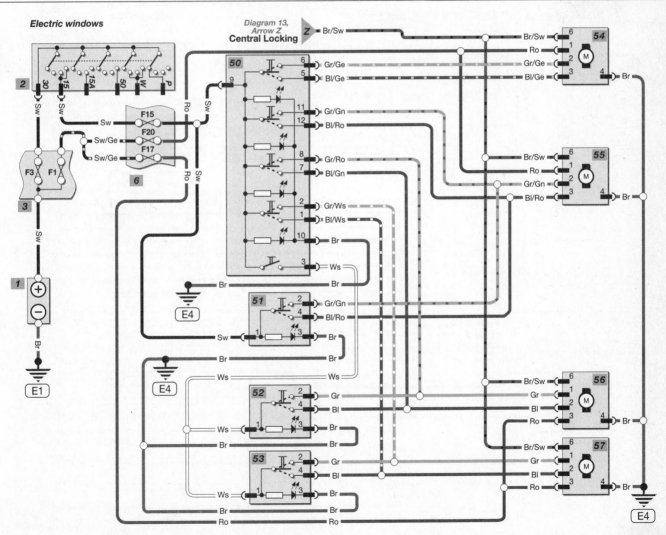

Wire colours

Bl	Blue	**Pu**	Purple
Br	Brown	**Ro**	Red
Ge	Yellow	**Sw**	Black
Gr	Grey	**Vi**	Violet
Gn	Green	**Ws**	White
Or	Orange		

Key to items

1 Battery
2 Ignition switch
3 Engine fuse box
8 Diagnostic connector
31 Camshaft position sensor
32 Fuel pump relay
33 fuel pump

34 Fuel injector cylinder 1
35 Fuel injector cylinder 2
36 Fuel injector cylinder 3
37 Fuel injector cylinder 4
38 Ignition coil
39 Spark plugs
40 Canister purge solenoid valve

41 Oxygen sensor
42 EGR solenoid valve
44 Throttle position sensor
45 Coolant temperature sensor
47 Knock sensor
49 Crankshaft sensor
59 Simtec control unit

60 Intake manifold
   change-over valve
61 Air mass meter

Zafira 1998 on - Diagram 5

Note: prefix 1/ = X57 multi plug
prefix 2/ = X58 multi plug

MTS
H31955

Ignition and injection X18XE1 engine

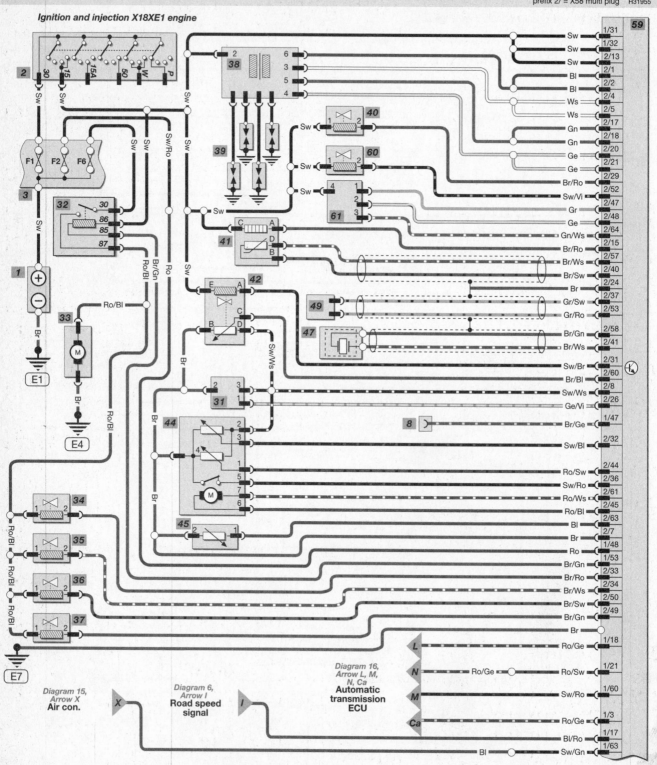

Wire colours

Bl	Blue	Pu	Purple
Br	Brown	Ro	Red
Ge	Yellow	Sw	Black
Gr	Grey	Vi	Violet
Gn	Green	Ws	White
Or	Orange		

Key to items

1 Battery
2 Ignition switch
3 Engine fuse box
8 Diagnostic connector
59 Simtec control unit
62 ABS with traction control module

63 LH front wheel speed sensor
64 RH front wheel speed sensor
65 LH rear wheel speed sensor
66 RH rear wheel speed sensor
67 Traction control switch
69 Vehicle speed sensor

Zafira 1998 on - Diagram 6

Note: prefix 1/ = X57 multi plug
prefix 2/ = X58 multi plug

MTS
H31956

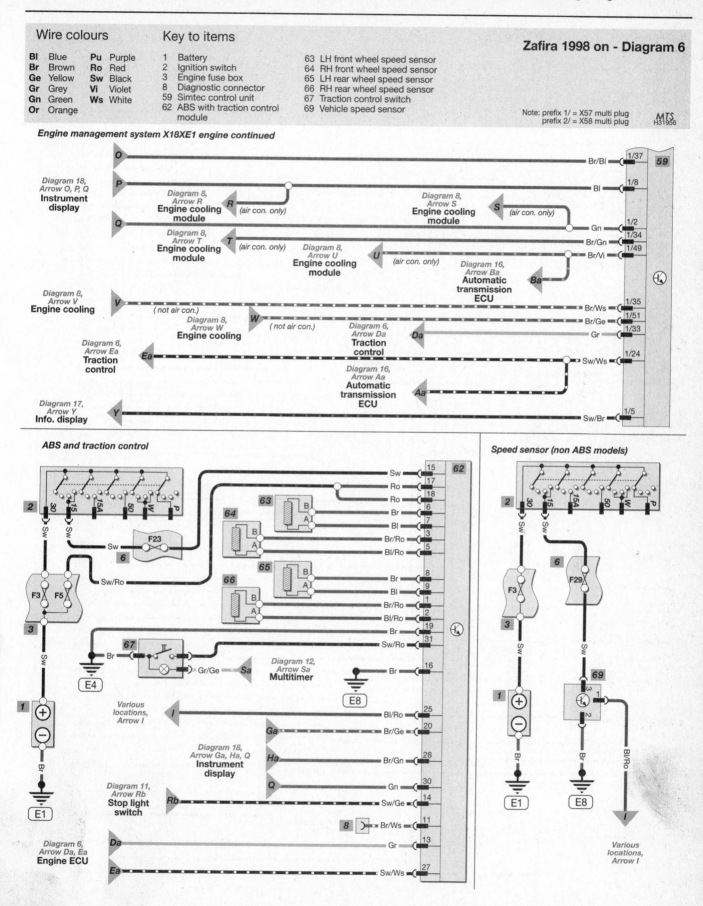

Engine management system X18XE1 engine continued

ABS and traction control

Speed sensor (non ABS models)

Wire colours

Bl	Blue	**Pu**	Purple
Br	Brown	**Pk**	Pink
Ge	Yellow	**Ro**	Red
Gr	Grey	**Sw**	Black
Gn	Green	**Vi**	Violet
Or	Orange	**Ws**	White

Key to items

1 Battery
2 Ignition switch
3 Engine fuse box
71 Headlight washer relay
72 Headlight washer pump
73 Wash/wipe switch

74 Windscreen washer pump
75 Windscreen wiper relay
76 Windscreen wiper motor
77 Rear wiper relay
78 Rear wiper motor
179 Auxiliary heater

Zafira 1998 on - Diagram 7

MTS
H31957

Wash/Wipe

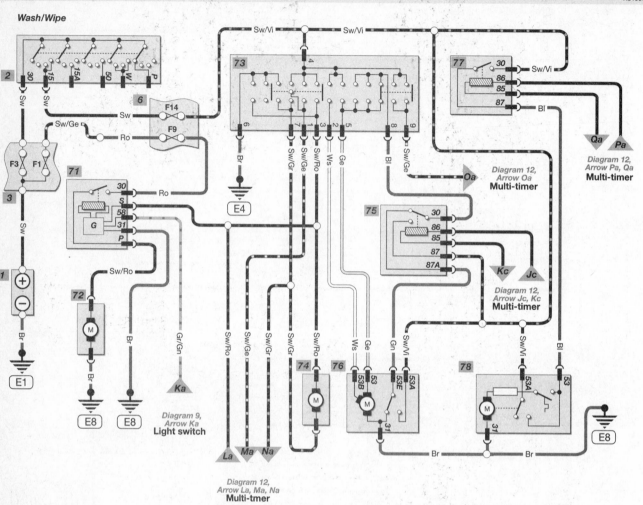

Auxiliary heating

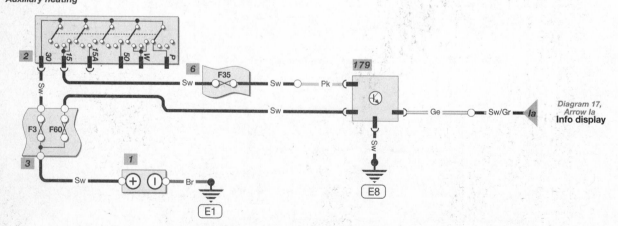

Wire colours

Bl	Blue	**Pu**	Purple
Br	Brown	**Ro**	Red
Ge	Yellow	**Sw**	Black
Gr	Grey	**Vi**	Violet
Gn	Green	**Ws**	White
Or	Orange		

Key to items

1   Battery
2   Ignition switch
3   Engine fuse box
8   Diagnostic connector
79   Engine cooling control unit
80   Air con. pressure sensor

81   Radiator blower motor
82   Air con. compressor clutch
83   Radiator blower motor relay
84   Triple info display
85   Outside temperature sensor

Zafira 1998 on - Diagram 8

Note: prefix 1/ = X63 multi plug
prefix 2/ = X64 multi plug

MTS
H31958

Typical engine cooling (air con.)

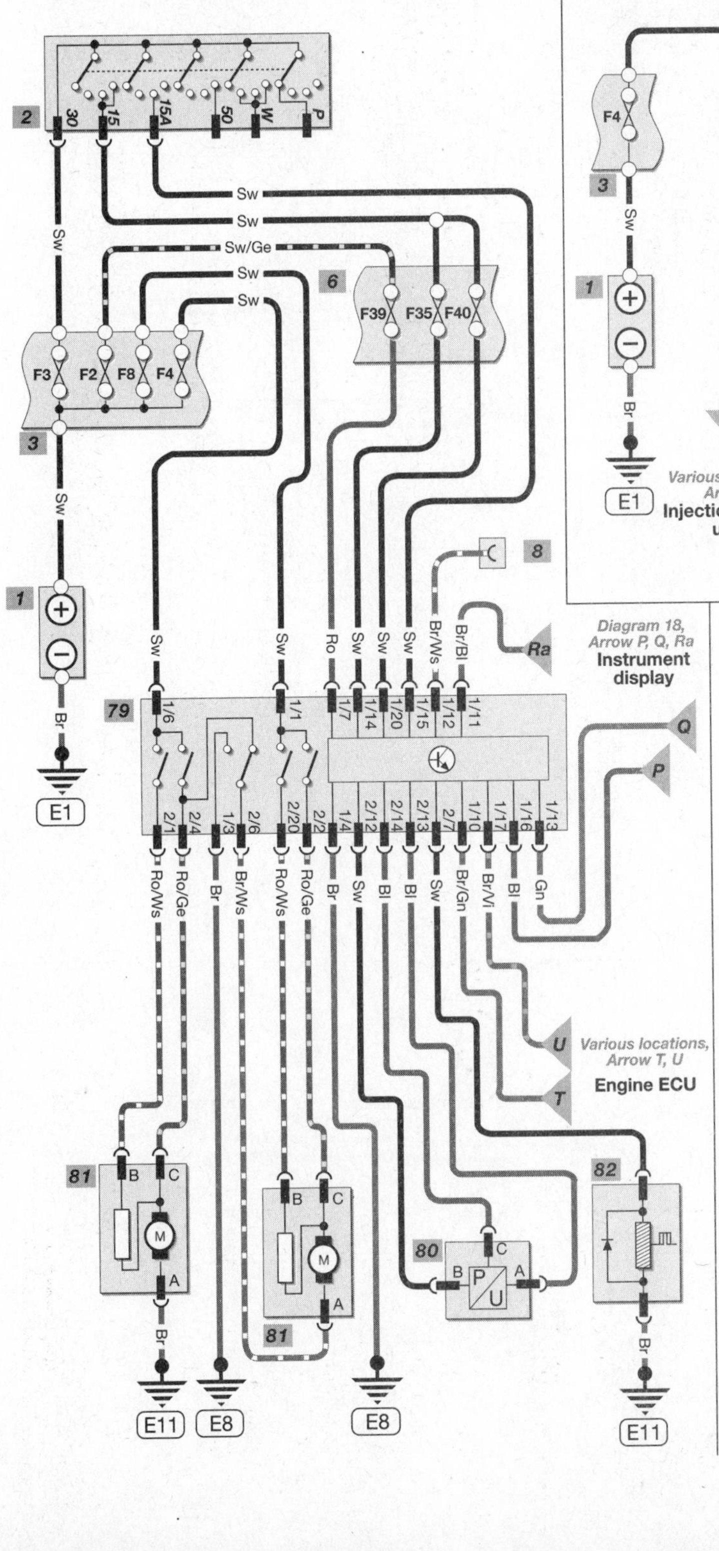

Engine cooling (not air con.)

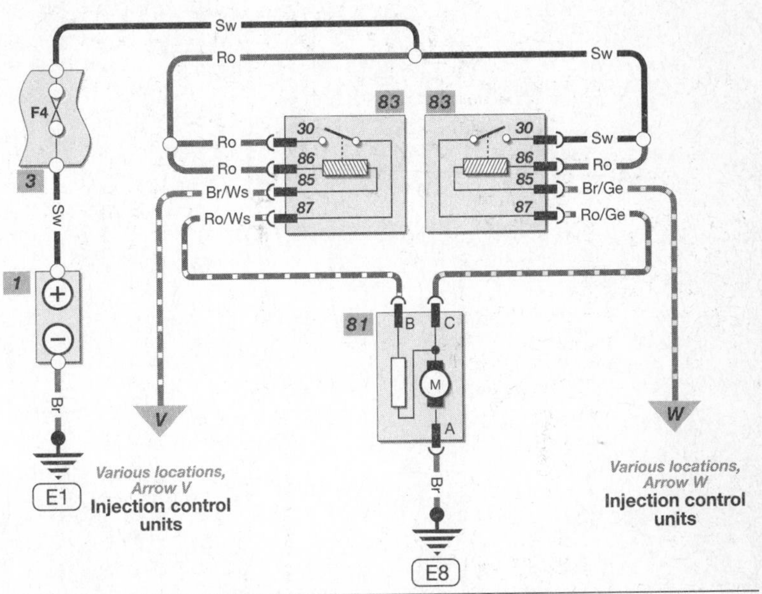

Various locations,
Arrow V
Injection control
units

Various locations,
Arrow W
Injection control
units

Diagram 18,
Arrow P, Q, Ra
Instrument
display

Triple info. display

Various locations,
Arrow T, U
Engine ECU

Diagram 12,
Arrow Sa
Multi-timer

Diagram 6,
Arrow I
Road speed
signal

Diagram 2,
Arrow F, G, H, J
Radio

Diagram 15,
Arrow Kc
Automatic
transmission
ECU

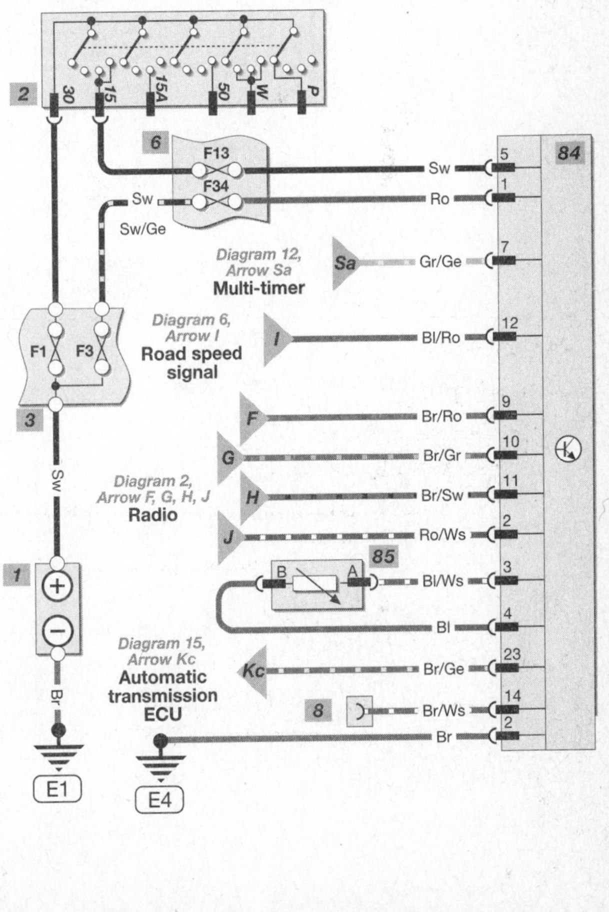

Wire colours

Bl	Blue	**Pu**	Purple
Br	Brown	**Ro**	Red
Ge	Yellow	**Sw**	Black
Gr	Grey	**Vi**	Violet
Gn	Green	**Ws**	White
Or	Orange		

Key to items

1 Battery
2 Ignition switch
3 Engine fuse box
6 Main fuse box
86 Main beam switch
87 Main beam relay
88 Light switch
89 LH headlight leveller

90 RH headlight leveller
91 LH front lights
   a) direction indicator
   b) main beam
   c) dipped beam
   d) side lights
   e) fog lights

92 RH front lights (as 91)
93 Trailer connection

Zafira 1998 on - Diagram 9

MTS
H31959

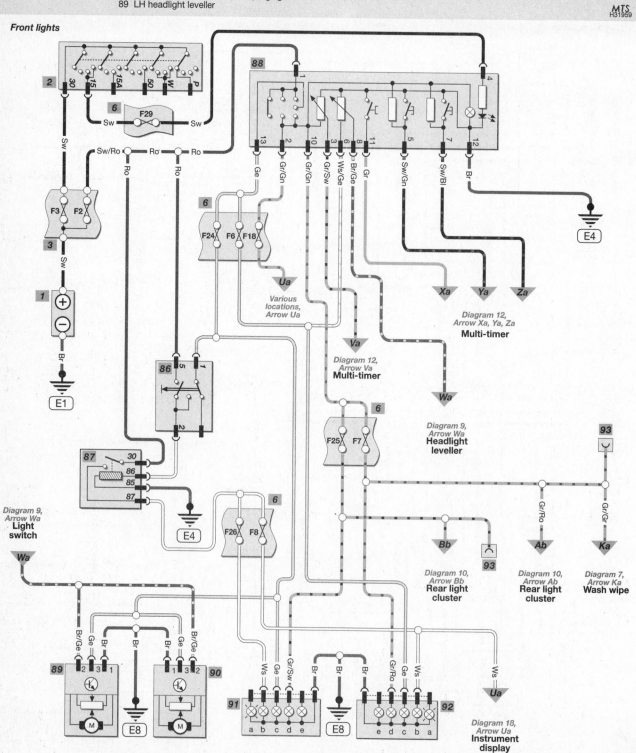

Wire colours

Bl	Blue	Pu	Purple
Br	Brown	Ro	Red
Ge	Yellow	Sw	Black
Gr	Grey	Vi	Violet
Gn	Green	Ws	White
Or	Orange		

Key to items

1 Battery
2 Ignition switch
3 Engine fuse box
6 Main fuse box
91 LH front light cluster
  a) direction indicator
  b) main beam
c) dipped beam
d) side lights
e) fog lights
92 RH front light cluster (as 91)
93 Trailer connection
94 Front fog light relay
95 Rear fog light relay
96 LH rear light cluster
  a) direction indicator
  b) stop light
  c) tail light
  d) reversing light
  e) fog light
97 RH rear light cluster (as 96)
98 Trailer socket switch
99 LH direction indicator relay
100 RH direction indicator relay
101 LH indicator side repeater
102 RH indicator side repeater
103 Reversing light switch

Zafira 1998 on - Diagram 10

MTS
H31960

Fog lights, tail lights

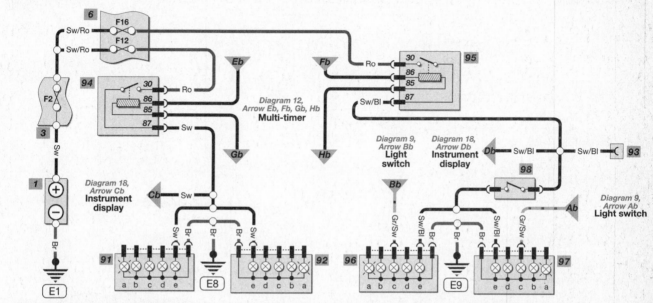

Direction indicators

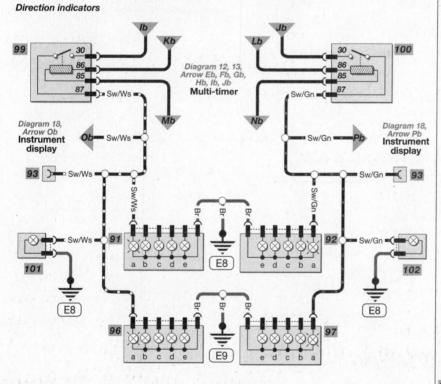

Reversing lights

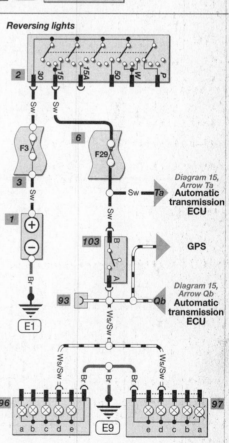

Wire colours

Bl	Blue	Pu	Purple
Br	Brown	Ro	Red
Ge	Yellow	Sw	Black
Gr	Grey	Vi	Violet
Gn	Green	Ws	White
Or	Orange		

Key to items

1 Battery
2 Ignition switch
3 Engine fuse box
6 Main fuse box
93 Trailer connector
96 LH rear light cluster
 a) direction indicator
 b) stop light

c) tail light
d) reversing light
e) fog light
97 RH rear light cluster (as 96)
105 LH number plate light
106 RH number plate light
108 Brake pedal/stop light switch

109 Cruise control clutch switch
110 High level stop light
111 Heated rear window relay
112 Heated rear window
113 Drivers door switch
114 Passenger door switch
115 LH rear door switch

116 RH rear door switch
117 Passenger compartment light with time delay
118 Rear reading light
120 Luggage compartment light
121 Tailgate switch
122 Cigarette lighter

Zafira 1998 on - Diagram 11

MTS
H31961

Number plate lights

Diagram 9, Arrow Ua
Light switch
Gr/Gn
105   106
Br
E10

Heated rear window

6   F3   Sw/Ge
F1
3   Sw   1
111   30   Ro   Vb
86   Diagram 12, Arrow Vb, Wb
85   **Multi-timer**
87   Sw   Wb
Diagram 14, Arrow Xb
Heating   Xb   Sw   Sw   Yb
Diagram 15, Arrow Yb **Air con.**
112
Br
E10

Brake lights

2   30   15   15A   50   W   P
Sw   6
F1   Sw   F38   Sw   Sw (CC only)
3   Sb (CC only)   Sw/Gr   109
1   Diagram 14, Arrow Sb, Tb   B
+   **Cruise control**   108   A
−   Tb   Gr
Br   Diagram 14, Arrow Ub
E1   Rb   **Cruise control**   Ub
Various locations Arrow Rb   Sw/Ro   Sw/Ge   Sw/Ge
110   B
Sw/Ge   A
96   Br   97
Sw/Ge   Br   Br   Sw/Ge
E9   E9
a b c d e   e d c b a

Interior lighting

6   F28   Sw/Ge
F1   Ro   Ro   Ro
3   117   118   120
Diagram 12, Arrow Zb, Ac, Cc
1   **Multi-timer**   Gr   Br/Ws
+   Zb   Ac   Cc   121
−   Bl   Gr   Gr   Gr   Gr   Br
Br   Bl   Bl   Gr   Gr   Gr   Gr   Br
E1   Bc   113   114   115   116   E4
Diagram 13, Arrow Bc **Central locking**

Cigarette lighter

2   30   15   15A   50   W   P
Sw   6
F3   Sw   F36
3   Gr/Ge
1   Sw   Sa   122
+   Diagram 12, Arrow Sa
−   **Multi-timer**
Br   Br
E1   E4

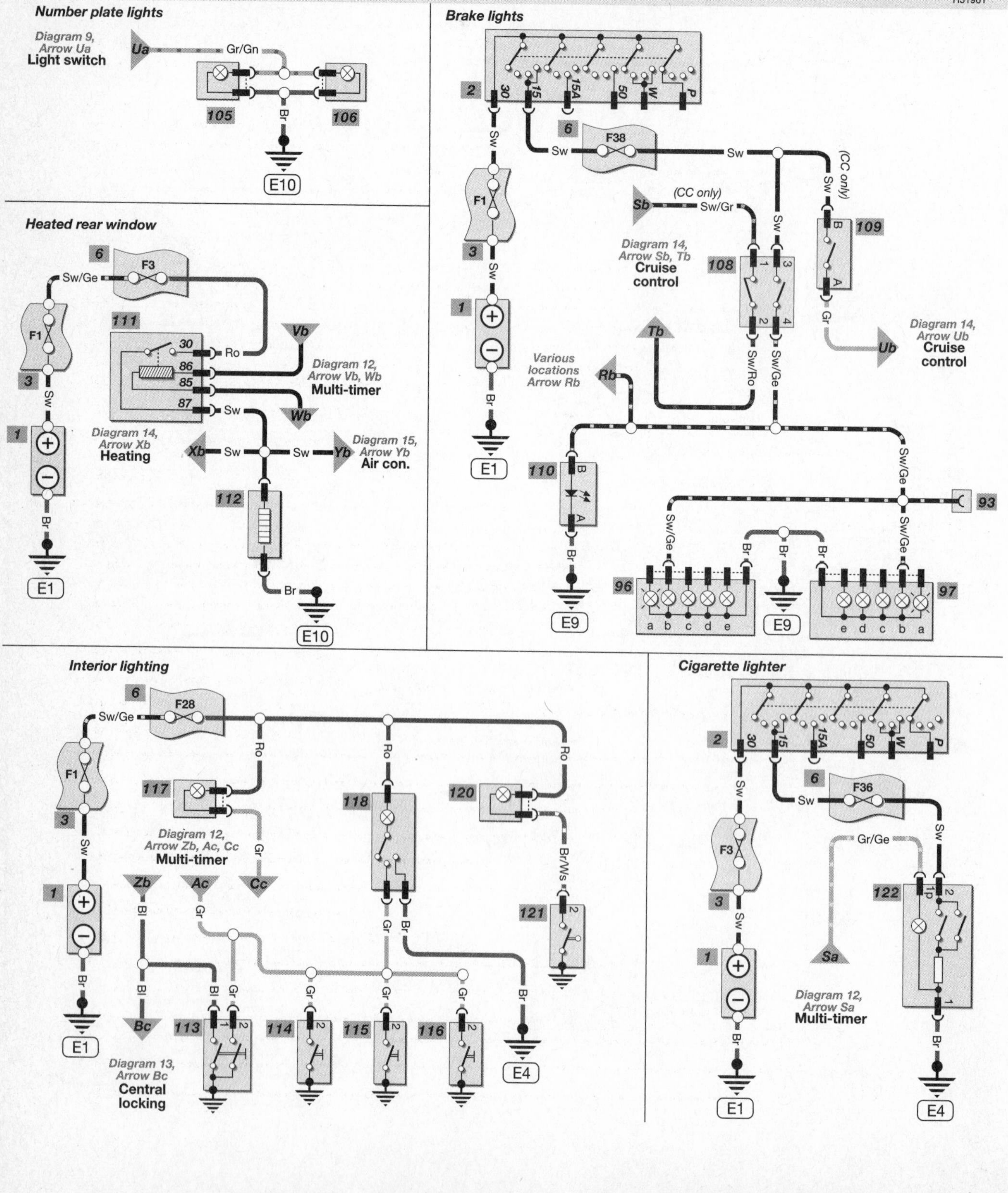

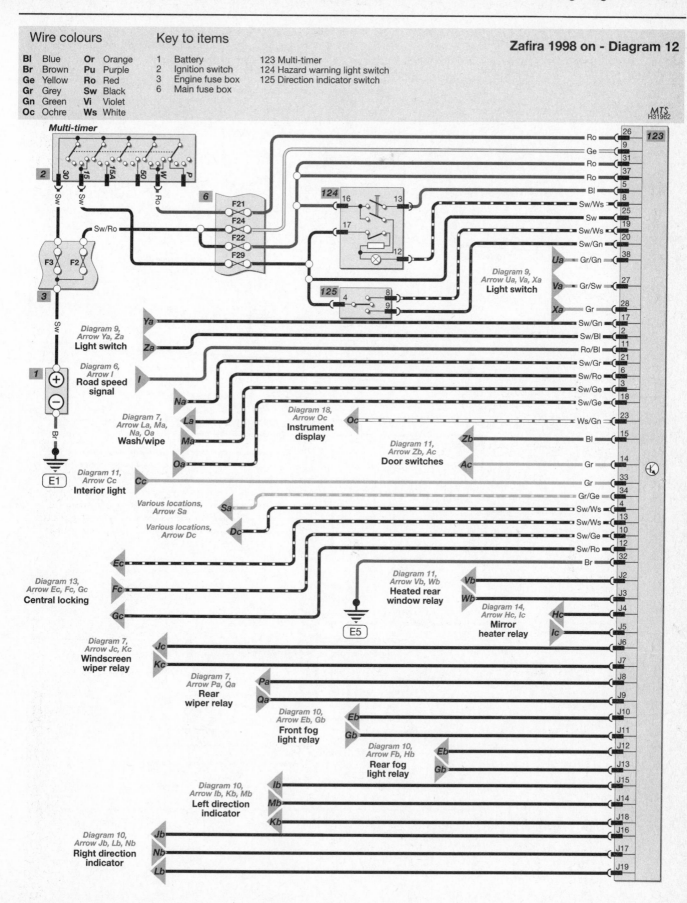

Wire colours

Bl	Blue	**Or**	Orange
Br	Brown	**Pu**	Purple
Ge	Yellow	**Ro**	Red
Gr	Grey	**Sw**	Black
Gn	Green	**Vi**	Violet
Oc	Ochre	**Ws**	White

Key to items

1 Battery
2 Ignition switch
3 Engine fuse box
6 Main fuse box

123 Multi-timer
124 Hazard warning light switch
125 Direction indicator switch

Zafira 1998 on - Diagram 12

MTS
H31962

Multi-timer

2

30 15 15A 50 W P

6

F21
F24
F22
F29

124 16 13
17 12

125 4 8
9

F3 F2

3

Sw/Ro

Diagram 9,
Arrow Ua, Va, Xa
Light switch

1

Diagram 9,
Arrow Ya, Za
Light switch

Ya
Za

Diagram 6,
Arrow I
**Road speed
signal**

I

Na
La
Ma

Diagram 7,
Arrow La, Ma,
Na, Oa
Wash/wipe

Diagram 18,
Arrow Oc
**Instrument
display**

Oc

Diagram 11,
Arrow Zb, Ac
Door switches

Zb
Ac

Oa

E1

Diagram 11,
Arrow Cc
Interior light

Cc

Sa

Various locations,
Arrow Sa

Dc

Various locations,
Arrow Dc

Ec

Diagram 13,
Arrow Ec, Fc, Gc
Central locking

Fc

Gc

Diagram 11,
Arrow Vb, Wb
**Heated rear
window relay**

Vb
Wb

E5

Diagram 14,
Arrow Hc, Ic
**Mirror
heater relay**

Hc
Ic

Diagram 7,
Arrow Jc, Kc
**Windscreen
wiper relay**

Jc
Kc

Diagram 7,
Arrow Pa, Qa
**Rear
wiper relay**

Pa
Qa

Diagram 10,
Arrow Eb, Gb
**Front fog
light relay**

Eb
Gb

Diagram 10,
Arrow Fb, Hb
**Rear fog
light relay**

Eb
Gb

Diagram 10,
Arrow Ib, Kb, Mb
**Left direction
indicator**

Ib
Mb
Kb

Diagram 10,
Arrow Jb, Lb, Nb
**Right direction
indicator**

Jb
Nb
Lb

123

Ro 26
Ge 9
Ro 31
Ro 37
Bl 5
Sw/Ws 8
Sw 25
Sw/Ws 19
Sw/Gn 20
Gr/Gn 38
Gr/Sw 27
Gr 28
Sw/Gn 17
Sw/Bl 2
Ro/Bl 11
Sw/Gr 21
Sw/Ro 6
Sw/Ge 3
Sw/Ge 18
Ws/Gn 23
Bl 15
Gr 14
Gr 33
Gr/Ge 34
Sw/Ws 4
Sw/Ws 13
Sw/Ge 10
Sw/Ro 12
Br 32
J2
J3
J4
J5
J6
J7
J8
J9
J10
J11
J12
J13
J15
J14
J18
J16
J17
J19

Wire colours

Bl	Blue	Pu	Purple
Br	Brown	Ro	Red
Ge	Yellow	Sw	Black
Gr	Grey	Vi	Violet
Gn	Green	Ws	White
Or	Orange		

Key to items

1 Battery
2 Ignition switch
3 Engine fuse box
6 Main fuse box
8 Diagnostic connector
24 Steering wheel clock spring
124 Horn switch

125 Horn relay
126 Horn
127 Glovebox light/switch
128 Central locking module
129 Drivers door lock motor
130 Passenger door lock motor
131 LH rear door lock motor

132 RH door lock motor
133 Tailgate lock motor
134 Filler flap lock motor
135 Sunroof motor
136 Sunroof switch

Zafira 1998 on - Diagram 13

Note: prefix 1/ = X61 multi plug
prefix 2/ = X62 multi plug

MTS
H31963

Horn

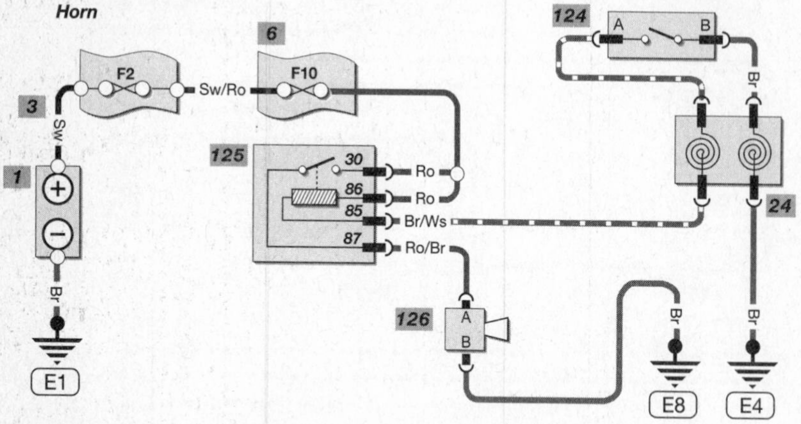

F2 Sw/Ro F10
3
125 30 Ro 86 Ro 85 Br/Ws 87 Ro/Br
1 + − Sw Br
E1
126 A B
E8 E4

124 A B Br
24
E4

Glovebox light

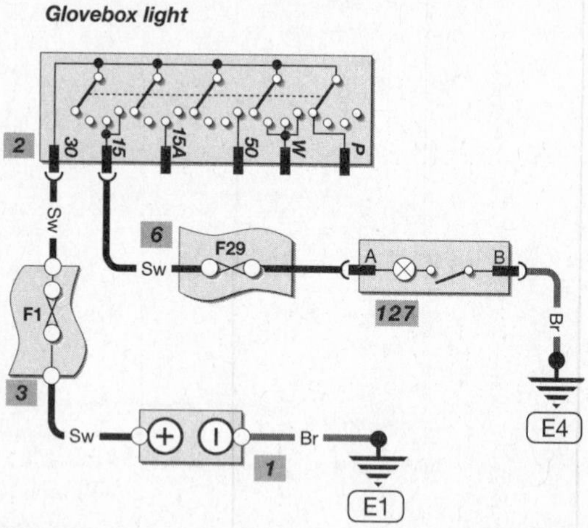

2 30 15 15A 50 W P
Sw
6 F29 Sw
F1
3
Sw + I Br
1
E1

127 A B Br
E4

Central locking

2 30 15 15A 50 W P
Sw Sw Ro
F1 F2 F3
3
Sw
1 + − Br
E1

136 3 Sw/Bl 5 Sw/Ws 4
135 Ro Sw 2 3 6 1 4
132 M
E4

6 F21 F15 F11 F30
Br
E4

129 7 9 6 2 8 4 Sw/Bl 5 Sw/Ge 3 Sw/Ro M
130 9 10 8 Sw/Bl Sw/Ge Sw/Ro M
131 Sw/Bl Sw/Ge Sw/Ro M
132 Sw/Bl Sw/Ge Sw/Ro M

Diagram 12, Arrow Ec
Multi-timer Ec

Diagram 11, Arrow Ec
Door switches Bc

133 A B Sw/Ge Sw/Ro M
134 A B Sw/Ge Sw/Ro M

8 Br/Ws 1/21
Bl Gr/Ws 1/15

Ro 2/3
Ro 2/9
Br/Ws 2/6
Br/Ro 2/2
Ro/Bl 1/1
Ro/Ws 1/2
Sw/Bl 1/10
Sw/Ge 2/7
Sw/Ro 2/8
Sw/Ws 1/14

128

Sw/Ge Fc
Sw/Ro Gc

Diagram 12, Arrow Fc, Gc
Multitimer

Ro/Ge Br/Sw
Diagram 4, Arrow Z
Electric windows Z

Br/Sw 1/24
Br/Sw 2/11
Br
E4

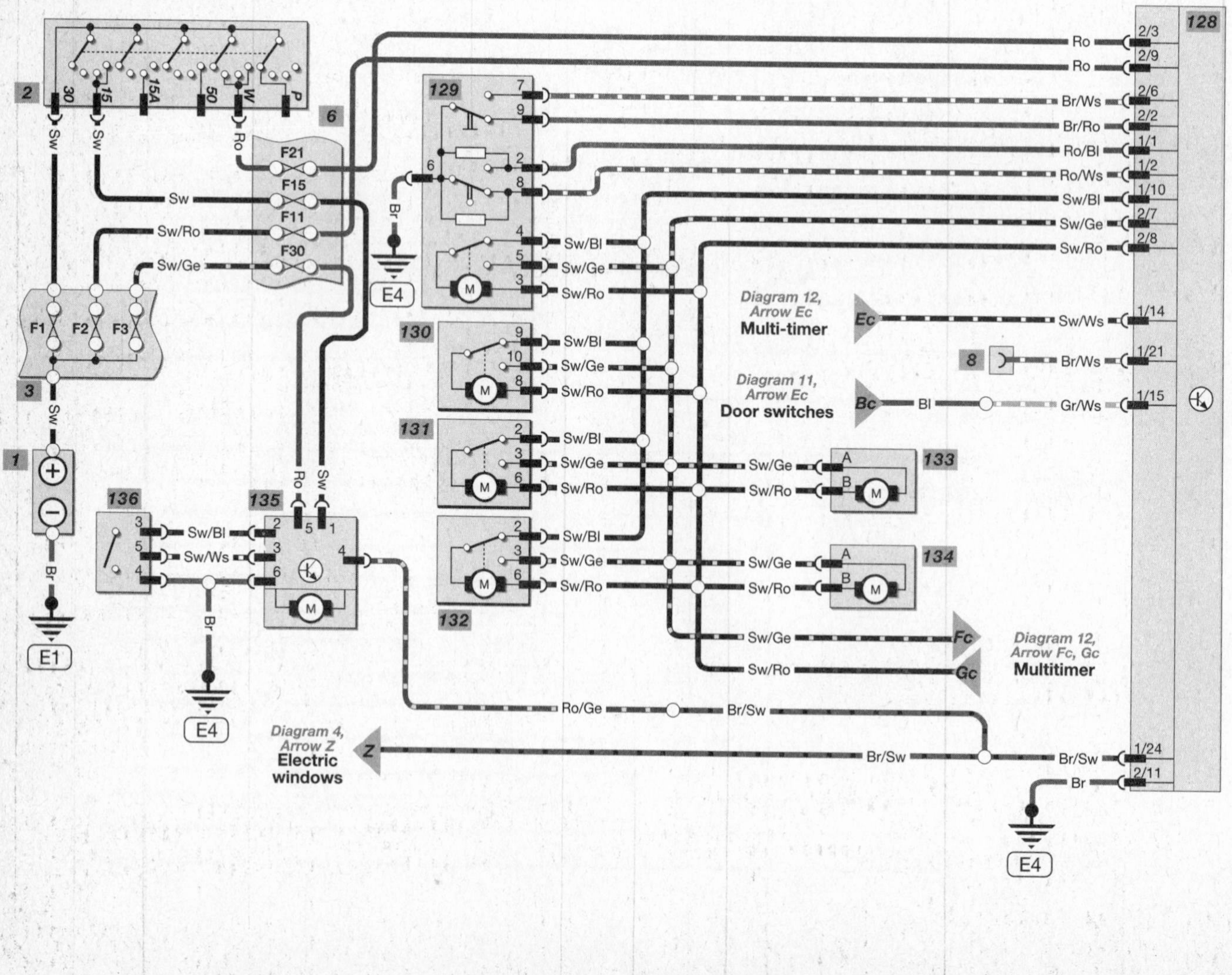

Wire colours

Bl	Blue	Pu	Purple
Br	Brown	Ro	Red
Ge	Yellow	Sw	Black
Gr	Grey	Vi	Violet
Gn	Green	Ws	White
Or	Orange		

Key to items

1 Battery
2 Ignition switch
3 Engine fuse box
6 Main fuse box
8 Diagnostic connector
137 Power steering motor
138 Heated mirror relay
139 Electric mirror switch

140 Driver' exterior door mirror
141 Passenger exterior door mirror
142 Cruise control switch
143 Cruise control module
144 Heater control module
145 Circulation flap motor
146 Heater blower motor resistor
147 Heater blower motor

178 Aux. heater passenger compartment

Zafira 1998 on - Diagram 14

MTS
H31984

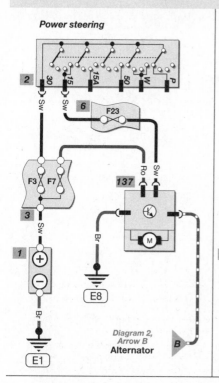
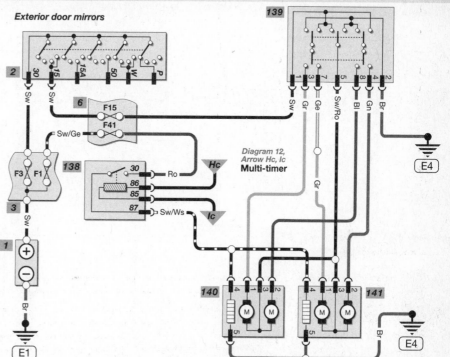
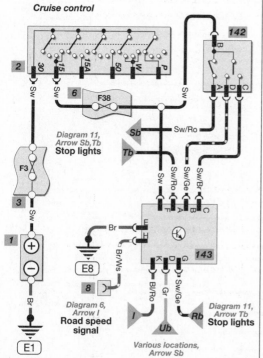
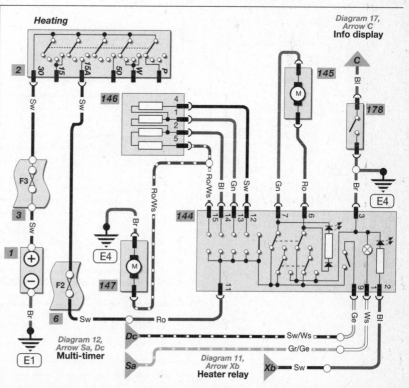

Wire colours

Bl	Blue	Pu	Purple
Br	Brown	Pk	Pink
Ge	Yellow	Ro	Red
Gr	Grey	Sw	Black
Gn	Green	Vi	Violet
Or	Orange	Ws	White

Key to items

1 Battery
2 Ignition switch
3 Engine fuse box
6 Main fuse box
8 Diagnostic connector
145 Circulation flap motor
146 Heater blower motor resistor
147 Heater blower motor
148 Air conditioning module
149 Coolant actuator
150 Anti freeze protection switch
151 Automatic transmission selector
152 Automatic transmission control unit
153 Selector display
154 Start assist switch
178 Aux. heater passenger compartment

Zafira 1998 on - Diagram 15

MTS
H31965

Air conditioning

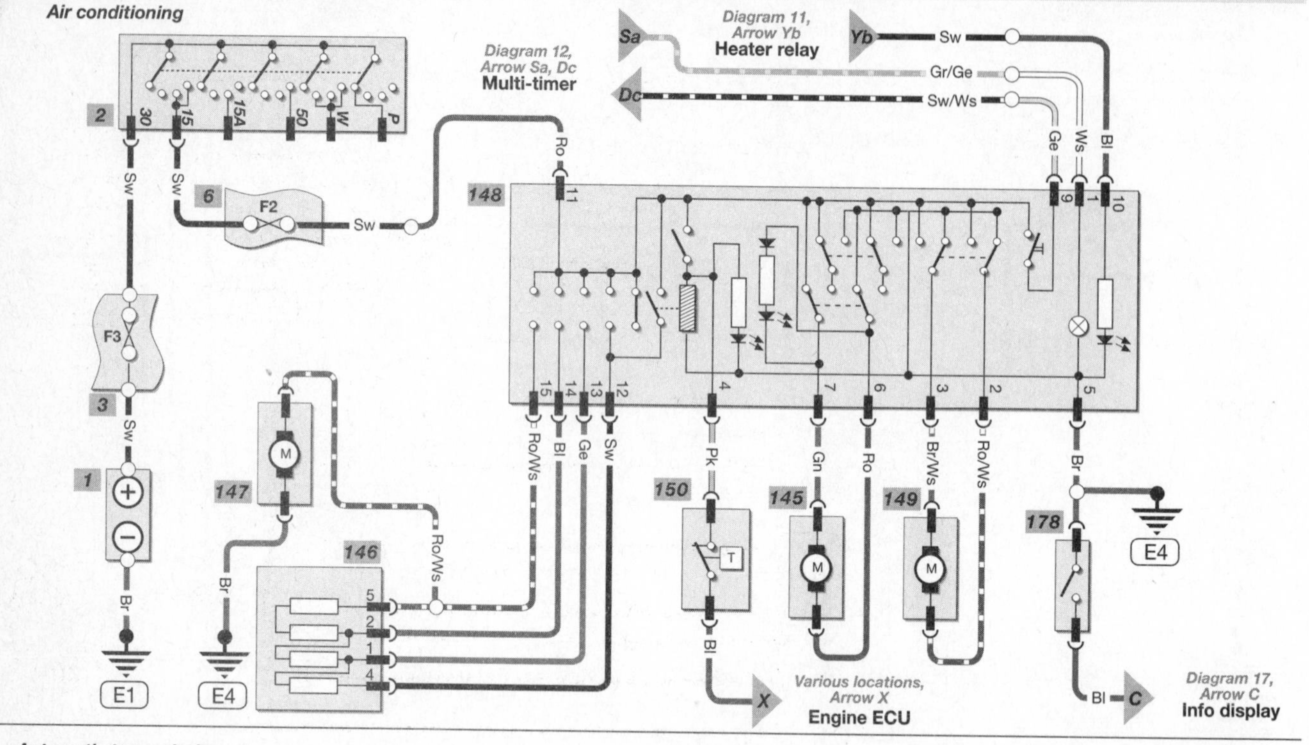

Diagram 12,
Arrow Sa, Dc
Multi-timer

Diagram 11,
Arrow Yb
Heater relay

147
146
148
150
145
149
178
E4

Various locations,
Arrow X
Engine ECU

Diagram 17,
Arrow C
Info display

Automatic transmission

Diagram 10,
Arrow Qb, Ta
Reversing lights

Diagram 2,
Arrow D, E
Starter motor

Diagram 9,
Arrow Ua
F18

Diagram 11,
Arrow Ub
Brake pedal switch

Diagram 12,
Arrow Sa
Multi-timer

153

151

152

Diagram 8, 17,
Arrow Kc
**Info display,
triple info
display**

Diagram 18,
Arrow Lc, Mc
**Instrument
display**

154

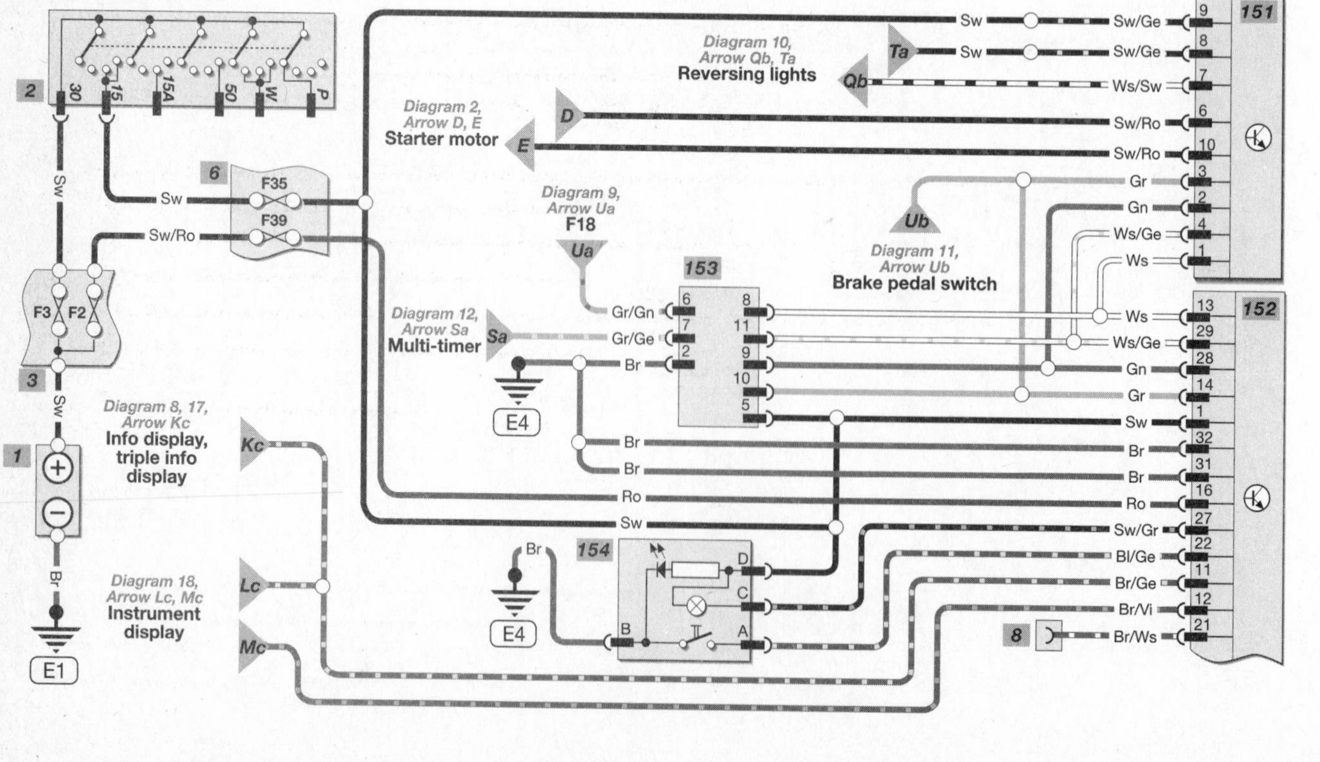

Wire colours

Bl	Blue	Pu	Purple
Br	Brown	Ro	Red
Ge	Yellow	Sw	Black
Gr	Grey	Vi	Violet
Gn	Green	Ws	White
Or	Orange		

Key to items

1 Battery
2 Ignition switch
3 Engine fuse box
6 Main fuse box
152 Automatic transmission
control unit
155 Ignition key locking magnet
156 Ignition key locking magnet switch
157 Transmission mode button
158 Selector lever magnet switch
159 Kickdown switch
160 Neutral control solenoid valve
161 Transmission solenoid valve block
162 Transmission input sensor
163 Transmission output sensor
164 Transmission oil temp. sensor
179 Selector lever magnet

Zafira 1998 on - Diagram 16

H31966

Automatic transmission continued

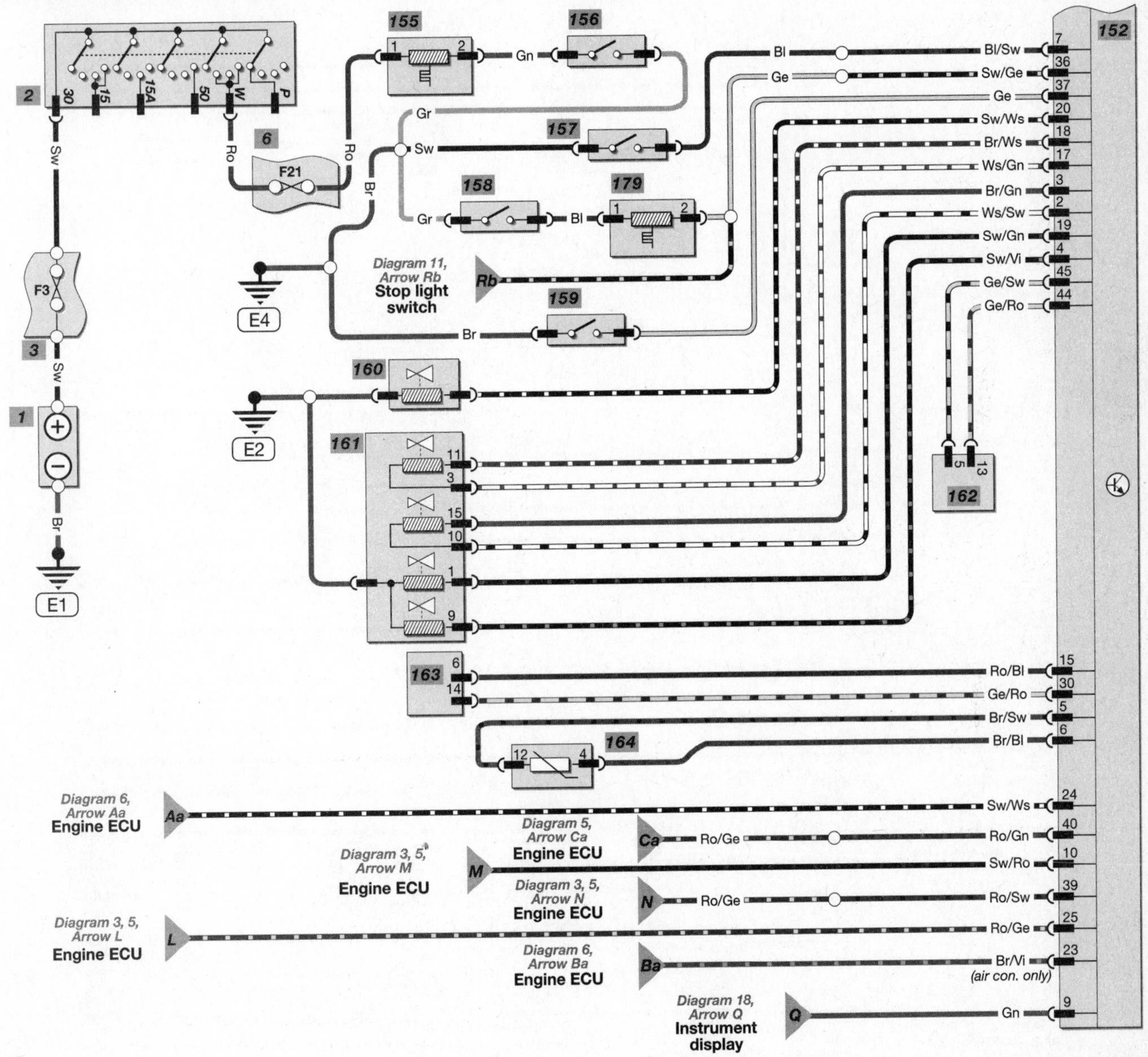

Wire colours

Bl	Blue	Pu	Purple
Br	Brown	Ro	Red
Ge	Yellow	Sw	Black
Gr	Grey	Vi	Violet
Gn	Green	Ws	White
Or	Orange		

Key to items

1 Battery
2 Ignition switch
3 Engine fuse box
6 Main fuse box
8 Diagnostic connector
165 Multi info display
166 LH front brake pad
     warning sensor

167 RH front brake pad
     warning sensor
168 Low washer fluid level switch
169 Low coolant level switch
170 Low oil level switch
171 Outside temperature sensor
172 Info display switch

Zafira 1998 on - Diagram 17

MTS
H31967

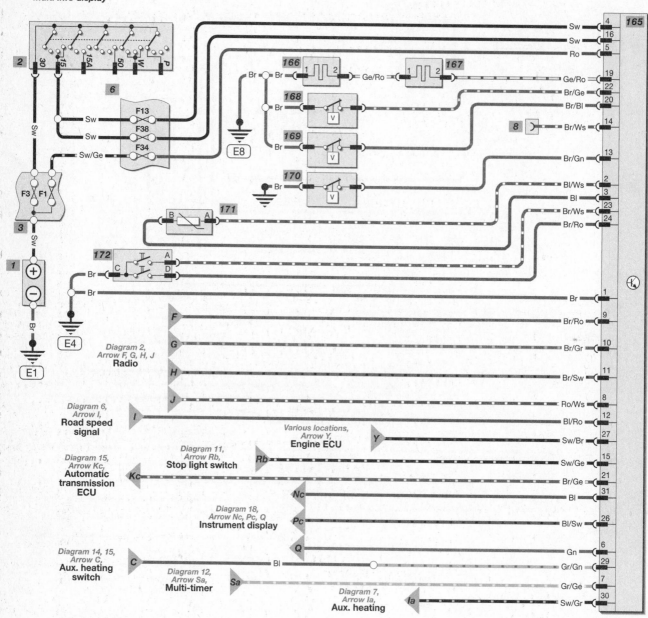

Multi info display

Wire colours

Bl	Blue	**Pu**	Purple
Br	Brown	**Ro**	Red
Ge	Yellow	**Sw**	Black
Gr	Grey	**Vi**	Violet
Gn	Green	**Ws**	White
Or	Orange		

Key to items

1 Battery
2 Ignition switch
3 Engine fuse box
6 Main fuse box
8 Diagnostic connector
173 Instrument panel
  a) alternator warning
  b) oil pressure warning
  c) airbag warning
  d) ABS warning

173 Instrument panel cont.
  e) engine warning
  f) automatic program power
  g) traction control warning
  h) automatic transmission
  i) engine cooling light
  j) brake system warning
  k) trailer turning signal
  l) coolant temp. gauge
  m) fuel reserve warning

173 Instrument panel cont.
  n) fuel gauge
  o) tachometer
  p) speedometer
  q) coolant temp warning
  r) instrument illumination
  s) rear fog light warning
  t*) high beam warning
  t) high beam warning
    (tachometer only)

173 Instrument panel cont.
  u*)front fog light warning
  u) front fog light warning
    (tachometer only)
  v) LH indicator
  w) RH indicator
174 Oil pressure switch
175 Brake fluid switch
176 Parking brake switch
177 Fuel tank sender

Zafira 1998 on - Diagram 18

MTS
H31968

Instrument display

Diagram 2, Arrow A
Alternator

Diagram 2, Arrow K
Air bag

Diagram 6, Arrow Ga
ABS

Various locations, Arrow O
Engine ECU

Diagram 15, Arrow Mc
Automatic transmission ECU

Diagram 6, Arrow Ha
Traction control

Diagram 15, Arrow Lc
Automatic transmission ECU

Diagram 8, Arrow Ra
Engine cooling

Diagram 12, Arrow Oc
Multi-timer

Various locations, Arrow P

Diagram 17, Arrow Nc, Pc
Multi info display

Various locations, Arrow Q

Diagram 6, Arrow L
Road speed signal

Diagram 12, Arrow Sa
Multi-timer

Diagram 10, Arrow Db,
Rear fog lights

Diagram 9, Arrow Ua,
Main beam

Diagram 10, Arrow Cb,
Front fog lights

Diagram 10, Arrow Ob,
LH indicator

Diagram 10, Arrow Pb,
RH indicator

Bl/Ws, Bl/Gn, Br/Ge, Br/Ge, Br/Bl, Br/Vi, Br/Gn, Br/Ge, Br/Bl, Br/Ws, Ws/Gn, Br/Ws, Bl, Bl/Sw, Br

Sw, Sw/Ro, Br, Br, Br/Ws

Sw/Bl, Ws, Sw, Sw/Ws, Sw/Gn, Gr/Ge, Ro, Sw

E1, E8, E9, E5, E8

F13, F22, F3, F2

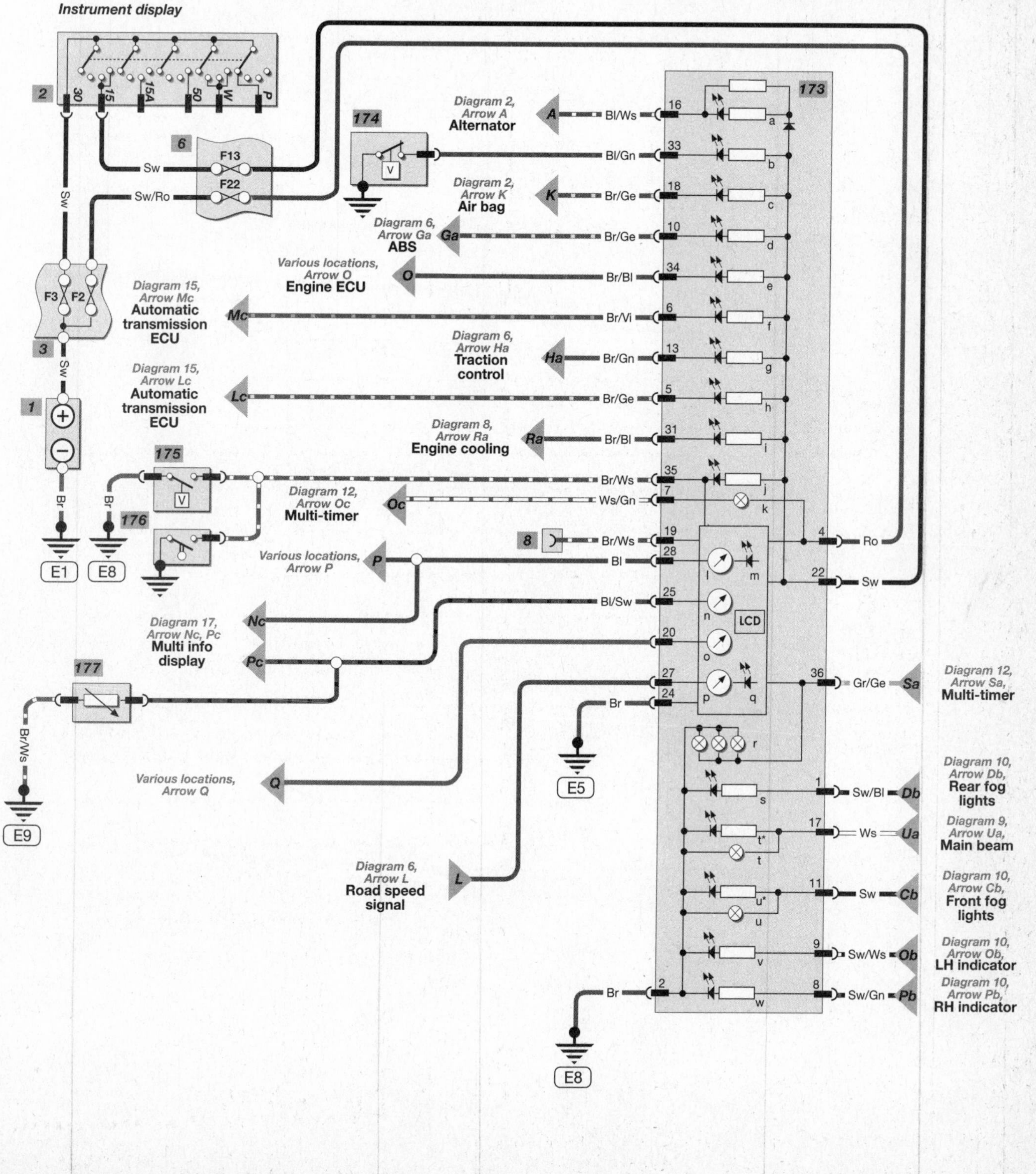

Notes

Dimensions and weights . . . .**REF•1**
Conversion factors . . . .**REF•2**
Buying spare parts . . . .**REF•3**
Vehicle identification . . . .**REF•3**
General repair procedures . . . .**REF•4**
Jacking and vehicle support . . . .**REF•5**

Disconnecting the battery . . . .**REF•5**
Tools and working facilities . . . .**REF•6**
MOT test checks . . . .**REF•8**
Fault finding . . . .**REF•12**
Glossary of technical terms . . . .**REF•19**
Index . . . .**REF•23**

Dimensions and weights

Note: *All figures are approximate, and vary according to model. Refer to manufacturer's data for exact figures.*

Dimensions

Overall length:
Astra Hatchback and Saloon	4110 mm
Astra Estate	4288 mm
Zafira	4317 mm

Overall width:
Excluding wing mirrors	1709 mm
Including wing mirrors	1989 mm

Overall height (unladen):
Astra Hatchback and Saloon	1425 mm
Astra Estate	1510 mm
Zafira	1634 mm

Wheelbase:
Astra	2614 mm
Zafira	2694 mm

Track width:

Front:
Astra	1464 mm
Zafira	1470 mm

Rear:
Astra	1452 mm
Zafira	1487 mm

Weights

Kerb weight*:

1.4 litre engine models:
Hatchback	1160 kg
Estate	1220 kg

1.6 litre engine models:
Hatchback	1165 kg
Estate	1250 kg

1.8 litre engine models:
Hatchback	1195 kg
Estate	1270 kg

2.0 and 2.2 litre engine models:
Hatchback	1235 kg
Estate	1320 kg

For automatic transmission add 30 kg. For air conditioning add 30 kg.

Maximum roof rack load

Astra	100 kg
Zafira	75 kg

Turning circle

Astra	10.8 metres
Zafira	11.1 metres

Length (distance)

Inches (in)	x 25.4	= Millimetres (mm)	x 0.0394	= Inches (in)	
Feet (ft)	x 0.305	= Metres (m)	x 3.281	= Feet (ft)	
Miles	x 1.609	= Kilometres (km)	x 0.621	= Miles	

Volume (capacity)

Cubic inches (cu in; in³)	x 16.387	= Cubic centimetres (cc; cm³)	x 0.061	= Cubic inches (cu in; in³)	
Imperial pints (Imp pt)	x 0.568	= Litres (l)	x 1.76	= Imperial pints (Imp pt)	
Imperial quarts (Imp qt)	x 1.137	= Litres (l)	x 0.88	= Imperial quarts (Imp qt)	
Imperial quarts (Imp qt)	x 1.201	= US quarts (US qt)	x 0.833	= Imperial quarts (Imp qt)	
US quarts (US qt)	x 0.946	= Litres (l)	x 1.057	= US quarts (US qt)	
Imperial gallons (Imp gal)	x 4.546	= Litres (l)	x 0.22	= Imperial gallons (Imp gal)	
Imperial gallons (Imp gal)	x 1.201	= US gallons (US gal)	x 0.833	= Imperial gallons (Imp gal)	
US gallons (US gal)	x 3.785	= Litres (l)	x 0.264	= US gallons (US gal)	

Mass (weight)

Ounces (oz)	x 28.35	= Grams (g)	x 0.035	= Ounces (oz)
Pounds (lb)	x 0.454	= Kilograms (kg)	x 2.205	= Pounds (lb)

Force

Ounces-force (ozf; oz)	x 0.278	= Newtons (N)	x 3.6	= Ounces-force (ozf; oz)
Pounds-force (lbf; lb)	x 4.448	= Newtons (N)	x 0.225	= Pounds-force (lbf; lb)
Newtons (N)	x 0.1	= Kilograms-force (kgf; kg)	x 9.81	= Newtons (N)

Pressure

Pounds-force per square inch (psi; lbf/in²; lb/in²)	x 0.070	= Kilograms-force per square centimetre (kgf/cm²; kg/cm²)	x 14.223	= Pounds-force per square inch (psi; lbf/in²; lb/in²)
Pounds-force per square inch (psi; lbf/in²; lb/in²)	x 0.068	= Atmospheres (atm)	x 14.696	= Pounds-force per square inch (psi; lbf/in²; lb/in²)
Pounds-force per square inch (psi; lbf/in²; lb/in²)	x 0.069	= Bars	x 14.5	= Pounds-force per square inch (psi; lbf/in²; lb/in²)
Pounds-force per square inch (psi; lbf/in²; lb/in²)	x 6.895	= Kilopascals (kPa)	x 0.145	= Pounds-force per square inch (psi; lbf/in²; lb/in²)
Kilopascals (kPa)	x 0.01	= Kilograms-force per square centimetre (kgf/cm²; kg/cm²)	x 98.1	= Kilopascals (kPa)
Millibar (mbar)	x 100	= Pascals (Pa)	x 0.01	= Millibar (mbar)
Millibar (mbar)	x 0.0145	= Pounds-force per square inch (psi; lbf/in²; lb/in²)	x 68.947	= Millibar (mbar)
Millibar (mbar)	x 0.75	= Millimetres of mercury (mmHg)	x 1.333	= Millibar (mbar)
Millibar (mbar)	x 0.401	= Inches of water (inH₂O)	x 2.491	= Millibar (mbar)
Millimetres of mercury (mmHg)	x 0.535	= Inches of water (inH₂O)	x 1.868	= Millimetres of mercury (mmHg)
Inches of water (inH₂O)	x 0.036	= Pounds-force per square inch (psi; lbf/in²; lb/in²)	x 27.68	= Inches of water (inH₂O)

Torque (moment of force)

Pounds-force inches (lbf in; lb in)	x 1.152	= Kilograms-force centimetre (kgf cm; kg cm)	x 0.868	= Pounds-force inches (lbf in; lb in)
Pounds-force inches (lbf in; lb in)	x 0.113	= Newton metres (Nm)	x 8.85	= Pounds-force inches (lbf in; lb in)
Pounds-force inches (lbf in; lb in)	x 0.083	= Pounds-force feet (lbf ft; lb ft)	x 12	= Pounds-force inches (lbf in; lb in)
Pounds-force feet (lbf ft; lb ft)	x 0.138	= Kilograms-force metres (kgf m; kg m)	x 7.233	= Pounds-force feet (lbf ft; lb ft)
Pounds-force feet (lbf ft; lb ft)	x 1.356	= Newton metres (Nm)	x 0.738	= Pounds-force feet (lbf ft; lb ft)
Newton metres (Nm)	x 0.102	= Kilograms-force metres (kgf m; kg m)	x 9.804	= Newton metres (Nm)

Power

Horsepower (hp)	x 745.7	= Watts (W)	x 0.0013	= Horsepower (hp)

Velocity (speed)

Miles per hour (miles/hr; mph)	x 1.609	= Kilometres per hour (km/hr; kph)	x 0.621	= Miles per hour (miles/hr; mph)

Fuel consumption*

Miles per gallon, Imperial (mpg)	x 0.354	= Kilometres per litre (km/l)	x 2.825	= Miles per gallon, Imperial (mpg)
Miles per gallon, US (mpg)	x 0.425	= Kilometres per litre (km/l)	x 2.352	= Miles per gallon, US (mpg)

Temperature

Degrees Fahrenheit = (°C x 1.8) + 32   Degrees Celsius (Degrees Centigrade; °C) = (°F - 32) x 0.56

It is common practice to convert from miles per gallon (mpg) to litres/100 kilometres (l/100km), where mpg x l/100 km = 282

Spare parts are available from many sources, including maker's appointed garages, accessory shops, and motor factors. To be sure of obtaining the correct parts, it will sometimes be necessary to quote the vehicle identification number. If possible, it can also be useful to take the old parts along for positive identification. Items such as starter motors and alternators may be available under a service exchange scheme – any parts returned should be clean.

Our advice regarding spare parts is as follows.

Officially appointed garages

This is the best source of parts which are peculiar to your car, and which are not otherwise generally available (eg, badges, interior trim, certain body panels, etc). It is also the only place at which you should buy parts if the vehicle is still under warranty.

Accessory shops

These are very good places to buy materials and components needed for the maintenance of your car (oil, air and fuel filters, light bulbs, drivebelts, greases, brake pads, tough-up paint, etc). Components of this nature sold by a reputable shop are of the same standard as those used by the car manufacturer.

Besides components, these shops also sell tools and general accessories, usually have convenient opening hours, charge lower prices, and can often be found close to home. Some accessory shops have parts counters where components needed for almost any repair job can be purchased or ordered.

Motor factors

Good factors will stock all the more important components which wear out comparatively quickly, and can sometimes supply individual components needed for the overhaul of a larger assembly (eg, brake seals and hydraulic parts, bearing shells, pistons, valves). They may also handle work such as cylinder block reboring, crankshaft regrinding, etc.

Tyre and exhaust specialists

These outlets may be independent, or members of a local or national chain. They frequently offer competitive prices when compared with a main dealer or local garage, but it will pay to obtain several quotes before making a decision. When researching prices, also ask what 'extras' may be added – for instance fitting a new valve and balancing the wheel are both commonly charged on top of the price of a new tyre.

Other sources

Beware of parts or materials obtained from market stalls, car boot sales or similar outlets. Such items are not invariably sub-standard, but there is little chance of compensation if they do prove unsatisfactory. In the case of safety-critical components such as brake pads, there is the risk not only of financial loss, but also of an accident causing injury or death.

Second-hand components or assemblies obtained from a car breaker can be a good buy in some circumstances, but his sort of purchase is best made by the experienced DIY mechanic.

Vehicle identification

Note: *When new, the car is provided with a Car Pass (similar to a credit card) having all the vehicle's data recorded on a magnetic strip.*

Modifications are a continuing and unpublicised process in vehicle manufacture, quite apart from major model changes. Spare parts manuals and lists are compiled upon a numerical basis, the individual vehicle identification numbers being essential to correct identification of the component concerned.

When ordering spare parts, always give as much information as possible. Quote the car model, year of manufacture, body and engine numbers as appropriate.

The *Vehicle Identification Number (VIN)* is stamped on a plate riveted to the engine compartment front crossmember, behind the radiator. It is also stamped into the body floor panel between the driver's seat and the door sill panel; lift the flap in the carpet to see it. On some non-UK models the plate may be attached to the front door frame **(see illustrations)**.

The *Engine number* is stamped on the front left-hand side of the cylinder block.

The Vehicle Identification Number (VIN) is stamped on a plate riveted to the engine compartment front crossmember

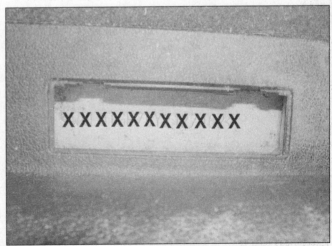

The VIN is also stamped into the body floor panel next to the driver's seat

Whenever servicing, repair or overhaul work is carried out on the car or its components, observe the following procedures and instructions. This will assist in carrying out the operation efficiently and to a professional standard of workmanship.

Joint mating faces and gaskets

When separating components at their mating faces, never insert screwdrivers or similar implements into the joint between the faces in order to prise them apart. This can cause severe damage which results in oil leaks, coolant leaks, etc upon reassembly. Separation is usually achieved by tapping along the joint with a soft-faced hammer in order to break the seal. However, note that this method may not be suitable where dowels are used for component location.

Where a gasket is used between the mating faces of two components, a new one must be fitted on reassembly; fit it dry unless otherwise stated in the repair procedure. Make sure that the mating faces are clean and dry, with all traces of old gasket removed. When cleaning a joint face, use a tool which is unlikely to score or damage the face, and remove any burrs or nicks with an oilstone or fine file.

Make sure that tapped holes are cleaned with a pipe cleaner, and keep them free of jointing compound, if this is being used, unless specifically instructed otherwise.

Ensure that all orifices, channels or pipes are clear, and blow through them, preferably using compressed air.

Oil seals

Oil seals can be removed by levering them out with a wide flat-bladed screwdriver or similar implement. Alternatively, a number of self-tapping screws may be screwed into the seal, and these used as a purchase for pliers or some similar device in order to pull the seal free.

Whenever an oil seal is removed from its working location, either individually or as part of an assembly, it should be renewed.

The very fine sealing lip of the seal is easily damaged, and will not seal if the surface it contacts is not completely clean and free from scratches, nicks or grooves. If the original sealing surface of the component cannot be restored, and the manufacturer has not made provision for slight relocation of the seal relative to the sealing surface, the component should be renewed.

Protect the lips of the seal from any surface which may damage them in the course of fitting. Use tape or a conical sleeve where possible. Lubricate the seal lips with oil before fitting and, on dual-lipped seals, fill the space between the lips with grease.

Unless otherwise stated, oil seals must be fitted with their sealing lips toward the lubricant to be sealed.

Use a tubular drift or block of wood of the appropriate size to install the seal and, if the seal housing is shouldered, drive the seal down to the shoulder. If the seal housing is unshouldered, the seal should be fitted with its face flush with the housing top face (unless otherwise instructed).

Screw threads and fastenings

Seized nuts, bolts and screws are quite a common occurrence where corrosion has set in, and the use of penetrating oil or releasing fluid will often overcome this problem if the offending item is soaked for a while before attempting to release it. The use of an impact driver may also provide a means of releasing such stubborn fastening devices, when used in conjunction with the appropriate screwdriver bit or socket. If none of these methods works, it may be necessary to resort to the careful application of heat, or the use of a hacksaw or nut splitter device.

Studs are usually removed by locking two nuts together on the threaded part, and then using a spanner on the lower nut to unscrew the stud. Studs or bolts which have broken off below the surface of the component in which they are mounted can sometimes be removed using a stud extractor. Always ensure that a blind tapped hole is completely free from oil, grease, water or other fluid before installing the bolt or stud. Failure to do this could cause the housing to crack due to the hydraulic action of the bolt or stud as it is screwed in.

When tightening a castellated nut to accept a split pin, tighten the nut to the specified torque, where applicable, and then tighten further to the next split pin hole. Never slacken the nut to align the split pin hole, unless stated in the repair procedure.

When checking or retightening a nut or bolt to a specified torque setting, slacken the nut or bolt by a quarter of a turn, and then retighten to the specified setting. However, this should not be attempted where angular tightening has been used.

For some screw fastenings, notably cylinder head bolts or nuts, torque wrench settings are no longer specified for the latter stages of tightening, "angle-tightening" being called up instead. Typically, a fairly low torque wrench setting will be applied to the bolts/nuts in the correct sequence, followed by one or more stages of tightening through specified angles.

Locknuts, locktabs and washers

Any fastening which will rotate against a component or housing during tightening should always have a washer between it and the relevant component or housing.

Spring or split washers should always be renewed when they are used to lock a critical component such as a big-end bearing retaining bolt or nut. Locktabs which are folded over to retain a nut or bolt should always be renewed.

Self-locking nuts can be re-used in non-critical areas, providing resistance can be felt when the locking portion passes over the bolt or stud thread. However, it should be noted that self-locking stiffnuts tend to lose their effectiveness after long periods of use, and should then be renewed as a matter of course.

Split pins must always be replaced with new ones of the correct size for the hole.

When thread-locking compound is found on the threads of a fastener which is to be re-used, it should be cleaned off with a wire brush and solvent, and fresh compound applied on reassembly.

Special tools

Some repair procedures in this manual entail the use of special tools such as a press, two or three-legged pullers, spring compressors, etc. Wherever possible, suitable readily-available alternatives to the manufacturer's special tools are described, and are shown in use. In some instances, where no alternative is possible, it has been necessary to resort to the use of a manufacturer's tool, and this has been done for reasons of safety as well as the efficient completion of the repair operation. Unless you are highly-skilled and have a thorough understanding of the procedures described, never attempt to bypass the use of any special tool when the procedure described specifies its use. Not only is there a very great risk of personal injury, but expensive damage could be caused to the components involved.

Environmental considerations

When disposing of used engine oil, brake fluid, antifreeze, etc, give due consideration to any detrimental environmental effects. Do not, for instance, pour any of the above liquids down drains into the general sewage system, or onto the ground to soak away. Many local council refuse tips provide a facility for waste oil disposal, as do some garages. If none of these facilities are available, consult your local Environmental Health Department, or the National Rivers Authority, for further advice.

With the universal tightening-up of legislation regarding the emission of environmentally-harmful substances from motor vehicles, most vehicles have tamperproof devices fitted to the main adjustment points of the fuel system. These devices are primarily designed to prevent unqualified persons from adjusting the fuel/air mixture, with the chance of a consequent increase in toxic emissions. If such devices are found during servicing or overhaul, they should, wherever possible, be renewed or refitted in accordance with the manufacturer's requirements or current legislation.

OIL CARE

FOLLOW THE CODE

OIL BANK LINE
0800 66 33 66
www.oilbankline.org.uk

Note: It is antisocial and illegal to dump oil down the drain. To find the location of your local oil recycling bank, call this number free.

The jack supplied with the vehicle tool kit should only be used for changing the roadwheels – see *Wheel changing* at the front of this manual. Ensure that the jack head is correctly engaged before attempting to raise the vehicle **(see illustration)**. When carrying out any other kind of work, raise the vehicle using a hydraulic trolley jack, and always supplement the jack with axle stands positioned under the vehicle jacking points.

When using a trolley jack or axle stands, always position the jack head or axle stand head under, or adjacent to one of the relevant wheel changing jacking points under the sills. Use a block of wood between the jack or axle stand and the sill – the block of wood should have a groove cut into it, in which the welded flange of the sill will locate **(see illustration)**.

Do not attempt to jack the vehicle under the front crossmember, the sump, or any of the suspension components.

Never work under, around, or near a raised vehicle, unless it is adequately supported in at least two places.

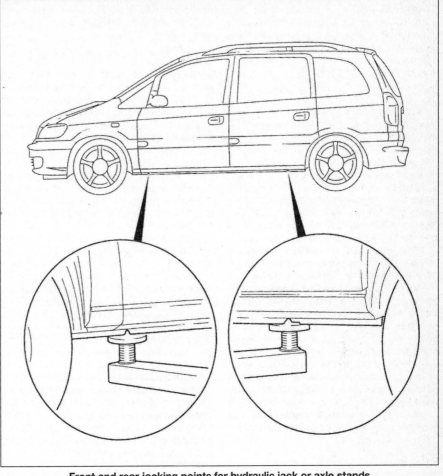

Front and rear jacking points for hydraulic jack or axle stands

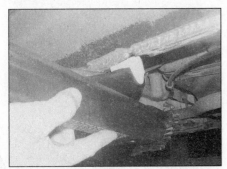

Using the jack supplied with the vehicle

Disconnecting the battery

Several systems fitted to the vehicle require battery power to be available at all times, either to ensure their continued operation (such as the clock) or to maintain control unit memories which would be erased if the battery were to be disconnected. Whenever the battery is to be disconnected therefore, first note the following, to ensure that there are no unforeseen consequences of this action:

a) First, on any vehicle with central locking, it is a wise precaution to remove the key from the ignition, and to keep it with you, so that it does not get locked in if the central locking should engage accidentally when the battery is reconnected.

b) If a security-coded audio unit is fitted, and the unit and/or the battery is disconnected, the unit will not function again on reconnection until the correct security code is entered. Details of this procedure, which varies according to the unit fitted, are given in the vehicle owner's

handbook. Ensure you have the correct code before you disconnect the battery. If you do not have the code or details of the correct procedure, but can supply proof of ownership and a legitimate reason for wanting this information, a Vauxhall dealer may be able to help.

c) The engine management system electronic control unit is of the 'self-learning' type, meaning that as it operates, it also monitors and stores the settings which give optimum engine performance under all operating conditions. When the battery is disconnected, these settings are lost and the ECU reverts to the base settings programmed into its memory at the factory. On restarting, this may lead to the engine running/idling roughly until the ECU has re-learned the optimum settings. This process is best accomplished by taking the vehicle on a road test (for approximately 15 minutes), covering all

engine speeds and loads, concentrating mainly in the 2500 to 3500 rpm region.

Devices known as 'memory-savers' (or 'code-savers') can be used to avoid some of the above problems. Precise details vary according to the device used. Typically, it is plugged into the cigarette lighter, and is connected by its own wires to a spare battery; the vehicle's own battery is then disconnected from the electrical system, leaving the memory-saver to pass sufficient current to maintain audio unit security codes and any other memory values, and also to run permanently-live circuits such as the clock.

⚠ **Warning: Some of these devices allow a considerable amount of current to pass, which can mean that many of the vehicle's systems are still operational when the main battery is disconnected. If a memory saver is used, ensure that the circuit concerned is actually 'dead' before carrying out any work on it!**

Introduction

A selection of good tools is a fundamental requirement for anyone contemplating the maintenance and repair of a motor vehicle. For the owner who does not possess any, their purchase will prove a considerable expense, offsetting some of the savings made by doing-it-yourself. However, provided that the tools purchased meet the relevant national safety standards and are of good quality, they will last for many years and prove an extremely worthwhile investment.

To help the average owner to decide which tools are needed to carry out the various tasks detailed in this manual, we have compiled three lists of tools under the following headings: *Maintenance and minor repair*, *Repair and overhaul*, and *Special*. Newcomers to practical mechanics should start off with the *Maintenance and minor repair* tool kit, and confine themselves to the simpler jobs around the vehicle. Then, as confidence and experience grow, more difficult tasks can be undertaken, with extra tools being purchased as, and when, they are needed. In this way, a *Maintenance and minor repair* tool kit can be built up into a *Repair and overhaul* tool kit over a considerable period of time, without any major cash outlays. The experienced do-it-yourselfer will have a tool kit good enough for most repair and overhaul procedures, and will add tools from the *Special* category when it is felt that the expense is justified by the amount of use to which these tools will be put.

Maintenance and minor repair tool kit

The tools given in this list should be considered as a minimum requirement if routine maintenance, servicing and minor repair operations are to be undertaken. We recommend the purchase of combination spanners (ring one end, open-ended the other); although more expensive than open-ended ones, they do give the advantages of both types of spanner.

☐ *Combination spanners:*
  Metric - 8 to 19 mm inclusive
☐ *Adjustable spanner - 35 mm jaw (approx.)*
☐ *Spark plug spanner (with rubber insert) - petrol models*
☐ *Spark plug gap adjustment tool - petrol models*
☐ *Set of feeler gauges*
☐ *Brake bleed nipple spanner*
☐ *Screwdrivers:*
  Flat blade - 100 mm long x 6 mm dia
  Cross blade - 100 mm long x 6 mm dia
  Torx - various sizes (not all vehicles)
☐ *Combination pliers*
☐ *Hacksaw (junior)*
☐ *Tyre pump*
☐ *Tyre pressure gauge*
☐ *Oil can*
☐ *Oil filter removal tool*
☐ *Fine emery cloth*
☐ *Wire brush (small)*
☐ *Funnel (medium size)*
☐ *Sump drain plug key (not all vehicles)*

Repair and overhaul tool kit

These tools are virtually essential for anyone undertaking any major repairs to a motor vehicle, and are additional to those given in the *Maintenance and minor repair* list. Included in this list is a comprehensive set of sockets. Although these are expensive, they will be found invaluable as they are so versatile - particularly if various drives are included in the set. We recommend the half-inch square-drive type, as this can be used with most proprietary torque wrenches.

The tools in this list will sometimes need to be supplemented by tools from the *Special* list:

☐ *Sockets (or box spanners) to cover range in previous list (including Torx sockets)*
☐ *Reversible ratchet drive (for use with sockets)*
☐ *Extension piece, 250 mm (for use with sockets)*
☐ *Universal joint (for use with sockets)*
☐ *Flexible handle or sliding T "breaker bar" (for use with sockets)*
☐ *Torque wrench (for use with sockets)*
☐ *Self-locking grips*
☐ *Ball pein hammer*
☐ *Soft-faced mallet (plastic or rubber)*
☐ *Screwdrivers:*
  Flat blade - long & sturdy, short (chubby), and narrow (electrician's) types
  Cross blade – long & sturdy, and short (chubby) types
☐ *Pliers:*
  Long-nosed
  Side cutters (electrician's)
  Circlip (internal and external)
☐ *Cold chisel - 25 mm*
☐ *Scriber*
☐ *Scraper*
☐ *Centre-punch*
☐ *Pin punch*
☐ *Hacksaw*
☐ *Brake hose clamp*
☐ *Brake/clutch bleeding kit*
☐ *Selection of twist drills*
☐ *Steel rule/straight-edge*
☐ *Allen keys (inc. splined/Torx type)*
☐ *Selection of files*
☐ *Wire brush*
☐ *Axle stands*
☐ *Jack (strong trolley or hydraulic type)*
☐ *Light with extension lead*
☐ *Universal electrical multi-meter*

Sockets and reversible ratchet drive

Brake bleeding kit

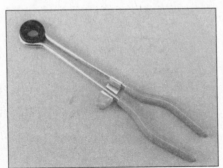

Torx key, socket and bit

Hose clamp

Angular-tightening gauge

Special tools

The tools in this list are those which are not used regularly, are expensive to buy, or which need to be used in accordance with their manufacturers' instructions. Unless relatively difficult mechanical jobs are undertaken frequently, it will not be economic to buy many of these tools. Where this is the case, you could consider clubbing together with friends (or joining a motorists' club) to make a joint purchase, or borrowing the tools against a deposit from a local garage or tool hire specialist. It is worth noting that many of the larger DIY superstores now carry a large range of special tools for hire at modest rates.

The following list contains only those tools and instruments freely available to the public, and not those special tools produced by the vehicle manufacturer specifically for its dealer network. You will find occasional references to these manufacturers' special tools in the text of this manual. Generally, an alternative method of doing the job without the vehicle manufacturers' special tool is given. However, sometimes there is no alternative to using them. Where this is the case and the relevant tool cannot be bought or borrowed, you will have to entrust the work to a dealer.

- ☐ Angular-tightening gauge
- ☐ Valve spring compressor
- ☐ Valve grinding tool
- ☐ Piston ring compressor
- ☐ Piston ring removal/installation tool
- ☐ Cylinder bore hone
- ☐ Balljoint separator
- ☐ Coil spring compressors (where applicable)
- ☐ Two/three-legged hub and bearing puller
- ☐ Impact screwdriver
- ☐ Micrometer and/or vernier calipers
- ☐ Dial gauge
- ☐ Stroboscopic timing light
- ☐ Dwell angle meter/tachometer
- ☐ Fault code reader
- ☐ Cylinder compression gauge
- ☐ Hand-operated vacuum pump and gauge
- ☐ Clutch plate alignment set
- ☐ Brake shoe steady spring cup removal tool
- ☐ Bush and bearing removal/installation set
- ☐ Stud extractors
- ☐ Tap and die set
- ☐ Lifting tackle
- ☐ Trolley jack

Buying tools

Reputable motor accessory shops and superstores often offer excellent quality tools at discount prices, so it pays to shop around.

Remember, you don't have to buy the most expensive items on the shelf, but it is always advisable to steer clear of the very cheap tools. Beware of 'bargains' offered on market stalls or at car boot sales. There are plenty of good tools around at reasonable prices, but always aim to purchase items which meet the relevant national safety standards. If in doubt, ask the proprietor or manager of the shop for advice before making a purchase.

Care and maintenance of tools

Having purchased a reasonable tool kit, it is necessary to keep the tools in a clean and serviceable condition. After use, always wipe off any dirt, grease and metal particles using a clean, dry cloth, before putting the tools away. Never leave them lying around after they have been used. A simple tool rack on the garage or workshop wall for items such as screwdrivers and pliers is a good idea. Store all normal spanners and sockets in a metal box. Any measuring instruments, gauges, meters, etc, must be carefully stored where they cannot be damaged or become rusty.

Take a little care when tools are used. Hammer heads inevitably become marked, and screwdrivers lose the keen edge on their blades from time to time. A little timely attention with emery cloth or a file will soon restore items like this to a good finish.

Working facilities

Not to be forgotten when discussing tools is the workshop itself. If anything more than routine maintenance is to be carried out, a suitable working area becomes essential.

It is appreciated that many an owner-mechanic is forced by circumstances to remove an engine or similar item without the benefit of a garage or workshop. Having done this, any repairs should always be done under the cover of a roof.

Wherever possible, any dismantling should be done on a clean, flat workbench or table at a suitable working height.

Any workbench needs a vice; one with a jaw opening of 100 mm is suitable for most jobs. As mentioned previously, some clean dry storage space is also required for tools, as well as for any lubricants, cleaning fluids, touch-up paints etc, which become necessary.

Another item which may be required, and which has a much more general usage, is an electric drill with a chuck capacity of at least 8 mm. This, together with a good range of twist drills, is virtually essential for fitting accessories.

Last, but not least, always keep a supply of old newspapers and clean, lint-free rags available, and try to keep any working area as clean as possible.

Micrometers

Dial test indicator ("dial gauge")

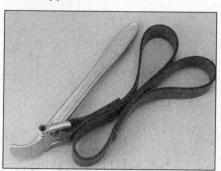
Strap wrench

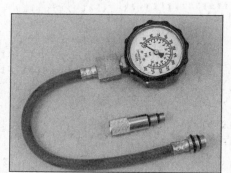
Compression tester

Fault code reader

This is a guide to getting your vehicle through the MOT test. Obviously it will not be possible to examine the vehicle to the same standard as the professional MOT tester. However, working through the following checks will enable you to identify any problem areas before submitting the vehicle for the test.

Where a testable component is in borderline condition, the tester has discretion in deciding whether to pass or fail it. The basis of such discretion is whether the tester would be happy for a close relative or friend to use the vehicle with the component in that condition. If the vehicle presented is clean and evidently well cared for, the tester may be more inclined to pass a borderline component than if the vehicle is scruffy and apparently neglected.

It has only been possible to summarise the test requirements here, based on the regulations in force at the time of printing. Test standards are becoming increasingly stringent, although there are some exemptions for older vehicles.

An assistant will be needed to help carry out some of these checks.

The checks have been sub-divided into four categories, as follows:

1 Checks carried out **FROM THE DRIVER'S SEAT**

2 Checks carried out **WITH THE VEHICLE ON THE GROUND**

3 Checks carried out **WITH THE VEHICLE RAISED AND THE WHEELS FREE TO TURN**

4 Checks carried out on **YOUR VEHICLE'S EXHAUST EMISSION SYSTEM**

---

1 Checks carried out **FROM THE DRIVER'S SEAT**

Handbrake

☐ Test the operation of the handbrake. Excessive travel (too many clicks) indicates incorrect brake or cable adjustment.
☐ Check that the handbrake cannot be released by tapping the lever sideways. Check the security of the lever mountings.

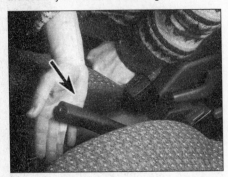

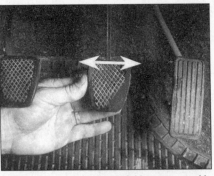

☐ Check that the brake pedal is secure and in good condition. Check also for signs of fluid leaks on the pedal, floor or carpets, which would indicate failed seals in the brake master cylinder.
☐ Check the servo unit (when applicable) by operating the brake pedal several times, then keeping the pedal depressed and starting the engine. As the engine starts, the pedal will move down slightly. If not, the vacuum hose or the servo itself may be faulty.

Steering wheel and column

☐ Examine the steering wheel for fractures or looseness of the hub, spokes or rim.
☐ Move the steering wheel from side to side and then up and down. Check that the steering wheel is not loose on the column, indicating wear or a loose retaining nut. Continue moving the steering wheel as before, but also turn it slightly from left to right.
☐ Check that the steering wheel is not loose on the column, and that there is no abnormal

movement of the steering wheel, indicating wear in the column support bearings or couplings.

Windscreen, mirrors and sunvisor

☐ The windscreen must be free of cracks or other significant damage within the driver's field of view. (Small stone chips are acceptable.) Rear view mirrors must be secure, intact, and capable of being adjusted.

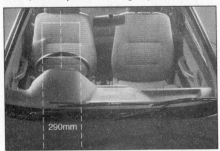

290mm

☐ The driver's sunvisor must be capable of being stored in the "up" position.

Footbrake

☐ Depress the brake pedal and check that it does not creep down to the floor, indicating a master cylinder fault. Release the pedal, wait a few seconds, then depress it again. If the pedal travels nearly to the floor before firm resistance is felt, brake adjustment or repair is necessary. If the pedal feels spongy, there is air in the hydraulic system which must be removed by bleeding.

Seat belts and seats

Note: *The following checks are applicable to all seat belts, front and rear.*

☐ Examine the webbing of all the belts (including rear belts if fitted) for cuts, serious fraying or deterioration. Fasten and unfasten each belt to check the buckles. If applicable, check the retracting mechanism. Check the security of all seat belt mountings accessible from inside the vehicle.

☐ Seat belts with pre-tensioners, once activated, have a "flag" or similar showing on the seat belt stalk. This, in itself, is not a reason for test failure.

☐ The front seats themselves must be securely attached and the backrests must lock in the upright position.

Doors

☐ Both front doors must be able to be opened and closed from outside and inside, and must latch securely when closed.

2 Checks carried out WITH THE VEHICLE ON THE GROUND

Vehicle identification

☐ Number plates must be in good condition, secure and legible, with letters and numbers correctly spaced – spacing at (A) should be at least twice that at (B).

☐ The VIN plate and/or homologation plate must be legible.

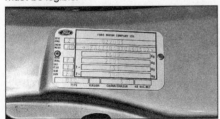

Electrical equipment

☐ Switch on the ignition and check the operation of the horn.

☐ Check the windscreen washers and wipers, examining the wiper blades; renew damaged or perished blades. Also check the operation of the stop-lights.

☐ Check the operation of the sidelights and number plate lights. The lenses and reflectors must be secure, clean and undamaged.

☐ Check the operation and alignment of the headlights. The headlight reflectors must not be tarnished and the lenses must be undamaged.

☐ Switch on the ignition and check the operation of the direction indicators (including the instrument panel tell-tale) and the hazard warning lights. Operation of the sidelights and stop-lights must not affect the indicators - if it does, the cause is usually a bad earth at the rear light cluster.

☐ Check the operation of the rear foglight(s), including the warning light on the instrument panel or in the switch.

☐ The ABS warning light must illuminate in accordance with the manufacturers' design. For most vehicles, the ABS warning light should illuminate when the ignition is switched on, and (if the system is operating properly) extinguish after a few seconds. Refer to the owner's handbook.

Footbrake

☐ Examine the master cylinder, brake pipes and servo unit for leaks, loose mountings, corrosion or other damage.

☐ The fluid reservoir must be secure and the fluid level must be between the upper (**A**) and lower (**B**) markings.

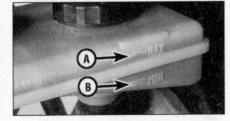

☐ Inspect both front brake flexible hoses for cracks or deterioration of the rubber. Turn the steering from lock to lock, and ensure that the hoses do not contact the wheel, tyre, or any part of the steering or suspension mechanism. With the brake pedal firmly depressed, check the hoses for bulges or leaks under pressure.

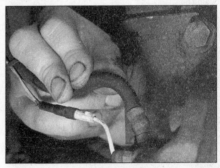

Steering and suspension

☐ Have your assistant turn the steering wheel from side to side slightly, up to the point where the steering gear just begins to transmit this movement to the roadwheels. Check for excessive free play between the steering wheel and the steering gear, indicating wear or insecurity of the steering column joints, the column-to-steering gear coupling, or the steering gear itself.

☐ Have your assistant turn the steering wheel more vigorously in each direction, so that the roadwheels just begin to turn. As this is done, examine all the steering joints, linkages, fittings and attachments. Renew any component that shows signs of wear or damage. On vehicles with power steering, check the security and condition of the steering pump, drivebelt and hoses.

☐ Check that the vehicle is standing level, and at approximately the correct ride height.

Shock absorbers

☐ Depress each corner of the vehicle in turn, then release it. The vehicle should rise and then settle in its normal position. If the vehicle continues to rise and fall, the shock absorber is defective. A shock absorber which has seized will also cause the vehicle to fail.

Exhaust system

☐ Start the engine. With your assistant holding a rag over the tailpipe, check the entire system for leaks. Repair or renew leaking sections.

3 Checks carried out
WITH THE VEHICLE RAISED AND THE WHEELS FREE TO TURN

Jack up the front and rear of the vehicle, and securely support it on axle stands. Position the stands clear of the suspension assemblies. Ensure that the wheels are clear of the ground and that the steering can be turned from lock to lock.

Steering mechanism

☐ Have your assistant turn the steering from lock to lock. Check that the steering turns smoothly, and that no part of the steering mechanism, including a wheel or tyre, fouls any brake hose or pipe or any part of the body structure.
☐ Examine the steering rack rubber gaiters for damage or insecurity of the retaining clips. If power steering is fitted, check for signs of damage or leakage of the fluid hoses, pipes or connections. Also check for excessive stiffness or binding of the steering, a missing split pin or locking device, or severe corrosion of the body structure within 30 cm of any steering component attachment point.

Front and rear suspension and wheel bearings

☐ Starting at the front right-hand side, grasp the roadwheel at the 3 o'clock and 9 o'clock positions and rock gently but firmly. Check for free play or insecurity at the wheel bearings, suspension balljoints, or suspension mountings, pivots and attachments.
☐ Now grasp the wheel at the 12 o'clock and 6 o'clock positions and repeat the previous inspection. Spin the wheel, and check for roughness or tightness of the front wheel bearing.

☐ If excess free play is suspected at a component pivot point, this can be confirmed by using a large screwdriver or similar tool and levering between the mounting and the component attachment. This will confirm whether the wear is in the pivot bush, its retaining bolt, or in the mounting itself (the bolt holes can often become elongated).

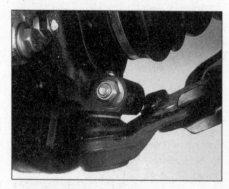

☐ Carry out all the above checks at the other front wheel, and then at both rear wheels.

Springs and shock absorbers

☐ Examine the suspension struts (when applicable) for serious fluid leakage, corrosion, or damage to the casing. Also check the security of the mounting points.
☐ If coil springs are fitted, check that the spring ends locate in their seats, and that the spring is not corroded, cracked or broken.
☐ If leaf springs are fitted, check that all leaves are intact, that the axle is securely attached to each spring, and that there is no deterioration of the spring eye mountings, bushes, and shackles.

☐ The same general checks apply to vehicles fitted with other suspension types, such as torsion bars, hydraulic displacer units, etc. Ensure that all mountings and attachments are secure, that there are no signs of excessive wear, corrosion or damage, and (on hydraulic types) that there are no fluid leaks or damaged pipes.
☐ Inspect the shock absorbers for signs of serious fluid leakage. Check for wear of the mounting bushes or attachments, or damage to the body of the unit.

Driveshafts (fwd vehicles only)

☐ Rotate each front wheel in turn and inspect the constant velocity joint gaiters for splits or damage. Also check that each driveshaft is straight and undamaged.

Braking system

☐ If possible without dismantling, check brake pad wear and disc condition. Ensure that the friction lining material has not worn excessively, (A) and that the discs are not fractured, pitted, scored or badly worn (B).

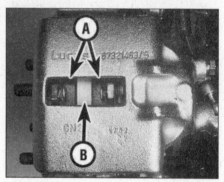

☐ Examine all the rigid brake pipes underneath the vehicle, and the flexible hose(s) at the rear. Look for corrosion, chafing or insecurity of the pipes, and for signs of bulging under pressure, chafing, splits or deterioration of the flexible hoses.
☐ Look for signs of fluid leaks at the brake calipers or on the brake backplates. Repair or renew leaking components.
☐ Slowly spin each wheel, while your assistant depresses and releases the footbrake. Ensure that each brake is operating and does not bind when the pedal is released.

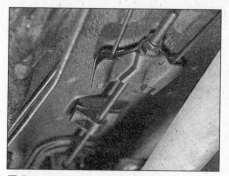

□ Examine the handbrake mechanism, checking for frayed or broken cables, excessive corrosion, or wear or insecurity of the linkage. Check that the mechanism works on each relevant wheel, and releases fully, without binding.

□ It is not possible to test brake efficiency without special equipment, but a road test can be carried out later to check that the vehicle pulls up in a straight line.

Fuel and exhaust systems

□ Inspect the fuel tank (including the filler cap), fuel pipes, hoses and unions. All components must be secure and free from leaks.

□ Examine the exhaust system over its entire length, checking for any damaged, broken or missing mountings, security of the retaining clamps and rust or corrosion.

Wheels and tyres

□ Examine the sidewalls and tread area of each tyre in turn. Check for cuts, tears, lumps, bulges, separation of the tread, and exposure of the ply or cord due to wear or damage. Check that the tyre bead is correctly seated on the wheel rim, that the valve is sound and properly seated, and that the wheel is not distorted or damaged.

□ Check that the tyres are of the correct size for the vehicle, that they are of the same size and type on each axle, and that the pressures are correct.

□ Check the tyre tread depth. The legal minimum at the time of writing is 1.6 mm over at least three-quarters of the tread width. Abnormal tread wear may indicate incorrect front wheel alignment.

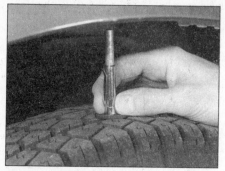

Body corrosion

□ Check the condition of the entire vehicle structure for signs of corrosion in load-bearing areas. (These include chassis box sections, side sills, cross-members, pillars, and all suspension, steering, braking system and seat belt mountings and anchorages.) Any corrosion which has seriously reduced the thickness of a load-bearing area is likely to cause the vehicle to fail. In this case professional repairs are likely to be needed.

□ Damage or corrosion which causes sharp or otherwise dangerous edges to be exposed will also cause the vehicle to fail.

4 Checks carried out on YOUR VEHICLE'S EXHAUST EMISSION SYSTEM

Petrol models

□ Have the engine at normal operating temperature, and make sure that it is in good tune (ignition system in good order, air filter element clean, etc).

□ Before any measurements are carried out, raise the engine speed to around 2500 rpm, and hold it at this speed for 20 seconds. Allow the engine speed to return to idle, and watch for smoke emissions from the exhaust tailpipe. If the idle speed is obviously much too high, or if dense blue or clearly-visible black smoke comes from the tailpipe for more than 5 seconds, the vehicle will fail. As a rule of thumb, blue smoke signifies oil being burnt (engine wear) while black smoke signifies unburnt fuel (dirty air cleaner element, or other carburettor or fuel system fault).

□ An exhaust gas analyser capable of measuring carbon monoxide (CO) and hydrocarbons (HC) is now needed. If such an instrument cannot be hired or borrowed, a local garage may agree to perform the check for a small fee.

CO emissions (mixture)

□ At the time of writing, for vehicles first used between 1st August 1975 and 31st July 1986 (P to C registration), the CO level must not exceed 4.5% by volume. For vehicles first used between 1st August 1986 and 31st July 1992 (D to J registration), the CO level must not exceed 3.5% by volume. Vehicles first

used after 1st August 1992 (K registration) must conform to the manufacturer's specification. The MOT tester has access to a DOT database or emissions handbook, which lists the CO and HC limits for each make and model of vehicle. The CO level is measured with the engine at idle speed, and at "fast idle". The following limits are given as a general guide:

At idle speed -
CO level no more than 0.5%
At "fast idle" (2500 to 3000 rpm) -
CO level no more than 0.3%
(Minimum oil temperature 60°C)

□ If the CO level cannot be reduced far enough to pass the test (and the fuel and ignition systems are otherwise in good condition) then the carburettor is badly worn, or there is some problem in the fuel injection system or catalytic converter (as applicable).

HC emissions

□ With the CO within limits, HC emissions for vehicles first used between 1st August 1975 and 31st July 1992 (P to J registration) must not exceed 1200 ppm. Vehicles first used after 1st August 1992 (K registration) must conform to the manufacturer's specification. The MOT tester has access to a DOT database or emissions handbook, which lists the CO and HC limits for each make and model of vehicle. The HC level is measured with the engine at "fast idle". The following is given as a general guide:

At "fast idle" (2500 to 3000 rpm) -
HC level no more than 200 ppm
(Minimum oil temperature 60°C)

□ Excessive HC emissions are caused by incomplete combustion, the causes of which can include oil being burnt, mechanical wear and ignition/fuel system malfunction.

Diesel models

□ The only emission test applicable to Diesel engines is the measuring of exhaust smoke density. The test involves accelerating the engine several times to its maximum unloaded speed.

Note: *It is of the utmost importance that the engine timing belt is in good condition before the test is carried out.*

□ The limits for Diesel engine exhaust smoke, introduced in September 1995 are:
Vehicles first used before 1st August 1979:
Exempt from metered smoke testing, but must not emit "dense blue or clearly visible black smoke for a period of more than 5 seconds at idle" or "dense blue or clearly visible black smoke during acceleration which would obscure the view of other road users".
Non-turbocharged vehicles first used after 1st August 1979: 2.5m⁻¹
Turbocharged vehicles first used after 1st August 1979: 3.0m⁻¹

□ Excessive smoke can be caused by a dirty air cleaner element. Otherwise, professional advice may be needed to find the cause.

Engine

- [ ] Engine fails to rotate when attempting to start
- [ ] Engine rotates, but will not start
- [ ] Engine difficult to start when cold
- [ ] Engine difficult to start when hot
- [ ] Starter motor noisy or excessively-rough in engagement
- [ ] Engine starts, but stops immediately
- [ ] Engine idles erratically
- [ ] Engine misfires at idle speed
- [ ] Engine misfires throughout the driving speed range
- [ ] Engine hesitates on acceleration
- [ ] Engine stalls
- [ ] Engine lacks power
- [ ] Engine backfires
- [ ] Oil pressure warning light illuminated with engine running
- [ ] Engine runs-on after switching off
- [ ] Engine noises

Cooling system

- [ ] Overheating
- [ ] Overcooling
- [ ] External coolant leakage
- [ ] Internal coolant leakage
- [ ] Corrosion

Fuel and exhaust systems

- [ ] Excessive fuel consumption
- [ ] Fuel leakage and/or fuel odour
- [ ] Excessive noise or fumes from the exhaust system

Clutch

- [ ] Pedal travels to floor – no pressure or very little resistance
- [ ] Clutch fails to disengage (unable to select gears)
- [ ] Clutch slips (engine speed increases, with no increase in vehicle speed)
- [ ] Judder as clutch is engaged
- [ ] Noise when depressing or releasing clutch pedal

Manual transmission

- [ ] Noisy in neutral with engine running
- [ ] Noisy in one particular gear
- [ ] Difficulty engaging gears
- [ ] Jumps out of gear
- [ ] Vibration
- [ ] Lubricant leaks

Automatic transmission

- [ ] Fluid leakage
- [ ] Transmission fluid brown, or has burned smell
- [ ] Engine will not start in any gear, or starts in gears other than Park or Neutral
- [ ] General gear selection problems
- [ ] Transmission will not downshift (kickdown) with accelerator pedal fully depressed
- [ ] Transmission slips, shifts roughly, is noisy, or has no drive in forward or reverse gears

Driveshafts

- [ ] Vibration when accelerating or decelerating
- [ ] Clicking or knocking noise on turns (at slow speed on full-lock)

Braking system

- [ ] Vehicle pulls to one side under braking
- [ ] Noise (grinding or high-pitched squeal) when brakes applied
- [ ] Excessive brake pedal travel
- [ ] Brake pedal feels spongy when depressed
- [ ] Excessive brake pedal effort required to stop vehicle
- [ ] Judder felt through brake pedal or steering wheel when braking
- [ ] Pedal pulsates when braking hard
- [ ] Brakes binding
- [ ] Rear wheels locking under normal braking

Steering and suspension

- [ ] Vehicle pulls to one side
- [ ] Wheel wobble and vibration
- [ ] Excessive pitching and/or rolling around corners, or during braking
- [ ] Wandering or general instability
- [ ] Excessively-stiff steering
- [ ] Excessive play in steering
- [ ] Lack of power assistance
- [ ] Tyre wear excessive

Electrical system

- [ ] Battery will not hold a charge for more than a few days
- [ ] Ignition/no-charge warning light remains illuminated with engine running
- [ ] Ignition/no-charge warning light fails to come on
- [ ] Lights inoperative
- [ ] Instrument readings inaccurate or erratic
- [ ] Horn inoperative, or unsatisfactory in operation
- [ ] Windscreen/tailgate wipers inoperative, or unsatisfactory in operation
- [ ] Windscreen/tailgate washers inoperative, or unsatisfactory in operation
- [ ] Electric windows inoperative, or unsatisfactory in operation
- [ ] Central locking system inoperative, or unsatisfactory in operation

Introduction

The vehicle owner who does his or her own maintenance according to the recommended service schedules should not have to use this section of the manual very often. Modern component reliability is such that, provided those items subject to wear or deterioration are inspected or renewed at the specified intervals, sudden failure is comparatively rare. Faults do not usually just happen as a result of sudden failure, but develop over a period of time. Major mechanical failures in particular are usually preceded by characteristic symptoms over hundreds or even thousands of miles. Those components which do occasionally fail without warning are often small and easily carried in the vehicle.

With any fault finding, the first step is to decide where to begin investigations. Sometimes this is obvious, but on other occasions, a little detective work will be necessary. The owner who makes half a dozen haphazard adjustments or replacements may be successful in curing a fault (or its symptoms), but will be none the wiser if the fault recurs, and ultimately may have spent more time and money than was necessary. A calm and logical approach will be found to be more satisfactory in the long run. Always take into account any warning signs or abnormalities that may have been noticed in the period preceding the fault – power loss, high or low gauge readings, unusual smells, etc – and remember that failure of components such as fuses or spark plugs may only be pointers to some underlying fault.

The pages which follow provide an easy-reference guide to the more common problems which may occur during the operation of the vehicle. These problems and their possible causes are grouped under headings denoting various components or systems, such as Engine, Cooling system, etc. The general Chapter which deals with the problem is also shown in brackets; refer to the relevant part of that Chapter for system-specific information. Whatever the fault, certain basic principles apply. These are as follows:

Verify the fault. This is simply a matter of being sure that you know what the symptoms are before starting work. This is particularly important if you are investigating a fault for someone else, who may not have described it very accurately.

Don't overlook the obvious. For example, if the vehicle won't start, is there fuel in the tank? (Don't take anyone else's word on this particular point, and don't trust the fuel gauge either!) If an electrical fault is indicated, look for loose or broken wires before digging out the test gear.

Cure the disease, not the symptom. Substituting a flat battery with a fully-charged one will get you off the hard shoulder, but if the underlying cause is not attended to, the new battery will go the same way. Similarly, changing oil-fouled spark plugs for a new set will get you moving again, but remember that the reason for the fouling (if it wasn't simply an incorrect grade of plug) will have to be established and corrected.

Don't take anything for granted. Particularly, don't forget that a 'new' component may itself be defective (especially if it's been rattling around in the boot for months), and don't leave components out of a fault diagnosis sequence just because they are new or recently-fitted. When you do finally diagnose a difficult fault, you'll probably realise that all the evidence was there from the start.

Engine

Engine fails to rotate when attempting to start

☐ Battery terminal connections loose or corroded (see *Weekly checks*).
☐ Battery discharged or faulty (Chapter 5A).
☐ Broken, loose or disconnected wiring in the starting circuit (Chapter 5A).
☐ Defective starter solenoid or switch (Chapter 5A).
☐ Defective starter motor (Chapter 5A).
☐ Starter pinion or flywheel ring gear teeth loose or broken (Chapters 2 and 5A).
☐ Engine earth strap broken or disconnected (Chapter 5A).

Engine rotates, but will not start

☐ Fuel tank empty.
☐ Battery discharged (engine rotates slowly) (Chapter 5A).
☐ Battery terminal connections loose or corroded (see *Weekly checks*).
☐ Ignition components damp or damaged (Chapters 1 and 5B).
☐ Broken, loose or disconnected wiring in the ignition circuit (Chapters 1 and 5B).
☐ Worn, faulty or incorrectly-gapped spark plugs (Chapter 1).
☐ Fuel injection system faulty (Chapter 4A).
☐ Major mechanical failure (eg, camshaft drive) (Chapter 2).

Engine difficult to start when cold

☐ Battery discharged (Chapter 5A).
☐ Battery terminal connections loose or corroded (see *Weekly checks*).
☐ Worn, faulty or incorrectly-gapped spark plugs (Chapter 1).
☐ Fuel injection system faulty (Chapter 4A).
☐ Other ignition system fault (Chapters 1 and 5B).
☐ Low cylinder compressions (Chapter 2).

Engine difficult to start when hot

☐ Air filter element dirty or clogged (Chapter 1).
☐ Fuel injection system faulty (Chapter 4A).
☐ Low cylinder compressions (Chapter 2).

Starter motor noisy or excessively-rough in engagement

☐ Starter pinion or flywheel ring gear teeth loose or broken (Chapters 2 and 5A).
☐ Starter motor mounting bolts loose or missing (Chapter 5A).
☐ Starter motor internal components worn or damaged (Chapter 5A).

Engine starts, but stops immediately

☐ Loose or faulty electrical connections in the ignition circuit (Chapters 1 and 5B).
☐ Vacuum leak at the throttle body or inlet manifold (Chapter 4A).
☐ Blocked injector/fuel injection system fault (Chapter 4A).

Engine idles erratically

☐ Air filter element clogged (Chapter 1).
☐ Vacuum leak at the throttle body, inlet manifold or associated hoses (Chapter 4A).
☐ Worn, faulty or incorrectly-gapped spark plugs (Chapter 1).
☐ Uneven or low cylinder compressions (Chapter 2).
☐ Camshaft lobes worn (Chapter 2).
☐ Timing belt incorrectly fitted (Chapter 2).
☐ Blocked injector/fuel injection system fault (Chapter 4A).

Engine misfires at idle speed

☐ Worn, faulty or incorrectly-gapped spark plugs (Chapter 1).
☐ Faulty spark plug HT leads (Chapter 1).
☐ Vacuum leak at the throttle body, inlet manifold or associated hoses (Chapter 4A).
☐ Blocked injector/fuel injection system fault (Chapter 4A).
☐ Uneven or low cylinder compressions (Chapter 2).
☐ Disconnected, leaking, or perished crankcase ventilation hoses (Chapter 4B).

Engine misfires throughout the driving speed range

☐ Fuel filter choked (Chapter 1).
☐ Fuel pump faulty, or delivery pressure low (Chapter 4A).
☐ Fuel tank vent blocked, or fuel pipes restricted (Chapter 4A).
☐ Vacuum leak at the throttle body, inlet manifold or associated hoses (Chapter 4A).
☐ Worn, faulty or incorrectly-gapped spark plugs (Chapter 1).
☐ Faulty spark plug HT leads (Chapter 1).
☐ Faulty ignition coil (Chapter 5B).
☐ Uneven or low cylinder compressions (Chapter 2).
☐ Blocked injector/fuel injection system fault (Chapter 4A).

Engine hesitates on acceleration

☐ Worn, faulty or incorrectly-gapped spark plugs (Chapter 1).
☐ Vacuum leak at the throttle body, inlet manifold or associated hoses (Chapter 4A).
☐ Blocked injector/fuel injection system fault (Chapter 4A).

Engine stalls

☐ Vacuum leak at the throttle body, inlet manifold or associated hoses (Chapter 4A).
☐ Fuel filter choked (Chapter 1).
☐ Fuel pump faulty, or delivery pressure low (Chapter 4A).
☐ Fuel tank vent blocked, or fuel pipes restricted (Chapter 4A).
☐ Blocked injector/fuel injection system fault (Chapter 4A).

Engine (continued)

Engine lacks power

☐ Timing belt/chain incorrectly fitted or tensioned (Chapter 2).
☐ Fuel filter choked (Chapter 1).
☐ Fuel pump faulty, or delivery pressure low (Chapter 4A).
☐ Uneven or low cylinder compressions (Chapter 2).
☐ Worn, faulty or incorrectly-gapped spark plugs (Chapter 1).
☐ Vacuum leak at the throttle body, inlet manifold or associated hoses (Chapter 4A).
☐ Blocked injector/fuel injection system fault (Chapter 4A).
☐ Brakes binding (Chapters 1 and 9).
☐ Clutch slipping (Chapter 6).

Engine backfires

☐ Timing belt incorrectly fitted or tensioned (Chapter 2).
☐ Vacuum leak at the throttle body, inlet manifold or associated hoses (Chapter 4A).
☐ Blocked injector/fuel injection system fault (Chapter 4A).

Oil pressure warning light illuminated with engine running

☐ Low oil level, or incorrect oil grade (Weekly checks).
☐ Faulty oil pressure sensor (Chapter 5A).
☐ Worn engine bearings and/or oil pump (Chapter 2).
☐ High engine operating temperature (Chapter 3).
☐ Oil pressure relief valve defective (Chapter 2).
☐ Oil pick-up strainer clogged (Chapter 2).

Engine runs-on after switching off

☐ Excessive carbon build-up in engine (Chapter 2).
☐ High engine operating temperature (Chapter 3).
☐ Fuel injection system faulty (Chapter 4A).

Engine noises

Pre-ignition (pinking) or knocking during acceleration or under load

☐ Ignition timing incorrect/ignition system fault (Chapters 1 and 5B).
☐ Incorrect grade of spark plug (Chapter 1).
☐ Incorrect grade of fuel (Chapter 4A).
☐ Vacuum leak at the throttle body, inlet manifold or associated hoses (Chapter 4A).
☐ Excessive carbon build-up in engine (Chapter 2).
☐ Blocked injector/fuel injection system fault (Chapter 4A).

Whistling or wheezing noises

☐ Leaking inlet manifold or throttle body gasket (Chapter 4A).
☐ Leaking exhaust manifold gasket or pipe-to-manifold joint (Chapter 4A).
☐ Leaking vacuum hose (Chapters 4, 5 and 9).
☐ Blowing cylinder head gasket (Chapter 2).

Tapping or rattling noises

☐ Worn valve gear or camshaft (Chapter 2).
☐ Ancillary component fault (coolant pump, alternator, etc) (Chapters 3, 5, etc).

Knocking or thumping noises

☐ Worn big-end bearings (regular heavy knocking, perhaps less under load) (Chapter 2).
☐ Worn main bearings (rumbling and knocking, perhaps worsening under load) (Chapter 2).
☐ Piston slap (most noticeable when cold) (Chapter 2).
☐ Ancillary component fault (coolant pump, alternator, etc) (Chapters 3, 5, etc).

Cooling system

Overheating

☐ Insufficient coolant in system (Weekly Checks).
☐ Thermostat faulty (Chapter 3).
☐ Radiator core blocked, or grille restricted (Chapter 3).
☐ Electric cooling fan or thermostatic switch faulty (Chapter 3).
☐ Inaccurate temperature gauge sender unit (Chapter 3).
☐ Airlock in cooling system (Chapter 3).
☐ Expansion tank pressure cap faulty (Chapter 3).

Overcooling

☐ Thermostat faulty (Chapter 3).
☐ Inaccurate temperature gauge sender unit (Chapter 3).

External coolant leakage

☐ Deteriorated or damaged hoses or hose clips (Chapter 1).
☐ Radiator core or heater matrix leaking (Chapter 3).
☐ Pressure cap faulty (Chapter 3).
☐ Coolant pump internal seal leaking (Chapter 3).
☐ Coolant pump-to-block seal leaking (Chapter 3).
☐ Boiling due to overheating (Chapter 3).
☐ Core plug leaking (Chapter 2).

Internal coolant leakage

☐ Leaking cylinder head gasket (Chapter 2).
☐ Cracked cylinder head or cylinder block (Chapter 2).

Corrosion

☐ Infrequent draining and flushing (Chapter 1).
☐ Incorrect coolant mixture or inappropriate coolant type (see Weekly checks).

Fuel and exhaust systems

Excessive fuel consumption

☐ Air filter element dirty or clogged (Chapter 1).
☐ Fuel injection system faulty (Chapter 4A).
☐ Ignition timing incorrect/ignition system faulty (Chapters 1 and 5B).
☐ Tyres under-inflated (see Weekly checks).

Fuel leakage and/or fuel odour

☐ Damaged or corroded fuel tank, pipes or connections (Chapter 4A).

Excessive noise or fumes from the exhaust system

☐ Leaking exhaust system or manifold joints (Chapters 1 and 4A).
☐ Leaking, corroded or damaged silencers or pipe (Chapters 1 and 4A).
☐ Broken mountings causing body or suspension contact (Chapter 1).

Clutch

Pedal travels to floor – no pressure or very little resistance

- ☐ Air in hydraulic system/faulty master or slave cylinder (Chapter 6).
- ☐ Faulty hydraulic release system (Chapter 6).
- ☐ Broken clutch release bearing or arm (Chapter 6).
- ☐ Broken diaphragm spring in clutch pressure plate (Chapter 6).

Clutch fails to disengage (unable to select gears)

- ☐ Air in hydraulic system/faulty master or slave cylinder (Chapter 6).
- ☐ Faulty hydraulic release system (Chapter 6).
- ☐ Clutch disc sticking on gearbox input shaft splines (Chapter 6).
- ☐ Clutch disc sticking to flywheel or pressure plate (Chapter 6).
- ☐ Faulty pressure plate assembly (Chapter 6).
- ☐ Clutch release mechanism worn or incorrectly assembled (Chapter 6).

Clutch slips (engine speed increases, with no increase in vehicle speed)

- ☐ Faulty hydraulic release system (Chapter 6).

- ☐ Clutch disc linings excessively worn (Chapter 6).
- ☐ Clutch disc linings contaminated with oil or grease (Chapter 6).
- ☐ Faulty pressure plate or weak diaphragm spring (Chapter 6).

Judder as clutch is engaged

- ☐ Clutch disc linings contaminated with oil or grease (Chapter 6).
- ☐ Clutch disc linings excessively worn (Chapter 6).
- ☐ Faulty or distorted pressure plate or diaphragm spring (Chapter 6).
- ☐ Worn or loose engine or gearbox mountings (Chapter 2).
- ☐ Clutch disc hub or gearbox input shaft splines worn (Chapter 6).

Noise when depressing or releasing clutch pedal

- ☐ Worn clutch release bearing (Chapter 6).
- ☐ Worn or dry clutch pedal pivot (Chapter 6).
- ☐ Faulty pressure plate assembly (Chapter 6).
- ☐ Pressure plate diaphragm spring broken (Chapter 6).
- ☐ Broken clutch friction plate cushioning springs (Chapter 6).

Manual transmission

Noisy in neutral with engine running

- ☐ Input shaft bearings worn (noise apparent with clutch pedal released, but not when depressed) (Chapter 7A).*
- ☐ Clutch release bearing worn (noise apparent with clutch pedal depressed, possibly less when released) (Chapter 6).

Noisy in one particular gear

- ☐ Worn, damaged or chipped gear teeth (Chapter 7A).*

Difficulty engaging gears

- ☐ Clutch faulty (Chapter 6).
- ☐ Worn or damaged gear linkage (Chapter 7A).
- ☐ Worn synchroniser units (Chapter 7A).*

Jumps out of gear

- ☐ Worn or damaged gear linkage (Chapter 7A).
- ☐ Worn synchroniser units (Chapter 7A).*
- ☐ Worn selector forks (Chapter 7A).*

Vibration

- ☐ Lack of oil (Chapter 1).
- ☐ Worn bearings (Chapter 7A).*

Lubricant leaks

- ☐ Leaking oil seal (Chapter 7A).
- ☐ Leaking housing joint (Chapter 7A).*

The above information should be helpful in isolating the cause of the condition, so that the owner can communicate clearly with a professional mechanic.

Automatic transmission

Note: *Due to the complexity of the automatic transmission, it is difficult for the home mechanic to properly diagnose and service this unit. For problems other than the following, the vehicle should be taken to a dealer service department or automatic transmission specialist. Do not be too hasty in removing the transmission if a fault is suspected, as most of the testing is carried out with the unit still fitted.*

Fluid leakage

- ☐ Automatic transmission fluid is usually dark in colour. Fluid leaks should not be confused with engine oil, which can easily be blown onto the transmission by airflow.
- ☐ To determine the source of a leak, first remove all built-up dirt and grime from the transmission housing and surrounding areas using a degreasing agent, or by steam-cleaning. Drive the vehicle at low speed, so airflow will not blow the leak far from its source. Raise and support the vehicle, and determine where the leak is coming from.

Transmission fluid brown, or has burned smell

- ☐ Transmission fluid level low, or fluid in need of renewal (Chapter 1 and 7B).

Engine will not start in any gear, or starts in gears other than Park or Neutral

- ☐ Incorrect starter/inhibitor switch adjustment (Chapter 7B).
- ☐ Incorrect selector cable adjustment (Chapter 7B).

General gear selection problems

Chapter 7B deals with checking and adjusting the selector cable on automatic transmissions. The following are common problems:
- a) Engine starting in gears other than Park or Neutral.
- b) Indicator panel indicating a gear other than the one actually being used.
- c) Vehicle moves when in Park or Neutral.
- d) Poor gear shift quality or erratic gearchanges.

Transmission will not downshift (kickdown) with accelerator pedal fully depressed

- ☐ Low transmission fluid level (Chapter 1).
- ☐ Incorrect selector cable adjustment (Chapter 7B).

Transmission slips, shifts roughly, is noisy, or has no drive in forward or reverse gears

- ☐ There are many probable causes for the above problems, but the home mechanic should be concerned with only one possibility – fluid level.

Driveshafts

Vibration when accelerating or decelerating

☐ Worn inner constant velocity joint (Chapter 8).
☐ Bent or distorted driveshaft (Chapter 8).
☐ Worn intermediate bearing – where applicable (Chapter 8).

Clicking or knocking noise on turns (at slow speed on full-lock)

☐ Worn outer constant velocity joint (Chapter 8).
☐ Lack of constant velocity joint lubricant, possibly due to damaged gaiter (Chapter 8).

Braking system

Note: *Before assuming that a brake problem exists, make sure that the tyres are in good condition and correctly inflated, that the front wheel alignment is correct, and that the vehicle is not loaded with weight in an unequal manner. Apart from checking the condition of all pipe and hose connections, any faults occurring on the anti-lock braking system should be referred to a Vauxhall dealer for diagnosis.*

Vehicle pulls to one side under braking

☐ Worn, defective, damaged or contaminated front or rear brake pads/shoes on one side (Chapters 1 and 9).
☐ Seized or partially-seized front or rear brake caliper/wheel cylinder piston (Chapter 9).
☐ A mixture of brake pad/shoe lining materials fitted between sides (Chapter 9).
☐ Brake caliper or rear brake backplate mounting bolts loose (Chapter 9).
☐ Worn or damaged steering or suspension components (Chapters 1 and 10).

Noise (grinding or high-pitched squeal) when brakes applied

☐ Brake pad friction lining material worn down to audible warning sensor (Chapter 9).
☐ Brake pad/shoe friction lining material worn down to metal backing (Chapters 1 and 9).
☐ Excessive corrosion of brake disc or drum – may be apparent after the vehicle has been standing for some time (Chapters 1 and 9).
☐ Foreign object (stone chipping, etc) trapped between brake disc and shield (Chapters 1 and 9).

Excessive brake pedal travel

☐ Faulty rear drum brake self-adjust mechanism (Chapter 9).
☐ Faulty master cylinder (Chapter 9).
☐ Air in hydraulic system (Chapter 9).
☐ Faulty vacuum servo unit (Chapter 9).

Brake pedal feels spongy when depressed

☐ Air in hydraulic system (Chapter 9).
☐ Deteriorated flexible rubber brake hoses (Chapters 1 and 9).
☐ Master cylinder mountings loose (Chapter 9).
☐ Faulty master cylinder (Chapter 9).

Excessive brake pedal effort required to stop vehicle

☐ Faulty vacuum servo unit (Chapter 9).
☐ Disconnected, damaged or insecure brake servo vacuum hose (Chapters 1 and 9).
☐ Primary or secondary hydraulic circuit failure (Chapter 9).
☐ Seized brake caliper or wheel cylinder piston(s) (Chapter 9).
☐ Brake pads/shoes incorrectly fitted (Chapter 9).
☐ Incorrect grade of brake pads/shoes fitted (Chapter 9).
☐ Brake pads/shoe linings contaminated (Chapter 9).

Judder felt through brake pedal or steering wheel when braking

☐ Excessive run-out or distortion of brake disc(s) or drum(s) (Chapter 9).
☐ Brake pad/shoe linings worn (Chapters 1 and 9).
☐ Brake caliper or rear brake backplate mounting bolts loose (Chapter 9).
☐ Wear in suspension or steering components or mountings (Chapters 1 and 10).

Pedal pulsates when braking hard

☐ Normal feature of ABS – no fault

Brakes binding

☐ Seized brake caliper/wheel cylinder piston(s) (Chapter 9).
☐ Incorrectly-adjusted handbrake cable (Chapter 9).
☐ Faulty master cylinder (Chapter 9).

Rear wheels locking under normal braking

☐ Rear brake pad/shoe linings contaminated (Chapters 1 and 9).
☐ Rear brake discs/drums warped (Chapters 1 and 9).

Steering and suspension

Note: *Before diagnosing suspension or steering faults, be sure that the trouble is not due to incorrect tyre pressures, mixtures of tyre types, or binding brakes.*

Vehicle pulls to one side

- [ ] Defective tyre (see *Weekly checks*).
- [ ] Excessive wear in suspension or steering components (Chapters 1 and 10).
- [ ] Incorrect front wheel alignment (Chapter 10).
- [ ] Accident damage to steering or suspension components (Chapters 1 and 10).

Wheel wobble and vibration

- [ ] Front roadwheels out of balance (vibration felt mainly through the steering wheel) (Chapter 10).
- [ ] Rear roadwheels out of balance (vibration felt throughout the vehicle) (Chapter 10).
- [ ] Roadwheels damaged or distorted (Chapter 10).
- [ ] Faulty or damaged tyre (*Weekly Checks*).
- [ ] Worn steering or suspension joints, bushes or components (Chapters 1 and 10).
- [ ] Wheel bolts loose (Chapter 1 and 10).

Excessive pitching and/or rolling around corners, or during braking

- [ ] Defective shock absorbers (Chapters 1 and 10).
- [ ] Broken or weak coil spring and/or suspension component (Chapters 1 and 10).
- [ ] Worn or damaged anti-roll bar or mountings (Chapter 10).

Wandering or general instability

- [ ] Incorrect front wheel alignment (Chapter 10).
- [ ] Worn steering or suspension joints, bushes or components (Chapters 1 and 10).
- [ ] Roadwheels out of balance (Chapter 10).
- [ ] Faulty or damaged tyre (*Weekly Checks*).
- [ ] Wheel bolts loose (Chapter 10).
- [ ] Defective shock absorbers (Chapters 1 and 10).

Excessively-stiff steering

- [ ] Seized track rod end balljoint or suspension balljoint (Chapters 1 and 10).
- [ ] Broken or incorrectly adjusted auxiliary drivebelt (Chapter 1).
- [ ] Incorrect front wheel alignment (Chapter 10).
- [ ] Steering gear damaged (Chapter 10).

Excessive play in steering

- [ ] Worn steering column universal joint(s) (Chapter 10).
- [ ] Worn steering track rod end balljoints (Chapters 1 and 10).
- [ ] Worn steering gear (Chapter 10).
- [ ] Worn steering or suspension joints, bushes or components (Chapters 1 and 10).

Lack of power assistance

- [ ] Broken or incorrectly-adjusted auxiliary drivebelt (Chapter 1).
- [ ] Incorrect power steering fluid level (*Weekly Checks*).
- [ ] Restriction in power steering fluid hoses (Chapter 10).
- [ ] Faulty power steering pump (Chapter 10).
- [ ] Faulty steering gear (Chapter 10).

Tyre wear excessive

Tyres worn on inside or outside edges

- [ ] Tyres under-inflated (wear on both edges) (*Weekly Checks*).
- [ ] Incorrect camber or castor angles (wear on one edge only) (Chapter 10).
- [ ] Worn steering or suspension joints, bushes or components (Chapters 1 and 10).
- [ ] Excessively-hard cornering.
- [ ] Accident damage.

Tyre treads exhibit feathered edges

- [ ] Incorrect toe setting (Chapter 10).

Tyres worn in centre of tread

- [ ] Tyres over-inflated (*Weekly Checks*).

Tyres worn on inside and outside edges

- [ ] Tyres under-inflated (*Weekly Checks*).
- [ ] Worn shock absorbers (Chapters 1 and 10).

Tyres worn unevenly

- [ ] Tyres/wheels out of balance (*Weekly Checks*).
- [ ] Excessive wheel or tyre run-out (Chapter 10).
- [ ] Worn shock absorbers (Chapters 1 and 10).
- [ ] Faulty tyre (*Weekly Checks*).

Electrical system

Note: *For problems associated with the starting system, refer to the faults listed under 'Engine' earlier in this Section.*

Battery will not hold a charge for more than a few days

- [ ] Battery defective internally (Chapter 5A).
- [ ] Battery electrolyte level low – where applicable (*Weekly Checks*).
- [ ] Battery terminal connections loose or corroded (*Weekly Checks*).
- [ ] Auxiliary drivebelt worn – or incorrectly adjusted, where applicable (Chapter 1).
- [ ] Alternator not charging at correct output (Chapter 5A).
- [ ] Alternator or voltage regulator faulty (Chapter 5A).
- [ ] Short-circuit causing continual battery drain (Chapters 5 and 12).

Ignition/no-charge warning light remains illuminated with engine running

- [ ] Auxiliary drivebelt broken, worn, or incorrectly adjusted (Chapter 1).
- [ ] Internal fault in alternator or voltage regulator (Chapter 5A).
- [ ] Broken, disconnected, or loose wiring in charging circuit (Chapter 5A).

Ignition/no-charge warning light fails to come on

- [ ] Warning light bulb blown (Chapter 12).
- [ ] Broken, disconnected, or loose wiring in warning light circuit (Chapter 12).
- [ ] Alternator faulty (Chapter 5A).

Electrical system (continued)

Lights inoperative

- ☐ Bulb blown (Chapter 12).
- ☐ Corrosion of bulb or bulbholder contacts (Chapter 12).
- ☐ Blown fuse (Chapter 12).
- ☐ Faulty relay (Chapter 12).
- ☐ Broken, loose, or disconnected wiring (Chapter 12).
- ☐ Faulty switch (Chapter 12).

Instrument readings inaccurate or erratic

Instrument readings increase with engine speed

- ☐ Faulty voltage regulator (Chapter 12).

Fuel or temperature gauges give no reading

- ☐ Faulty gauge sender unit (Chapters 3 and 4A).
- ☐ Wiring open-circuit (Chapter 12).
- ☐ Faulty gauge (Chapter 12).

Fuel or temperature gauges give continuous maximum reading

- ☐ Faulty gauge sender unit (Chapters 3 and 4A).
- ☐ Wiring short-circuit (Chapter 12).
- ☐ Faulty gauge (Chapter 12).

Horn inoperative, or unsatisfactory in operation

Horn operates all the time

- ☐ Horn contacts permanently bridged or horn push stuck down (Chapter 12).

Horn fails to operate

- ☐ Blown fuse (Chapter 12).
- ☐ Cable or cable connections loose, broken or disconnected (Chapter 12).
- ☐ Faulty horn (Chapter 12).

Horn emits intermittent or unsatisfactory sound

- ☐ Cable connections loose (Chapter 12).
- ☐ Horn mountings loose (Chapter 12).
- ☐ Faulty horn (Chapter 12).

Windscreen/tailgate wipers inoperative, or unsatisfactory in operation

Wipers fail to operate, or operate very slowly

- ☐ Wiper blades stuck to screen, or linkage seized or binding (Weekly Checks and Chapter 12).
- ☐ Blown fuse (Chapter 12).
- ☐ Cable or cable connections loose, broken or disconnected (Chapter 12).
- ☐ Faulty relay (Chapter 12).
- ☐ Faulty wiper motor (Chapter 12).

Wiper blades sweep over too large or too small an area of the glass

- ☐ Wiper arms incorrectly positioned on spindles (Chapter 12).
- ☐ Excessive wear of wiper linkage (Chapter 12).
- ☐ Wiper motor or linkage mountings loose or insecure (Chapter 12).

Wiper blades fail to clean the glass effectively

- ☐ Wiper blade rubbers worn or perished (Weekly Checks).
- ☐ Wiper arm tension springs broken, or arm pivots seized (Chapter 12).
- ☐ Insufficient windscreen washer additive to adequately remove road film (Weekly Checks).

Windscreen/tailgate washers inoperative, or unsatisfactory in operation

One or more washer jets inoperative

- ☐ Blocked washer jet (Chapter 12).
- ☐ Disconnected, kinked or restricted fluid hose (Chapter 12).
- ☐ Insufficient fluid in washer reservoir (Weekly Checks).

Washer pump fails to operate

- ☐ Broken or disconnected wiring or connections (Chapter 12).
- ☐ Blown fuse (Chapter 12).
- ☐ Faulty washer switch (Chapter 12).
- ☐ Faulty washer pump (Chapter 12).

Washer pump runs for some time before fluid is emitted from jets

- ☐ Faulty one-way valve in fluid supply hose (Chapter 12).

Electric windows inoperative, or unsatisfactory in operation

Window glass will only move in one direction

- ☐ Faulty switch (Chapter 12).

Window glass slow to move

- ☐ Regulator seized or damaged, or in need of lubrication (Chapter 11).
- ☐ Door internal components or trim fouling regulator (Chapter 11).
- ☐ Faulty motor (Chapter 11).

Window glass fails to move

- ☐ Blown fuse (Chapter 12).
- ☐ Faulty relay (Chapter 12).
- ☐ Broken or disconnected wiring or connections (Chapter 12).
- ☐ Faulty motor (Chapter 12).

Central locking system inoperative, or unsatisfactory in operation

Complete system failure

- ☐ Blown fuse (Chapter 12).
- ☐ Faulty relay (Chapter 12).
- ☐ Broken or disconnected wiring or connections (Chapter 12).
- ☐ Faulty motor (Chapter 11).

Latch locks but will not unlock, or unlocks but will not lock

- ☐ Faulty switch (Chapter 12).
- ☐ Broken or disconnected latch operating rods or levers (Chapter 11).
- ☐ Faulty relay (Chapter 12).
- ☐ Faulty motor (Chapter 11).

One solenoid/motor fails to operate

- ☐ Broken or disconnected wiring or connections (Chapter 12).
- ☐ Faulty motor (Chapter 11).
- ☐ Broken, binding or disconnected lock operating rods or levers (Chapter 11).
- ☐ Fault in door lock (Chapter 11).

A

ABS (Anti-lock brake system) A system, usually electronically controlled, that senses incipient wheel lockup during braking and relieves hydraulic pressure at wheels that are about to skid.

Air bag An inflatable bag hidden in the steering wheel (driver's side) or the dash or glovebox (passenger side). In a head-on collision, the bags inflate, preventing the driver and front passenger from being thrown forward into the steering wheel or windscreen.

Air cleaner A metal or plastic housing, containing a filter element, which removes dust and dirt from the air being drawn into the engine.

Air filter element The actual filter in an air cleaner system, usually manufactured from pleated paper and requiring renewal at regular intervals.

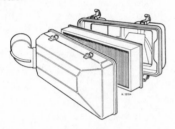

Air filter

Allen key A hexagonal wrench which fits into a recessed hexagonal hole.

Alligator clip A long-nosed spring-loaded metal clip with meshing teeth. Used to make temporary electrical connections.

Alternator A component in the electrical system which converts mechanical energy from a drivebelt into electrical energy to charge the battery and to operate the starting system, ignition system and electrical accessories.

Ampere (amp) A unit of measurement for the flow of electric current. One amp is the amount of current produced by one volt acting through a resistance of one ohm.

Anaerobic sealer A substance used to prevent bolts and screws from loosening. Anaerobic means that it does not require oxygen for activation. The Loctite brand is widely used.

Antifreeze A substance (usually ethylene glycol) mixed with water, and added to a vehicle's cooling system, to prevent freezing of the coolant in winter. Antifreeze also contains chemicals to inhibit corrosion and the formation of rust and other deposits that would tend to clog the radiator and coolant passages and reduce cooling efficiency.

Anti-seize compound A coating that reduces the risk of seizing on fasteners that are subjected to high temperatures, such as exhaust manifold bolts and nuts.

Asbestos A natural fibrous mineral with great heat resistance, commonly used in the composition of brake friction materials. Asbestos is a health hazard and the dust created by brake systems should never be inhaled or ingested.

Axle A shaft on which a wheel revolves, or which revolves with a wheel. Also, a solid beam that connects the two wheels at one end of the vehicle. An axle which also transmits power to the wheels is known as a live axle.

Axleshaft A single rotating shaft, on either side of the differential, which delivers power from the final drive assembly to the drive wheels. Also called a driveshaft or a halfshaft.

B

Ball bearing An anti-friction bearing consisting of a hardened inner and outer race with hardened steel balls between two races.

Bearing The curved surface on a shaft or in a bore, or the part assembled into either, that permits relative motion between them with minimum wear and friction.

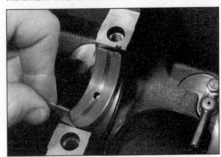

Bearing

Big-end bearing The bearing in the end of the connecting rod that's attached to the crankshaft.

Bleed nipple A valve on a brake wheel cylinder, caliper or other hydraulic component that is opened to purge the hydraulic system of air. Also called a bleed screw.

Brake bleeding Procedure for removing air from lines of a hydraulic brake system.

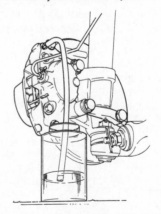

Brake bleeding

Brake disc The component of a disc brake that rotates with the wheels.

Brake drum The component of a drum brake that rotates with the wheels.

Brake linings The friction material which contacts the brake disc or drum to retard the vehicle's speed. The linings are bonded or riveted to the brake pads or shoes.

Brake pads The replaceable friction pads that pinch the brake disc when the brakes are applied. Brake pads consist of a friction material bonded or riveted to a rigid backing plate.

Brake shoe The crescent-shaped carrier to which the brake linings are mounted and which forces the lining against the rotating drum during braking.

Braking systems For more information on braking systems, consult the *Haynes Automotive Brake Manual*.

Breaker bar A long socket wrench handle providing greater leverage.

Bulkhead The insulated partition between the engine and the passenger compartment.

C

Caliper The non-rotating part of a disc-brake assembly that straddles the disc and carries the brake pads. The caliper also contains the hydraulic components that cause the pads to pinch the disc when the brakes are applied. A caliper is also a measuring tool that can be set to measure inside or outside dimensions of an object.

Camshaft A rotating shaft on which a series of cam lobes operate the valve mechanisms. The camshaft may be driven by gears, by sprockets and chain or by sprockets and a belt.

Canister A container in an evaporative emission control system; contains activated charcoal granules to trap vapours from the fuel system.

Canister

Carburettor A device which mixes fuel with air in the proper proportions to provide a desired power output from a spark ignition internal combustion engine.

Castellated Resembling the parapets along the top of a castle wall. For example, a castellated balljoint stud nut.

Castor In wheel alignment, the backward or forward tilt of the steering axis. Castor is positive when the steering axis is inclined rearward at the top.

Catalytic converter A silencer-like device in the exhaust system which converts certain pollutants in the exhaust gases into less harmful substances.

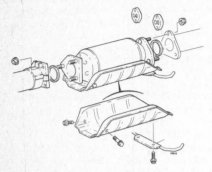

Catalytic converter

Circlip A ring-shaped clip used to prevent endwise movement of cylindrical parts and shafts. An internal circlip is installed in a groove in a housing; an external circlip fits into a groove on the outside of a cylindrical piece such as a shaft.

Clearance The amount of space between two parts. For example, between a piston and a cylinder, between a bearing and a journal, etc.

Coil spring A spiral of elastic steel found in various sizes throughout a vehicle, for example as a springing medium in the suspension and in the valve train.

Compression Reduction in volume, and increase in pressure and temperature, of a gas, caused by squeezing it into a smaller space.

Compression ratio The relationship between cylinder volume when the piston is at top dead centre and cylinder volume when the piston is at bottom dead centre.

Constant velocity (CV) joint A type of universal joint that cancels out vibrations caused by driving power being transmitted through an angle.

Core plug A disc or cup-shaped metal device inserted in a hole in a casting through which core was removed when the casting was formed. Also known as a freeze plug or expansion plug.

Crankcase The lower part of the engine block in which the crankshaft rotates.

Crankshaft The main rotating member, or shaft, running the length of the crankcase, with offset "throws" to which the connecting rods are attached.

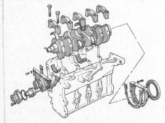

Crankshaft assembly

Crocodile clip See Alligator clip

D

Diagnostic code Code numbers obtained by accessing the diagnostic mode of an engine management computer. This code can be used to determine the area in the system where a malfunction may be located.

Disc brake A brake design incorporating a rotating disc onto which brake pads are squeezed. The resulting friction converts the energy of a moving vehicle into heat.

Double-overhead cam (DOHC) An engine that uses two overhead camshafts, usually one for the intake valves and one for the exhaust valves.

Drivebelt(s) The belt(s) used to drive accessories such as the alternator, water pump, power steering pump, air conditioning compressor, etc. off the crankshaft pulley.

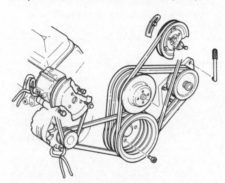

Accessory drivebelts

Driveshaft Any shaft used to transmit motion. Commonly used when referring to the axleshafts on a front wheel drive vehicle.

Drum brake A type of brake using a drum-shaped metal cylinder attached to the inner surface of the wheel. When the brake pedal is pressed, curved brake shoes with friction linings press against the inside of the drum to slow or stop the vehicle.

E

EGR valve A valve used to introduce exhaust gases into the intake air stream.

Electronic control unit (ECU) A computer which controls (for instance) ignition and fuel injection systems, or an anti-lock braking system. For more information refer to the *Haynes Automotive Electrical and Electronic Systems Manual*.

Electronic Fuel Injection (EFI) A computer controlled fuel system that distributes fuel through an injector located in each intake port of the engine.

Emergency brake A braking system, independent of the main hydraulic system, that can be used to slow or stop the vehicle if the primary brakes fail, or to hold the vehicle stationary even though the brake pedal isn't depressed. It usually consists of a hand lever that actuates either front or rear brakes mechanically through a series of cables and linkages. Also known as a handbrake or parking brake.

Endfloat The amount of lengthwise movement between two parts. As applied to a crankshaft, the distance that the crankshaft can move forward and back in the cylinder block.

Engine management system (EMS) A computer controlled system which manages the fuel injection and the ignition systems in an integrated fashion.

Exhaust manifold A part with several passages through which exhaust gases leave the engine combustion chambers and enter the exhaust pipe.

F

Fan clutch A viscous (fluid) drive coupling device which permits variable engine fan speeds in relation to engine speeds.

Feeler blade A thin strip or blade of hardened steel, ground to an exact thickness, used to check or measure clearances between parts.

Feeler blade

Firing order The order in which the engine cylinders fire, or deliver their power strokes, beginning with the number one cylinder.

Flywheel A heavy spinning wheel in which energy is absorbed and stored by means of momentum. On cars, the flywheel is attached to the crankshaft to smooth out firing impulses.

Free play The amount of travel before any action takes place. The "looseness" in a linkage, or an assembly of parts, between the initial application of force and actual movement. For example, the distance the brake pedal moves before the pistons in the master cylinder are actuated.

Fuse An electrical device which protects a circuit against accidental overload. The typical fuse contains a soft piece of metal which is calibrated to melt at a predetermined current flow (expressed as amps) and break the circuit.

Fusible link A circuit protection device consisting of a conductor surrounded by heat-resistant insulation. The conductor is smaller than the wire it protects, so it acts as the weakest link in the circuit. Unlike a blown fuse, a failed fusible link must frequently be cut from the wire for replacement.

G

Gap The distance the spark must travel in jumping from the centre electrode to the side electrode in a spark plug. Also refers to the spacing between the points in a contact breaker assembly in a conventional points-type ignition, or to the distance between the reluctor or rotor and the pickup coil in an electronic ignition.

Adjusting spark plug gap

Gasket Any thin, soft material - usually cork, cardboard, asbestos or soft metal - installed between two metal surfaces to ensure a good seal. For instance, the cylinder head gasket seals the joint between the block and the cylinder head.

Gasket

Gauge An instrument panel display used to monitor engine conditions. A gauge with a movable pointer on a dial or a fixed scale is an analogue gauge. A gauge with a numerical readout is called a digital gauge.

H

Halfshaft A rotating shaft that transmits power from the final drive unit to a drive wheel, usually when referring to a live rear axle.

Harmonic balancer A device designed to reduce torsion or twisting vibration in the crankshaft. May be incorporated in the crankshaft pulley. Also known as a vibration damper.

Hone An abrasive tool for correcting small irregularities or differences in diameter in an engine cylinder, brake cylinder, etc.

Hydraulic tappet A tappet that utilises hydraulic pressure from the engine's lubrication system to maintain zero clearance (constant contact with both camshaft and valve stem). Automatically adjusts to variation in valve stem length. Hydraulic tappets also reduce valve noise.

I

Ignition timing The moment at which the spark plug fires, usually expressed in the number of crankshaft degrees before the piston reaches the top of its stroke.

Inlet manifold A tube or housing with passages through which flows the air-fuel mixture (carburettor vehicles and vehicles with throttle body injection) or air only (port fuel-injected vehicles) to the port openings in the cylinder head.

J

Jump start Starting the engine of a vehicle with a discharged or weak battery by attaching jump leads from the weak battery to a charged or helper battery.

L

Load Sensing Proportioning Valve (LSPV) A brake hydraulic system control valve that works like a proportioning valve, but also takes into consideration the amount of weight carried by the rear axle.

Locknut A nut used to lock an adjustment nut, or other threaded component, in place. For example, a locknut is employed to keep the adjusting nut on the rocker arm in position.

Lockwasher A form of washer designed to prevent an attaching nut from working loose.

M

MacPherson strut A type of front suspension system devised by Earle MacPherson at Ford of England. In its original form, a simple lateral link with the anti-roll bar creates the lower control arm. A long strut - an integral coil spring and shock absorber - is mounted between the body and the steering knuckle. Many modern so-called MacPherson strut systems use a conventional lower A-arm and don't rely on the anti-roll bar for location.

Multimeter An electrical test instrument with the capability to measure voltage, current and resistance.

N

NOx Oxides of Nitrogen. A common toxic pollutant emitted by petrol and diesel engines at higher temperatures.

O

Ohm The unit of electrical resistance. One volt applied to a resistance of one ohm will produce a current of one amp.

Ohmmeter An instrument for measuring electrical resistance.

O-ring A type of sealing ring made of a special rubber-like material; in use, the O-ring is compressed into a groove to provide the sealing action.

Overhead cam (ohc) engine An engine with the camshaft(s) located on top of the cylinder head(s).

Overhead valve (ohv) engine An engine with the valves located in the cylinder head, but with the camshaft located in the engine block.

Oxygen sensor A device installed in the engine exhaust manifold, which senses the oxygen content in the exhaust and converts this information into an electric current. Also called a Lambda sensor.

P

Phillips screw A type of screw head having a cross instead of a slot for a corresponding type of screwdriver.

Plastigage A thin strip of plastic thread, available in different sizes, used for measuring clearances. For example, a strip of Plastigage is laid across a bearing journal. The parts are assembled and dismantled; the width of the crushed strip indicates the clearance between journal and bearing.

Plastigage

Propeller shaft The long hollow tube with universal joints at both ends that carries power from the transmission to the differential on front-engined rear wheel drive vehicles.

Proportioning valve A hydraulic control valve which limits the amount of pressure to the rear brakes during panic stops to prevent wheel lock-up.

R

Rack-and-pinion steering A steering system with a pinion gear on the end of the steering shaft that mates with a rack (think of a geared wheel opened up and laid flat). When the steering wheel is turned, the pinion turns, moving the rack to the left or right. This movement is transmitted through the track rods to the steering arms at the wheels.

Radiator A liquid-to-air heat transfer device designed to reduce the temperature of the coolant in an internal combustion engine cooling system.

Refrigerant Any substance used as a heat transfer agent in an air-conditioning system. R-12 has been the principle refrigerant for many years; recently, however, manufacturers have begun using R-134a, a non-CFC substance that is considered less harmful to the ozone in the upper atmosphere.

Rocker arm A lever arm that rocks on a shaft or pivots on a stud. In an overhead valve engine, the rocker arm converts the upward movement of the pushrod into a downward movement to open a valve.

Rotor In a distributor, the rotating device inside the cap that connects the centre electrode and the outer terminals as it turns, distributing the high voltage from the coil secondary winding to the proper spark plug. Also, that part of an alternator which rotates inside the stator. Also, the rotating assembly of a turbocharger, including the compressor wheel, shaft and turbine wheel.

Runout The amount of wobble (in-and-out movement) of a gear or wheel as it's rotated. The amount a shaft rotates "out-of-true." The out-of-round condition of a rotating part.

S

Sealant A liquid or paste used to prevent leakage at a joint. Sometimes used in conjunction with a gasket.

Sealed beam lamp An older headlight design which integrates the reflector, lens and filaments into a hermetically-sealed one-piece unit. When a filament burns out or the lens cracks, the entire unit is simply replaced.

Serpentine drivebelt A single, long, wide accessory drivebelt that's used on some newer vehicles to drive all the accessories, instead of a series of smaller, shorter belts. Serpentine drivebelts are usually tensioned by an automatic tensioner.

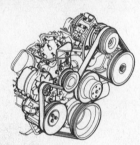

Serpentine drivebelt

Shim Thin spacer, commonly used to adjust the clearance or relative positions between two parts. For example, shims inserted into or under bucket tappets control valve clearances. Clearance is adjusted by changing the thickness of the shim.

Slide hammer A special puller that screws into or hooks onto a component such as a shaft or bearing; a heavy sliding handle on the shaft bottoms against the end of the shaft to knock the component free.

Sprocket A tooth or projection on the periphery of a wheel, shaped to engage with a chain or drivebelt. Commonly used to refer to the sprocket wheel itself.

Starter inhibitor switch On vehicles with an automatic transmission, a switch that prevents starting if the vehicle is not in Neutral or Park.

Strut See MacPherson strut.

T

Tappet A cylindrical component which transmits motion from the cam to the valve stem, either directly or via a pushrod and rocker arm. Also called a cam follower.

Thermostat A heat-controlled valve that regulates the flow of coolant between the cylinder block and the radiator, so maintaining optimum engine operating temperature. A thermostat is also used in some air cleaners in which the temperature is regulated.

Thrust bearing The bearing in the clutch assembly that is moved in to the release levers by clutch pedal action to disengage the clutch. Also referred to as a release bearing.

Timing belt A toothed belt which drives the camshaft. Serious engine damage may result if it breaks in service.

Timing chain A chain which drives the camshaft.

Toe-in The amount the front wheels are closer together at the front than at the rear. On rear wheel drive vehicles, a slight amount of toe-in is usually specified to keep the front wheels running parallel on the road by offsetting other forces that tend to spread the wheels apart.

Toe-out The amount the front wheels are closer together at the rear than at the front. On front wheel drive vehicles, a slight amount of toe-out is usually specified.

Tools For full information on choosing and using tools, refer to the *Haynes Automotive Tools Manual.*

Tracer A stripe of a second colour applied to a wire insulator to distinguish that wire from another one with the same colour insulator.

Tune-up A process of accurate and careful adjustments and parts replacement to obtain the best possible engine performance.

Turbocharger A centrifugal device, driven by exhaust gases, that pressurises the intake air. Normally used to increase the power output from a given engine displacement, but can also be used primarily to reduce exhaust emissions (as on VW's "Umwelt" Diesel engine).

U

Universal joint or U-joint A double-pivoted connection for transmitting power from a driving to a driven shaft through an angle. A U-joint consists of two Y-shaped yokes and a cross-shaped member called the spider.

V

Valve A device through which the flow of liquid, gas, vacuum, or loose material in bulk may be started, stopped, or regulated by a movable part that opens, shuts, or partially obstructs one or more ports or passageways. A valve is also the movable part of such a device.

Valve clearance The clearance between the valve tip (the end of the valve stem) and the rocker arm or tappet. The valve clearance is measured when the valve is closed.

Vernier caliper A precision measuring instrument that measures inside and outside dimensions. Not quite as accurate as a micrometer, but more convenient.

Viscosity The thickness of a liquid or its resistance to flow.

Volt A unit for expressing electrical "pressure" in a circuit. One volt that will produce a current of one ampere through a resistance of one ohm.

W

Welding Various processes used to join metal items by heating the areas to be joined to a molten state and fusing them together. For more information refer to the *Haynes Automotive Welding Manual.*

Wiring diagram A drawing portraying the components and wires in a vehicle's electrical system, using standardised symbols. For more information refer to the *Haynes Automotive Electrical and Electronic Systems Manual.*

Note: *References throughout this index are in the form - "Chapter number" • "Page number"*

A

Accelerator cable – 4A•4
Accelerator pedal – 4A•4
   position sensor – 4A•24
Acknowledgements – 0•6
Aerial – 12•22
Air conditioning system – 3•15, 3•16
   switch – 4A•17, 4A•18, 4A•20, 4A•23, 4A•25
Air filter – 1•14, 4A•3
Air temperature control system – 4A•3
Air temperature sensor – 4A•18, 4A•20, 4A•22
Air vents – 3•11
Airbags – 0•5, 12•23, 12•24
Alarm system – 12•22
Alternator – 5A•4
   brushes – 5A•5
Anti-lock Braking System – 9•18, 9•19
Anti-roll bar – 10•9
Anti-theft alarm system – 12•22
Asbestos – 0•5
Automatic transmission – 7B•1 *et seq*
   control system – 7B•4
   fault finding – REF•15
   fluid – 0•18, 1•14, 7B•2, 7B•5
   fluid cooler – 7B•4
Auxiliary drivebelt – 1•11
   tensioner – 5A•3

B

Backrest – 11•21
Balancer unit – 2B•22
Balance shaft – 2C•15
Battery – 0•5, 0•16, 5A•2, 5A•3, REF•5
Big-end bearings – 2D•17, 2D•21
Bleeding
   brakes – 9•3
   clutch – 6•2
   power steering – 10•16
Blower motor resistor – 3•11
Body corrosion – 1•11, REF•11
Body electrical systems – 12•1 *et seq*
Bodywork and fittings – 11•1 *et seq*
Bonnet – 11•6, 11•7
Boot lid – 11•13, 11•14, 11•17
Brake fluid – 0•15, 0•18, 1•18
Braking system – 1•13, 9•1 *et seq*,
   REF•9, REF•10
   fault finding – REF•16
Bulbs – 12•6, 12•9
   cigarette lighter – 12•11
   clock illumination – 12•11
   direction indicator light – 12•7
   foglight – 12•7
   glovebox light – 12•10
   headlight – 12•6
   heater control illumination – 12•11
   high-level stop-light – 12•9
   instrument panel illumination – 12•11
   interior light – 12•9, 12•10
   light switch illumination – 12•11
   luggage compartment interior light – 12•10
   multi-function display unit illumination – 12•11
   number plate light – 12•8
   reading light – 12•11
   rear light cluster – 12•7, 12•8
   sidelight – 12•6
   warning light bulbs – 12•11
Bumpers – 11•4
Burning – 0•5
Buying spare parts – REF•3

C

C-pillar – 11•29
Cables
   accelerator – 4A•4
   bonnet release – 11•7
   handbrake – 9•17
   selector – 7B•2, 7B•3
   sunroof – 11•19
Calipers – 9•12, 9•13
Camshaft – 2A•8, 2A•9, 2B•13, 2C•10
Camshaft cover – 2A•4, 2B•6, 2C•4
Camshaft oil seal – 2A•8, 2B•13
Camshaft sensor – 4A•18, 4A•20, 4A•22
Camshaft sprockets – 2A•7, 2B•11
Carpets – 11•2
Cassette player – 12•20
Catalytic converter – 4B•2
CD player – 12•20
Central locking system – 11•16
Centre console – 11•30
Charcoal canister – 4B•1
Charging – 5A•2, 5A•3
Cigarette lighter – 12•15
   bulb – 12•11
Clock illumination bulb – 12•11
Clutch – 6•1 *et seq*
   fault finding – REF•15
   fluid – 0•15, 0•18
Coil spring – 10•11
Compression test – 2A•3, 2B•5, 2C•3
Compressor – 3•16
Condenser – 3•17
Connecting rods – 2D•14, 2D•15, 2D•21
Console – 11•30
Conversion factors – REF•2
Coolant – 0•13, 0•18, 1•18
Coolant residue sensor – 12•15
*Cooling, heating and air conditioning
   systems* – 3•1 *et seq*
   fault finding – REF•14
Courtesy light switch – 12•5
Cowl panel – 11•5
Crankcase emission control – 4B•0, 4B•1
Crankshaft – 2D•14, 2D•16, 2D•19
   oil seals – 2A•15, 2B•21, 2C•15
   pulley – 2A•5, 2B•8, 2C•4
   sensor – 4A•18, 4A•20, 4A•22, 4A•25
   sprocket – 2A•8, 2B•13
   vibration damper – 2C•4

Crushing – 0•5
Cylinder block – 2D•15
Cylinder head – 2A•10, 2B•15, 2C•11,
   2D•11, 2D•12, 2D•13

D

Dents in bodywork – 11•3
Depressurisation of fuel system – 4A•10
Diesel injection equipment – 0•5
Dimensions – REF•1
Direction indicators – 12•4, 12•7, 12•11,
   12•12
Disconnecting the battery – REF•5
Discs – 1•11, 1•12, 9•10
*DOHC petrol engine in-car repair
   procedures* – 2B•1 *et seq*
Doors – 11•7, 11•8, 11•9, 11•10, 11•11,
   11•13, 11•17, REF•9
   mirror – 11•17, 11•18
   side strip – 11•20
Drivebelt – 1•11, 5A•3
Driveplate – 2A•15, 2B•20, 2C•16
Driveshafts – 8•1 *et seq*, REF•10
   fault finding – REF•16
   gaiter – 1•14, 8•4
   oil seals – 7A•5, 7B•3
Drivetrain – 1•13
Drum – 9•12

E

Earth fault – 12•3
Electric shock – 0•5
Electrical equipment – 1•13, REF•9
Electrical systems – 0•17, 1•11
   fault finding – 12•2, REF•19, REF•20
Electronic control units (ECU) – 4A•17,
   4A•18, 4A•20, 4A•23, 4A•25, 7B•5, 9•19,
   11•16, 12•25
*Emission control
   systems* – 4B•0 *et seq*, REF•11
Engine fault finding – REF•13, REF•14
Engine immobiliser – 12•22
Engine oil – 0•13, 0•18, 1•9
   level sensor – 12•15
*Engine removal and overhaul
   procedures* – 2D•1 *et seq*
Environmental considerations – REF•4
Evaporative emission control – 4B•1
Evaporator – 3•16
Exhaust emission – 1•11, 4B•0, 4B•1
Exhaust gas recirculation (EGR)
   system – 4B•1, 4B•2
Exhaust manifold – 4A•29
Exhaust system – 4A•30, REF•10, REF•11

F

Facia – 11•29, 11•31
Fan – 3•6, 3•17

Fault finding – REF•12 *et seq*
  automatic transmission – REF•15
  braking system – REF•16
  clutch – REF•15
  cooling system – REF•14
  driveshafts – REF•16
  electrical system – 12•2, REF•17, REF•18
  engine – REF•13, REF•14
  fuel and exhaust systems – REF•14
  manual transmission – REF•15
  steering and suspension – REF•17
Filling and respraying – 11•3
Filters
  air – 1•14, 4A•3
  fuel – 1•15
  oil – 1•9
  pollen – 1•12
Fire – 0•5
Flywheel/driveplate – 2A•15, 2B•20, 2C•16
Foglight – 12•12
  bulb – 12•7
  switch – 12•5
Footbrake – REF•8
Fuel and exhaust systems – 4A•1 *et seq*
  fault finding – REF•14
Fuel filler flap – 11•17, 11•20
Fuel filter – 1•15
Fuel gauge sender – 4A•12
Fuel injection systems – 4A•5
Fuel injector – 4A•15, 4A•17, 4A•18, 4A•20, 4A•23
Fuel pressure
  regulator – 4A•16, 4A•17, 4A•19, 4A•21, 4A•24
Fuel pump – 4A•11
  relay – 4A•17, 4A•19, 4A•22, 4A•24
Fuel rail – 4A•17, 4A•18, 4A•20, 4A•23
Fuel system – REF•11
Fuel tank – 4A•12
Fume or gas intoxication – 0•5
Fuses – 12•3

G

Gaiters
  driveshaft – 1•14, 8•4
  steering gear – 10•15
Gashes in bodywork – 11•3
Gaskets – REF•4
Gearchange mechanism – 7A•2, 7A•3
General repair procedures – REF•4
Glass – 11•11
Glossary of technical
  terms – REF•19 *et seq*
Glovebox – 11•31
  light bulb – 12•10
Grille – 11•5

H

Handbrake – 9•16, 9•17, REF•8
  'on' warning light switch – 9•18
Hazard warning switch – 12•5
Headlight – 12•11
  beam alignment – 12•13
  bulb – 12•6
  washer system – 12•19, 12•20

Heating system – 3•11
  blower motor – 3•11, 12•5
  control panel – 3•12, 12•11
  main housing – 3•13
  matrix – 3•13
  switch – 3•15
High-level stop-light bulb – 12•9
Hinge and lock lubrication – 1•13
Horn – 12•16
Hoses – 1•12, 3•4, 9•4
Hot Film Mass airflow meter – 4A•22
Hubs – 10•4, 10•10
Hydraulic tappets – 2A•9
Hydrofluoric acid – 0•5

I

Idle speed control
  motor – 4A•16, 4A•19, 4A•22
Idler pulleys – 2B•13
Ignition switch – 12•4
Ignition system – 1•17, 5B•1 *et seq*
Immobiliser – 12•22
Injectors – 4A•15, 4A•17, 4A•19, 4A•23
Inlet manifold – 4A•25
  valve – 4A•23
Input shaft
  speed sensors – 7B•5
  oil seal – 7A•5
Instrument panel – 12•13
  bulbs – 12•11
Instruments and electrical
  equipment – 1•13
Interior light bulb – 12•9, 12•10
Introduction – 0•6

J

Jacking and vehicle support – REF•5
Joint mating faces – REF•4
Jump starting – 0•8

K

Kickdown switch – 7B•5
Knock sensor – 4A•18, 4A•20, 4A•23, 4A•25

L

Leaks – 0•10, 1•12
Level control system – 1•12, 10•12
Light switch illumination bulb – 12•11
Lighting switch – 12•5
Locks
  bonnet – 11•6
  bootlid – 11•14, 11•17
  central locking – 11•16
  door – 11•9, 11•10, 11•11, 11•17
  fuel filler flap – 11•17
  lubrication – 1•13
  tailgate – 11•15, 11•17
Locknuts, locktabs and washers – REF•4
Loudspeakers – 12•21
Lower arm – 10•9
  balljoint – 10•10
Lubricants and fluids – 0•18

Luggage compartment
  interior light bulb – 12•10
  switch – 12•5

M

Main and big-end bearings – 2D•17, 2D•19
Manifold Absolute Pressure (MAP)
  sensor – 4A•17, 4A•18, 4A•20, 4A•24
Manifolds – 4A•25, 4A•29
Manual transmission – 7A•1 *et seq*
  fault finding – REF•15
  oil – 0•18, 7A•2, 7A•8
Master cylinder
  brakes – 9•14
  clutch – 6•3
Mirrors – 11•17, 11•18, REF•8
MOT test checks – REF•8 *et seq*
Motor factors – REF•3
Mountings – 2A•15, 2B•22, 2C•16
Multi-function display unit – 12•14
  illumination bulb – 12•11

N

Navigation control – 12•20, 12•21
Number plate light – 12•8, 12•13

O

Oil
  engine – 0•13, 0•18, 1•9
  manual transmission – 0•18, 7A•2, 7A•8
Oil filter – 1•9
Oil level sensor – 2B•19, 5A•7, 12•15
Oil pressure warning light switch – 5A•6
Oil pump – 2A•13, 2B•19, 2C•14
Oil seals – REF•4
  camshaft – 2A•8, 2B•13
  crankshaft – 2A•15, 2B•21, 2C•15
  driveshaft – 7A•5, 7B•3
  input shaft – 7A•5
  selector rod – 7A•6
  torque converter – 7B•3
Open-circuit – 12•2
Outside temperature sensor – 12•15
Oxygen sensor – 4B•1

P

Pads – 1•11, 1•12, 9•4, 9•6
Passenger seat sensor mat – 12•25
Pipes and hoses – 9•4
Piston rings – 2D•18
Piston/connecting rod
  assembly – 2D•14, 2D•15, 2D•21
Plastic components – 11•4
Poisonous or irritant substances – 0•5
Pollen filter – 1•12
Power steering fluid – 0•16, 0•18
Power steering pump – 10•16
Project vehicles – 0•6
Proportioning valve – 9•19
Pump relay fuel – 4A•17, 4A•20
Puncture – 0•9
Purge valve renewal – 4B•1

Q

Quarter panel – 11•28
Quarter window glass – 11•19

R

Radiator – 3•4
  grille – 11•5
Radio – 12•20
  aerial – 12•22
  remote control switches – 12•21
Reading light bulb – 12•11
Rear light cluster – 12•12
  bulb – 12•7, 12•8
Rear quarter side strip – 11•20
Rear window – 11•19
Receiver-dryer – 3•17
Relays – 12•3
  fuel pump – 4A•117, 4A•19, 4A•22, 4A•24
Release cylinder – 6•4
Remote control battery – 1•18
Respraying – 11•3
Reversing light switch – 7A•6, 7B•4
Road test – 1•13
Roadside repairs – 0•7 et seq
Roof trim strip – 11•20
Routine maintenance and
  servicing – 1•1 et seq
  bodywork and underframe – 11•2
  upholstery and carpets – 11•2
Rust holes or gashes in bodywork – 11•3

S

Safety first! – 0•5, 0•15
Scalding – 0•5
Scratches in bodywork – 11•3
Screen washer fluid – 0•16
Screw threads and fastenings – REF•4
Sealer check – 11•2
Seat belts – 11•22, 25
Seats – 11•20, 11•21
Selector
  cable – 7B•2, 7B•3
  lever – 7B•3
  rod oil seal – 7A•6
Service indicator – 1•9
Servo unit – 9•15, 9•16
Shock absorbers – 1•14, 10•10, REF•9,
  REF•10
Shoes – 9•8
Short-circuit – 12•2
Sidelight bulb – 12•6
SOHC petrol engine in-car repair
  procedures – 2A•1 et seq
Spark plug – 1•16
Speedometer sensor – 12•23
Sport mode switch – 7B•4
Springs – REF•10
Start up after overhaul – 2D•22
Starter inhibitor/reversing light
  switch – 7B•4
Starter motor – 5A•6

Starting and charging
  systems – 5A•1 et seq
Steering – 1•13, REF•9, REF•10
  angles – 10•18
  column – 10•13, 12•4, REF•8
  fault finding – REF•17
  gear – 10•15
  wheel – 10•13, REF•8
Stop-light switch – 9•18
Strut – 10•7
Subframe – 10•5
Sump – 2A•12, 2B•17, 2C•13
Sunroof
  glass panel – 11•19
  switch – 12•6
Suspension and steering – 1•13, 1•14,
  10•1 et seq, REF•9, REF•10
  fault finding – REF•17
  level control system – 1•12
Switches – 3•8, 12•4
  courtesy light – 12•5
  direction indicator – 12•4
  electric window – 11•17
  foglight – 12•5
  handbrake 'on' warning light – 9•18
  hazard warning – 12•5
  heater blower motor – 12•5
  ignition – 12•4
  kickdown – 7B•5
  lighting – 12•5
  luggage compartment switch – 12•5
  mirror – 11•18
  reversing light – 7A•6, 7B•4
  sport mode – 7B•4
  steering column lock cylinder – 12•4
  stop-light – 9•18
  sunroof – 12•6
  winter mode – 7B•4
  wipers – 12•4

T

Tailgate – 11•14, 11•15, 11•17, 11•28
  washer system – 12•19
  wiper arm – 12•17
  wiper motor – 12•18
Tappets – 2A•9, 2C•10
Temperature sensor – 3•8, 4A•17, 4A•18,
  4A•20, 4A•22, 12•15
Thermostat – 3•5
Throttle body/housing – 4A•13
Throttle potentiometer – 4A•16, 4A•19,
  4A•22, 4A•24
Throttle valve adjuster – 4A•21
Throttle valve servo motor – 4A•24
Timing belt – 2A•6, 2B•9
  covers – 2A•5, 2B•8
  idler pulleys – 2B•11
  tensioner and sprockets – 2A•7, 2B•11
Timing chain – 2C•7
  cover – 2C•5
  tensioners – 2C•6
Timing (ignition) – 5B•2
Tools and working
  facilities – REF•4, REF•6 et seq

Top dead centre (TDC) for No 1 piston –
  locating – 2A•4, 2B•5, 2C•3
Torque converter oil seal – 7B•3
Torsion beam – 10•11, 10•12
Towing – 0•10
Track-rod – 10•17
Traction Control systems – 9•18, 9•19
Trailing arms – 10•11
Trim panels – 11•25, 11•29
Tyres – REF•11
  condition and pressure – 0•14, 0•18
  specialists – REF•3

U

Underbody sealer check – 11•2
Underbonnet check points – 0•11, 0•12
Underframe – 11•2
Unleaded petrol – 4A•5
Upholstery and carpets – 11•2

V

Vacuum servo unit – 9•15, 9•16
Valves – 2D•12
Valve timing – 2C•4
Vehicle identification – REF•3, REF•9
Vehicle support – REF•5
Ventilation system – 3•11

W

Warning light bulbs – 12•11
Washer fluid – 0•16
  level sensor – 12•15
  pump – 12•19
  reservoir – 12•19
Washer nozzle – 12•19, 12•20
Weekly checks – 0•11 et seq
Weights – REF•1
Wheel alignment and steering
  angles – 10•18
Wheel bearings – 10•4, 10•10, REF•10
Wheel bolt tightness – 1•12
Wheel changing – 0•9
Wheel cylinder – 9•14
Wheel sensor – 9•19
Wheelarch liners – 11•19
Wheels – REF•11
Wind deflector – 11•19
Window motors – 11•17
Window regulator – 11•13
Windscreen – 11•19, REF•8
  cowl panel – 11•5
  washer nozzle – 12•19
  washer system – 12•19
  wiper motor and linkage – 12•17
Winter mode switch – 7B•4
Wiper arm – 12•16
Wiper blades – 0•17
Wiper motor – 12•18
Wiper switch assembly – 12•4
Wiring diagrams – 12•26 et seq
Working facilities – REF•7

Haynes Manuals – The Complete List

Title	Book No.
ALFA ROMEO Alfasud/Sprint (74 - 88) up to F *	0292
Alfa Romeo Alfetta (73 - 87) up to E *	0531
AUDI 80, 90 & Coupe Petrol (79 - Nov 88) up to F	0605
Audi 80, 90 & Coupe Petrol (Oct 86 - 90) D to H	1491
Audi 100 & 200 Petrol (Oct 82 - 90) up to H	0907
Audi 100 & A6 Petrol & Diesel (May 91 - May 97) H to P	3504
Audi A3 Petrol & Diesel (96 - May 03) P to 03	4253
Audi A4 Petrol & Diesel (95 - Feb 00) M to V	3575
AUSTIN A35 & A40 (56 - 67) up to F *	0118
Austin/MG/Rover Maestro 1.3 & 1.6 Petrol (83 - 95) up to M	0922
Austin/MG Metro (80 - May 90) up to G	0718
Austin/Rover Montego 1.3 & 1.6 Petrol (84 - 94) A to L	1066
Austin/MG/Rover Montego 2.0 Petrol (84 - 95) A to M	1067
Mini (59 - 69) up to H *	0527
Mini (69 - 01) up to X	0646
Austin/Rover 2.0 litre Diesel Engine (86 - 93) C to L	1857
Austin Healey 100/6 & 3000 (56 - 68) up to G *	0049
BEDFORD CF Petrol (69 - 87) up to E	0163
Bedford/Vauxhall Rascal & Suzuki Supercarry (86 - Oct 94) C to M	3015
BMW 316, 320 & 320i (4-cyl) (75 - Feb 83) up to Y*	0276
BMW 320, 320i, 323i & 325i (6-cyl) (Oct 77 - Sept 87) up to E	0815
BMW 3- & 5-Series Petrol (81 - 91) up to J	1948
BMW 3-Series Petrol (Apr 91 - 96) H to N	3210
BMW 3-Series Petrol (Sept 98 - 03) S to 53	4067
BMW 520i & 525e (Oct 81 - June 88) up to E	1560
BMW 525, 528 & 528i (73 - Sept 81) up to X *	0632
BMW 5-Series 6-cyl Petrol (April 96 - Aug 03) N to 03	4151
BMW 1500, 1502, 1600, 1602, 2000 & 2002 (59 - 77) up to S *	0240
CHRYSLER PT Cruiser Petrol (00 - 03) W to 53	4058
CITROËN 2CV, Ami & Dyane (67 - 90) up to H	0196
Citroën AX Petrol & Diesel (87 - 97) D to P	3014
Citroën Berlingo & Peugeot Partner Petrol & Diesel (96 - 05) P to 55	4281
Citroën BX Petrol (83 - 94) A to L	0908
Citroën C15 Van Petrol & Diesel (89 - Oct 98) F to S	3509
Citroën C3 Petrol & Diesel (02 - 05) 51 to 05	4197
Citroën CX Petrol (75 - 88) up to F	0528
Citroën Saxo Petrol & Diesel (96 - 04) N to 54	3506
Citroën Visa Petrol (79 - 88) up to F	0620
Citroën Xantia Petrol & Diesel (93 - 01) K to Y	3082
Citroën XM Petrol & Diesel (89 - 00) G to X	3451
Citroën Xsara Petrol & Diesel (97 - Sept 00) R to W	3751
Citroën Xsara Picasso Petrol & Diesel (00 - 02) W to 52	3944
Citroën ZX Diesel (91 - 98) J to S	1922
Citroën ZX Petrol (91 - 98) H to S	1881
Citroën 1.7 & 1.9 litre Diesel Engine (84 - 96) A to N	1379
FIAT 126 (73 - 87) up to E *	0305
Fiat 500 (57 - 73) up to M *	0090
Fiat Bravo & Brava Petrol (95 - 00) N to W	3572
Fiat Cinquecento (93 - 98) K to R	3501
Fiat Panda (81 - 95) up to M	0793
Fiat Punto Petrol & Diesel (94 - Oct 99) L to V	3251
Fiat Punto Petrol (Oct 99 - July 03) V to 03	4066
Fiat Regata Petrol (84 - 88) A to F	1167
Fiat Tipo Petrol (88 - 91) E to J	1625
Fiat Uno Petrol (83 - 95) up to M	0923
Fiat X1/9 (74 - 89) up to G *	0273
FORD Anglia (59 - 68) up to G *	0001

Title	Book No.
Ford Capri II (& III) 1.6 & 2.0 (74 - 87) up to E *	0283
Ford Capri II (& III) 2.8 & 3.0 V6 (74 - 87) up to E	1309
Ford Cortina Mk III 1300 & 1600 (70 - 76) up to P *	0070
Ford Escort Mk I 1100 & 1300 (68 - 74) up to N *	0171
Ford Escort Mk I Mexico, RS 1600 & RS 2000 (70 - 74) up to N *	0139
Ford Escort Mk II Mexico, RS 1800 & RS 2000 (75 - 80) up to W *	0735
Ford Escort (75 - Aug 80) up to V *	0280
Ford Escort Petrol (Sept 80 - Sept 90) up to H	0686
Ford Escort & Orion Petrol (Sept 90 - 00) H to X	1737
Ford Escort & Orion Diesel (Sept 90 - 00) H to X	4081
Ford Fiesta (76 - Aug 83) up to Y	0334
Ford Fiesta Petrol (Aug 83 - Feb 89) A to F	1030
Ford Fiesta Petrol (Feb 89 - Oct 95) F to N	1595
Ford Fiesta Petrol & Diesel (Oct 95 - Mar 02) N to 02	3397
Ford Fiesta Petrol & Diesel (Apr 02 - 05) 02 to 54	4170
Ford Focus Petrol & Diesel (98 - 01) S to Y	3759
Ford Focus Petrol & Diesel (Oct 01 - 04) 51 to 54	4167
Ford Galaxy Petrol & Diesel (95 - Aug 00) M to W	3984
Ford Granada Petrol (Sept 77 - Feb 85) up to B *	0481
Ford Granada & Scorpio Petrol (Mar 85 - 94) B to M	1245
Ford Ka (96 - 02) P to 52	3570
Ford Mondeo Petrol (93 - Sept 00) K to X	1923
Ford Mondeo Petrol & Diesel (Oct 00 - Jul 03) X to 03	3990
Ford Mondeo Diesel (93 - 96) L to N	3465
Ford Orion Petrol (83 - Sept 90) up to H	1009
Ford Sierra 4-cyl Petrol (82 - 93) up to K	0903
Ford Sierra V6 Petrol (82 - 91) up to J	0904
Ford Transit Petrol (Mk 2) (78 - Jan 86) up to C	0719
Ford Transit Petrol (Mk 3) (Feb 86 - 89) C to G	1468
Ford Transit Diesel (Feb 86 - 99) C to T	3019
Ford 1.6 & 1.8 litre Diesel Engine (84 - 96) A to N	1172
Ford 2.1, 2.3 & 2.5 litre Diesel Engine (77 - 90) up to H	1606
FREIGHT ROVER Sherpa Petrol (74 - 87) up to E	0463
HILLMAN Avenger (70 - 82) up to Y	0037
Hillman Imp (63 - 76) up to R *	0022
HONDA Civic (Feb 84 - Oct 87) A to E	1226
Honda Civic (Nov 91 - 96) J to N	3199
Honda Civic Petrol (Mar 95 - 00) M to X	4050
HYUNDAI Pony (85 - 94) C to M	3398
JAGUAR E Type (61 - 72) up to L *	0140
Jaguar MkI & II, 240 & 340 (55 - 69) up to H *	0098
Jaguar XJ6, XJ & Sovereign; Daimler Sovereign (68 - Oct 86) up to D	0242
Jaguar XJ6 & Sovereign (Oct 86 - Sept 94) D to M	3261
Jaguar XJ12, XJS & Sovereign; Daimler Double Six (72 - 88) up to F	0478
JEEP Cherokee Petrol (93 - 96) K to N	1943
LADA 1200, 1300, 1500 & 1600 (74 - 91) up to J	0413
Lada Samara (87 - 91) D to J	1610
LAND ROVER 90, 110 & Defender Diesel (83 - 95) up to N	3017
Land Rover Discovery Petrol & Diesel (89 - 98) G to S	3016
Land Rover Freelander Petrol & Diesel (97 - 02) R to 52	3929
Land Rover Series IIA & III Diesel (58 - 85) up to C	0529
Land Rover Series II, IIA & III 4-cyl Petrol (58 - 85) up to C	0314
MAZDA 323 (Mar 81 - Oct 89) up to G	1608
Mazda 323 (Oct 89 - 98) G to R	3455
Mazda 626 (May 83 - Sept 87) up to E	0929
Mazda B1600, B1800 & B2000 Pick-up Petrol (72 - 88) up to F	0267

Title	Book No.
Mazda RX-7 (79 - 85) up to C *	0460
MERCEDES-BENZ 190, 190E & 190D Petrol & Diesel (83 - 93) A to L	3450
Mercedes-Benz 200D, 240D, 240TD, 300D & 300TD 123 Series Diesel (Oct 76 - 85) up	1114
Mercedes-Benz 250 & 280 (68 - 72) up to L *	0346
Mercedes-Benz 250 & 280 123 Series Petrol (Oct 76 - 84) up to B *	0677
Mercedes-Benz 124 Series Petrol & Diesel (85 - Aug 93) C to K	3253
Mercedes-Benz C-Class Petrol & Diesel (93 - Aug 00) L to W	3511
MGA (55 - 62) *	0475
MGB (62 - 80) up to W	0111
MG Midget & Austin-Healey Sprite (58 - 80) up to W *	0265
MINI Petrol (July 01 - 05) Y to 05	4273
MITSUBISHI Shogun & L200 Pick-Ups Petrol (83 - 94) up to M	1944
MORRIS Ital 1.3 (80 - 84) up to B	0705
Morris Minor 1000 (56 - 71) up to K	0024
NISSAN Almera Petrol (95 - Feb 00) N to V	4053
Nissan Bluebird (May 84 - Mar 86) A to C	1223
Nissan Bluebird Petrol (Mar 86 - 90) C to H	1473
Nissan Cherry (Sept 82 - 86) up to D	1031
Nissan Micra (83 - Jan 93) up to K	0931
Nissan Micra (93 - 02) K to 52	3254
Nissan Primera Petrol (90 - Aug 99) H to T	1851
Nissan Stanza (82 - 86) up to D	0824
Nissan Sunny Petrol (May 82 - Oct 86) up to D	0895
Nissan Sunny Petrol (Oct 86 - Mar 91) D to H	1378
Nissan Sunny Petrol (Apr 91 - 95) H to N	3219
OPEL Ascona & Manta (B Series) (Sept 75 - 88) up to F *	0316
Opel Ascona Petrol (81 - 88)	3215
Opel Astra Petrol (Oct 91 - Feb 98)	3156
Opel Corsa Petrol (83 - Mar 93)	3160
Opel Corsa Petrol (Mar 93 - 97)	3159
Opel Kadett Petrol (Nov 79 - Oct 84) up to B	0634
Opel Kadett Petrol (Oct 84 - Oct 91)	3196
Opel Omega & Senator Petrol (Nov 86 - 94)	3157
Opel Rekord Petrol (Feb 78 - Oct 86) up to D	0543
Opel Vectra Petrol (Oct 88 - Oct 95)	3158
PEUGEOT 106 Petrol & Diesel (91 - 04) J to 53	1882
Peugeot 205 Petrol (83 - 97) A to P	0932
Peugeot 206 Petrol & Diesel (98 - 01) S to X	3757
Peugeot 306 Petrol & Diesel (93 - 02) K to 02	3073
Peugeot 307 Petrol & Diesel (01 - 04) Y to 54	4147
Peugeot 309 Petrol (86 - 93) C to K	1266
Peugeot 405 Petrol (88 - 97) E to P	1559
Peugeot 405 Diesel (88 - 97) E to P	3198
Peugeot 406 Petrol & Diesel (96 - Mar 99) N to T	3394
Peugeot 406 Petrol & Diesel (Mar 99 - 02) T to 52	3982
Peugeot 505 Petrol (79 - 89) up to G	0762
Peugeot 1.7/1.8 & 1.9 litre Diesel Engine (82 - 96) up to N	0950
Peugeot 2.0, 2.1, 2.3 & 2.5 litre Diesel Engines (74 - 90) up to H	1607
PORSCHE 911 (65 - 85) up to C	0264
Porsche 924 & 924 Turbo (76 - 85) up to C	0397
PROTON (89 - 97) F to P	3255
RANGE ROVER V8 Petrol (70 - Oct 92) up to K	0606
RELIANT Robin & Kitten (73 - 83) up to A *	0436
RENAULT 4 (61 - 86) up to D *	0072

* Classic reprint

Title	Book No.
Renault 5 Petrol (Feb 85 - 96) B to N	1219
Renault 9 & 11 Petrol (82 - 89) up to F	0822
Renault 18 Petrol (79 - 86) up to D	0598
Renault 19 Petrol (89 - 96) F to N	1646
Renault 19 Diesel (89 - 96) F to N	1946
Renault 21 Petrol (86 - 94) C to M	1397
Renault 25 Petrol & Diesel (84 - 92) B to K	1228
Renault Clio Petrol (91 - May 98) H to R	1853
Renault Clio Diesel (91 - June 96) H to N	3031
Renault Clio Petrol & Diesel (May 98 - May 01) R to Y	3906
Renault Clio Petrol & Diesel (June 01 - 04) Y to 54	4168
Renault Espace Petrol & Diesel (85 - 96) C to N	3197
Renault Laguna Petrol & Diesel (94 - 00) L to W	3252
Renault Laguna Petrol & Diesel (01 - 05) X to 05	4283
Renault Mégane & Scénic Petrol & Diesel (96 - 98) N to R	3395
Renault Mégane & Scénic Petrol & Diesel (Apr 99 - 02) T to 52	3916
Renault Megane Petrol & Diesel (Oct 02 - 05) 52 to 55	4284
Renault Scenic Petrol & Diesel (Sept 03 - 06) 53 to 06	4297
ROVER 213 & 216 (84 - 89) A to G	1116
Rover 214 & 414 Petrol (89 - 96) G to N	1689
Rover 216 & 416 Petrol (89 - 96) G to N	1830
Rover 211, 214, 216, 218 & 220 Petrol & Diesel (Dec 95 - 99) N to V	3399
Rover 25 & MG ZR Petrol & Diesel (Oct 99 - 04) V to 54	4145
Rover 414, 416 & 420 Petrol & Diesel (May 95 - 98) M to R	3453
Rover 45 / MG ZS	4384
Rover 618, 620 & 623 Petrol (93 - 97) K to P	3257
Rover 75 / MG ZT Petrol & Diesel (Feb 99 - 05) T to 05	4292
Rover 820, 825 & 827 Petrol (86 - 95) D to N	1380
Rover 3500 (76 - 87) up to E *	0365
Rover Metro, 111 & 114 Petrol (May 90 - 98) G to S	1711
SAAB 95 & 96 (66 - 76) up to R *	0198
Saab 90, 99 & 900 (79 - Oct 93) up to L	0765
Saab 900 (Oct 93 - 98) L to R	3512
Saab 9000 (4-cyl) (85 - 98) C to S	1686
Saab 9-5 4-cyl Petrol (97 - 04) R to 54	4156
SEAT Ibiza & Cordoba Petrol & Diesel (Oct 93 - Oct 99) L to V	3571
Seat Ibiza & Malaga Petrol (85 - 92) B to K	1609
SKODA Estelle (77 - 89) up to G	0604
Skoda Fabia (00 - 06) W to 06	4376
Skoda Favorit (89 - 96) F to N	1801
Skoda Felicia Petrol & Diesel (95 - 01) M to X	3505
Skoda Octavia Petrol & Diesel (98 - Apr 04) R to 04	4285
SUBARU 1600 & 1800 (Nov 79 - 90) up to H *	0995
SUNBEAM Alpine, Rapier & H120 (67 - 74) up to N *	0051
SUZUKI SJ Series, Samurai & Vitara (4-cyl) Petrol (82 - 97) up to P	1942
Suzuki Supercarry & Bedford/Vauxhall Rascal (86 - Oct 94) C to M	3015
TALBOT Alpine, Solara, Minx & Rapier (75 - 86) up to D	0337
Talbot Horizon Petrol (78 - 86) up to D	0473
Talbot Samba (82 - 86) up to D	0823
TOYOTA Avensis Petrol (Nov 97 - Jan 03) R to 52	4264
Toyota Carina E Petrol (May 92 - 97) J to P	3256
Toyota Corolla (80 - 85) up to C	0683

Title	Book No.
Toyota Corolla (Sept 83 - Sept 87) A to E	1024
Toyota Corolla (Sept 87 - Aug 92) E to K	1683
Toyota Corolla Petrol (Aug 92 - 97) K to P	3259
Toyota Corolla Petrol (June 97 - 01) P to 51	4286
Toyota Hi-Ace & Hi-Lux Petrol (69 - Oct 83) up to A	0304
Toyota Yaris Petrol (99 - 05) T to 05	4265
TRIUMPH GT6 & Vitesse (62 - 74) up to N *	0112
Triumph Herald (59 - 71) up to K *	0010
Triumph Spitfire (62 - 81) up to X *	0113
Triumph Stag (70 - 78) up to T *	0441
Triumph TR2, TR3, TR3A, TR4 & TR4A (52 - 67) up to F *	0028
Triumph TR5 & 6 (67 - 75) up to P *	0031
Triumph TR7 (75 - 82) up to Y *	0322
VAUXHALL Astra Petrol (80 - Oct 84) up to B	0635
Vauxhall Astra & Belmont Petrol (Oct 84 - Oct 91) B to J	1136
Vauxhall Astra Petrol (Oct 91 - Feb 98) J to R	1832
Vauxhall/Opel Astra & Zafira Petrol (Feb 98 - Apr 04) R to 04	3758
Vauxhall/Opel Astra & Zafira Diesel (Feb 98 - Apr 04) R to 04	3797
Vauxhall/Opel Calibra (90 - 98) G to S	3502
Vauxhall Carlton Petrol (Oct 78 - Oct 86) up to D	0480
Vauxhall Carlton & Senator Petrol (Nov 86 - 94) D to L	1469
Vauxhall Cavalier Petrol (81 - Oct 88) up to F	0812
Vauxhall Cavalier Petrol (Oct 88 - 95) F to N	1570
Vauxhall Chevette (75 - 84) up to B	0285
Vauxhall/Opel Corsa Diesel (Mar 93 - Oct 00) K to X	4087
Vauxhall Corsa Petrol (Mar 93 - 97) K to R	1985
Vauxhall/Opel Corsa Petrol (Apr 97 - Oct 00) P to X	3921
Vauxhall/Opel Corsa Petrol & Diesel (Oct 00 - Sept 03) X to 53	4079
Vauxhall/Opel Frontera Petrol & Diesel (91 - Sept 98) J to S	3454
Vauxhall Nova Petrol (83 - 93) up to K	0909
Vauxhall/Opel Omega Petrol (94 - 99) L to T	3510
Vauxhall/Opel Vectra Petrol & Diesel (95 - Feb 99) N to S	3396
Vauxhall/Opel Vectra Petrol & Diesel (Mar 99 - May 02) T to 02	3930
Vauxhall/Opel 1.5, 1.6 & 1.7 litre Diesel Engine (82 - 96) up to N	1222
VOLKSWAGEN 411 & 412 (68 - 75) up to P *	0091
Volkswagen Beetle 1200 (54 - 77) up to S	0036
Volkswagen Beetle 1300 & 1500 (65 - 75) up to P	0039
Volkswagen Beetle 1302 & 1302S (70 - 72) up to L *	0110
Volkswagen Beetle 1303, 1303S & GT (72 - 75) up to P	0159
Volkswagen Beetle Petrol & Diesel (Apr 99 - 01) T to 51	3798
Volkswagen Golf & Jetta Mk 1 Petrol 1.1 & 1.3 (74 - 84) up to A	0716
Volkswagen Golf, Jetta & Scirocco Mk 1 Petrol 1.5, 1.6 & 1.8 (74 - 84) up to A	0726
Volkswagen Golf & Jetta Mk 1 Diesel (78 - 84) up to A	0451
Volkswagen Golf & Jetta Mk 2 Petrol (Mar 84 - Feb 92) A to J	1081
Volkswagen Golf & Vento Petrol & Diesel (Feb 92 - Mar 98) J to R	3097
Volkswagen Golf & Bora Petrol & Diesel (April 98 - 00) R to X	3727
Volkswagen Golf & Bora 4-cyl Petrol & Diesel (01 - 03) X to 53	4169

Title	Book No.
Volkswagen LT Petrol Vans & Light Trucks (76 - 87) up to E	0637
Volkswagen Passat & Santana Petrol (Sept 81 - May 88) up to E	0814
Volkswagen Passat 4-cyl Petrol & Diesel (May 88 - 96) E to P	3498
Volkswagen Passat 4-cyl Petrol & Diesel (Dec 96 - Nov 00) P to X	3917
Volkswagen Passat Petrol & Diesel (Dec 00 - May 05) X to 05	4279
Volkswagen Polo & Derby (76 - Jan 82) up to X	0335
Volkswagen Polo (82 - Oct 90) up to H	0813
Volkswagen Polo Petrol (Nov 90 - Aug 94) H to L	3245
Volkswagen Polo Hatchback Petrol & Diesel (94 - 99) M to S	3500
Volkswagen Polo Hatchback Petrol (00 - Jan 02) V to 51	4150
Volkswagen Scirocco (82 - 90) up to H *	1224
Volkswagen Transporter 1600 (68 - 79) up to V	0082
Volkswagen Transporter 1700, 1800 & 2000 (72 - 79) up to V *	0226
Volkswagen Transporter (air-cooled) Petrol (79 - 82) up to Y *	0638
Volkswagen Transporter (water-cooled) Petrol (82 - 90) up to H	3452
Volkswagen Type 3 (63 - 73) up to M *	0084
VOLVO 120 & 130 Series (& P1800) (61 - 73) up to M *	0203
Volvo 142, 144 & 145 (66 - 74) up to N *	0129
Volvo 240 Series Petrol (74 - 93) up to K	0270
Volvo 262, 264 & 260/265 (75 - 85) up to C *	0400
Volvo 340, 343, 345 & 360 (76 - 91) up to J	0715
Volvo 440, 460 & 480 Petrol (87 - 97) D to P	1691
Volvo 740 & 760 Petrol (82 - 91) up to J	1258
Volvo 850 Petrol (92 - 96) J to P	3260
Volvo 940 Petrol (90 - 96) H to N	3249
Volvo S40 & V40 Petrol (96 - Mar 04) N to 04	3569
Volvo S70, V70 & C70 Petrol (96 - 99) P to V	3573
Volvo V70 / S80 Petrol & Diesel (98 - 05) S to 55	4263

AUTOMOTIVE TECHBOOKS

Title	Book No.
Automotive Air Conditioning Systems	3740
Automotive Electrical and Electronic Systems Manual	3049
Automotive Gearbox Overhaul Manual	3473
Automotive Service Summaries Manual	3475
Automotive Timing Belts Manual – Austin/Rover	3549
Automotive Timing Belts Manual – Ford	3474
Automotive Timing Belts Manual – Peugeot/Citroën	3568
Automotive Timing Belts Manual – Vauxhall/Opel	3577

DIY MANUAL SERIES

Title	Book No.
The Haynes Air Conditioning Manual	4192
The Haynes Manual on Bodywork	4198
The Haynes Manual on Brakes	4178
The Haynes Manual on Carburettors	4177
The Haynes Car Electrical Systems Manual	4251
The Haynes Manual on Diesel Engines	4174
The Haynes Manual on Engine Management	4199
The Haynes Manual on Fault Codes	4175
The Haynes Manual on Practical Electrical Systems	4267
The Haynes Manual on Small Engines	4250
The Haynes Manual on Welding	4176

* Classic reprint

CL20.3/06

Preserving Our Motoring Heritage

< The Model J Duesenberg Derham Tourster. Only eight of these magnificent cars were ever built – this is the only example to be found outside the United States of America

Almost every car you've ever loved, loathed or desired is gathered under one roof at the Haynes Motor Museum. Over 300 immaculately presented cars and motorbikes represent every aspect of our motoring heritage, from elegant reminders of bygone days, such as the superb Model J Duesenberg to curiosities like the bug-eyed BMW Isetta. There are also many old friends and flames. Perhaps you remember the 1959 Ford Popular that you did your courting in? The magnificent 'Red Collection' is a spectacle of classic sports cars including AC, Alfa Romeo, Austin Healey, Ferrari, Lamborghini, Maserati, MG, Riley, Porsche and Triumph.

A Perfect Day Out

Each and every vehicle at the Haynes Motor Museum has played its part in the history and culture of Motoring. Today, they make a wonderful spectacle and a great day out for all the family. Bring the kids, bring Mum and Dad, but above all bring your camera to capture those golden memories for ever. You will also find an impressive array of motoring memorabilia, a comfortable 70 seat video cinema and one of the most extensive transport book shops in Britain. The Pit Stop Cafe serves everything from a cup of tea to wholesome, home-made meals or, if you prefer, you can enjoy the large picnic area nestled in the beautiful rural surroundings of Somerset.

> John Haynes O.B.E., Founder and Chairman of the museum at the wheel of a Haynes Light 12.

< Graham Hill's Lola Cosworth Formula 1 car next to a 1934 Riley Sports.

The Museum is situated on the A359 Yeovil to Frome road at Sparkford, just off the A303 in Somerset. It is about 40 miles south of Bristol, and 25 minutes drive from the M5 intersection at Taunton.

Open 9.30am - 5.30pm (10.00am - 4.00pm Winter) 7 days a week, *except Christmas Day, Boxing Day and New Years Day*

Special rates available for schools, coach parties and outings Charitable Trust No. 292048